# Animal Sacrifice in the Roman Empire (31 BCE–395 CE)

# Animal Sacrifice in the Roman Empire (31 BCE–395 CE)

*Power, Communication, and Cultural Transformation*

J. B. RIVES

**OXFORD**
UNIVERSITY PRESS

Oxford University Press is a department of the University of Oxford. It furthers
the University's objective of excellence in research, scholarship, and education
by publishing worldwide. Oxford is a registered trade mark of Oxford University
Press in the UK and certain other countries.

Published in the United States of America by Oxford University Press
198 Madison Avenue, New York, NY 10016, United States of America.

© Oxford University Press 2024

All rights reserved. No part of this publication may be reproduced, stored in
a retrieval system, or transmitted, in any form or by any means, without the
prior permission in writing of Oxford University Press, or as expressly permitted
by law, by license, or under terms agreed with the appropriate reproduction
rights organization. Inquiries concerning reproduction outside the scope of the
above should be sent to the Rights Department, Oxford University Press, at the
address above.

You must not circulate this work in any other form
and you must impose this same condition on any acquirer.

Library of Congress Control Number: 2024001942

ISBN 978–0–19–764891–9

DOI: 10.1093/oso/9780197648919.001.0001

Printed by Integrated Books International, United States of America

*For John, of course*

# Contents

*Acknowledgments* ix

*Abbreviations* xiii

1. Introduction  1

PART I. *The Practice of Animal Sacrifice in the Roman Empire*

Prologue: The Sacrifices of Nestor (*Odyssey* 3.5–66 and 418–72)  21

2. The Economics of Animal Sacrifice  26
3. Animal Sacrifice and Euergetism in the Roman Empire  41
4. Animal Sacrifice and Graeco-Roman Culture  81
5. Animal Sacrifice and the Roman Emperor  114

Epilogue  147

PART II. *Discourses of Animal Sacrifice in Graeco-Roman Culture and Early Christianity*

Prologue: Paul and Barnabas at Lystra (Acts 14.8–18)  153

6. Theorizing Animal Sacrifice I: From Hesiod to Plutarch (c. 700 BCE–c. 100 CE)  157
7. The Early Christian Displacement of Animal Sacrifice (c. 50–c. 150 CE)  186

8. Theorizing Animal Sacrifice II: From Apollonius to
   Iamblichus (c. 100–c. 300 CE) — 214

   Epilogue — 241

## PART III. *Transformations of Animal Sacrifice in Late Antiquity*

Prologue: The Decree of Decius (*SB* I.443) — 247

9. The Obligations of Empire: Decius to the Tetrarchs
   (250–313 CE) — 251

10. From Roman to Pagan: Constantine to Theodosius I
    (313–395 CE) — 291

    Epilogue — 332

11. The End of Animal Sacrifice? — 336

*References* — 353
*Index* — 387

# *Acknowledgments*

THIS BOOK HAS been long in the making. I see from my CV that the first paper conceived as part of this larger research project was one that I presented in January 2008, although my interest in the social and cultural significance of animal sacrifice in the Graeco-Roman world extends back at least a decade before that. In the years since then, I have accumulated many debts, of which I can here acknowledge only the most important. I began working in earnest on this project in 2009–10, during a year of research leave in the idyllic surroundings of the School of Historical Studies at the Institute for Advanced Study in Princeton, New Jersey. I owe many thanks to the Institute and its faculty and staff, and also to the National Endowment for the Humanities and the Andrew W. Mellon Foundation, which provided the funding that made my stay there possible. In November and December 2013, I was Directeur d'Études Invité in the Section des Sciences Religieuses of the École Pratique des Hautes Études in Paris. It was in this context that I was able to present for the first time, in a series of four lectures, an overview of my project as it existed at that time. I am grateful to Nicole Belayche and Jean-Daniel Dubois for their invitation to be a visiting member of this extraordinary institution and to all those who attended the lectures for their questions and comments. Thereafter, work on the project slowed considerably during my eight years as Chair of the Department of Classics at the University of North Carolina at Chapel Hill. During this time, I made progress largely by orienting all the invitations that I received to present lectures or participate in conferences and panels toward my research on animal sacrifice. I am much indebted to the organizers and participants of all these events, which gave me the opportunity to consider my subject from many different angles and receive valuable feedback from colleagues in a wide range of disciplines. In 2021–22, I was fortunate to have another year of research leave, which enabled me to pull together all my previous work and complete a full draft of the book. I am grateful to the friends and colleagues who wrote in support of my applications for fellowships: Jan Bremmer, Bart Ehrman, David Frankfurter, and Celia Schultz. I am particularly grateful to the Loeb Classical Library Foundation and the Office of the Provost at the University of North Carolina at Chapel Hill for funding this year of leave. I also owe thanks to the College of Arts and Sciences for its financial support of all my research leaves and to all my colleagues in the Department of Classics for accommodating them; no one could ask for better colleagues.

I have benefited over the years from the thoughtful feedback that I have received from many colleagues. I must here thank especially those who read and commented on drafts of various chapters: Marc Domingo Gygax on an early draft of Chapter 3, Katie Tardio on Chapter 2, and Paula Fredriksen on Chapters 7, 9, and 10. The Working Group in Ancient Religion (2021–22) devoted one of its sessions to Chapter 4 and gave me much food for thought; I am grateful to Lindsay Driediger-Murphey, Ailsa Hunt, Ted Kaizer, Duncan MacRae, Claudia Moser, Gil Renberg, and Celia Schultz for our many stimulating meetings. I owe particular thanks to Jan Bremmer, Fred Naiden, and Bill Race, who heroically read through the entire manuscript and offered much valuable advice. All these colleagues have helped me correct mistakes, rectify omissions, and improve the clarity of my arguments and presentation. Their generosity in assisting me with this project does not in any way make them liable for the errors and idiosyncrasies that remain. I am likewise very grateful to my two research assistants. Emily Lime did all the work of locating and obtaining permissions for the images that appear in the book; I also owe thanks to my colleague Hérica Valladares for her advice and guidance on this process. Matt Sherry undertook the formidable task of verifying the myriad primary references and checking the consistency of my citations, which he did with meticulous care. I could not have finished this project as soon as I did without their assistance.

I thank the staff of Oxford University Press in New York for their work in making this book a reality. My commissioning editor, Stefan Vranka, played an important role in helping me refine my ideas of the book's shape and make the transition from a loosely imagined study to an actual book. The anonymous readers for the Press provided many helpful comments and suggestions, for which I am grateful. I am also grateful to Alex Rouch, my project editor, and Vinothini Thiruvannamalai and Balaji Padmanaban, my project managers, who guided me through key stages of the production process, and to Wendy Keebler, for her careful work in copy-editing the manuscript. I am also grateful to my friend Elizabeth Matheson for taking my author photograph and to my friend Ippy Patterson for creating the art that appears behind me in the photograph.

Support for research comes in many forms, and as anyone who has ever completed a major project is well aware, one of the most important is the personal and emotional support provided by family and friends. I am extremely fortunate in having many wonderful friends, to all of whom I am very grateful. I thank in particular Elizabeth and Bob Babcock, Jeffery Beam and Stanley Finch, Jimmy Holcomb and Fred Stewart, Larry Logan and Mark Pandick, Sara Mack, Steven Petrow, Diane and Bill Race, my sister Carol Rives, Laurie Thorp, and Cecil Wooten. My deepest thanks go to John Johnston, Executive Director and Chef de Cuisine of the Mangum Institute for Advanced Study and, not incidentally, my husband. Those who know us have some sense of how much I owe him; he and I alone know the full reckoning.

Durham, North Carolina
April 1, 2023

# Abbreviations

ABBREVIATIONS OF THE names of ancient authors and works are based on those in *The Oxford Classical Dictionary* (4th edition, 2012) and *The SBL Handbook of Style* (2nd edition, 2014). Other abbreviations are noted below.

| | |
|---|---|
| *AE* | *L'année épigraphique*. Paris: E. Leroux, 1888–. |
| *BDAG* | Walter Bauer, *A Greek-English Lexicon of the New Testament and Other Early Christian Literature*. 3rd ed. Edited by Frederick W. Danker, William F. Arndt, and F. Wilbur Gingrich. Chicago: University of Chicago Press, 2000. |
| *BHG* | *Bibliotheca Hagiographica Graeca*. 3rd ed. Edited by François Halkin. Brussels: Société des Bollandistes, 1957. |
| *BHG Auct.* | *Auctarium Bibliothecae Hagiographicae Graecae*. Edited by François Halkin. Brussels: Société des Bollandistes, 1969. |
| *BHL* | *Bibliotheca Hagiographica Latina Antiquæ et Mediæ Aetatis*. Brussels: Société des Bollandistes, 1898–1901. |
| *BHL NS* | *Bibliotheca Hagiographica Latina Antiquæ et Mediæ Aetatis*. Novum Supplementum. Edited by Henricus Fros. Brussels: Société des Bollandistes, 1986. |
| *CIL* | *Corpus Inscriptionum Latinarum*. Berlin: Akademie der Wissenschaften, 1863–. |
| *DK* | *Die Fragmente der Vorsokratiker*. 6th ed. Edited by Hermann Diels and Walther Kranz. Berlin: Weidmann, 1952. |
| *EDCS* | Epigraphik-Datenbank Clauss-Slaby. http://www.manfredclauss.de/. |
| *EDH* | Epigraphic Database Heidelberg. https://edh.ub.uni-heidelberg.de/home. |
| *EDR* | Epigraphic Database Roma. http://www.edr-edr.it/default/index.php. |
| *FGrH* | *Die Fragmente der griechischen Historiker*. Edited by Felix Jacoby. Berlin: Weidmann, 1923–. |
| *HJP* | Emil Schürer, *A History of the Jewish People in the Age of Jesus Christ*. Revised and edited by Geza Vermes, Fergus Millar, Matthew Black, and Martin Goodman. 3 vols. Edinburgh: T&T Clark, 1973–1987. |

| | |
|---|---|
| *IG* | *Inscriptiones Graecae*. Berlin: G. Reimer, 1873–. |
| *IGRom.* | *Inscriptiones Graecae ad Res Romanas Pertinentes*. Edited by René Cagnat, Jules Toutain, and Georges LaFaye. Paris: E. Leroux, 1906–1927. |
| *ILS* | *Inscriptiones Latinae Selectae*. Edited by Hermann Dessau. Berlin: Weidmann, 1892–1916. |
| *I. Perge* | *Die Inschriften von Perge*. Edited by Sencer Şahin. Bonn: Rudolf Habelt, 1999. |
| *I. Sestos* | *Die Inschriften von Sestos und der thrakischen Chersones*. Edited by Johannes Krauss. Bonn: Rudolf Habelt, 1980. |
| K-A | *Poetae Comici Graeci*. Edited by Rudolf Kassel and Colin Austin. Berlin: De Gruyter, 1983–. |
| *LRER* | *Les lois religieuses des empereurs romains de Constantin à Théodose II (312–438)*. Translated by Jean Rougé, introduction and notes by Roland Delmaire. 2 vols. Paris: Éditions du Cerf, 2005–2009. |
| LXX | *Septuaginta*. 2nd ed. Edited by Alfred Rahlfs, revised by Robert Hanhart. Stuttgart: Deutsche Bibelgesellschaft, 2006. |
| m. | Mishnah. |
| *NETS* | *A New English Translation of the Septuagint*. Edited by Albert Pietersma and Benjamin C. Wright. Oxford: Oxford University Press, 2007. |
| NRSV | Bible, New Revised Standard Version. |
| OCRE | Online Coins of the Roman Empire. http://www.numismatics.org/ocre/. |
| *OGIS* | *Orientis Graecae Inscriptiones Selectae*. Edited by Wilhelm Dittenberger. Leipzig: S. Hirzel, 1903–1905. |
| *ORF* | *Oratorum Romanorum Fragmenta Liberae Rei Publicae*. Edited by Henrica Malcovati. Turin: Paravia, 1953. |
| *PLRE* 1 | A. H. M. Jones, J. R. Martindale, and John Morris, *The Prosopography of the Later Roman Empire,* Vol. 1: *A.D. 260–395*. Cambridge: Cambridge University Press, 1971. |
| *P.Lips.* II | *Griechische Urkunden der Papyrussammlung zu Leipzig*, Vol. 2. Edited by Ruth Duttenhöfer. Munich: K. G. Saur, 2002. |
| *P.Oxy.* | *The Oxyrhynchus Papyri*. London: Egypt Exploration Society, 1898–. |
| PSI VII | *Papiri greci e latini*, Vol. 7. Edited by G. Vitelli and M. Norsa. Florence: Pubblicazioni della Società Italiana per la Ricerca dei Papiri Greci e Latini in Egitto, 1925. |
| *RIC*[1] | *The Roman Imperial Coinage*. 1st ed. Edited by Harold Mattingly, E. A. Sydenham, C. H. V. Sutherland, and R. A. G. Carson. London: Spink, 1923–1981. |
| *RIC* 1[2] | *The Roman Imperial Coinage,* Vol 1: *From 31 BC to AD 69*. 2nd ed. Edited by C. H. V. Sutherland. London: Spink, 1984. |

| | |
|---|---|
| RIC 2.1² | *The Roman Imperial Coinage*, Vol. II.1: *From AD 69 to AD 96, Vespasian to Domitian*. 2nd ed. Edited by Ian A. Carradice and Theodore V. Buttrey. London: Spink, 2007. |
| RIC 2.3² | *The Roman Imperial Coinage*, Vol II.3: *From AD 117 to AD 138: Hadrian*. 2nd ed. Edited by Richard A. Abdy, with a contribution by Peter F. Mittag. London: Spink, 2019. |
| SB | *Sammelbuch griechischer Urkunden aus Ägypten*. Edited by Friedrich Preisigke et al. Strassburg: K. J. Trübner, 1915–. |
| SEG | *Supplementum Epigraphicum Graecum*. Leiden: Brill, 1923–. |

# I

# Introduction

## 1a. An Altar from Pompeii

At some point in the first century CE, someone in Pompeii commissioned a workshop to construct an altar for a small public sanctuary.[1] As was normal, the altar stood outside, in front of the temple that housed the cult statue. Its front panel is adorned with an elaborate marble relief that represents the sacrifice of a bull (see Figure 1.1). The large animal, flanked by three attendants, takes up the right half of the panel. The attendants are all stripped to the waist in preparation for the bloody business of slaughtering and butchering that is to come; the one in the foreground carries the axe that he will use to stun the animal prior to the slaughter. Crowded together in the left half of the panel are the other participants in the ritual. The most prominent member of this group, the only full-size figure depicted in his entirety, is the man who presides over the sacrifice. He has a fold of his toga draped over his head in the manner prescribed by Roman tradition for those who presided over sacred rites and is depicted in the act of pouring a liquid offering, which most viewers would have understood to be wine, over a fire in a tall three-legged brazier. To his left are two other attendants, one a young boy holding a jug and another libation dish and the other an adult carrying a small platter. Immediately to the officiant's right, behind the brazier, is a musician playing a tibia, the double-barreled reed pipe whose music normally accompanied an animal sacrifice.

The style of the relief is so naturalistic that it is tempting to interpret it as the depiction of an actual event. This is a temptation that we should resist.

---

1. Ryberg 1955, 81–84; Gradel 2002, 79–80, 91–93. The dating is disputed, with arguments for both an Augustan and a Flavian date.

**FIGURE 1.1.** Front panel relief from the altar of the Temple of Vespasian, Pompeii. Art Resource, NY

Although animal sacrifices may in actuality have taken place at this altar, and although those sacrifices are likely to have involved the same sorts of personnel and implements that are depicted here, we can be reasonably certain that none of them would have looked quite like this. On the contrary, the sculptor, a skillful artist, carefully arranged his composition in order to highlight certain themes that most contemporary viewers would have perceived without too much conscious effort. First and foremost among these is piety. In the Roman tradition, animal sacrifice had served since time immemorial as an important way of demonstrating piety toward the gods. The depiction of that ritual in a marble relief on an altar thus constituted an enduring public signifier of piety. Another prominent theme is wealth. No one in the ancient Mediterranean world would have needed to be told that a fully grown bull was a very expensive animal, far beyond most people's means. To slaughter such an animal as a gift to the gods was accordingly as much a demonstration of wealth as it was of piety. The relief does not indicate whose wealth had paid for the animal, but most viewers were likely to have associated it, directly or indirectly, with the figure who presides over the sacrifice. Although they would not have been able to identify him precisely without some further marker such as an inscription, the altar's setting and their own familiarity with normal practice would have led them to regard him as some sort of official, a priest or a magistrate. The men (rarely women) who held such offices were by definition wealthy, and that wealth was readily apparent in this relief, not only in the costly animal but also in the cluster of specialized personnel involved in the sacrifice. A related theme is that of benefaction. An adult bovine produced a great deal of edible meat, which for many people would have been something of a luxury; moreover, in the case of any animal judged fit to serve as an offering to a god, that meat was likely to be of a higher quality than what was often available. As a result, many ancient viewers would have perceived the potential for largesse implicit in this scene. Lastly, the relief signaled conformity to widely acknowledged cultural norms. Although the specifics of the sacrificial procedure depicted here are distinctively Roman, practices akin to Roman animal sacrifice were traditional among many of the peoples brought under Roman hegemony, and although viewers from other cultural backgrounds may have been struck by details that were unfamiliar to them, most would have easily recognized a practice that was normative across the empire.

Although we know nothing about the individual or group who commissioned this relief, it is likely enough that the themes enumerated above were the ones that they wanted to convey, and so to that extent, we can say that these themes constituted the relief's message. Yet while most ancient viewers were likely to have registered them more or less automatically, some viewers, depending on their backgrounds and interests, would have seen other meanings in this image as well. To a resident Judaean, it may have been a reminder of the exclusive devotion to her own god that she was expected to maintain even amid a world of gentiles. Someone with philosophical interests may have appreciated the adherence to ancestral modes of piety but at the same time have reflected on the folly of those who believed that costly offerings, rather than moral conduct, were what pleased the gods. An early follower of the cult of the risen Christ may have interpreted the scene as one of fellowship with spirits hostile to humanity, those beings called *daimones* in Greek. Viewers from later centuries might have regarded the relief as signifying either allegiance to the Roman Empire or adherence to paganism, although by that time, the altar would have long since been buried in volcanic ash.

As this one example suggests, animal sacrifice in the ancient Graeco-Roman world did a great deal of cultural work. My project in this book is to analyze some aspects of that work. It is by no means intended to be a comprehensive study of animal sacrifice in Graeco-Roman antiquity, and it accordingly omits a number of important topics. My goal is instead to illuminate particular aspects of its social function and cultural significance and to trace the way these developed and changed over the course of the first four centuries CE. This introductory chapter sets out the project's parameters and analytical framework by explicating the key terms in the book's title and subtitle, beginning with animal sacrifice itself.

## *1b. Animal Sacrifice*

For the purposes of this book "animal sacrifice" designates a ritualized practice involving the slaughter of an animal, of which the whole or parts were offered to perceived superhuman powers for the sake of winning their favor. We may begin fleshing out the bare bones of this definition by considering its major components in more detail.

By "a ritualized practice" I mean one that is distinguished from other practices by a set of rules that dictate details of its performance but that often appear arbitrary; when a practice is ritualized, there is a right way and a wrong way to do it. Participants in a ritualized practice are aware that they are engaged in a rule-bound activity, even when they are uncertain of the specific rules, and commonly perceive it as traditional, highly formal, unvarying, and capable of indefinite repetition. All these characteristics apply to animal sacrifice in Graeco-Roman antiquity, which consisted of a complex series of actions that had to be performed in specific ways in a specific sequence. Failure to perform an animal sacrifice correctly was thought to entail the risk of dire consequences. I use the phrase "ritualized practice" instead of "ritual" to emphasize that animal sacrifice was not a sui generis phenomenon but rather a particular type of social and cultural practice.[2] I say more about the meaning of "practice" in a later section of this chapter.

---

2. The best introduction to the study of ritual remains Bell 1997; see especially 80–83 on the idea of ritualized practice and 138–69 on the characteristics of ritualization. For a good brief overview of animal sacrifice in the Graeco-Roman tradition, see Ekroth 2014a; for a bibliographical survey, Naiden and Rives 2016; for a survey of recent work on sacrifice in the ancient

## Introduction

By "perceived superhuman powers" I mean the beings that the peoples of the ancient Graeco-Roman world believed to be present and active in their world and to have power over their lives that was greater than that which they could exercise themselves. As shorthand, both ancient and modern commentators often refer to these beings as "gods" (Greek *theoi*, Latin *di*), although, in fact, people in the Graeco-Roman world distinguished numerous different categories of such beings and employed a wide range of terms to designate them. People generally took it for granted that these perceived superhuman powers behaved in ways similar to those of humans in the society with which they were familiar. Consequently, it was thought possible, and indeed advisable, to win their favor by offering them gifts and other tokens of esteem, so that they would use their power to help rather than harm those who made the offering. For most people in the Graeco-Roman world, this was the true raison d'être of animal sacrifice and other cult offerings.[3] It was for this reason that they regarded prayer as a key element of sacrificial practice, since it was by means of prayer that they could articulate their reasons for approaching the deity.

The verb "offered" is accordingly a crucial part of my definition, whose significance is greater than it may initially appear to be. In using the term "sacrifice," I unavoidably evoke a long-standing and complex debate. Over the years, scholars have tried to identify the essential nature and function of sacrifice: as a type of gift, a form of communion, an act of atonement, and so forth. This is a debate with which, for the most part, I do not engage. It rests on the premise that the term "sacrifice" denotes some unitary transhistorical and transcultural phenomenon that is capable of having an essence, a premise that in my view is highly problematic.[4] My own concern is not with "sacrifice" in any abstract or absolute sense but rather with a range of specific practices

---

Mediterranean, Ullucci 2015; for Greek sacrifice in particular, see also the valuable overview of Bremmer 2019b.

3. It is one of the great merits of Naiden 2013 that it rightly restores the gods to a central place in the ancient Greek understanding of sacrifice; on prayer, see 25. For a cogent and rigorous analysis of the centrality of belief in Roman religion, see Mackey 2022, especially 371–93 on the role of belief in the gods in sacrificial practice.

4. For a useful overview of theories, see Carter 2003; for a thoughtful survey focusing on the ancient Mediterranean, Knust and Várhelyi 2011, 3–18; see also Reed 2014, 115–21, who situates early theories of animal sacrifice in the context of the progressive removal of animal slaughter and meat production from the everyday experience of people in European societies. Criticism of "sacrifice" as a category for analysis: McClymond 2008, 25–34, who proposes a polythetic definition of sacrifice instead of a single defining essence; see further Frankfurter 2011 and, for a survey of recent critiques, Ullucci 2015, 390–99.

in the Graeco-Roman world. As extant texts make clear, ancient Greeks and Romans regularly conceptualized these practices in one or both of two ways: as offerings and, in some cases, as meals shared between superhuman and human participants.[5] The characterization of these practices as offerings both distinguishes them from other ritualized practices that involved the slaughter of animals but were not offerings and at the same time associates them with other types of offerings that did not involve the slaughter of animals. The former include various oath ceremonies, battlefield rituals, and purification practices that existed in both the Greek and the Roman traditions and that are sometimes described as "quasi-sacrifices." These are not my concern in this book, and I do not consider them further.[6] I do, however, need to say more about other types of offerings and the place of animal sacrifice in relation to them.

The ancient Greeks and Romans had an astonishingly rich repertory of practices meant to win the favor of the gods. A reasonably complete enumeration would include, along with animal and vegetal offerings, the dedication of durable objects (statues, altars, and shrines, as well as a virtually limitless range of smaller objects) and various types of verbal and nonverbal performances (processions, songs, dances, athletic competitions, and theatrical performances). Greek and Roman terminology generally distinguished animal and vegetal offerings from these other practices and thus marked them as a more or less discrete category. One important class of vegetal offerings consisted of liquids (especially wine but also milk, oil, honey, and even water), which the worshiper poured out over an altar or simply onto the ground; there existed a specialized set of terms to designate these liquid offerings, conventionally called libations in modern scholarship. Other vegetal offerings included incense, small cakes and other prepared foods, and flowers, often in the form of garlands. Although there were also specialized Greek and Latin nouns to denote animal victims, the two languages did not otherwise make a sharp distinction between animal and vegetal offerings; instead, most of the relevant terminology applied to both types of offerings, suggesting that people regarded them as more or less equivalent in terms of their efficacy in

---

5. E.g., Hes. *Theog.* 535–57; Pl. *Euthyphr.* 14c–e (with Casabona 1966, 129); Cato *Agr.* 131–32, 134.

6. It is worth noting, however, that the process of distinguishing between these quasi-sacrifices and sacrifices that are more obviously offerings is often messy and complex; see, e.g., Georgoudi 2017.

winning the goodwill of the gods. Animal sacrifice, as distinct from vegetal offerings, is thus more a modern than an ancient category.[7]

What, then, is the justification for treating animal sacrifice as a distinct category? There is a long-standing and highly influential scholarly tradition that emphasizes violence as the key factor that distinguishes animal sacrifice from vegetal offerings. To some extent, this seems self-evident; after all, animal sacrifice by definition involves the deliberate slaughter of an animal, and it is reasonable enough to regard slaughter as a form of violence. More recent scholars, however, have offered a cogent critique of this traditional emphasis on violence as the defining feature of animal sacrifice.[8] In this book, I accept this critique and do not regard the act of slaughter as the crucial distinguishing feature of animal sacrifice. Instead, I stress two interrelated features, which I summarize here and analyze in more detail in Chapter 2.

First, animal sacrifice required a significant expenditure of economic resources in a way that vegetal offerings did not. Although the scale of expenditure varied considerably, animal victims on the whole were more expensive than vegetal offerings. The latter must have been vastly more common in practice, even though they are less well attested in our evidence and have received much less attention in modern scholarship. Many people who could not have afforded to slaughter an animal could have afforded to weave a garland of flowers, offer a small cake, or pour out a little wine. Vegetal offerings must accordingly have been standard in most circumstances, whereas animal sacrifice marked special occasions and large-scale events.

Second, unlike vegetal offerings, animal sacrifice typically generated a significant quantity of a valuable consumer good: high-quality meat. There were forms of animal sacrifice in Graeco-Roman tradition in which the entire animal was burned on the altar, a practice that modern scholars conventionally denote by the term "holocaust," derived from an ancient Greek adjective

---

7. Rudhardt 1992 [1958], 213–302, and especially Casabona 1966 provide detailed studies of Greek terminology; I know of no comparable studies of Latin terminology, but see Schultz 2016, especially 69–73. The Greek noun ἱερεῖον was used only of animal victims (Casabona 1966, 28–38), as were the nouns *hostia* and *victima* in Latin; I owe thanks to an anonymous reader for Oxford University Press for pointing this out. In Greek, the largest word group used to designate offerings, that connected with the verb θύω, had a much more extensive range (Casabona 1966, 69–154); cf. *sacrifico* in Latin. On the lack of a significant distinction between vegetal and animal offerings, see further Naiden 2013, especially 70–81, 103, 118–20, 140–41, on the Greek tradition, and Scheid 2019 [2011], 155–62, on the Roman tradition.

8. On violence as the essential characteristic of animal sacrifice, see especially Burkert 1983 [1972] and Girard 1977 [1972]. Critique: e.g., McClymond 2008, 44–64; Schultz 2016, 61–63.

meaning "wholly burned."[9] These, however, were the exception. The norm was a sacrifice in which only a small portion of the animal victim was offered to the divine recipient and burned on the altar, while the rest of the flesh was reserved for human consumption. This is the practice that modern scholars often term "alimentary animal sacrifice." What happened to the meat from such sacrifices varied considerably. It could be eaten on the spot by a smaller or larger group of participants, distributed among them for later consumption, or sold in public markets. In all cases, however, alimentary animal sacrifice produced a valuable commodity in a way that vegetal offerings did not.[10]

As I argue in Part I, these two characteristics combined to endow alimentary animal sacrifice with social and cultural functions that other types of offerings lacked. Another characteristic also played an important role, even though it was not limited to animal sacrifice. In common with other kinds of offerings, animal sacrifice structured relationships among the participants. We can identify three basic roles: the party who offered the sacrifice, the party to whom the sacrifice was offered, and the party on whose behalf the sacrifice was offered. The first and third of these roles could coincide but often did not.

The first of these roles had some distinctive features in Graeco-Roman tradition. In many traditions of animal sacrifice, ordinary worshipers require the mediation of specialized cultic personnel. Henri Hubert and Marcel Mauss incorporated this fact into their general theory of sacrifice by making a distinction between the *sacrifiant*, the person who offers the sacrifice and thus obtains the favor of the gods, and the *sacrificateur*, the person who is needed to perform some or all of the actions and thus officiates.[11] This distinction did not exist in Graeco-Roman tradition. There were, to be sure, various cultic personnel whom we conventionally term "priests" in English and who had a wide range of functions. One function that they did not have, however, was a monopoly on officiating at sacrifices. Instead, virtually anyone was able to officiate at a sacrifice. In many cases, especially when the victim was a larger animal, the person presiding used the services of an expert slaughterer and butcher, termed a *mageiros* in Greek and a *victimarius* in Latin, but this expert was generally of lower social status than the officiant; the reason for his involvement was more practical than ritual, and his role was closer to that of a hired assistant than that of a priest. In this book, I use the term "sacrificant"

---

9. Ekroth 2017.

10. On animal sacrifice and meat production, see Naiden 2013, 232–50; cf. Van Andringa 2007.

11. Hubert and Mauss 1968 [1899], 201–2, 217–18.

to designate the person who presided over the ritual and thus offered the sacrifice.

A sacrificant could offer the sacrifice on behalf of him/herself, of a group that he/she represented, or of some third party. If on behalf of a group, the sacrificant was normally the person in the group with the greatest authority or social prominence, for example, heads of households in domestic contexts and officeholders or benefactors in civic and collegial contexts.[12] In this book, I have a particular although not exclusive concern with public animal sacrifice, in which the political community was the party on whose behalf the sacrifice was offered and a public official served as sacrificant.

## 1c. The Roman Empire

As the title indicates, this book is about animal sacrifice in the Roman Empire. The focus on a specific historical context is crucial to my project. Some of the most influential treatments of animal sacrifice in Graeco-Roman antiquity tend to treat its social function and cultural significance as more or less fixed and unchanging, the expression of deep-seated psychological dispositions or cultural patterns. My own goal is to examine animal sacrifice not as an expression of timeless structures but rather as a practice embedded within a specific historical context, whose function and significance shifted over time in tandem with other economic, social, and cultural changes.[13]

The book's chronological parameters are thus broadly those of the Roman imperial period, from the beginning of Augustus's sole rule in 31 BCE to the death in 395 CE of Theodosius I, the last emperor to rule over both the eastern and the western empire. By that point, the trajectory that I trace had reached its conclusion, although in the short final chapter, I briefly sketch a few later developments. It is more difficult to adhere closely to a precise start date, since it is not always possible to understand developments in the imperial period without some awareness of what happened before. For example, the euergetic

---

12. Although some scholars have argued that women were ritually incapable of presiding over animal sacrifices, others have cogently refuted their arguments: on the Greek side, see Detienne 1979b and, contra, Osborne 1993; on the Roman side, see de Cazanove 1987 and Flemming 2007. Nevertheless, given that women rarely had the greatest authority in a group, in practice they no doubt rarely presided over group sacrifices; see Rives 2013. The intersection of animal sacrifice and gender is one of several important topics that I do not address in this book.

13. Timeless structures: notably Burkert 1983 [1972]; Detienne 2007 [1972]; Detienne 1977, briefly summarized in Detienne 1979a. For another study that highlights the diachronic dimension of animal sacrifice, see Naiden 2013, especially 229–31.

system that prevailed in the Greek cities of the eastern Mediterranean during the imperial period originated in the Hellenistic period, and so in Chapter 3, my analysis begins in the late fourth century BCE. In an even greater departure from the stated chronological limits, Chapter 6 focuses almost entirely on the fifth and fourth centuries BCE, in order to locate in the proper perspective the discourses of animal sacrifice that developed in the imperial period.

These exceptions to my chronological parameters reflect another aspect of the Roman Empire that is important to my project, namely, the fact that, culturally speaking, it was not all Roman. Not only did the empire incorporate a stunningly wide range of peoples with distinctive cultural traditions of their own, but the eastern half of the empire was culturally always more Greek than Roman. Although the elites of the eastern empire gradually acquired Roman citizenship and adopted some distinctively Roman practices, the dominant language and cultural norms remained Greek. Chapter 4 addresses the part played by animal sacrifice in constructing a normative Graeco-Roman culture that at the empire's height allowed for a significant degree of integration across its eastern and western halves.

## 1d. Power

The title of my book identifies its subject; the subtitle signals my analytical framework and particular focus. As I have already noted, most people in the Graeco-Roman world took it for granted that the fundamental purpose of animal sacrifice and other cult offerings was to win the favor of the gods. This fact is crucial to understanding the role of animal sacrifice in Graeco-Roman antiquity, but it is not my focus in this book. My focus is instead on the ways that animal sacrifice functioned to shape and maintain relationships of social power.

Social power, to adopt the definition of sociologist Michael Mann, is "the ability to pursue and attain goals through mastery of one's environment," especially "mastery exercised over other people." Mann further makes a distinction, useful for my project, between authoritative and diffused power. Whereas authoritative power is explicit and direct, involving "definite command and conscious obedience," diffused power "spreads in a more spontaneous, unconscious, decentered way throughout a population, resulting in similar social practices that embody power relations but are not explicitly commanded. It typically comprises, not command and obedience, but an understanding that these practices are natural or moral or result from self-evident common interest." Examples of diffused power include normative economic systems such as capitalism and ideologies such as nationalism.[14] Although I deal with some instances of authoritative power in this book, especially in Chapters 9 and 10, I am for the most part concerned with diffused power.

In the ancient Graeco-Roman world, there were multiple sources of social power and, as a consequence, different types of power relationships that intersected in a range of ways. Since it is not my purpose to analyze these systematically, I here limit myself to a few observations that are important for my specific topic. As in most societies, one crucial source of social power was control over economic resources. In the Graeco-Roman world, the most important of these economic resources was land, which was the essential source of most other economic goods, notably food; although from an early date there were other forms of wealth as well, landownership remained throughout antiquity by far the most important. Ownership of land and other forms of wealth was always unequally distributed, albeit to different degrees at different times and places, with a smaller percentage of the population controlling a larger percentage of the economic resources. Although this unequal distribution existed as far back as the evidence allows us to go, it generally increased under Roman rule, since Roman authorities tended to distrust any form of socioeconomic egalitarianism. Chapters 2 and 3 analyze some of the ways the practice of animal sacrifice was intimately bound up with the particular form that economic power took in the Graeco-Roman world.

Another crucial source of social power was control over physical force, which intersected and often aligned with control over economic resources. The Roman Empire, with respect to both its territorial extension and its increasingly autocratic organization, was largely built on a foundation of military might. Control over physical force was also essential to the system of enslaved labor that played so large a part in Graeco-Roman economy and society. For the issues addressed in this book, however, physical force was generally a less important source of social power; the chief exceptions occur in connection with the enforcement of the imperial directives that I discuss in Chapters 9 and 10, and even in those instances diffused power was often more important.

For my purposes, much more important than control of physical force as a source of social power was ideology. In my analysis, I distinguish between

---

14. Definition of social power: Mann 2012 [1986], 6; authoritative and diffused power: 8. My framework for analyzing social power owes much to Mann, even though it employs only a fraction of his complex and sophisticated model. My interest in the interrelationship of social power and religious institutions was first sparked by Asad 1983, revised as Asad 1993.

two different forms of ideological power, which Mann terms immanent and transcendent.[15] Immanent ideologies involved the propagation and naturalization of preexisting power hierarchies, particularly those based on the unequal distribution of economic resources. Ideologies of this sort reinforced the status quo by making those social relationships appear normal and natural. An example is the system of euergetism discussed in Chapter 3, in which the wealthy inhabitants of Graeco-Roman cities expended their private resources on public benefactions in exchange for superior social standing and greater political power within their community. Another example is the normative Graeco-Roman culture analyzed in Chapter 4, which served to forge an impressive degree of social and ideological coherence among the local elites on whom Roman authorities depended for the successful running of the empire.

Transcendent ideological power, by contrast, was much more autonomous and often functioned not to reinforce preexisting social structures but rather to fashion alternative structures. This form of ideological power was generally based on claims to a true understanding of the world, an understanding that only a privileged few possessed but that, according to its proponents, had significant implications for the way people in general needed to conduct their lives in order to understand and attain their true goals. When those who made such claims were able to persuade others of their truth, they acquired a degree of power over them, since their followers came to believe that a failure to heed them would have dire personal consequences. An ability to persuade others, especially by means of verbal discourse, was thus a crucial element of transcendent ideological power. The discourses surveyed in Part II were all forms of transcendent ideology, even though some social actors were much more effective than others in maximizing their potential for social power. In Part III, I chart the ways the transcendent ideology of the developing Christian tradition intersected with the authoritative power of Roman emperors to generate the cultural transformations of animal sacrifice in the third and fourth centuries CE. These two forms of ideological power, immanent and transcendent, broadly correlated with practice and discourse, the two main forms of communication that I discuss in the following section.

Before leaving the subject of ideological power, I need to say a few words about another term that I occasionally employ: "identity." Although as a category for analysis, "identity" has rightly been criticized for meaning both too much and too little, I generally use it in the limited sense of self-identification,

---

15. Mann 2012 [1986], 23–24.

that is, an explicit or implicit claim on the part of an individual or group of allegiance to or association with a larger-scale institution, tradition, or class.[16] Identity claims of this sort functioned in effect as an ideology, a form of diffused power that served to increase solidarity within sets of social actors and reinforce certain social structures. Although the force of such claims was all the greater when they were backed by a strong emotional commitment on the part of the people who made them, they could be effective even without such a commitment, insofar as they generated social expectations for conformity to certain standards of behavior.

## 1e. Communication

Communication is the second key component of my analytical framework. Although ancient peoples themselves associated animal sacrifice first and foremost with communication between the human and divine spheres, my own interest lies instead in its role within the human sphere. I use the term "communication" in a broad and loose sense, to describe the propagation of diffused power, especially in the form of ideologies. Communication in this sense thus involved not merely the transmission of information but also the process of establishing, shaping, and maintaining structures of social power; how it did this is a topic that I address in Part I. For the purposes of my analysis, I distinguish between two major modes of communication: practice and discourse. Both terms are currently used in such capacious senses that it is equally possible to describe practice as a type of discourse and discourse as a type of practice. It is accordingly important to define how I use them in this book.

For my purposes, practice is a mode of communication that is primarily nonverbal, in contrast to discourse, which is primarily verbal. Each involves its own distinctive dynamic. Practice does its work of communication and construction through its very performance, whereas discourse does so by utilizing the medium of language. Practice is generally flexible and open-ended, so that individuals can often adapt particular practices as needed to fit with a range of identity claims and allegiances. Discourse, by contrast, has the ability to generate much greater precision and specificity; where practice can remain indeterminate and undefined, verbal discourse can specify and define. This not to say that verbal discourse necessarily entails greater precision; some forms of

---

16. For criticism, see Brubaker and Cooper 2000, especially 14–17 on the utility of "identification," as opposed to "identity," as an analytical term that emphasizes agency and process.

verbal discourse rely extensively on ambiguity and allusiveness. Nevertheless, discourse, as a mode of communication, has inherently greater potential than practice to specify, to make distinctions, to formulate questions and provide answers, to promote some interpretations and reject others. For all their differences, practice and discourse are not autonomous but can and often do interact with each other. Practice allows for and even invites discursive interpretations on the part of participants and observers, while discourse can lead to the alteration of established practices or the generation of new ones.[17]

In the Graeco-Roman world, the dynamics of this interaction were closely connected with and largely shaped by the acquisition and exercise of different forms of social power. As I have already noted, there was a broad correlation of practice and discourse with, respectively, immanent and transcendent forms of ideological power. Those with established social power, typically based on control of economic resources and physical force, generally prioritized practice as the favored mode of communication in matters relating to the gods. That is, they endorsed and promoted cults, not doctrines. One reason they could do this was that numerous cult practices, animal sacrifice chief among them, could so readily serve to communicate and construct the types of social relationships and identity claims that established elites favored, notably hierarchies based on wealth and self-identification with normative Graeco-Roman culture. Since animal sacrifice and other cult practices fulfilled this function through their very performance, public authorities could afford to leave ample room for multiple and competing discursive interpretations of these practices, even though these might result in critiques of established practices or attempts to replace them with new ones. Public authorities tended not to interfere with the people who propagated such discourses unless they perceived them as having a negative impact on the community. To describe in deliberately simplistic terms the normal workings of public cult, priests and magistrates regarded it as their job to oversee what people did, and they left it to poets and philosophers to argue about what it meant.

---

17. My use of the term "practice" is loosely informed by what is often labeled "practice theory," briefly surveyed in Bell 1997, 76–83. In practice theory, "ritual is more complex than the mere communication of meanings and values; it is a set of activities that construct particular types of meanings and values in specific ways. Hence, rather than ritual as the vehicle for the *expression* of authority, practice theorists tend to explore how ritual is a vehicle for the *construction* of relationships of authority and submission" (Bell 1997, 82, emphasis in original). My distinction between practice and discourse owes much to Stowers's distinction between the religion of everyday social exchange and the religion of literate culture producers (Stowers 2011b).

By contrast, those who lacked social power sufficient to meet their goals often utilized discourse as an effective strategy for acquiring and augmenting it. This does not mean that such people consciously regarded the discourses that they propagated simply as a means to an end, a mere tool for aggrandizing their own social power. Although that may have been true in some cases, it is likely enough that most of them genuinely believed that whatever they were advocating was valuable and beneficial for their audience. Such people tended to favor discourse over practice as the primary mode of communication in matters relating to the divine world. They worked to persuade others of a particular understanding of the world and of their place within it, an understanding to which they laid a privileged and exclusive claim.[18] This does not mean that they rejected cult practices per se but rather that they located their value not in their performance but in their interpretation. They insisted, for example, that people could grasp the real implications of animal sacrifice only when they had a proper appreciation of its place within a correct understanding of the world. As we will see, some of those who advanced discursive interpretations of animal sacrifice regarded it as an acceptable cult practice and insisted only that people understand it properly; others argued that it was inherently flawed and must be transformed or even abandoned.

## 1f. Cultural Transformation

It may be helpful to begin discussion of the last term in my subtitle by saying something about another term that might be expected to appear in the title but does not. That is "religion." A number of scholars have questioned the assumption that "religion" is a universally applicable category for analyzing human society and have argued in particular that it is an inappropriate and misleading category for analyzing ancient Graeco-Roman culture.[19] This is an argument with which I am largely in agreement. Despite the fact that it has been almost impossible to formulate a satisfactory scholarly definition of religion, the word as it is commonly used in contemporary anglophone societies (and as its cognates are used in other European languages) tends to carry a number of connotations that do not apply at all well to the ancient Graeco-Roman world. For example, many people in contemporary societies take it for

---

18. Wendt 2016, especially 1–73.

19. See especially Nongbri 2013, with the critique of Frankfurter 2015, and Barton and Boyarin 2016.

granted that their practices and beliefs regarding the divine world constitute a distinctive aspect of their public self-identification, which they can label by using an established set of distinctive terms: Christian, Muslim, Hindu, and so forth. That was not the case in the ancient Graeco-Roman world, where such terms were rare and few people separated their practices and beliefs regarding the divine from other aspects of their public self-identification. Similarly, although there existed in that world a few institutions that people primarily identified in terms of practices and beliefs about the divine, along the lines of contemporary churches, mosques, and temples, those were the exception rather than the rule. Instead, people's interactions with the divine world were in most circumstances mediated by the same social and political institutions that dominated other aspects of life: household and kinship groups, voluntary and professional associations, civic institutions, and so forth. A third example: outside Judaean tradition, it is difficult to identify any Greek or Roman texts that fit the commonly accepted notion of "sacred scriptures." This list could be extended further, but I hope that the examples already provided suffice to demonstrate my overall point: many of the connotations of the word "religion" that are widespread in contemporary society are misleading when we are talking about the ancient Graeco-Roman world. I have accordingly downplayed the term, not only in my title but throughout the book, and in its place I have tried to use more precise terms whenever I could do so easily and efficiently. I have not, however, struggled to avoid the word at all costs and have freely used the terms "religion" and "religious" whenever that seemed the most effective option. When I do use them, I generally mean beliefs about perceived superhuman powers as well as any associated practices that people employed to win their assistance and/or goodwill.

By the late fourth century CE, however, the end of the period covered in this book, there existed something much closer to "religion," as the term is commonly used in many contemporary societies. Practices and beliefs regarding perceived superhuman powers had by that point come to constitute a separable aspect of a person's public self-identification, for which there was an extensive set of distinctive labels (some used for labeling both oneself and others, some used only for labeling others): Christian, Judaean, Hellene, pagan, heretic, and so forth. There were highly elaborate institutions, separate from those of secular life, that mediated interactions with the divine world and that claimed something approaching a monopoly on such mediation. There were sacred scriptures, not only in the Christian and Judaean traditions but even in the Hellenic, "pagan" tradition. As a result, I use the terms "religion" and "religious" more frequently in Part III, since it deals with a cultural milieu in which we can more appropriately apply them. It is the dynamics of this transformation, from a culture in which there was no "religion" to one in which there was, that I hope to illuminate through my examination of animal sacrifice. My underlying argument is thus not merely that the social function and cultural significance of animal sacrifice changed during the first four centuries CE but, more important, that they changed because the social and cultural framework that shaped the practice's function and significance also changed.

## 1g. Overview

This book is organized in three main parts, each consisting of two or more chapters and dealing with different aspects of the social and cultural role of animal sacrifice in the Roman Empire. Part I deals with animal sacrifice as a practice and a source of immanent ideological power. As such, it functioned to propagate and reinforce some of the key social structures that enabled the smooth operation of the empire: the socioeconomic hierarchies of Graeco-Roman cities, the normative Graeco-Roman culture that bound together urban elites, and the ideological role of the Roman emperor. Part II takes up the discourses of animal sacrifice that developed from the fifth century BCE to the fourth century CE and the way individuals and groups deployed those discourses as a source of transcendent ideological power. In both these parts, my concern is primarily with animal sacrifice in relation to forms of diffused power. In Part III, by contrast, my concern is primarily with authoritative power, as both Roman authorities and Christian leaders enacted policies on animal sacrifice, policies that in some cases were shaped by the discourses traced in Part II. Each of the three parts opens with a prologue, in which I use a particular text to open up the main issues addressed in that part, and likewise ends with an epilogue, which sums up those issues. The final chapter provides a brief glance at later developments and some retrospective reflections on my overall approach.

One final observation: throughout the book, I stick very closely to the data. In stressing this point, I do not mean to suggest that I am simply "letting the evidence speak for itself." On the contrary, I have sought in this introductory chapter to be as explicit as possible about the analytic framework that I bring to bear on my data. Nevertheless, I consider a data-centered approach crucial to any project focusing on animal sacrifice, since ancient animal sacrifice, as a social practice and a lived experience, must necessarily remain inaccessible; all that we really have are the traces that the practice has left in different contexts and in different media, such as the relief from the altar in Pompeii with which I began. In the end, this is a book not so much about animal sacrifice as about the evidence for animal sacrifice. If I can make an effective case concerning some of the things that we can and cannot learn from that evidence about the changing role of animal sacrifice in the Roman Empire, I will have accomplished my purpose.

# PART I

## *The Practice of Animal Sacrifice in the Roman Empire*

# Prologue

## THE SACRIFICES OF NESTOR
## (*ODYSSEY* 3.5–66 AND 418–72)

In Book 3 of the *Odyssey*, Odysseus's son Telemachus, grown to adulthood, has at the prompting of the goddess Athena set off in search of news about his father, about whom he has had no reliable information for many years. The first of his father's old comrades from the Trojan War whom he visits is Nestor, the ruler of Pylos in the Peloponnese. As Telemachus and his men arrive, "the townsfolk on the shore of the sea were offering sacrifice of black bulls to the dark-haired Earth-shaker [Poseidon]. Nine companies there were, and five hundred men sat in each, and in each they held nine bulls ready for sacrifice."[1] Homer does not pause to describe the sacrifice but fast-forwards to its conclusion, when Telemachus and his companion Mentor, who unbeknownst to him is Athena herself in disguise, disembark from their ship and are invited by Nestor to join the sacrificial feast. When they have eaten their fill, Telemachus asks Nestor what he knows of his father's fate. After a long conversation, Nestor invites the two visitors to be his guests for the night, but the disguised Athena declines, changes into an eagle, and flies away. The astonished Nestor responds to this revelation by promising to sacrifice a heifer to her the following morning. As the day dawns, Nestor gives instructions for the preparation of the sacrifice, at which he himself presides, assisted by his sons. Homer describes this sacrifice in great detail:

> Stratius and noble Echephron led the heifer by the horns, and Aretus came from the chamber, bringing them water for the hands in a basin embossed with flowers, and in the other hand he held barley grains in a basket; and Thrasymedes, steadfast in fight, stood by, holding in

---

1. Hom. *Od.* 3.5–8, in the Loeb translation of A. T. Murray, revised by George E. Dimock.

his hands a sharp axe, to fell the heifer; and Perseus held the bowl for the blood. Then the old man, Nestor, driver of chariots, began the opening rite of hand-washing and sprinkling with barley grains, and earnestly he prayed to Athena cutting off as first offering the hair from the head, and casting it into the fire. Now when they had prayed, and had strewn the barley grains, at once the son of Nestor, Thrasymedes, high of heart, came near and dealt the blow; and the axe cut through the sinews of the neck, and loosened the strength of the heifer, and the women raised the sacred cry, the daughters and the sons' wives and the revered wife of Nestor, Eurydice, the eldest of the daughters of Clymenus. Then the men raised the heifer's head from the broadwayed earth and held it, and Peisistratus, leader of men, cut the throat. And when the black blood had flowed from her and the life had left the bones, at once they cut up the body and straightway cut out the thigh pieces all in due order, and covered them with a double layer of fat, and laid the raw bits upon them. Then the old man burned them on billets of wood, and poured over them sparkling wine, and beside him the young men held in their hands the fivepronged forks. But when the thigh pieces were wholly burned, and they had tasted the inner parts, they cut up the rest and spitted and roasted it, holding the pointed spits in their hands.[2]

The account concludes with Nestor, his household, and his guests sitting down to enjoy the feast.

This passage is not only one of the earliest surviving descriptions of an animal sacrifice from the ancient Greek and Roman world, but it is also one of the most detailed and for that reason has often been used to illustrate archaic Greek sacrificial practice. Of particular importance for our purposes here is the close connection implicit in this account between piety toward the gods, control of economic resources, and the structuring of social hierarchies. An ancient audience would have been well aware that a heifer was a valuable commodity. That Nestor is able to sacrifice it to Athena and then share its meat with his household and guests is as much a demonstration of his wealth as it is of his piety. It is likewise a demonstration of his social status, since in sharing the meat with the others, he is bestowing on them a distinctive benefaction. The same is true of the sacrifice to Poseidon with which the book opens, although that sacrifice is on a much grander scale, as befits its context.

---

2. Hom. *Od.* 3.439–63, Loeb translation.

The nine companies of five hundred men are perhaps meant to represent the military force of Pylos, and Nestor, as their leader, is by implication the one who has provided each company with its nine black bulls for sacrifice. We should note that Nestor presides over these sacrifices not because he has any particular cultic status as a priest but rather in his capacity as the head of the household and the leader of the community.

In all these respects, the sacrifices depicted in *Odyssey* Book 3 are paradigmatic for sacrificial practice down into late antiquity. The connections between wealth, status, and the construction of sociopolitical hierarchies that are so readily observable here are the main focus of Part I. I begin in Chapter 2 by examining the economic dimensions of animal sacrifice. Although stock raising was an integral part of the ancient Mediterranean economy, environmental factors meant that the sorts of large domestic animals that were normally sacrificed were valuable resources that most people in most circumstances did not consume very often. Only the wealthy would have had enough surplus animals that they could afford to sacrifice them with any regularity; likewise, only the wealthy would have been able to sacrifice prestige victims such as the bovines that feature so prominently in the sacrifices of Nestor. Animal sacrifice was thus a practice that, through its very performance, both communicated and reinforced economic and social status. Moreover, because the most common form of animal sacrifice in the Graeco-Roman tradition was alimentary, it also provided an opportunity for articulating the unequal relationship that existed between those with greater and lesser economic resources, since the wealthy had the means to distribute meat of a quality and on a scale beyond what was possible for the majority of people.

The fact that in the Graeco-Roman tradition, those with the resources to sponsor animal sacrifices were also normally the ones who presided over them is the focus of Chapter 3. In the archaic society that the *Odyssey* portrays in an idealized form, the wealthy could employ animal sacrifice in a fairly direct way to transform their control of economic resources into positions of sociopolitical authority. With the development of the Graeco-Roman city-state in the archaic period, the personal relationships apparent in the sacrifices of Nestor became mediated and to some extent obscured by the institutions of the polis. Public cults, through which the community established favorable relations with the divine world, were an essential element of every ancient city, and the offering of animal victims was an essential element of most public cults. Ideally, the community collectively covered the cost of the victims that it offered to its gods. Despite this collectivist ideal, however, there was an ongoing tendency for the wealthy to lay claim to a greater role within the community. By the third century BCE, this tendency had become formalized in the system of unequal exchange that modern scholars conventionally label euergetism, from the Greek word *euergetēs*, "benefactor." In the euergetic system, local elites expended their economic resources on civic benefactions in return for control of public affairs and public recognition of their superior status within the community. In Chapter 3, I analyze the distinctive place of public animal sacrifice in the euergetic system. By giving benefactors a highly visible public role as sacrificants, animal sacrifice allowed them to enact in a particularly vivid form their relationship with their fellow citizens.

The importance of euergetism, however, was not limited to its role in individual cities. Historians have often remarked that at its height, the Romans were able to rule their vast empire with a remarkably small governing apparatus and, except in certain frontier areas, a minimal military presence. What enabled this highly efficient imperial system was the reliance of imperial authorities on the cooperation of local urban elites, who effectively took upon themselves most of the burdens of local administration. The euergetic system, which provided the incentives for local elites to shoulder these burdens, was thus essential to the smooth functioning of the empire. Accordingly, the institution of public animal sacrifice contributed not only to the structuring of local sociopolitical hierarchies but ultimately to the functioning of the Roman Empire as a whole.

In another way as well, animal sacrifice played a role in the structuring of the Roman Empire. The euergetic system, with the sociopolitical hierarchies that it helped construct, was just one element in a larger complex of normative practices and institutions that we may label Graeco-Roman culture. This shared Graeco-Roman culture was not simply a historical given but was rather the product of a gradual and complex process of negotiation between Greek and Roman elites, who ultimately found it to their mutual advantage to emphasize their similarities more than their differences. Animal sacrifice, as a highly charged cult practice common to both the Greek and the Roman traditions, played a distinctive role in this process. Moreover, because some form of ritualized slaughter of animals in honor of the gods was also traditional among virtually all the peoples brought under Roman hegemony, it provided local elites across the empire with a readily available and supple instrument that they could use to negotiate a place for themselves in the empire-wide networks of social power. It is on this aspect of animal sacrifice that I focus in Chapter 4. Since the details vary according to the specific context, I follow a brief general discussion with two contrasting case studies, in which I examine the role of animal sacrifice among Gauls and Judaeans.

The most important shared element in the empire, one of the few things that bound all parts alike to the center, was the figure of the emperor himself. Given the role of animal sacrifice in structuring sociopolitical hierarchies and its distinctive place in the shared Graeco-Roman culture of the imperial elite, it not surprisingly also did important work in creating consensus around the figure of the emperor. As I noted in Section 1b, the practice of animal sacrifice involves three different parties: the one offering the sacrifice, the one to whom the sacrifice is offered, and the one on whose behalf the sacrifice is offered. In Chapter 5, I show how the emperor was able to fill any one of these roles in an animal sacrifice and sometimes filled more than one of them simultaneously. As a result, the practice of animal sacrifice provided a means of defining the emperor's relationship to his subjects that was flexible enough to allow all the various peoples of the empire to participate in ways that were meaningful and acceptable to everyone involved.

One final caveat. It is not my intention to exaggerate the significance of animal sacrifice in the Roman Empire. It was by no means the unique and indispensable linchpin of the imperial system. What I hope to demonstrate instead is that its distinctive features as a social and cultural practice made it an effective instrument for communicating and reinforcing some of the structures and institutions that were central to the effective functioning of the empire and that it did this not through any verbally articulated discourse but through the practice itself. I revert to these themes in the epilogue to this part.

# 2
# The Economics of Animal Sacrifice

## 2a. The Ancient Mediterranean and Its Diet

Like many social practices, Graeco-Roman animal sacrifice was grounded in the physical environment. To state the obvious, animal sacrifice required animals, and animals required expenditure of resources. Since the most important victims in mainstream Graeco-Roman sacrifice were domestic animals, especially sheep, pigs, and bovines, the practice of animal sacrifice in the Graeco-Roman world was closely integrated with the agrarian economy and the practice of animal husbandry.[1] In order to understand the place of animal sacrifice in the Roman Empire, it is accordingly useful to have some sense of the environmental and economic factors that influenced animal production. These varied widely over the vast expanse of the Roman Empire, and I make no attempt to cover the full range of variations. My focus is instead on the chief homelands of Graeco-Roman culture: mainland Greece, the Aegean islands, the Aegean coast of Asia Minor, the Italian peninsula, and Sicily. The environmental conditions of those areas helped determine the cultural values that were encoded in the practice of animal sacrifice, and those values remained encoded in that practice even when it was carried into other areas with different environmental conditions.

The Mediterranean region, as has often been observed, constitutes a very distinctive environment. It is defined most obviously by the Mediterranean Sea itself, which both divides and connects the lands that adjoin it. It is also defined by other features that are less obvious but just as important. The

---

1. My initial inspiration for this chapter was the classic article of Jameson 2014 [1988]. Smaller domestic animals, especially fowl, were also sacrificed (see n. 35 below) but were ideologically less important.

Mediterranean is a region of intense tectonic activity, straddling the contact zone between two continental tectonic plates, the Eurasian and the African, which are moving toward each other at the rate of some two centimeters a year, and encompassing a number of smaller plates (Levantine, Turkish, Aegean, Ionian, and Adriatic).[2] One result is that the terrain surrounding the Mediterranean Sea is typically hilly or mountainous; for example, less than 25 percent of Italy, only 15 percent of Provence, and a mere 11 percent of Spain lie below 300 meters or could be described as plain.[3] Much of the landscape is dominated by evergreen shrubs, and large and well-watered plains, such as the Po Valley in northern Italy, are very much the exception. Contributing to the irregularity of the landscape is the fact that much of the bedrock in the Mediterranean basin consists of limestone. Because limestone is soluble in mildly acidic water, it erodes easily, creating gullies, escarpments, caves, and karst. Territory that lies on limestone bedrock also tends not to support much groundwater, since the cracks and crevices that form in the bedrock allow for subterranean drainage. Combined with the fact that the hilly and fragmented terrain limits catchment areas, this means that large rivers and lakes are rare; the Nile is the only really large river that drains into the Mediterranean, and it receives its water from sources outside the Mediterranean basin. Smaller rivers and streams, pools, and marshlands are common but depend on local rainfall and so, given the easy drainage, fluctuate dramatically not only from season to season but even from year to year.

The Mediterranean climate is characterized by hot, dry summers and mild, wet winters; hence, streams and marshlands that are abundant in winter often dry up in summer. In addition, there can be extreme interannual variation in precipitation, by as much as 500 millimeters in the space of two years.[4] Runs of years that are above or below the mean precipitation are not uncommon, leading to periods of agricultural abundance or shortage. But droughts and the consequent food shortages are not the only sources of insecurity. In addition to the volcanoes and earthquakes that are common in areas of intense tectonic activity, severe floods can occur; the flooding of the Tiber was a problem that occupied Roman authorities for years. Flooding in some cases leads to benefits, since the silt deposited in a flood can produce new and highly fertile agricultural land, but the exploitation of that land always depends on the

---

2. Lewin and Woodward 2009, 294, fig. 10.6(a).

3. Delano Smith 1979, 160.

4. Horden and Purcell 2000, 13.

vagaries of the climate. For all these reasons, the Mediterranean environment is characterized by extreme diversity, fragmentation, and variability, both geographical and temporal; conditions can vary dramatically even over short distances and short spans of time.[5] All these elements of the Mediterranean environment have an impact on food production, especially stock raising.

The staples of the ancient Mediterranean diet were cereals, primarily barley and wheat; olives, especially in the form of oil; and grapes, especially in the form of wine. All three are well suited to the distinctive Mediterranean environment, and together they constituted the "Mediterranean triad." Of these, cereals were by far the most important source of nutrition in antiquity; one detailed study suggests that for most people, cereals may have supplied as much as 70 percent to 75 percent of their caloric needs.[6] Olive oil and wine were the main supplements, along with pulses such as broad beans, peas, chickpeas, and lentils; pulses were a crucial source of nutrients in which cereals are deficient. Beyond that, there were minor supplements such as vegetables, greens, fish, fowl, small game, dairy products, and meat from domesticated animals. The wealthier one was, the more access one had to a variety of foodstuffs, so that the rich would have enjoyed as regular parts of their diet items such as meat that for many people must have been occasional supplements. Nevertheless, there is a consensus among modern scholars that meat, for most people at most times, played a relatively minor part in the diet.[7]

There are two main reasons this should have been the case. First, meat production is an expensive proposition in any agrarian context. The mere process of converting plant calories into animal calories is inherently wasteful; it is much more efficient for people to eat plant products directly than to feed them to animals and then eat the animals. For example, in today's world, it requires almost 120 square meters of land to produce 1,000 kilocalories of beef and almost 117 square meters to produce an equivalent in mutton or lamb; in contrast, it takes less than 1.5 square meters to produce 1,000 kilocalories in wheat or rye. Similarly, to produce 100 grams of protein requires almost

---

5. For a detailed description of the Mediterranean environment, see Woodward 2009; Delano Smith 1979 is more limited but geared to historians; Sallares 2009 provides a succinct overview. Horden and Purcell 2000 put fragmentation and variability at the center of their analysis of Mediterranean history; see especially 77–80, 175–82.

6. Foxhall and Forbes 1982, 74.

7. For a brief overview of diet, see Garnsey 1999, 12–21; see further, with specific reference to preservation and storage, Thurmond 2006 and the detailed surveys in Erdkamp and Holleran 2019. Meat consumption and social class: MacKinnon 2004, 225–26.

185 square meters for sheep and almost 164 for cattle but only 4.6 for grains. Consequently, in any agricultural society where the majority of the people are operating at or not far above subsistence level, as was certainly the case in the ancient Mediterranean, there are inherent pressures on people with limited resources to focus on crops rather than stock raising, while only those with fairly extensive landholdings are able to devote any significant amount of it to animal husbandry. Second, the particular ecological conditions of the Mediterranean generally hinder animal husbandry on a large scale. In many areas, the growing season is short, so that natural pastures tend to dry out, and the usual sorts of fodder run short; water supplies fluctuate dramatically, making irrigation a highly uncertain process. The Roman agricultural writer Columella, for example, says that it is best to feed cattle on the kind of green pasture that is available in well-watered districts but seems to assume that this would be the exception rather than the rule. He has much more to say about various types of fodder, recommending vetch and chickpea in particular, and considers it normal to resort in late summer and early fall to the foliage of trees: elm, ash, and poplar while they last but oak and fig if the others run out.[8]

Yet to conclude that meat production was practiced on only a limited scale would be a gross and ultimately untenable generalization. We must keep in mind that a number of different variables come into play. First, the diversity and variability of the Mediterranean environment mean that some regions are more suited than others to animal husbandry on a middling or even large scale, if never on the scale of the North American middle west or the South American pampas. As Timothy Howe has demonstrated, even within mainland Greece, the conditions for stock raising differed dramatically between Athens and Sparta, Thessaly and Arcadia; consequently, we ought to speak not generically of animal husbandry in the ancient Mediterranean but rather of "systems of animal husbandry as discrete historical and regional entities, differing from each other in significant and observable ways."[9] Moreover, conditions that allowed for animal husbandry on a small scale existed in virtually all parts of the Mediterranean world, so that domestic animals must

---

8. Land requirements for meat and grain: Ritchie 2021; note that these figures assume modern rather than ancient species and so cannot be applied directly to the ancient world. Columella *Rust.* 6.3.2–8; the practice of feeding tree foliage to both cows and sheep is likewise mentioned by the elder Cato (*Agr.* 6.3, 30, 54) and Varro (*Rust.* 1.15).

9. Howe 2008, 50; see in general 49–75.

almost always have been a normal part of the landscape.[10] Second, the different categories of edible domestic animals had very different needs. Fowl and small mammals such as rabbits, which were an important source of meat for those with less resources, could be raised even in an urban setting. Even the three major groups of larger species (cattle, sheep/goats, and pigs) had significantly different requirements for their production and offered significantly different benefits to their producers. Third, the goals and priorities of producers at different economic levels must have varied significantly. The two last points warrant more detailed consideration.

## 2b. *The Major Groups of Edible Domestic Animals*

Cattle require fertile and well-watered plains of a sort that, as we have seen, is relatively uncommon in the Mediterranean basin; such land as was suitable for pasture or for the kinds of fodder that cattle required was often equally well suited for raising cereals or other crops for human consumption. In most contexts, then, cattle were in direct competition with humans for relatively scarce resources, and it is hardly surprising that cattle usually lost out. Only large landowners could afford to raise cattle on any significant scale, so that possession of a herd of cattle was throughout Graeco-Roman antiquity a sign of elite status. At the same time, cattle provided some important and even unique benefits. When slaughtered, an adult cow yields significantly more meat than an adult sheep or pig; its hide is also an important source of leather, a crucial commodity that had a wide range of uses in antiquity. Yet cattle were an even more valuable resource while alive. Many people today are apt to think first and foremost of their milk, the source of a wide range of dairy products (cream, butter, cheese) that figure largely in European cuisines. But the peoples of the ancient Mediterranean did not drink much fresh milk and preferred sheep's or goat's milk for their soured-milk products and cheeses.[11] For them, cattle would instead have been important primarily for their labor. Lacking the technology that allowed them to exploit other sources of power on a significant scale, people relied to a large extent on muscle power for their

---

10. On the practicalities of animal husbandry in Mediterranean antiquity, see White 1970, 199–223, 272–327, who relies largely on the Roman agricultural writers, and Isager and Skydsgaard 1992, 83–107, who draw on Aristotle. For a recent assessment that stresses the sophistication of ancient animal husbandry, see Kron 2014.

11. See Arist. *Hist. an.* 522a.25–30 and Varr. *Rust.* 2.11.1–3; Columella (*Rust.* 7.2.1–2, 7.3.13, 7.8) repeatedly associates dairy products with sheep and goats, never with cattle. On the dairy products of sheep, see Frayn 1982, 127–41; more generally, see Thurmond 2006, 189–207.

energy needs, and cattle, particularly oxen (that is, castrated adult males), were the animals of choice for big jobs such as plowing and pulling heavy carts.[12] Agricultural writers from Hesiod onward clearly regarded them as standard and essential equipment in a well-stocked farm.[13]

How many farmers would have been able to maintain an ox or two is another question. Not all farmers would have owned farms large enough to support an ox, and even those who did might have found various alternatives more attractive. Working the land by hand with a hoe or a spade is more labor-intensive than plowing but also tends to increase productivity and can better utilize the available human labor pool. Donkeys and mules, whose dietary requirements are less demanding than those of oxen, provided a cheaper alternative for plowing and were no doubt widely used, especially where soils were more easily worked. There were also options available to farmers who wanted to employ oxen for plowing without the expense of maintaining them themselves. Some small farmers would have been tenants, who might have had access to oxen as part of their tenancy agreement; others might have preferred to rent oxen as needed rather than maintain them themselves year-round. Some neighbors might have pooled their resources to support a yoke of oxen between them; the Roman legal writer Ulpian can imagine a scenario in which two neighbors own one ox each, which they take turns using as a team. Although it is impossible to quantify, it is likely that on a small scale, cattle must have been relatively common.[14]

The second main category of edible domestic animals consisted of sheep and goats. Although sheep thrive on the same sorts of pasture and fodder as cattle, they can also be maintained on drier pasture, a great advantage in the context of the Mediterranean. In addition, they can feed on the vegetation that comes up after the first plowing of a field, as recommended by Columella, or on the stubble left over after harvest, as recommended by

---

12. Although horses are stronger than oxen, they seem rarely to have been used in the Graeco-Roman world for labor, being reserved instead for prestige activities such as chariot racing and equestrian combat. Donkeys and mules, by contrast, were in great demand as beasts of burden.

13. Hes. *Op.* 405. Columella, for example, devotes the better part of a book to a discussion of cattle (*Rust.* 6) but is clearly thinking of oxen as labor animals; hence, he has a long section on breaking them in (*Rust.* 6.2) as well as one on castration (*Rust.* 6.26) and separate sections on bulls and heifers, whose main purpose is obviously breeding (*Rust.* 6.20–24).

14. On all these issues, see MacKinnon 2004, 95–96. Hand cultivation: Hodkinson 1988, 39–40. Asses: Varro *Rust.* 1.20.4–5; Columella *Rust.* 7.1.2; Plin. *Nat.* 8.167. Tenancy agreements: Foxhall 1990, 107, 112. Ulpian: *Dig.* 19.5.17.3. MacKinnon 2004, 90–91, notes that cattle remains make up about 10 percent of mammalian remains from excavated rural sites in Italy.

Varro. Goats prefer leaves and shrubbery and can be grazed even in scrubland. Being smaller and, especially in the case of goats, more sure-footed than cattle, they can be grazed on hillier terrain, another advantage in many parts of the Mediterranean. Moreover, while alive, they are more productive than cattle. Although of virtually no use as a source of labor, they do supply milk, which, as noted above, was generally preferred to cow's milk. They were also valued for their manure, a crucial product in a world without artificial fertilizers; as with milk, sheep and goat manure was generally preferred to that of cattle.[15] The elder Cato includes 100 sheep among the standard equipment for an olive farm of 240 *iugera* (about 60 hectares), as well as three donkeys for carrying manure. Sheep were important above all for their wool. Sheep's wool was by far the largest source of textiles in the Graeco-Roman world, with linen a fairly distant second; sheep raising would thus have been attractive both to those at the subsistence level, who were trying to meet their needs from limited resources, and to the well-off, for whom wool could be a good source of income.[16] For all these reasons, small flocks of sheep and goats must have been ubiquitous throughout the Roman world, and even large-scale production would have been relatively common. It is also worth noting that sheep and goats have an advantage over cattle in terms of fertility, so that a larger number can be slaughtered without threatening the integrity of the herd. Columella, for example, recommends that the managers of estates close to towns sell lambs to butchers, keeping only one in five for the maintenance of the herd.[17]

Lastly, there are pigs. Pigs are unique among the domesticated animals of the ancient Mediterranean in that they are of virtually no use while they are alive: they cannot be used as a source of labor and provide neither milk nor wool. Even their manure was poorly regarded; Columella considered it the "worst of all." It is only when they are slaughtered that their value is realized, in the form of their hides, bristles, fat, and especially meat. Hence, in the Graeco-Roman world, pigs, and pigs alone, were raised primarily for

---

15. Feeding sheep: Columella *Rust.* 7.3.20–22; Varro *Rust.* 2.2.12. Grazing goats: Varro *Rust.* 2.1.16, 2.3.6–7. Manure: Varro *Rust.* 1.38.2–3; Columella *Rust.* 2.14.4; see further White 1970, 125–35.

16. Cato *Agr.* 10.1. Varro notes that sheep provide a profit from their wool as used for clothing (*Rust.* 2.11.22); Pliny (*Nat.* 8.190–97) has a discussion of wools that leads very naturally into a survey of textiles, indicating the close association of the two in his mind.

17. Columella *Rust.* 7.3.13. On sheep production in Italy, see in general MacKinnon 2004, 120–33.

their meat, a fact widely acknowledged: "what, indeed, does a pig offer except food?" asks Cicero. According to a saying of Aesop, pigs squeal whenever anyone touches them, because, since they produce only meat, they know how they become profitable to others and consequently expect to be slaughtered.[18] As a source of meat, however, pigs present some unique advantages. Unlike cattle, sheep, and even goats, pigs are true omnivores, readily eating both plant and animal produce. Their snouts and tusks allow them to root effectively, and in the wild, their typical habitat is the forest, where they forage for roots, nuts, fruits, insects, and worms. In the countryside, accordingly, pig keeping allowed people to exploit areas such as woodlands that in terms of productivity were otherwise useless; Columella points out that pigs can feed in any type of country, mountain or plain, although woodlands provide the best grazing. More important, pigs can also be fed on waste from garden, kitchen, and table. People accordingly did not need access to extensive land in order to raise pigs but could keep them in a fairly small area in close proximity to human habitations; indeed, Aristotle describes pigs, along with dogs, as "animals that live with humans."[19] Pigs are also extremely fertile. Sows reach sexual maturity before the age of one year, have a gestation period of something less than four months, and can produce litters of eight or more piglets once or twice a year. Consequently, pigs constitute a very efficient means of transforming waste products into high-quality food; Cicero proposed that "nature has produced nothing more fertile than pigs, because they are suited to human consumption." Suckling pigs, in particular, were regarded as a great delicacy, and Columella recommends selling them as a way to encourage the sow to bear another litter more quickly; piglets must have been regularly culled. Given these advantages, it is not surprising that Varro could ask, "who of our people tends a farm without keeping pigs?"[20]

In sum, the different sorts of domestic animals had very different requirements in terms of their production and also offered a wide variety of benefits to their producers. Cattle were important enough as a source of labor

---

18. Columella *Rust.* 2.14.4; Cicero *Nat. D.* 2.160; Aesop, Ael. *VH* 10.5; cf. Clem. Al. *Strom.* 7.6.33.3.

19. Columella *Rust.* 7.9.6; Aristotle *Hist. an.* 542a27–29. Pigs do require fairly abundant water, however, not only for drinking but also for wallowing, which is crucial for their regulation of body heat; hence, they tended to be less common in the drier parts of the Mediterranean to the south and east.

20. Cicero *Nat. D.* 2.160; Columella *Rust.* 7.9.4; Varro *Rust.* 2.4.3. On pig production in Italy, see in general MacKinnon 2004, 153–59.

that most farmers who could afford it would have been willing to devote the necessary resources to maintaining an ox or two, and the demand for oxen would obviously have encouraged the local raising of cattle. Nevertheless, cattle production on anything more than a very small scale would generally have been beyond the means of all but the wealthy. Sheep and goats provided valuable resources while alive, in the form of milk, manure, and especially wool; they also allowed for the maximum exploitation of otherwise nonproductive land. Pigs could similarly be used to exploit marginal land and were even more valuable as an efficient way of transforming garbage into food. Because they were less demanding in terms of resources, we would expect that in most areas, the raising of sheep, goats, and pigs was more widespread than that of cattle.[21]

## 2c. *Peasant and Elite Production*

These differences in the production of larger domestic animals need to be kept in mind when we consider the different goals and priorities of producers at different economic levels. Peasant farmers would have been concerned first of all with meeting their own immediate subsistence needs and secondly with generating small surpluses that could be stored, traded, sold, or used to meet other obligations (such as demonstrating piety toward the gods). For these farmers, animal husbandry on a small scale would have constituted a valuable option, since domestic animals would have provided important options to people facing what Peregrine Horden and Nicholas Purcell describe as the "ineluctable triple imperative" of survival in an environment as fragmented and variable as that of the Mediterranean: diversification, storage, and redistribution.[22] Animal husbandry allowed not only for a more thorough exploitation of resources but also for a greater diversification of resources and consequently for a reduction of risk; for example, a period of unusually low precipitation that could prove ruinous for crops might have relatively little impact on animals. Animals also constituted a highly effective form of food storage. In a culture that had relatively few techniques for preserving foodstuffs, an animal was an excellent way to maintain a food supply that would not spoil, at least as

---

21. This is a very broad generalization. Patterns of meat production and consumption, which were affected as much by social and cultural concerns as by environmental and economic factors, varied significantly across different regions of the empire; see King 1999.

22. Horden and Purcell 2000, 178.

long as it remained alive.[23] Lastly, the various benefits that animals provided, whether labor, manure, leather, wool, milk, or meat, meant that animals and their products could be readily exchanged in a redistribution system, either as items of barter or as commodities in a market. For all these reasons, we can reasonably expect that animal husbandry on a small scale was omnipresent. As Horden and Purcell have argued, "animal husbandry lies at the heart of the Mediterranean agrosystem."[24]

Elite agricultural production, in contrast, involved a very different set of concerns. Members of the elite were primarily concerned with exploiting their economic resources in order to maintain their social status.[25] To some extent, stock raising in and of itself could serve as a means to this end. Horse breeding provides a particularly clear example. Horses, to a greater degree even than cattle, require rich and extensive pastureland or high-quality fodder; to raise horses successfully, especially in most areas of the ancient Mediterranean, was proof that one could command the resources required to do so and thus a public demonstration of one's wealth. It is thus not surprising that activities centered on horses were accorded high levels of prestige: in the Greek world, we might think of the value placed on chariot racing in the Panhellenic games; in Rome, there is the fact that the highest traditional census category was that of *eques*, literally, "horse-man."

What was true of horses was true of other livestock as well, especially cattle but also sheep and even pigs, if raised in suitably large numbers. The swineherd Eumaeus, for example, boasts that his master Odysseus has twelve herds each of cattle, sheep, pigs, and goats on the mainland, as well as additional goats and pigs on Ithaca itself. To some extent, this method of calculating wealth no

---

23. Note the well-known saying attributed variously to Chrysippus (Cic. *Nat. D*. 2.160; Porph. *Abst*. 3.20.1) and Cleanthes (Clem. Al. *Strom*. 7.6.33.3) that pigs were given a soul in place of salt, simply as a means of preserving their meat (cf. Cic. *Fin*. 5.13; Varro *Rust*. 2.4.10; Plin. *Nat*. 8.207; Plut. *Quaest. conv*. 5.10.3, 685C). The peoples of the Roman world also had a range of techniques for preserving meat, especially pork; see Thurmond 2006, 209–22.

24. Horden and Purcell 2000, 200. This is a strong statement of what is often described as the agropastoralist position, the argument that in the ancient Mediterranean, animal husbandry and agricultural production were closely integrated. Earlier scholars argued that environmental conditions were such that stock raising depended on seasonal transhumance, which effectively divorced it from agriculture. Although the debate on agropastoralism versus transhumance is not fully settled, advocates of the former are now in a clear majority; see Howe 2008, 13–25, for a useful summary of the debate.

25. See especially Finley 1985, 35–61. Although Finley's overall interpretation of the ancient economy has been the subject of much debate, his views on the social motivations of the elite have never been seriously challenged.

doubt reflects the particular conditions of the archaic period,[26] but it retained its significance in later periods as well. The freedman C. Caecilius Isidorus, who for generations remained famous for his wealth, was said to have left on his death in 8 BCE an estate that comprised 4,116 slaves, 3,600 yoke of oxen, and 257,000 other herd animals, as well as 60 million sesterces in cash. In terms of demonstrating social status, extensive herds were in some ways even more useful than hard cash. Throughout antiquity, land remained the most respectable—and to a large extent the only respectable—form of wealth; as much as the elite might actually be involved in trade and manufacturing, their self-image was predominantly that of landowners. In this context, the number of animals people owned was a reliable indicator of the amount and quality of land they owned and thus constituted a claim to respectability that a mere abundance of cash could not provide. For all these reasons, the raising of large animals such as horses or cattle and the raising of other herd animals in large numbers could in itself serve to establish or maintain the elite status of the producer.[27]

In more strictly economic terms, stock raising could also effectively fill the need for a cash crop. Elite landowners had to realize a sizable and reliable profit in order to maintain their status, and that entailed a concentration of resources on products for which there was a ready market. The cash crops for which we have most evidence were grapes and olives; the profits from cereal cultivation were normally lower and more uncertain. That stock raising could also be regarded as a good investment is suggested by a well-known anecdote about the elder Cato. When asked about the most profitable type of agricultural investment, he is supposed to have responded "good grazing"; when asked what was next, he responded "reasonably good grazing"; when asked what was third, he responded "poor grazing" and allowed cereal cultivation only fourth place. Although the anecdote may lack any historical basis, it is in any case a useful index of attitudes at the time when it was in circulation.[28]

---

26. Hom. *Od.* 14.96–104. That herd animals signified wealth in archaic Rome is indicated by the fact that *pecunia*, the Latin word for "money," derives from *pecus*, "cattle," a fact noted by the Romans themselves: Varro *Ling.* 5.95; cf. Varro *Rust.* 2.1.11; Columella *Rust.* 6.*praef*.4.

27. Caecilius Isidorus: Plin. *Nat.* 33.135. On the social importance of the ownership of land, see especially de Ste. Croix 1981, 120–33. On "animals as gentlemanly wealth" in archaic and classical Greece, see Howe 2008, 27–47, and, on competitive displays involving animals, 99–123; see also the concise summary of this argument in Howe 2014.

28. Cic. *Off.* 2.89; Columella *Rust.* 6.*praef*.45; Plin. *Nat.* 18.29. On animals as a cash crop for the wealthy, see Howe 2014, 144–50, who emphasizes in particular the market for sacrificial victims, especially in the Greek world.

## 2d. Conclusion: Animal Sacrifice in the Ancient Mediterranean Context

These, then, are some of the key environmental, economic, and social factors that affected the production of animals in the ancient Mediterranean. Keeping these factors in mind, we may consider in more detail the two features of alimentary animal sacrifice that distinguish it from other types of offerings. One is the expenditure of economic resources. As we have seen, only the wealthy would have regularly engaged in stock raising on a scale large enough to produce a surplus of animals available for slaughter or would have had the financial resources to purchase sacrificial victims on a regular basis. The vast majority of people would normally have expressed their piety to the gods through vegetal offerings and would have offered an animal sacrifice only on important occasions, if ever. Animal sacrifice, accordingly, was a practice that not only demonstrated one's piety to the gods but also helped define one's economic and social status. The emphasis on animal sacrifice that is so familiar from ancient art and literature is thus not so much a reflection of actual practice as an expression of elite ideology, privileging a kind of offering that only the wealthy could afford on a regular basis.

In addition, different types of sacrificial victims commanded greater or lesser prestige, which was generally in a clear inverse correlation with their availability and cost.[29] Given the recurring need to cull the young of sheep and especially pigs, lambs and piglets were more readily available and thus more affordable sacrificial victims; fully grown adults, by contrast, were more expensive and hence more prestigious. Likewise, the greater resources required to raise bovines rendered them more prestigious victims. For similar reasons, uncastrated male animals were much less common and thus more prestigious than castrated victims. Most male sheep would have been castrated when they were young, since wethers not only are easier to manage than rams but provide more and better wool and tastier meat. Likewise, most male bovines would have been castrated in order to make them more tractable as plow or draft animals; uncastrated adult males would have been kept only for purposes of breeding, an activity that must to a large extent have been

---

[29]. Our clearest evidence comes from the inscribed festival calendars of classical Athens, which specify the victims for the different public sacrifices and often include prices. Full-grown cattle cost between 40 and 90 drachmas, pigs between 20 and 40, sheep and goats between 10 and 17. Young animals are cheaper: calves cost 25, lambs between 4 and 7 depending on age, piglets only 3 (Van Straten 1995, 171–78). See further Hermary et al. 2004, 101–3.

confined to the economic elite.[30] There was accordingly a hierarchy of victims in terms of prestige, with piglets at the bottom, adult sheep in the middle, and bulls, uncastrated adult male bovines, at the very top, as what the elder Pliny called "the choicest victims and the most sumptuous appeasement of the gods." The fact that bulls, and cattle more generally, regularly appear as sacrificial victims in literature and art is thus another reflection not of actual practice but of elite values.[31]

In another way as well, animal sacrifice was geared toward the wealthy. We know from a variety of sources that animals offered to the gods were supposed to be unblemished and in perfect condition; in some cases, they also had to meet particular requirements as to species, sex, color, and fertility (for example, uncastrated males or pregnant females).[32] There were, moreover, traditions that working cattle, which would have been the only type available to most people, were specifically excluded from sacrifice. It was much easier to fulfill such conditions if one could draw on a large pool of animals and even set aside certain animals from an early age as potential sacrificial victims. Poorer people would not have been consistently able to meet these conditions and probably sacrificed or at least slaughtered and ate old, sick, and lame farm animals.[33] In public contexts and among the elite, however, the observance of such rules seems to have received great stress and been regarded as an important index of piety. For all these reasons, then, animal sacrifice, as an expression of piety toward the gods, was a social practice that was inherently geared toward the wealthy and served in many ways to mark elite status.

The other distinctive feature of animal sacrifice is its alimentary dimension. Given the relative infrequency of holocausts, there was a high rate of correlation between the practice of animal sacrifice and the production of edible meat. Exactly how high the rate of correlation was has been a topic of considerable debate, especially in the last decade or so. There was for a time a

---

30. On castration, see especially Ekroth 2014b.

31. Plin. *Nat.* 8.183. As Van Straten has argued, cattle are the most common victims in scenes of animal sacrifice from classical Attic vases not because they were the most common victims but because the artists deliberately emphasized more costly sacrifices as having more appeal to potential purchasers (Van Straten 1995, 170–81, especially 179). See further McInerney 2010 for a wide-ranging discussion of the cultural importance of cattle from the Bronze Age to the fourth century BCE. On the prestige of bulls over other bovines, see Ekroth 2014b, 159–63.

32. See in general Ziehen 1939, 592–97, and Hermary et al. 2004, 97–101, on the Greek tradition; Wissowa 1912, 412–16, and Huet et al. 2004, 199–201, on the Roman tradition. On pregnant victims, see Bremmer 2005.

33. See Rosivach 1994, 161–63; cf. Jameson 2014 [1988], 198–99.

tendency to assume a very high rate indeed; Marcel Detienne went so far as to declare that in ancient Greece, "l'alimentation carnée coïncide absolument avec la pratique sacrificielle."[34] Many scholars now reject such an extreme position. In most contexts, a considerable amount of edible meat must have been available that did not come from sacrifices. For one thing, most people had access to a wide range of animals, both wild and farmed, that did not typically serve as sacrificial victims, including fowl, fish, shellfish, game, and small mammals. For the wealthy, such foodstuffs often had a notable place in luxury dining, while the poor would undoubtedly have taken advantage of whatever sources of nutrition were available to them.[35] Even meat from animals that typically did serve as victims may not always have come from animals that had actually been sacrificed, although this is much debated. It also depends to some extent on what we mean by "actually sacrificed." Some scholars have argued that the slaughtering of animals always involved some minimal acknowledgment of the divine, such as was apparently common in many aspects of Greek and Roman life, so that the slaughtering of domesticated animals was roughly analogous to the production of kosher or halal meat today.[36]

Yet the extent to which this was true is not of much importance for my analysis here. It is clear that when people did sacrifice animals, they usually ended up with a great deal of edible meat. If we assume a portion of meat equivalent to that in a Big Mac, which we may take as a standard serving size in much of the contemporary world, and using even a low estimate of the size of domestic animals in antiquity, an adult sheep would have produced enough meat for 100 portions, a pig 110, and a cow 675.[37] Moreover, given

---

34. Detienne 1979a, 10. For the Roman world, compare the similar but more limited conclusion of John Scheid (e.g., 2007, 26: "à Rome, le bétail était en fait toujours sacrifié").

35. See in general Ekroth 2007 and Parker 2010. Chickens and to a lesser extent geese were sacrificed with some frequency (see most recently Villing 2017), no doubt in part because they were less expensive than other victims, as the women in Herodas's mime explain apologetically to Asklepios (Herod. 4.14–17). Fish were also sacrificed (Carboni 2016) but only exceptionally, whereas they were commonly eaten. Game animals, both large and small, must have been eaten with some regularity but again appear only exceptionally as sacrificial victims (see, e.g., Larsen 2017). Small mammals were regularly eaten (see Varro *Rust*. 3.12–15 for suburban estates that produced rabbits and dormice for the Roman market) but to my knowledge never sacrificed.

36. On meat from non-sacrificed animals, see Naiden 2013, 232–50. For the comparison with kosher or halal meat, see Ekroth 2014a, 343–44 (contra, Naiden 2013, 274). This is more or less Scheid's position; see, e.g., Scheid 2005, 250–54, and Scheid 2007, 24–26.

37. I am assuming that a Big Mac contains two patties of about 1.6 ounces or 45 grams each; see    https://www.today.com/food/how-choose-healthy-fast-food-burgers-mcdonald-s-bur

expectations about the sorts of victims that were most acceptable to the divine recipients, we can expect that the meat produced by formal, full-dress sacrifices was generally of a higher quality than would normally have been available to most people.[38] For all these reasons, those who could afford to sacrifice an animal were ipso facto in a position to bestow a significant benefaction on others. The circumstances in which and the reasons for which they might choose to do so is the subject of Chapter 3.

---

ger-king-t127754 for the former and https://www.mcdonalds.com/gb/en-gb/help/faq/whats-the-average-weight-in-grams-of-a-big-mac.html for the latter (McDonald's does not specify the weight on its US website). I have used the calculations of the amount of meat available from ancient domestic animals that are made by Naiden 2013, 252–53, 258–59.

38. McDonough 2004 makes a case that sacrificial meat was sold at higher prices than meat from unsacrificed animals because it was of a higher quality. See further Ekroth 2007, 270–71, with additional references.

# 3
# Animal Sacrifice and Euergetism in the Roman Empire

## 3a. Introduction

We saw in Chapter 2 that given the environmental, economic, and social factors that affected the production of animals in the ancient Mediterranean, animal sacrifice was a way of expressing piety to the gods that could simultaneously serve to mark elite status. Furthermore, the fact that most animal sacrifices were alimentary, in which the bulk of the sacrificed animal was reserved for human consumption, meant that those who offered an animal sacrifice generated a significant quantity of a valuable consumer good: high-quality meat. These two features, combined with the fact that in the Graeco-Roman tradition, animal sacrifice did not require the mediation of a cult specialist but allowed people to preside over their own offerings, meant that alimentary animal sacrifice could function as a particularly efficient instrument for structuring sociopolitical hierarchies. Through participation in a traditional practice that served to win the favor of the gods for their community, the wealthy were able to transform their economic control of animal resources into a position of sociopolitical authority. This is an important aspect of animal sacrifice in the Greek tradition that is attested from the beginning of the literary record, as we saw, for example, in the sacrifices over which Nestor presides in Book 3 of the *Odyssey*. Nevertheless, I would argue that it took on new force in the Hellenistic and Roman periods, when public animal sacrifice came to be integrated into the system of unequal exchange that modern scholars label euergetism. In this chapter, I argue that although these benefactions took a wide variety of forms, public animal sacrifice provided a particularly potent context in which benefactors enacted their relationship with their community.

## 3b. Euergetism in the Graeco-Roman World

The phenomenon of euergetism has been a focus of scholarly interest for several decades.[1] Although initially seen as a development of the Hellenistic period, Marc Domingo Gygax has more recently made a strong case that it originated in the archaic Greek practice of *xenia*, institutionalized friendship between elite citizens of different poleis that was marked by the formalized exchange of gifts. These foreign "friends" gradually developed into benefactors of entire communities, for which they were awarded public honors. During the classical period, citizens began to benefit their own communities in similar ways and accordingly receive similar honors. Therefore, scholars now commonly analyze euergetism as a form of gift exchange, in which wealthy members of the community bestowed benefits on their fellow citizens in exchange for public honors and recognition of their superior status. This exchange in turn served to legitimate the control that the wealthy members of the community came to exercise over public affairs during the late Hellenistic and imperial periods, which saw an increasing concentration of economic resources and political power in the hands of a small number of citizens. It was only under the economic and social strains of the third century CE that this euergetic system gradually began to break down.[2]

Inscriptions constitute by far the most important type of evidence for euergetic practice, and most studies of euergetism rely on them almost exclusively. Given their importance, it is useful to be aware from the start that Greek and Latin inscriptions recording the gifts of benefactors display some significant differences. Those from the Greek-speaking eastern provinces are often lavishly detailed, describing at sometimes considerable length the exact nature of the benefaction and the actions of the parties involved. They also elaborate

---

1. The study of euergetism was initiated by Veyne 1976, translated in abridged form as Veyne 1990; for a thoughtful assessment, see Garnsey 1991. Important later studies include Gauthier 1985; Quass 1993; Zuiderhoek 2009; Domingo Gygax 2016. It is important to note that most major studies of euergetism have focused on the Greek world; of those cited here, Veyne is the only one to include discussion of Rome, and he is insistent that Roman republican practice differed fundamentally from the euergetism of the Greek tradition. For a brief general discussion of euergetism in the Roman Empire that focuses on the west, see Eck 1997.

2. On gift exchange, see Domingo Gygax 2016, especially 12–57, 251–58. On euergetism as legitimation, see Zuiderhoek 2009, especially 113–53, and on its decline, 154–59.

in great detail on the moral qualities involved, highlighting the benefactor's *philotimia*, "love of honor"; *philodoxia*, "love of renown"; and *megalophrosynē* or *megalopsychia*, "magnanimity."[3] Those from the Latin-speaking western provinces are generally more laconic about these topics but at the same time are generally more explicit about the financial and legal aspects of the benefaction, often including specific sums and indicating the context in which the gift was made; consequently, many of the technical terms that scholars use to describe the institutional framework of euergetism are Latin.[4] As we will see, it is not always easy to distinguish the extent to which these differences in epigraphic convention reflect differences in practice or merely in presentation.

We can distinguish a range of contexts in which members of local elites expended their resources on their fellow citizens. Not surprisingly, given the role of euergetism in legitimating their control of public affairs, many of these were directly related to the holding of public office. In the most direct and no doubt earliest form of benefaction, officeholders undertook to pay the expenses of the public amenities for which they were responsible out of their own private resources. Over time, it seems, such contributions came to be expected, so that what had begun as voluntary largesse on the part of the elite became in practice obligatory. In the Greek cities of the eastern provinces, the assumption of the expenses of an office, whether voluntary or obligatory, continued to be one of the most common forms of euergetism.[5] In the western empire, obligatory financial contributions began early on to take the form of set fees for the holding of the different municipal offices. This kind of fee is well documented in Latin inscriptions, where it is often termed a *summa honoraria*, "payment for honor/office" (the Latin word *honor* carries both meanings). It seems likely that it originated as a contribution made by officials toward the expense of public festivals for which they were responsible, a practice that was established in republican Rome and was eventually imported into Roman colonies. In time, the payment of a *summa honoraria* was apparently extended to most magistracies and priesthoods, and over the course of the second century CE, it seems to have become required even for membership in local city councils.[6] It is also worth noting that in Roman law, quite

---

3. Zuiderhoek 2009, 122–33.

4. See, e.g., the lists of inscriptions in Duncan-Jones 1982, especially 102–10 for North Africa and 171–209 for Italy.

5. See the detailed discussion of Quass 1993, 275–328, with many examples.

6. Garnsey 1971a; see also Briand-Ponsart 1999 for North Africa. Although Greek inscriptions lack an equivalent term, they do record payment *anti*, "in exchange for," or *huper*, "on behalf

apart from the issue of entrance fees, the members of local city councils, the decurions, constituted a distinct order, with defined privileges and membership requirements, including a minimum property qualification. Although this technically applied only to cities with the juridical status of a Roman *colonia* or *municipium*, the same principle must have existed, if only on an ad hoc basis, in most cities. Those who held public office were thus by definition members of the local economic elite.[7]

As the payment of entry fees and the financial contributions of officeholders became standard, those who wished to establish a reputation for real munificence had to supplement them with some further benefaction. There is abundant epigraphic evidence in the Latin west for gifts made *ob honorem*, "on account of the honor/office." Although some of these may represent *summae honorariae*, it is likely that most do not. Some holders of public office chose not to make a gift at the time of their appointment but instead made a pledge to fund a particular benefaction in the future, indicated in Latin inscriptions by the verb *polliceri*, "promise." Although these pledges, conventionally described as *pollicitationes*, were in theory voluntarily undertaken, in the early second century CE, they became legally binding under Roman law, so that a man's heirs could be obliged to fulfil his *pollicitatio* if he had failed to do so. Lastly, wealthy members of a community could also present their fellow citizens with benefactions completely unconnected with the holding of public office.[8]

Elite benefactions took a wide range of forms. Perhaps the most popular, in both the eastern and the western empire, was funding the construction of a new public building or monument or, less ambitiously, the repair, improvement, or adornment of a preexisting structure. Also popular was sponsoring a distribution of cash or some other good, known in Latin as *sportulae*, to all citizens or to some subsection thereof, such as the city councilors. Many benefactors chose to pay for events of various kinds, such as civic festivals or performances or public banquets.[9] Although these are the most commonly attested benefactions, a great variety of others appear less frequently: subsidies

---

of," an office, which perhaps indicates an equivalent practice; see Quass 1993, 328–34. See further Garnsey 1971a, 309–13; Briand-Ponsart 1999, 324–35; Camia 2011, 50n44.

7. The minimum property qualification is usually said to be 100,000 sesterces, although that is explicitly attested only for the northern Italian city of Comum (Plin. *Ep.* 1.19.2); the amount probably varied from city to city. On the transformation of city councils in Greek cities into a distinct economic order, see Quass 1993, especially 382–94.

8. Gifts *ob honorem*: Briand-Ponsart 1999, 218–19. *Pollicitationes*: Garnsey 1971b, especially 116–18 for an overview and 120 for their being made legally binding.

9. On banquets, see Schmitt Pantel 1992 for the Greek world, Donahue 2017 for the Roman.

for the grain supply, embassies to the emperor, the upkeep of aqueducts and baths, and so forth.[10] It was common for benefactors to sponsor different kinds of gifts in conjunction with one another; for example, someone might construct a temple and then pay for a banquet and a distribution at its dedication. Many benefactions were one-time gifts, especially those made in connection with the holding of public office, but people with sufficient means sometimes established foundations, bestowing a certain amount of capital to generate an annual income that would fund their gift in perpetuity; numerous foundations are attested in both the eastern and the western empire.

Although public benefactions took such a wide range of forms, many of which did not involve animal sacrifice at all, in this chapter, I make a case that public animal sacrifice played a distinctive role in the euergetic system. I examine evidence first from the Greek cities of the eastern empire and then from Rome and the Latin-speaking cities of the west, before concluding with an overall assessment.[11]

## 3c. The Greek East

With the rise of the polis, the straightforward relationship between animal sacrifice and elite patronage that existed in the archaic period, as we see it depicted in the Homeric accounts of the sacrifices of Nestor, became much more complex and indirect.[12] Although individual members of the elite continued to pay for and preside over sacrifices and to feast their households, friends, and fellow citizens on the meat of the victims, public cult superseded private piety as the dominant context for large-scale animal sacrifices. From the late archaic through the early Hellenistic periods, it was apparently standard practice throughout the Greek world for public sacrifices to be funded from public sources and not by individual sponsors. This was particularly true in

---

10. Duncan-Jones 1982, in his list of inscriptions from North Africa that mention specific sums, includes eleven examples of banquets, ten of games, and thirty of *sportulae* (104–6); in his comparable list from Italy (188–206), he includes some 250 examples of *sportulae*, eleven of games, twenty-eight of banquets and distributions of oil, and thirty-eight of commemorative rites; it is important to note that many of these inscriptions include more than one benefaction. Zuiderhoek 2009, 76–77, in a sample of 529 inscriptions from Asia Minor, calculates that 58 percent involve public buildings, 17 percent distributions, 13 percent games and festivals, and 12 percent miscellaneous; again, the gifts are not mutually exclusive.

11. My exploration of the relationship between animal sacrifice and euergetism was inspired by Gordon 1990, 219–31; see also Petropoulou 2008, 75–86, who covers many of the examples I discuss in this section, along with her useful collection of relevant inscriptions, 111–16.

12. This section includes material that appeared in earlier form in Rives 2019a.

democratic Athens, where the role of public sacrifices in affirming the bond between community and deity and in articulating the structure of the community made it ideologically problematic for any private individual to fund them. Athens was, of course, exceptional in both the rigor of its egalitarian ethos and the scale of its resources, but to the extent that the limited evidence allows us to draw any conclusions, public funding for public sacrifices seems to have been the norm throughout the Greek world.[13]

Starting in the late fourth century BCE, however, we start to see a shift in this pattern, even in Athens. An inscription of c. 300 BCE records a public resolution made by the deme of Eleusis, one of the wards into which the polis of Athens was divided, to extend various honors to a local notable named Euthydemos because as demarch, or "deme president," he had among other things "offered the sacrifice to Dionysus on behalf of the health and well-being of his fellow demesmen at his own expense and displayed his love of honor (*philotimia*) towards them and increased the public revenue."[14] Similarly, at some point in the late fourth century BCE, the deme of Lamptrae honored a man named Philokedes, who had moved there from the deme of Acharnae, because of the "love of honor" (*philotimia*) that he showed "with respect to the sacrifices and the public affairs of which he has a share in the deme" by voting him "freedom from public duties" and a share in public sacrificial meat equal to that of the demesmen. As David Whitehead has demonstrated, *philotimia* in this context refers to a substantial financial contribution, usually made by an outsider, so that in effect, as Howe observes, "this Acharnian used his animal resources to gain acceptance in his new deme, as a local man of some importance."[15] Other references to *philotimia* in similar contexts suggest that by the end of the fourth century BCE, it was becoming relatively common in the Attic demes for the wealthy to contribute directly toward the cost of the victims for public sacrifices.[16]

---

13. On Athens, see especially Rosivach 1994; for other cities, see Migeotte 2014, 360–72, and Domingo Gygax 2016, 160–61. The sources of public funds for cults could, however, include liturgies; Migeotte 2014, 286–91.

14. Threpsiades 1939, with quotation from ll. 8–12.

15. *IG* II/III².1204, with quotation from ll. 3–7; see Whitehead 1983 on the connotation of *philotimia*; quotation from Howe 2008, 122.

16. See Rosivach 1994, 129–31, for other references. Parker 1996, 247–48, points out that in general, it is in the late fourth century BCE that we find significant private patronage of public cult for the first time since the sixth century BCE. See also Domingo Gygax 2016, 218–50, for the development of the euergetic system in fourth-century BCE Athens.

Over the course of the following century, the practice seems to have become more widespread. As just one example, we may consider the case of Epinomides, a wealthy citizen of Minoa on the Aegean island of Amorgos sometime in the mid- to late third century BCE. The major festival in this city was in honor of Athena Itonia, and like all such festivals, it centered on a procession and a sacrifice. Traditionally, this sacrifice had been funded by the interest on property belonging to the goddess. When Epinomides served as president of this festival, however, "keen that the goddess's sacrifice and procession be as splendid as possible," he turned that income over to the cult's managing board, so that they could spend it on construction work in the sanctuary; Epinomides himself, out of his own resources, paid for the sacrificial victim, in this case a cow, and covered all the other expenses as well. Moreover, those who took part in the sacrificial banquet that followed had in the past bought a ticket to help defray the cost; Epinomides forfeited this contribution and again absorbed the full expense, even though the number of attendees amounted to 550 people. It is not surprising that the cult's managing board voted to honor Epinomides "for his excellence and *philotimia*" by presenting him with a garland and by publicly proclaiming this honor.[17] In this case, although there was an established source of public funding for the sacrifice and banquet, Epinomides chose not to make use of it but instead redirected one part of it to other needs of the cult and remitted another part to the participants.

Although public funding for sacrifices continued, it also became increasingly common for wealthy men like Epinomides to display their "love of honor" by supplementing or even replacing public funds with their own. The increasing importance of the role played by wealthy benefactors in the funding of civic festivals, and of the sacrifices and banquets that were their central feature, is vividly illustrated by two inscriptions from the small city of Acraephia on the shores of Lake Copais in Boeotia that concern the worship of the local god Apollo Ptoios. This was an ancient cult that dated back at least to the late seventh century BCE and perhaps originated when a local oracular deity became identified with the Panhellenic Apollo. The cult flourished during the archaic period and continued into the Hellenistic period. By then, the shrine seems to have functioned as an official oracle of the Boeotian confederacy, even though it apparently remained the particular property of Acraephia. Inscriptions dating to 228–226 BCE attest to the existence of a quadrennial

---

17. *IG* XII.7.241, with the discussion of Delamarre 1896, 75–76; for the festival, see Nilsson 1906, 89–90; Quass 1993, 282–83.

musical competition in honor of the god, called the Ptoia, to which a number of other Boeotian cities sent official delegates. We may easily guess from all this how important the cult and its chief festival were to the Acraephians' sense of local identity and civic pride.[18]

By the late Hellenistic period, however, the city, and indeed the region as a whole, was no longer as wealthy as it had been, and in the early first century CE, the Ptoia ceased to be held altogether, no doubt for lack of funds. It was only after a gap of some thirty years that a wealthy benefactor named Epaminondas was appointed agonothete, "president of the games," and took it upon himself to revive the festival. Epaminondas had already proved his worth as a benefactor, not only serving in other public offices but also undertaking an important embassy to Rome in order to congratulate the new emperor, Caligula, on behalf of all the Achaeans. But as agonothete, he shone even more brightly, "surpassing in his magnanimity and general excellence all those before him and even surpassing himself in respect to the love of renown (*philodoxia*) and the pleasure of doing good." The emperor now joined Apollo as the honoree, so that the festival became known as the Great Ptoia and Kaisareia. Epaminondas himself, "immediately upon assuming the office, carried out the sacrifices and the oracles of the god; feasting magistrates and councilors five times with magnificent annual banquets and supplying the city with a dinner (*ariston*) for a stretch of five years, he never once put off a sacrifice or expenditure." The inscription describes in loving detail the various meals and distributions of food that he and his wife sponsored. At the end of his tenure, when Epaminondas returned from the sanctuary to the city, the people met him en masse to demonstrate their gratitude. Even then, "he did not forget his magnanimity (*megalophrosynē*), but in the city sacrificed a bull to Zeus the Greatest and at once invited those who had come together to the feast of thanksgiving."[19]

Unfortunately, the good times inaugurated by Epaminondas did not last. From another inscription, we learn that just a few years later, public funds were again insufficient to pay for the sacrifice to Apollo Ptoios and the emperor that was at the heart of the Ptoia. Once more, two benefactors stepped

---

18. For an overview of the cult and its history, see Schachter 1981, 52–73.

19. *IG* VII.2712, republished with improved readings and an English translation as Inscription B in Oliver 1971. I have quoted ll. 53–54, 59–63, and 84–87, using Oliver's translation with slight modifications; in particular, I have substituted "dinner" for his rendering of *ariston* as "breakfast," since it appears from other inscriptions that an *ariston* often followed a sacrifice and could thus be a substantial midday meal (Schmitt Pantel 1992, 263–65). On the difficulties of this region during the Roman period, see Fossey 1979.

in and "promised to provide the customary dinner (*ariston*) out of their own resources." That times were particularly hard is clear from the fact that the same benefactors went on to hold several magistracies simultaneously, apparently because no one else could be found. There is reason to think that unusual circumstances were involved; a reference in the inscription to "loss of territory" has suggested to some scholars that the dikes that held back the waters of Lake Copais had collapsed, resulting in a major flood. Yet even granting unusual circumstances, these two inscriptions vividly reveal the extent to which the maintenance of a public cult could come to depend on the generosity of benefactors.[20]

As I noted in Section 3b, euergetism encompassed far more than animal sacrifice, including the construction of public buildings, the funding of public entertainments, and the maintenance of public amenities. I would nevertheless argue that animal sacrifice in the Greek tradition provided an unusually potent site for euergetic activity. On the one hand, it inserted the benefactor into a particularly dense nexus of associations that were crucial to the self-identity of local communities. On the other hand, it allowed the benefactor to display his largesse in a very immediate and face-to-face way, by sponsoring and presiding over a ritual that resulted in what for most people must have been the luxury of eating high-quality meat. In order to develop this analysis further, it is helpful to consider in detail a few additional examples of what I call sacrificial euergetism. I have chosen three examples that cover the heyday of euergetism, from the latter part of the second century BCE to the first part of the second century CE.

A long inscription from the city of Sestos allows us to observe civic euergetism at the point when it began to crystallize into a system. Sestos was one of the major Greek settlements on the Thracian Chersonese, the narrow peninsula that forms the European coast of the Hellespont. In the Hellenistic period, it passed from the control of one regional ruler to another, ending with the Attalid kings of Pergamum from 188 BCE. In the latter years of Attalid control, the city came under military pressure from the Thracians, who in 144 BCE captured and destroyed the city of Lysimacheia just north of Sestos. It was in this context that a local citizen named Menas began to make his mark as a benefactor: by undertaking numerous embassies to the Attalid

---

20. Robert 1935, 438–40 = *SEG* 15.330, with the additional comments of Roos 1938; I have paraphrased Robert's observation (1935, 442) that "on voit clairement comme, à cette époque, le culte n'est assuré que par les générosités d'un évergète." "Provide the dinner": ll. 16–24; "loss of territory": l. 47, with the discussion of Fossey 1979, 558–59.

kings, by establishing good relations with the commander of the Attalid troops in the Thracian Chersonese, and by serving as the priest of the Attalids in Sestos itself, he helped to ensure that Attalid military power would be used to protect the city against its Thracian enemies. The death of the last Attalid king in 133 BE, however, created a power vacuum in the area, and as a result, the city seems for a number of years to have been thrown back on its own resources to defend itself against the Thracians, who at one point prevented the inhabitants from cultivating the fields and so brought about a serious grain shortage.

In this difficult situation, Menas was urged by his fellow citizens to serve as gymnasiarch, the superintendent of the public training institution for boys and young men. Despite the fact that he had already held this position several years previously and was in financial difficulties himself, he readily agreed and, as his fellow citizens had no doubt anticipated, acquitted himself splendidly. On entering office, he offered a sacrifice to Hermes and Herakles, the normal patron gods of the gymnasium, and organized races and contests in javelin throwing and archery for the young men; on the next day, having sacrificed again, he invited to the banquet not only the youths enrolled in the gymnasium but everyone else as well, even giving a share of the meat to noncitizens. These sacrifices and competitions he repeated every month, although the monthly banquets were apparently limited to the young men who took part in the competitions. Finally, presumably at the end of his year in office, he organized athletic competitions in honor of Hermes and Herakles, concluding with another sacrifice and a banquet that he opened to resident aliens as well as the youths in the gymnasium. In gratitude, the city voted him a number of public honors, with the explicit aim of encouraging others to emulate him: every year at the games, he was to be crowned with a golden garland, and a statue with an accompanying testimonial was to be erected in the gymnasium.

Menas came to the aid of his city under conditions that became increasingly uncommon. As the most recent editor of the inscription points out, his administration of the gymnasium was presumably intended in part to revive its old function as a training ground for citizen-soldiers, since in the absence of any royal army, the people of Sestos needed to defend themselves against the Thracians. The contests that he organized in javelin throwing and archery thus had an immediate practical purpose. His sacrifices and banquets served the same end; the inscription is explicit that "through love of renown (*philodoxia*) of this sort he exhorted the young men to discipline and diligence." On the more basic level of nutrition, we should not neglect the contribution that the meat from the sacrificial victims made to the diet of the city's inhabitants, especially the young men who were in training to defend it; its value was all the greater given the scarcity of grain at the time. By funding and presiding over these animal sacrifices, then, Menas was providing an immediate and important benefit to his fellow citizens.[21]

Relatively few benefactors of the Hellenistic and Roman periods would have been called upon to cope with military pressures as Menas was. Much more typical is the case of Apollonios, a distinguished citizen of the small city of Kalindoia in Mygdonia, about 35 kilometers east of Thessalonica. An honorific inscription dating to the year 1 CE records that Apollonios had voluntarily assumed the priesthood of Zeus, Rome, and Augustus and in that office had demonstrated such magnanimity (*megalophrosynē*) "as to omit no excess of expenditure on the gods and his native city." First, he used his own resources to fund a monthly sacrifice to Zeus and Augustus, treating the populace on each occasion to a lavish feast. Second, he oversaw the annual festival for Zeus and Augustus, which involved a procession and competition as well as more sacrifices and banquets. These sacrifices normally took place at public expense, but Apollonios made a special request that he be allowed to provide the funds himself. Lastly, as a permanent memorial "of the beneficence (*euergesia*) of Augustus to all mankind," and no doubt of his own *euergesia* as well, he also paid for a statue of the emperor. In return, "in order that other citizens might be rendered eager to seek honor and to contribute generously to their native city," the people of Kalindoia voted to crown him with a garland (prominently depicted in the middle of the inscription) and to erect statues of Apollonios and his father and mother in whatever place he chose. Apollonios graciously accepted this honor and moreover took over the expense of the statues himself, a type of benefaction that would become common in the imperial period.[22]

Typical, too, but also revealing other facets of euergetism, is an inscription from the city of Thyatira in Asia, some 60 kilometers southeast of Pergamum, dating probably to the 130s CE.

---

21. *OGIS* 339 = *I. Sestos* 1, especially ll. 53–86 for Menas's second term as gymnasiarch; I have relied heavily on Johannes Krauss's detailed discussion in *I. Sestos*. "Love of renown": ll. 70–71. On gymnasiarchs as benefactors, see generally Quass 1993, 286–91, 317–23, especially 290–91 on their importance in wartime.

22. *SEG* 35.744; English translation and brief discussion in Millar 1993, 248–49; I have quoted ll. 36–37 and 46–48 in Millar's translation.

The council and the people honor Dionysios son of Menelaos, a boy (παῖς), first agonothete of the first Augustan and Tyrimnean festival to be held by the city, piously and magnanimously. In all things he enacted his love of honor (*philotimia*) for his native city: he produced from his own resources the prizes of the contests and the honoraria for those putting on displays; he accomplished the pious sacrifices for the god, public and splendid, for the auspicious feasts, the very first ones; he provided a banquet for the council and the people.[23]

An agonothete was the civic official charged with the oversight of athletic or musical competitions (*agōnes*); since these were always held in honor of a deity, agonothetes typically also presided over the public sacrifices that accompanied them. Hence the responsibilities of Dionysios the agonothete were not much different from those of Apollonios the priest, although the office of the latter extended over the entire year rather than being confined to a single event. Dionysios had the particular honor of being the first person to preside over a newly established festival, one dedicated to both the Roman emperor and the traditional patron deity of Thyatira, Apollo Tyrimnos. Tyrimnos was apparently a native Lydian sun god who in the Hellenistic period became identified with Apollo; coins depict him with the long hair and garland of Apollo, carrying a laurel branch in his left hand and a double axe in his right.[24]

What is particularly striking is that Dionysios held this position while still a boy (*pais*), presumably no older than his early teens. Since he could hardly have earned this honor by his own merits, we may reasonably assume that it was due instead to the social position and wealth of his family. Corroboration comes from another inscription, which reveals that it was in fact Dionysios's paternal uncle Markos Ioulios Attikianos who funded the early benefactions of Dionysios and also of his brother. This Attikianos was clearly both wealthy and also prominent enough to have obtained Roman citizenship by the first decades of the second century CE. He was in addition obviously ambitious for his family, so that he used his wealth to ensure that his nephews had an

---

23. *IGRom.* IV.1270, republished in corrected form by Robert 1948, 73. The date can be extrapolated from the fact that Dionysios's son, M. Ioulios Menelaos, was strategos sometime before 180 CE and hosted the emperor Caracalla in 215 CE (*OGIS* 516; see further Buckler 1913, 308–9).

24. Tyrimnos: Schmidt 1948; Lambrinudakis 1984, 245–46. Festival: Keil and von Premerstein 1911, 33–35. Duties of agonothetes: Robert 1948, 72–79; Quass 1993, 310–13.

early and impressive entrance into public life; he may also have adopted them, thereby extending Roman citizenship to them. At any rate, it was as Markos Ioulios Dionysios Akylianos that Dionysios went on to have an extremely distinguished career both in his hometown and beyond, eventually holding the highest position in the province as high priest and Asiarch. Over the course of his career, he must have presided over, and no doubt funded, many sacrifices and public banquets; in this respect, his first public position, as agonothete of the newly established festival of Apollo Tyrimnos and the emperor, set the pattern for all that would follow.[25]

The benefactions of Apollonios and Dionysios, and even those of Epaminondas discussed earlier, may appear to have been less urgent than those of Menas, given that they did not contribute to the safety and preservation of the city in a time of military threat. In their own way, however, they were every bit as important. A major civic festival like those that we have been considering constituted a dense nexus of associations so tightly interwoven that they are difficult to disengage from one another. First, it involved the worship of one of the city's chief deities, typically its patron deity, one whose associations with that particular community were unique and extended back into its legendary and, in some cases, pre-Greek past; we see this very clearly with Apollo Tyrimnos in Thyatira but also with Apollo Ptoios in Acraephia. Festivals celebrating gods like these evoked a strong sense both of the community's unique identity and of its continuity through time. Second, by the imperial period, most festivals also honored the Roman emperor, as we see with the Ptoia in Acraephia, the festival for Zeus and Augustus in Kalindoia, and the "Augustan and Tyrimnean festival" in Thyatira.[26] These demonstrations of devotion to the emperor were not mere exercises in public relations but served to balance a city's sense of its own unique identity with an equally strong sense of its participation in the wider community of the Roman Empire. Third, many festivals involved competitions of some sort, either athletic or artistic or both. Those in the Ptoia were solely musical, those at Thyatira both athletic and artistic. The festival for Zeus and Augustus at Kalindoia also involved competitions, although the inscription does not indicate what kind. Those that Menas sponsored in Sestos were limited to the youths enrolled in the gymnasium but were for that reason no less an

---

25. Attikianos: Buckler 1913, 307–10, no. 7. Adoption: Robert 1948, 74n1. For Dionysios's further career, see Buckler 1913, 315–16, no. 10, and *OGIS* 516.

26. For an overview of this phenomenon, see Buraselis 2012; further examples in Quass 1993, 309–10.

important civic event. Competitions like these showcased the physical and intellectual skills that had been crucial to Greek cultural identity since the archaic period and thus served to affirm a city's claim to that identity.[27]

The symbolic dimensions of these festivals were powerfully reinforced by their social, psychological, and even physiological aspects. The fact that people of every social status took part would have reinforced people's sense of community and their affective bonds with their fellows. This does not mean that civic festivals were carnivalesque affairs in which social distinctions were eradicated; no doubt, general merrymaking did have that effect to some extent, but on the whole, the more organized elements of a festival tended, if anything, to emphasize the community's social hierarchy rather than break it down. Yet the hierarchy that it emphasized was nonetheless that of the community as a whole. Furthermore, the good spirits that naturally accompany a break from day-to-day life, the pleasure taken in the performances and spectacles, and the sense of physical well-being that comes from the sort of meal that one does not regularly enjoy all provided a powerful psychological reinforcement for the evocation of civic identity that I have been delineating. Last but not least, there was the meat of the victims eaten in the banquets. Since high-quality meat was for many people a luxury rather than a staple, a good serving of it represented a significant addition to one's diet. The monthly banquets that Menas provided for the youth of Sestos no doubt played an important part in giving them the nutrition that their athletic and military training required; similarly, the monthly feasts funded by Apollonios must have represented a substantial contribution to the dietary requirements of the poorer elements in Kalindoia. And at the very center of this rich and complex network of symbolic and affective associations was the figure of the *euergetēs*, acting as sacrificant; it was his beneficence and his wealth, embodied quite literally in the expensive animal or animals about to be slaughtered and shared out among the people and their gods, that made it all possible.

The ideological importance of animal sacrifice in the euergetic system thus did not depend on the extent to which it was an essential element in any single act of euergetism. As I have indicated, not all public benefactions involved sacrificial banquets, nor in fact did all public meals and distributions of food; some were light meals, equivalent to tea or "wine and dessert," that would not have included meat. Likewise, not all public sacrificial banquets

---

27. Ptoia: Schachter 1981, 52–73. Thyateira: Robert 1948, no. 25, ll. 13–15. Kalindoia: *SEG* 35.744, l. 22. On the cultural significance of competitions, see Van Nijf 2001, especially 314–18; Camia 2011, 41–46.

were due to some benefactor's munificence; it was normal for public sacrifices to be funded from public revenues, and although these may at times have been insufficient, as they were at one point in Acraephia, that would not always have been the case. It was rather the unique place of animal sacrifice in the dense nexus of associations that I have mapped out that endowed it with its ideological weight. Animal sacrifice, which had always served to reaffirm communal bonds and delineate the citizen body, came in the Hellenistic and Roman periods also to define the unique role of benefactors; their economic and social prominence as the ones who funded these civic events took on concrete form in their ritual prominence as the ones who presided over the sacrifice and the distribution of meat. In important ways, therefore, public animal sacrifice served to embody the entire euergetic system.[28]

By the imperial period, the euergetic system had become integral to the sociopolitical organization of the Greek polis, and public animal sacrifice, as I have argued, had become tightly integrated into the euergetic system. Two further developments in the late Hellenistic and Roman periods meant that the sort of sacrificial euergetism that I have been sketching here became much more widely and frequently practiced. First, the institutions of the Greek polis became increasingly widespread. Alexander the Great had set a precedent for founding Greek poleis in areas where they had not previously existed, a policy maintained by the Hellenistic monarchs who succeeded him. The Romans, if anything, accelerated the practice and actively promoted the establishment of new Greek-style cities in areas that had previously lacked any significant urbanization. Given that public animal sacrifice had become an integral element of the Greek polis, it necessarily became more widespread along with the polis itself. The second phenomenon has less to do with the policies of the Roman overlords and more with the rivalry and ambitions of the cities themselves. With the incorporation of individual cities into the larger polities of the Hellenistic kingdoms and later the Roman Empire, the military and political spheres lost much of their earlier importance as sites for competition, whether between elite citizens within cities or between different cities. Almost in compensation, social and cultural forms such as monumental urban centers and public festivals gained in importance. There was thus constant pressure to increase the frequency and lavishness of public festivals and, correspondingly, of the animal sacrifices that were so central to

---

28. On the varieties of public meals and the food served in them, see in general Schmitt Pantel 1992, 261–89, 334–55. On the mix of private and public funding of festivals in the Roman period, see Camia 2011, 49–75.

them.[29] As a result of these two developments, sacrificial euergetism not only became more widespread but even penetrated into rural areas. Two examples will give some sense of its spread.

A long and complex inscription from the Lycian city of Oenoanda in southwest Asia Minor provides a dossier of documents relating to the establishment of a new festival. In 124 CE, a man named Gaios Ioulios Demosthenes made a formal promise to his fellow citizens that he would fund a quadrennial festival, to be called the Demostheneia in his honor, involving an extensive series of musical and literary competitions. Demosthenes's family had long been among the elite of the city; his name suggests that more than a century and a half previously, one of his ancestors had been granted Roman citizenship by Julius Caesar. Demosthenes himself had by this time already had a career in the Roman imperial service, as a military officer in Syria and as a procurator of Trajan in Sicily. Rather than continuing with his imperial career, however, he returned to his hometown to hold local and provincial office. At the time of his gift to Oenoanda, he was serving as a magistrate and secretary to the city council, and he would go on to be provincial priest of Lycia. Not surprisingly, Demosthenes was no stranger to euergetic practice, having provided annual subsidies to his hometown to maintain a low price for grain and having spent 15,000 denarii on a public building complex comprising a market and porticoes. His funding of a new festival was presumably meant to cap his career as a benefactor and to function at the same time as an ongoing commemoration of his own benevolence.[30]

The inscription that records his gift consists of five separate documents, including both the original promise made by Demosthenes and the preliminary proposal for its implementation. It is interesting to note that Demosthenes's original promise, although including very detailed instructions for the competitions themselves, provides no details at all about the sacrifices that were normally so central to this kind of event: although two days are set aside for sacrifices to "ancestral Apollo," nothing is said about funding, types of victims, or public banquets. The city council's immediate response to Demosthenes's offer was to set up a committee to formulate a more detailed proposal. The process took almost a year, and in the end, evidently after considerable consultation with the council and the people, they presented

---

29. On the increase of festivals in the Hellenistic and Roman periods, see Chaniotis 1995.

30. Inscription: Wörrle 1988, 4–17 (with German translation); see further Mitchell 1990 (with English translation); Rogers 1991. Citizenship: Wörrle 1988, 57. Career: *IGRom.* III.487 and 500 II, ll. 52–60, with Wörrle 1988, 55–63. Earlier benefactions: ll. 9–11.

a proposal that elaborated on Demosthenes's original promise in some significant ways. Some of their additions ensured a heightened presence for the Roman emperor, whose role was now apparently equal to that of ancestral Apollo, while others expanded on the brief references to sacrifices. All the officials of the city were to take part in an elaborate procession, each accompanying one or more bulls as offerings for a common sacrifice. In addition, all the villages (*kōmai*) in the city's outlying territory were also to contribute assigned numbers of bulls; village leaders (*kōmarchai*), appointed by the agonothete the previous year, were to be responsible for providing the victims, just as their civic counterparts were. All these officials were apparently expected to pay for the victims out of their own resources; although the inscription does not spell this out, it is clearly implied by the following provision that anyone who refused to take part in the joint sacrifice would have to pay a fine of 300 drachmas. Nothing is said even in this expanded proposal about banquets, but we can only assume that they must have followed the sacrifice as usual and have been on an unusually large scale: at least twenty-seven bulls were slaughtered, enough for some eight thousand portions of meat.[31]

Two things are worth stressing about the sacrifices of the Demostheneia. One is that they were not funded by the benefactor, as were those in most of the cases discussed earlier in this section, but were instead added to his original proposal, presumably at the insistence of the council and people of Oenoanda. The elite of the city evidently regarded them as important enough that they were willing to take on the burden, as future officeholders, of paying for the expensive victims themselves; in this way, the large-scale voluntary euergetism of Demosthenes prompted a smaller-scale obligatory euergetism on the part of the elite as a whole. This modification of the original proposal thus demonstrates the crucial value of animal sacrifices for civic self-presentation. The second striking thing is the incorporation of the surrounding villages into this civic festival; just as the procession and the joint sacrifice gave visual expression to the social and administrative hierarchy of the city, so, too, they enacted the unity of the urban core and its rural territory.[32] It is impossible to say whether the impetus for the inclusion of the

---

31. Original promise: ll. 6–46, with the sacrifices to Apollo at ll. 42–43. Proposal by the committee: ll. 46–102, with the involvement of the civic and village officials in ll. 68–85. Consultation: Rogers 1991. Portions of meat: Wörrle 1988, 254–55. The victims are described simply as *boes*, "cattle," but evidence for the cult of Apollo elsewhere suggests that Mitchell 1990 and Rogers 1991 are surely right to translate this as "bulls."

32. Or, perhaps more accurately, the domination of the former over the latter; see Ando 2017.

villages came from the city or from the villages themselves, but in either case, the result was the extension of sacrificial euergetism from a Hellenized urban context into a probably much less Hellenized rural context. Although in this case, the villagers engaged in sacrificial euergetism in an urban context, in Oenoanda itself and not back in Elbessos or Nigyrassos, a pair of inscriptions from the territory of Perge, a city of Pamphylia just to the east of Lycia, indicate that sacrificial euergetism could also be enacted in villages themselves.

The inscriptions were carved on the wall of a stone tower some 8 to 9 kilometers northwest of Perge, in what was evidently the village of the Lyrbotai. One of them, prefaced with a dedication to the emperor Hadrian and Apollo of the Lyrbotai, reads as follows:

> I Mouas, son of Stasias, son of Trokondas, being alive and of sound mind, bequeath to my mother for the duration of her life the individual farm in the place Baris and 600 mature olive trees, and olive shoots at the place Three Olive Trees, and in another place called 'by Kallikleis' Armax'; and after my mother's end I bequeath them to the god Apollo of the Lyrbotai, on condition that the annually chosen village leaders (κωμάρχαι) make provision that the aforementioned properties be leased out and that the annual income from them be used for Apollo's sacrifices and the purchase of wine and bread, so that days of contests be held for me every year on the third of the ninth month and that, while all the inhabitants of the village (κώμη) enjoy the banquet on that day, they remember me and my brother Kotes son of Stasias and my mother Kille daughter of Mouas.

The second inscription concerns a very similar bequest, made by Menneas son of Timotheos son of Menneas, of 1,500 denarii for the purchase of a piece of land to be used for the very same purposes; this bequest was carried out by Les, his sister and heir.[33]

The obviously indigenous names of the people involved, the nonstandard spelling and grammar of the Greek (e.g., nominative used for accusative), and the way Mouas identifies the properties all suggest that we have here some not-very-Hellenized members of the rural well-to-do, the sort of people who in the Demostheneia of Oenoanda might have been chosen to contribute

---

33. Mouas: *I. Perge* 77. Menneas: *I. Perge* 78. Cf. the epitaphs of Kille and Les, *I. Perge* 421–22. The place name Baris (which may also be either Baros or Barios) designated a fortified place and thus presumably referred to the area of the tower; see Şahin 1995, 20–22.

the bulls for the joint sacrifice. Yet there is rather more to their story. The tower on which their bequests were engraved was originally dedicated to the emperor Domitian and to "inviolable" (*asylos*) Artemis of Perge by a woman named Arete, the daughter of Demetrios; sometime later, it was refurbished by her grandson Timotheos, the son of Menneas, acting through his mother and guardian, Kille, the daughter of Mouas. The two benefactors thus turn out to be related: Menneas, the son of Timotheos, was the grandson of Kille by her first husband, Menneas, the son of Arete, and Mouas was Kille's son by her second husband, Stasias. Moreover, Arete herself belonged to one of the most distinguished families of Perge. Her father, Demetrios, along with his brother Apollonios, had funded one of the city's great public monuments, an arch that, like Arete's tower, was dedicated to Domitian and the "inviolable" Artemis of Perge. "Inviolable" here refers to the much-prized honor of *asylia*, official recognition that those seeking asylum in the goddess's sanctuary would be safe from seizure by their oppressors. It was apparently through the efforts of Demetrios and Apollonios that Artemis of Perge had been granted this honor, or perhaps had it reconfirmed, by Domitian. Both brothers had very distinguished public careers in Perge, and Apollonios had also been awarded Roman citizenship and had held public office in Rome itself. Yet their family seems to have originated from, or at least to have had ancestral estates in, the area where Arete built her tower and Mouas made his bequest. Thus, all the branches of the family belonged to the landed elite of the village of the Lyrbotai; some bore Greek names and pursued public careers in the urban center, whereas other bore indigenous names and apparently focused on their home village. Elite families like this were in a perfect position to import the sorts of euergetic activities that had become common in Hellenized urban contexts into less Hellenized rural contexts.[34]

Let me now sum up the case I have developed here and elaborate on the significance of public animal sacrifice in the Greek cities of the Roman Empire. As I argued in Section 2d, the distinctive features of animal sacrifice rendered it a highly effective instrument for the construction of sociopolitical hierarchies. Those wealthy enough to afford large-scale sacrifices used them not only to communicate their superior piety but also to reinforce their superior social status. It was thus perhaps inevitable that animal sacrifice would play a part in the euergetic system as it developed from the fourth century

---

34. For the activities, relations, and origins of this family, I rely on the careful study of Şahin 1995. Tower in village: *I. Perge* 65 + 76. Arch in Perge: *I. Perge* 56. Apollonios's career: *I. Perge* 58. On *asylia*, see in general Rigsby 1996, 1–29, with 449–52 on Artemis of Perge in particular.

BCE onward. To use the semiotic terminology of C. S. Peirce, its relationship to euergetism was that of an index, "a sign which is fit to serve as such by virtue of being in a real reaction with its object."[35] When benefactors presided over public animal sacrifices and the subsequent distribution of meat, they were not so much symbolically representing their relationship with the fellow citizens as physically enacting it in a particularly vivid and concentrated form. It was their wealth and their willingness to use that wealth for public benefactions that entitled them to act on behalf of the community as its magistrates and priests. In a public animal sacrifice, the members of the community could see, hear, smell, and sometimes even taste that wealth as it was embodied, quite literally, in the sacrificial victim.[36]

## 3d. *The Latin West*

It is thanks to long and detailed inscriptions such as those examined in the previous section that we are able to recreate with such vividness the practice of sacrificial euergetism in the Greek cities of the eastern empire. When we turn to the cities of the Latin west, we immediately encounter a very different situation, at least as far as the evidence is concerned. The differences are well illustrated by an inscription from Forum Clodii, a town some 35 kilometers northwest of Rome on the shores of the Lago di Bracciano; I translate it here in full, attempting to retain some of the awkwardness that characterizes the original:

> In the year when Tiberius Caesar for the third time and Germanicus Caesar for the second time were consuls [18 CE], and when Gnaeus Acceius Rufus Lutatius son of Gnaeus of the Arnensian tribe and Titus Petillius son of Publius of the Quirinian tribe were *duoviri* [the two chief magistrates of Forum Clodii],
>
> Decrees:

---

35. C. Peirce 1998, 306, in an essay written in 1904. Peirce continues: "For example, a weathercock is such a sign. It is fit to be taken as an index of the wind for the reason that it is physically connected with the wind. A weathercock conveys information; but this it does because in facing the very quarter from which the wind blows, it resembles the wind in this respect." Much the same could be said, mutatis mutandis, of animal sacrifice and the socioeconomic structure of the Graeco-Roman world. For further discussion and examples of indexes, see his earlier essay in the same volume, C. Peirce 1998, 13–16.

36. On the potentially intense sensory impact of an animal sacrifice, see Weddle 2013.

a shrine and these statues, a victim for the dedication; [that] on the birthday of Augustus, September 24, the two victims that are customarily sacrificed in perpetuity, be sacrificed on September 23 and 24 at the altar that has been dedicated to the Numen Augustum [the Augustan Godhead]; [that] likewise on the birthday of Tiberius Caesar [November 16], who will act in perpetuity, the decurions [city councilors] and people dine—since Quintus Cascellius Labeo promises this expense in perpetuity, that thanks be given to his munificence—and that every year on that birthday a bull calf be sacrificed; and that on the birthdays of Augustus and Tiberius Caesar, before the decurions go to dine, their *genii* [tutelary spirits] be invited by wine and incense to dine at the altar of the Numen Augustum.

The altar of the Numen Augustum we arranged to be built at our own expense; *ludi* [games] for six days, starting from August 13, we arranged to be held at our own expense. On the birthday of Augusta [Augustus's wife Livia, January 30] we gave at our own expense sweet wine and pastry to the neighborhood ladies near Bona Dea. Likewise, at the dedication of the statues of the Caesars and Augusta we gave at our own expense sweet wine and pastries to the decurions and people; and we have testified that we will make that gift in perpetuity on the day of that dedication; and so that it may every year be more thronged, we will observe that day, March 10, on which Tiberius Caesar was with great good fortune made *pontifex maximus*.

There is enough in both the content and the format of this inscription to show that we are dealing with the same sort of document that provided the bulk of the evidence in the previous section. Yet the contrast with the long and lavishly detailed inscriptions in honor of Epaminondas of Acraephia or Menas of Sestos is striking. Although it does provide some details, it leaves much more unsaid; the original audience was no doubt able to fill in the gaps easily enough, but for us it raises more questions than it answers.

The first half of the inscription apparently records extracts from municipal decrees regulating civic celebrations in honor of Augustus and Tiberius; although the inscription itself dates to four years after the death of Augustus, the decrees were probably passed while he was still alive, since he is not given the title of *divus*, "the Deified," that he was officially granted after his death. These extracts are given in greatly abbreviated form, so much so that the first clause provides nothing more than bare headings. Nevertheless, we may deduce that the local council had voted to erect a shrine and statues, presumably of Augustus and Tiberius, and to establish or perhaps reorganize public sacrifices and banquets on their birthdays. Both the monuments and the celebrations were presumably meant in general to be publicly funded, since the inscription makes a point of noting that one specific person will fund one specific item, the annual banquet on Tiberius's birthday; although our inscription says nothing about the identity of this Quintus Cascellius Labeo, an inscription from Rome suggests that he was of equestrian status and served as a chief engineer in the army. The second half of the inscription shifts abruptly to a series of statements of what "we" have done, without any indication of who "we" were; the most likely guess is that they were the *duoviri* named in the heading. These men were responsible for a variety of benefactions associated with these celebrations: they took on the expense of constructing the altar, presumably a part of the previously mentioned shrine; they sponsored six days of games; they paid for two sets of public refreshments, one specifically for women and another, on the occasion of the statues' dedication, for the decurions and the people in general; and they made arrangements for the latter to be an annual event.[37]

There is much in all this that is familiar from the last section: the general context of a civic festival, the particulars of what is to take place, the careful documentation of elite benefactions. We might even see in Cascellius Labeo's benefaction an example of the sacrificial euergetism that was so characteristic of cities in the Greek east, although the inscription's brevity and lack of detail make it much more difficult to document that nexus with any certainty. What is most striking about this inscription, however, is not how frustratingly brief and obscure it is in comparison with the Greek inscriptions discussed in the previous section but the fact that in the amount of detail that it does provide about the role of public animal sacrifice, it has very few parallels in the cities of the Latin west. Although there is abundant epigraphic evidence for the funding of both public festivals and public banquets by members of the local elites, almost none of it includes explicit reference to animal sacrifice. For example, of the 275 inscriptions from the Latin west attesting to public banquets that have been collected by John Donahue, only one explicitly mentions a sacrifice. This inscription, from the town of Macomades in Numidia, celebrates the benefaction of Gaius Valerius Valentinus, who in 265 CE refurbished a

---

37. *CIL* XI.3303 = *ILS* 154 = EDR153071, with Gradel 2002, 240–45, and Scheid 2005, 238–45. Gasperini 2008 discusses in detail the different phases of the shrine and provides (121–28) recent photographs and minor corrections to the transcription in *CIL*; cf. Koortbojian 2013, 172–79. Cascellius Labeo: *CIL* VI.3510, with Gradel 2002, 249–50.

shrine to Deus Pluto Augustus and dedicated it "with victims duly rendered to the god and a banquet (*epulum*) provided for his fellow citizens and an annual banquet established for the priests in perpetuity."[38] Here we encounter the sort of sacrificial euergetism that in the previous section I was able to document so abundantly for the cities of the eastern empire, but it is difficult to come up with others. A much more typical example is an honorific inscription of the late second century CE from the town of Corfinium in central Italy that celebrates the career of a local grandee named Quintus Avelius Priscus. This Priscus, in the course of an illustrious but strictly local career, had presented his fellow citizens with a wide range of benefactions including a gladiatorial show, theatrical performances (*ludi scaenici*), further performances (*ludi*) in honor of the otherwise unknown local goddess Vetidina, a subsidy for the public grain supply, and the construction of a women's bathhouse, as well as "frequent banquets (*epulationes*) and distributions of cash to all the citizens, out of his own resources." The townspeople accordingly voted to erect an inscription "on account of his notable zeal toward the community," the expense of which he "honorably" (*honore usus*) took upon himself. The overall scenario here is familiar enough, but the inscription lacks the sorts of details that are crucial for understanding the role of animal sacrifice. Did any of the events that he sponsored involve sacrifices? We may reasonably suppose that the performances in honor of Vetidina did, but can we also suppose that the sacrifice was followed by a public banquet? Did any of the banquets that he funded involve meat, and if so, did the meat come from a preceding public sacrifice over which Priscus himself presided? The inscription gives us no basis to answer such questions.[39]

In short, the rich epigraphic evidence that allows us to trace in such detail the workings of sacrificial euergetism in the cities of the Greek east simply does not exist for the cities of the western empire. Although we may suppose that to some extent this merely reflects differences in the epigraphic habit between Greek and Roman culture, the paucity of references to animal sacrifice is in itself an indication that at the very least, most people did not regard it as something that deserved special mention in inscriptions celebrating benefactions. Should we therefore infer that animal sacrifice was not as important an element in civic life or that the close connection between public

---

38. Valentinus: *AE* 1905, no. 35 = Donahue 2017, no. 73 = EDH HD030138, with the quotation from ll. 9–13. See Donahue 2017, 166–227; the thirty-six additional inscriptions in the expanded edition (241–50) include no further examples of sacrificial euergetism.

39. *CIL* IX.7242 = EDCS 10700952 = EDR074260 = EDH HD017797.

animal sacrifice and euergetism did not exist in the western empire as it did in the eastern? In what follows, I argue for a negative answer to both these questions, although my approach will necessarily be more indirect than it was in the previous section. I first survey the evidence for public animal sacrifice in the city of Rome, which, although atypical in many ways, provides by far the most extensive evidence. I then consider the more limited evidence for the other cities of the Latin west and lastly return to the relationship between public animal sacrifice and euergetism in the western empire.

Thanks to numerous fragments of inscribed calendars, or *fasti*, and to the remains of a rich historical and antiquarian tradition, our evidence for the role of public animal sacrifice in Rome is both abundant and relatively detailed.[40] Even though it provides no answers to many of the questions we would like to ask, it makes it clear that animal sacrifice was deeply enmeshed in the fabric of civic life and took place in a wide range of contexts. On a small scale, it seems to have been a regular part of many archaic rituals. For example, in the Agonalia, celebrated four times every year, the *rex sacrorum*, the "king of sacred rites," sacrificed a ram in the Regia, the "Royal House," a structure just off the Forum that housed a number of sacred antiquities and served as the official residence of the *pontifex maximus*, the head of the Roman cultic hierarchy.[41] There is evidence for a number of similar annual sacrifices, all of them small-scale affairs performed by specialized priests in locations not readily accessible to the general public.[42] The main exception was the Saturnalia in December, which, although mostly celebrated in a domestic context, seems to have opened at the Temple of Saturn with a sacrifice and *lectisternium*, a ritual banquet at which the gods were represented by their images, which was

---

40. Degrassi 1963 is the standard edition of the *fasti*; it also includes a survey that collects all the relevant literary and epigraphic evidence for each event, on which I have relied heavily in many of the following notes. Scullard 1981 is similar but less comprehensive. For a thorough study of the *fasti*, see Rüpke 1995, translated in abridged form as Rüpke 2011.

41. Agonalia: Varro *Ling.* 6.12; Ov. *Fast.* 1.317–36; Paul. Fest. 9.15 Lindsay 1913; see further Scullard 1981, 60–61.

42. For example, the Lupercalia (Plut. *Rom.* 21.4–5; cf. Val. Max. 2.2.9), the Robigalia (Ov. *Fast.* 4.905–42; Columella *Rust.* 10.342–43; cf. Varro *Ling.* 6.16 and Paul. Fest. 325.7–8 Lindsay 1913), the Vinalia (Varro *Ling.* 6.16), the Consualia (Tert. *Spect.* 5.7; cf. Varro *Ling.* 6.20), and the Volturnalia (Paul. Fest. 519.19–20 Lindsay 1913). There were also similar monthly sacrifices on the Kalends (Macrob. *Sat.* 1.15.19) and Ides (Ov. *Fast.* 1.56 and 587–88; Paul. Fest. 93.3 Lindsay 1913; Macrob. *Sat.* 1.15.16) as well as on the weekly market days, the *nundinae* (Macrob. *Sat.* 1.16.30).

followed by a public banquet.[43] Most of the priests who presided over these sacrifices were members of one of the main colleges of public priests in Rome, the *pontifices*, and there is some evidence that the *pontifices* themselves also presided over some sacrifices. Ovid, for example, says that they were the ones who sacrificed a pregnant heifer at the festival of Fordicidia on May 15, and there is equally explicit evidence that they presided over sacrifices to the ancient and obscure goddesses Acca Larentia and Angerona.[44]

Our best source of information for these kinds of small-scale sacrifices, and indeed for Roman ritual in general, are the *commentarii*, the inscribed records, of the Arval Brothers. This priestly college was originally dedicated to the worship of the ancient and obscure goddess Dea Dia, whose cult centered on a sacred grove outside Rome, although in the imperial period, it came to focus on the emperor as well. The *commentarii* of this priesthood allow us to reconstruct in great detail the elaborate three-day annual sacrifice for Dea Dia, performed partly in Rome in the home of the college's president and partly at the sacred grove. It is likely enough that some of the other archaic rituals noted in the previous paragraph, for which our evidence is much scantier, were similarly elaborate. In addition, the Arval Brothers offered sacrifice in a number of other contexts: expiatory sacrifices for violations of the grove's sacral integrity, annual and extraordinary vows on behalf of the emperors, and sacrifices marking other regular and extraordinary imperial events. The *commentarii* also frequently refer to banquets, although the extent to which these featured meat from the sacrificial victims is not clear. All the Arval rites seem to have been fairly intimate affairs, involving only the priests and their assistants and generally taking place outside the public eye.[45]

In addition to these small-scale sacrifices, there were also public animal sacrifices that had a much higher profile. For example, every January 1, the new chief magistrates of the year, the two consuls, presided over a large-scale ritual in honor of Jupiter Optimus Maximus. Accompanied by great crowds, they ascended to the Capitol, Jupiter's great temple and one of the symbolic hearts of the city, and there solemnly contracted a vow with the god to sacrifice two

---

43. Livy 22.1.19–20, describing the reformed festival of 217 BCE; on the Saturnalia as a domestic festival, see Dolansky 2011.

44. *Pontifices*: Van Haeperen 2002, 215–41 on their expertise and 342–425 on their participation in rituals. Fordicidia: Ov. *Fast.* 4.629–30. Acca Larentia: Cic. *Ad Brut.* 1.15.8. Angerona: Macrob. *Sat.* 1.10.7.

45. See Scheid 1990 for an analysis, especially 484–503 and 551–639 for the annual sacrifice and 316–39 and 384–426 for other sacrifices; definitive publication of the texts in Scheid 1998.

white oxen the following New Year's day if he would protect the res publica over the course of the year and then sacrificed two oxen to fulfill the vow made by the previous year's consuls.[46] Another high-profile sacrifice occurred less regularly but, at least in certain periods, more frequently. The traditional Roman ritual of purification, the lustration, involved a circular procession around the persons or places being purified and climaxed with a *suovetaurilia*, the sacrifice to Mars of a pig (*sus*), sheep (*ovis*), and bull (*taurus*). The most celebrated lustration during the republican period was the one that took place at the conclusion of the quadrennial census, in which special magistrates, the censors, reviewed all the citizen rolls as well as those of the various orders (senate, *equites*, etc.), although the ritual was performed in a wide variety of other contexts as well.[47] There is no evidence that any of these sacrifices were followed by public banquets.[48]

Similarly high-profile were the sacrifices connected with the great games, or *ludi*: the Ludi Romani and Ludi Plebeii in honor of Jupiter and other *ludi* in honor of Apollo, Ceres, Magna Mater, and Flora. Unlike Greek festivals, which encompassed a wide range of athletic, musical, and theatrical competitions, the Roman games were of two main types: chariot races, called *ludi circenses* or "circus games" because the race course where they took place was called a *circus*, and theatrical performances or *ludi scaenici*. The Ludi Romani were very ancient, dating back to the mid-fourth or even the late sixth century BCE; the others were established in the period extending from the late third to the early second century BCE.[49] Like the festivals of the Greek cities in the east, the Roman games were large-scale public events in which a significant percentage of the population took part. The calendars indicate that, at least by the Augustan period, they consisted of several days

---

46. Ov. *Fast.* 1.71–88; *Pont.* 4.4.29–34; *Pont.* 4.9.29–30 and 49–50; cf. Livy 41.14.7; see further Scullard 1981, 52–53.

47. Lustration: Baudy 1998, especially 103–25 on Cato *Agr.* 141, the most detailed description of the ritual. Tib. 2.1.27–30 may allude to a feast at the conclusion of the lustration of a farm, but he refers explicitly only to drinking the health of his patron Messalla; cf. Baudy 1998, 137–39.

48. Another high-profile sacrifice was the one that occurred at the conclusion of a triumph (see the account of Aemilius Paullus's triumph in 167 BCE: Plut. *Aem.* 33.2; cf. Diod. Sic. 31.8.12; also that of Vespasian and Titus in 79 CE: Joseph. *BJ* 7.155–56). This was apparently traditionally followed by feasts on the Capitol for select groups of elite Romans, although starting in the late republic, we hear of occasional public feasts (see Kajava 1998, 125–31; Beard 2007, 257–63).

49. Origins of Ludi Romani: Bernstein 1998, 23–78, with English summary in Bernstein 2007, 223–25. Other *ludi*: Bernstein 1998, 157–225, with English summary in Bernstein 2007, 226–27.

of unspecified *ludi*, presumably theatrical performances, followed by one or more days of chariot races in the Circus Maximus.

The public officials tasked with organizing the great games in Rome were not priests or agonothetes, as in the Greek east, but magistrates: originally, for the most part, aediles, lower-tier magistrates concerned with supervising the markets and maintaining the urban infrastructure, although the Ludi Apollinares were assigned to the urban praetor, a second-tier magistrate responsible in particular for legal administration. These magistrates received public funds for the purpose.[50] From an early date, however, it apparently became customary for the presiding magistrate to supplement the allotted public funds out of his own resources. Aediles were junior magistrates, and the men who served as aediles typically had ambitions to be elected to more senior positions. One way they could make their mark was by staging particularly elaborate and memorable games. Already in 182 BCE, a law was passed limiting the amount of private money that could be spent on the games, presumably in an attempt to curb competitive spending; despite such efforts, the aedileship had by the first century BCE become proverbial as a drain on financial resources. Finally, in 22 BCE, Augustus overhauled the entire system, turning oversight of all public games over to the praetors, assigning them public funds, and forbidding any one of them to spend more from his own resources than the others; four years later, however, he is said to have allowed any praetor who wished to spend three times the amounts allotted from the public treasury. By that time, the sums involved were very considerable: a version of the calendar dating to the period 23–37 CE records that 380,000 sesterces were allotted to the Ludi Apollinares, 760,000 to the Ludi Romani, and 600,000 to the Ludi Plebeii.[51]

Since all these *ludi* were presented as offerings to specific deities, it is reasonable to assume that at some stage of the proceedings, someone offered a sacrifice to the deity in question. Corroboration comes from the historian Livy, who relates that the Ludi Apollinares were instituted in 212 BCE after

---

50. According to Dionysius of Halicarnassus (*Ant. Rom.* 7.71.2), the original amount was 500 *mnai* of silver, a sum usually interpreted as 200,000 sesterces; cf. Pseudo-Asconius *Verr.* 1.31 = Stangl 1912, 217.8–9, with the discussion in Bernstein 1998, 143–46. When the senate established the Ludi Apollinares in 212 BCE, by contrast, it assigned the praetor a mere 12,000 asses, equivalent to 3,000 sesterces, although it also directed that the people who attended the games make a contribution toward their cost (Livy 25.12.12 and 14).

51. Financial drain: e.g., Cic. *Off.* 2.57–58, with discussion in Bernstein 1998, 300–305. Augustan regulations: Dio Cass. 54.2.3–4 and 17.4. Calendar: Fasti Antiates minores = Degrassi 1963, no. 26, at July 6, September 4, and November 4; date: Rüpke 1995, 139.

a prophecy that surfaced at the height of the Second Punic War advised the Romans to establish games for Apollo and sacrifice victims to him. The senate voted that the games be held under the presidency of the urban praetor and that he be allotted public funds and two "major" sacrificial victims; another decree ordered the *decemviri sacris faciundis*, the "ten men for performing sacred rites," to sacrifice an ox and two goats to Apollo and a heifer to his mother, Latona. Animal sacrifices were thus an integral part of the Ludi Apollinares from their inception. The same was presumably true of the other *ludi publici* as well.[52] Although Livy says nothing about the specific context in which the sacrifices took place, another source provides a bit more information. Dionysius of Halicarnassus, a Greek scholar working in Rome during the reign of Augustus, preserves what purports to be a description of the procession that preceded the games vowed by the dictator Aulus Postumius in the very early fifth century BCE, which he claims he took from the work of Quintus Fabius Pictor, a Roman historian writing in Greek in the early second century BCE. According to Dionysius, the procession ended in the circus where the games were to take place; the consuls headed the procession and at its conclusion "forthwith" presided over a sacrifice of cattle, presumably in the circus itself. Such a procession, known in Latin as a *pompa circensis*, was apparently a standard feature of all circus games, even though it is explicitly attested only for the Ludi Apollinares and the Ludi Cereales.[53] Although we have no other reference to sacrifices following the *pompa circensis*, that is the most plausible context for them, especially if we assume that the Roman games were to some extent based on Greek models, in which the sequence procession-sacrifice-games was standard. In the republican period, the magistrates who led the procession and presided over the sacrifices were not necessarily the ones who organized them but a more senior magistrate, often one of the two consuls.[54]

---

52. Livy 25.12.8–13; cf. Macrob. *Sat.* 1.17.27–9. For other *ludi*, note Dion. Hal. *Ant. Rom.* 2.19.4, a reference to "sacrifices and games" for Magna Mater; and Tert. *Spect.* 7, a general allusion to sacrifices at the start, in the course of, and at the end of circus games.

53. On the *pompa circensis*, see Bernstein 1998, 254–68, and the thorough study of Latham 2016. Dionysius: *Ant. Rom.* 7.71–72, especially 72.1 for consuls at head of procession and 72.15 for the concluding sacrifice; on the problems of the passage as evidence, see Latham 2016, 21–25. *Pompa circensis* at Ludi Apollinares: Livy 30.38.11; at Ludi Cereales: Ov. *Fast.* 4.391; cf. Suet. *Calig.* 15.1, implying that a *pompa* was a regular feature of all circus games. *Ludi scaenici* were likewise preceded by a *pompa theatralis*, although much less is known of it; see Latham 2016, 161–71.

54. Sacrifices: Latham 2016, 27–28. Latham notes Cicero's reference (*Mil.* 65) to a *popa . . . de circo maximo*; since a *popa* was a sacrificial attendant who performed the actual slaughter, this

As we saw in the previous section, it was also common in Greek festivals for the sacrifice that followed a procession to be followed in turn by a public banquet. This seems not to have been the case for the Roman games. Livy refers to people dining in the open air in connection with the Ludi Apollinares, but no other source makes any references to banquets or distributions of food in connection with *ludi circenses*.[55] Since it is unlikely that such total silence is merely the result of chance, it seems best to conclude either that there was no sacrificial banquet at all or that it was a small-scale event open to only a limited number of participants. As it happens, we know that a sacrificial banquet with limited participation was indeed associated with two of the games. By the reign of Augustus, both the Ludi Romani and the Ludi Plebeii were scheduled around an event described in the calendars as the *epulum Iovi*, the "feast for Jupiter": after nine days of theatrical performances (the 4th through the 12th of September and November, respectively), the "feast for Jupiter" took place on the 13th, that is, the Ides, which were sacred to Jupiter, followed by the "inspection of horses" on the 14th and then several days of circus games. This "feast for Jupiter" was held on the Capitol, presumably in the area of Jupiter's temple, and was open only to senators; it was, in fact, a distinctive senatorial perquisite that they had the right to dine on these occasions at public expense. Although ancient writers connect the banquet with sacrifice, they provide no details about the sacrifice itself. It was apparently not the sacrifice that concluded the *pompa circensis*, since the feast of Jupiter occurred two days before the first day of circus games, when the procession presumably took place.[56]

If the meat from these sacrifices was not consumed in large-scale public banquets, what happened to it? It is important to keep in mind that there were a great many public sacrifices in Rome, not only those connected with the games. Together, these must have generated substantial amounts

---

suggests regular sacrifices in the Circus Maximus. Presiding magistrate: Latham 2016, 25, with further references in n. 34.

55. Livy 25.12.15; Kajava 1998, 118, interprets this as a sacrificial banquet, but the connection with the sacrifice is not as clear as he implies.

56. Schedule: Degrassi 1963, 506–7 and 528–29, compiling the relevant evidence from the calendars. Senators dining on the Capitol: Livy 38.57.5 and 45.39.13; Dio Cass. 39.30.4 and 48.52.2; Mart. 12.48.11–12; right to dine at public expense: Suet. *Aug.* 35.2. Connection with sacrifice: Cic. *De or.* 3.73 refers to *illud ludorum epulare sacrificium*, "that alimentary sacrifice of the games"; Gell. *NA* 12.8.2 relates an anecdote set *cum . . . epulum Ioui libaretur atque ob id sacrificium senatus in Capitolio epularetur*, "when . . . the feast was being offered to Jupiter and on account of that sacrifice the senate was feasting on the Capitoline."

of high-quality meat. Some of this may have been consumed by a limited number of participants, as was probably the case with the sacrifices of the Arval Brothers, or by elite subsections of the populace, as in the *epulum Iovi*.[57] The scholarly consensus, however, is that meat left over from public sacrifices was mostly sold to vendors, who in turn resold it to the general public in markets. The evidence for this practice falls into three distinct groups. First are passages indicating that early Christians were concerned about buying meat in the marketplace that came from sacrificial victims. The most frequently cited are from Paul's first letter to Christ followers in Corinth, which I discuss in more detail in Section 7b, and the younger Pliny's letter to Trajan regarding his handling of people accused of being Christians in the province of Bithynia (now the north coast of Turkey).[58] Second, there is evidence from Italy that public officials sold the hides and possibly other remains of sacrificial victims and turned over the proceeds to public funds.[59] Lastly, passages from three fairly obscure texts, the *Life of Aesop*, the dictionary of the Latin scholar Festus, and the fourth-century CE grammarian Servius's commentary on Vergil's *Aeneid*, apparently refer to the practice dof buying or selling the meat from sacrificial victims.[60] Although all this evidence is rather circumstantial, it seems likely that in both the Greek and the Roman traditions, it was common practice for sacrificial meat to be sold in public markets.[61] Furthermore, the fact that large-scale sacrificial banquets seem to have been

---

57. Substantial amounts of meat: Scheid 2005, 229–34, with some *exempli gratia* quantifications. Banquets with limited participants: Scheid 2005, 257–59.

58. Paul 1 Cor. 10.25–28 and Plin. *Ep.* 10.96.10, both extensively discussed. Passages from later Christian authors include Tert. *Jejun.* 15.5 and Jer. *Ep.* 64.2.

59. An inscription of 58 BCE from the town of Furfo in central Italy (*CIL* IX.3513 = *ILS* 4906 = EDR167161), recording the regulations of the Temple of Jupiter Liber, specifies that the pelts and hides of any victims sacrificed there are the property of the temple, presumably meaning that they were sold for profit. According to Valerius Maximus (2.2.8), in Rome the *quaestores aerarii*, treasury officials, sold the *exta*, the innards, of sacrificial victims; since in Roman tradition, the *exta* were normally the part of the victim offered to the gods, some scholars amend it to *pelles*, "hides," in conformity with the Furfo inscription; see, e.g., Scheid 2005, 261 with n. 32.

60. *Life of Aesop* 51 and 54, with Isenberg 1975 and Naiden 2013, 237–41; Festus 478.22-34 Lindsay 1913 (cf. Paul. 479.8–12), with Scheid 2005, 261–62; Servius at *Aen.* 8.183, with McDonough 2004.

61. For the Greek tradition, see, e.g., Naiden 2013, 232–58, especially 249 and 257–58; for the Roman, see, e.g., Scheid 1985, 203–5, and Scheid 2005, 261–62. Van Andringa 2007 recreates the meat trade in Pompeii from sacrifice to sale; see especially his observation (66) that in many cities of the western empire, the market, *macellum*, is adjacent to the forum and the main temples; see also Van Andringa 2008, 35–39.

less common in the Roman than in the Greek tradition suggests that the sale of sacrificial meat may have been more common in the western empire than in the eastern.[62]

Although the evidence is scattered and often scrappy and indirect, it nevertheless demonstrates that public animal sacrifice was a frequent, almost constant, element of Roman civic life just as it was in the Greek cities of the eastern Mediterranean. Although some of the sacrifices that I have surveyed probably did not loom large in the consciousness of the populace at large, others undoubtedly did. Those that took place in the context of major public events, such as the annual vows or the great games, must have had a particularly high profile. The great *ludi* present striking similarities to the civic festivals of Greek cities, in that they provided members of the elite with the opportunity of presiding over a high-profile public animal sacrifice within a context of euergetic expenditure. But the differences are just as striking. Although direct evidence is slight, we may infer that, with the significant exception of the great games, the funding for all these events was public, leaving little room for direct elite benefactions. Even more strikingly, with the exception of the Saturnalia, there is no evidence that any of these public sacrifices were followed by large-scale public banquets. The scanty evidence indicates that sacrificial banquets were normally limited to groups of elite participants, whether smaller, as in the case of the Arval Brothers, or larger, as in the case of the senate at the *epulum Iovi*, and that otherwise the meat from sacrificial victims was sold to markets.

Rome was, of course, anomalous, since its wealth and power allowed it to maintain a range of public cults that would have been far beyond the capability of any other city in the western empire. Nevertheless, we can with due caution extrapolate from the information we have gleaned about public animal sacrifice in Rome, because just as cities in the eastern empire generally took the form of a Greek polis, so, too, did those in the western empire generally followed the model of Rome. This is apparent even on the level of their spatial layout and public buildings, which generally featured a central forum bounded by temples, basilicas, and markets, and prominent entertainment venues such as baths, theaters, and, in wealthier cities, amphitheaters and circuses. In terms of civic organization as well, there was a tendency to follow the model of Rome, with a city council comparable to the senate,

---

62. It is worth noting that there is a striking correlation between the lack of textual evidence for large-scale public sacrificial banquets and the scarcity of zooarchaeological evidence for large-scale public sacrifice from Roman Mediterranean sites: MacKinnon 2023, 201–7.

administrative and executive officials, and public priests. This was particularly true of cities that attained the juridical status of a *municipium* or a *colonia*, which brought with it varying degrees of Roman citizenship. Such cities were issued civic charters or constitutions that determined many aspects of their public organization. As we saw in Section 3b, the members of the city council, the decurions, constituted a distinct order, with a minimum property qualification and defined privileges and obligations. Although the configuration of the administrative officials varied, the most common pattern was that of two annual executive magistrates comparable to the Roman consuls, the *duoviri* or *duumviri* (literally "two men"); aediles, with responsibilities analogous to those of their Roman namesakes; and sometimes financial officers called quaestors like those in Rome. Of the attested public priests, some were clearly modeled on those at Rome, notably *pontifices*, while others were more distinctively local.[63]

Our most expansive source of evidence about the organization of public cult are the extant examples of civic charters found in Spain, supplemented by a few other epigraphic and literary sources. Two of the civic charters are especially useful for our purposes: that of the Roman colony at Urso, about 70 kilometers east of Seville, which in substance dates to the colony's foundation in probably 44 BCE, and that issued to the town of Irni, some 20 kilometers south of Urso, when it became a *municipium* in the late first century CE. These sources make it clear that the cities of the western empire had annual cycles of public sacrifices and games similar to, although much more limited than, that of Rome. The Urso charter specifies that the *duoviri*, at the beginning of their year in office, must raise the issue of public festivals with the city council, which is to determine how many public festivals there will be, on what days they will fall, which gods will be honored, and who will preside. The charter also specifies three annual festivals: the *duoviri* are to organize a four-day festival for Jupiter Optimus Maximus, Juno, and Minerva; and the aediles are to organize a three-day festival for the same deities and a one-day festival for Venus.[64]

---

63. Laurence, Esmonde Cleary, and Sears 2011 provides a good overview, especially of the physical space. On the organization of public cult, see Rives 1995b, 28–39; Rüpke 1995, 533–46; Scheid 1999, especially 390–93; Rüpke 2006. See further Ando 2007 and Woolf 2009 for important cautions and qualifications.

64. Urso charter: *ILS* 6087 = Crawford 1996, no. 25, with English translation and commentary; section 64 on the selection of festivals, 70 on the games given by the *duoviri*, 71 on those given by the aediles.

Inscriptions from Italy provide other specific examples of public cults. The *fasti* from Praeneste, a town some 25 kilometers east of Rome, has under April 10 the following fragmentary entry: "[ . . . ] of/for Fortuna Primigenia; on whichever of these days the oracle is open, the *duoviri* sacrifice a bull-calf." Fortuna Primigenia was the chief deity of Praeneste, and her temple housed a well-known oracle that was consulted by the random drawing of lots. A fragmentary local *feriale*, or festival list, from the town of Ameria some 75 kilometers north of Rome contains a list of deities who receive animal sacrifices, presumably arranged by day: Vesta, Jupiter Optimus Maximus, Apollo, Mercury, and, on three separate occasions, Fortuna. The inscription does not specify the type of victim, although three entries apparently indicate that there were to be five of them. Another *feriale*, which dates to the period 4–14 CE, comes from the town of Cumae in the Bay of Naples and lists a number of imperial anniversaries connected with Augustus and his family; some seventeen entries are preserved, extending from late August to late May. Each entry consists of a date, the nature of the anniversary, and the type of observance; the last is almost always a *supplicatio*, an offering of wine and incense, except for the birthday of Augustus on September 23, when an animal victim was sacrificed to the emperor. It is somewhat surprising that more local cult calendars do not survive from the western empire, but the scarcity perhaps results from the practice in Romanized towns of posting the dates of local festivals on an annual basis, either orally or on some perishable material, as suggested by the prescription in the Urso charter cited in the previous paragraph.[65]

Although the calendars and festival lists are too laconic to indicate what these sacrifices involved, other evidence provides some hints. A section of the Urso charter refers explicitly to *ludi circenses*, sacrifices, and *pulvinaria*, couches used for images of the gods at ritual banquets.[66] The numerous circuses and even more numerous theaters found in the cities of the western empire provide further evidence that *ludi circenses* and *scaenici* along the lines of those in Rome must have been relatively common. Presumably, these would also have involved the processions and sacrifices attested in Rome. Indeed, the Christian author Tertullian, writing in Carthage around 200 CE, implies that the *pompa circensis*, complete with sacrifices, was a familiar

---

65. Praeneste: Degrassi 1963, no. 17, with Rüpke 1995, 121–22 and 356. Ameria: Degrassi 1963, no. 45, with Rüpke 1995, 357n107. Cumae: *CIL* X.8375 = *ILS* 108 = Degrassi 1963, no. 44. Annual posting: Rüpke 1995, 533–37.

66. Urso charter, section 98.

feature of provincial cities.[67] The Irni charter provides a further glimpse of the forms that local festivals might take when it declares that legal business shall not take place "on the days on which shows (*spectacula*) are presented in that *municipium* by decree of the decurions, a banquet (*epulum*) or distribution of meat (*visceratio*) is given to the citizens or a dinner (*cena*) to the decurions at public expense." Although it does not connect these banquets and distributions with sacrifices, the fact that they are publicly funded suggests that they were tied to festivals. Another section of the same charter makes this association more explicit: "The *duumviri* who are in charge of administering justice in that *municipium* are to raise with the decurions or *conscripti* as soon as possible how much should be disbursed on the expenses of sacred rites and games and how much on dinners that are given to the citizens or decurions or *conscripti* in common."[68] Although some of these publicly funded dinners were limited to the decurions, just as the *epulum Iovi* in Rome was limited to senators, others were apparently open to the citizen body in general, suggesting that large-scale sacrifices may have been offered in the context of large-scale public events.

We may reasonably assume that the magistrates who staged the games in Urso also presided over any sacrifices that were associated with them. The Urso charter, in fact, suggests that acting as sacrificants was one of these magistrates' regular duties, since among the publicly paid attendants assigned to them were a *haruspex*, a diviner who inspected the entrails of sacrificial victims, and a *tibicen*, a pipe player, whose services would have been needed only at sacrifices. As further corroboration, we may note that Tertullian argues that Christians cannot serve as magistrates, because a magistrate cannot avoid "sacrificing or lending his authority to sacrifices, awarding contracts for sacrificial victims, delegating the oversight of temples, administering their revenue, producing shows with his own or public money, or presiding over them when they are produced."[69] Most cities also had public priests of various sorts. The Urso charter includes references to *pontifices* and augurs, both of which are attested epigraphically in a number of western cities. We may guess that the

---

67. *Spect.* 7.2–5, with discussion in Latham 2016, 159–61. Tertullian likewise alludes to sacrifices in the context of the *pompa theatralis* in *Spect.* 10.2.

68. Irni charter: González 1986, with English translation by Michael Crawford = *AE* 1986, no. 333, with French translation; section 92 on the prohibition of legal business and section 77 (cf. 79) on consultation of decurions.

69. Attendants of magistrates: Urso charter, section 62, with Scheid 1999, 389–90. Tertullian on duties of magistrates: *Idol.* 17.3.

duties of the *pontifices* included presiding over public sacrifices, as they did in Rome, even though there is little specific evidence. In some cities, there were also public priesthoods of individual deities, such as the annual priesthood of Ceres in Carthage, which was clearly a very prestigious position. Although the evidence provides virtually no information about these priests' duties, it is likely enough that they presided over major festivals for the goddess, including public animal sacrifices.[70]

The remarks of Tertullian quoted in the previous paragraph suggest that the expenses of festivals were covered by a mix of public and private funds. We have seen that the Irni charter required the city council to allot public funds for rituals and games, just as the senate in Rome did for the great games there. The Urso charter, in contrast, specifies that income from fines collected in connection with public revenue be spent on public rituals and on nothing else, thus establishing a stable and designated source of funding. Yet it also stipulates that the expenses of the major festivals be met in part by the magistrates who presided over them: for the staging of the games in honor of Jupiter, Juno, and Minerva, the *duoviri* are required to spend no less than 2,000 sesterces of their own money, although they are also allowed to draw on up to the same amount of public funds; the same requirement is made of the aediles, although they are limited to only 1,000 sesterces of public money. Two other Latin inscriptions, one from Pompeii dating to the late 80s BCE and another from Knossos on Crete dating to some point after its refoundation as a Roman colony in 36 BCE, also seem to refer to a similar requirement that magistrates spend a set amount of their own money on public games. Such requirements, which some scholars regard as an early form of *summa honoraria*, were probably fairly common.[71]

Although the evidence for public animal sacrifice in the cities of the western empire is even more scattered and scrappy than that for the city of Rome, there is enough for us to get some sense of its importance in civic life. It is likely that any community that aspired to respectable civic status would have had an annual cycle of public festivals and animal sacrifices, similar to that in Rome but much simplified, including, for those that could afford it, *ludi scaenici* and *circenses*. The people who presided over these festivals and sacrifices were local public officials, either magistrates or priests. As in Rome,

---

70. Gascou 1987; Rives 1995b, 45–50, 158–61.

71. Funding of public rituals by fines: Urso charter, section 65; cf. section 69. Funding of games: Urso charter, sections 69–70. Pompeii: *CIL* X.829 = *ILS* 5706 = EDR150879. Knossos: *CIL* III.12042 = *ILS* 7210.

however, the expenses for these festivals and sacrifices was generally covered by public funds, with only the magistrates who presided over games providing additional funding from their private resources. Likewise, we may assume that in most cases, the meat from animal sacrifices either was consumed in banquets limited to elite subgroups or was sold in the markets.

We are now in a position to address the second question that I posed at the beginning of this section. Although we may readily grant that animal sacrifice was just as important an aspect of public life in the cities of the Latin west as it was in those of the Greek east, can we also conclude that it had as close a connection with euergetism as I argued it had in the east? At first glance, it would seem that it did not: references to animal sacrifice are almost completely lacking in the honorific inscriptions of the Latin west; there seem to have been few opportunities for members of the elite to pay for public animal sacrifices, which were instead typically covered by public funds; and public sacrifices were not normally followed by large-scale public banquets. In these circumstances, it is not so easy to draw a vivid scene of public benefactors presiding over the sacrifice of victims that embodied the wealth they were expending on their fellow citizens or to interpret public animal sacrifice as an index of the euergetic system.

Yet to conclude that public animal sacrifice did not serve as an index of euergetism does not necessarily mean that there was no significant correlation between the two. I would argue that in the western empire, there was an equally important relationship between animal sacrifice and euergetism but that it took the form of metonymy more than an index. As we have seen, the people who presided over public animal sacrifices were typically magistrates or public priests. They were by definition members of the order of decurions, and as such they acted as public benefactors throughout their public careers, necessarily, through the payment of *summae honorariae*, and, at least in some cases, also voluntarily, through additional benefactions made *ob honorem*. Although they may not have directly paid for the victims over which they

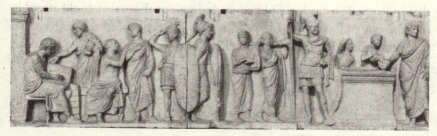

**FIGURE 3.1A.** The "census" panel from the Altar of Domitius Ahenobarbus, Louvre, Paris. Marie-Lan Nguyeusen/Creative Commons, CC0

presided, indirectly they did, insofar as their financial contributions were a major source of public funds. Moreover, visually and gesturally, acting as a sacrificant was one of the most distinctive and easily recognizable actions that magistrates and priests regularly performed and could thus function as visual metonymy for the holding of public office.

We find a good example of this visual metonymy in a splendid relief panel originally found in the southern Campus Martius in Rome and now in the Louvre. According to a long-standing hypothesis, this panel and another in Munich, depicting the marriage of Neptune and Amphitrite, were originally part of a single monument, conventionally known as the Altar of Domitius Ahenobarbus, which has been variously dated from 123 to 28 BCE. The panel is largely taken up with a scene of animal sacrifice, bounded on the left and right by small groups of soldiers (see Figure 3.1). Between them, the animal victims and their attendants process from the right to an altar near the center of the panel, which is surrounded by the sacrificant and another set of attendants. The sacrificant is just to the right of the altar, balanced by another figure in full armor immediately opposite. The far left of the panel is taken up by a separate and much smaller scene of four male figures in togas, one of whom is writing on a large tablet. The fact that the victims are a bull, a ram, and a pig indicates that the sacrifice is a *suovetaurilia*, which normally marked the conclusion of a lustration. On the basis of its iconography, scholars identify the armored figure to the left of the altar as Mars, the most common recipient of a *suovetaurilia*, visually paired with the sacrificant to the right (see Figure 3.2). The latter is shown with a fold of his toga pulled over his head, a pose prescribed in the Roman tradition for people performing sacred acts and conventionally described as *capite velato*, "with veiled head." With his right hand, he is pouring a libation over the altar while an attendant refills his libation bowl, or *patera*, as part of the *praefatio*, the initial stage of Roman sacrificial procedure that consisted of a preliminary offering of incense and wine. The composition is arranged so that the sacrificant is at the precise center of the

**FIGURE 3.1B.** The "census" panel from the Altar of Domitius Ahenobarbus, Louvre, Paris. Marie-Lan Nguyeusen/Creative Commons, CC0

FIGURE 3.2. Altar of Domitius Ahenobarbus, detail of altar scene, Louvre, Paris. Marie-Lan Nguyeusen/Creative Commons, CC0

panel, the focal point of the entire complex scene. Who is he, and what is the context for his sacrifice? The most common interpretation is that the scene represents the lustration that concluded the census and that the sacrificant is one of the two censors. More recently, Dominik Maschek has made a cogent case for rejecting the traditional interpretation and understanding the scene instead as a *deductio*, or ritual foundation, of a Roman colony, perhaps that of Neptunia in 123 BCE, and the sacrificant as one of the three officials charged with establishing the new colony.[72]

On either reading, the panel demonstrates that by the late republic, at least one member of the Roman elite chose to depict himself in the role of sacrificant as the most effective way of commemorating his public office. If we accept the traditional interpretation of the scene as the conclusion of a census, it serves to highlight the authority of the censor, presiding over the enrollment of the Roman people in both their civilian and military aspects, an authority reinforced by his pairing with the god Mars. If we accept Maschek's interpretation, the sacrificant is only one of three men equally empowered to establish the new colony, the other two being the seated man with the tablet at the far left and the man carrying the banner amid the sacrificial victims on

---

72. See Maschek 2018 for detailed discussion of the monument, its history, and earlier scholarship.

the right. Yet the sacrificant is the one of the three who most commands the viewer's attention, a vivid demonstration of the visual potential that inhered in the role of sacrificant to a much greater extent than in many other activities that public officials characteristically performed.

Given the limitations of our evidence, it is impossible to determine how widespread the imagery of public officials as sacrificants actually was. Given what we know about their roles in the cities of the western empire, however, it must have been imagery that many people would have implicitly understood. They would have likewise understood that the holding of public office necessarily involved public benefactions. In this way, I suggest, the link between public animal sacrifice and euergetism, while not normally as immediate and direct in the cities of the Latin west as in those of the Greek east, was nevertheless just as strong.

## 3e. Conclusion

Although the intersection of animal sacrifice and euergetism took rather different forms in the western and eastern parts of the Roman Empire, we should be careful not to exaggerate those differences. We can document a few cases in the western empire in which animal sacrifice functioned as an index of euergetism in much the same way as it did in the east, such as the benefaction of Gaius Valerius Valentinus in Macomades and perhaps that of Quintus Cascellius Labeo in Forum Clodii. The differences in epigraphic conventions between east and west may well mean that sacrificial euergetism of this sort was common enough in practice but rarely documented in inscriptions. Likewise, the metonymic relationship between animal sacrifice and euergetism that I argued for in the western empire was no doubt just as strong in the east. The differences that I have sketched were a matter of degree more than of an absolute distinction.

I should also be clear that I am not claiming that animal sacrifice was an essential element of euergetism. Euergetism did not by any means require animal sacrifice. On the contrary, in both east and west, benefactions involving animal sacrifice were probably a distinct minority of the total. I am instead arguing that animal sacrifice, as a result of the inherent features that I have identified (its connection to wealth and meat production, the prominent public role that it afforded the sacrificant), served as a particularly potent site for enacting the relationship between benefactor and beneficiary, whether it did so as an index or as metonymy. It was its ideological power as a social practice that made it such an integral element of the euergetic system.

But if public animal sacrifice had become by the imperial period an integral element of the euergetic system, the euergetic system had itself become integral to the sociopolitical organization of the Graeco-Roman city, and the city, in turn, had become integral to the organization of the Roman Empire. As is well known, the Romans were able to govern their empire only because of their co-option of local elites, who took on themselves much of the business of local governance. The type of sociopolitical organization that the Romans most favored was naturally that to which they were themselves accustomed, that of an urbanized civic community in which political and religious power was concentrated in the hands of a socioeconomic elite. The practice of public animal sacrifice, by helping to structure the social and political role of local elites in these cities and their surrounding territories, thus contributed to the structuring of the Roman Empire as a whole.

# 4

# Animal Sacrifice and Graeco-Roman Culture

## 4a. Introduction

In Chapter 3, I argued that animal sacrifice, which was organized in such a way as to reflect the unequal distribution of economic resources in Graeco-Roman society, played an important role in structuring socioeconomic hierarchies in Graeco-Roman cities and consequently in reinforcing the social and political order of the empire as a whole. Yet there was a further reason for the importance of animal sacrifice in the Roman Empire: it served as a key element in the common Graeco-Roman culture that elites across the empire used in negotiating a place for themselves in the network of social power. It is this social and cultural function of animal sacrifice that I explore in this chapter. After a brief discussion of Graeco-Roman culture and the role of animal sacrifice within it, I develop my argument through two case studies: in northern Gaul, local elites employed animal sacrifice as a tool for managing the process of cultural change and continuity that resulted from their incorporation into the Roman Empire, while elites in Judaea mobilized it as a crucial point of overlap between their own highly distinctive local culture and the generalized Graeco-Roman culture of the wider empire.

## 4b. A Shared Cultural Practice

Although omnipresent in modern scholarship, the term "Graeco-Roman" has no equivalent in either Greek or Latin. Indeed, it is difficult to imagine that it could have had much meaning for speakers of either language had they encountered it. Those who identified as Greeks or Romans were highly conscious of their cultural differences and for the most part highly protective of their distinct cultural identities. As modern observers, however, we can fairly easily identify something that we might reasonably describe as "Graeco-Roman" culture, especially in contrast to other major cultural traditions of Mediterranean antiquity, such as Egyptian, Persian, Punic, or Celtic. For all their differences, elite Greeks and Romans came increasingly to share a set of assumptions about cultural norms that, in the view of those who wielded social and political power in the Roman Empire, defined civilization. A number of complex historical processes lay behind this development, including the early, significant, and ongoing influence of Greek culture on Roman society and the gradual but steady incorporation of Greek elites into Roman power structures, but I am here concerned not with its causes but with its effects. Graeco-Roman culture, as a shared set of cultural norms and expectations, served to provide a framework for mutual recognition and hence cohesion among the local elites on whom Roman authorities depended for the functioning of the empire.[1]

We can readily identify the key features of this shared Graeco-Roman culture, and I have already touched on many of them. First and foremost, Graeco-Roman culture was an urban culture. As we have seen, Roman imperial administration depended on the institutions of the Graeco-Roman city, so that Roman authorities regularly encouraged and promoted urban culture. To be sure, the countryside was of crucial economic importance, as the most important source of elite wealth, and likewise held an important place in the Graeco-Roman imagination as a locus of old-fashioned virtues and rural simplicity. But although the wealthy might at times retreat to their country estates, these were in effect oases of urbanity amid a rustic wasteland. A proper city, moreover, meant more than mere density of population; a proper city had to meet certain expectations as to both physical appearance and sociopolitical organization. Physically, a city was ideally expected to have an ordered plan and include some minimum of the typical structures: paved streets, plazas, and porticoes; a water distribution system involving aqueducts, fountains, and baths; civic buildings such as council halls, basilicas, and gymnasia; sacred spaces such as temples, sanctuaries, and altars; and entertainment venues such as theaters, amphitheaters, and circuses. So, too, there were expectations about building materials (stone, brick, concrete), construction techniques

---

[1]. For cultural negotiations between Greeks and Romans, see, e.g., Woolf 1994; Swain 1996; Madsen 2009. It is important to add that neither "Greek" nor "Roman" was in itself a stable identity.

(columns, arches, vaults), architectural styles, and decorative embellishments. Sociopolitically, a city implied a hierarchical social structure based largely on wealth; administrative institutions such as a city council, civic officials, and public priests; and associations with membership based on local, professional, or devotional criteria. Lastly, Graeco-Roman culture involved a certain degree of adherence to shared intellectual, literary, artistic, and performance traditions, which were to some extent embodied in the physical apparatus of the city. Indeed, all these elements were to some extent imbricated with one another. It was on the institutions that defined urban Graeco-Roman culture that elite benefactors throughout the empire chose to expend their resources, since these institutions were crucial to their negotiating a place for themselves in the empire-wide network of social power.[2] Although the details varied from city to city and region to region, and although the variation in detail was very important to contemporary participants, the commonalities were what defined a baseline imperial culture and so allowed the variations to acquire significance.

Together with the other features that I have identified, Graeco-Roman culture also involved a certain way of structuring relations with the divine world, the key features of which we can likewise readily identify. The gods were thought to enjoy marks of esteem and honor much as humans did and to bestow their benefits on those who demonstrated their esteem, again much as did the human benefactors whose activities we considered in Chapter 3. That, at least, is the logic underlying such traditional cult acts as offering gifts to the gods (shrines, dedications, sacrifices), staging performances in their honor (processions and games), praising them in hymns, and requesting their blessings in prayers. Cities sponsored and organized these sorts of activities on behalf of the community, in order to win the divine favor for the community as a whole, just as individuals and groups did for themselves. Authority over civic cult lay with the same people who had authority over other aspects of civic life: the members of the socioeconomic elite, in their roles as city councilors, magistrates, and priests. We have already seen how animal sacrifice provided a particularly potent context in which they could enact their authority; we may now consider why it was also a particularly potent component of the shared Graeco-Roman culture that local elites were for the most part eager to adopt and propagate.

---

2. For good overviews of cities in the eastern and western parts of the empire, see, respectively, Gleason 2006 and Edmondson 2006. Benefactors: Zuiderhoek 2009, 71–77, 92–93.

To begin with, unlike a number of cultural practices that spread throughout the Roman world and were marked as distinctively Greek or Roman, such as athletic competitions or gladiatorial games, animal sacrifice had been integral to both the Greek and the Roman traditions since time immemorial. Moreover, sacrificial practice in the two traditions shared many common features. The types of victims were the same, with cattle, sheep, and pigs the most usual and a range of others acceptable in particular circumstances. The procedure also involved the same basic elements. The sacrificant, participants, and victims processed to the altar, where the sacrificant performed a set of preliminary rites and pronounced the prayers. The sacrificant or an attendant then slaughtered the animal, and after inspecting the victim's remains, the sacrificant offered the god's portion by burning it on the altar. Lastly, attendants prepared the rest of the carcass for human consumption, either on the spot or for later. The social and institutional framework in which animal sacrifice took place was likewise much the same in both traditions. As I discussed in Section 1b, the person who acted as sacrificant did so not because of cultic or ritual qualifications but rather because of social qualifications: those with authority in a group acted as sacrificants on its behalf.

At the same time, there were also numerous differences between Greek and Roman sacrificial practice.[3] The preliminary rites at the altar, for example, differed considerably. In Greek tradition, the sacrificant threw barley over the victim, prayed, cut hairs from the victim's forehead, and burned them on the altar. A Roman sacrificant, in contrast, opened the proceedings with the *praefatio*, the preliminary offering of wine and incense at a portable brazier, and then initiated the offering of the victim by pouring wine on its forehead, sprinkling it with a special salted meal, and drawing a knife along its spine. In Roman tradition, a sacrificant covered his head with a fold of his toga, as we saw on the Altar of Domitius Ahenobarbus, in the style conventionally labeled *capite velato*, "with veiled head," whereas participants in a Greek sacrifice wore garlands on their otherwise bare heads. In Greek tradition, the god normally received the victim's thigh bones, folds of fat, and tail; in Roman tradition, the god received the *exta*, the innards, which in Greek tradition went instead to the inner circle of human participants. Despite these manifest differences in their sacrificial procedure, however, I would argue that more

---

3. The following comparison draws on standard scholarly accounts of Greek and Roman sacrificial procedures, which tend to conflate information from a wide range of sources; in neither tradition was there actually one single normative procedure. Nevertheless, we may reasonably speak of practices that on average seem to have been more common.

often than not, both Greeks and Romans found it advantageous to emphasize the similarities. In support, I note just two examples.

The first concerns the Greek scholar Dionysius of Halicarnassus, who worked in Rome during the reign of Augustus. As I noted in Section 3d, Dionysius is one of our best sources for the *pompa circensis*, the procession that preceded the Roman circus games and concluded with the presiding officials performing a sacrifice of cattle. He describes in some detail the sacrificial procedure, which he insists he had personally observed. Dionysius claims explicitly that the Romans' "manner of performing the sacrifices was the same as with us [Greeks]," a claim that he goes on to support with quotations from Homeric descriptions of sacrifice. His claim about the identity of Roman and Greek sacrificial practice is, in fact, his reason for including this description and, indeed, the whole account of the procession. He explains that he includes it not as a mere embellishment but in order to "win credence for an essential matter of history, namely, that the peoples which joined in founding the city of Rome were Greek colonies sent out from the most famous places, and not, as some believe, barbarians and vagabonds." Dionysius's desire to demonstrate that the Romans were in origin Greek apparently affected his observation of Roman sacrificial practice, since some of the Homeric passages that he cites in support, such as that in which the sacrificant cuts hair from the forehead of the victim, describe actions that were not actually a normal part of Roman sacrificial procedure. Yet the very fact that a well-informed Greek observer such as Dionysius could make such a claim indicates how easy it was for him to regard Roman sacrificial practice as effectively the same as Greek.[4]

My second example concerns Roman priests rather than Greek scholars. Priestly tradition required that those who presided over sacrifices in certain cults perform them *Graeco ritu*, "in Greek fashion." The scanty evidence does not allow us to determine what precisely sacrifice "in Greek fashion" entailed, although our sources consistently remark that the sacrificant kept his head bare, rather than covering it with a fold of his toga (*capite velato*). It is impossible to determine at what point Roman priests instituted this practice, although it must have been at an early date. We know that sacrifice *Graeco ritu* was the norm in two very ancient cults, those of Saturn and of Hercules at the Ara Maxima, and it was presumably already well established when it

---

4. Dion. Hal. *Ant. Rom.* 7.72.15–18 for the discussion of sacrificial practice (citing *Od.*14.422 for the hair cutting) and 7.70.1–5 for his purpose; quotations from 7.72.15 and 70.1, trans. Earnest Cary, Loeb. Background: Gabba 1991, especially 107–18, 134–36. Analysis: Mackey 2022, 373–76, 388–92.

was specified for the sacrifices to Apollo in the Ludi Apollinares that were instituted in the late third century BCE.[5]

It is important to note that in both these examples, claims about similarity and difference in sacrificial practice were embedded within and to some extent determined by larger and more complex claims regarding political power and cultural authority. Dionysius, writing in the center of an imperial power than had dominated the Greek world for more than a century, was in effect attempting to establish Greek claims to cultural authority over its imperial rulers. In providing Rome with what Greeks at least would regard as a respectable pedigree, he was simultaneously making an implicit case that Romans owed Greeks the sort of respect that a colony owed its metropolis. The Roman priestly convention of sacrifice *Graeco ritu* is an even more striking example. Superficially, it appears to emphasize the differences between Greek and Roman sacrificial practice by isolating and labeling them. At the same time, by reducing those differences to something as simple and easily changed as a head covering, it makes a deeper claim to similarity, presenting Greek sacrificial practice as merely a minor variation of Roman practice and thus just as easily subsumed within Roman ritual praxis as Greek polities had been subsumed within Roman imperium.

These negotiations of similarity and difference in sacrificial procedure were facilitated by another principle that was common to both the Greek and the Roman traditions, namely, that in matters of cult, difference in detail was the norm: each deity, each cult, each shrine was expected to have its own specific rules. The principle could not be extended indefinitely; as we will see, Roman authorities treated some practices, no matter how traditional, as fundamentally unacceptable. Nevertheless, the shared principle of local variation made it easier for Greeks and Romans to regard animal sacrifice as a practice that they had in common and consequently as both normal and natural. Its apparent naturalness was heightened by two other factors. First, as an important way of expressing piety toward the gods, it was both a familiar part of life and simultaneously imbued with special significance. For most people, animal sacrifice would have been part of their experience for as long as they could remember, even if they associated it with special occasions and not regular worship. Second, precisely because animal sacrifice was a practice and not a verbal discourse, it did not require translation: Romans who did not understand Greek could have easily taken a meaningful part in a Greek sacrifice,

---

5. Saturn: Cato *ORF* F 77; Macrob. *Sat.* 1.8.2. Hercules: Livy 1.7.3; Macrob. *Sat.* 3.6.17. Apollo: Livy 25.12.10 and 13. On sacrifices *Graeco ritu*, see further Scheid 1995.

and vice versa. Although they may well have been struck by aspects of the procedure that differed from that with which they were familiar, they could with little difficulty have accepted these as normal variations on a shared and natural practice.

For all these reasons, elite Greeks and Romans could alike regard animal sacrifice as a Graeco-Roman practice par excellence, a practice emblematic of the shared Graeco-Roman culture that defined the standards of civilized life in the Roman Empire. Further evidence for its cultural significance can be found in the fact that those with social and political power often treated major deviations from the norms of Graeco-Roman sacrificial practice as markers of deviation from civilized behavior. The choice of sacrificial victim provides a good example. As we have seen, normal victims in the Graeco-Roman tradition were larger domesticated species that served as major sources of edible meat: primarily cattle, sheep, and pigs and to a lesser extent goats and domestic fowl. At the same time, in particular contexts, acceptable victims could include domesticated species that were not normally eaten, such as horses and dogs, and wild animals that were eaten, such as deer and fish. Human victims, by contrast, were always and everywhere unacceptable, even though there were a few practices in Roman tradition, that Romans themselves regarded as tantamount to human sacrifice. Stories about human sacrifice thus served to mark off various groups and individuals who were thought to lack or deliberately reject the normal standards of civilization, such as barbarians, witches, revolutionaries, and tyrants. There are many examples dating back to archaic Greece, but we may note in particular its use to characterize foreign enemies, Carthaginians and Gauls especially. Whether Carthaginians and Gauls actually did engage in human sacrifice is a question that scholars have hotly debated but one that is not very important to my argument. Whatever the actual situation, the Romans prided themselves on putting an end to the practice wherever they encountered it, a policy that they regarded as paradigmatic of their civilizing mission. Strabo, for example, speaking of the Gauls, says that "the Romans made them desist . . . from sacrificial and divinatory practices that are opposed to our norms" (note his incidental acknowledgment of the shared standards of Graeco-Roman culture). Pliny patriotically waxes more eloquent: "It is beyond calculation how great is the debt owed to the Romans, who swept away the monstrous rites, in which to kill a man was the highest religious duty and for him to be eaten a passport to health!"[6]

---

6. Stories about human sacrifice: Rives 1995a; Schultz 2010 (which also treats relevant Roman practices); see further Frankfurter 2021 for the broader discursive work done by such

By the same token, sacrificial practices that were closer to the Graeco-Roman norm could serve as a valuable resource in the cultural and political negotiations that took place when new peoples were incorporated into Roman hegemony. It is one of the most striking aspects of ancient Mediterranean history that Greek and Roman cultural hegemony and political domination steadily grew over time to incorporate more and more peoples and traditions that had previously been outside it, a process that reached its climax with the Roman Empire. This incorporation of other peoples into the Graeco-Roman sphere entailed a complex process of cultural integration that scholars have long debated. Without entering into the specifics of that debate, I want to make a case that animal sacrifice played an important part in these cultural and political negotiations.[7] Many of these peoples had their own traditions of honoring the gods through practices involving the slaughter of animals. Perhaps the only major cultural tradition within the sphere of Roman hegemony that did not put significant emphasis on animal sacrifice was that of Egypt, and even it included practices that Greek observers as early as Herodotus were able to interpret as the sort of animal sacrifices to which they were accustomed.[8] By adapting their traditional practices, highlighting similarities with Graeco-Roman sacrificial procedure, and downplaying differences, local elites could employ the practice of animal sacrifice as an effective and supple tool when negotiating a place for themselves within empire-wide structures of social power.

---

stories. Human sacrifice among the Carthaginians: most recently, Shaw 2016; McCarty 2017; D'Andrea 2018; among the Gauls: Brunaux 2000, 150–71; Watson 2007, 149–65; Marco Simón 2007, 158–63. Roman pride in ending human sacrifice: Strabo 4.4.5 (my translation); Plin. *Nat.* 30.13 (trans. W. H. S. Jones, Loeb); cf. Plut. *Quaest. Rom.* 83, 283F–284C, who focuses more on the Romans' own practice of human sacrifice. The Romans' civilizing mission: e.g., Woolf 1998, 48–76. Stories about deviant sacrifice were not limited to those that involved human victims; see, e.g., Köster 2021 on flamingo sacrifices.

7. The debate over what is often called Romanization has in recent decades been both extensive and highly complex; for some key discussions, see, e.g., D. Mattingly 1997; Woolf 1998, 1–23; Ando 2000, 1–70; Hingley 2005. Moreover, most studies focus on the western empire and do not fully engage with the fact that in the eastern Mediterranean, Roman rule generally led to the adoption of Greek, even more than Roman, institutions and practices; exceptions include Ando 2000 and Zuiderhoek and Vanacker 2017.

8. Sacrifice in the traditions of the ancient Mediterranean: Johnston 2004, 325–48. Animal sacrifice in Egypt: Frankfurter 2011; Rutherford 2017. Herodotus on Egyptian animal sacrifice: 2.39–42, 47.

In the remainder of this chapter, I analyze two contrasting case studies of such negotiations: Gauls, especially those north of the Seine, and Judaeans.[9] The Judaeans were a people organized around a monumental temple of the sort common in Near Eastern culture; they had a written tradition extending back hundreds of years and long-standing interactions with the major political powers and dominant cultures of the eastern Mediterranean. By contrast, the peoples of northern Gaul were organized tribally, had very limited literacy and a fairly low level of urbanism, and prior to the mid-first century BCE had had minimal direct (although some indirect) contacts with the Mediterranean world. In terms of their religious traditions, these two peoples also differed in the degree to which they could readily accommodate themselves to Graeco-Roman norms, especially in sacrificial practice. They also provide a useful contrast in terms of the available evidence. In the case of the northern Gauls, there are two main types of evidence: on the one hand, Greek and Roman accounts of Gallic society in general and, on the other, archaeological evidence from the specific region of northern France. In the case of Judaeans, there is an extensive body of texts from their own tradition, extending over a period of centuries. Although these two case studies cannot be regarded as exemplary of all the peoples of the empire, I hope that they at least give some sense of the range.

## 4c. Gauls

The two main bodies of evidence for animal sacrifice among the peoples of northern Gaul are very different. One consists of Greek and Roman ethnographic accounts, which extend back to the fifth century BCE but begin in earnest with the Greek scholar Posidonius, who visited Gaul in person in the early first century BCE. Although his description of the Gauls is largely lost, it was used by later Greek writers such as Diodorus Siculus (mid-first century BCE) and Strabo (under Augustus), although Strabo in particular had other sources as well. The most important extant source is Julius Caesar's account of his conquest of Gaul in the 50s BCE, since he had more opportunity to observe Gallic society at first hand than any other Greek or Roman

---

9. It is a much-debated question whether to translate the Greek and Latin term *Ioudaios/ Iudaeus* (itself a borrowing from Aramaic) as "Jew" (the English derivative) or as "Judaean"; see, e.g., Mason 2007; Law and Halton 2014; and D. Schwartz 2014. For the purposes of my argument here, I have preferred "Judaean," since it highlights the geographical and ethnic connotations of the term that would have been prominent in the Graeco-Roman frame of reference.

writer. Although Caesar had no doubt read Posidonius's account of the Gauls, scholars today consider his account to be largely independent.[10] The other body of evidence is archaeological, the result of excavations extending back a century and a half and continuing up to the present day. I focus on one particular region, the area north of the Seine and the Marne that corresponds roughly to the historical region of Picardy and was in antiquity the territory of peoples whom Caesar classed as Belgae.[11] This region is unusually rich in sanctuaries that have been well excavated and carefully published, that were in continuous use from the period of Gallic independence into the era of Roman rule, and that provide evidence for animal sacrifice. The most important site is the rural sanctuary of Gournay-sur-Aronde, which lies some 80 kilometers northeast of Paris on a minor tributary of the Oise. I also refer to other comparable sites in northern Gaul, all within an 80-kilometer radius of Gournay, especially Bennecourt, Fesques, Longueil-Sainte-Marie, and Ribemont-sur-Ancre, as well as the site of Vertault in central Gaul.[12]

The sanctuary at Gournay-sur-Aronde was excavated by Jean-Louis Brunaux in the 1970s and 1980s and was the first of its kind to be so carefully excavated and fully published. Brunaux and his colleagues identified six phases in the development of the sanctuary, four dating to the pre-Roman period and two to the period after the Roman conquest. In the earliest phase, at the beginning of the third century BCE, the sanctuary consisted simply of a rectangular site of some 38 by 45 meters marked off by a ditch 2.5 meters wide and 2 meters deep, with a bank beyond it and an entrance some 3 meters wide. In the middle of the third century, a large oval pit, some 3 by 4 meters with a depth of 2 meters, was dug in the center of the enclosure, with nine smaller pits around it; the walls of these pits, like those of the ditch, were apparently lined with wooden planks. At about the same time, a wooden palisade was constructed on the bank outside the ditch, probably with some sort of porch at the entrance. In a third phase, at the start of the second century BCE, the

---

10. Posidonius F 67–69, 274–75 Edelstein and Kidd 1972; Diod. Sic. 5.24–32; Strabo 4.3–4; Caes. *Bell. Gall.* 6.11–20. Earlier scholars tended to regard the later accounts simply as meager summaries of Posidonius (see especially Tierney 1960, 201–24), but later scholars convincingly argued that the relationship between these texts is likely to be much more complex (see, e.g., Nash 1976, especially 111–19).

11. Caes. *Bell. Gall.* 1.1; see Wightman 1985, 1–25, and Roymans 1990, 11–15, for modern evaluations of this classification.

12. Brunaux and Malagoli 2003 provide a useful overview of Gallic sanctuaries in northern France, including a catalog of sites (47–73); see also Brunaux 2000, 83–85, on the importance of Gournay.

pit was covered by a roofed shelter supported by wooden poles. A major reconstruction took place in the course of the second century BCE, when the shelter was replaced by a more substantial wooden structure with rammed-earth walls on the two sides and back. This fourth phase ended around the end of the second century BCE with the burning of the wooden structures, the filling in of the central pit, and the leveling of the interior.[13]

The perimeter ditch of the sanctuary yielded many remains of animal bones, mostly dating to the second century BCE. The excavators identified a number of distinct groups. The most striking are two clusters of cattle bones, one on each side of the entrance porch, representing four separate deposits of some dozen animals each. Close examination of the bones allowed the excavators to reconstruct in some detail the elaborate process that resulted in their deposition in the ditch. The participants first killed the animal by a blow to its head with an iron axe, which they inflicted while it was standing. They then threw the corpse into the central pit, where they allowed it to decompose; there are no indications that they butchered or burned any part of the victim. After the flesh had rotted away and the bones had become disjointed, they removed first the skull, which they may have used to adorn the entrance porch, and then the rest of the bones; the fact that only three very tiny bones were found in the pit indicates the care with which they cleared it out. They then deposited the bones in the ditch, where they continued to be exposed to the open air, and lastly added the skulls, before starting the whole process over again. The animal remains indicate that they maintained this practice with little variation for a period of some fifty years. The elaborate and apparently consistent precision with which they carried it out strongly suggests that it constituted a prescribed ritual, one that we might reasonably describe as an animal sacrifice. In addition to this cattle sacrifice, the ditch yielded remains of four horses that had undergone a similar treatment, with some minor differences. Lastly, there are two sets of remains from animals that, unlike the cattle and horse sacrifices, had been butchered and eaten; the earlier one, from the second century BCE, consisted of lambs and some pigs. Although the state of the bones did not allow for many other deductions about how the animals were slaughtered or handled, the fact that their remains were deposited in the same perimeter ditch as those of cattle and horses that had been ritually slaughtered led the excavators to conclude they were

---

13. The original publication is Brunaux, Méniel, and Poplin 1985; I have followed the summary of Derks 1998, 170–73, supplemented by Brunaux 2000, 91–101, and Moser 2016, 177–78.

the remains of a different type of sacrificial ritual, an alimentary sacrifice of the sort familiar from the Graeco-Roman tradition.[14]

How typical was the sanctuary at Gournay? In physical form, it seems to have been highly typical. Since its excavation, archaeologists have identified and excavated a number of similar sanctuaries. The use of a ditch to mark off the sacred area seems to have been more or less universal, and most sanctuaries have a similar quadrangular arrangement. A number of them have a central pit or pits similar to those at Gournay, in some cases in almost exactly the same arrangement.[15] The presence of these pits suggests the same sacrificial practice of deposition and decomposition of the victims' bodies that is documented at Gournay, although none of them has yielded any clear evidence of it. We know, however, that the practice was not unique to Gournay. Outside northern France, the sanctuary at Vertault, some 85 kilometers northwest of Dijon, has yielded deposits of horses, dogs, and a few sheep that were slaughtered in a similar fashion and laid out intact in pits, with the bodies carefully oriented. Although the dogs seem to have been buried immediately, the bodies of the horses were apparently left to decompose for a period of days or weeks before being rearranged. Despite the obvious differences, the practice at Vertault has a clear affinity with that at Gournay.[16] Much more common in the sanctuaries of northern Gaul (and indeed elsewhere) are the remains of animals that had been eaten, usually interpreted, as at Gournay, as evidence for alimentary sacrifice. The perimeter ditch at Bennecourt, for example, on the north bank of the Seine some 80 kilometers southwest of Gournay, has yielded large numbers of bones, chiefly of pigs (some two-thirds of the total) and sheep (somewhat less than a third), with a few from cattle, dogs, and birds. The remains from Ribemont-sur-Ancre, some 60 kilometers north of Gournay, are similar: pigs make up some three-quarters, sheep some 13 percent, with the rest coming from cattle and dogs. Overall, pigs, sheep,

---

14. Méniel 1992, 25–27, 47–68, 101–5; more briefly, Brunaux 2000, 138–41, and Moser 2016, 177–78. Sheep and pig bones as remains of alimentary sacrifice: Méniel 1992, 91–92; Brunaux 2000, 137–38; most recently, Méniel 2008, 149.

15. See Roymans 1990, 68–70, and Brunaux and Malagoli 2003, 16–23, for summaries of the physical layout and structures of the sanctuaries of northern Gaul. Bennecourt, a single large pit: Brunaux and Malagoli 2003, 43–44. Fesques, a large pit surrounded by smaller pits, later replaced by a single large pit: 56–59. Saint-Maur, a large pit surrounded by nine smaller ones: 69–71. Vendeuil-Caply, a large pit surrounded by smaller ones in groups of threes: 71. La Villeneuve-au-Châtelot, a single large pit: 71–73.

16. Vertault: Méniel 1992, 71–88; more briefly, Lepetz and Méniel 2008, 159–60, and Moser 2016, 178–79. Méniel 2008, 148, notes in passing that similar practices are attested at other sites.

and dogs are the most common remains from alimentary sacrifices, with cattle a distant fourth. Horses, in contrast, seem never to have been eaten in ritual contexts.[17]

There is much about the sacrificial practice of northern Gaul that would have been familiar to Greek and Roman observers, although they would no doubt have been most struck by the deviations from normative Graeco-Roman practice. The rituals at Gournay-sur-Aronde that involved throwing the carcasses of the sacrificial victims into pits and letting them decompose would probably have seemed particularly unusual, even though similar practices were not unknown in the Greek tradition. Likewise, there is evidence that the Romans sacrificed both horses and dogs in particular contexts, although neither was ever a typical sacrificial victim.[18] Nevertheless, our hypothetical Graeco-Roman observers would have had no difficulty in concluding that the peoples of northern Gaul, despite some idiosyncrasies, engaged in more or less the same practice of animal sacrifice that they themselves accepted as the normal and natural expression of piety. Even the more deviant aspects of Gallic practice fell comfortably within the spectrum of variations that were acceptable under the principle that each shrine had its own cultic rules. It is thus not surprising that, in contrast to their lurid accounts of human sacrifice among the Gauls, Greek and Roman writers have little to say about animal sacrifice, suggesting that they regarded it as normal and thus unremarkable.[19]

They did, however, have a great deal to say about the social and institutional context of Gallic animal sacrifice, something not discernible in the archaeological record. We have seen that one of the distinguishing features of animal sacrifice in the Graeco-Roman tradition was that, in effect, anyone was ritually able to preside over a sacrifice; the choice of sacrificant was generally determined by considerations of social and political status rather

---

17. Remains of alimentary sacrifices: Méniel 1992, 91–110, 141–43, especially 93–100 on Bennecourt and 100–102 on Ribemont. Preferred species: Brunaux and Malagoli 2003, 24, who claim that remains of alimentary sacrifices, in greater or lesser quantities, have been found at all cult sites in the region; see further the survey in Watson 2007, 165–72. Absence of horses: Méniel 2008, 153.

18. In the Thesmophoria, a festival of Demeter, the celebrants sacrificed piglets and threw their bodies into a ditch to rot, although for only a period of time. In Rome, a horse was sacrificed in the rite of the Equus October, and a dog was sacrificed at the festival of the Robigalia: Scullard 1981, 193–94, 108–9.

19. See, e.g., Caes. Bell. Gall. 6.17.3 and Diod. Sic. 5.31.3. On the tendency of the Greeks and Romans who wrote on Gallic cult to emphasize the exotic and pass over the familiar, see especially Marco Simón 2007.

than by ritual requirements. The situation in Gaul was apparently quite different. Julius Caesar claims that among the Gauls were two distinct groups of leading men, whose authority had very different bases. One group, whom he describes with the Latin word *equites*, "horse-men," derived their power from their birth and their control of resources, which they used to acquire followers (*clientes*) in the warfare that was endemic in Gallic society. Presumably because this was a social category that was readily understandable to his Roman audience, he has little to say about them.[20] The other group, in contrast, he discusses at considerable length, presumably because they were difficult to fit into familiar Graeco-Roman social categories. It was no doubt for the same reason that to label them, he resorts to the Celtic word "druids." The druids, he declares, functioned as ritual experts, as judges with authority to resolve public and private disputes, and as teachers responsible for the maintenance and transmission of traditional lore; it was no doubt the last of these roles that led other Graeco-Roman writers to describe them as philosophers. According to Caesar, the druids enjoyed special privileges and had great influence and consequently attracted many students.[21] Among much else, they exercised authority over sacrifices. Caesar reports that "they are involved in matters relating to the gods, have charge of sacrifices public and private, interpret issues of religious observance," and can forbid those who do not accept their judgments from participating in sacrifices, which he calls the most severe punishment in Gaul. Other major Graeco-Roman accounts of the druids agree on this point: Diodorus Siculus states categorically that "it is a custom among them that no one perform a sacrifice without a philosopher" (i.e., a druid), and Strabo similarly observes that the Gauls "would not sacrifice without druids."[22] Although we have no evidence for the precise role that druids played in sacrifices, it would appear that Gallic sacrificial tradition, in requiring the participation of a ritual specialist, differed significantly from the Graeco-Roman norm.

---

20. See Caes. *Bell. Gall.* 6.13.1–3 for the two groups and 6.15 for the *equites*; see Roymans 1990, 17–47, for an anthropological analysis of their social role that is very much in keeping with Caesar's account.

21. Caes. *Bell. Gall.* 6.13.4–14.6; other major ancient accounts are Diod. Sic. 5.31 and Strabo 4.4.4, both of whom associate druids with philosophy. There have been many studies of the druids; Piggott 1968 remains a balanced overview; the most recent are Brunaux 2006 and Aldhouse-Green 2010.

22. Role in sacrifices: Caes. *Bell. Gall.* 6.13.4 and 6–7; Diod. Sic. 5.31.4; Strabo 4.4.5.

Such was the practice of animal sacrifice among the peoples of northern Gaul at the time of the Roman conquest in the mid-first century BCE. The conquest inevitably brought significant social and cultural changes, as the indigenous peoples gradually adapted to the norms of the Roman conquerors. The Romans introduced a new language, new cultural practices, new economic networks, and new social structures. Above all, they introduced the model of the Roman city, in both its physical and its institutional dimensions, as the essential organizing principle of civilized life. These changes naturally affected the traditional practice of animal sacrifice in ways that gradually brought it into even closer conformity with Graeco-Roman norms than it had been before.[23] We may begin exploring these changes by returning briefly to Gournay-sur-Aronde. After the sanctuary's destruction at the end of the second century BCE, it seems to have remained out of use for a time. Then, in the second half of the first century BCE, that is, shortly after the Roman conquest, it was rebuilt from the ground up. A hearth was now constructed on the site of the central pit, surrounded by a structure with stone foundations on three sides and probably open on the fourth. This phase seems to have ended in the early to mid-first century CE. In the sixth and last phase, a Gallo-Roman temple was constructed in stone, with an enclosed central hall surrounded on all four sides by a portico. The excavators dated this phase to the mid-fourth century CE, on the basis of two coins found in the rubble layer of the temple foundation. As Ton Derks has pointed out, however, the construction of a new Gallo-Roman temple at such a late date is virtually unparalleled. If we can explain the coins as the result of later activity on the site, we might redate this sixth phase to the mid-first century CE and place it in direct continuity with the previous phase.[24]

Similar transformations occurred at other sites in northern Gaul. At Fesques, some 65 kilometers northwest of Gournay, the central pit altar with its wooden shelter was replaced in the Augustan period by a more substantial building, which was in turn replaced, probably in the late first century CE, by a stone Gallo-Roman temple and portico. At Ribemont-sur-Ancre, what apparently began as a sort of military trophy in the third century BCE was replaced in the Augustan period by a Gallo-Roman temple, which over the course of the next two centuries was gradually elaborated and extended

---

23. Changes brought by Roman conquest: Woolf 1998, especially 106–41 on urbanism. On northern Gaul in particular, see Wightman 1985, especially 75–100 on urbanism. On changes in religion, see especially Woolf 1998, 206–37; Derks 1998; Van Andringa 2002; Watson 2007.

24. Derks 1998, 173–75; cf. Moser 2016, 182–83.

into a monumental complex.[25] The transformation in the physical space of these sanctuaries must have been accompanied by changes in sacrificial ritual. Although no Roman-era animal remains have been documented at Gournay, the replacement of the central pit by a hearth suggests a change from a ritual centered on the decomposition and relocation of the animal remains to one that involved burning, much more in keeping with Graeco-Roman norms. A similar shift to a hearth can also be observed at Bennecourt and other sites. At the same time, rituals involving decomposition did not entirely disappear. A site near Longueil-Sainte-Marie, some 20 kilometers south of Gournay, which can be dated by pottery remains to the third century CE, has yielded the bones of some forty horses, along with four dogs. The jumbled state of the bones and the absence of smaller bones have led researchers to conclude that they are probably the result of a process of decomposition and relocation similar to that attested at Gournay and Vertault.[26] Nevertheless, such practices seem to have remained comparatively rare in the Roman period. Much more common in Roman-era sanctuaries is evidence for feasting and thus presumably for alimentary sacrifices. As we have seen, this practice was already common in the pre-Roman period, and it continued into the Roman period with only minor changes. The remains from one deposit near the Gallo-Roman temple at Ribemont, for example, dating to the first and second centuries CE, consist of some 60 percent pigs, 18 percent sheep, and slightly less fowl. Similar patterns can be observed at the Roman-period sanctuaries of Bennecourt, Fesques, and other sites. The chief differences from the alimentary deposits of the pre-Roman period are an increase in domestic fowl and a disappearance of dogs.[27]

Although incorporation into the Roman Empire had a significant impact on rural sanctuaries such as that at Gournay-sur-Aronde, an even more important development was the appearance and spread of Graeco-Roman urbanism, which, as we have seen, was fundamental to Graeco-Roman civilization. Physically, Gallic settlements were gradually transformed into Roman cities, through the application of Roman urban design, the use of

---

25. Fesques and Ribemont: summaries in Van Andringa 2002, 91. There were similar developments at Vendeuil-Caply and Bennecourt (Van Andringa 2002, 91, 94) and at La Villeneuve-au-Châtelot (Brunaux and Malagoli 2003, 71–73); see also Roymans 1990, 70–73, and the survey in Watson 2007, 103–44.

26. Hearths: Van Andringa 2002, 96. Longueil-Sainte-Marie: Lepetz and Méniel 2008, 162.

27. Ribemont: Fercoq du Leslay and Lepetz 2008, 203; general trends: Brunaux and Malagoli 2003, 42–46; Méniel 2008, 149; Moser 2016, 179–80.

Roman construction techniques, and the adoption of Roman building types. Institutionally, the old Gallic warrior aristocracy, Caesar's *equites*, reinvented itself as a Roman order of decurions, with typical magistracies (*duoviri*, aediles) and civic priesthoods. By far the most widely attested priestly titles are ones associated with the worship of the Roman emperor: *sacerdos Augusti* or *sacerdos Romae et Augusti*, "priest of Augustus" or "priest of Rome and Augustus," and (using a different Latin term for priest) *flamen Augusti/ Augustalis*. Although the native priestly title of *gutuater* survived in a few places, it was assimilated into the Roman hierarchy of public priesthoods and magistracies. The spread of Graeco-Roman urbanism, in both its physical and institutional dimensions, would necessarily have involved the spread of the Graeco-Roman practice of public animal sacrifice, which, as we saw in Chapter 3, was so deeply integrated with it.[28]

Accompanying the spread of Graeco-Roman urban institutions was the suppression of one of the most distinctive Gallic social institutions, the order of druids. Ancient writers attest that Roman authorities gradually outlawed the druids, although the evidence is slight and inconsistent. According to the elder Pliny, "the reign of Tiberius Caesar did away with their [i.e., the Gauls'] druids and this class of seers and healers"; according to Suetonius, it was the emperor Claudius who "completely wiped out the cult of the druids among the Gauls, a matter of dreadful savagery that under Augustus had merely been forbidden to citizens." Although the precise sequence of events is uncertain, it nevertheless seems clear that starting in the Augustan period, Roman authorities came to regard druidic tradition as incompatible with Roman identity and that thenceforth, elite Gauls who aspired to positions of power and prestige had to choose between druidic training and Roman citizenship; we may readily guess which choice proved more popular. The reason for the suppression of the druids is debated. Roman writers emphasize their association with human sacrifice, which, as we have seen, Roman authorities prided themselves on stamping out. Martin Goodman, however, has plausibly argued that they were equally motivated by a suspicion of social structures that did not conform to those with which they were familiar. Whatever the reason, by the later first century CE, druids seem to have lost their central role

---

28. Spread of Graeco-Roman urbanism: Wightman 1985, 75–100; Woolf 1998, 106–41. Transformation of Gallic aristocracy: Roymans 1990, 44–45, 268–69. Priesthoods in Roman Gaul: Van Andringa 2002, 207–31, with 217–18 on the title *gutuater*.

in Gallic society and become marginalized.[29] Taken together, the suppression of the druids and the development of a Roman order of decurions amounted to a policy on the part of Roman authorities to discourage structures of social power that did not suit their needs and encourage those that did. As a result, they effectively eliminated one of the most anomalous aspects of Gallic sacrificial practice and brought it more into line with the Graeco-Roman norm, in which acting as sacrificant was linked not with the mastery of traditional wisdom but rather with elite social status based on wealth.

The incorporation of Gaul into the Roman Empire, and the concomitant assimilation of Gallic society and culture to Graeco-Roman norms, resulted ultimately in a distinctive regional culture that scholars conventionally label "Gallo-Roman." As the label suggests, this culture was the result of a complex process that involved both continuity and change. Since we have already considered a number of changes in matters of cult, we may now briefly consider some examples of continuity. The one most easily documented is continuity of place. As we have seen, a number of rural Gallic sanctuaries in northern Gaul, including those at Gournay-sur-Aronde, Bennecourt, and Fesques, continued in use into the Roman period. These examples were not the exception but rather the rule. As scholars have observed, virtually every known rural sanctuary of the pre-Roman period remained active under Roman rule, lasting in some cases down into the fourth century CE.[30] We must be careful not to exaggerate this continuity. On the one hand, shrines were certainly constructed in the Roman period that have no known Gallic antecedents, especially in the new Roman-style cities. On the other hand, since the presence of Roman-era remains makes it easier to identify rural cult sites, it may be that those that fell out of use and did not receive a Roman makeover have gone undetected. Nevertheless, there remains a striking degree of continuity in cult places from the pre-Roman to Roman periods.

A corollary of this continuity in place is continuity in deity. In general, most people in the ancient world tended to associate specific deities very closely with specific places. There was at the same time a countervailing tendency to associate local deities with more abstractly conceived generalized

---

29. Plin. *Nat.* 30.13; Suet. *Claud.* 25.5. Last 1949 makes the best case that human sacrifice was the issue, effectively accepting the Romans' presentation of themselves as a civilizing power. See, *contra*, Goodman 1987, 239–44, who aptly observes that the essential problem for Roman authorities was that "Druids enjoyed extremely high status among the Gallic and British populations even though many of them were not rich" (242).

30. For example, Roymans 1990, 68.

deities or, in what amounts to much the same thing, to interpret local deities as specific manifestations of universal deities. To take two examples from Section 3c, we saw that the Boeotian cult of Apollo Ptoios probably originated when a local oracular deity was assimilated to the Panhellenic Apollo and that the cult of Apollo Tyrimnos in Thyatira resulted from the identification of the Lydian sun god Tyrimnos with the Greek Apollo.[31] The same tendencies seem to have been in operation in Gaul. People conceived of deities first and foremost in association with specific locales and only secondarily identified them with more widely worshiped figures. As evidence for the importance of local deities, scholars point to the abundance of divine names and epithets attested in the inscriptions of Roman Gaul, of which there are hundreds, many of them known from only a single inscription. Some of these names occur independently, while others are paired with a Graeco-Roman divine name. Thus, alongside Apollo Ptoios and Apollo Tyrimnos we may place Lenus Mars of the Treveri (around modern Trier), Mars Camulus of the Remi (modern Rheims), and Mars Cicolluis of the Lingones (modern Langres).[32]

Yet is it really accurate to speak of continuity in cult places and deities? Worship may have continued in the same place, but was the place really the same if it had undergone a greater or lesser degree of physical transformation? Was a deity really the same if worshipers endowed it with new names, new attributes, and new associations? That is, should we place the emphasis on continuity or change? Earlier scholars of Gallo-Roman religion tended to stress continuity, inviting us to imagine Gauls of Roman times maintaining the worship of their ancestral deities under a superficially Roman veneer. William Van Andringa, in one of the most important studies of Gallo-Roman religion in the last twenty-five years, pushed back against this tendency and instead stressed the fundamental transformation of Gallic culture, and specifically its religious culture, that resulted from its incorporation into the Roman order. For Van Andringa, apparent continuity masked underlying change. In contrast, Claudia Moser argues for ongoing significance of place: "even with these Roman transformations in architecture and practices, a strong locative

---

31. The phenomenon of identifying deities from different linguistic or cultural traditions and transferring names, epithets, and iconographic attributes from one to another is conventionally described as *interpretatio Romana* (or *Graeca*, etc.), a phrase that originates with Tacitus (*Germ.* 43.3). The best discussion is Ando 2005 = Ando 2008, 43–58; see also Rives 2011b.

32. Deities and place in Roman tradition: Ando 2008, 120–48; in Gallic tradition: Brunaux 2000, 72–73. For the Gallo-Roman deities noted here, see Van Andringa 2002, 141–49; cf. Derks 1998, 91–118.

continuity persists, a privileging, in the new performance spaces above, of the location of the old places beneath."[33]

The only possible resolution to this debate is to acknowledge that continuity and change are in effect opposite sides of the same coin; one can scarcely exist without the other. Whether a person wishes to emphasize one or the other depends on his or her priorities, goals, and frame of reference. Gallic elites, I would argue, deployed animal sacrifice as an effective tool for achieving change while simultaneously maintaining a degree of continuity. It was a practice long established in Gallic tradition that, by virtue of its numerous similarities with Graeco-Roman practice, they could both retain as ancestral and readily refashion as Roman. It is telling that the most far-reaching changes involved not the procedures of sacrificial practice, despite the apparent shift from rituals centered on decomposition to rituals that involved burning, but its institutional context, as authority over sacrifices shifted from specialists in traditional lore to an urbanized economic elite. As a result, in Gaul as elsewhere, animal sacrifice increasingly came to structure the sorts of socioeconomic hierarchies that were normative in the Roman Empire. Yet even as these elites brought Gallic structures of social power into increasing conformity with Graeco-Roman norms, the ancestral practice of offering animal sacrifices to ancestral gods allowed them to claim a distinctively Gallic identity.

## 4d. *Judaeans*

In sharp contrast to the Gauls, most of the evidence for Judaean sacrificial practice comes from an extensive and quite varied body of texts that for the most part emanate from within Judaean tradition.[34] We can distinguish three main groups: biblical texts, texts from the later Second Temple period (second century BCE to late first century CE), and early rabbinic texts, especially the Mishnah (compiled in the early third century CE). The most important of the biblical texts come from the Torah, especially the detailed regulations for offerings in Leviticus. These texts are the result of a long and complex process of historical development and redaction, the details of which are much debated but do not concern us here. The process was probably substantially

---

33. Van Andringa 2002, e.g., 97: "En somme, le constat de continuité, lorsqu'il est avéré, masque l'essential, c'est à dire la reformulation drastique des espaces sacrés opérée progressivement à partir de l'époque augustéenne." Moser 2016, quotation from 185.

34. This section contains material that appeared in an earlier form in Rives 2014.

complete by the early Second Temple period, around the fifth century BCE, and Judaeans thereafter increasingly came to accept the Torah as authoritative.[35] The writings from the later Second Temple period are very various. For our purposes, the most important are the works in Greek of the Judaean philosopher Philo of Alexandria (mid-first century CE) and the historian Josephus, who commanded Judaean troops in the rebellion against Rome, was taken prisoner, and was eventually given citizenship and brought to Rome in the retinue of the emperor Vespasian after the destruction of Jerusalem in 70 CE; it was there in the following decades that he wrote his account of the Judaean war and his history of the Judaean people. Lastly, the Mishnah is a compilation of rabbinic opinions on the interpretation of Judaean law and custom that were originally issued and transmitted orally and only later redacted into a written text. The opinions quoted often explicitly contradict one another, so that the Mishnah as a whole documents points of disagreement as well as areas of general agreement. All these sources are to varying degrees as much prescriptive as descriptive, amalgamating accounts of the way sacrificial ritual was carried out with opinions about the way it ought to be carried out. This is especially true of the Mishnah, which dates to a period after the destruction of the Jerusalem Temple, when Judaeans were no longer able to conduct actual sacrifices, and sacrifice had as a result become a primarily discursive construct.[36] In drawing on all three of these very different bodies of evidence in the following analysis, I am inevitably making generalizations about matters that require greater nuance. My concern, however, is with broad differences between Judaean and Graeco-Roman tradition, which I hope I do not seriously misrepresent.

Judaean sacrificial practice differed considerably more than Gallic practice from the Graeco-Roman norm. As a result, Judaeans could not employ it to the same degree or in quite the same ways to integrate themselves into the Graeco-Roman mainstream. Nevertheless, I argue that animal sacrifice, as a point of cultural overlap between a highly distinctive local tradition and the normative Graeco-Roman tradition, constituted a crucial site for cultural and political negotiation. In what follows, I first survey the key differences between Judaean and Graeco-Roman sacrificial practice and analyze their

---

35. The main set of regulations is Lev. 1–7, attributed to the Priestly source, but others appear in the so-called Holiness Code (Lev. 17–26) and elsewhere in the Torah. De Vaux 1964 remains a classic discussion; more recently, see Marx 2005.

36. Second Temple sources: J. Schwartz 2014. For the Mishnah, I have relied on Danby 1933, together with the important study of Balberg 2017.

implications.[37] I then turn to the similarities between the two and examine the ways Judaean elites used their tradition of animal sacrifice to foster good relationships with their non-Judaean overlords.

The most fundamental difference between Judaean and Graeco-Roman sacrificial practice was the fact that Judaeans refused to participate in sacrifices to gods other than their own. This was simply one facet of the general Judaean rejection of all alien worship, and it is by no means clear that animal sacrifice constituted an area of particular concern. Rabbinic opinion suggests that it did not; thus, for example, we read in the Mishnah the view that "'The idolater' [is culpable] no matter whether he worships or sacrifices or burns incense or pours out a libation or bows himself down to it or accepts it as his god or says to it 'Thou art my god.'"[38] The Damascus Document, one of the "Dead Sea Scrolls" discovered at the site of Qumran, specifically forbids the sale of clean animals to gentiles for fear that they might offer them in sacrifice, but this is only one of several kinds of prohibited commercial interactions with gentiles, and in later rabbinic tradition, a concern with selling gentiles animals that could be sacrificed is not particularly prominent.[39] Likewise, although the refusal of Judaeans to participate in the worship of other gods was one of the chief objections that their non-Judaean neighbors had against them, I find little evidence for a concern with the refusal to sacrifice in particular. The limitation of sacrifice to only one god, although viewed by Judaeans and non-Judaeans alike as a distinctive feature of Judaean sacrificial practice, was thus only one aspect of their general rejection of alien worship.

Equally distinctive was the fact that in Judaean tradition, sacrifices could take place in only one location, the Temple in Jerusalem. In Graeco-Roman tradition, a person could offer a sacrifice more or less anywhere; to sacrifice to Jupiter Optimus Maximus, for example, one did not need to go to his chief temple on the Capitoline Hill in Rome or even to one of the many other temples dedicated to him. The fact that Judaeans who wanted to sacrifice to their god had to do so in the Temple in Jerusalem must have struck non-Judaean observers as peculiar. There is, to be sure, some slight and uncertain

---

37. See also Petropoulou 2008, 118–20, especially 119–20 on the lack of sacrificial euergetism in Judaean tradition.

38. m. Sanh. 7.6, trans. Danby 1933.

39. Damascus Document: CD 12.9–10. Rabbinic views on this issue seem to have been less strict than those found in the Qumran texts; two passages in the Mishnah that are sometimes interpreted as evidence for a specific concern with gentile sacrifice (m. 'Abod. Zar. 1.5–6) seem to me to suggest the reverse.

evidence that some Judaeans of the diaspora may, in fact, have performed sacrifices, especially the Passover lamb, at other locations.[40] Set against this, however, is the much more abundant evidence that all Judaean sacrifices, including that for Passover, took place in the Jerusalem Temple. Certainly, this was what Judaean law required, and the large number of pilgrims who poured into Jerusalem for Passover suggests that this was what most Judaeans did. The known exceptions appear to prove the rule. Jodi Magness has made a strong case that the sectarians at Qumran offered sacrifices in their own community, but if they did, it was in the context of their explicit rejection of the Temple cult in Jerusalem as corrupt and no longer legitimate. The Judaean temple founded in Leontopolis in Egypt by the high priest Onias III in about 168 BCE housed a regular sacrificial cult until it was finally closed by order of Vespasian in 73 CE, yet none of the abundant Judaean literature produced in Alexandria explicitly refers to it, and later rabbinic sources accord it only a grudging and very limited recognition.[41]

The restriction of Judaean sacrifice to the Jerusalem Temple has further implications as well, since it was a space from which non-Judaeans were strictly excluded. The Temple was a massive complex consisting of multiple courtyards with the Temple building itself at the heart. Non-Judaeans were permitted only in the outermost courtyard, known accordingly as the Court of the Gentiles, which was in effect an agora-like space exterior to the Temple complex proper. Animal sacrifices, however, took place in the innermost courtyard, at an altar immediately adjacent to the Temple building, to which only priests had access and which was accordingly known as the Court of the Priests.[42]

The priesthood itself constitutes another way in which Judaean practice differed from Graeco-Roman. In Judaean tradition, as in Gallic tradition, a

---

40. Philo (*Mos.* 2.224; *Decal.* 159; *Spec.* 2.145) implies that Judaeans resident in Alexandria sacrificed Passover lambs in their homes; see Petropoulou 2008, 183–85, and especially Rosenblum 2013. Josephus (*AJ* 14.259–61) records a decree of the city council of Sardis in Asia that refers to sacrifices offered in the Judaeans' assembly hall: some scholars attribute this to a misunderstanding, but Cohen 1987, 165–66, argues that we should take it literally.

41. Qumran: Magness 2016. Temple of Onias: see Piotrkowski 2019, especially 102–4 on the date of its foundation and 401 on its sacrificial cult. Josephus is the only Judaean writing in Greek to mention it explicitly, although there may be oblique references in a few other texts: Piotrkowski 2019, 209–322. Limited recognition: m. Menah. 13.10, the only reference in the Mishnah.

42. Exclusion of gentiles: Philo *Legat.* 212; Joseph. *BJ* 5.193–94 and 6.124–26, *AJ* 15.417; Acts 21.28–29; m. Kelim 1.8. Two copies survive of the inscription posted at the Temple perimeter prohibiting entry to gentiles: *OGIS* 598 and *SEG* 8.169, with Llewelyn and Van Beek 2010.

valid animal sacrifice required the participation of someone from a strictly defined group of people, in this case, a member of the hereditary clan of Aaronite priests. Although any adult male Israelite, with certain exceptions, was ritually able to slaughter a victim, only priests could perform the essential acts of splashing the blood on the altar, flaying and cutting up the carcass, and burning the appropriate parts. It was thus only priests who could effectively act as sacrificants. Indeed, we can trace in Judaean tradition the progressive marginalization of the sponsor of the sacrifice in favor of the priests.[43] As we have seen, this was in sharp contrast to Graeco-Roman tradition, in which the role of sacrificant was generally determined more by wealth and social status than by cultic status.

Another important difference is that in Judaean tradition, there were virtually no large-scale public sacrifices that produced significant quantities of edible meat. The vast majority of the sacrifices offered on behalf of the Judaean people as a whole were burnt offerings, equivalent to Greek holocausts, in which the entire animal was burned on the altar; these were accompanied by smaller-scale "sin offerings," the meat of which was consumed by the priests within the Temple. Individuals also offered a range of sacrifices on their own behalf, many of which were also burnt offerings and sin offerings.[44] Thus, only a few sacrifices actually produced meat that ordinary Judaeans could eat. The most important of these were the "peace offering" or thanks offering, which Josephus explicitly characterizes as "performed with the intention of providing a feast for those who have offered it," and the Passover sacrifice, which held an anomalous place in the biblical sacrificial system. The feasts connected with these sacrifices, however, seem to have been limited to a small circle of family and/or friends, such as the group of Jesus and his twelve followers that we find in the synoptic accounts of the Last Supper; Josephus assumes that some ten to twenty people typically shared a Passover lamb.[45]

---

43. Lev. 1–7; cf. Joseph. *AJ* 3.226–27; m. Zebah. 3.1; m. Menahot 9.8. Progressive marginalization of the sponsor: see Marx 2005, 89–142, for the Priestly source in Leviticus 1–7 and Balberg 2017, 27–64, for the rabbinic tradition.

44. See in general the classification of sacrifices in Philo (*Spec.* 1.194–97), Josephus (*AJ* 3.224–32), and the Mishnah (m. Zebah. 5.1–7), with Sanders 1992, 103–18. Public sacrifices as burnt offerings and sin offerings: Num. 28–29; cf. Philo, *Spec.* 1.190; Joseph. *AJ* 3.237–54. Priests eating the meat from sin offerings: Lev. 6.26, 6.29–30, 7.6–7; Philo, *Spec.* 1.239–40. Public peace offerings did exist, but the meat from them was also eaten by the priests, not by the wider community (Lev. 23.19–20; m. Zebah. 5.5).

45. Quotation from Josephus: *AJ* 3.225, trans. H. St. J. Thackeray, Loeb.; cf. Philo *Spec.* 1.212. Passover as anomalous: Balberg 2017, 142–50. Last Supper: Matt. 26.17–20; Mark 14.12–17; Luke 22.7–16. Ten to twenty people per Passover lamb: Joseph. *BJ* 6.423.

Judaean tradition, then, at least in the late Second Temple period, did not provide any occasion for large-scale public sacrifices that produced meat for general consumption.

Lastly, for funding public sacrifices, the Jerusalem Temple could draw on sources of revenue that far surpassed those available to most Graeco-Roman civic cults. In addition to various other tithes and contributions, every male Israelite over the age of twenty was required to make an annual contribution of a half shekel (interpreted as two drachmas in Greek currency) to the Temple's funds; these funds were apparently used to purchase the victims and other materials needed for the regular public sacrifices.[46] They were collected not only in Judaea and surrounding regions but from the entire diaspora; we have specific evidence for Alexandria, Cyrene, various cities in Asia Minor, Rome, and even the territory beyond the Euphrates. The sums collected were sufficient to attract the ill will of these Judaean communities' non-Judaean neighbors, who resented the fact that so much wealth was being shipped off to a distant region; both Philo and Josephus attest that Roman authorities had to intervene repeatedly in order to uphold the rights of Judaeans to collect these funds and send them to Jerusalem, although on occasion, Roman authorities themselves prevented the money from being sent. This Temple tax meant that there must normally have been ample money to fund the public sacrifices of the Judaean people and that consequently there were fewer opportunities for elite benefactors to assume their expense.[47]

As a result of these differences from normative Graeco-Roman practice, animal sacrifice was a much more limited instrument for integrating Judaeans into the Graeco-Roman mainstream than it was for Gauls. We can identify two major issues. First, the exclusivity of Judaean cult tended to impede the adaptations of cult practices that we can document among Gauls. Judaeans

---

46. Philo *Spec.* 1.77–78; Joseph. *BJ* 7.218, *AJ* 18.312–13; Matt. 17.24; m. Šeqal. 4.1; see further Safrai 1981, 70–71. The origin of the custom was referred back to Exod. 30.11–16 (cf. Joseph. *AJ* 3.194-96), even though that passage seems to describe something rather different. The period in which the annual tax became established is uncertain; many scholars have dated it to the start of the Second Temple period (cf. Neh. 10.32–33), although Liver 1963 has argued strongly that it does not antedate the late Hasmonean period; see further Balberg 2017, 112–14.

47. Alexandria: Philo *Spec.* 1.77–78. Cyrene: Joseph. *AJ* 16.169–70. Asia Minor: Cic. *Flac.* 68; Philo *Legat.* 315; Joseph. *AJ* 16.167–73. Rome: Philo *Legat.* 156–57. Beyond the Euphrates: Philo *Legat.* 216; Joseph. *AJ* 18.312. Support of Roman authorities: Philo *Legat.* 312–15; Joseph. *AJ* 16.28 and 45, 16.162–73; opposition: Cic. *Flac.* 66–69. Hayim Lapin, in a detailed and rigorous study of the cost and funding of the Temple cult, argues that, depending on population estimates and compliance rates, the Temple tax could easily have covered the costs of the biblically mandated sacrifices but not the total operating costs of the temple. Lapin 2017, 422–24; cf. 436.

could not participate in the worship of gentile deities or even associate their deity with those of others without compromising their claims to Judaean identity. Likewise, the fact that core Judaean cult practices, notably animal sacrifice, could take place only in a space from which non-Judaeans were excluded effectively limited the latter's participation in Judaean cult.

The second issue is less obvious but equally important: Judaean tradition provided much less opportunity for the sort of sacrificial euergetism that I argued in Chapter 3 was so important in the Graeco-Roman tradition. There were several reasons for this: an extensive system of public funding for public sacrifices, an absence of large-scale public sacrifices that produced meat for general consumption, an emphasis on the role of the priest over that of the sponsor. The few known cases of sacrificial euergetism seem to prove the rule. For example, Josephus claims that Herod celebrated the completion of his work on the Temple by sacrificing three hundred oxen, but since he says nothing about feasts, we are perhaps meant to infer that these sacrifices were holocausts. It is also important that, since Herod was not a priest, he would not have been able to preside over his sacrifices in person, unlike benefactors in the Graeco-Roman tradition. Even priests, who could preside over sacrifices, could do so only in the inner courtyard of the Temple, which significantly limited the opportunity for public spectacle. In short, Judaean sacrificial practice simply did not lend itself to structuring the sorts of socioeconomic hierarchies that were so prominent in Graeco-Roman cities. On the contrary, the social location of animal sacrifice in the two traditions provides a perfect illustration of what Seth Schwartz has identified as a broad and fundamental difference in ideology between Judaean and Graeco-Roman culture, with the egalitarian solidarity espoused by the former in tension with the unequal reciprocity characteristic of the latter.[48] As we have seen, the most drastic intervention that Roman authorities made in Gallic sacrificial practice, the suppression of the druids, had the effect of bringing it into line with Graeco-Roman institutional norms. In the case of the Judaeans, however, there were even greater structural obstacles to the assimilation of their sacrificial practice.

Yet even though the differences in sacrificial practice between the Judaean and Graeco-Roman traditions were both numerous and significant, I would

---

48. Joseph. *AJ* 15.422–23. On Herod as a benefactor on the Graeco-Roman model, see S. Schwartz 2010, 99–102, and on Judaean egalitarian solidarity in tension with Graeco-Roman institutionalized reciprocity, 7–20, 166–75. Balberg 2017, 108–25, argues cogently that the rejection of euergetism in favor of the collective funding of sacrifices is an ideologically motivated innovation of the rabbis; for the reasons I outline here, I would add that they built on earlier tendencies.

argue that a number of crucial similarities allowed both Judaeans and non-Judaeans alike to employ it as a tool for cultural and political negotiation. There is, first of all, the basic fact that in both traditions, the ritualized slaughter of animals was an important cult practice. Second, the class of victims was essentially the same: edible domestic animals that had to be unblemished and free of imperfections. There were, to be sure, some specific differences: most obviously, Judaean tradition prohibited pigs absolutely and apparently placed more emphasis on birds; similarly, sacrifices in which the entire animal was burned on the altar were regular in Judaean tradition but exceptional in Graeco-Roman tradition.[49] As we have seen, however, observers could readily understand such variations on the general principle that each sanctuary had its own specific sacrificial rules. Third, sacrificial procedures in the two traditions were very similar: the animals were presented at an altar, had their throats cut, were flayed and butchered, and then were partly or wholly burned on the altar; the parts that were not burned were eaten. We can even identify similarities in specific details, such as the fact that in both Judaean and Greek tradition, it was very important that blood be splashed on the altar, although most non-Judaeans were probably not aware of this.[50]

These similarities in sacrificial procedure were important in a situation where both Judaeans and people in the Graeco-Roman mainstream not infrequently regarded each other with bafflement, suspicion, and distaste.[51] It is worth noting that, despite the considerable evidence for both Graeco-Roman criticism of Judaean tradition and Judaean criticism of gentile worship, almost nowhere in either body of material do we find criticisms of animal sacrifice. Non-Judaeans resented the Judaean refusal to worship other gods and more generally their perceived aloofness; they mocked their abstention from pork and found the practice of circumcision repulsive.[52] Among Judaeans, there was a long-established tradition, extending back at least to the time of

---

49. As noted by Theophrastus (in Porph. *Abst.* 2.26), although in a form that is exaggerated and misinterpreted to suit his argument. Holocausts in Greek tradition: Ekroth 2017; see also Ekroth 2018 for a comparison of Greek and Levantine holocaustic practice.

50. Blood in Judaean tradition: Balberg 2017, 67–85, who demonstrates that its importance was emphasized even more by the rabbis; in Greek tradition: Ekroth 2005.

51. It is impossible to quantify tensions between Judaeans and non-Judaeans. There is ample evidence for a variety of amicable relations, e.g., Feldman 1993, 57–69, 342–82; Barclay 1996, 103–24, 320–35; Harland 2003, 200–210, 219–28. At the same time, there is also ample evidence for tensions of a sort that are not so easily documented for other groups; see, e.g., Feldman 1993, 107–23; Barclay 1996, 48–81; Schäfer 1997, 163–95.

52. See Feldman 1993, 123–76, and, in general, Schäfer 1997.

the Babylonian exile, of deriding the gods of gentiles as mere idols, man-made objects that had no power for good or evil. Later texts built on this foundation by emphasizing the fundamental error of worshiping the creation rather than the creator and by identifying idolatry as the cause of all immorality.[53] Notably absent from all these polemics, however, is any reference to animal sacrifice, a practice that both sides accepted as an appropriate mode of worship.[54] The only real exception known to me also provides some of the best evidence for this accord. The Alexandrian grammarian Apion, in his now-lost polemic against Judaeans, apparently did in some way criticize their practice of animal sacrifice; Josephus tartly responds by pointing out that this was a custom that Judaeans held in common with all the rest of humanity and that Apion's criticism is simply further proof of his own status as an Egyptian and thus a cultural outsider.[55]

The fact that animal sacrifice provided common ground between these two otherwise very different traditions meant that, despite the limitations discussed in the first part of this section, both Judaeans and non-Judaeans were able to employ it as a valuable resource in forging and maintaining positive relations with each other. Although Judaeans could not participate in non-Judaean sacrifice, non-Judaeans could participate in Judaean sacrifice, even if in only a limited way. They could not preside over a sacrifice or, it seems, eat the meat from it or even be present at its performance, but they could be honored by sacrifices offered to the Judaean god on their behalf.[56] They could also take a more active role by sponsoring sacrifices themselves.

---

53. The classic versions of this critique are in Second Isaiah (especially 44.6–20; cf. 40.18–20 and 46.6–7) and Jeremiah (10.1–16); later elaborations include Wisdom of Solomon 13–15, the "letter of Jeremiah" (= Bar. 6), and Philo *Decal*. 52–69.

54. See especially Sibylline Oracle 3.545–600, which attacks the Greeks for sacrificing to idols (547–49) but praises the Judaeans who offer animal sacrifices at the Temple of the great God (575–79); the author foretells that the Greeks, too, will one day offer holocausts at the Temple (564–70).

55. Joseph. *Ap*. 2.137–38. Barclay 2007, 240n499, points out that Apion is unlikely to have criticized animal sacrifice as such and plausibly suggests that his criticisms may have been more like those leveled by Tacitus, *Hist*. 5.4.2, who claims that Judaeans sacrifice bulls and rams as an insult to Apis and Ammon, respectively.

56. Non-Judaeans were explicitly prohibited from sharing in the Passover offering (Exod. 12.43–49). According to rabbinic tradition, they could make vow offerings and free-will offerings (m. Šeqal. 1.5), but these presumably could only have taken the form of burnt offerings (cf. M. Šeqal. 7.6), since gentiles would have been prevented from eating the meat from shared offerings by the requirement that those who do so be ritually clean (Lev. 7.19–21, 22.1–6), an impossibility for gentiles; see *HJP* 2.309–10. D. Schwartz 1992 argues that victims supplied by gentiles were regarded not even as sacrifices but merely as gifts.

Although it is impossible to determine how frequently non-Judaeans actually did that, passages in both Josephus and the Mishnah suggest that it was not uncommon.[57]

Animal sacrifice seems to have had particular importance in maintaining good relationships between Judaeans and their non-Judaean overlords. There are numerous examples, in texts ranging from the biblical book of Ezra to Josephus, both of non-Judaean rulers demonstrating their respect for the Judaean god by sponsoring sacrifices, either in absentia or in person, and of Judaeans demonstrating their respect for their non-Judaean rulers by offering sacrifices on their behalf.[58] Although some of these episodes are certainly not historical, for the purposes of my argument, their historicity matters less than the insight they provide into Judaean ideas about the role of animal sacrifice in constructing positive relationships with gentile rulers. Three specific passages illustrate the range of possibilities.

The first comes from the book of Ezra, written probably in the fourth century BCE, which quotes what purports to be a letter of the Persian king Darius. In it, Darius confirms a decree issued by his predecessor Cyrus, granting the Judaeans the right to rebuild their Temple and promising to subsidize the work with particular tax revenues. Darius augments these directives by instructing his governors that "whatever is needed—young bulls, rams, or sheep for burnt offerings to the God of heaven, wheat, salt, wine, or oil, as the priests in Jerusalem require—let that be given to them day by day without fail, so that they may offer pleasing sacrifices to the God of heaven, and pray for the life of the king and his children."[59] In this account, the initiative comes from the gentile overlord, who not only bestows benefactions on the Temple but also acknowledges the power of the Judaean god and the privileged role of the Judaean people by requesting that they offer sacrifices and prayers on his behalf. A very different pattern is found in the opening chapter of Baruch, in which the exiled Judaeans in Babylon are said to have collected money to send to the high priest in Jerusalem with the following instructions: "Here we send you money; so buy with the money burnt offerings and sin offerings and incense, and prepare a grain offering, and offer them on the altar of the Lord our God; and pray for the life of King Nebuchadnezzar of Babylon, and

---

57. Joseph. *BJ* 2.409–16 and 5.15–18; M. Šeqal. 1.5 and 7.6; see further Safrai 1981, 107–11.

58. For a brief overview, see *HJP* 2.309–13.

59. Letter of Darius: Ezra 6.6–12, with quotation from 6.9–10 (NRSV translation); cf. 1 Esd. 6.27–33; Joseph. *AJ* 11.12–7 and 99–103. On the historicity of these documents, see Grabbe 2004–8, 1.76–78, 209–16.

for the life of his son Belshazzar, so that their days on earth may be like the days of heaven. The Lord will give us strength, and light to our eyes; we shall live under the protection of King Nebuchadnezzar of Babylon, and under the protection of his son Belshazzar, and we shall serve them many days and find favor in their sight." In this case, the initiative lies with the Judaeans, who demonstrate their loyalty to their ruler by offering sacrifices on his behalf and hope thereby to gain his goodwill.[60] Lastly, the Hellenistic Letter of Aristeas combines these two patterns, so that an initiative from the ruler meets with an appropriate response from the ruled. Here, Ptolemy II writes to the high priest in Jerusalem to announce various benefactions, request men to translate the scriptures, and send a hundred talents of silver for sacrifices; in his response, the high priest reports that he has "offered sacrifices on behalf of you, your children, and your Friends, and all the people prayed that your plans might prosper continually and that Almighty God might preserve your kingdom in peace with glory."[61]

Although none of these texts is easy to date, none is likely to be later than the second century BCE. We can thus say that at least by the mid-Hellenistic period, the role of animal sacrifice in forging good relationships with gentile overlords was a familiar idea to Judaean communities both in Judaea itself and in the diaspora. It was an idea, moreover, that people actually put into practice, even if none of these particular episodes was historical.[62]

Given this earlier background, it is not surprising that in the Roman period, the animal sacrifices of the Temple came to play an important role in maintaining good relations between Judaeans and their Roman rulers. At least some Roman authorities offered sacrifice at the Temple in person, such

---

60. Bar. 1.10–12 (NRSV translation); the events described here are widely acknowledged not to be historical. The text's date and provenance are very uncertain: *HJP* 3.735–36.

61. Let. Aris. 35–46, with quotation from 45, trans. White and Keddie 2018. The content of the book is widely accepted as legendary; the author was almost certainly a Judaean resident in Alexandria, writing sometime between the mid-second and mid-first century BCE: White and Keddie 2018, 32–39.

62. For other episodes that are possibly or probably historical, see Joseph. *Ap.* 2.48 on Ptolemy III offering sacrifice in 241 BCE; Joseph. *AJ* 12.138–44, with Grabbe 2004–8, 2.324–26, for a letter of Antiochus III from shortly after his conquest of Jerusalem in 200 BCE promising funding for the Temple cult; 2 Macc. 3.2–3 on Seleucus IV Philopator (187–175 BCE) providing funding; 1 Macc. 7.33, with *HJP* 1.168–70, for sacrifices on behalf of Demetrius I Soter in 161 BCE; and Joseph. *AJ* 13.241–44, with *HJP* 1.202–4, for Antiochus VII Sidetes providing victims for a sacrifice in the 130s BCE (while in the process of besieging Jerusalem, no less).

as Marcus Agrippa in 15 BCE and the governor Vitellius in 37 CE.[63] Most famous, and most important, Judaean priests offered a daily sacrifice on behalf of the emperor and the Roman people, a practice that according to Philo was instituted in the reign of Augustus. The sources contradict each other as regards the funding of these sacrifices: Philo says explicitly that Augustus paid for them out of his own revenues, whereas Josephus says equally explicitly that they were provided at the expense of the Judaean community, although he elsewhere implies that the funding came from Roman sources. Although it is possible that the funds derived from provincial taxes and so might reasonably be described as either Judaean or imperial, it is perhaps slightly more likely that Josephus was massaging the facts when he claimed that the Judaeans provided the funding.[64] In addition to these daily sacrifices, additional sacrifices were offered on special occasions. When the Alexandrian ambassador to the emperor Caligula accused Judaean ambassadors from Alexandria of disloyalty, they were quick to respond that they had offered hecatombs on three occasions: at his accession, after his recovery from illness, and before his expedition to Germania. Josephus responds in a very similar vein to Apion's charge of disloyalty, arguing that rather than blaming the Judaeans, he should admire "the magnanimity and moderation of the Romans, since they do not compel their subjects to transgress their ancestral laws, but accept such honors as it is pious and legitimate for their donors to offer."[65] In general, the demonstrations of mutual respect that the practice of animal sacrifice afforded both Judaeans and Romans seem to have worked reasonably well to maintain good relations.

By the same token, it was the cessation of the regular sacrifices for the emperor that both signaled and contributed to the breakdown of good relations. Josephus, in describing the buildup to the Judaean revolt against Rome, reports that at one point, the captain of the Temple in Jerusalem persuaded the officiating priests to accept no gift or sacrifice from a foreigner, with the result that the sacrifices on behalf of the emperor and the Roman people ceased to be offered. Josephus even goes so far as to describe this action as

---

63. Agrippa: Joseph. *AJ* 16.12–15, with *HJP* 1.292; cf. Philo *Legat*. 291, 294–97, although he does not mention sacrifice. Vitellius: Joseph. *AJ* 18.122, with *HJP* 1.350.

64. Philo *Legat*. 157, 317; see Smallwood 1961, 240–41, for the suggestion of provincial taxes. Josephus's evidence is inconsistent: at *Ap*. 2.77, he says that the sacrifices were offered "at the common expense of all Judaeans" (cf. *BJ* 2.197), but at *BJ* 2.409–10, he implies that the funding came from Roman sources; for the suggestion that his claim in *Ap*. is not accurate, see Barclay 2007, 210–11n268.

65. Philo *Legat*. 355–57; Joseph. *Ap* 2.72–77, with the quotation from 2.73, trans. Barclay 2007.

"the foundation of the war against the Romans."[66] Although we cannot know for certain whether Roman authorities at the time viewed the cessation of sacrifices on behalf of the emperor in the same way that Josephus later did, the overall social and political significance attached to animal sacrifice in this period suggests that they very well may have.

With the destruction of the Jerusalem Temple and the concomitant end of Judaean sacrificial cult, animal sacrifice ceased to play an important role in shaping relations between Judaeans and non-Judaeans.[67] Its significance, however, by no means came to an end. As Mira Balberg has demonstrated in cogent detail, the practice of animal sacrifice continued to be a central concern for the early rabbis, who lavished considerable care on the elaboration of the rules governing its performance. Sacrifice was for them not a mere metaphor, a symbolic means of attributing value to another practice such as prayer or charity, but rather a specific ritual act, even if it existed in the discursive rather than material sphere. Nor was this ongoing emphasis on animal sacrifice simply a peculiarity of the rabbis, since images of sacrifice also occur in visual sources such as the paintings from the synagogue in Dura-Europus.[68] Many Judaeans continued to refuse to sacrifice to other gods, and since they could no longer sacrifice to their own god, they, like Christians, did not sacrifice at all. Christians, however, came to regard the practice of animal sacrifice as intrinsically wrong, as we will see in Chapters 7 and 8. In striking contrast, most Judaeans, it seems, never questioned the central place of animal sacrifice in the worship of their god. It was perhaps for this reason that, as we will see in Chapter 9, whereas the Christian refusal to sacrifice became a central issue in Roman hostility toward Christians, the Judaean refusal, as far as we know, had no repercussions. Indeed, the emperor Julian, in arguing that Judaean tradition had more in common with Hellenic tradition than Christianity, gave pride of place to the Judaean practice of animal sacrifice; according to later Christian accounts, it was his desire to see the Judaeans revive their

---

66. *BJ* 2.408–9, with further elaboration at 410–17.

67. Although it is not certain that Judaean sacrificial practice came to an end with the destruction of the Temple, majority opinion holds that it did; see, e.g., *HJP* 1.521–23; *contra*, Hutt 2018–19, 252–64.

68. Balberg 2017, especially 223–34. Dura-Europus: Hachlili 1998, 117–18 with plate III-11, and 131–33, 149–50 with plates III-23 and III-24.

sacrificial cult that led him to order the restoration of the Jerusalem Temple.[69] As Balberg has argued, the rabbis continued throughout the imperial period to present Judaeans as "people who sacrifice" and thus as participants in the shared Graeco-Roman culture of the Roman Empire.[70]

## 4e. Conclusion

In the cultural context of the Roman Empire, animal sacrifice had a number of distinctive features. As a cult practice that existed from an early date in both the Greek and the Roman traditions, it was an important element in the Graeco-Roman culture that served to define the norms of civilized life in the Roman Empire. People in both the Greek and the Roman traditions could easily regard it as not only normal but also natural, a proper and expected way of demonstrating piety to the gods. At the same time, thanks to the principle that it was normal for specific cults and shrines to have their own particular procedures, there was considerable flexibility in what could count as a proper animal sacrifice. As a result, when new peoples were brought under Roman hegemony, their elites could employ their own traditions of animal sacrifice as an effective tool for negotiating cultural and political interactions and integration. As we have seen, peoples with cultural traditions as different as Gauls and Judaeans did precisely that. For the peoples of northern Gaul, animal sacrifice provided a supple instrument for achieving social and cultural change while simultaneously maintaining continuity in ancestral traditions. For Judaeans, it served as a crucial point of overlap between their own highly distinctive tradition and Graeco-Roman norms. These are just two examples of the ways elites across the empire could employ the practice of animal sacrifice to forge a place for themselves within the empire-wide structures of social power. Yet although the specifics of these negotiations varied significantly depending on the particular culture involved, there was one factor that was common to the whole empire. That is the focus of Chapter 5.

---

69. Julian *Contra Galil.* 299A–C + 305B, D + 306A-B (= Loeb 3.402–6). Later accounts: Rufin. *Hist. eccl.* 10.38–40; Sozom. *Hist. eccl.* 5.22; Socrates *Hist. eccl.* 3.20; Theodoret *Hist. eccl.* 3.20. See further Section 10c herein. Porphyry (in August. *Ep.* 102.16) evidently made a similar point.

70. "People who sacrifice": Balberg 2017, 228.

# 5

# *Animal Sacrifice and the Roman Emperor*

## 5a. Introduction

In Chapters 3 and 4, we examined the ways animal sacrifice helped shape and maintain two of the systems that provided the Roman Empire with a degree of unity and enabled it to function as smoothly as, at its height, it did. Thanks to the distinctive characteristics of Graeco-Roman sacrificial practice, public animal sacrifice served to structure the normative socioeconomic hierarchies of Graeco-Roman cities that allowed Roman authorities to sustain their vast empire with maximum efficiency and minimum investment of resources. At the same time, as an important element in the shared Graeco-Roman culture that defined imperial standards of civilization, as well as a practice that was in some form already traditional among many of the peoples brought under Roman hegemony, it provided local elites with an effective and flexible tool for negotiating their cultural and political integration into the empire. In this chapter, we will consider some of the ways animal sacrifice played a similar role in shaping and maintaining the most crucial unifying feature of the empire, the figure of the Roman emperor.[1]

As has often been observed, the emperor was one of the few things that was truly common to the entire empire. The unique status of the emperor within the empire was expressed through his unique status vis-à-vis the divine, in what is usually labeled "imperial cult." Although this label is so convenient that we may not easily dispense with it, it can also be seriously

---

[1]. This chapter expands, corrects, and refines arguments that I previously advanced in Rives 2019b.

misleading. Two points are crucial. The first is a question that for many years was implicit in all scholarly discussions of imperial cult: how could anyone seriously regard another human being as a god? The implicit answer was always that no thoughtful person could. As a result, most people tended to dismiss phenomena that they labeled "imperial cult" as mere political stratagems devoid of true religious significance, empty conventions at best and servile flattery at worst. Over the last half century, however, scholars have increasingly moved beyond the often simplistic assumptions that underpinned this dismissive approach and have instead focused on the way imperial cult drew on traditional practices and imagery as a means of defining the role of the emperor. The second point is closely related. Although the phrase "imperial cult" encourages us to imagine a coherent and unified system, it is, in fact, merely a conventional modern label for what was in reality a congeries of quite varied cultic, verbal, and iconographic practices, strategies, and institutions that in different and sometimes contradictory ways brought the emperor into a distinctive association with the divine. The fact that imperial cult was not a unified system was, in fact, one of its strengths, since its variety and flexibility provided the peoples of the empire with a wide range of options for engaging in it.[2]

Given the social and political importance of animal sacrifice that I have already described, it should come as no surprise that it had an important place in this range of practices and strategies. To analyze its significance, I employ the framework of the three different roles inherent in sacrificial practice that I outlined in Section 1b: the one who offers the sacrifice, the one on whose behalf it is offered, and the one to whom it is offered. For many years, the role that attracted the most scholarly attention was the third, the one to whom a sacrifice is offered, since it seemed to define the emperor as a god. As we shall see, however, the actual situation was a great deal more complex than that. The emperor could, and did, take any of the three roles in a sacrifice. Although the role of sacrificant has received less attention than the other two, I argue that it was at least as important, since it located the emperor in the tightly woven connections between public animal sacrifice and euergetism discussed in Chapter 3. Above all, the very fact that the emperor could fill different roles in sacrificial procedure, and in some cases more than one role

---

2. Unique status of the emperor: Hopkins 1978 is a classic essay; Ando 2000, especially 206–73, is one of the most thorough treatments. Price 1984 remains fundamental for modern scholarship on imperial cult, although there has been much important work since then; for a good recent summary, see Frija 2019.

at the same time, was what rendered the practice of animal sacrifice so well suited to the creation of a broad consensus around the figure of the emperor. In what follows, I look first at sacrifices on behalf of and to the emperor and then at the emperor as sacrificant, the one who offers the sacrifice.

## 5b. *Sacrifices for the Emperor*

Animal sacrifice was a regular and central element in the worship of the Roman emperor. Although the evidence is less abundant than we might expect, the general picture is nevertheless clear enough. Sacrifices for the emperor took place both on a recurring annual basis (for example, annual vows and imperial anniversaries) and on special occasions (for example, accessions, victories, threats to health and security). In this section, I focus especially on annual sacrifices.

Sacrifices for the emperor played an important role in defining his position from the start. Already in January 29 BCE, shortly after Augustus had defeated his rival Marcus Antonius and established himself as the sole ruler of the Roman world, the senate decreed that "the day on which he entered the city be glorified by public sacrifices and considered sacred for all time"; when Augustus entered the city that summer, the consul Valerius Potitus "publicly and in person, on behalf of both the people and the senate, presided over a sacrifice of cattle at Caesar's arrival, which had previously never been done for anyone." A decade later, annual public sacrifices marking notable events in Augustus's reign began to be instituted and offered at monuments specifically constructed for that purpose. Augustus himself records two of these in his *Res Gestae*, the long account of his accomplishments that he had inscribed outside his tomb. In October 19 BCE, to mark his return from a tour of the eastern provinces, the senate decreed an altar to Fortuna Redux, "Fortune Who Leads Back Home," at which the *pontifices* and Vestal Virgins were to offer an annual sacrifice. A few years later, in 13 BCE, "when I returned to Rome from Hispania and Gallia . . ., the senate decreed that an altar of Pax Augusta [Augustan Peace] should be consecrated for my return on the Campus Martius, at which it directed the magistrates and priests and Vestal Virgins to offer an annual sacrifice." The poet Ovid, who may well have witnessed this sacrifice, confirms that it was offered to Pax Augusta, and iconographic evidence suggests that the victims included both cows and sheep.[3] Over the

---

3. 29 BCE: Dio Cass. 51.20.3 and 21.1–2. Fortuna Redux: *Res Gestae* 11. Pax Augusta: *Res Gestae* 12.2; Ov. *Fast.* 1.709–22.

course of Augustus's reign, the practice of marking imperial anniversaries with public offerings became well established, and it soon spread to other parts of the empire.

Before examining it in more detail, however, I first want to note another practice that also involved annual sacrifices for the emperor: the vows for the emperor's well-being. A vow (Latin *votum*, plural *vota*) was a well-established practice in both the Greek and the Roman traditions. It was essentially a form of contract between a person or persons and a deity. The mortal party made a specific request of the divine party and undertook to make a specific offering if that request were granted. In Rome, the most important public vow was that made every January 1, when, as noted in Section 3d, the new consuls prayed to Jupiter Maximus Optimus for the well-being of the res publica throughout the coming year. In an annual vow like this, the new vow was preceded by the sacrifice that discharged the previous year's vow. Early in the reign of Augustus, these traditional vows were altered to include the emperor as well as the Roman people, and by the reign of Caligula, the emperor had effectively displaced the res publica, of which he was now the embodiment, and the ritual had come to be spread over two days, with the sacrifice discharging the previous year's vows on January 1, in keeping with long-standing tradition, and the new vows for the year to come made on January 3. We can deduce further details about the specific procedures for these vows from the *commentarii* of the Arval Brothers. These preserve the actual wording of the vows undertaken by that priesthood, as well as indicating the deities and victims involved, usually an ox for Jupiter Optimus Maximus and heifers for Juno Regina, Minerva, and Salus Publica, the "Well-Being of the People."[4]

We know that vows on behalf of the well-being of the emperor were made in provincial cities just as they were in Rome, although our evidence is slight. The younger Pliny, in his correspondence with Trajan from Bithynia, twice notes that "we have undertaken and likewise discharged solemn vows on behalf of your safety," and a few fragmentary inscriptions recording such vows have been found in Cyrenaica and Dacia. Enough survives of these inscriptions to show that the language of the vows was close to that found in the Arval *commentarii* in Rome and that they similarly involved sacrifices of

---

4. Traditional vows on January 1: Ov. *Fast.* 1.71–88; *Pont.* 4.4.29–34; *Pont.* 4.9.29–30 and 49–50; cf. Livy 41.14.7; see further Scullard 1981, 52–53. Reign of Augustus: Dio Cass. 51.19.7. Date of January 3: Plut. *Cic.* 2.1; Gaius at *Dig.* 50.16.233.1. Evolution of the ritual: Scheid 1990, 298–309. Arval Brothers: Scheid 1990, 316–63, especially 323 for the deities and victims (citing *CIL* VI.2065 = Scheid 1998 no. 55, ll. 18–21, from 87 CE).

cattle. Who presided over them is unknown. Pliny's letters suggest that the governor presided when he was present, but the governor could be present in only one city of the province at a time. We may reasonably suppose on the basis of what was done in Rome that in other cities, a local magistrate or other official presided, although we have no specific evidence for this at all.[5]

The best evidence for offerings on imperial anniversaries comes from two sources. One is the *commentarii* of the Arval Brothers in Rome, and the other is a text known as the Feriale Duranum, a papyrus from the site of Dura-Europus on the Euphrates that contains a list of the festivals observed by a Roman military unit stationed there in the 220s CE. Together these documents make it clear that the most important imperial anniversaries were birthdays, followed by anniversaries of accessions and other major events. The choice of anniversaries seems to have shifted over time according to the emperor and dynasty in power, although the Feriale Duranum indicates that birthdays could be celebrated indefinitely and so could accumulate over the years. The two sources differ noticeably in the offerings that they specify for these anniversaries. Whereas the Arval Brothers observed all imperial anniversaries with sacrifices of cattle, the Feriale Duranum restricts cattle sacrifices to major anniversaries and prescribes *supplicationes*, offerings of incense and wine, for lesser occasions, such as the birthdays of imperial women.[6]

A few inscriptions show that similar but much less extensive cycles existed in individual cities of the western empire, although virtually all our evidence comes from the first two decades CE. The inscribed festival list or *feriale* from Cumae, dating to the period 4–14 CE, contains a number of imperial anniversaries connected with Augustus and his family. As in the Feriale Duranum, each entry consists of a date, the anniversary being observed, and the type of offering prescribed; in this case, it is almost always a *supplicatio*, except for the birthday of Augustus, when an animal victim (the precise type is not specified) was sacrificed to the emperor. There are also the detailed regulations for the altar of the Numen Augusti at Narbo in Gaul (modern Narbonne), dating to the year 11 CE; these require that a board of three *equites* and three freedmen offer victims (likewise unspecified) and provide

---

5. Plin. *Ep.* 10.35; cf. *Ep.* 10.36 and 100–101. Inscriptions: Reynolds 1962 and Reynolds 1965 on Cyrenaica; Marghitan and Petolescu 1976 on Dacia; cf. Saquete Chamizo et al. 2011 on an inscription from Spain recording vows undertaken on an imperial birthday. Plutarch (*Cic.* 2.1) says that *archontes* led the vows, a term that could refer equally to Roman governors and local magistrates.

6. Arval Brothers: Scheid 1990, 384–439. Feriale Duranum: P. Dura 54, first published with extensive commentary in Fink, Hoey, and Snyder 1940.

the people with incense and wine for *supplicationes* on three important anniversaries: Augustus's birthday, the day of his first receiving legal power, and the day on which he resolved a local conflict. Lastly, there is the inscription of 18 CE from Forum Clodii discussed in Section 3d, which directs that two victims (again unspecified) be sacrificed on the birthday of Augustus and a bull calf on that of Tiberius, with wine and pastries distributed to married women on the birthday of Livia.[7]

Although a scarcity of evidence precludes firm conclusions, it seems that it was common for cities of the western empire to have regular cycles of imperial anniversaries, like those in the *commentarii* of the Arval Brothers and the Feriale Duranum but on a much smaller scale, which they observed with public offerings. Since these cities generally used the Roman calendar, it was relatively simple for them to adapt the "official" cycle of imperial festivals. The inscriptions surveyed here suggest that the pattern of offerings found in the Feriale Duranum was typical: animal sacrifice for the emperor seems normally to have been limited to only the most important occasions, whereas lesser anniversaries were observed with *supplicationes*; when there was an animal sacrifice, the typical victim was the most prestigious one, that is, a bovine. We may guess, however, that there was considerable variety of offerings, depending on the wealth and ambition of the community involved.[8] As to who presided, we have relatively little to go on. The *feriale* from Cumae gives no indication whatsoever; in Forum Clodii, it was apparently the *duoviri*, the local chief magistrates, although the inscription is not clear on this point; in Narbo, it was a special board of *equites* and freedmen. All these inscriptions date to a very early period in the development of imperial cult, however, and it seems likely enough that as its institutions developed, the local imperial priests, who appear so regularly in the epigraphic record, became the ones normally responsible.

The Greek cities of the eastern empire present a very different picture. There the sacrifices and festivals honoring the emperor and his family

---

7. Cumae: *CIL* X.8375 = *ILS* 108 = Degrassi 1963, no. 44; see further Fishwick 1987–92, 2.1.490 and 509–10, and Gradel 2002, 96–97. Narbo: *CIL* XII.4333 = *ILS* 112 = EDH HD063725; see further Gradel 2002, 239–40, and Fishwick 2007. Forum Clodii: *CIL* XI.3303 = *ILS* 154 = EDR 153071. For a general discussion of sacrifice in imperial cult in the Latin west, with a full survey of the evidence, see Fishwick 1987–92, 2.1.501–28, with 588–89 for a brief hypothetical reconstruction; see also Fishwick 2002–5, 3.247–58.

8. Cf. Fishwick 1987–92, 2.1.515: "Expense will undoubtedly have been a major concern and one would expect the sacrifice of a victim to have been limited to a few major feast days, with other anniversaries observed by the cheaper rite of the supplication."

were more often geared to the local context than to the cycle of imperial anniversaries, although those could also be observed. Some of these festivals were entirely new and devised specifically for the emperor, while in other cases, the emperor and members of his family were integrated into preexisting cults. A long inscription from the small city of Gythium in Laconia, dating to the first years of Tiberius's reign (14–19 CE), provides a good example of a new festival established specifically for the emperor and his family. The beginning and the end of the inscription are lost, but from what survives, we learn that this was a multiday festival consisting of *agōnes thymelikoi*, musical and literary competitions conducted in the theater. The first day was devoted to "the god Caesar Augustus, son of the god, Savior and Liberator," the second day to Tiberius, the third to Livia, and so on. After six days dedicated to illustrious Romans, an additional two days of competitions were dedicated to local benefactors. The festival opened with a procession that began at the sanctuary of Asklepios and Hygieia and proceeded to the Kaisareion, the imperial shrine, where the ephors, the chief magistrates, sacrificed a bull; various civic bodies also sacrificed in the agora. In addition, statues of Augustus, Tiberius, and Livia were erected in the theater, before which the city councilors and magistrates burned incense prior to the entrance of the competitors. The official charged with making the arrangements for the festival was the agoranomos, the magistrate responsible for the market and public order.[9] As for festivals for local deities to which the emperor was added, we have already encountered several examples in Section 3c: in Acraephia in Boeotia, the traditional festival of Apollo Ptoios had by the early first century CE become the Great Ptoia and Kaisareia, and in Thyatira in Asia, the "first Augustan and Tyrimnean festival" over which Dionysios son of Menelaos presided in the 130s CE was presumably a continuation of an earlier festival dedicated to the local god Apollo Tyrimnos. The association of the emperor with traditional deities could also occur in the context of new festivals, such as that established in Oenoanda by Gaios Ioulios Demosthenes, which in its original form included two days for sacrifices to "ancestral Apollo" but which in its final form gave the emperor a place equal to that of Apollo. Overall, the integration of emperors and their families into traditional cults seems to have been a common phenomenon across the Greek world.[10]

---

9. *SEG* 11.923, with Seyrig 1929, and for the broader regional context, Camia and Kantiréa 2010.

10. Acraephia, Thyatira, Oenoanda: see Section 3c. Integration into traditional cults: Buraselis 2012; Camia 2012.

This brief selection of examples is meant not to be representative in any systematic way but only to give some sense of the range of possibilities. Even more than in the cities of the western empire, diversity is the hallmark of imperial sacrifices in the cities of the east. As in the western empire, there is considerable variety in the officials who presided over imperial festivals. In several of those noted here, the presiding official is a specially appointed agonothete, as in Acraephia, Thyatira, and Oenoanda. At Oenoanda, however, the agonothete is not the only sacrificant: all the civic officials, as well as officials from the villages in the city's territory, preside over the same types of sacrifices as he. Similarly, although at Gythium the agoranomos is in charge of the festival, the ephors are the ones who actually conduct the sacrifices in the agora. Moreover, although the small sample I have considered here does not include an example, another very important category of officiant was the priests of the Sebastoi, a collective term that encompassed the reigning emperor, his family, and his predecessors. In some cases, these priests served ex officio as agonothetes of imperial festivals, but they could also preside over sacrifices for the emperor in other contexts.[11]

As regards the types of festivals and the occasions that they celebrate, we find even greater variety in the east than in the west. Although there are examples of Greek cities celebrating the imperial birthdays and other anniversaries found in the "official" calendar that dominated in the cities of the western empire, local priorities seem more often to have prevailed, especially when the emperor was integrated into a preexisting cult or festival, as happened at Acraephia and Thyatira.[12] Lastly, although there was a range of offerings, the most common victims seem, as we might expect, to have been the most extravagant, bovines and in particular bulls. This is especially emphatic at Oenoanda, where the various officials collectively sacrifice at least twenty-seven bulls, although bulls are also specified as the victims in Acraephia and Gythium. The fact that a number of inscriptions use the compound verb *bouthuteuein*, "to sacrifice cattle," is a further indication that they were the standard victim in imperial sacrifices.[13]

---

11. See Camia 2016, 255–59, for a brief overview of imperial priests in Achaea, especially 257–58 for priests as agonothetes. See Frija 2012 for priests in Asia Minor, especially 145–50 for their role in sacrifices and 156–59 for priests as agonothetes.

12. See, e.g., the summary in Camia 2016, 259–65, for festivals in Achaea.

13. Bulls at Oenoanda: Wörrle 1988, ll. 68–79; at Acraephia: Oliver 1971, inscription B, ll. 84–87; at Gythium: *SEG* 11.923, ll. 28–32. *Bouthuteuein*: Frija 2012, 148; cf. the compound verb *taurothutein*, "to sacrifice bulls," in the Acraephia inscription.

It seems safe to conclude that most inhabitants of the empire, certainly all those who lived in or near urban centers, would have been familiar with sacrifices for the emperor, and sacrifices of cattle in particular. So far, however, I have deliberately hedged on a much-debated issue. When I refer to sacrifices "for" the emperor, what precisely do I mean? Was the emperor the party to whom the sacrifice was offered or rather the party on whose behalf it was offered? In fact, we find both phrasings in our sources, as well as others that are more indeterminate. For example, the inscription from Gythium states explicitly that the bull that the ephors sacrificed in front of the Kaisareion was offered not to the emperor but rather on his behalf, although it does not indicate to whom they were, in fact, offered. In contrast, the inscription from Acraephia includes two references to sacrifices offered explicitly "to" the Sebastoi. The first of these is in an account of a gymnastic competition sponsored by the agonothete Epaminondas. Since the passage occurs just at the point where the inscription becomes fully legible, we cannot be sure of all the details, but it is clear that he sacrificed a bull to the Sebastoi together with Hermes and Herakles; it is notable that the inscription does not distinguish the Sebastoi, either grammatically or in any other way, from the two traditional gods. A few lines later, it records another sacrifice to the Sebastoi that was followed by a public feast. Lastly, there are some references to sacrifices that are simply said to be "of" the emperors. For example, an honorific inscription from Philadelphia in the province of Asia praises the honorand and his family for their outstanding management of the sacrifices "of the Sebastoi."[14]

There was also variety in the western empire, although it took a rather different form. Augustus established a firm precedent that "good" emperors refused to accept honors equivalent to those given to traditional gods, such as animal sacrifices or *supplicationes* of wine and incense. Such offerings were acceptable, however, if offered not to the emperor himself but to his *genius* or *numen*. The *genius*, a noun related to the verb *gigno*, "to beget," was originally a kind of divine embodiment of a man's life force, although over time, the concept was also applied to a wide range of corporate bodies and places; the *genius* of the head of the household had long been the object of domestic cult. *Numen* had a range of meanings, many of which evoked an association with divine power; it was often used with the name of a deity in the genitive. In addition, an emperor who had been formally deified after his death by a decree of the senate and received the title *divus* could also receive divine offerings.

---

14. Gythium: ll. 29–32; Acraephia: ll. 22–23, 30–31; Philadelphia: *IGRom.* IV.1615, ll. 17–18.

Deification of this sort was not automatic but reserved for those who had the support of their successor and/or the senate.[15]

The limitation of animal sacrifice to the *genius* or *numen* of the living emperor or to deified former emperors was for the most part carefully observed in official Roman contexts. The Arval Brothers, for example, generally celebrated imperial anniversaries by sacrifices of bovines to some combination of traditional deities, deified emperors, and the *genius* of the current emperor. For example, on the anniversary of Nero's taking power in 58 CE, their *commentarii* record the sacrifice of an ox to Jupiter; heifers to Juno, Minerva, and Felicitas; a bull to Nero's *genius*; oxen to Divus Augustus and Divus Claudius; and a heifer to Diva Augusta (i.e., Livia). Some century and a half later, the Feriale Duranum, an official document of a Roman army unit, directs that oxen be offered to deified emperors on their birthdays. For the anniversaries of the reigning emperor, Severus Alexander, practices differ. On March 13, the anniversary of his taking power, there was a sacrifice of bovines to Jupiter, Juno, Minerva, and Mars; lesser occasions are marked by *supplicationes*. In contrast, the entry for June 26, the day on which he came of age and was named Caesar, specifies that a bull be sacrificed to his *genius*.[16] These conventions, although in theory obligatory only for Roman citizens, naturally carried considerable weight and so can be observed more widely. For example, although the regulations for the cult at Narbo do not explicitly specify the recipient of the offerings, the fact that they take place at an altar dedicated to the *numen* of Augustus leaves little doubt. The cult at Forum Clodii similarly centered on an altar dedicated to the Numen Augustum. Nevertheless, it is clear that in the western empire, just as in the east, people also made offerings directly to the living emperor, not only in private contexts but in public contexts as well. For example, the *feriale* from Cumae uses the same grammatical construction used for *supplicationes* directed toward traditional deities, noun plus the name of the deity in the dative case, also for the animal sacrifice for Augustus.

The general category of sacrifices "for" the emperor thus encompasses a wide range of different strategies, whose precise significance has been much discussed. In a seminal paper published more than forty years ago, Simon Price argued that the Greeks of the imperial period used these details of sacrificial practice to highlight the emperor's ambiguous status by characterizing him as

---

15. *Genius* and *numen*: Fishwick 1987–92, 2.1.375–96; Gradel 2002, 37–44, 77–81, 209–12, 234–50; Flower 2017, 299–310. *Divus*: Gradel 2002, 63–68, 261–371.

16. Arval Brothers: *CIL* VI.2041 = Scheid 1998 no. 27, ll. 9–12; in general, Scheid 1990, 384–426. Feriale Duranum: P. Dura 54, col. i, ll. 23–26; col. ii, ll. 16–17.

similar to but not precisely the equivalent of the traditional gods. Sacrifices "on behalf of" the emperor, he concluded, were much more common than sacrifices "to" the emperor, and even when the latter did occur, they did not establish the same kind of relationship as did sacrifices to traditional gods. Although his analysis has remained fundamental for subsequent work, later scholars have critiqued and modified it. Steven Friesen, for example, countered that "sacrifices to the emperor and those on behalf of the emperor were not in tension with each other," because "sacrifice was not so much a means for expressing divinity as a way of demonstrating and maintaining a variety of relationships." "It was appropriate for the inhabitants to sacrifice to the emperors because the emperors functioned like gods in relationship to them. It was also correct for the inhabitants of the empire to sacrifice to the gods on behalf of the emperors because the emperors were not independent of the gods." Ittai Gradel made a similar point, effectively highlighting the fact that, in my terms, sacrifice was a practice and not a discourse. He argued, for example, that "state sacrifices to Jupiter were not performed simply because he was a god" but rather because "his immense power over the well-being of Rome gave him divine status in the Roman 'constitution.' His divine status was thus relative to the body honouring him, and it was 'constructed' by the honours accorded him by this body. Jupiter's nature, the aspect of absolute divinity, hardly mattered in this connection; it was irrelevant to the *relative* status system constructed in cultic rites."[17]

What I would like to emphasize is that animal sacrifice, when used as a practice to define the relationship of the emperor to his subjects, was characterized above all by its potential for flexibility and indeterminacy. As I noted in Section 1e, this was an essential feature of social practice as opposed to verbal discourse and one of its great advantages. For most people, the point of a cult practice like animal sacrifice was to establish and define relationships among the various parties involved, on both the human and the superhuman level. It was this practical focus that resulted in much of the ambiguity that we have noted. While the relative rarity of sacrifices offered explicitly "to" the living emperor may reflect a reluctance to treat him exactly the same as traditional gods, the practice of offering sacrifices that were in one way or another "for" the emperor made it clear that emperors, and members of the imperial family more generally, were not to be treated exactly the same as ordinary humans, either. Beyond that, I would suggest that most people were

---

17. Price 1980; Price 1984, 207–33; Friesen 1993, 146–52, with quotations from 149–50; Gradel 2002, quotation from 28–29; see also Frija 2012, 149–50.

not particularly concerned about whether the emperor was the one on whose behalf sacrifices were offered or the one to whom they were offered. As we will see in the next section, the flexibility and indeterminacy of animal sacrifice in constructing the figure of the emperor extended beyond even these two roles, since the emperor could also figure as the one who offered sacrifices.

## 5c. The Emperor as Sacrificant

Roman emperors must in practice have often presided over animal sacrifices in a wide range of contexts. The position that we conventionally describe as that of "emperor" was one that Augustus, the "first emperor," cobbled together out of bits and pieces of earlier republican offices and that thereafter gradually coalesced and evolved over time. An important element in the initial cobbling together was the assumption of traditional Roman priesthoods. Augustus was a member of all four major priestly colleges as well as several minor ones and was in addition *pontifex maximus*, the highest-ranked member of the most prestigious and powerful college and the effective head of Roman public cult. The same was true of all his successors down to the late third century CE. It was not only as priests, however, that emperors would have presided over animal sacrifices. As we have seen, in the Graeco-Roman tradition, a person did not need to be a priest in order to act as a sacrificant. The basic principle was rather that those with positions of authority within a community acted as its representative in its interactions with the gods and thus served as sacrificants in group sacrifices; although the precise nature of the office they held varied from one context to another, the basic principle was a constant. We would thus expect that as the position of emperor became more established over time and as the emperor was more and more readily accepted as the supreme representative of the Roman Empire as a whole, it must have become increasingly normal for the emperor to act as sacrificant simply by virtue of his being emperor. Yet it is not on the emperor's role as an actual sacrificant that I wish to focus here but rather on the image of emperor as sacrificant.[18]

We begin our survey with one of the most famous monuments of Augustus's reign, the Ara Pacis Augustae, the Altar of Augustan Peace. This is a large open-air marble altar on a base 11.6 by 10.6 meters, enclosed by marble

---

18. Emperor as priest: Stepper 2003; see especially her brief but perceptive argument (105–6) that representations of the emperor as sacrificant relate more to his role as benefactor than as priest. The fundamental study of such representations remains Gordon 1990, 202–19, to which my own discussion is greatly indebted.

walls 6.3 meters high. The enclosure walls, which on the east and west sides are interrupted by large entrances, feature highly elaborate reliefs on the outside. These reliefs are divided into an upper and a lower register by a meander band. Below the band on all sides are sumptuous vegetal motifs; above the band are figurative reliefs. The two long sides, north and south, feature scenes of a procession. The east and west sides each have two smaller panels, one on either side of the entrance. On the east facade, an allegorical scene of a seated woman on the left evokes themes of peace and prosperity; on the right, a now mostly lost panel depicted the personified Roma seated on pile of weapons. On the west facade, the discovery of Romulus and Remus on the left is paired with a sacrifice on the right. Within the enclosure, the altar itself, facing the west entrance and enclosed on north and south by two large slabs or "wings," also featured reliefs, of which survive only the frieze on the north wing and small fragments from that on the south wing. After a lengthy process of recovery and reconstruction, the Ara Pacis is now one of the best-preserved and best-known monumental works of art from Augustan Rome. The attention lavished on it by modern scholars is in keeping with its importance in its own day. As we have seen, Augustus devoted a section of his *Res Gestae* to it and the annual sacrifices that took place there. As *pontifex maximus*, Augustus himself must have taken part in these sacrifices, as did his successors for as long as the altar remained in use.[19]

Given the magnificence of this monument and the interest that Augustus obviously took in it, it is striking that its many reliefs do not seem to have included any depictions of the emperor as sacrificant, such as that on the so-called Altar of Domitius Ahenobarbus discussed in Section 3d. It does depict a sacrificial procession: the surviving section of the frieze on the north wing of the altar portrays on the long outer face a procession of victims, two cows and a sheep, with a number of attendants carrying sacrificial implements, and on the shorter inner face the six Vestal Virgins, as specified in the *Res Gestae*. The only surviving fragment from the inner face of the south wing depicts a male figure with veiled head, but the correspondence with the opposite relief of Vestals suggests that this frieze, too, represented figures in a procession. The corresponding field directly above the altar may have included an altar scene, but we can do no more than guess. Yet even if the small altar relief did depict Augustus as a sacrificant, its scale and location in the monument's interior would hardly have made it a dramatic public statement.

---

19. For a useful and well-illustrated overview, see Rossini 2008. Few of the many discussions of the Ara Pacis consider it as a site of animal sacrifice; the best is Elsner 1991.

The large reliefs on the exterior of the enclosure wall, by contrast, provided a space that was exactly suited to such a statement, but they definitely did not include an image of Augustus as sacrificant. Augustus does appear in these reliefs, about two-thirds in from the left in the procession on the south side, balanced by the figure of his right-hand man, Agrippa, about two-thirds in from the right. Both are depicted *capite velato*, with veiled heads, in the guise appropriate for a sacrificant. Unfortunately, the figure of Augustus is fragmentary; we can see that his right arm is extended, but the loss of his hand prevents us from knowing what he was doing. Although it is tempting to think that he was holding a *patera*, a libation bowl, as does the sacrificant in the Altar of Domitius Ahenobarbus, the fact that he is depicted in the midst of a procession and not at an altar makes that unlikely. Moreover, in Roman tradition, people veiled their heads not only when presiding over a sacrifice but also when performing other ritual acts, particularly the rituals of the distinctive Roman form of divination known as augury. A veiled head was thus a visual marker of a sacral, but not necessarily sacrificial, role.[20] Lastly, it is by no means clear what precisely the procession depicted on the two long sides of the enclosure walls is meant to represent. It is not obviously a sacrificial procession, however, since it has none of the standard iconographic markers of such a scene, such as victims and sacrificial attendants. Moreover, the normal convention in depicting sacrificial processions was to represent the sacrificant already at the altar while the victims and attendants process toward him, as on the Altar of Domitius Ahenobarbus.[21] Although viewers were perhaps intended to interpret it as a continuation of the sacrificial procession that appears on the altar relief, the differences in location and scale present significant visual obstacles. Given that the friezes adorn the enclosure of a monumental altar, casual viewers were quite likely to associate them loosely with the sacrifices performed there, but such an association was at best indirect.

An indirect association of Augustus with animal sacrifice also characterizes the one definite altar scene on the monument. The panel to the right of the west entrance, just beside the steps that lead up to the altar, depicts a

---

20. Veiled heads in augury: Livy 1.18.7, 1.36.5, 10.7.10; cf. Dion. Hal. *Ant. Rom.* 3.71.5 and Plut. *Num.* 7.2. In other rituals: Cic. *Dom.* 124 and *Nat. D.* 2.10; Livy 1.32.6; Varro *Ling.* 5.84. For images, see, e.g., the Vicus Sandalarius altar depicting an augur *capite velato*: Ryberg 1955, 60–61 with fig. 31.

21. See Billows 1993 for a survey of the possibilities, especially 80–81 for the lack of iconographic markers of a sacrificial procession; he himself argues that it represents the *supplicatio* held in 13 BCE in thanksgiving for Augustus's return. Contrast Elsner 1991, 50–52, who stresses the inadequacy of all such historicizing interpretations.

historical/mythical scene of sacrifice (see Figure 5.1). The most prominent figure is that of a man with a full beard, wearing a toga with no tunic underneath and *capite velato*. His right hand is extended over an altar of unworked stones; although the hand is lost, in this case it almost certainly held a *patera*. On the other side of the altar are two youthful attendants, one in charge of the sacrificial victim, a full-grown pig. To the right of the sacrificant was another figure; although mostly lost, what remains shows that he wears a cloak over a long-sleeved tunic and holds a long staff in his right hand. Abundant visual cues would have prompted ancient viewers to interpret this as a scene of the distant past: the rustic altar; the sacrificant's lack of a tunic under his toga, which Romans considered their most ancient form of dress; the long-sleeved tunic of the figure on the right, which viewers would have interpreted as non-Roman garb. The identity of the sacrificant has been much debated. Majority opinion has long held that he is Aeneas and that the sacrifice is that of the white sow described by Vergil in the *Aeneid*. More recently, scholars have forcefully rejected that interpretation and argued instead that he is Romulus's successor Numa Pompilius, or Titus Tatius, the king of the Sabines who joined Romulus in his rule. For our purposes, the precise identification does not matter, just as it probably did not matter to most ancient

FIGURE 5.1. Sacrifice panel from the Ara Pacis Augustae, 13–9 BCE, Museo dell'Ara Pacis, Rome.
Miguel Hermoso Cuesta/Creative Commons, CC BY-SA 3.0

viewers: whatever name they attached to the figure, if any, they would certainly have regarded him as a paradigmatic Roman leader from the early days of the city. As such, the scene would have evoked a highly effective resonance with Augustus, who was regularly represented as a new founder of Rome.[22]

Although it is possible that Augustus was depicted on other monuments as a sacrificant in his own person, there is little evidence for it. A highly decorated room at the end of the northwestern portico of the Forum of Augustus housed a colossal statue that has sometimes been identified as Augustus in the guise of a sacrificant, but that is unlikely.[23] More definite is a statue of Augustus discovered near the Via Labicana in Rome and now in the Palazzo Massimo alla Terme, which depicts him *capite velato* and with his right arm outstretched. As a comparison with altar scenes on reliefs makes clear, this pose is appropriate for a person in the act of pouring a libation, but the loss of the hand once again precludes certainty. Another statue, however, now in the Vatican's Museo Pio-Clementino and fortunately intact, has almost precisely the same pose and does indeed hold a *patera* (see Figure 5.2); although it has been identified not as Augustus but as his grandson and heir Gaius Caesar, it was very probably based on an Augustan model, such as the Via Labicana statue.[24] Lastly, we may note that some twenty to twenty-five portrait statues of Augustus *capite velato* have been found, mostly in Italy but also throughout the provinces, although as busts and heads, they naturally did not represent him in any specific act.[25] Indirect evidence for the representation of Augustus as sacrificant is found on a monument erected in his honor in 9/8 BCE by Marcus Julius Cottius, the ruler of a number of Alpine tribes who

---

22. Clothes: Gell. *NA* 6.12; cf. Plin. *Nat.* 34.23 on togas without tunics. Majority opinion: e.g., Ryberg 1955, 40–41; Gordon 1990, 209–10; Rossini 2008, 30. Virgil: *Aen.* 3.389–93, 8.42-45 and 81–85; cf. Dion. Hal. *Ant. Rom.* 1.56–57.1 and Varro *Ling.* 5.144. Numa Pompilius: Rehak 2001. Titus Tatius: Flower 2017, 320–28.

23. More precisely, the suggestion is that the colossus represented the *genius* of Augustus, depicted like the *genius paterfamilias* in wall paintings from Pompeii as a togated figure *capite velato* holding a cornucopia and pouring a libation. Spannagel 1999, 303–16, provides a full discussion and convincingly argues that the statue instead represented Divus Iulius; see further Spannagel 2017.

24. Via Labicana statue: Boschung 1993, no. 165. Gaius Caesar: Pollini 1987, 57–59, with Gaius no. 15 in the catalog.

25. Boschung 1993, 6n57, provides a full list; examples definitely found outside Italy include those at Alcúdia on Mallorca (no. 6), Osor in Croatia (no. 21), Conimbriga in Portugal (no. 89), Heraklion on Crete (no. 104), Kyme on the Aegean coast of Turkey (now in Istanbul, no. 106), Corinth in Greece (no. 114), Mérida in Spain (no. 130), and Gigthis in North Africa (now in Paris, no. 148).

FIGURE 5.2. Statue of Gaius Caesar pouring a libation, Museo Pio-Clementino, Musei Vaticani, Rome.

Marie-Lan Nguyeusen/Creative Commons, CC0

traded his royal title for that of a Roman prefect. This is a single-span arch that straddles a north-south road outside the town of Segusio (modern Susa), some 45 kilometers west of Turin. The friezes above the architrave on both the north and south facades depict a *suovetaurilia* with the sacrificant, presumably Cottius himself and/or a legate of Augustus, depicted *capite velato* in the center of the scene next to an altar. Regardless of the precise identity of the sacrificants, Cottius's adoption of this imagery suggests that it was well known in the power networks over which Augustus presided.[26]

The evidence, such as it is, thus suggests that Augustus made relatively little effort to adopt the precedent of the Altar of Domitius Ahenobarbus. Although the sacrificial reliefs on Cottius's arch are suggestive, not a single unambiguous representation of Augustus as sacrificant is extant. Images of Augustus *capite velato* are fairly common, but the extent to which viewers associated them with animal sacrifice would have depended on the extent to which they were familiar with Roman ritual protocol, since the practice of veiling one's head while presiding over a ritual was distinctively Roman. Representations of Augustus pouring a libation would probably have evoked a stronger association with animal sacrifice: although a libation could be a stand-alone offering, altar scenes such as those on the Altar of Domitius Ahenobarbus and the Ara Pacis suggest that those familiar with Roman sacrificial procedure would have readily interpreted a libation as the *praefatio* that proceeded the slaughter. Yet we have little reason to think that representations of Augustus offering a libation were common, since the Via Labicana statue is the only extant example, and even it is uncertain. We are thus left with the Ara Pacis, which makes very effective use of sacrificial imagery to represent Augustus's authority but does so in a more nuanced and oblique manner than the Altar of Domitius Ahenobarbus. It is tempting to associate this hesitation to depict Augustus directly as a sacrificant with the careful crafting of his position as "first among equals" rather than the holder of supreme power that he actually was. Yet just as his successors gradually solidified the position of emperor, so, too, they developed the imagery of emperor as sacrificant much more directly and extensively.

The first moves in that direction may, in fact, have occurred in the latter part of Augustus's own reign. We have already noted the statue of Gaius Caesar pouring a libation, which many viewers would have associated with the act of presiding over an animal sacrifice. A much more explicit scene of

---

26. Arch of Segusio: Cornwell 2015 for rich contextualization. Identity of sacrificant(s): e.g., Gordon 1990, 213–14; Letta 2006–7.

an imperial heir acting as sacrificant appears on one of two silver cups that were part of a treasure hoard discovered in the late nineteenth century in a large villa near the modern village of Boscoreale on the southeastern slopes of Mount Vesuvius. The cups, already damaged in antiquity, were carefully documented for their original 1899 publication but suffered further damage while they were in private hands for most of the twentieth century. Each cup is decorated with highly elaborate figurative reliefs: on one cup were two scenes of Augustus enthroned amid his honor guard, receiving the homage of barbarians; the other has scenes of Tiberius celebrating a triumph and presiding over the sacrifice of a bovine. In the latter, the figure of Tiberius had already been damaged in antiquity, and more of the scene was lost in the twentieth century; a sketch, however, records its state at the time of the cup's discovery (see Figure 5.3). In the original scene, Tiberius faced the tripod brazier at which the *praefatio* normally took place. To the right of the tripod is a scene of the slaughter: an attendant to the right of the victim pulls down its head, a second stands behind with axe raised to strike the blow, and a third crouches to the left holding the sacrificial knife. This is the earliest known example of a stereotyped scene that, with some variations, appears in a range of reliefs and coins over the next two centuries. There is general agreement that the scenes on the cups are copies of reliefs on a large-scale monument that is now lost; they seem too elaborate to have been devised solely for such small objects, and the fact that the arrangement of the sacrifice scene seems

**FIGURE 5.3.** Silver cup from Boscoreale, sketch of its state at time of discovery, Louvre, Paris.

R. Cagnat, "Triumphus," in *Dictionnaire des antiquités grecques et romaines*, edited by C. Daremberg and E. Saglio (Paris: Hochette, 1919), Vol. 5, 490 /Creative Commons, CC0

to have influenced later reliefs suggests that it was well known. This monument apparently celebrated a successful military campaign of Tiberius, but since Tiberius celebrated two triumphs, one in 8/7 BCE and another in 12 CE, there is debate over its date. For many years, majority opinion held that the later triumph was the one in question, and some scholars argued that the original reliefs adorned a now-lost arch of Tiberius and Germanicus erected in 16 CE. Ann Kuttner, however, in the most detailed analysis of the cups, has argued strongly that the scenes must instead refer to events in the time of Tiberius's first triumph and that the original reliefs were located on the base of a monument such as a column. Whatever the monument and its date, it evidently included the earliest known scene of an emperor (or an imperial heir) presiding over an animal sacrifice, one that eventually provided a model for future emperors.[27]

It was not, however, a model that either Augustus's Julio-Claudian successors or Vespasian and his sons seem to have adopted, since there is no evidence for images of emperors as sacrificants on any monuments of the first century CE. Reliefs on a monumental altar erected probably in the reign of Claudius included at least one and probably two or more scenes of animal sacrifice, as we know from the surviving fragments that have been attributed to it, but none of them suggests a sacrificial role for Claudius himself. Given that it was apparently modeled on the Augustan Ara Pacis, we may guess that Claudius's associations with sacrifice were, like those of Augustus, more oblique. The so-called Arch of Titus, dedicated by his brother and successor Domitian shortly after Titus's death in 81 CE, features a sacrificial procession in the frieze above the architrave; although only partially extant, its layout seems to preclude an altar scene with a sacrificant. Given our imperfect knowledge of Julio-Claudian and Flavian monuments, there may well have been scenes of emperors as sacrificants that have left no trace, but the available evidence suggests that such imagery did not play a major role.[28]

We can find some confirmation for this conclusion in the evidence of coinage. In contrast to monumental reliefs, coins have survived in abundance and have moreover been extensively cataloged. It is thus significant that there are very few coin types of the first century CE that feature emperors as

---

27. Kuttner 1995, especially 6–9 on the history of the cups, 131–42 on the sacrifice scene, and 193–98 on the date and nature of the original monument. Arch of Tiberius: Ryberg 1955, 141–44; rejected by De Maria 1988, 275–76.

28. Claudian altar: briefly, Rossini 2008, 100–103; see further Pollini 2012, 309–53. Arch of Titus: Ryberg 1955, 146–48; De Maria 1988, 287–89.

sacrificants. The earliest example is a sesterce of Caligula, issued throughout his short reign (37–41 CE), which depicts on the obverse the seated figure of Pietas and on the reverse an elaborate sacrificial scene. A sacrificant, *capite velato*, pours a libation over a small altar in front of a temple; a bovine is behind the altar to the left, its head held by an attendant, and another attendant to the right of the sacrificant carries sacrificial implements. The legend on the reverse, DIVO AVG, "to Divus Augustus," has led scholars to identify the temple as that of Divus Augustus, Caligula's deified great-grandfather, and the sacrificant as Caligula himself. The pairing of this image with that of the personified Pietas on the obverse highlights the role that imagery of animal sacrifice could play as an emblem of piety.[29] Almost fifty years later, Domitian issued a series of sesterces in the years 85–89 CE that have on the reverse a scene of the emperor, *capite velato*, pouring a libation over an altar before a shrine with a statue of Minerva, to whom Domitian was especially devoted.[30] In 88 CE, he issued another series of coins to publicize the great games, the Ludi Saeculares, over which he presided in that year. The reverse of these coins features a much more elaborate scene of sacrifice than that in the earlier series: Domitian pours a libation over an altar in the company of sacrificial attendants and an animal victim (see Figure 5.4). All these coins are small bronze or copper denominations (sesterces, dupondii, asses), which means that they would have circulated widely in everyday use.[31]

Domitian's deployment of sacrificial imagery on his coinage proved to be a harbinger of developments in the second century CE, when representations of the emperor as sacrificant became much more widespread. The key innovator was Trajan, especially in the last few years of his reign. It is from this period that we have the first definite evidence for depictions of the emperor as sacrificant on public monuments since the one to which the Boscoreale cups attest about a century before. In Rome, the centerpiece of the magnificent new Forum that Trajan built was a massive column, some 29.5 meters high, dedicated in 113 CE and decorated from bottom to top with a spiral series of reliefs depicting his wars in Dacia (101–2 and 105–6 CE). Among these reliefs are no fewer than eight scenes of animal sacrifice: three show Trajan,

---

29. *RIC* 1² = OCRE Gaius nos. 36 (37–38 CE), 44 (39–40 CE), and 51 (40–41 CE).

30. *RIC* 2.1² = OCRE Domitian nos. 277, 355, 399 (85 CE), 467 (86 CE), 637 (88–89 CE). Devotion to Minerva: B. Jones 1992, 100. A poorly attested sesterce of Vespasian from 71 CE (*RIC* 2.1² = OCRE Vespasian no. 212) apparently provided a precedent.

31. *RIC* 2.1² = OCRE Domitian nos. 612–14 (sesterces), 618–21 and 628 (dupondii), 623–27 (asses; all 88 CE). Ludi Saeculares: B. Jones 1992, 102–3.

**FIGURE 5.4.** Sesterce of 88 CE, reverse: Domitian presiding over the sacrifice of a pig (OCRE Domitian no. 613), Münzkabinett, Staatliche Museen, Berlin.
Münzkabinett–Staatliche Museen zu Berlin/Creative Commons, CC BY-SA 4.0

*capite velato*, performing the *praefatio* before a *suovetaurilia* at the establishment of a fortified army camp; five depict sacrifices connected with Trajan's arrival or departure, in which Trajan himself is again normally portrayed as the sacrificant. The repetition of such scenes, which account for some 5 percent of the 155 scenes on the column, suggests the importance of sacrificial imagery.[32] Outside Rome, an arch in the southern Italian town of Beneventum (modern Benevento), dedicated to Trajan by the senate in 114 CE, features a pictorial program that likewise places great stress on sacrificial imagery. As on

---

32. Column of Trajan, *suovetaurilia*: Scenes 8, 53, and 103 (Ryberg 1955, 109–13 with figs. 55-57); arrivals and departures: Scenes 84–85, 86, 98–99, 100–101, 102 (Ryberg 1955, 121–27 with figs. 63–67). Scholars have long connected the sacrifice on the Extispicium Relief, known from two substantial fragments found in the Forum of Trajan and now in the Louvre, with the Dacian Wars as well (e.g., Ryberg 1955, 128–30), but a recent reassessment suggests that it instead dates to the third or fourth century CE: Sobocinski and Thill 2018.

**FIGURE 5.5.** Arch of Trajan, 114 CE: Trajan presiding over the sacrifice of a bovine, Benevento.
Carole Raddato/Creative Commons, CC BY-SA 2.0

the Arch of Titus in Rome, the frieze above the architrave depicts a triumphal procession, in which sacrificial victims and attendants have a prominent place. The scene of the actual sacrifice appears in one of the large reliefs in the passageway (see Figure 5.5): Trajan, *capite velato*, performs the *praefatio* at a tripod, accompanied by sacrificial attendants, while to the left, two attendants are about to slaughter a bovine, in an arrangement very similar to that on the Boscoreale cup.[33]

In coinage as well, Trajan initiated a development that was to play a central role in propagating the image of the emperor as sacrificant, even though only one minor issue actually depicted him as a sacrificant, a dupondius dating to the period 103–111 CE. More important, sometime in the period 114–117 CE, he issued a series of large-denomination coins, gold aurei and silver denarii, with the reverse legend VOTA SVSCEPTA, "vows undertaken." This is a reference to vows for the emperor's well-being, either the annual ones on January 3 or ad hoc ones marking some notable event. The image on the reverse depicts a lighted altar between two figures: on the left, a man in a toga gestures to the altar with his right hand; on the left, a male figure with a mantle around his hips holds a cornucopia with his left arm and pours a libation over the altar

---

33. Ryberg 1955, 150–56 with figs. 82–84; De Maria 1988, 232–35; Gordon 1990, 202–4.

**FIGURE 5.6.** Aureus of 133–135 CE, reverse: Hadrian presiding over the sacrifice of a bovine (cf. OCRE Hadrian, no. 2035), Kunsthistorisches Museum, Vienna.

Kunsthistorisches Museum Wien/Creative Commons, CC BY-NC-SA 3.0 AT

with his right. These two figures are usually identified as personifications of the senate and the *genius* of the emperor, respectively.[34] Trajan was the first emperor to publicize the imperial *vota* on his coins, and it is striking that he did so by employing sacrificial imagery. His successor Hadrian, who followed his lead, heightened this imagery further. In 133–135 CE, he issued a series of coins, including both gold aurei and bronze sesterces, with the legend VOTA PVBLICA, "public vows," and a scene of sacrifice on the reverse (see Figure 5.6). Unlike the Trajanic scene, this was explicitly an animal sacrifice: to the left of the tripod, a sacrificial attendant is about to strike a bovine victim, while other attendants face the sacrificant to the right of the tripod. The latter is not an allegorical figure as on the Trajanic issue but rather the emperor himself, *capite velato*, performing the *praefatio*. Hadrian's reworking of the scene thus

---

34. Dupondius: *RIC* 2¹ = OCRE Trajan no. 548. Vota Suscepta series: *RIC* 2¹ = OCRE Trajan nos. 371–74.

presents the emperor himself as the sacrificant in the public vows undertaken for his own welfare. Hadrian's successor Antoninus Pius codified the practice of publicizing imperial *vota* in this way by issuing two extensive series of coins in all denominations, from gold aurei to copper asses, to mark his *decennalia*, the tenth anniversary of his reign, in 147–48 CE and his *vicennalia*, the twentieth anniversary, in 157–58 CE. The reverse of each coin features a scene of Antoninus Pius offering a libation over a tripod, sometimes including the victim and sometimes not. Such issues thereafter became standard for all emperors down to the death of Septimius Severus's son Caracalla in 217 CE.[35]

Later emperors likewise adopted the Trajanic practice of celebrating military accomplishments with monuments that feature scenes of emperors as sacrificants. Marcus Aurelius's wars with the Marcomanni and Quadi in 168–73 CE, for which he celebrated a triumph in 176 CE, prompted the construction of at least two major monuments in Rome. One of these, preserved more or less intact, is the Column of Marcus Aurelius in the northern Campus Martius, which was perhaps decreed at the time of his triumph and completed by 193 CE. Obviously modeled on the Trajanic column, whose dimensions it replicates, it features similar scenes of sacrifice, although they are fewer in number (only three in total) and less emphatically presented. The other monument is known solely through a series of eleven relief panels (presumably out of an original twelve), eight incorporated into the Arch of Constantine and three, preserved separately, that are now in the Palazzo dei Conservatori in Rome. Although nothing is known of their original setting and arrangement, scholars generally agree that they probably adorned an arch erected to celebrate the triumph. The panels depict in highly compressed and stylized form the course of the campaigns, from the emperor's departure from Rome to his triumph on his return, and include two scenes of sacrifices over which Marcus Aurelius presides in person: a *suovetaurilia* for the purification of the army (see Figure 10.1 in Chapter 10) and the sacrifice to Jupiter that concluded the

---

35. Hadrian: *RIC* 2.3² = OCRE nos. 2035 (aureus), 2141-42 (sesterces), 2325-30 (denarii). Antoninus Pius *decennalia*: e.g., *RIC* 3¹ = OCRE nos. 170A and B (aurei), 843-44 (sesterces), 849 (dupondius), 852A-C (asses); *vicennalia*: e.g., nos. 156Aa and b (aurei), 157 (denarius), 283, 291A and B (aurei), 306-7 (denarii), 792-94 (sesterces), 1008-12 (sesterces), 1018-20 (dupondii), 1026-28 (asses). Later emperors (I list only a few examples for each), Marcus Aurelius: *RIC* 3¹ = OCRE nos. 247-51 (aurei and denarii), 1014-18 (sesterces and dupondii); Commodus: *RIC* 3¹ = OCRE nos. 99A–C and 115 (aurei and dupondii), 433 (as), 441 and 602-3 (sesterces); Pertinax: *RIC* 4.1¹ = OCRE nos. 13a-b (aurei), 24 (sesterces), 31A (dupondius), 39 (as); Septimius Severus: *RIC* 4.1¹ = OCRE nos. 149 (aureus), 172, 186, 306–10 (denarii); Caracalla: *RIC* 4.1¹ = OCRE nos. 150–51, 178–81 (denarii), 204–5 (aurei and denarii); Geta: *RIC* 4.1¹ = OCRE nos. 24–26 (aurei and denarii); see also Elagabalus *RIC* 4.2¹ = OCRE nos. 202–3 (denarii). The fundamental study of the coinage remains H. Mattingly 1950 and 1951; see further Rachat 1980; Chastagnol 1984a and 1984b.

triumph (see Figure 5.7).[36] Again, the fact that two of the twelve panels featured animal sacrifice highlights its importance. Septimius Severus continued the use of sacrificial imagery on military monuments. Although he did not employ it on the arch he constructed in Rome, the four-sided arch that he erected in his hometown of Lepcis Magna on the coast of what is now western Libya includes two scenes of sacrifice: a large relief on one of the four sides of the attic, with reliefs of a triumphal procession on the two adjacent sides and two smaller reliefs on the interior of one of the pylons.[37]

Images of the emperor as sacrificant continued in the third century CE, although with some shifts in iconography. The sacrificial scene marking imperial *vota* that first appears under Hadrian effectively disappears after about 220 CE, but new types appear to take its place. I note here just two examples. Pescennius Niger, who along with Septimius Severus was one of the three claimants to the throne after the assassination of Commodus, issued a denarius in Antioch in 193–94 CE that on the reverse depicts him pouring a libation over an altar with the legend PIETATI AVG, "to Augustan Piety"; Severus countered by issuing a similar coin of his own from the mint in Emesa the next year. Picking up a motif last seen on the coin of Caligula, such coins spell out the significance of serving as a sacrificant. Severus also used sacrificial imagery in a very different way in a series of coins that depict him in military garb, holding a spear in his left hand and pouring a libation over a tripod with his right, with the legend RESTITVTOR VRBIS, "Restorer of the City." With such new variants, images of emperors as sacrificants continue to feature on coins, if more sporadically, throughout the third century CE.[38]

---

36. Column: Beckmann 2012; Griebel 2013. Scenes of sacrifice: Ryberg 1955, 113–15 and 127–28 with figs. 58 and 67–68; Griebel 2013, 107–13, scenes 13, 30, 75. Relief panels: Boschung 2012, 309–12, for a brief overview; Ryberg 1955, 115 with fig. 59 for the *suovetaurilia* and 157–58 with fig. 86 for the triumphal sacrifice; De Maria 1988, 303–5, for the arch.

37. Ryberg 1955, 134–36 with figs. 73a–b for the pylon reliefs, 160–62 with figs. 88–89a–b for the attic relief.

38. Pietas: *RIC* 4.1¹ = OCRE Pescennius Niger no. 68; Septimius Severus no. 413 (both denarii). Restitutor: *RIC* 4.1¹ = OCRE Septimius Severus nos. 140–140A, 167A–168B, 288–89, 512A (aurei and denarii), 753, 755 (sesterces and dupondii). The Restitutor type was adopted, with variations, by later emperors: e.g., *RIC* 4.1¹ = OCRE Caracalla nos. 41 and 323A, *RIC* 4.2¹ = OCRE Macrinus no. 81, *RIC* 5.1¹ = OCRE Gallienus (Salonina no. 83), *RIC* 5.1¹ = OCRE Claudius Gothicus nos. 188–89. On the ongoing popularity of images of emperors as sacrificants on coins, see Manders 2012, 135–37, especially the bar graph in fig. 136; she calculates that such images account for about 5 percent of coins under Septimius Severus, a little more than 4 percent for Caracalla, about 4 percent for Severus Alexander, more than 5 percent for Gordian III, about 3 percent for Philip, and less than 3 percent for later emperors down to 270 CE. Images of emperors as sacrificants also occurs in the early to mid-270s CE on coins of Aurelian (*RIC* 5.1¹ = OCRE Aurelian nos. 319-22) and the Gallic emperor Tetricus (*RIC* 5.2¹ = OCRE Tetricus I nos. 114, 214–15).

FIGURE 5.7. Relief panel from a lost monument (arch?) in Rome (late 170s CE?): Marcus Aurelius presiding over the sacrifice of a bovine, Palazzo dei Conservatori, Musei Capitolini, Rome.

White Images Scala/Art Resource, NY

Having briefly surveyed the evidence for representations of the emperor as sacrificant, we may now consider its significance. Two points bear consideration. The first concerns the clear chronological pattern. Although sacrificial imagery had a significant place in the iconographic repertoire developed to support the Augustan regime, there is scant evidence that Augustus himself was much represented as a sacrificant. Sacrificial imagery instead evoked the emperor is less direct ways, as on the Ara Pacis. A few exceptions aside, that seems to have remained standard practice for the next century. Domitian was the first to be depicted more regularly as a sacrificant in his coinage, and Trajan seems to have begun a trend to include such imagery in monumental reliefs. Thereafter, it remained a common motif in both coinage and monuments well into the third century CE. After the early third century, it disappeared from public monuments, and from the middle of the century, it became rarer on coins, until, as we shall see in Section 9d, there was a dramatic if short-lived revival in the 290s CE. I would suggest that this chronological pattern in the imagery of emperor as sacrificant corresponds to broader developments in the role of the emperor. It is well known that over time, emperors became less closely connected with the city of Rome and more representative of the empire as a whole. At the same time, and in a parallel process, the empire was increasingly integrated, becoming less an empire ruled by Rome and more an empire of Romans; the spread of Roman citizenship is one index of that change. The peripatetic Hadrian, who not only traveled throughout the empire but repeatedly publicized that fact, is often seen as a pivotal figure in these developments. It is no coincidence, I would suggest, that the increase in representations of the emperor as sacrificant took place at the same time.[39]

The reason this should have been so brings me to my second point. Representations of the emperor as sacrificant could be found across the empire, even if they were more concentrated in some locations and at some social levels than others. Although most of the surviving monumental reliefs come from Rome, some are attested elsewhere, and since only a tiny fraction of such reliefs have survived, especially from provincial sites, we may suppose that they were more plentiful in antiquity.[40] Coins provide a more reliable

---

39. See in general Ando 2000, especially 316–20 on Hadrian. Citizenship: Sherwin-White 1973, 221–394. Further on Hadrian: Boatwright 2000.

40. In addition to those noted in the text, other monumental reliefs from outside Rome that portray emperors as sacrificants include two panels from the "Parthian monument" in Ephesus that depict Hadrian and Antoninus Pius (Ryberg 1955, 133–34 with figs. 72a–b; Schörner 2011, 86–91) and a relief from the theater of Sabratha depicting Septimius Severus (Ryberg 1955, 136–37 with fig. 74).

marker of the spread of such imagery, since they circulated so widely. The coins on their own suffice to make it clear that one of the guises in which people throughout the empire would have known the emperor was that of sacrificant. Given the fact that, as we have seen, most people in urban contexts would have been familiar at first hand with the practice of public animal sacrifice, they would have understood the significance of this guise without need of explanation. Just as local benefactors enacted their positions in their communities through their roles as sacrificants, so, too, did the emperor in the community of the empire as a whole. Yet, although a live ritual could serve to structure the sociopolitical hierarchy in a relatively small community such as a city, it simply could not function in the same way on an imperial scale. What became important for the emperor was not so much actually serving as sacrificant as being represented in that guise. In this context, animal sacrifice was transformed from a practice into a symbol, one that translated into a compact yet highly charged image the work of social structuring that the practice of animal sacrifice performed on the local level. It was thus not as an actual but as a virtual sacrificant, depicted as the paradigmatic officiant in coins and reliefs across the empire, that the vast majority of his subjects came to experience the Roman emperor.

## *5d. Conclusion*

In this chapter, I have tried to demonstrate that one of the things that made animal sacrifice such a valuable tool for the creation of consensus around the figure of the emperor was that it allowed for maximum variety and flexibility. The emperor could figure as the sacrificant, the one who offered the sacrifice, or as the beneficiary, the one on whose behalf the sacrifice was offered, or yet again as the recipient, the one to whom the sacrifice was offered. Each of these roles provided a different strategy for modeling the relationship between the emperor and his subjects. As sacrificant, the emperor appeared as a participant in the ritual and a member of a human community, mediating between that community and its gods. In the emperor's case, that community was increasingly understood as the entire Roman Empire, so that images of the emperor as sacrificant implicitly located him at the pinnacle of the empire's sociopolitical hierarchy. The practice of offering sacrifices to the gods on behalf of the emperor also represented him as a member of the human community, depending like everyone else on the power of the gods, yet at the same time created a rather different relationship among the three parties: people made offerings to win the blessings of the gods for the emperor, so that the emperor in turn might convey those blessings to the people. Lastly, the practice of offering sacrifices directly to the emperor located him outside the ritual and above the community, as the one who provided the inhabitants of the empire with the benefits of peace, stability, and prosperity. Taken together, these strategies constituted contrasting yet complementary ways of communicating and constructing the superior power and status of the emperor in relation to his subjects. Although, as modern observers, we might be struck by the tensions between these different strategies or even regard them as contradictory, that does not seem to have been an issue for contemporaries. Two final examples will serve to highlight the importance of this variety and flexibility as well as its limits.

The first example concerns the peripatetic emperor Hadrian. As we have seen, his Vota Publica coin issues depict the emperor as the paradigmatic officiant at the sacrifices offered on behalf of his own well-being. Their imagery accordingly effects the convergence of two different roles in sacrificial procedure: the emperor is both the one who makes the offering and the one on whose behalf it is made. At the same time, the conventions of public animal sacrifice meant that viewers were also able to read his role as representing the empire as a whole: he was simultaneously the essential intermediary between the gods and the people of the empire and the essential recipient of their favor. The Vota Publica issues thus provide a good example of the multifaceted relationship between emperor and people that the imagery of animal sacrifice could communicate. Yet this was not the only example of sacrificial imagery on Hadrian's coinage. To commemorate his travels across the empire, he issued four different series of coins featuring personifications of the provinces, of which the one that concerns us is known as the Adventus series. The Latin noun *adventus* simply means "a coming to, an arrival," but it became a technical term for an official state visit of an emperor, an event that over time became increasingly formalized and replete with ceremonial protocols. Hadrian's Adventus issues, which date mostly to the years 130–33 CE, celebrate his visits to individual provinces. The reverse features the legend ADVENTVI AVG AFRICAE (or HISPANIAE, etc.), "For the Imperial Visit to Africa" (or "Hispania," etc.), along with a stereotyped but complex scene of an altar flanked by two figures (see Figure 5.8). On the left is Hadrian himself, his right hand raised in a gesture of address, his left hand holding a scroll. Facing him on the right is a personification of the province in question, pouring a libation over the altar with her right hand and holding in her left a symbolic object that varies from province to province (stalks of grain in the case of Africa). Many of the coins in this series also include the small figure of

**FIGURE 5.8.** Aureus of 130–33 CE, reverse: Hadrian facing a personification of the province of Africa, who presides over the sacrifice of a bovine (cf. OCRE Hadrian no. 1553–54), Kunsthistorisches Museum, Vienna.

Kunsthistorisches Museum Wien/Creative Commons, CC BY-NC-SA 3.0 AT

a bovine just to the right of the altar, in an obvious allusion to the sort of sacrifice that was particularly associated with the emperor. The Adventus issues encompass both a limited series of gold aurei, featuring Africa, Hispania, and Italia as well as the key city of Alexandria, and a much more extensive series of bronze sesterces and dupondii that depict more than fifteen different provinces.[41] In the Adventus series, in contrast to the Vota Publica series, Hadrian is not the sacrificant; that role is filled by the personification of the province. Is he, then, the one on whose behalf the sacrifice is offered or the one to whom it is offered? The image allows the viewer to pose that question, but it does

---

41. *RIC* 2.3² = OCRE Hadrian nos. 1552–62 (aurei), 1715–1800 (sesterces and dupondii); see in general Ando 2000, 316–20.

not and cannot provide an answer to it. Rather, viewers were able to pose and answer the question as they wished.

If the coinage of Hadrian provides an example of the way sacrificial imagery could be deployed to fashion the figure of the emperor with maximum flexibility and indeterminacy, my second example illustrates the limits to that flexibility. Many of the sacrificial roles that these coins assign to Hadrian would have been unacceptable to Judaeans. No gentile could possibly officiate at a sacrifice to the Judaean god, a role that was restricted to Aaronite priests. For Judaean viewers, accordingly, images of the emperor as sacrificant were not primarily representations of his piety or his role as intermediary between the people of the empire and the gods but rather a reminder of his status as a gentile. Even more emphatically, an emperor could not be the recipient of sacrifices, since that would usurp one of the privileges of their god. In the Hellenistic and imperial periods, as best as we can determine, most Judaeans regarded it as a major offense to offer to any other being the worship that they owed to their god alone, an offense that in times past had repeatedly aroused their god's anger. In Judaean tradition, then, there were strict limits on the range of ways animal sacrifice could be deployed to shape the relationship between the emperor and his subjects. It was, however, perfectly acceptable to honor the emperor by offering sacrifices to their god on his behalf, in much the same way as the citizens of Gythium did, and as we saw in Section 4d, there is ample evidence that they, in fact, did so. The flexibility of animal sacrifice as a way of defining the emperor's distinctive status was thus great enough that even Judaeans could employ it in a way acceptable to all parties.

Nevertheless, there were limits to this flexibility on both sides. Philo, in his account of the embassy that the Judaeans of Alexandria sent to the emperor Caligula, describes how Caligula, in response to their enumeration of all the sacrifices they had offered on his behalf, replied testily, "Granted that this is true and that you have offered sacrifices. But it was to another god, even if it was on my behalf. What is the good of that? You have not sacrificed to me." Although in this respect, as in so many others, Caligula was not a typical emperor, the anecdote makes it clear that to some Romans, the distinction between *sacrifices on behalf of* and *sacrifices to* was important enough that it could complicate the ability of Judaeans to participate in the empire-wide practice of honoring the emperor through animal sacrifice. On the Judaean side, it was the cessation of the regular sacrifices for the emperor that both signaled and contributed to the breakdown of good relations between Judaeans and their Roman overlords. Although Josephus, our source for this story, does not explain the reasoning behind this decision, some scholars have suggested that those responsible regarded sacrifices funded by and offered on behalf of gentiles as too great a compromise of the exclusive devotion that they owed their god. These exceptions show that the use of animal sacrifice to create cultural consensus around the emperor was an ongoing process, not a stable state.[42]

Keeping in mind these limitations, we can nevertheless conclude that animal sacrifice proved so useful in creating consensus around the figure of the emperor because it was both widespread and highly flexible. As a practice that in one form or another was traditional to virtually all groups within the empire, it provided a means of structuring and communicating relationships that was understandable by all the parties involved. Moreover, the wide range of ways in which animal sacrifice was able to structure the relationship of the emperor to his subjects meant that it provided a language that virtually all the people of the empire, regardless of their particular cultural allegiances, could employ. Animal sacrifice thus played an important part in the ongoing process of constructing the figure of the Roman emperor and consequently in constructing the empire itself.

---

42. Caligula: Philo *Legat.* 355–57, trans. Smallwood 1961. Cessation of sacrifice: Joseph. *BJ* 2.408–17.

# Epilogue

The environmental and economic factors involved in animal production in the ancient Mediterranean world, especially in the core areas of Greek and Roman culture, meant that animal sacrifice, in ways that were inherent in the practice and not reliant on any associated verbal discourse, communicated certain information about wealth and thus helped construct relationships of social power. It operated in effect at the intersection of economic power and ideology and accordingly had a distinctive role in shaping and maintaining the social, cultural, and political structures on which the smooth functioning of the Roman Empire depended. In Part I, we have explored three areas in which we can observe the work it did along these lines. Within the framework of the Graeco-Roman city, public animal sacrifice allowed members of the local elite to enact their relationship with their fellow citizens in a particularly vivid way and thus, as a distinctive element in the euergetic system, served to fashion the sociopolitical hierarchies normative in Graeco-Roman cities. In addition, as a socially charged practice common to both the Greek and the Roman traditions, it had a distinctive place in the shared culture that defined the standards of civilization within the empire; moreover, since in some form or another it was likewise traditional for virtually all the peoples brought under Roman rule, it provided their elites with an effective and flexible tool for negotiating their integration into the empire-wide networks of social power. Lastly, animal sacrifice also served as an effective and highly flexible instrument for constructing the figure of the Roman emperor in relation to his subjects.

These three areas were closely interrelated, so that the work done by animal sacrifice in one area intersected with and reinforced the work it did in the other two. For example, the sorts of sociopolitical hierarchies that Graeco-Roman animal sacrifice served to fashion and reinforce were precisely the sorts of hierarchies on which Roman authorities relied for the efficient administration of the empire. It was no coincidence that animal sacrifice was a distinctive element of the normative Graeco-Roman culture that became dominant in the empire and thus a practice that local elites could deploy in negotiating their own place within that system. Although a certain amount of variability in sacrificial practice was acceptable and even expected, deviations from normative Graeco-Roman sociopolitical hierarchies were generally curtailed. In Gaul, for example, where we can trace a significant continuity in sacrificial practice in terms of locations and deities, we also observe a significant change in the institutional framework, as the authority of the druids was gradually suppressed and animal sacrifice came instead to reinforce the sorts of sociopolitical hierarchies that Roman authorities favored. The ideological power of normative Graeco-Roman sacrificial practice coincided with the authoritative power of Roman administrative structures. So, too, it is no coincidence that animal sacrifice served to define and reinforce both local hierarchies and those that obtained in the empire as a whole, especially the all-encompassing hierarchy between the emperor and his subjects. The same local elites who used public animal sacrifice to construct their relationship to their fellow citizens also used it to construct their relationship with the emperor; as we have seen, many of the sacrifices over which they presided were sacrifices for the emperor. Moreover, not only did the imagery of emperor as sacrificant rely in part for its efficacy on viewers' familiarity with the sociopolitical role of sacrificants in their own communities, but it in turn served as a model for that role: the two were in a mutually reinforcing circular relationship.

All this might make it appear that animal sacrifice was of unique cultural and political importance, the indispensable sine qua non that held the empire together and kept it functioning. As I noted in the prologue to Part I, this is not what I mean to argue. Animal sacrifice was not an inherent element of euergetism; it was not the singular defining element of Graeco-Roman culture or the crucial tool for cultural and political integration; it was not even an essential element of imperial cult. What makes animal sacrifice interesting and worth our sustained attention is not that it was unique or indispensable but that it was operative in all these varied contexts simultaneously and often in ways that were highly distinctive. Animal sacrifice was characterized by a flexibility and adaptability that allowed it to be effective and meaningful across a wide range of social, cultural, and performative contexts. That flexibility and adaptability, in turn, resulted from the fact that it was a practice and not a doctrine or a dogma or any other type of verbally articulated discourse. It was through its very performance that animal sacrifice communicated and reinforced the sorts of social, cultural, and political norms that the ruling elites of the Roman world wanted to promote. As we will see in Part II, however, animal sacrifice was also the subject of verbally articulated discourses, discourses that ultimately contributed to a fundamental transformation of its cultural significance.

# PART II

*Discourses of Animal Sacrifice in Graeco-Roman Culture and Early Christianity*

# *Prologue*

## PAUL AND BARNABAS AT LYSTRA (ACTS 14.8–18)

The author of the Acts of the Apostles in the New Testament, in his account of the apostle Paul's first mission to Asia Minor, describes an episode that took place when Paul and his companion Barnabas had come to the city of Lystra, in what is now south-central Turkey, and were proclaiming their message of salvation.[1]

> In Lystra there was a man sitting who could not use his feet and had never walked, for he had been crippled from birth. He listened to Paul as he was speaking. And Paul, looking at him intently and seeing that he had faith to be healed, said in a loud voice, "Stand upright on your feet." And the man sprang up and began to walk. When the crowds saw what Paul had done, they shouted in the Lycaonian language, "The gods have come down to us in human form!" Barnabas they called Zeus, and Paul they called Hermes, because he was the chief speaker. The priest of Zeus, whose temple was just outside the city, brought bulls and garlands (ταύρους καὶ στέμματα) to the gates; he wanted to offer sacrifice (ἤθελεν θύειν) with the crowds. When the apostles Barnabas and Paul heard of it, they tore their clothes and rushed out into the crowd, shouting, "Friends, why are you doing this? We are mortals just like you, and we bring you good news, that you should turn from these worthless things (ἀπὸ τούτων τῶν ματαίων) to the

---

1. For a more detailed discussion of this passage and its significance, see Rives 2018, 71–78, on which I have drawn for the following.

living God, who made the heaven and the earth and the sea and all that is in them. In past generations he allowed all the nations to follow their own ways; yet he has not left himself without a witness in doing good—giving you rains from heaven and fruitful seasons, and filling you with food and your hearts with joy." Even with these words, they scarcely restrained the crowds from offering sacrifice to them.[2]

Although the historical value of this account is highly uncertain, for my purposes the issue is largely unimportant. What is most interesting to me is how the author, presumably a well-informed observer of c. 100 CE, chose to represent the interactions between an early bearer of the Christian message and the normative worship traditions of the Graeco-Roman world.[3] The people of Lystra respond to the perception that they are in the presence of gods very much as we might expect, through the practice of animal sacrifice. The priest of Zeus, whom the author and his audience would have understood to be a member of the local elite, brings bulls, the costliest victims possible, and prepares to preside over a public sacrifice on behalf of the community. Paul and Barnabas, however, react to this entirely normal behavior with dismay and try their best to prevent the sacrifice from taking place. They do this by attempting to persuade the Lystrans that their beliefs are wrong—not merely their belief that Paul and Barnabas are gods but the entire understanding of the divine realm that informs their actions. Paul characterizes these beliefs as "worthless," *mataios*, a word that in Judaean-Greek literature is often associated with the gentile worship of false gods, and insists that in reality, there is a single universal god who created the world; according to the author, even in this sudden crisis, Paul had the wherewithal to adduce specific arguments to support his assertion. In other words, Paul counters the practice of sacrifice with a verbally articulated discourse about the nature of the world, of whose truth he hopes to persuade his audience. If he succeeds,

---

2. Acts 14.8–18. All quotations from biblical texts throughout this part are from the NRSV translation, sometimes lightly adapted.

3. The most detailed and thorough attempt to relate the episode to the historical milieu of its setting is Breytenbach 1993; in contrast, Pervo 2009, 248–49, concludes that "Acts 13–14 is, by all important criteria, narrative fiction." Scholars have dated Acts anywhere from the early 60s CE to c. 140 CE; see the survey in Pervo 2006, 259–63. The consensus is for a date of c. 85 CE (Pervo 2006, 5), although Pervo himself (2006, 343–46) argues forcefully for a date of c. 115 CE. For my purposes, a general dating to the late first or early second century CE is sufficient.

or so the narrative suggests, the Lystrans will understand that their wish to sacrifice is wrong.[4]

Verbal discourses about animal sacrifice are the subject of Part II. In Part I, we explored some of the ways the practice of animal sacrifice functioned to articulate and reinforce key sociopolitical relationships in the Roman Empire. As I argued, one of the chief reasons for its effectiveness along these lines was precisely that it was a practice, which through its very performance communicated particular structures of social power. Yet, as we will see in Part II, there were from an early date people who assigned it other meanings that supplemented or even displaced those messages about social power. They did so by articulating alternative frameworks for understanding the true nature of the world, within which the practice of animal sacrifice had quite a different significance from that which it traditionally had in Graeco-Roman culture. Those who developed these alternative frameworks were generally people who lacked established forms of social power based on control of economic resources and physical force, unlike local elites and Roman officials, but were instead in the process of creating positions of authority for themselves by persuading others to accept these alternative worldviews, of which they claimed a privileged understanding.

This is not to say that the writers and thinkers discussed in this part were concerned solely or even self-consciously with advancing their own social power. Some perhaps were, but most were no doubt primarily concerned with promoting an understanding of the world that they regarded as true and beneficial to those who accepted it. In order to do this, however, they had to persuade others that their claims were true, and in that process, they inevitably had to persuade others of their own authority. In Part I, we saw that, although shaping and reinforcing sociopolitical hierarchies were not what the peoples of the Graeco-Roman world regarded as the primary goal of animal sacrifice, it nevertheless did do these things and that people at the top of the sociopolitical hierarchy at times consciously exploited that fact. So, too, here in Part II: those who developed discourses about animal sacrifice may not have been primarily concerned with using those discourses to advance their own social power, yet they nevertheless needed to do that in order to persuade people of what they regarded as the true significance of animal sacrifice.

I begin my survey in Chapter 6 with the Greek philosophical tradition, focusing on developments in the fifth and fourth centuries BCE. Although this material is outside the chronological parameters indicated in the book's title, it is essential to

---

4. *Mataios*: e.g., LXX Jer. 2.5 and 8.19, 3 Kgdms. 16.2, 4 Kgdms. 17.15, Esth. 4.17p, 3 Macc. 6.11; see further Breytenbach 1993, 397; Pervo 2006, 273. For more detailed analysis of this passage, see Pervo 2009, 345–58.

have a clear sense of the way the classical philosophical schools dealt with the topic of animal sacrifice in order to appreciate the significance of later developments. Chapter 7 focuses on the place of animal sacrifice in the extant accounts of the earliest followers of Christ, from the apostle Paul in the mid-first century CE down to the mid-second century CE. By the end of that period, many Christian leaders, it seems, had come to appropriate and repurpose the vocabulary of sacrifice and at the same time to reject the actual practice of animal sacrifice in toto. This development, however, was neither linear nor inevitable but rather contingent and haphazard. Lastly, in Chapter 8, I trace two interrelated discourses about animal sacrifice that developed over the course of the second and third centuries CE: the notion of a hierarchy of offerings correlated with a hierarchy of divine beings and the belief that animal sacrifice provided sustenance to a particular class of superhuman entities that humans ought to avoid. Both discourses, I argue, worked to undermine the social significance of animal sacrifice explored in Part I.

# 6

# *Theorizing Animal Sacrifice I*

FROM HESIOD TO PLUTARCH (C. 700 BCE–C. 100 CE)

## *6a. Introduction*

Animal sacrifice was a topic of verbal discourse in the Greek world as far back as our evidence extends. The earliest extant example is also one of the best known, the story of Prometheus's deception of Zeus that Hesiod included in *Theogony*, his grand synthetic account of the origins of the cosmic order. "When the gods and mortal men were reaching a settlement at Mekone," he tells us, Prometheus divided an ox into two portions and set them before Zeus with the intention of deceiving him. In one portion, he put the meat and the innards, covering them with the stomach, and in the other, he placed the bones, covering them with "gleaming fat." He then offered Zeus his choice. According to Hesiod, Zeus recognized the deception in advance but nevertheless chose the portion that Prometheus had presumably meant him to choose, the bones covered by the rich fat. "And ever since then the tribes of human beings upon the earth burn white bones upon smoking altars for the immortals."[1] In its original form, this story was almost certainly a simple etiological narrative that served to explain one particular element of traditional Greek sacrificial practice, the fact that the gods received a portion of the sacrificial victim that, from the human point of view, was much less desirable than the portion that went to the human participants. We thus have evidence that some Greeks from a very early date conceptualized the practice of animal sacrifice as a shared meal between gods and mortals and then tried to explain aspects of the practice that, when conceptualized in that way, appeared

---

1. Hes. *Theog.* 535–57, trans. Glenn W. Most, Loeb.

anomalous.[2] As was typical of archaic Greek culture, these early discourses about animal sacrifice took a narrative rather than an analytical form.[3]

Although Hesiod's story of Prometheus and Zeus involves no critique of animal sacrifice, other early discourses did, especially those associated with the mythic poet Orpheus and the semi-legendary wise man Pythagoras. In the first section of this chapter, I assess the nature and extent of these early critiques, examining in turn the evidence for the Orphic and Pythagorean traditions and lastly the pre-Socratic philosopher Empedocles. Given the limitations of our evidence, it is difficult to determine whether these early critiques took more of a narrative form, such as we find in Hesiod, or an analytical form; the best guess is that they probably fell somewhere in between. The development of the classical philosophical schools in Athens over the course of the fourth and third centuries BCE, by contrast, established a standard for more rigorously articulated analytical discourse. In the second section, I briefly survey the evidence for the theorization of sacrificial practice in the four major schools: Academic, Peripatetic, Stoic, and Epicurean. I close with a brief consideration of philosophical discourse on animal sacrifice as it had evolved by the first century CE.[4]

## 6b. *Early Critiques*

In venturing to explore early Orphic and Pythagorean discourses, we are entering a morass in which virtually no foothold is entirely secure. Yet it is a morass that we cannot skirt, since it contains the earliest discourses about animal sacrifice that apparently conceptualized it in such a way as to entail its rejection. In order to traverse this treacherous terrain, we must keep in mind two fundamental points. First, these discourses were neither monolithic nor tightly bounded but were instead multifaceted, capacious, and highly fluid. Second, and consequently, they seem to have steadily changed and developed over time, shifting, expanding, and adapting according to the goals of those

---

2. I am assuming that Hesiod altered the story by insisting that Zeus was not, in fact, deceived, a change that fits with his emphasis throughout the poem on that god's matchless wisdom: West 1966, 321, at l. 551. In the process, however, he also transformed the story into an account of the fundamental division between divine and mortal; see especially Vernant 1979.

3. Another early example is the episode in the *Homeric Hymn to Hermes* (105–41) where Hermes slaughters and cooks two of the cattle that he has stolen from Apollo; for a recent discussion, see Thomas 2017.

4. This chapter develops ideas that I presented in an earlier form in Rives 2011c.

who either advocated or attacked them. Generally speaking, our fullest sources are also the latest in date, from the third century CE and later, and they inevitably reflect the conditions of their day. I accordingly carefully consider the nature and date of each bit of evidence, focusing as far as possible on sources that can be more or less securely dated to the classical period. Most of these represent the views of outsiders, that is, of people who did not themselves hold the positions that they describe. Hence the surviving quotations from the work of Empedocles are all the more valuable, since they provide us with the writings of someone who himself advanced a version of these discourses and whom we can date with a fair degree of confidence. I argue that if we pay close attention to the evidence, we can see that these early critiques of animal sacrifice were in certain respects more limited than they are often thought to have been.

Although modern scholarship closely associates an abstinence from eating meat with the name Orpheus, the ancient evidence for this association consists of only a handful of passages. The earliest comes from Euripides's *Hippolytus*, securely dated to 428 BCE. When Hippolytus defends himself against his father Theseus's accusation of having raped his stepmother, Theseus sneers at his son's claim to purity: "now pride yourself and through inanimate food (δι' ἀψύχου βορᾶς) be a huckster with your food and, having Orpheus as your lord, act as a Bacchant, honoring the smoke of many writings." As commentators have pointed out, there is a certain absurdity in having Theseus charge the avid hunter Hippolytus with vegetarianism, but it is his attribution of the practice to the authority of Orpheus that concerns us.[5] Next, from a little more than two decades later, Aristophanes includes Orpheus in a list of poet-teachers, with the claim that he taught initiations and abstinence from slaughter (φόνων ἀπέχεσθαι). The fullest testimony comes from Plato's *Laws*, when the Athenian declares that some peoples made only vegetal offerings to the gods, "and from flesh they abstained as though it were unholy to eat it or to stain with blood the altars of the gods; instead of that, those of us men who then existed lived what is called an 'Orphic life,' keeping wholly to inanimate

---

5. Eur. *Hipp.* 952–54 (= Bernabé 2004–5, no. 627 T), my translation; see further Linforth 1941, 50–60. The chorus in Euripides's lost play *Cretans* (F 472 Kannicht 2004), in a passage quoted by Porphyry (*Abst.* 4.19.2), also claims to have "set my guard against the eating of animate food" (τὴν τ' ἐμψύχων βρῶσιν ἐδεστῶν; trans. Clark 2000) but amid a welter of claims to purity and mystic practices and without any clear reference to Orpheus (but see Bernabé 2004–5, no. 567 T).

food (ἀψύχων ἐχόμενοι) and, contrariwise, abstaining wholly from things animate (ἐμψύχων ἀπεχόμενοι)."[6]

That is the sum of evidence from the fifth and fourth centuries BCE attesting to an Orphic abstinence from animal flesh and virtually the total sum of evidence from all periods. Apart from a brief reference in Jerome, writing in the late fourth century CE, the only other extant writer who attests to it is Plutarch, once in a passing reference and at greater length in a passage from one of his two essays against eating meat.[7] The text of these essays survives only in mutilated form, so there are gaps and uncertainties. Nevertheless, the passage as we have it is worth setting out in full. After presenting a range of arguments against eating meat, Plutarch declares: "I still hesitate, however, to attempt a discussion of the principle underlying my opinion, great as it is, and mysterious and incredible." He then quotes some lines of Empedocles, now missing from the text, and explains that in them the poet allegorizes the doctrine "that human souls are imprisoned in mortal bodies as a punishment for murder, the eating of animal flesh, and cannibalism (φόνων καὶ βρώσεως σαρκῶν καὶ ἀλληλοφαγίας δίκην τίνουσαι)." He continues: "This doctrine, however, seems to be even older, for the stories told about the sufferings and dismemberment of Dionysus and the outrageous assaults of the Titans upon him, and their punishment and blasting by thunderbolt after they had tasted his blood—all this is a myth which in its inner meaning has to do with rebirth (παλιγγενεσίαν)." Unfortunately, after one more sentence, the text breaks off, and so we have little idea how Plutarch developed this observation. The story to which Plutarch refers is one that many modern scholars have regarded as the central myth of a distinctive and long-lasting Orphic theology: that the Titans dismembered the infant Dionysus, ate his flesh, and were destroyed by Zeus with a thunderbolt. This essay of Plutarch is the only extant text to make a connection between this myth and abstinence from killing and eating

---

6. Aristophanes: *Ran.* 1032; cf. the similar but more explicit phrasing at Hor. *Ars P.* 391–92, "caedibus et victu foedo deterruit Orpheus" (= Bernabé 2004–5, no. 626 T). Plato: *Leg.* 6.782c–d (= Bernabé 2004–5, no. 625 T), trans. R. G. Bury, Loeb; an obscure fragment of the roughly contemporary comic playwright Antiphanes (F 178 K-A) may also refer to an Orphic vegetarian diet (see Bernabé 2004–5, no. 631 V).

7. Jer. *Adv. Jovinian.* 2.14 (= Bernabé 2004–5, no. 630 F): "Orpheus in carmine suo esum carnium penitus detestatur." Plutarch's passing mention: Plut. *Conv. sept. sap.* 16, 159C (= Bernabé 2004–5, no. 629 F).

animals, although the passage in its current state does not make explicit the precise nature of that connection.[8]

When we turn to the Pythagorean tradition, the evidence is more abundant, but our problems in assessing it are no fewer. In the introduction to this chapter, I referred to Pythagoras as "semi-legendary," not because there is any significant doubt about his existence but rather because reliable information about the historical Pythagoras is meager in the extreme. Although the biographical tradition about Pythagoras that dates to the third century CE and later is rich and detailed, much of it is certainly the result of later elaboration and speculation. That said, there seems no good reason to reject the barebones outline of his life as presented there. He was born on the Greek island of Samos in the mid-sixth century BCE, migrated in adulthood to the Greek city of Croton in southern Italy, founded a society that at least at times had some political influence, and, after an upheaval, died in old age at the nearby city of Metapontum. From the earliest extant evidence, which dates to the late sixth and fifth centuries BCE, we may deduce that Pythagoras strongly impressed his contemporaries with his distinctive teachings, in which the fate of the soul after death seems to have played a prominent part. Beyond that, things quickly become very controversial. The core problem is that the later sources portray him sometimes as a rigorous philosopher and mathematician and sometimes as a shaman-like religious leader. The task of reconciling these different portraits has been an ongoing scholarly challenge. The uncertainty is compounded by the fact that Pythagoras himself, as is now generally agreed, left no writings, despite the variety of texts that over the years came to bear his name. In my brief discussion here, I make no attempt to engage with all the

---

8. Plut. *De esu* 1.7, 995F–996C, trans. Harold Cherniss and William C. Helmbold, Loeb; cf. Bernabé 2004–5, nos. 313 F and 318 F. Orphic theology: for example, Detienne 1977, 161–217. Radcliffe Edmonds, building on the work of Linforth 1941, has challenged this traditional view, sparking a heated debate; for the main lines, see Edmonds 1999; Bernabé 2002; Edmonds 2013, 296–391; Parker 2014. Without delving into the details, I note only that I sympathize with Edmonds's analysis of this theology as largely a construct of modern scholarship and with his polythetic redefinition that stresses the labeling process (Edmonds 2013, 6–10, 71–92). In any case, evidence for the myth is relatively late: the earliest writers to refer to it date to the third century BCE (Callimachus F 643 Pfeiffer 1949 and Euphorion F 14 Lightfoot 2009 = Bernabé 2004–5, no. 36 V; cf. Euphorion F 40 Lightfoot 2009); Euphorion is also the earliest writer to identify it as Orphic (Henrichs 2011), followed by Diodorus Siculus (3.62.6–8 = Bernabé 2004–5, nos. 58 F and 59 F iii); on Pausanias's attribution of the story to the sixth-century BCE writer Onomacritus (Paus. 8.37.5; cf. Hdt. 7.6), see Linforth 1941, 350–53.

debates about the early Pythagorean tradition but instead focus on material relevant to animal sacrifice.[9]

By the imperial period, the Pythagorean position on this topic was clearly articulated and, it seems, widely known. According to this tradition, Pythagoras taught that the souls of living creatures continue to exist after death and are reincarnated in new bodies, which could be those of either humans or other animals; this is the doctrine that became known as metempsychosis or the transmigration of souls. In such circumstances, killing and eating animals is tantamount to murder and cannibalism, potentially of one's own family members, and so animal sacrifice, which necessarily involves killing and eating animals, must be strictly avoided. The earliest explicit statement of this doctrine, however, dates only to the mid-first century BCE, in a brief report in Diodorus Siculus's history, followed a few decades later by a lengthier and more elaborate exposition in the last book of Ovid's *Metamorphoses*. Although it thereafter becomes a standard piece of cultural knowledge, the earlier evidence is much patchier and more inconsistent.[10]

The earliest references to a Pythagorean concern with abstinence from animal flesh date to the fourth century BCE, when there seems to have been an explosion of interest in followers of Pythagoras; although none of the relevant texts survives in full, numerous citations in later writers give us some idea of their contents. Two main bodies of texts are relevant: on the one hand, Aristotle and his associates wrote more or less serious treatises on the Pythagoreans; on the other hand, a favorite butt of the comic playwrights of the day was people who were said to "Pythagorize." This fourth-century evidence includes many references to Pythagorean practices and beliefs that are

---

9. The fundamental modern study remains Burkert 1972 [1962]; Kahn 2001 and Riedweg 2005 are useful brief introductions; Huffman 2014a is a valuable survey that provides a vivid sense of the range of scholarly disagreement; Macris 2018 provides a comprehensive overview and bibliography. Earliest evidence: Lloyd 2014, 28–32.

10. Diod. Sic.10.6.1: "Pythagoras believed in the transmigration of souls (μετεμψύχωσιν) and considered the eating of flesh (κρεοφαγίαν) as an abominable thing, saying that the souls of all living creatures pass after death into other living creatures" (trans. C. H. Oldfather, Loeb); this passage is also the earliest extant example of the word *metempsychōsis*. Ovid: *Met.* 15.75–478, especially 75–175 and 453–78. The most striking testimony to the later familiarity with this Pythagorean doctrine is a school exercise from the third century CE that involved ringing grammatical changes on the set text "The philosopher Pythagoras, having disembarked and teaching letters, counselled his students to abstain from things with blood in them (ἐναιμόνων ἀπέχεσθαι)"; Kenyon 1909, 29–31.

relevant to animal sacrifice, although it is full of inconsistencies and outright contradictions.[11]

One important strand attributes to Pythagoras not a total abstinence from killing and eating animals but rather a complex of more specific dietary rules. Several later writers concur that Aristotle stated that Pythagoreans abstained from certain body parts (the heart and the womb are most often mentioned) and from certain animals (especially certain types of fish and seafood); although the reports differ in detail, they all imply that Pythagoreans did not reject the consumption of meat in general. Aristotle's associate Aristoxenus went further and declared explicitly that Pythagoras abstained only from plow oxen and rams but assented to the consumption of all other animals; according to Aulus Gellius, Aristoxenus even reported that Pythagoras liked to dine on tiny piglets and tender young kids.[12]

In stark contrast, it was one of the hallmarks of the Pythagorists of the comic stage that they abstained totally from all living creatures. Antiphanes, in a play titled *Kōrukos* (a leather bag for provisions), had one character say of another, "First of all, he acts like a Pythagorean and eats nothing that's alive (ἐσθίει ἔμψυχον οὐδέν), but buys a black piece of the biggest barley-cake he can get for an obol and gnaws on it." Alexis, in *The Men from Tarentum* (another southern Italian city associated with Pythagoreans), wrote, "Because the Pythagoreans, according to what we hear, don't eat fish or anything else that's alive (ἔμψυχον); and they're the only people who don't drink wine." Aristophon, in a play actually titled *The Pythagorist*, claims that "their food is just greens, and to wet it pure water is all that they drink; and the want of a bath, and the vermin, and their old threadbare coats so do stink that none of the rest will come near them." Finally, Mnesimachus in *Alcmaeon* included the following lines, presumably spoken by some Pythagorists: "To Loxias we sacrifice: Pythagoras his rite, / Of nothing that is animate we ever take a bite" (ἔμψυχον οὐδὲν ἐσθίοντες παντελῶς).[13] These extracts, to which others could

---

11. Aristotle and associates: Huffman 2014b. Comic "Pythagorists": the extracts are chiefly preserved by Athenaeus (4.161) and Diogenes Laertius (8.37–38); cf. Burkert 1972 [1962], 198–201.

12. Aristotle: F 194 Rose 1886 = Gell. *NA* 4.11.11–13, Diog. Laert. 8.19, and Porph. *Vit. Pyth.* 45; cf. F 195 Rose 1886 = Diog. Laert. 8.34. Aristoxenus: F 29a Wehrli 1967b = Diog. Laert. 8.20; Gellius: *NA* 4.11.6–7. Gellius also reports that Aristoxenus likewise claimed that Pythagoras, far from prohibiting beans, as most sources assert, actually recommended them as an aid to digestion; Huffman 2014b, 285–95, makes a case for Aristoxenus's reliability.

13. Antiphanes (F 133 K-A) and Alexis (F 223 K-A): Ath. *Deipn.* 4.161a–b, trans. E. Douglas Olson, Loeb. Aristophon (F 13 K-A) and Mnesimachus (F 1 K-A): Diog. Laert. 8.37–38, trans. R. D. Hicks, Loeb.

be added, give us a fairly good sense of how the comic playwrights portrayed these Pythagorists: as eccentric misfits who rejected the accepted standards of civilized society and were consequently avoided by all right-thinking people.

This comic caricature may, in fact, have been closer to real-life exemplars than we might assume. Athenaeus, writing in the second century CE, quotes a passage from Archestratus, the fourth-century BCE author of a poem on gastronomy, in which he declares that people who raise moral objections to certain foodstuffs should "keep company with vegetables and go to the wise Diodorus and temperately play the Pythagorean (πυθαγορίζειν) along with him." The speaker adds that "this Diodorus was an Aspendian by birth, and was thought to be a Pythagorean but lived as you Cynics do, growing his hair long and going dirty and barefoot" and goes on to quote the fourth-century BCE historian Timaeus to the same effect: "Diodorus, an Aspendian by birth, introduced their strange way of life and pretended to have been associated with the Pythagoreans."[14] Archestratus's gibe strongly suggests that Diodorus abstained from animal flesh, a practice that other sources of the period explicitly associate with Pythagoras. The mathematician and astronomer Eudoxus is quoted as saying that Pythagoras "practiced such great purity, especially in avoiding slaughter and those who slaughter, that he not only abstained from living creatures (τῶν ἐμψύχων ἀπέχεσθαι) but also never drew near butchers and hunters." Onesicritus, Alexander the Great's pilot on his sea voyage back from India, wrote in his account of his travels that in conversation with one of the ascetic wise men of India, he declared that the doctrines of Pythagoras were similar to those of his host and that Pythagoras also bade people to abstain from living creatures (ἐμψύχων ἀπέχεσθαι).[15]

Although scholars have advanced various schemes to reconcile this contradictory evidence, such as a shift in practice over time or the existence of different groups of Pythagoreans with different practices, for my purposes, the issue does not much matter.[16] What does matter is the fact that by the fourth century BCE, at least some people strongly associated followers of

---

14. Diodorus of Aspendus: Ath. *Deipn.* 4.163d-f, trans. E. Douglas Olson, Loeb; Archestratus: F 24.18–20 Olson and Sens 2000; Timaeus: *FGrH* 566 F16; see further Burkert 1972 [1962], 202–4.

15. Eudoxus: F 325 Lasserre 1966 = Porph. *Vit. Pyth.* 7. Onesicritus: *FGrH* 134 F 17a = Strabo 15.1.65, 716. In the third century BCE, Callimachus likewise claimed that Pythagoras taught abstinence from creatures that breathe (νηστεύειν τῶν ἐμπνεόντων): *Iambus* 1, F 191.59–62 Pfeiffer 1949 = Diod. Sic. 10.6.4; cf. Diog. Laert. 1.25.

16. Shift over time: e.g., Burkert 1972 [1962], 180–83; cf. Kahn 2001, 9. Different groups: Detienne 2007 [1972], 63–70; cf. Riedweg 2005, 69.

Pythagoras with abstinence from killing and eating animals. Before assessing the evidence further, however, we must consider one final body of material, which also happens to be the earliest that can be securely dated.

These are texts and teachings attributed to Empedocles. Here we are on much firmer ground than with either the Pythagorean or the Orphic material, since Empedocles did leave writings that, even though they survive only in fragments, provide us with some standard for assessing later reports of his teachings. We have little secure information about his life but can be confident that he was born into an elite family in the Greek city of Akragas on the southern coast of Sicily and that he was active in the middle of the fifth century BCE. Like several other early Greek thinkers, he used poetry rather than prose as the vehicle for expressing his ideas. Later writers preserve a number of direct quotations, as well as summaries and allusions, that address a wide range of topics. Many of these deal in some way with the typical concerns of pre-Socratic philosophy and show clear signs that Empedocles was familiar with and responding to the arguments of his predecessors. Others, by contrast, are couched in mystical language and include claims to extraordinary wisdom and abilities. The long-standing consensus that Empedocles composed two different poems, one titled *Nature* (*Ta Physika*) and another titled *Purifications* (*Katharmoi*), might help explain the differences in the topic and tone of the extant quotations. More recent scholars have proposed that Empedocles, in fact, wrote only one work, to which later authors referred under different names. Yet whether he wrote two poems or only one, the challenge of identifying the underlying unity of his thought remains. The challenge is in many ways similar to that of understanding the Pythagorean tradition, and it is not surprising that later writers closely associated Empedocles with Pythagoras, some of them going so far as to claim that he was Pythagoras's student.[17]

In exploring Empedocles's views on animal sacrifice, we may begin with a passage of Sextus Empiricus, a philosopher of the Skeptical school who in

---

17. For a useful overview of Empedocles and his thought, see Inwood 2001, 6–79, especially 6–8 on his life, 8–19 on his works, and 21–24 on his intellectual context; all fragments of Empedocles and related testimonia are in Inwood's translation, unless otherwise noted. Student of Pythagoras: Diog. Laert. 8.54–55, citing Timaeus (*FGrH* 566 F14) and Neanthes (*FGrH* 84 F26), historical writers active in the later fourth century BCE; Diogenes himself presents Empedocles as in effect Pythagoras's successor. Modern scholars generally reject the claim that Empedocles was a student of Pythagoras, while allowing for some degree of Pythagorean influence.

the late second century CE wrote a work against philosophers who advanced positive dogmas. According to Sextus,

> the followers of Pythagoras and Empedocles and the rest of the Italian group say that we have a kind of communion (τινα κοινωνίαν) not only with each other and the gods but also with irrational animals. For there is one spirit penetrating the entire cosmos, like a soul, which also unites us with them. That is why if we kill them and feed on their flesh we will be committing injustice and impiety (ἀδικήσομέν τε καὶ ἀσεβήσομεν), by destroying our kin. So these philosophers also recommended abstinence from living things (ἀπέχεσθαι τῶν ἐμψύχων) and said that men committed impiety "by staining red the altar of the blessed ones with hot blood" and Empedocles somewhere says "Will you not desist from harsh-sounding bloodshed? Do you not see that you are devouring each other in the heedlessness of your understanding?" and "A father lifts up his dear son, who has changed his form, and prays and slaughters him, in great folly, and they are at a loss as they sacrifice (θύοντες) the suppliant. But he, on the other hand, deaf to the rebukes, sacrificed him in his halls, and prepared himself an evil meal. In the same way, a son seizes his father and the children their mother, and tearing out their life-breath devour their own dear flesh."

Although the first of Sextus's two quotations from Empedocles could refer only to the slaughter of other humans, the second makes it clear that Empedocles was, in fact, referring to the slaughter of animals as well.[18]

Two points are worth stressing. First, there is ample evidence to confirm that Sextus, who had access to more of the text than we do, was correct in asserting that the reason for Empedocles's opposition to killing and eating animals was his belief that souls after death pass between the bodies of humans and animals. Although none of the extant passages from his work states that explicitly, the theory of transmigration of souls was well known in his day, since Xenophanes, Pindar, and Herodotus, writers contemporary with or a generation older than Empedocles, all explicitly refer to it.[19] More important, Empedocles himself clearly implies it in two other passage from his work.

---

18. Sext. Emp. *Math.* 9.127–29 = Inwood 2001, CTXT 103a. Quotations of Empedocles: DK 31 B 136 and 137 = F 126 and 128 Inwood 2001; the first two lines of the latter are also quoted by Plutarch (*Superst.* 171C) and Origen (*Cels.* 5.49).

19. Xenophanes DK 21 B 7; Pind. *Ol.* 2.56–83; Hdt. 2.123.

In one, he asserts that "whenever one, in his sins, stains his dear limbs with blood . . . he wanders for three ten thousand seasons away from the blessed ones, growing to be all sorts of forms of mortal things through time"; the quotation ends with Empedocles declaring, "I too am now one of these, an exile from the gods and a wanderer, trusting in mad strife." In a separate quotation, he claims, "I have already become a boy and a girl and a bush and a bird and a [corrupt text] fish from the sea."[20]

Second, Empedocles's primary concern was the general practice of killing and eating animals and not the specific practice of animal sacrifice. This seems clear from a passage quoted by Porphyry: "Woe is me! That the pitiless day did not destroy me before I devised with my claws terrible deeds for the sake of food."[21] Of course, since the practice of animal sacrifice necessarily involves killing animals and (in mainstream Greek tradition) eating their flesh, Empedocles was necessarily concerned with it as well. He, in fact, seems to have been the first to advance a history of cult practice in which a lost golden age was characterized by vegetal offerings only: "her [Aphrodite] they worshiped with pious images, painted pictures and perfumes of varied odors, and sacrifices of unmixed myrrh and fragrant frankincense, dashing onto the ground libations of yellow honey . . . [her] altar was not wetted with the unmixed blood of bulls, but this was the greatest abomination among men, to tear out their life-breath and eat their goodly limbs."[22] Yet even here, Empedocles's focus is on the slaughter and consumption of animals; his concern with sacrificial practice follows from that. It is true that sacrificial imagery features prominently in the passage quoted by Sextus, with its pathetic description of a father unwittingly slaughtering his son at an altar, but I would suggest that Empedocles is here doing the same thing as the tragedians who

---

20. DK 31 B 115 and 117 = F 11 and 111 Inwood 2001. The former passage was particularly well known, being cited by Plutarch, Celsus, Plotinus, and Porphyry, as well as the Christian antiheretical treatise usually attributed to Hippolytus: Inwood 2001, CTXT 10. The last of these, like Sextus Empiricus, interprets the passage with explicit reference to Empedocles's belief in the transmigration of souls: "because of this kind of organization of this divided cosmos, [created by] destructive strife, Empedocles calls on his students to refrain from all living things (ἐμψύχων ἀπέχεσθαι). For he says that the bodies of animals which are eaten are the dwelling of punished souls" ([Hippol.] *Haer.* 7.29.22; cf. 7.30.4). On Empedocles's ideas about reincarnation, see further Inwood 2001, 55–68.

21. DK 31 B 139 = F 124 Inwood 2001, ll. 5–6.

22. DK 31 B 128 = F 122 Inwood 2001, ll. 4–10.

were his contemporaries, using sacrificial imagery to heighten the emotional impact of the issue that he is confronting.[23]

Keeping in mind these conclusions about Empedocles, we are now in a position to assess the early Greek critiques of animal sacrifice. Despite the scattered and indirect evidence, several points seem clear. First, by the fifth century BCE, there were people who promoted the idea that it was wrong for humans to kill and eat animals. Some apparently cited the authority of Orpheus and others that of Pythagoras, while still others, like Empedocles, fashioned themselves as authorities. The characteristic terminology that writers of the fifth and fourth centuries BCE used to describe this idea, regardless of the authority invoked, highlights the importance of the *psychē*, "soul": people should not consume food that is *empsychos*, "ensouled" or "animate," but should instead eat only that which is *apsychos*, "soulless" or "inanimate." This suggests that by the fourth century BCE, this terminology had become standard for describing this particular dietary regime.[24]

Second, this standard terminology provides some hint of the thinking behind the regime. In all cases, the goal, obviously, was to avoid eating anything with a *psychē*. Although none of the extant sources concerning Pythagorean or Orphic practice provides any explanation for this goal, in the case of Empedocles, it clearly followed from a belief in the transmigration of souls between humans and animals. We can be reasonably confident that this was also true of Pythagorean practice. Later writers from Ovid on associated Pythagorean abstinence from animal flesh with the doctrine of transmigration, and although the earlier evidence is both less explicit and more inconsistent, it suggests that at least some people associated the doctrine

---

23. Sacrificial imagery in tragedy: e.g., Zeitlin 1965 and Henrichs 2000. When Plutarch writes that Empedocles criticized those who sacrifice animals (*Superst.* 171C, τῶν τὰ ζῷα θυόντων καθαπτόμενος), he does so with reference to these specific lines.

24. This terminology occurs in both the key passages referring to the Orphic way of life (Euripides uses the phrase δι' ἀψύχου βορᾶς, Plato the expression ἀψύχων μὲν ἔχεσθαι, ἐμψύχων δὲ ἀπέχεσθαι) and regularly in those describing the Pythagorean way of life, both serious (Aristoxenus, Eudoxus, and Onesicritus all use a version of the phrase ἐμψύχων ἀπέχεσθαι) and comic (Antiphanes, Alexis, and Mnesimachus all use the phrase ἐσθίειν ἔμψυχον οὐδέν); for the details, see the earlier notes. Empedocles apparently did not employ it but seems instead to have used the term *daimōn* in the place of *psychē* (see Inwood 2001, 56); later writers such as Aristotle (*Rhet.* 1373b6–17), however, do use the terminology of *empsychos* in reference to his teachings. The most dramatic example of how established this terminology became is its application to the Buddhist practices of the third century BCE Mauryan emperor Aśoka (ἀπέχεται βασιλεὺς τῶν ἐμψύχων) in an inscription found near Kandahar in present-day Afghanistan; see Schlumberger et al. 1958, with the comments of Louis Robert at 14–16.

of transmigration with the Pythagorean tradition from an early date.[25] The same is likely to have been true of Orphic tradition as well, even though the evidence in this case is very uncertain. The specific framing of this belief in the transmigration of souls seems to have varied, with some relying more on mythic discourses and others more on analytical discourses, but our evidence is too uncertain to be more precise.

Third, contemporary observers and later writers alike seem to have regarded this set of interrelated discourses and practices as outside the mainstream of Greek culture. The socially deviant Pythagorists of the comic stage are the most obvious case in point, but many of the other references also involve a greater or lesser degree of marginalization. The perceived marginality of one group reinforced that of the others, since there was a long-lasting tendency to perceive connections among them. As we have seen, writers from the late fourth century BCE on regarded Empedocles as a student of Pythagoras, and those of imperial date regularly associated the two as promoting the same teachings; similarly, already in the fifth century BCE, there were writers who connected the categories "Pythagorean" and "Orphic."[26] Another indicator of the perceived marginality of these beliefs and practices is the fact that several Greek writers attributed similar beliefs to foreign peoples, with the implication that there was something "non-Greek" about them.[27] In various ways, then, observers consistently positioned this complex of beliefs and practices on the margins of normative Greek society and culture.

---

25. For example, Xenophanes DK 21 B 7. Several fourth-century BCE writers apparently referred to Pythagoras's earlier incarnations, which presupposes a belief in transmigration: Heraclides Ponticus (F 89 Wehrli 1969 = Diog. Laert. 8.4–5), Aristoxenus (F 12 Wehrli 1967b), and Dicaearchus (F 36 Wehrli 1967a = Gellius 4.11.14). Aristotle (*De an.* 407b20) is explicit that Pythagoreans believe that any soul can pass into any body. For a careful discussion, see Huffman 2009.

26. Pythagoras and Empedocles: Cic. *Rep.* 3.19; Plut. *De esu* 2.3, 997F–998A; Ath. *Deipn.* 1.3e; Sext. Emp. *Math.* 9.127. Pythagorean and Orphic: Hdt. 2.81 and Ion of Chios DK 36 B 2 = Diog. Laert. 8.8; a later example: Plut. *Quaest. conv.* 2.3.1, 635E; see further Betegh 2014. Tertullian similarly associates Empedocles with Orphic tradition: Tert. *An.* 15.5 with DK 31 B 105.3.

27. Herodotus (2.123.1) believed the idea of transmigration was Egyptian in origin; Megasthenes, writing in the late fourth century BCE, claimed that the Brahmans abstained from animate food (*FGrH* 715 F 33 = Strabo 15.1.59, 712: ἀπεχομένους ἐμψύχων); Onesicritus (*FGrH* 134 F 17 = Strabo 15.65, 716) implied that the Indian gymnosophists held beliefs similar to those of Pythagoras. A different association with "foreignness" informs the story that Zalmoxis taught the Pythagorean doctrine of abstaining from animate foods to the Getae, who still preserved it centuries later (Strabo 7.3.5, 298).

What about insiders, those who proclaimed and advocated for these practices and beliefs? Although we have no real access to the self-presentation of those who invoked the authority of Pythagoras or Orpheus, we do have some access to that of Empedocles. The surviving passages of his work in which he talks about himself emphasize the extraordinary nature of his insights and abilities.[28] On the one hand, this put him at odds with mainstream Greek society and so encouraged and reinforced people's perception of his marginality. At the same time, his extraordinariness is what provided the basis for his authority. It was precisely his claim to offer uncommon insights about the nature of the cosmos, and consequently to provide unique guidance about how people should best conduct their lives, that justified his claim to their attention and respect. The evidence that we have for those who claimed to follow Orpheus or Pythagoras suggests that they, too, made similar claims.

Last, and for our purposes most important, none of the early evidence suggests that the practice of animal sacrifice per se was a focus of attention for any of these figures or groups. As I argued in the case of Empedocles, traditional Greek animal sacrifice was of concern insofar as it by definition involved killing and eating animals. Plato associates the Orphic life with vegetal offerings, and the comic writers made similar observations about the Pythagorists. Yet we have no warrant for reversing the logic of their concerns as it appears in the evidence. Although in the later imperial period, both Orpheus and Pythagoras were regarded as great religious teachers with a specific interest in sacrificial practice, that does not seem to have been as true in the fourth and third centuries BCE.[29] At least on the available evidence, none of these figures was concerned with theorizing sacrifice as a cult act. Instead, the teachings about sacrificial practice that we have surveyed appear only as a corollary of the fundamental concern with killing and eating animals.[30]

---

28. See especially DK 31 B 112 = F 1 Inwood 2001, where he describes himself as a god with multitudes of people seeking his guidance.

29. To my knowledge, the only significant evidence to the contrary is in Isocrates's *Busiris* (28–29), dating to the early fourth century BCE, where he claims that Pythagoras had a particularly notable interest in matters of sacrifice and ritual purity (τὰς θυσίας καὶ τὰς ἁγιστείας τὰς ἐν τοῖς ἱεροῖς).

30. On this point, I sharply disagree with Marcel Detienne's influential structuralist analysis, which interprets the essence of both Orphism and Pythagoreanism as a rejection of the normative Greek sacrificial system and consequently of the overall political-religious system; see especially Detienne 1977, 139–60. Detienne's elegant construction is intellectually stimulating and aesthetically compelling but historically problematic, since it relies on a selective and arbitrary combination of scraps of evidence divorced from their literary, social, and cultural contexts.

## 6c. The Classical Philosophical Schools

When we turn to the major philosophical schools of the classical and Hellenistic periods (Academic, Peripatetic, Stoic, and Epicurean), we encounter a rather different situation. On the one hand, we find more explicit discussion of sacrifice than we do in the early critiques examined in Section 6b. On the other hand, there is very little in these discussions to suggest that any philosopher of the four main schools, with one notable exception, had much interest in theorizing sacrificial practice. To the extent that there is any substantive engagement with the topic at all, it lies in an insistence that the moral character of the worshiper is more important than the actual offering. Otherwise, most philosophers seem to have accepted sacrifice largely as a traditional practice. The notable exception is the Peripatetic Theophrastus, whose treatise on piety included a number of forceful arguments for rejecting animal sacrifice altogether. I begin my survey with Plato, whose comments on sacrifice are more numerous than those of any other extant philosopher of this period; after a brief glance at what little can be gleaned about the other schools, I close by examining the remains of Theophrastus's treatise.[31]

Plato's extant works all take the form of dialogues with real-world settings, some described in more detail than others, and it is worth noting that he chose more than once to include a sacrifice in his scenario. *Lysis* opens with Socrates meeting some youths outside a wrestling school; after some conversation, they enter to find the youths inside finishing a sacrifice. Similarly, when Socrates and his companions go to the house of Cephalus at the opening of *Republic*, they encounter him still garlanded after having sacrificed in the courtyard.[32] Sacrifice in these scenes appears as a customary part of Greek life, and it was a part that Plato readily included in the ideal communities that he constructed in his two longest works, *Republic* and *Laws*. In the former, in contrast to the elaborate case he makes for excluding traditional myth, he has little to say about traditional cult practice but seems to accept as a matter of course that sacrifice will be part of life in his polis.[33] In the latter, communal sacrifices play an important role in articulating the main spatial, temporal, and social structures of the polis envisioned by the Athenian. For example, he declares that the lawgivers shall assign each subdivision of the polis "the name of a god

---

31. Useful overviews: Mikalson 2010, 55–83; Ullucci 2012, 34–42.

32. *Lysis* 206d and 207d; *Resp.* 1.328c and 331d.

33. Critique of traditional myth: *Resp.* 2.377a–383c. Socrates refers to sacrifices accompanying approved marriages in his ideal polis: 5.460a and 461a.

or a child of gods, and bestow on it altars and all that belongs thereto; and at these we shall appoint two assemblies every month for sacrifice (θυσιῶν πέρι ξυνόδους) . . .; the object of these shall be, first, to offer thanksgiving to the gods and to do them service, and secondly, as we should assert, to promote fellowship amongst ourselves and mutual acquaintance and association of every sort." The opportunity for social interaction on these occasions is particularly useful for establishing the sorts of connections that lead to marriage, which are themselves accompanied by sacrifices. The Athenian repeatedly emphasizes the social benefits that accrue from public sacrifices: the lawgiver will allot property to the patron deity or hero of each subdivision, so that "when assemblies of each of the sections take place at the appointed times, they may provide an ample supply of things requisite, and the people may fraternize with one another at the sacrifices (μετὰ θυσιῶν) and gain knowledge and intimacy, since nothing is of more benefit to the state than this mutual acquaintance."[34]

Sacrifice was thus a traditional part of Greek culture that Plato for the most part accepted without critique, in striking contrast to his strong objections to traditional myth. His rejection of the latter rested on his conviction that it misrepresented the gods, who, according to Plato, were as perfect morally as they were physically; insofar as he critiqued any aspect of traditional sacrificial practice, he did so on the same grounds. He took issue in particular with the traditional view that, as Homer put it, "the gods themselves can be moved by supplication, and humans, with sacrifices and soothing prayers, with libations and sacrifices, turn their wills by prayer, when anyone has overstepped the mark and offended." Plato has Adeimantus quote these lines in a key passage in *Republic*, when he and Glaucon challenge Socrates to prove to them that the just man is always better off than the unjust man, regardless of circumstances. If Homer is right, Glaucon argues, it is much better to be unjust than just: "for if we are just we will merely escape punishment from the gods, but at the same time we will be rejecting the profits which would come from our injustice; but if we are unjust we will both profit and, provided we

---

34. Quotations from *Leg.* 6.771c–d (cf. 771e–772a on connections leading to marriage) and 5.738d–e, trans. R. G. Bury, Loeb, lightly adapted; sacrifice at marriages: 6.784a. Other examples of the role of sacrifice in articulating the structures of the polis: 7.799b–800b, 7.809d, 8.828a–d; see further Mikalson 2010, 79–81. McPherran 2000, 102–6, argues that Plato's endorsement of traditional cult practice here extends beyond the recognition of its social utility to an appreciation of its role as a sort of spiritual training: "In the operations of Platonic cult . . . the prescribed external motions are inducements and models for developing matching internal movements that aim at a harmonious relationship between the soul's parts" (105).

make our supplications as transgressors and wrongdoers, will be able to win them over and get off unpunished."³⁵

For Plato, the notion that the gods could be bribed by gifts to disregard injustice was completely unacceptable. Although Socrates's eventual demonstration in *Republic* that the just man is always better off than the unjust man provides an implicit refutation of Adeimantus's proposition about sacrifice, it is not until Book 10 of *Laws* that Plato addresses the problem explicitly and at length. That entire book is devoted to the issue of correct belief in the gods, which the Athenian presents as a matter of fundamental importance to a well-run polity: "No one who believes, as the laws prescribe, in the existence of the gods has ever yet done an impious deed voluntarily or uttered a lawless word: he that acts so is in one or other of these three conditions of mind— either he does not believe [that the gods exist]; or, secondly, he believes that the gods exist, but have no care for men; or, thirdly, he believes that they are easy to win over when bribed by offerings and prayers (ἢ τρίτον εὐπαραμυθήτους εἶναι θυσίαις τε καὶ εὐχαῖς παραγομένους)." The bulk of the book is taken up with an elaborate refutation of the first two positions, whereas the third is dispatched more briefly. The book concludes with an enumeration of the appropriate penalties for the various forms of impiety, *asebeia*, with some of the worst reserved for those who promise "to persuade the gods by bewitching them, as it were, with sacrifices, prayers and incantations (ὡς θυσίαις τε καὶ εὐχαῖς καὶ ἐπῳδαῖς γοητεύοντες)."³⁶

A passage from the second of the two dialogues titled *Alcibiades*, generally considered not to be a work of Plato himself, presents a more popular version of the same point. The subject of the dialogue is prayer, and Socrates, in praising the prayers of the Spartans, who simply ask the gods to grant them what is beneficial, says that the Athenians, in the war with Sparta, became annoyed at the fact that, although they presented the gods with "more and finer sacrifices (πλείστας ... θυσίας καὶ καλλίστας) than any of the Greeks," they lost every battle to the Spartans, who are "so neglectful in their behavior to the gods, that they make a practice of sacrificing defective victims (ἀνάπηρα

---

35. *Resp.* 2.362c–367e, with quotations from 364d–e (Hom. *Il.* 9.497 and 499–501) and 366a, trans. Chris Emlyn-Jones and William Preddy, Loeb, lightly adapted. Adeimantus singles out Orphic initiators, who "persuade not only individuals but cities that they really can have atonement and purification for their wrongdoing through sacrifices and playful delights while they are still alive and equally after death; these they actually call initiations, which free us from evils in the next world, while terrible things await those who neglect their sacrifices" (364e–365a).

36. Quotations from *Leg.* 10.885b and 909b, trans. R. G. Bury, Loeb, lightly adapted; for the refutation of the idea that gods can be bribed, see 905d–907b.

θύουσιν)." They accordingly sent an embassy to the oracle of Zeus Ammon to determine why. The god's only response was that "I would rather have the reverent reserve (εὐφημίαν) of the Spartans than all the ritual of the Greeks." Socrates deduces that by "reverent reserve" the god must have meant their restrained prayer. Most Greeks, he argues, present the gods with "bulls with gilded horns" and costly offerings but then pray for whatever they happen to want, whether it is good or bad; the gods, accordingly, hearing them engaging in this insulting speech (βλασφημούντων ... ἀκούοντες), reject their costly offerings. "For it would be a strange thing (δεινόν)," he concludes, "if the gods had regard to our gifts and sacrifices (τὰ δῶρα καὶ τὰς θυσίας) instead of our soul, whether it is in fact pious and just (ὅσιος καὶ δίκαιος)."[37]

In general, then, Plato displays relatively little interest in sacrifice or cult practice more broadly. His profound concern with propagating a correct understanding of the gods led him to condemn the popular belief that people could win them over by means of sacrifices and other offerings; the gods, he insisted, were much more interested in their worshipers' moral qualities than in their gifts.[38] Beyond that, he seems to have accepted the practice of sacrifice largely on the basis of tradition, with a certain appreciation for its social utility. The fact that he never discusses the specifics of sacrificial practice or even distinguishes between different types of sacrificial offerings, which he almost always refers to simply as *thusiai*, demonstrates his lack of interest in theorizing the practice. A particularly telling indication of his indifference to cult practice is the Athenian's insistence in *Laws* that the founders of his new city should consult the oracle at Delphi and thereby allow the gods themselves to determine what sacrifices are to be offered to what deities. Although on a superficial level this deference demonstrates a reverence for the gods, it also has the effect of dismissing cult practice as a topic for serious philosophical analysis. What really matters is not what we do but our frame of mind when we do it.[39]

---

37. 2 *Alc.* 148d–151b, with quotations from 148e, 149a–c, and 149e, trans. W. R. M. Lamb, Loeb, adapted. On the importance of *euphēmia* in connection with sacrifices, see also *Leg.* 7.800b–801a.

38. In this respect, Plato was very much in line with a long tradition of Greek thought that emphasized the importance of the worshiper's behavior outside the cult act itself: Naiden 2013, especially 82–83, 104–9, 132, 153–63, 225–29.

39. *Leg.* 5.738c and 8.828a; see further Mikalson 2010, 130–39, although I disagree with his conclusion that Plato's deference to oracles in such matters expresses his belief "that not *all* matter of human life can be explained solely by human reason" (137).

Plato's respectful if somewhat indifferent acceptance of sacrifice and other traditional cult practices may go back to his master Socrates, who was suspected of impiety and ultimately executed in part on those grounds. It is worth noting that Xenophon, who, like Plato, was a devotee of Socrates, although one with very different priorities and commitments, made a point of defending him against the charge of impiety by emphasizing his punctilious observance of traditional cult practices. Xenophon insists that Socrates "often offered sacrifices (θύων) and made no secret of it, now in his home, now at the communal altars of the state," and that "his deeds and words were clearly consistent with the answer given by the Priestess at Delphi to those who inquire about their duty regarding sacrifice," that is, "that those who follow the custom of the state (νόμῳ πόλεως) would act piously." That, Xenophon declares, is how Socrates himself always acted and how he advised others to act. Although Socrates's offerings were modest, given his limited means, he believed that it was not the value of the offering that mattered; rather, "the greater the piety of the giver, the greater was the delight of the gods in the gift." Regardless of the extent to which these sentiments represent the views of the historical Socrates, they seem to have established the baseline for all four of the classical philosophical schools.[40]

Aristotle seems, if anything, to have had even less interest in sacrifice than Plato; he several times refers to it in passing as a customary practice but never discusses it. Perhaps his most telling reference is a passage in *Nicomachean Ethics* where he distinguishes between two types of political justice, one founded on nature (τὸ φυσικόν) and the other on convention (τὸ νομικόν). "A rule of justice is natural," he explains, "that has the same validity everywhere, and does not depend on our accepting it or not. A rule is conventional that in the first instance may be settled in one way or the other indifferently, though having once been settled it is not indifferent: for example, . . . that a sacrifice shall consist of a goat and not of two sheep."[41] Although Aristotle's classification of sacrificial practice as a matter of convention rather than nature is on the surface completely different from Plato's insistence that oracles determine the public sacrifices of his ideal polis, the two are alike, I would suggest,

---

40. Xen. *Mem.* 1.1.1–2 on the charge of impiety and Socrates's frequent sacrifices, and 1.3.1–3 on Socrates's views about sacrifice; quotations from 1.1.2, 1.3.1, and 1.3.3, trans. E. C. Marchant, rev. Jeffrey Henderson, Loeb, lightly adapted. On Socrates's views of traditional cult practice, see further McPherran 2000, 90–102.

41. Arist. *Eth. Nic.* 5.7.1, 1134b19–24, trans. H. Rackham, Loeb. See also the long discussion of public sacrifice as a matter of convention in the pseudo-Aristotelian *Rhetorica ad Alexandrum*, 1423a30–1424a9.

in treating the specifics of sacrificial practice as more or less arbitrary. In the fragmentary remains of the early Stoics, there is no reference to sacrifice at all. It would be interesting to know whether Zeno discussed public sacrifice in *Politeia*, his now-lost treatise on sociopolitical organization, since according to later writers he rejected many traditional institutions of the Greek polis, including temples; but we can only speculate. By the imperial period, at any rate, Stoics seem to have adopted the standard line on cult practices, if we can regard Epictetus as typical: "In piety toward the gods, I would have you know, the chief element is this, to have right opinions about them, as existing and as administering the universe well and justly.... But it is always appropriate to make libations and sacrifices and to give of the first fruits after the manner of our fathers (σπένδειν δὲ καὶ θύειν καὶ ἀπάρχεσθαι κατὰ τὰ πάτρια)."[42]

Somewhat surprisingly, Epicurus also seems to have upheld traditional sacrificial practice. He was as concerned as Plato that people have a correct understanding of the gods' nature, even though his understanding differed profoundly from Plato's: Epicurus's gods were completely untroubled by any concerns and were thus entirely indifferent to human affairs. Although his conception of the gods would logically have rendered traditional cult practices entirely pointless, there is solid evidence that Epicurus, in fact, resoundingly endorsed them. According to Philodemus, an Epicurean philosopher who lived and worked in the Bay of Naples in the mid-first century BCE and scraps of whose writings were preserved by the lava flow from the eruption of Vesuvius, Epicurus declared that "to pray is natural for us, not because the gods would be hostile if we did not pray, but in order that, according to the understanding of beings surpassing in power and excellence, we may realize our fulfillments and social conformity with the laws." In the same way, "let us sacrifice to the gods devoutly and fittingly (θύωμεν ... ὁσίως καὶ καλῶς) on the proper days, and let us fittingly perform all the acts of worship in accordance with the laws (κατὰ τοὺς νόμους), in no way disturbing ourselves with opinions in matters concerning the most excellent and august of beings." Epicurus's critics pounced on the perceived contradiction between his endorsement of traditional cult practices and what they regarded as his atheism and regarded the former as simply the result of timidity and hypocrisy. Plutarch, for example, declared that "if the god is not present at the sacrifice as master of rites (so to speak), what is left bears no mark of sanctity or holy day and leaves the spirit untouched by the divine influence; rather let us

---

42. Zeno's *Politeia*: Diog. Laert. 7.4 and 32–34; on temples, see also Plut. *Stoic. rep.* 1034B; cf. Ullucci 2012, 39. Epictetus: *Ench.* 31.1 and 5, trans. W. A. Oldfather, Loeb.

say for such a man the occasion is distasteful and even distressing. For out of fear of public opinion he goes through a mummery of prayers and obeisances that he has no use for and pronounces words that run counter to his philosophy." Such a man leaves a sacrifice quoting the line of Menander, "I sacrificed to gods who heed me not." This, Plutarch concludes, "is the comedy that Epicurus thinks we should play." Polemic aside, however, it seems that in his respectful acceptance of traditional cult practices as a matter of convention, Epicurus was squarely in the mainstream of classical philosophy.[43]

The available evidence thus suggests that no philosopher of the major classical schools had any significant critical interest in the practice of sacrifice. We must remember, however, that the available evidence is very limited. The chance survival of selections from Theophrastus's treatise on piety raises the possibility that there may have been more philosophical discussion of the topic than we are aware of. Theophrastus was a somewhat younger associate of Aristotle who in 323 BCE succeeded him as the head of the Lyceum, a position he held until his death around 288/287 BCE. His range matched that of his mentor, whose work in many areas he continued and not infrequently modified. His output, like Aristotle's, was enormous, although, apart from his work on botany and metaphysics and a scattering of minor treatises, much of it is now known only through later citations. His treatise on piety is a case in point. We have something of this work only because Porphyry, in the treatise on abstinence from animals that he wrote probably in the last third of the third century CE, draws at length on arguments of Theophrastus against the practice of animal sacrifice. Although Porphyry does not provide the title of the work from which he took his material, a chance reference preserved in Byzantine literary scholarship confirms that it is indeed the treatise on piety, *Peri Eusebeias*, whose title is preserved by Diogenes Laertius.[44] Since we have no other information about its contents, we can say nothing about its overall structure and thesis; it is even possible that the arguments against animal sacrifice constituted merely one side of a debate. Nevertheless, we may be reasonably confident that Porphyry, despite some omissions, additions,

---

43. Philodemus: *Piet.* F 26, 737–51, and F 31, 879–89 Obbink 1996. Plutarch: *Suav. viv.* 21, 1102A–D, with quotations from 1102B–C, trans. Benedict Einarson and Phillip H. De Lacy, Loeb.

44. Diog. Laert. 5.50. An ancient note on a line of Aristophanes's *Birds* (scholia vetera ad *Av.* 1354) provides an etymology for an obscure term that it credits to "Theophrastus in *On Piety*" (also cited, without title, by Photius *Lex.* s.v. Κύρβεις, K 1234) and that appears in more or less identical form in Porph. *Abst.* 2.21.1.

and summaries, has reproduced Theophrastus's arguments with some fidelity, since they differ noticeably from his own in both focus and vocabulary.[45]

On the evidence of Porphyry, Theophrastus seems to have advanced a wide variety of arguments against animal sacrifice. Although we cannot be sure how they fit together in the original work, we can nevertheless identify a few dominant themes. One that Theophrastus apparently developed at some length is an argument from cultural history. Elaborating on a schema that, as we have seen, went back at least to Empedocles, Theophrastus saw animal sacrifice as a late development in human culture. Originally, all offerings were vegetal, although over time, they gradually evolved from wild plants to cultivated grains to cakes. The origin of animal sacrifice was yet later, and "its cause is not a benefit, as for the sacrifice of crops, but a problem arising from famine or some other misfortune." He then recounted an etiological story about the first sacrifice of pigs in Athens, just as he elsewhere (at least in Porphyry's reworking) described at greater length the origin of the sacrifice of bovines. In yet another passage, he outlined an elaborate narrative according to which animal sacrifice was a later modification of human sacrifice, which was itself the result of people's resort to cannibalism in a terrible famine. Although it is not easy to make all his claims cohere, the overall point is clear: not only is animal sacrifice a late development, but its origins lie in misery and crime.[46]

Another idea that Theophrastus explores is that animal sacrifice is inherently contrary to what is *hosios*, "religiously correct," and *dikaios*, "just," and is thus not an appropriate way to honor the gods. His first argument along these lines is that animal sacrifice constitutes theft and so cannot be *hosios*. "For sacrifice (θυσία) is by definition (κατὰ τοὔνομα) *hosios*, but no one is *hosios* if he returns favors (ἀποδίδωσι χάριτας) out of other people's possessions without their consent, not even if he takes crops of plants. How could it be *hosios*,

---

45. Omissions, additions, and summaries: Porph. *Abst.* 2.32.3. Differences between Theophrastus and Porphyry: Bouffartigue and Papillon 1979, 19–20; we may also note that whereas Porphyry typically uses the term *empsychos*, Theophrastus seems instead to use the phrase *ta zōa*, "living things" (e.g., Porph. *Abst.* 2.12.3, 13.3, 14.1, 22.2). There nevertheless remains disagreement over the details of what is Theophrastus and what is Porphyry, e.g., Bouffartigue and Papillon 1979, 20–29. The most recent full discussion of Theophrastus's treatise is Fortenbaugh 2003. All quotations from Porphyry's treatise, including his extracts from Theophrastus, are in the translation of Clark 2000, sometimes adapted.

46. History of vegetal offerings: Porph. *Abst.* 2.5–6; cf. 2.20.3 on a similar history of libations. Animal sacrifice as the result of misfortunes: 2.7.1–2.9.2, with quotation from 2.9.1 and the first pig sacrifice at 2.9.2; for arguments that 2.9.1–2 are Theophrastean, see Bouffartigue and Papillon 1979, 21–22. First cattle sacrifice: 2.29–30 (a much-discussed passage). Animal sacrifice as a development from human sacrifice: 2.27. On Theophrastus's history of sacrifice, see Obbink 1988 and Fortenbaugh 2003, 174–78.

when injustice is done to those who are robbed? A man who takes crops from another cannot sacrifice in a religiously correct manner (ὁσίως); so much more so with someone who takes life from another, which is much more valuable.... So it is not fitting to take it away by sacrificing animals (θύοντα τὰ ζῷα)."[47] The second argument he develops at greater length, in the form of a dilemma. We agree, he declares, that it is right to kill people whose nature inclines them to harm those whom they encounter; by the same token, it is perhaps likewise right to kill animals that are similarly "unjust by nature and evil-doers." Yet "it must be unjust (ἄδικον) to exterminate and kill those of the other animals that do nothing unjust (τὰ δὲ μηθὲν ἀδικοῦντα) and are not impelled by their nature to do harm, as it is unjust to kill people like that." On the other hand, we should not sacrifice to the gods creatures that really deserve to be killed, since they are bad by nature; that would be no different from sacrificing defective animals. Accordingly, we must sacrifice those that do us no wrong. It has already been established, however, that it is unjust to kill those kinds of animals. "If, then, neither these nor the evil-doers should be sacrificed, is it not obvious that we should in all cases abstain, and that none of the other animals should be sacrificed?"[48] These arguments are particularly interesting, since they seem to imply that a kinship (οἰκειότης) exists between humans and other animals, a position that Theophrastus argues explicitly in a passage quoted by Porphyry elsewhere. If that is so, then the same relationships of justice and injustice that exist among humans also exist between humans and other animals. This was the topic of much debate among philosophers of the fourth and third centuries BCE. Theophrastus's position, which was one of the points on which he was at odds with Aristotle, was perhaps that of a minority, but it was by no means unparalleled.[49]

The third type of argument rests on the nature of piety, *eusebeia*. According to Theophrastus, "things which are inexpensive and easy to get are more *hosios*

---

47. Porph. *Abst.* 2.12.4–13.3, with quotation from 2.12.4. In translating *hosios* as "religiously correct," I follow Mikalson 2010, 11–12, 140–52; cf. Peels 2016, 66–67.

48. Porph. *Abst.* 2.22.2–2.23.2; Theophrastus restates the argument in more elaborate form at 2.24; see further Fortenbaugh 2003, 183–88. The perception of a relationship between "religiously correct" and "just" goes back at least to the time of Aeschylus (*Supp.* 404; cf. Peels 2016, 124–27) and was developed dialectically by Plato (*Euthyphr.* 11e–12e); see further Mikalson 2010, 29–32, 187–207; in more detail, Peels 2016, 107–48.

49. Theophrastus on the kinship of humans and animals: Porph. *Abst.* 3.25; see *contra* Brink 1956, 124–29, who argues that Theophrastus's arguments at *Abst.* 2.22.2–2.23.2 do not rest on the notion of shared kinship. Philosophical debate: Sorabji 1993, 122–33. Aristotle denied that relationships of justice can exist between humans and animals: *Eth. Nic.* 8.11, 1161b2–3.

and pleasing to the gods (ὁσιώτερον καὶ θεοῖς κεχαρισμένον) than things which are difficult to get, and that which is easiest for the sacrificers is at hand to show uninterrupted piety (πρὸς συνεχῆ εὐσέβειαν)." That principle excludes animal sacrifice, since many people cannot afford animals fit for sacrifice, and those who live in cities have difficulty acquiring them. Agricultural products, by contrast, are less expensive and easier to acquire, even for those in cities, and "inexpensive things which are easy to get contribute to uninterrupted piety and to the piety of everyone." After recounting an anecdote about an oracle of Apollo at Delphi that revealed the god's preference for inexpensive offerings over cattle and hecatombs, he concludes with a striking aphorism: "inexpensive things are dear to the gods, and divinity considers rather the character of the sacrificers (τὸ τῶν θυόντων ἦθος) than the quantity of the sacrifice (τὸ τῶν θυομένων πλῆθος)."[50]

In advancing this argument, Theophrastus was drawing on a current of thought that was already widespread among his contemporaries. As we have seen, Xenophon attributed to Socrates the idea that the gods cared more for the piety of the giver than the price of the gift, and it was well established in Platonic circles; the passage from *2 Alcibiades* cited earlier in this section has many similarities with Theophrastus's argument, even down to the appeal to an oracle, although the two writers invoke somewhat different principles. It was moreover an idea not limited to works of philosophy. After presenting Theophrastus's arguments, Porphyry elaborates on them by adding a further example from the historian Theopompus (yet another anecdote involving an oracle) and appropriate quotations from the comic playwrights Antiphanes and Menander.[51] At the same time, Theophrastus developed this commonplace idea along distinctive lines, with his stress on uninterrupted piety. What he seems to have meant by this were offerings that could be made on a regular basis, daily or even several times a day, in contrast to expensive offerings that in most circumstances could be made only infrequently. As I suggest in Section 9a, Theophrastus was here expressing a view that may have acquired a more widespread popular currency in the centuries to come.

Although at first sight, Theophrastus's treatise appears to have been a unique example of serious philosophical engagement with animal sacrifice, closer examination reveals that in certain respects, it was, in fact, fairly typical

---

50. Porph. *Abst.* 2.13.4–2.15.3, with quotations from 2.13.4, 14.3, and 15.3.

51. Theopompus: Porph. *Abst.* 2.16 = *FGrH* 115 F 344; Antiphanes: *Abst.* 2.17.3 = F 162 K-A; Menander: *Abst.* 2.17.4 = *Dys.* 449–51.

in its interests and arguments, as best as we can judge from the extant remains. Certainly, his argument that the gods are more concerned with the character of the sacrificant than with the costliness of the sacrifice was very much in keeping with the mainstream of his day, even though his emphasis on uninterrupted piety seems to have been his own distinctive contribution. It is true that Theophrastus was, as far as we can determine, the only philosopher of the four main classical schools to discuss animal sacrifice as a distinctive type of offering and the only one to discuss it in the context of a treatise on piety. Yet it seems likely that his concern with animal sacrifice grew out of his belief that a kinship, *oikeiotēs*, existed between humans and other animals. Once that point was granted, it followed that killing innocent animals could never be anything other than unjust, and injustice, as Plato had already forcefully argued, could never be acceptable to the gods. In this respect as well, then, Theophrastus's views fit comfortably within the philosophical mainstream of his day. It is impossible to say more without knowing more about the contents of his treatise on piety, but on the available evidence, it is not clear that Theophrastus had much more interest in theorizing sacrificial practice than any other philosopher of his day.

The evidence thus suggests that the philosophers of the major classical schools, while all deeply concerned with people's conception of the gods, were much less concerned with the practices that they employed in their actual worship.[52] As Epictetus put it, the chief element in piety toward the gods was to hold the right opinions about them. This central concern did have some implications for views about cult practice, particularly the idea that in a sacrifice, the gods were concerned above all with the moral character of the sacrificant. Hence Plato devoted considerable care to disproving the idea that sacrifices could function as bribes that would persuade the gods to overlook injustice. The same idea underpins Theophrastus's argument that animal sacrifice is inherently unjust and consequently can never be religiously correct. The insistence on the primacy of the sacrificant's morality most commonly took the form of assertions that, as Theophrastus memorably put it, the gods looked more to the character of the sacrificant than to the quantity of the sacrifice; we encounter similar statements in Xenophon's *Memorabilia* and

---

52. See the valuable survey in Mikalson 2010, 43–109. The great exception is divination, which was of particular interest to the Stoics and became the topic of heated philosophical debate. Our best evidence for this debate is Cicero's dialogue *On Divination*, in which he draws on the arguments and counterarguments that had been developed over the preceding two or three centuries. The absence of anything comparable regarding sacrificial practice is telling.

the Platonic *2 Alcibiades*. In this form, the idea became a commonplace and was often attributed to the gods themselves in anecdotes about oracles such as we find in *2 Alcibiades*, Theophrastus, and Theopompus. This tendency to emphasize the moral character of the sacrificant over the costliness of the sacrifice had the potential to undercut the role of animal sacrifice in reinforcing the sociopolitical hierarchies of the Graeco-Roman city, which, as we saw in Part I, was in part predicated on the costliness of animal sacrifices relative to other types of offerings. The philosophers we have considered here, however, seem to have had little interest in pursuing this type of social critique.

There is otherwise little evidence for serious philosophical engagement with sacrificial practice. On the contrary, we can detect an underlying assumption that cult practice was not really a suitable subject for philosophical analysis. Both Plato's proposal that oracles should determine the cult practices of his ideal polis and Aristotle's classification of sacrifices as a matter of human convention can be understood as different ways of articulating that assumption. There consequently seem to have been few attempts to theorize sacrificial practice. Theophrastus may have done so in his treatise on piety, although the extant remains provide little evidence of it, and other writers may have done so in the now-lost treatises with similar titles.[53] The general consensus seems rather to have been that the observance of customary cult practices was an appropriate way of demonstrating one's respect for the gods and that the main reason to observe them was simply the fact that they were customary. That idea is implicit in Plato's account of the cult practices of his ideal polis in *Laws* and explicit in the repeated injunctions that in their offerings to the gods, people should follow ancestral custom.[54]

## 6d. Conclusion: From Theophrastus to Plutarch

Down to the death of Theophrastus in the early third century BCE, philosophical engagement with the practice of animal sacrifice seems to have been largely limited to the question of whether or not it was right for people to kill and eat animals, whether this was framed in terms of the transmigration of souls between humans and animals, as in the case of Empedocles and those who invoked Pythagoras and Orpheus, or a more vaguely defined kinship

---

53. For such treatises, see Obbink 1996, 82–83.

54. E.g.: Xen. *Mem.* 1.3.1 (νόμῳ πόλεως); Epicurus ap. Phld. *Piet.* F 31, 883–84 Obbink 1996 (κατὰ τοὺς νόμους); Epictetus *Ench.* 31.5 (κατὰ τὰ πάτρια).

between humans and animals, as in the case of Theophrastus. Otherwise, we find little interest in theorizing cult practices but rather a tendency to endorse them on the basis of tradition. Over the next three centuries or so, this overall pattern seems to have changed little. Theophrastus's arguments against animal sacrifice, the most focused and extensive known to us, appear to have had little impact; apart from a few scraps of learning that made their way into literary scholarship, there is no clear trace of his treatise until the late third century CE, when Porphyry drew on it.[55] I have already noted the views of Philodemus and Epictetus, representatives of the Epicurean and Stoic schools in the mid-first century BCE and the early second century CE, respectively, which conform very closely to those of earlier philosophers. The same can be said of Cicero and Plutarch, both of whom were well read in the philosophical tradition and had a serious interest in religion in practice as well as theory. As an Academic skeptic, Cicero was hesitant to commit to any fixed dogma about the nature of the gods but had no hesitation at all about endorsing traditional cult practices. Although Plutarch often explained unusual cult practices by employing allegory, he generally took more mainstream practices for granted.

Yet if there seems to have been little actual theorization of sacrificial practice prior to the time of Plutarch, the framework within which such a theorization could take place had become well established. An essential development was the forging of a form of social power that was effectively independent of the control of economic resources and physical force. Unlike the traditional socioeconomic elite of the Greek city, and despite the fact that some like Plato actually came from that class, philosophers based their claims to authority on their ability to use verbal discourse to persuade others to accept views of the world that differed from and in some cases were radically at odds with the views implicit in traditional Greek culture. These alternative views usually had significant implications for the way people conducted their lives, and their acceptance almost inevitably entailed recognizing the authority of those who propagated them. The possibility that people might deploy these techniques to promote an alternative understanding of sacrificial practice was thus a very real one, and one that in the imperial period

---

55. For example, Sextus Empiricus's exposition of Pythagorean and Empedoclean doctrine (*Math.* 9.127–29) is framed in broadly Theophrastean terms but lacks his characteristic vocabulary. Eusebius later cites Theophrastus through Porphyry (*Praep. evang.* 1.9.6–7, 4.14.1–7, 4.16.10, and 9.2.1), and Theodoret, later still, cites him through Eusebius (*Graecarum affectionum curatio* 7.38–41, quoting Euseb. *Praep. evang.* 4.14.1–3, and 7.41–42, quoting 4.16.1–9). Scraps of learning: e.g., scholia vetera ad Ar. *Av.* 1354, Photius *Lex.* s.v. Κύρβεις, K 1234.

became fully actualized. Two developments played an important part in that actualization.

One was an apparent increase in interest among intellectuals in abstaining from animal flesh. The practice presumably continued throughout the Hellenistic period, although we have few clear references to it. Starting in the later first century BCE, however, there is a noticeable increase in our evidence. For example, Ovid framed his lengthy exposition of Pythagorean doctrine in the last book of his *Metamorphoses* with the philosopher's urgent exhortations to avoid killing and eating animals. Whether or not Ovid knew of contemporaries who actually followed that teaching is not clear, but it is quite possible that he did. The younger Seneca reports that in his youth, during the late 10s CE, he was inspired by his teacher Sotion to give up eating meat; he kept it up for a year, until hostility toward foreign cult practices that involved abstinence from particular animals caused him to resume his regular diet. According to Seneca, Sotion expounded not only the Pythagorean doctrine of metempsychosis but also the teaching of the Roman philosopher Quintus Sextius, who advocated abstinence from animal flesh for the sake of avoiding cruelty and luxury. If Pythagoras is right, Sotion argued, we must abstain from animal food in order to remain innocent of crime; but even if he is wrong, it is nevertheless a beneficial form of austerity.[56] Somewhat later in the century, the youthful Plutarch also went through a period of enthusiasm for vegetarianism, during which time he apparently wrote the two essays against eating meat to which I have already referred.[57] Like Seneca's teacher Sotion, although with greater rhetorical exuberance, he invoked a full battery of arguments, including the Pythagorean/Empedoclean/Orphic theory of metempsychosis, considerations of mental and physical health, and humanitarian concerns. Although Plutarch, like Seneca, seems eventually to have given up his vegetarian diet, the fact that abstinence from animal flesh had such appeal for these two young men, both philosophically inclined members of the elite but otherwise very different in background and circumstances, suggests the extent to which it was "in the air" in the first century CE. Whatever the

---

56. Seneca: *Ep.* 108.17–22; Seneca dates the episode to the early part of Tiberius's reign, and his reference to hostility toward foreign cult practices suggests a more precise date of 19 CE (cf. Tac. *Ann.* 2.85). We cannot date Sextius very precisely, but he was old enough to stand for public office in the early 40s BCE (Sen. *Ep.* 98.13); Seneca held him in high esteem (*Ep.* 59.7 and 64.2–5, *Nat.* 7.32.2). On the interest in Pythagorean teachings in late republican and early imperial Rome, see Flinterman 2014, 343–53; on the debate over vegetarianism, see Martins 2018, 81–93.

57. Plutarch *De esu* 1 and 2.

reasons behind it, abstinence from animal flesh necessarily invited reflection on the practice of animal sacrifice.

The second development also dates back to the late classical period, and in particular to Plato. Despite Plato's evident lack of interest in theorizing sacrifice, he did make one contribution that would become crucial to the theorization of sacrifice in the imperial period: the idea of *daimones* as intermediaries between gods and humans in cult. The Greek word *daimōn*, whence modern English "demon," had a long and varied history prior to Plato; it generally denoted a superhuman force or being that was less well defined than a god or hero. Plato himself used the term in different ways in his various works, but the key passage for us is from Socrates's speech in *Symposium*, in which he purports to pass on to his audience what he learned in his youth from his teacher Diotima, that Eros is neither a god nor a mortal but a great *daimōn*; the sphere of *daimones*, Diotima explains, is intermediary between gods and mortals, and its function is to convey prayers and sacrifices from mortals to gods and orders and responses from gods to mortals. The mediation of *daimones*, Diotima asserts, is, in fact, what makes possible divination and the priestly craft of sacrifices and initiations and the like, since gods and humans do not interact directly. The theory of *daimones* as intermediaries between gods and humans was developed further by Plato's successors, notably Xenocrates, the head of the Academy from 339 to 314 BCE, whose work seems to have been an important influence on Plutarch. Plutarch himself relied on the theory extensively in his explication of various aspects of traditional cult practice, especially oracles.[58] Before we examine its role in the theorization of sacrificial practice, however, we need to consider an entirely separate discursive tradition in which animal sacrifice also played a central role. That is the subject of Chapter 7.

---

58. Eros as *daimōn*: Pl. *Symp*. 202d–203a. On *daimones*, see further Timotin 2012, especially 13–36 on pre-Platonic usage, 37–52 on the Platonic Eros, 93–99 on Xenocrates, and 163–201 on Plutarch. I have throughout chosen to transliterate the Greek term rather than translate it by its English derivative "demon," since the latter reflects a distinctively Christian understanding of a word whose meaning was, in fact, as discussed in Section 8c, the subject of heated debate.

# 7

# The Early Christian Displacement of Animal Sacrifice (c. 50–c. 150 CE)

## 7a. Introduction

By the time Plutarch was writing his treatises against eating meat, a quite separate movement was under way that would ultimately have a much more profound impact on the practice of animal sacrifice than any of the discourses discussed in Chapter 6. Its impact, however, was by no means inevitable but was rather the cumulative result of several originally unrelated and contingent developments. The purpose of this chapter is to trace some of these key developments in their earliest stages.[1]

The movement in question, of course, is what we would now describe as the beginnings of Christianity. This movement was from the start characterized by considerable diversity, to the extent that it can even be misleading to characterize it as a single movement. The most important unifying feature was an emphasis on the figure of Jesus as someone in a unique relationship with the one true God, usually identified as the God of Judaean tradition. At a very early date, possibly in his own lifetime, Jesus's followers gave him the title *Christos*, "the Anointed One," a Greek calque of the Hebrew *Mashiach* or Messiah. According to later tradition, the term *Christianoi* for his followers first arose in Antioch in the mid-first century CE, probably as a designation devised by Roman authorities, but it seems not to have become widely used by insiders until the second half of the second century CE.[2] Although it is

---

1. This chapter owes much to Ullucci 2012, even though I take somewhat different positions on the place of animal sacrifice in early Christian thought.

2. *Christos*: Allison 2010, 279–93. *Christianoi*: Acts 11.26; for a useful recent discussion, see Van der Lans and Bremmer 2017, 319–24.

anachronistic and to some extent misleading to apply it to the early adherents of this varied movement, in this chapter I do so for the sake of convenience.

Not much more is definitely known about the historical Jesus than is known about the historical Pythagoras, although the evidence has been subjected to even more intensive scholarly scrutiny. Without entering into the numerous controversies, we may note a few points that seem reasonably secure. He was a Judaean from the region of Galilee, north of Judaea proper, whose background was rural and working-class. At some point, he embarked on a career as an itinerant teacher and wonderworker; he was evidently highly charismatic and attracted a number of followers. Most of his career seems to have unfolded in the villages and small towns of Galilee and its environs, but he eventually transferred his activities to Jerusalem, where he attracted the unfavorable attention of local authorities and was executed on the orders of the Roman governor, probably sometime around the year 30 CE. His followers, however, remained devoted to his memory and very quickly, it seems, came to believe that after his execution, he had risen from the dead. The cult of the risen Christ rapidly began to attract new adherents, not only in Judaea but in other cities throughout the eastern Mediterranean, for many of whom the historical Jesus was an increasingly remote figure.[3]

The most famous of these new adherents is Paul, the self-styled "Apostle of Christ Jesus," whose surviving letters constitute our earliest evidence for the new movement. It is difficult to date Paul's correspondence very precisely, but there is a general consensus that he wrote the extant letters in the 50s CE, with one or two possibly dating to the 40s. They reveal a world in which groups of Christ followers existed in cities across the eastern Mediterranean: Corinth in Achaea, Thessalonica and Philippi in Macedonia, Ephesus in Asia, several unnamed cities in Galatia, and even Rome, as well as Jerusalem. They likewise reveal a considerable diversity of practice and belief among these communities, with various self-appointed leaders, such as Paul himself, vying to promote their own particular take on the Christian message. At the same time, there was extensive communication between these communities, as itinerant teachers moved from place to place and members of one group carried letters to others. In this unstructured and competitive environment, the use

---

3. Historical Jesus: Allison 2010. In my account of Jesus's career, I have followed the synoptic tradition; the Gospel of John differs significantly, in representing him as active in the villages of Judaea and Samaria as well as Galilee and visiting Jerusalem repeatedly. Since my interests lie elsewhere, in this chapter I do not engage with the issues that arise from attempts to assess whether such incidents as the "cleansing of the Temple" and the Last Supper have a historical basis.

of verbal discourse to persuade others of the truth of one's own particular views, and at the same time to establish one's own authority, was crucial. It is now widely accepted that it is historically more accurate to read Paul's letters as interventions in these ongoing interactions rather than systematic theological treatises. Paul clearly had complex ideas about the significance of Christ's death and resurrection, ideas that may to some extent have changed over time, but in his letters, he is applying them on an ad hoc basis to specific situations.[4]

Early Christians preserved a number of traditions about the words and deeds of Jesus, especially the events surrounding his death, and of his earliest followers, which were eventually incorporated into written texts. Three of the earliest accounts of Jesus, conventionally known as gospels, share enough common elements that they have long been known as the Synoptic Gospels. Although their relationship to one another has been much debated, the majority position is that the one attributed to Mark is the earliest, which was then expanded and elaborated in those attributed to Matthew and Luke. Luke continued his account of Jesus in a second volume devoted to the deeds of his earliest followers, now known as the Acts of the Apostles. The fourth canonical Gospel, attributed to John, differs radically from the three Synoptics in many respects and represents a significantly different tradition. Christian writers also continued to produce letters. Many of these were, like those of Paul, apparently composed to address specific situations in specific places, although some are effectively general treatises that to varying degrees adopt the conventions of the epistolary format; examples are the so-called letter to the Hebrews and the one attributed to Barnabas. Other genres, represented more sporadically, include apocalypse (the Revelation of John) and community manuals (the Didache). The vast majority of the earliest Christian texts are either anonymous (many of them later attributed to specific figures in the Christian tradition) or pseudonymous (notably, several letters deliberately written in the persona of Paul). There are a few exceptions: in addition to Paul, the author of Revelation identifies himself as John, writing on the Greek island of Patmos, and Ignatius, bishop of Antioch, wrote several letters under

---

4. The bibliography on Paul is overwhelming. For three very different recent studies, see Harrill 2012, Sanders 2015, and Fredriksen 2017; for a survey of earlier scholarship, Zetterholm 2009; for an overview of current research, Schellenberg and Wendt 2022. Apostle: e.g., 1 Cor. 1.1, 9.1–6, 15.9; 2 Cor. 1.1; Gal. 1.1; Rom. 1.1. Date of Paul's letters: e.g., Campbell 2022. Paul as self-appointed expert: Stowers 2011a; Wendt 2016, 146–89. Ad hoc nature of Paul's letters: e.g., Sanders 2015, 169–72.

his own name.[5] By the middle of the second century CE, although anonymous and pseudonymous texts continued to be produced in abundance, an increasing number of Christian texts can be attributed to named and datable authors. Important for our purposes is Justin, traditionally known as Justin "Martyr," who wrote in the 150s CE and thus stands at the end of the period under discussion here.

Christianity originated and developed in a world in which, for the most part, animal sacrifice was taken for granted; Jesus and his earliest followers were Judaeans at a time when the sacrificial cult of the Jerusalem Temple was still at the center of Judaean tradition, and the non-Judaean adherents of the risen Christ who were Paul's primary audience lived in Graeco-Roman cities where, as we saw in Part I, animal sacrifice to traditional deities was integral to the functioning of society. In the first section of this chapter, I survey what we can deduce about the relationship of the earliest Christians to these preexisting sacrificial traditions, both Judaean and non-Judaean. In the second section, I turn to the multiple ways in which early Christian writers drew on these traditions, especially Judaean tradition, as a source of metaphors and imagery for articulating the significance of the life and death of Jesus Christ. As we will see, their strategies varied significantly, although by the end of our period, they were starting to cohere into a more systematic set of ideas. These ideas, as I argue in the third section, combined with gradually developing cult practices, provided the framework within which Christian leaders eventually came to reject the practice of animal sacrifice in toto.

## 7b. Early Christians and the Practice of Animal Sacrifice

For many years, people took it for granted that Christians were from the start opposed to the practice of animal sacrifice; the origin of the opposition was attributed to Jesus himself, especially as attested in the account of his so-called cleansing of the Jerusalem Temple which, is found in all four Gospels. More recently, however, scholars have challenged this traditional view and have argued that there is, in fact, little evidence for opposition to the sacrificial cult of the Jerusalem Temple on the part of Jesus or his earliest followers.

---

5. John: Rev. 1.1, 4, 9, 22.8. Patmos: 1.9. Ignatius names himself in the preface of all seven of the letters generally regarded as authentic; the authenticity and the date of the Ignatian corpus are much debated; see most recently Bremmer 2021, with full references to earlier work.

According to Mark, the first thing that Jesus did after his triumphal entry into Jerusalem was to visit the Temple. On his return the next day, he "began to drive out those who were selling and those who were buying in the Temple, and he overturned the tables of the money changers and the seats of those who sold doves; and he would not allow anyone to carry anything through the temple. He was teaching and saying, 'Is it not written, "My house shall be called a house of prayer for all the nations"? But you have made it a den of robbers.'" Matthew and, more briefly, Luke follow Mark's account very closely, although they omit the obscure reference to carrying things through the Temple. John, who dates the episode to the beginning rather than the end of Jesus's career, has a more elaborate and dramatic version: he (somewhat improbably) adds cattle and sheep to the doves and has Jesus drive them all out with a whip. What none of the accounts makes explicit is that all the activities that attracted Jesus's ire were support services offered to pilgrims; since only one type of currency was acceptable for paying the tithe required of all adult Judaean males, the services of money changers were required, and most worshipers at the Temple would have needed to purchase their sacrificial victims on the spot. It was for this reason that many people have regarded Jesus's attack on the money changers and dove sellers as an attack on the Temple cult per se. Yet many other ways of interpreting this episode are equally possible. For example, we could see Jesus's actions not as evidence of hostility to the Temple cult per se but rather of a concern that it was unduly burdensome on the poor. Or we could interpret them as a symbolic enactment of a central part of his teaching: that the kingdom of God was at hand, when God would destroy the Temple built by Herod and replace it with the eternal temple of the end times.[6]

Apart from this one episode, there is very little in the Gospels or Acts that suggests opposition to the Temple and its sacrificial cult.[7] On the contrary, various stories indicate Jesus's endorsement of it. According to Mark, Jesus, after healing a leper, instructed him to go to the Temple, "show yourself to the

---

6. Mark 11.15–17, with Jesus quoting Isa. 56.7 and alluding to Jer. 7.11; cf. Matt. 21.12–14, Luke 19.45–46, John 2.14–17. Money changers and dove sellers as support for Temple cult: Sanders 1992, 85–92. For a thorough discussion of interpretations, see Klawans 2006, 223–36; Klawans himself suggests that Jesus's motivation was his concern for the poor (236–41). Symbolic enactment: Fredriksen 2015, 315–19, and Fredriksen 2018, 42–51, who stresses that such an action need not imply hostility to the Temple cult.

7. The speech of Stephen in Acts 7.2–53 is often read as a statement of opposition to the Jerusalem Temple and its cult (e.g., Daly 1978, 228–30), but that has been called into question (Ullucci 2012, 85–86); it does not, in any case, include any explicit antisacrificial sentiments.

priest, and offer for your cleansing what Moses commanded"; these offerings include two male lambs and one female or, for those of lesser means, one male lamb and two doves.[8] Matthew, in his compilation of Jesus's teachings conventionally known as the Sermon on the Mount, has him repeatedly stress the importance of moving beyond the letter of the law in order to monitor not only one's actions but also one's thoughts. For example: "You have heard that it was said to those of ancient times, 'You shall not murder'; and 'whoever murders shall be liable to judgment.' But I say to you that if you are angry with a brother, you will be liable to judgment." Jesus then illustrates his point with the following example: "So when you are offering your gift at the altar, if you remember that your brother has something against you, leave your gift there before the altar and go; first be reconciled to your brother, and then come and offer your gift."[9] The author of Luke-Acts, in the account of Jesus's birth and childhood that appears in no other Gospel, depicts his parents as pious observers of the Temple cult, who offer the sacrifice of two doves or pigeons to mark the end of impurity after childbirth, as required by Mosaic law, and who go to Jerusalem every year to celebrate Passover. He likewise presents Jesus's earliest followers as continuing to frequent the Temple after his death, going there to pray at the hour of the daily offering of a lamb, for example, even if he does not mention their offering sacrifices themselves.[10] Although the historicity of these anecdotes is very uncertain, we can at least say that the early followers of Jesus who shaped and transmitted them seem to have had little interest either in suppressing indications of respect for the Temple cult on the part of Jesus and his disciples or in documenting their opposition to it.

The author of Acts likewise records Paul's active participation in the Temple cult, although his reports are, again, of uncertain historical value. What about Paul's own writings? Although Paul makes few, if any, straightforward references to Judaean sacrificial cult in his letters, he often draws on it as a source of comparisons and metaphors for talking about other things. Yet drawing on a practice as a source for metaphors does not in itself imply any denigration of the actual practice, as many of Paul's interpreters have

---

8. Mark 1.40–45, with quotation from 1.44; Mark is followed closely by Matt. 8.1–4, Luke 5.12–16. Offerings: Lev. 14.10–32.

9. Matt. 5.21–24; "gift" here need not designate animal sacrifice but would certainly include it.

10. Jesus's parents and the dedication of the firstborn male: Luke 2.22–24, with Lev. 12.8 for the prescribed offering; and Passover: Luke 2.41–42. Jesus's followers and the Temple: e.g., Luke 24.53; Acts 2.46–47, 5.12, 42, and especially 3.1 for prayer at the hour of the daily offering (cf. HJP 2.300–301 with n. 30).

assumed; if anything, it constitutes an acknowledgment of the practice's power and importance. In fact, Paul's comparisons and metaphors generally treat Judaean sacrificial practice as the gold standard for establishing a positive relationship with God, the practice against which all others can be measured. As just one example, he closes his letter to the Christian community in Philippi by thanking them for their financial support during his time of need, which he praises as "a fragrant offering, a sacrifice (θυσία) acceptable and pleasing to God."[11]

There is thus little reason to think that either Jesus or his earliest followers rejected Judaean sacrificial cult.[12] Nevertheless, active participation in it was necessarily restricted: since it could take place only in the Temple in Jerusalem, Judaeans who lived outside that general vicinity would have taken part only occasionally, and non-Judaeans, as we saw in Section 4d, could participate only indirectly. Consequently, Judaean sacrificial cult inevitably had only a limited role in the lives of Christ followers, except those who were Judaeans living near the Jerusalem Temple.

Non-Judaean sacrificial cult, in contrast, was by definition forbidden to all Christ followers, Judaean and gentile alike. As we saw in Section 4d, Judaean tradition strictly prohibited direct participation in cult acts directed to deities other than the Judaean God. It seems that many early Christian leaders expected non-Judaeans to observe this principle as well. This was certainly true of Paul, who demanded that his followers avoid idolatry.[13] The general principle that Christ followers should not participate in the cult of gentile gods seems to have been widely accepted; at any rate, I know of no evidence for debates about it. What we do find evidence for is an extensive and widespread discussion about the propriety of eating meat from animals that had been sacrificed to gentile gods, if that is indeed what is meant by the

---

11. Paul in Acts: 21.17–26, 24.17–18. Comparisons and metaphors: Phil. 4.18; see also 1 Cor. 5.7, 9.13, 10.18; 2 Cor. 2.15; Phil. 2.17; Rom. 12.1; I discuss several of these passages in more detail later in this chapter. For a direct and highly positive reference to the Temple cult, see Rom. 9.4–5. On Paul's positive evaluation of the Judaean Temple cult, see Klawans 2002, 10–12; Fredriksen 2017, 151–54; Fredriksen 2018, 23–29.

12. See further Klawans 2006, 217–20. It is worth noting that some later Christians credited Jesus with an explicit rejection of animal sacrifice. The fourth-century CE heresiologist Epiphanius quotes a passage from the "Gospel of the Ebionites," which probably dates to the second century CE, in which Jesus declares, "I have come to abolish sacrifices (καταλῦσαι τὰς θυσίας) and if you do not stop sacrificing the wrath will not cease from you" (*Pan.* 30.16.4–5): see Joseph 2017, especially 103–4, whose text and translation I quote.

13. Avoiding idolatry: e.g., 1 Thess. 1.9, 1 Cor. 5.11 and 10.14; see further Fredriksen 2010, especially 240–44, and Fredriksen 2017, 86–91.

key term *eidōlothuton*, literally something like "an idol-sacrificial thing." This word does not occur in classical Greek, although it seems to be a variation of the classical adjective *hierothutos*, "sacrificial." It first appears in Judaean Greek texts dating to the mid-first century CE, most notably Paul's first letter to Christ followers in Corinth, where his discussion makes it clear that he uses the term to mean "meat from animals sacrificed to idols."[14]

In this letter, Paul repeatedly addresses problems of divisions within the community of Christ followers in Corinth. His train of thought in the passage in question is, as so often, highly elliptical and allusive, so that there is considerable uncertainty about his precise meaning.[15] Without entering into the complexities, I will simply note that the core issue was apparently that some in the Corinthian community claimed that since idols are merely inanimate objects, eating food that has been offered to them is a matter of indifference. Paul seems to concede the premise but disagrees with the conclusion, since eating *eidōlothuton* could present a stumbling block to fellow Christians who do not share their strength. Moreover, it is incumbent on Christ followers to avoid idolatry, which he suggests in some way involved the consumption of *eidōlothuton*. He insists that, even though idols themselves are nothing, "what they [i.e., the worshipers of idols] sacrifice, they sacrifice to *daimonia* and not to God. I do not want you to be partners with *daimonia*. You cannot drink the cup of the Lord and the cup of *daimonia*. You cannot partake of the table of the Lord and the table of *daimonia*." He goes on to modify this position, however, by concluding that gentile Christ followers at private meals do not need to inquire into the source of all their food, but if they are told that a dish comes from a sacrifice (*hierothuton*), they should avoid it for the sake of other believers who might be present.[16]

Concerns over the consumption of *eidōlothuton* by gentile Christ followers were by no means confined to Paul. The author of the Didache instructs his

---

14. *Hierothutos*: e.g., Ar. *Av.* 1266; Arist. [*Oec.*] 1349b13. *Eidōlothuton* seems a deliberate reworking of the earlier term intended to delegitimize it. Paul uses it repeatedly in 1 Cor. 8 and 10; the one time he uses *hierothuton* as an equivalent, he apparently puts it in the mouth of a gentile (10.28). Outside early Christian texts, *eidōlothuton* appears only in 4 Maccabees (5.2), dating probably to the second century CE (Bowersock 1995, 79; Bremmer 2021, 417–18).

15. For a thorough discussion, with references to earlier scholarship, see Fitzmyer 2008, 330–404; I draw here on my more detailed analysis at Rives 2019c, 8–10.

16. Idols as inanimate objects: 1 Cor. 8.4; stumbling block: 8.7–11; avoiding idolatry: 10.14; sacrifice to *daimonia*: 10:20–21; conclusion: 10.25–29. Paul makes similar points about food at Rom. 14.1–4 and 14–23, although it is not clear whether the problematic food there is *eidōlothuton*. The word *daimonion* is an alternative to *daimōn* and is generally the more common of the two in early Christian writing: BDAG s.v. δαιμόνιον and δαίμων.

audience to do what they can in matters of food but to keep strictly away from *eidōlothuton*. According to the author of Acts, this prohibition had an apostolic origin. Paul's conversion of gentiles sparked a debate over the extent to which these gentile Christ followers should be required to observe Mosaic law. Paul and his associate Barnabas accordingly went to meet with the apostles in Jerusalem (the so-called Council of Jerusalem) so that they could determine a common policy. In the end, James the brother of Jesus decided that gentile converts should not be required to observe Mosaic law but only a few fundamental requirements: avoidance of blood, things strangled, fornication, and *eidōlothuton*.[17] Although both the Didache and Acts treat the prohibition of *eidōlothuton* as beyond debate, there does seem, in fact, to have been debate. John of Patmos, in the letters addressed to Christian groups in seven cities of Asia that preface the account of his visions, expresses his anger at teachers in two of these cities (Pergamum and Thyatira) for enticing their followers into practicing fornication and eating *eidōlothuton*. Later writers, such as Justin Martyr and Irenaeus of Lyons, similarly assert that Christians whom they considered heretical wrongly regarded the consumption of *eidōlothuton* as a matter of indifference.[18]

We may conclude that, although there is little reason to believe that the earliest Christians rejected the practice of animal sacrifice per se, preexisting traditions of animal sacrifice had at most only a very limited place in their cultic life. The only Christ followers for whom the practice of sacrifice could have been important were Judaeans who lived in the environs of Jerusalem and could accordingly participate in the Temple cult. Judaeans who lived elsewhere, such as the apostle Paul, would have engaged in sacrificial cult only on those rare occasions when they were in Jerusalem; in their home communities, the prohibition on the worship of gentile gods meant that they would not have had participated in animal sacrifice at all. Early Christian leaders such as Paul seem to have applied this prohibition to gentile Christ followers as

---

17. Did. 6.3. "Council of Jerusalem": Acts 15. In his speech, James uses the term "things polluted by idols" (15.20), but the letter conveying the decision to the Christ followers of Antioch uses instead *eidōlothuton* (15.29). The list has similarities with the so-called Noachide laws that God imposed on Noah and his descendants, i.e., the entire human race: Gen. 9.4–6, later elaborated in b. Sanhedrin 56a.

18. John of Patmos: Rev. 2.14–16, to the group in Pergamum, and 2.20–23, to that in Thyatira. Later writers: Justin *Dial.* 34.8–35.3; Irenaeus *Haer.* 1.6.3, 2.14.5. Pliny, in his letter seeking the emperor Trajan's guidance on how to handle accusations of Christianity, notes that as a result of his policy so far, the meat from sacrificial victims is again finding buyers (*Ep.* 10.96.10), perhaps suggesting that commitment to this principle on the part of some Christians was uncertain.

well, and although it is impossible to determine how successful they were in enforcing it, it seems to have been widely accepted as a general principle. As a result, gentile Christians, like diaspora Judaeans, would in practice have been cut off from animal sacrifice.[19] It is surely significant that there is no evidence for debate over gentile participation in animal sacrifice but only over gentile consumption of *eidōlothuton*, a prohibition that goes even further in insulating Christ followers from the taint of gentile cult. Gentile Christ followers would thus have found themselves in a cultic environment in which animal sacrifice effectively had no place, something to which diaspora Judaeans had long grown accustomed. Moreover, the fact that Judaean sacrificial cult came to an end with the destruction of the Jerusalem Temple in 70 CE, just a few decades after Jesus's death, meant that animal sacrifice ceased to be a living practice even for Judaean Christ followers in Judaea.

Because animal sacrifice had so limited a role in early Christian cult practice, it is likely enough that many early Christ followers came to associate it primarily with the worship of gentile deities and thus to regard it as something to be avoided. Yet such an outcome was not inevitable; there was, at least initially, some possibility that they could have developed their own practices of animal sacrifice. As I argue in the next section, we can identify discourses in our earliest evidence that could, in fact, have provided a suitable conceptual framework for Christian animal sacrifice.

## 7c. Jesus as Sacrificial Victim

The strategy of making sense of Jesus's life and death by employing metaphors and other figures drawn from sacrificial practice seems to have been a very early development, as Christian leaders struggled to articulate its significance to the people whom they were trying to persuade of their message. The unstructured and competitive context in which they operated meant that their use of these metaphors initially took quite different forms and only gradually cohered into a more standardized doctrine. I do not here attempt any sort of

---

19. Cf. Klawans 2006, 221: "to a Gentile in the Diaspora, rejecting all sacrifice but the Jerusalem cult is little different from rejecting all sacrifice whatsoever." Ullucci 2012, 134: "for much of Paul's audience, however, living in places like Thessalonica, Corinth, and Galatia, their new-found beliefs meant de facto nonparticipation in animal sacrifice."

comprehensive survey of this complex development but simply note a few key strands.[20]

We may begin with the earliest examples, in the letters of Paul. His correspondence provides valuable insight into the early stages of the process, since we can observe him employing sacrificial metaphors "off the cuff," so to speak. I limit my discussion to the two most striking examples. One of these occurs in another passage of his letter to the Christian community in Corinth: "For our paschal lamb, Christ, has been sacrificed (τὸ πάσχα ἡμῶν ἐτύθη Χριστός)." Here Paul makes an explicit equivalence between Christ and the lamb that was slaughtered as the central element of the Passover feast, the point of comparison presumably being that both Jesus and the lamb were killed. Yet there is both less and more here than meets the eye. On the one hand, the comparison is by no means the focus of Paul's concern here but one that apparently occurs to him only in passing as a corollary of a different metaphor that is his main focus. His chief concern here is to reprimand his correspondents for their boasting, since boasting, he says, is like yeast: a small amount can leaven a whole batch of dough. He elaborates this metaphor by invoking the important role of yeast in the Passover festival as practiced in his day: "Clean out the old yeast so that you may be a new batch, as you really are unleavened. For our paschal lamb, Christ, has been sacrificed. Therefore, let us celebrate the festival, not with the old yeast, the yeast of malice and evil, but with the unleavened bread of sincerity and truth." On the other hand, the fact that it occurred to him in this connection to compare Christ with the paschal lamb may indicate that he was familiar with the tradition that Jesus's execution and last meal occurred at the time of the Passover festival; I discuss this tradition in more detail later in this section.[21]

The other key metaphor occurs in Paul's letter to the Christian community at Rome. Of all the extant writings of Paul, this letter comes the closest to a systematic exposition of his ideas about the significance of Christ's death and resurrection. At the same time, it contains some of his most densely allusive and elliptical writing and has consequently been for centuries the subject of intense scrutiny and debate. In the passage that concerns us, Paul is elaborating on the idea that all people have sinned and fallen short of God's

---

20. Daly 1978, 208–372, and Young 1979, 139–217, remain valuable overviews of the relevant material, although their theologically inflected approach differs significantly from my own. See more recently the careful study of Eberhart 2013, who argues that the application of sacrificial metaphors to Christ was not limited to or even primarily concerned with his death.

21. 1 Cor. 5.7–8. Passover: Sanders 1992, 132–38.

expectations but have now been "justified by his grace as a gift, through the redemption that is in Christ Jesus, whom God put forward as a sacrifice of atonement by his blood, effective through faith (ἱλαστήριον διὰ [τῆς] πίστεως ἐν τῷ αὐτοῦ αἵματι)." The crucial term, translated in the New Revised Standard Version as "a sacrifice of atonement," is *hilastērion*, the neuter of an adjective derived from the verb *hilaskomai*, "to appease or propitiate"; in the Septuagint, it was used to denote the cover on the Ark of the Covenant, which the high priest sprinkled with the blood of the sin offering on the Day of Atonement. Most commentators believe that Paul is here again referring metaphorically to Judaean sacrificial practice in his attempt to articulate the significance of Christ's life and death, although it is uncertain whether many in Paul's original audience would have caught that somewhat recherché reference. Stanley Stowers, in contrast, has argued cogently that the word is much more likely to have conveyed the more general sense of "conciliation" or "propitiation" and that there is no sacrificial reference here at all.[22]

Although Paul provides the earliest extant examples of applying sacrificial imagery to Jesus's life and death, the practice clearly predates him, as we know from another passage in his letter to the Corinthians. Paul here addresses a report that when the Christ followers of Corinth gather together to celebrate what he calls "the Lord's supper" (κυριακὸν δεῖπνον), there is a conspicuous absence of community spirit: "each of you goes ahead with your own supper, and one goes hungry and another becomes drunk." He rebukes them for this behavior and proceeds to remind them of the origin and model for their communal meals: "For I received from the Lord what I also handed on to you, that the Lord Jesus on the night when he was betrayed took a loaf of bread, and when he had given thanks, he broke it and said, 'This is my body that is for you. Do this in remembrance of me.' In the same way he took the cup also, after supper, saying, 'This cup is the new covenant in my blood. Do this, as often as you drink it, in remembrance of me.' For as often as you eat this bread and drink the cup, you proclaim the Lord's death until he comes." Accordingly, those who participate in this meal must do so in a proper state of mind: "Whoever, therefore, eats the bread or drinks the cup of the Lord in an unworthy manner will be answerable for the body and blood of the Lord.

---

22. Rom. 3.24–25. *Hilastērion*: BDAG, s.v.; LXX: see Exod. 25.17–22 for the description of the *hilastērion* and Ezek. 43.18–21 for its role in the atonement sacrifice; for detailed analysis of the *hilaskomai* word group used in reference to Christ, see Eberhart 2013, 157–77; for a nonsacrificial interpretation of this passage, see Stowers 1994, 206–13. It is worth noting that Paul employs sacrificial metaphors not only in talking about Christ but in other contexts as well, e.g., Phil. 2.17, Rom. 12.1.

Examine yourselves, and only then eat of the bread and drink of the cup." Those who are hungry should eat at home first, he concludes, so that they may then participate in the communal meal in an appropriate manner.[23]

Much about this passage is debated, but a few points seem clear enough. First, the meal to which Paul refers is not merely the consumption of a token amount of bread and drink but an actual meal (δεῖπνον). Second, he associates this communal meal with the story of Jesus's Last Supper, in which the bread and the cup likewise have a central place; he seems to treat the story as an etiology for the practice of the communal meal, which he here interprets as a commemoration of Jesus's death.[24] Third, the story and presumably the associated communal meal apparently constituted a preexisting tradition that Paul had previously learned and that he in turn passed on to the Corinthians. This tradition evidently goes back to a very early period, possibly even to an actual event at the end of Jesus's life. Fourth, in Paul's account, neither the story nor the communal meal involves any overt evocation of sacrificial practice; for that, we must look elsewhere.

Paul is the earliest source for the story of the "Last Supper," as it is conventionally known, but by no means the only one: all three Synoptic Gospels include accounts that, despite differences in detail, are very clearly versions of the same story. The one in Mark, usually regarded as the earliest, represents a somewhat different tradition from that found in Paul: "While they were eating, he [Jesus] took a loaf of bread, and after blessing it he broke it, gave it to them, and said, 'Take; this is my body.' Then he took a cup, and after giving thanks he gave it to them, and all of them drank from it. He said to them, 'This is my blood of the covenant, which is poured out for many. Truly I tell you, I will never again drink of the fruit of the vine until that day when I drink it new in the kingdom of God.'" Matthew follows Mark very closely, with some alterations and additions, while Luke's version is quite distinct and appears to combine elements from those of both Mark and Paul. What all three Synoptic writers have in common, in contrast with Paul, is that they locate the story within a broader narrative context and, in doing so, identify the meal as the feast marking the beginning of Passover. Thus, Mark opens his narrative as follows: "On the first day of Unleavened Bread, when people used to sacrifice the Passover lamb (ὅτε τὸ πάσχα ἔθυον), his disciples said to

---

23. 1 Cor. 11.17–34, with quotations from 11.21, 23–26, and 27–28. On Paul's use of the term "Lord's supper," see McGowan 2015. Paul also refers to the sharing of the bread and cup in his discussion of *eidōlothuton*: 1 Cor. 10.16–17.

24. McGowan 2010, 187–88.

him, 'Where do you want us to go and make the preparations for you to eat the Passover (φάγῃς τὸ πάσχα)?'" The crucial and distinctive element of the Passover meal was the lamb that was slaughtered on the day on which the festival began at sundown. The term *to pascha* is ambiguous, since it can refer to the festival as a whole, the feast with which it opened, or the lamb that was that meal's distinguishing feature, but the author of Mark, followed by Luke, uses it unambiguously in the last of these senses, when he says that people used to sacrifice the *pascha*; his subsequent references to "eating the *pascha*" thus strongly connote eating the lamb in particular.[25]

It is accordingly striking that in their description of what transpired during the meal, all three Synoptic writers omit entirely any reference to eating the lamb; indeed, they elide most of the meal in order to focus on the bread and the cup. In this context, Jesus's statements associating his flesh with the bread and his blood with the cup effectively function to figure him in the place of the lamb, whose flesh was normally consumed by the participants in the Passover meal. We must note, however, that the association of Jesus with the Passover lamb that this story effects is very loose and indirect, since the participants in the feast would certainly not have drunk the lamb's blood, something fundamentally at odds with Judaean law.[26]

Despite this loose association of Jesus with the sacrificial lamb of the Passover in the Synoptic accounts of the Last Supper, the authors never directly identify the two. Other texts, however, explicitly figure Christ as a lamb.[27] We have already noted Paul's seemingly off-the-cuff equation of Christ with the Passover lamb in his first letter to the Corinthians, and we find an equally explicit identification in a very different strand of early Christian tradition. Like the authors of the Synoptic Gospels, John begins his account of Jesus's career with the story of his encounter with John "the Baptist." Among the many ways in which his version differs from theirs, he has John twice

---

25. Accounts of the Last Supper: Mark 14.22–25 (quoted); cf. Matt. 26.26–30, Luke 22.14–21. Dating to Passover: Mark 14.12 (quoted with modifications to the NRSV translation); cf. Matt. 26.17 and Luke 22.7; Matthew omits the reference to the Passover lamb being sacrificed, thus downplaying its role. Eating/preparing the *pascha*: Mark 14.14, Matt. 26.18 and 19, Luke 22.8, 11, and 13; cf. Ullucci 2012, 80. That some readers interpreted the text to mean that Jesus ate of the lamb is indicated by the fact that they altered the account so that Jesus explicitly declares that he did not desire to eat meat at the Passover (Epiphan. *Pan.* 30.22.4; see Joseph 2017, 102–3).

26. Scholars have identified a wide range of potential sacrificial references in these texts, although, like the evocation of the Passover lamb, they are all indirect and allusive; see the recent survey of Kazen 2017.

27. For a systematic discussion, see Eberhart 2013, 178–201.

declare Jesus to be "the Lamb of God" (ὁ ἀμνὸς τοῦ θεοῦ). The first of these pronouncements is particularly marked, since it takes place on the first occasion in the narrative when John sees Jesus: "Here is the Lamb of God who takes away the sin of the world!"[28]

John of Patmos, in his account of his apocalyptic vision, employs this lamb imagery even more extensively. He begins by describing God enthroned amid twenty-four elders and four bizarre "living creatures" and then quickly introduces the Lamb: "I saw between the throne and the four living creatures and among the elders a Lamb standing as if it had been slaughtered (ἀρνίον ἑστηκὸς ὡς ἐσφαγμένον)." The living creatures and elders praise the Lamb, "because you were slaughtered and by your blood you ransomed for God (ὅτι ἐσφάγης καὶ ἠγόρασας τῷ θεῷ ἐν τῷ αἵματί σου) saints from every tribe and language and people and nation." The author goes on to refer repeatedly to the slaughter of the Lamb and the efficacy of its blood. Without going into all the details that make the identification clear, I note simply that the Lamb is obviously a figure for Christ, conceived as God's primary agent. The author never explicitly describes the Lamb as having been sacrificed, but the verb that he does use, *sphagein*, easily carries sacrificial connotations, and the emphasis on its blood has similar implications.[29]

Although neither author provides any hint to the significance of this identification of Christ as a lamb, scholars generally cite two possible sources, which later writers are likely to have combined. One of these we have already considered: the Synoptic accounts of the Last Supper in which Jesus seems symbolically to take the place of the Passover lamb. In this connection, it is worth noting that John's chronology of Jesus's trial and execution differs from that in the Synoptics. As we have seen, the latter all explicitly indicate that the Last Supper was the feast that took place at the start of Passover, which, like all Judaean festivals, began at sundown. On this chronology, Jesus was arrested during the following night and tried, condemned, and executed the next day. John shifts the time frame forward by one day, so that the trial and execution take place on the day of preparation for Passover; by the time of the Passover feast in the evening, Jesus is already dead. It is for this reason that John lacks any account of the Last Supper that corresponds to the one in Paul's letter to the Corinthians and the Synoptic Gospels. Yet, as a number of scholars have

---

28. John 1.29; cf. 1.35–36. John's further comments in the first passage (1.29–34) reveal that he has already encountered Jesus, but that encounter is described only retrospectively.

29. Quotations from Rev. 5.6 and 9. Other references to the Lamb's slaughter: 5.12, 13.8; to its blood: 7.14, 12.11.

pointed out, John as well, albeit in a different way, loosely associates the crucifixion of Jesus with the slaughter of the Passover lamb, since he times it to coincide with the period when people were busy sacrificing the lambs for that evening's feasts.[30]

The other possible source for the lamb imagery comes from the prophet Isaiah, a verse in the sequence conventionally known as the "Suffering Servant" passage: "He was oppressed, and he was afflicted, yet he did not open his mouth; like a lamb that is led to the slaughter (LXX: ὡς πρόβατον ἐπὶ σφαγήν), and like a sheep (ὡς ἀμνός) that before its shearers is silent, so he did not open his mouth." This passage was very popular with early Christian writers because of the ease with which it could be applied to the sufferings and subsequent exaltation of Jesus. There are two striking examples in extant texts of this particular verse being used in this way. The author of Acts, in his brief account of the apostle Philip, describes his encounter with an official of the queen of Ethiopia who was returning home after worshiping at the Temple in Jerusalem. The spirit moves Philip to approach him and ask whether he understands what he is reading; the man invites Philip to join him and explicate it. The verse turns out to be the one from Isaiah just quoted, and when the official asks Philip to whom it refers, Philip proclaims to him the good news about Jesus and baptizes him on the spot. The other example comes from the so-called letter of Barnabas. Here, the author is explaining the reason for Christ's suffering: "This is why the Lord allowed his flesh to be given over to corruption, that we might be made holy through the forgiveness of sins, which comes in the sprinkling of his blood. For some of the things written about him concern Israel; others concern us. And so it says: 'He was wounded because of our lawless acts and weakened because of our sins. By his bruising we were healed. He was led like a sheep going to slaughter; and like a lamb, silent before the one who shears it.'" It is worth stressing that the verse from Isaiah does not necessarily concern animal sacrifice; indeed, the second of the two images it contains explicitly does not, although the first could be applied to that context.[31]

---

30. Chronology of Jesus's execution: John 13.1, 18.28, and especially 19.14; for a careful discussion of the issues, see Brown 1994, especially 1369–73. Several details in the account of the crucifixion that are unique to John may allude to an identification with the Passover lamb: 19.29 and 33–37, with Brown 1994, 847. John does include an account of Jesus's last meal, but it features his washing of his followers' feet and says nothing of the bread and the cup (13.1–15).

31. "Suffering Servant": Isa. 52.13–53.12; quotation from 53.7. Philip: Acts 8.26–39. Barnabas: 5.1–2, quoting Isa. 53.5 and 7 (trans. Bart D. Ehrman, Loeb).

Regardless of its origin, the practice of employing sacrificial imagery in connection with Christ, especially figuring him as a lamb, with its potential sacrificial connotations, seems rapidly to have become widespread throughout many different strands of early Christian tradition. By the early second century CE, we find it in various forms in the letters of Paul, the Synoptic Gospels, the fourth Gospel, the apocalypse of John, and the so-called letter of Barnabas, as well as letters attributed to Peter and John.[32] Again, it is important to stress the looseness and the variety of these metaphors and allusions; it would be going far beyond the evidence to deduce from them any sort of systematic theology. On the contrary, some of them are in significant tension with one another. By the middle of the century, however, Christian thinkers were gradually crafting something more coherent out of these various bits and pieces. Justin Martyr, for example, elaborates on the comparison of Christ to the Passover lamb in much more systematic detail: "The mystery of the lamb (τὸ μυστήριον . . . τοῦ προβάτου), then, which God ordered you to sacrifice as the Passover (ὃ τὸ πάσχα θύειν ἐντέταλται ὁ θεός), was truly a type of Christ (τύπος . . . τοῦ Χριστοῦ), with whose blood the believers, in proportion to the strength of their faith, anoint their homes, that is, themselves." God's order to offer the Passover lamb was from the start only a temporary one, however, as can be determined from the fact that he directed it to take place only in the Jerusalem Temple, which he knew would someday be destroyed; at that point, all sacrifices would cease. In a later passage from the same work, Justin develops the comparison further by making an analogy between the blood of the Passover lamb, which averted death from those whose doors were marked with it, and the blood of Christ, which likewise averts death from those who believe; in support, he, too, quotes the passage from Isaiah, which we have already repeatedly encountered, about the sheep led to slaughter. These passages make it clear that for Justin, the Passover lamb was not simply a loose

---

32. 1 Pet. 1.18–19: "You know that you were ransomed from the futile ways inherited from your ancestors, not with perishable things like silver or gold, but with the precious blood of Christ, like that of a lamb (ὡς ἀμνοῦ) without defect or blemish." The author of 1 John twice describes Christ as "the atoning sacrifice for our sins (ἱλασμός . . . περὶ τῶν ἁμαρτιῶν ἡμῶν)" (2.2 and 4.10); the term *hilasmos*, literally "appeasement," is used in the LXX to denote an expiatory animal sacrifice, e.g., Num. 5.8, Ezek. 44.27 and 45.19; see further Eberhart 2013, 170–72. See also the (probably pseudo-)Pauline Eph. 5.2: "Christ loved us and gave himself up for us, a fragrant offering and sacrifice (θυσίαν) to God." Christ is likewise repeatedly figured as a sacrifice in the so-called letter to the Hebrews, which I discuss in the following section.

metaphor but a key to understanding the true significance of Christ's salvific suffering and death.[33]

What I would like to stress is the possibility that the widespread use of this sacrificial imagery, even before thinkers like Justin began developing it systematically, could have provided a conceptual framework for commemorating the death of Jesus with actual animal sacrifices. Although sacrificial practice played a very limited role in the cultic lives of the earliest Christ followers, in the culture of the Roman world more generally, Judaean as well as gentile, it was of central importance. I thus find nothing prima facie implausible in supposing that early Christ followers could have represented the death of Jesus, the "paschal lamb," by sacrificing a real lamb as the central element of their communal meal.[34] It seems all the more plausible given the fact that the etiology for that practice was a story that, at least by the late first century CE, centered on a meal whose most distinctive element was precisely a lamb. Yet from an early date, this was the road not taken. Instead, Christian leaders came more and more to reject the practice of animal sacrifice altogether. In the following section, I explore some of the circumstances that seem to have contributed to this outcome.

## 7d. The Early Christian Rejection of Animal Sacrifice

Two developments in particular seem to have militated against the possibility that the imagery of Jesus as a sacrificial victim could have led to the commemoration of his death through animal sacrifice. One is the fact that the Christian communal meal seems from a very early date to have marginalized or even excluded the consumption of meat. The other is an increasing tendency on the part of some (although not all) Christian leaders to define Christianity in contrast to Judaean tradition; in this context, some began to

---

33. *Dial.* 40.1–2, with quotation from 40.1 (trans. Falls 2003); later passage: 111.13, quoting Isa. 53.7. The interpretation of passages in the Judaean scriptures as symbolic prefigurations or "types" of Christ and other figures and events in early Christian history is often regarded as a distinctive mode of early Christian exegesis; for a recent critical re-evaluation, see Martens 2008.

34. My proposal may appear less far-fetched when we realize that at various times, some Christians have done precisely what I suggest here: Conybeare 1903, 84–86, and Kovaltchuk 2008, 173–75. On Christian rituals involving the slaughter of animals, see further Section 11c below. In my view, it requires considerably more mental gymnastics to figure Jesus's flesh as bread than as meat; see, e.g., John 6.22–59 (whether or not the author intended this as a reflection on Eucharistic practice).

dismiss or even condemn the practice of animal sacrifice that, as we have seen, had so central a place in that tradition.

The development of the early Christian communal meal, the practice that eventually developed into the ritual known as the Eucharist, has been much discussed and debated in recent decades, with an emphasis on locating it in wider traditions of communal and ritual meals in the ancient Mediterranean world. Two crucial points that have emerged from this recent work are worth stressing. First, there was no single form of early Christian meal that developed in a direct and linear fashion from the Last Supper, as was long taken for granted, but rather a diversity of practices. Second, despite this diversity, the evidence is consistent that early Christian communal meals, as we have already seen in Paul's letter to the Christian community in Corinth, were actual meals. It was only gradually that these diverse meal practices cohered into a single ritual involving the consumption of a token amount of bread and drink. Rather than trying to trace this complex development in any systematic way, I limit my discussion to a few key attestations from the first century of the Christian movement.[35]

The earliest evidence for Christian communal meals is in Paul's letter to the Christ followers of Corinth, dating to the 50s or possibly 40s CE, which was discussed in the previous section. As I noted there, it is clear that the practice in question was an actual communal meal, although its ritual center was the sharing of the bread and the cup.[36] In his initial stay in Corinth, Paul seems to have introduced the practice or at least helped shape it by passing on the story of the Last Supper, which functioned as both an etiology and a standard; as he notes, this was a tradition that had previously been passed on to him, presumably by other Christ followers. It was thus a very early tradition, possibly going back to an actual event at the end of Jesus's life.

Another cluster of references dates to the early second century CE. It is in these that we first find the term "Eucharist," literally "thanksgiving," used as a technical term to denote a specific ritual.[37] Ignatius of Antioch refers to it

---

35. For a survey of scholarship, see Bradshaw 2002, 61–72, 118–43; for a good recent overview, McGowan 2014, 19–55; for the current concern with contextualization, note the seventy-six wide-ranging papers collected in Hellholm and Sänger 2017.

36. I follow here the terminology of Paul himself (1 Cor. 11.25–27), who consistently uses the word "cup" (τὸ ποτήριον) without specifying its contents. Since wine was the normal drink in the ancient Mediterranean, usually mixed with water, we may assume that it was likely meant in this and other similar references, although there were groups that for ascetic purposes insisted on water: McGowan 1999a and cf. Bremmer 2019a.

37. BDAG s.v. εὐχαριστία; on terminology, see further McGowan 2015.

several times in the letters that he wrote to the Christian communities in various cities of the province of Asia. He provides little detail about what the ritual involves, presumably because he took it for granted that his addressees were familiar with it, but focuses more on linking it to some of his main concerns, the importance of correct beliefs and the authority of the bishop and clergy. So, for example, he encourages the Christian community at Philadelphia "to celebrate just one Eucharist (μιᾷ εὐχαριστίᾳ χρῆσθαι); for there is one flesh of our Lord Jesus Christ and one cup that brings the unity of his blood, and one altar, as there is one bishop together with the presbytery and the deacons." In his letter to the Christians of Smyrna, he warns against "those who spout false opinions" and who "abstain from the Eucharist and prayer, since they do not confess that the Eucharist is the flesh of our savior Jesus Christ, which suffered on behalf of our sins and which the Father raised in his kindness." True Christians should avoid such people and instead follow their bishop and presbyters; only the Eucharist that takes place under their authority is valid. Despite the lack of detail, it is clear that Ignatius regarded the Eucharist as a ritual closely tied to correct belief and for that reason needed to be under the authority of the community leaders.[38]

Unlike Ignatius, the early church manual known as the Didache, "The Teaching," provides point-by-point instructions for the proper conduct of the Eucharist: "And with respect to the thanksgiving meal (περὶ δὲ τῆς εὐχαριστίας), you shall give thanks as follows. First, with respect to the cup: 'We give you thanks, our Father, for the holy vine of David, your child, which you made known to us through Jesus your child. To you be the glory forever.' And with respect to the fragment of bread: 'We give you thanks, our Father, for the life and knowledge that you made known to us through Jesus your child. To you be the glory forever.'" In addition to these opening prayers over the cup and the bread, the author (or compiler) gives instructions for a concluding prayer of thanks as well. His emphasis in these prayers of thanksgiving is very much in keeping with the ritual's name, but it is striking that he nowhere alludes to the association of the bread and the cup with the flesh and blood of Christ, which is so prominent in Ignatius and other early sources. On the other hand, the Didache is the earliest extant text that refers to the Eucharist as a "sacrifice," and more specifically as a "pure sacrifice" (θυσία καθαρά), in ways that

---

38. Ignatius: Phld. 4 and Smyrn. 6–8, with quotations from 6.2 and 7.1 (trans. Bart D. Ehrman, Loeb). For the debate over the dating of these letters, see Bremmer 2021.

strongly suggest that the author regarded it as an equivalent to the animal sacrifices of the traditional Temple cult.[39]

Lastly, Justin Martyr provides a detailed discussion of the ritual and its meaning in the defense of Christianity that he addressed to the emperor Antoninus Pius.[40] After the participants in a Christian assembly have prayed and exchanged kisses of greeting, he explains, "then there is brought to the president of the brothers bread and a cup of wine mixed with water, and the president takes them and sends up praise and glory to the Father of all through the name of his Son and of the holy Spirit, and he makes thanksgiving at length for being considered worthy of these things by him." After the prayer, "those called deacons amongst us give to each of those present to partake of the eucharistized bread and wine and water." He goes on to explain that they call this food "Eucharist" and that it is no mere ordinary bread and drink but something much more profound: "just as Jesus Christ our Savior was made flesh by means of a word of God, and had flesh and blood for our salvation, just so we have been taught that the food which has been eucharistized through a word of prayer which comes from him is the flesh and blood of that Jesus who was made flesh." Justin concludes his account by retelling the story of the Last Supper as the origin of the practice.[41] In Justin, clearly, we encounter a much more developed theology of the Eucharist.

We may conclude this brief survey by highlighting a few points. A shared meal was a common element in social interactions in the ancient Mediterranean world, particularly in the meetings of voluntary associations. Given normative Graeco-Roman practice, such communal meals would regularly have involved some invocation of and offering to a deity, although

---

39. Guidelines for celebrating the Eucharist: Did. 9–10, with quotations from 9.1–3 (trans. Bart D. Ehrman, Loeb). Eucharist as a sacrifice: Did. 14.1–3; the author alludes to Jesus's command to settle any quarrels before making one's gift at the altar (Matt. 5.23–24, discussed here in Section 7b) and paraphrases God's request for "pure sacrifice" from the LXX version of the prophet Malachi (1.11); in its original context, that request appears in a complaint that the priests are sacrificing to God animals that are blind, maimed, and sick (Mal. 1.6–14).

40. Outsiders were aware that Christians gathered for communal meals, about which dark rumors circulated: McGowan 1994 and Rives 1995a, especially 65–66. Pliny had carefully interrogated those accused before him of being Christians and ascertained to his satisfaction that the meals were, in fact, innocuous (*Ep.* 10.96.7). All this may provide the context for Justin's detailed account in his defense.

41. Justin 1 *Apol.* 65–66, with quotations from 65.3, 65.5, and 66.2 (trans. Minns and Parvis 2009). It is worth noting that neither the Didache nor Justin include the "Words of Institution" attributed to Jesus in the accounts of the Last Supper found in Paul and the Synoptic Gospels as part of the ritual prayers; the earliest reference to them being used in this way comes from a text of the third century CE: McGowan 1999b, especially 75 and 83.

whether that took the form of an animal sacrifice would have depended on the specific group, particularly its members' economic resources.[42] What is striking about early Christian communal meals is that they seem not to have included the consumption of meat, although the limitations of our evidence mean that we cannot be entirely sure. The communal meals mentioned by Paul certainly could have included meat, and the debate over *eidōlothuton* suggests that they sometimes did. As far as I am aware, however, there is not a single explicit reference to the consumption of meat in the context of a Christian communal meal, although there are occasional references to other foodstuffs, including cheese, milk and honey, oil, and even fish.[43] In all cases, however, the ritual focus was from the start on the bread and the cup, which by the time of Justin seem to have constituted the whole of the ritual. The exclusion of meat can hardly have been an accident. What could have been the reasons for it?

It is tempting to interpret the choice to organize this key cult practice around bread and wine rather than meat as an implicit rejection of the whole framework of socioeconomic hierarchies and the dynamics of benefaction with which animal sacrifice, as we have seen, was so closely bound up, even though, as discussed in Section 4d, those dynamics were much less prominent in Judaean sacrificial tradition. Bread and wine, two of the elements in the basic "Mediterranean triad" of grain, grape, and olive, were much more affordable than meat and consequently much more accessible to a wider range of people.[44] The practice of centering communal meals on bread and wine rather than meat would thus have aligned very closely with the emphasis on the poorer classes and the criticism of the wealthy that are so prominent in the earliest Christian tradition. It is important to note, however, that if this was a major consideration behind the cultic emphasis on bread and wine, it is, to the best of my knowledge, never articulated in any extant early Christian text. What we find articulated instead is something quite different.

It is a truism to point out that the Christian movement originated within Judaean tradition. Jesus and his earliest followers were all Judaeans, with an apparently deep commitment to that tradition. The extent to which Jesus himself acted as a reformer or a critic of that tradition is a question that is much debated and ultimately impossible to answer, given that all the extant

---

42. A useful survey: Öhler 2014; see further the works cited in n. 35 above.

43. McGowan 1999a, 89–142.

44. McGowan 2010, 184–85; for the "Mediterranean triad," see Section 2a above.

evidence for his activities dates to several decades after his death. What is more certain is that by that time, especially after the destruction of the Jerusalem Temple, there was an increasing tendency on the part of some of the movement's leaders to define its distinctive qualities by contrasting it with Judaean tradition. The shifting relationship between the nascent Christian tradition and Judaean tradition, itself undergoing significant change during this time, is another complex and much-debated issue, but it is important for us largely because it was the context within which some Christian thinkers came to reject the practice of animal sacrifice per se.[45] This rejection took several different forms.

As I already noted in my survey of sacrificial imagery, many early Christian thinkers drew on Judaean sacred writings and cultic traditions in their attempts to articulate the significance of Jesus's life and death. In some instances, they did so by applying the tools of allegory. Allegory was a long-established interpretive strategy in Graeco-Roman culture, often employed by philosophers to reveal the "true" meaning behind traditional myths and cult practices, and it was adopted by early Christian thinkers from an early date; we have already encountered an example in Justin Martyr's exposition of the Passover lamb as a figure for Jesus. Some of these thinkers took the additional step of arguing that the allegorical interpretation of Judaean cult practices not only revealed their true significance but also rendered the practices themselves superfluous. I here note two examples that are particularly important for the evolving Christian understanding of sacrifice.

The most important, because it is the most thorough and systematic, is the anonymous treatise traditionally known as the "letter to the Hebrews." The central argument, whose development takes up much of the text, is that the high priesthood and sacrificial cult established by Mosaic law were merely an earthly foreshadowing of the heavenly and eternal high priesthood of Jesus Christ, whose self-sacrifice has perfected and thus replaced the old sacrificial cult. The author's argument is elaborate and complex, and I can here summarize only a few key points. The author introduces early on the idea of Jesus as high priest: in noting that the Son of God assumed mortal flesh so that through his own death he might save others, he adds that "he had to become like his brothers in every respect, so that he might be a merciful and faithful

---

45. On the process of Christian self-definition through the construction of a contrasting Judaean tradition, see, e.g., Boyarin 2004, especially 37–73 on Justin Martyr. On the Christian rejection of animal sacrifice, see Ullucci 2012, especially 65–136, and Petropoulou 2008, 264–74.

high priest in the service of God, to make a sacrifice of atonement for the sins of the people (εἰς τὸ ἱλάσκεσθαι τὰς ἁμαρτίας τοῦ λαοῦ)."[46] After a comparison of Christ with Moses, he elaborates further on this idea, focusing especially on the high priest's role in the sacrificial cult: "every high priest chosen from among mortals is put in charge of things pertaining to God on their behalf, to offer gifts and sacrifices for sins (ἵνα προσφέρῃ δῶρά τε καὶ θυσίας ὑπὲρ ἁμαρτιῶν)." Christ, however, is high priest of a different order, that of Melchizedek. Applying to Christ a passage from a Psalm ("you are a priest forever, according to the order of Melchizedek"), he argues on the basis of a brief episode in Genesis that Melchizedek is superior to Abraham and his descendants.[47] By the same token, Christ is superior to the high priests established by Mosaic law; accordingly, "unlike the other high priests, he has no need to offer sacrifices (θυσίας ἀναφέρειν) day after day, first for his own sins and then for those of the people; this he did once for all when he offered himself (ἑαυτὸν ἀνενέγκας)." The original tabernacle was merely "a sketch and shadow of the heavenly one," as was the ministry that it supported. "But Jesus has now obtained a more excellent ministry, and to that degree he is the mediator of a better covenant, which has been enacted through better promises. For if that first covenant had been faultless, there would have been no need to look for a second one." After quoting at length a passage from the prophet Jeremiah in the LXX translation ("The days are surely coming, says the Lord, when I will establish a new covenant with the house of Israel"), he declares that "in speaking of 'a new covenant,' he [i.e., the Lord] has made the first one obsolete. And what is obsolete and growing old will soon disappear." He then elaborates in extensive detail on the idea that the traditional sin offerings made by the high priests were merely imperfect anticipations of the perfect sin offering of Christ's self-sacrifice: "he entered once for all into the Holy Place, not with the blood of goats and calves, but with his own blood, thus obtaining eternal redemption."[48]

---

46. Heb. 2.17. Despite the NRSV translation, the verb *hilaskomai* does not necessarily connote a sacrifice (see n. 22 above); a more literal translation would be "to expiate the sins of the people." For a useful recent overview of issues raised by this text, see Eberhart and Schweitzer 2019, although their theological concerns are remote from my historical focus.

47. Christ as high priest: Heb. 4.14–5.10, with quotation from 5.1. Melchizedek: 5.6–10, quoting Ps. 110 (LXX 109).4, and 6.19–7.10, elaborating in 7.1–10 on Gen. 14.18–20.

48. Christ superior to traditional high priests: Heb. 7.11–28, with quotation from 7.27. Christ as mediator of a better covenant: 8.1–13, with quotations from 8.5, 6–8, and 13; the author cites Jeremiah 31.31–34, with quotation from 31.31. Traditional sin offerings as imperfect anticipations: 9–10, with quotation from 9.12.

The author's overall strategy is clear: explicating carefully selected passages from the Judaean scriptures, he interprets traditional sacrificial cult as a mere foreshadowing of the true sacrifice, in which Christ was both perfect high priest and perfect victim. As such, Christ is the mediator of a new covenant, which supersedes the old one. The old sacrificial cult, never sufficient, has consequently been rendered completely superfluous.

We find a very similar strategy in the so-called letter of Barnabas, much of which consists of an argument that Judaeans were wrong to take literally the ritual prescriptions of Mosaic law, which are, in fact, symbolic prefigurations of the reality embodied in Christ. The first issue the author tackles is animal sacrifice. "For through all the prophets he [i.e., God] has shown us that he has no need of sacrifices, whole burnt offerings, or regular offerings (οὔτε θυσιῶν οὔτε ὁλοκαυτωμάτων οὔτε προσφορῶν χρῄζει)." He then supports this assertion with a barrage of quotations from the prophets and Psalms, which he repurposes in order to make additional points. First, the sacrifices of Mosaic law have now been replaced: "he nullified these things that the new law of our Lord Jesus Christ, which is without the yoke of compulsion, should provide an offering not made by humans." The language here loosely evokes the argument of Hebrews that Christ has established a new dispensation and a new superior form of offering. The author, however, does not pause to elaborate on these ideas but quotes other passages that suggest that what God wants instead of sacrifices is ethical behavior and true devotion.[49] In two later passages, the author provides two detailed examples of his allegorical readings of Judaean ritual practices, the rites of the Day of Atonement and the ritual of the red heifer, to demonstrate that they actually refer to the suffering and death of Jesus and to the spread of his gospel. Many of the details in these regulations, he argues, are, in fact, symbols or, as he calls them, "types" of Jesus and his sacrifice for human sins.[50]

Like the author of the letter of Barnabas, Justin Martyr also argues that, despite all the prescriptions concerning animal sacrifice in Mosaic law, God

---

49. Barn. 2.4–10, with quotations from 2.4 and 6 (trans. Bart D. Ehrman, Loeb); the author quotes or paraphrases Isa. 1.11–13, Jer. 7.22, Zech. 8.17, and Ps. 51.17. As scholars have demonstrated, in their original context, these passages did not function as outright condemnations of sacrificial cult; for two rather different approaches, see Klawans 2006, 75–100, and Ullucci 2012, 42–48.

50. Day of Atonement: Barn. 7; cf. Lev. 16.2–28. Red heifer: Barn. 8; cf. Num. 19.1–10. Jesus's sacrifice: Barn. 7.3, "For the Lord gave the written commandment that 'Whoever does not keep the fast must surely die,' because he himself was about to offer the vessel of the Spirit as a sacrifice (θυσία) for our own sins."

never really wanted it at all. Rather than arguing that the Judaeans understood literally what they should have interpreted figuratively, however, he takes quite a different line: God instituted the sacrificial cult "not because he needed such sacrifices but because of the sins of your people [i.e., the Judaeans], especially their sins of idolatry." He, too, supports his argument with a battery of scriptural passages taken out of context and concludes by asserting that "your sacrifices are not acceptable to God, nor were you first commanded to offer them because of God's need of them, but because of your sins. The same can be said of the temple. . . . God called it his house or court, not as if he needed a house or a court, but because, by uniting yourselves to him in that place, you might abstain from the worship of idols." The sacrifices of which he does approve are those of the Christians, that is, the "pure sacrifice" of the bread and the cup of the Eucharist.[51]

## 7e. Conclusion

As this brief survey has demonstrated, during the first century or so of its existence, the Christian movement included a wide range of discourses and practices relevant to animal sacrifice. Of fundamental importance was the principle, derived from Judaean tradition, of rejecting all cult directed to gods other than the Judaean God. For the practical reasons discussed in Section 7b, even Judaean sacrificial cult could never have had more than a limited role in Christian practice, and the destruction of the Jerusalem Temple in 70 CE ended the possibility of even that. The practical exclusion of animal sacrifice from the cultic lives of early Christians is likely to have fostered an association of animal sacrifice with the worship of other gods and thus a perception of it as something to be avoided. Yet this contextual factor is not in itself sufficient to account for the increasing disdain for and eventual outright rejection of animal sacrifice that came to characterize much early Christian tradition. The same circumstances applied equally to Judaeans but never resulted in their rejection of sacrificial practice. As Mira Balberg has cogently argued, the rabbis continued to treat Judaeans as a people who sacrifice, and they devoted considerable time and energy to elaborating the rules of animal sacrifice and analyzing their significance and purpose. We know much less

---

51. Sacrificial cult as a concession to idolatrous tendencies: Justin *Dial.* 22, with quotations from 22.1 and 11 (trans. Falls 2003); Justin quotes Amos 5.18–6.7, Jer. 7.21–22, Ps. 50 (LXX 49).1–23, and Isa. 66.1. Eucharist: *Dial.* 41.1–3, taking the phrase "pure sacrifice" from Malachi (1.11; see n. 39 above); cf. *Dial.* 117.1–5.

about nonrabbinic Judaean tradition, but the biblical scenes of sacrifice from the third-century CE synagogue of Dura-Europus suggest that a continued identification with sacrificial cult was not limited to the rabbis.[52] Although the nascent Christian tradition lacked the same degree of commitment to the Judaean sacrificial tradition, it could have developed its own practice of animal sacrifice. As I have proposed, the tendency to understand the significance of Christ's life, death, and resurrection through the use of Judaean sacrificial imagery could have resulted in the commemoration of his sacrificial death with an actual animal sacrifice. Why did this not happen?

I have highlighted two additional factors that I would suggest tipped the balance against the possibility of Christian animal sacrifice. One was the effective exclusion of meat from Christian communal meals, one of the earliest Christian cult practices that we can identify. As noted in Section 7d, the reasons for this exclusion are not articulated in any extant Christian text. While it is very much in keeping with the early Christian sympathy with the poor and hostility to the wealthy, in the absence of any direct evidence, we can only speculate. Yet, whatever the reasons, it was a distinctive feature of the practice as far back as we can trace it; the Synoptic account of the Last Supper, which must date back to the first few decades after Jesus's death, already elides the consumption of the Passover lamb in favor of an emphasis on bread and cup. The other important factor was the attempt on the part of some early Christian thinkers, especially after the destruction of the Jerusalem Temple, to distance themselves from Judaean tradition. As we have seen, some utilized metaphorical or typological interpretations of Judaean sacred writings and ritual practices to demonstrate that Judaean sacrificial cult was in reality a prefiguration of Christ's life and death and accordingly either had now been superseded, as the author of Hebrews argues, or was from the start the result of misinterpretation, as the author of Barnabas argues. Others, such Justin Martyr, dismissed Judaean sacrificial cult as nothing more than a concession that God had made to a people with an inveterate inclination to idolatry. All these arguments provided people with conceptual frameworks that they could use to theorize the end of Judaean sacrificial cult not as a mere contingent event or a sign of God's anger but as proof of God's disinterest in or even hostility to animal sacrifice.

---

52. Scenes of animal sacrifice occur in the depiction of the consecration of the tabernacle and in the Elijah sequence: Hachlili 1998, 117–18 with plate III-11, and 131–3, 149–50 with plates III-23 and 24.

I would suggest that these three developments, in context, practice, and discourse, worked in tandem to shape the way that many early Christian leaders viewed animal sacrifice. As we have seen, early Christians, in the decades after the death of Jesus, came to draw in various ways on the imagery of animal sacrifice in the process of articulating the significance of his life and death. These by no means constituted any sort of coherent and consistent theology but functioned more as metaphors whose significance was often highly allusive and open-ended. Although this imagery could have lent itself to a practice of commemorative animal sacrifice, the marginalization of meat consumption in early Christian cult practice and the discursive move to define Christian tradition against Judaean tradition, with its emphasis on sacrificial cult, combined to work against such a development. Instead, these three factors had the cumulative effect of redefining the terminology and conceptual framework of sacrifice: what began as a set of metaphors eventually came to displace ritual practice as the real meaning of "sacrifice." Jesus's life and death, conceived as the one true and perfect sacrifice, came to occupy the same conceptual space, so to speak, as sacrificial practice, leaving no room for actual animal sacrifice. As we will see in Chapter 8, the Christian displacement of animal sacrifice and the associated hostility toward traditional sacrificial practice that Christian leaders came increasingly to adopt eventually intersected with a development in the Greek philosophical tradition to fashion a discourse about traditional Graeco-Roman animal sacrifice that justified an ever more fervent opposition to it.

# 8

# Theorizing Animal Sacrifice II

## FROM APOLLONIUS TO IAMBLICHUS
## (C. 100–C. 300 CE)

### 8a. Introduction

The same period that saw the beginnings of a distinctively Christian discourse of sacrifice also saw the beginnings of a new Greek philosophical discourse, one that no longer treated sacrificial practice merely as incidental to other concerns, as I argued was the case for the classical philosophical schools and even for the Orphic and Pythagorean traditions, but one that instead theorized it as a practice that had profound implications for the central goals of the philosophical project. A crucial part of this development was the reconceptualization of animal sacrifice as part of a hierarchy of offerings structured not by socioeconomic considerations such as cost and prestige but rather by metaphysical considerations, specifically the notion of a divine hierarchy of superhuman beings. At some point between 50 and 150 CE, this new philosophical discourse of sacrificial practice cross-fertilized with the developing Christian tendency to associate animal sacrifice with maleficent *daimones*, which we have already encountered in an early form in Paul's letter to the Christians in Corinth. This cross-fertilization eventually produced what we may call the Christian demonological discourse of animal sacrifice. In this chapter, I examine the development of these two new discourses.

### 8b. Divine Hierarchies and Ritual Practice

Since so many major philosophers of the imperial period are known to us only through secondhand reports and handfuls of often exiguous quotations, it is a tricky business to trace developments in the philosophical thought of this period. The new discourse on sacrificial practice is no exception. For the sake of clarity, I begin my exploration with two more or less complete texts of the late third and early fourth centuries CE, by the Platonic philosophers Porphyry of Tyre and Iamblichus of Chalcis, which give us a good sense of that discourse in its fully developed form. I then attempt, as much as the evidence allows, to trace its growth over the course of the previous two centuries.[1]

Although Porphyry was one of the most important intellectuals of his day, we have only a few definite data about his life. Born in Tyre, he was given his father's Phoenician name Malchus, based on a Semitic root meaning "king"; hence his Greek nicknames Basileus, "king," and Porphyrios, a reference to the purple dye, associated with kingship, for which his hometown was famous. He studied as a youth in Athens with some of the leading teachers of the day, notably the literary scholar Longinus. In 263 CE, when he was about thirty years old, he moved to Rome, where he trained with the Platonic philosopher Plotinus. He stayed with him for six years, gradually becoming his foremost follower. In 268 CE, he fell into a bout of serious depression and ill health, and on Plotinus's advice retired to the estate of a friend in Sicily to recuperate. At some point after Plotinus's death around 270 CE, Porphyry returned to Rome. He later married a woman named Marcella, the widow of a friend, to whom he addressed a primer of the philosophical life. In his sixty-eighth year, around 301 CE, he wrote a life of Plotinus as a preface to his edition of his former teacher's essays, a work now known as the *Enneads*, the only version of Plotinus's philosophy to survive antiquity. It was apparently just a few years later that Porphyry died. He was an extremely prolific writer whose works ranged widely in both subject matter and format, although only a few of them, and those mostly minor ones, survive intact; the majority of his extensive oeuvre is known only through quotations and paraphrases in later writers.[2]

Porphyry believed that the primary concern of philosophy was the salvation of the soul. Building on developments in Platonic thought that culminated with the teaching of Plotinus, Porphyry understood God as the transcendent One at the apex of a divine hierarchy, whose lower levels were increasingly more remote and diffuse emanations of that ultimate reality. Human souls had their origin in the transcendent realm of the supreme God

---

1. This section develops ideas that I first presented in Rives 2011c.

2. Life of Porphyry: Saffrey and Segonds 2012, xi–xxv; Johnson 2013, 14–21.

but had become entangled and, as it were, imprisoned in the world of matter. The purpose of philosophy was to enable souls to return to their origin and reunite with God. For Porphyry, as for most ancient philosophers, philosophy was not merely an intellectual activity but also, and perhaps first and foremost, a way of life. Although rigorous intellectual training was essential to the attainment of this goal, so, too, was a lifestyle that was conducive to freeing the soul from its entanglement in the world of matter. The true philosopher must avoid the pleasures of the flesh, which reinforce the hold that matter has on the soul, and adopt instead a simple and ascetic lifestyle, which helps to purify the soul and promote its separation from the material world. For Porphyry, abstinence from eating meat was an important element in such a lifestyle. As I noted in Section 6d, there had evidently been a resurgence of interest in vegetarianism in the first century CE, and this had continued down to Porphyry's own day. Porphyry reports that Plotinus had been so strict in his abstinence from meat that he even refused to use medicines that contained animal products.[3]

This is the context for the work of Porphyry on which I focus here. At some point, perhaps shortly after the death of Plotinus while Porphyry was still in Sicily, he learned that a friend of his named Firmus Castricius, who, like him, had been a devoted student of Plotinus, had "condemned fleshless food and reverted to consuming flesh." Porphyry's response was to compose an extensive treatise that would demonstrate to Castricius why he was wrong to do so and to refute the arguments that various philosophers had brought against abstinence from animal flesh. Over the course of four books, Porphyry addresses the issue of killing and consuming animals from many different angles, including the specific issue of animal sacrifice, to which he devotes the entirety of Book 2. That book falls into two roughly even halves. In the first half, Porphyry presents Theophrastus's arguments against animal sacrifice, which we have already examined in Section 6c. In the second half, he takes a very different approach, one that is much more closely aligned with his own philosophical commitments and priorities.[4]

---

3. Philosophy of Porphyry: Bouffartigue and Patillon 1977, xxxviii–lx; Johnson 2013, especially 102–21. Plotinus: Porph. *V. Plot.* 2.

4. Context and purpose: Porph. *Abst.* 1.1–3, with quotation from 1.1.1; all quotations from *De abstinentia* are in the translation of Clark 2000, sometimes lightly modified. Date of treatise and identity of Castricius: Bouffartigue and Patillon 1977, xviii–xx; Clark 2000, 4–8. Digeser 2012, 106–8, makes the intriguing suggestion that Castricius's return to eating meat was inspired by Iamblichus's favorable views of material offerings, as discussed later in this section,

Porphyry pivots from the first to the second half of Book 2 by insisting that, despite his arguments against animal sacrifice, "I am not trying to destroy the customs which prevail among each people: the state (πολιτεία) is not my present subject. But the laws by which we are governed allow the divine power to be honored even by very simple and inanimate things, so by choosing the simplest we shall sacrifice in accordance with the law of the city (νόμῳ πόλεως), and will ourselves strive to offer a fitting sacrifice, pure in all respects, when we approach the gods." It is on this basis that he enunciates his general principle: "we too [i.e., philosophers like Porphyry and Castricius] shall sacrifice. But we shall make, as is fitting, different sacrifices to different powers (διαφόρους τὰς θυσίας ὡς ἂν διαφόροις δυνάμεσι προσάγοντες)." He then goes on to explain which sacrifices are appropriate for which powers. "To the God who rules over all, as a wise man said (ὥς τις ἀνὴρ σοφὸς ἔφη), we shall offer nothing perceived by the senses, either by burning or in words"; that God, Porphyry declares, we must instead worship in silence and pure thought. The only sacrifice truly befitting him is our own striving to be joined with and become like him: "we must offer our own uplifting (ἀναγωγή) as a holy sacrifice (θυσία ἱερά) to the God," a sacrifice that we fulfill through "dispassion of the soul and contemplation of the God." Next, "for his offspring, the intelligible gods, hymn-singing in words should be added." After them, "for the gods within the heaven, the wandering and the fixed . . ., we should kindle fire which is already kin to them, and we shall do what the theologian (ὁ θεολόγος) says: . . . not a single animate (ἔμψυχον) creature should be sacrificed, but offerings should not go beyond barley-grains and honey and the fruits of the earth." He then concludes by pointing out that "someone concerned for piety knows that no animate creature is sacrificed to the gods, but to other *daimones*, either good or bad, and knows whose practice it is to sacrifice to them and to what extent these people need to do so."[5]

Porphyry's strategy in crafting this sacrificial program for philosophers is clear enough. He takes as its basis the premise of a divine hierarchy extending from the transcendent One down to the *daimones* who inhabit the level just above humans. To each level of this hierarchy we must offer the sacrifices that are appropriate to it, the basic principle being that of "like to like." He explicates this principle most fully in explaining why we should offer hymns

---

but the fact that Porphyry's overall focus in his treatise is the consumption of meat, not sacrificial practice, weighs against it. Overview of Book 2: Bouffartigue and Patillon 1979, 3–8.

5. Law of the city: *Abst*. 2.33.1. General principle: 2.34.1. Gods and appropriate offerings: 2.34.2–36.5, with quotations from 34.2–4 and 36.3–5.

to the intelligible gods: "for sacrifice is an offering (ἀπαρχή) to each god from what he has given, with which he sustains us and maintains our essence in being." Just as a farmer offers first fruits from his crops, so, too, we offer them beautiful thoughts about the intelligible gods, thanking them for the vision of those things they have given us and which truly nourish us. It is only at the lowest level of this divine hierarchy that animal sacrifices are appropriate.[6]

Yet this is not the end of it. After outlining an alternative divine hierarchy, Porphyry returns to the topic of *daimones*, who, he says, are commonly believed to harm those who arouse their anger by neglecting them but to benefit those who win their goodwill through prayers, supplication, and sacrifice. (It is worth noting that Porphyry's account of these beliefs corresponds very closely to the beliefs about the gods implicit in traditional myth.) Yet popular ideas about *daimones* are very confused, Porphyry complains, and hence he must provide a more accurate account of their nature. He then launches into a disquisition on *daimones* that takes up a full five chapters of the book. His main point is that we must distinguish between benevolent *daimones*, who administer the sublunary parts of the cosmos, and *daimones* who are controlled by the material element of their makeup and are consequently subject to passions and desires like those of humans. Such *daimones*, he asserts "may reasonably be called maleficent (κακοεργοί)." Although these maleficent *daimones* "are themselves responsible for the sufferings that occur around the earth," they "convince us that the responsibility lies with those who are responsible for just the opposite." They then "prompt us to supplications and sacrifices, as if the beneficent gods were angry." They do this partly to lead us astray in our conception of the divine but also because they themselves crave these traditional offerings: "it is they who rejoice in the 'drink offerings and smoking meat' on which their pneumatic part grows fat, for it lives on vapors and exhalations ... and it draws power from the smoke that rises from blood and flesh."[7]

Animal sacrifices, then, are not merely the lowest form of offering directed toward the lowest level of the divine hierarchy; they are positively dangerous for those whose goal is to free themselves from entanglements with the material world and return to the pure realm of the transcendent God. "An intelligent, temperate man will be wary of making sacrifices through which he

---

6. First fruits: *Abst.* 2.34.4–5.

7. Disquisition on *daimones*: *Abst.* 2.38–42, with quotations from 38.4, 40.1–2, and 42.3; the quotation in the last passage is from Hom. *Il.* 9.500.

will draw such beings to himself. He will work to purify his soul in every way, for they [i.e., the maleficent *daimones*] do not attack a pure soul, because it is unlike them." Porphyry then returns to the point at which he began, by reminding the reader that his prescriptions are directed specifically at philosophers, not the general population. "If it is necessary for cities to appease even these beings, that has nothing to do with us. In cities, riches and external and corporeal things are thought to be good and their opposites bad, and the soul is the least of their concerns." The philosopher, by contrast, whose chief concern is precisely his soul, will follow the sacrificial regimen that Porphyry has already outlined.[8]

Before I analyze in more detail Porphyry's theorization of animal sacrifice, it will be helpful to look at how another contemporary Platonist handled the same subject. Although Iamblichus is often described as a student of Porphyry, it is now generally agreed that he was only a decade or so younger. He was born into a very distinguished Syrian family that traced its lineage back to the ancient priest-kings of Emesa; his name, the Hellenized version of a Syriac name meaning "he is king," alludes to this heritage. At some point in his youth, he seems to have been a close associate of Porphyry, although we have little clear evidence for the precise nature of their relationship. He eventually returned to Syria and established his own school there, probably in Apamea. It was Iamblichus even more than Porphyry who shaped the future course of Platonic philosophy in late antiquity, since his pupils and their pupils in turn became its leading representatives in the fourth century. Like Porphyry, he believed that the primary purpose of philosophy was to enable the soul to ascend the divine hierarchy back to its original source in the realm of the transcendent God. The two sharply disagreed, however, on how that could be done. Porphyry insisted that it was only through mental discipline and abstract reasoning that philosophers could reach their goal. Iamblichus, in contrast, felt equally strongly that human reason could take one only so far. In order to advance further, he declared, philosophers must move beyond the intellect by engaging in suprarational activities that activate divine power; to use Iamblichus's own terminology, they must move beyond theology, "god

---

8. Implications of animal sacrifice: *Abst.* 2.43, with quotations from 43.1–2. Porphyry downplays animal sacrifice and extols bloodless offerings, especially that of striving to become like God, in other works as well, including *Philosophy from Oracles* (F 306 A. Smith 1993 = Firm. Mat. *Err. prof. rel.* 13.4–5, F 326 A. Smith 1993 = Euseb. *Praep. evang.* 4.22.15–4.23.6) and *Letter to Marcella* (16–19). Johnson 2013, 122–39, argues that Porphyry presents a negative or, at best, ambivalent attitude toward animal sacrifice that is consistent across his works.

talk," and engage in theurgy, "god work." It was in the context of this disagreement that Iamblichus wrote the work that concerns us.[9]

Porphyry, it appears, felt the need at some point to address in public his doubts about Iamblichus's focus on theurgy. The strategy he chose was to write an open letter in which he posed a series of specific questions about the nature of the divine, the process of divination, and especially the practice of theurgy. Instead of addressing this letter directly to Iamblichus, however, he addressed it to an Egyptian named Anebo. There has been considerable debate about whether this Anebo, for whom there is no other evidence, was a historical person or simply a fictional stand-in for Iamblichus; scholarly opinion now leans toward the latter, but there is in any case general agreement that Porphyry's questions were directed toward Iamblichean teachings. Porphyry's letter survives only in the quotations and paraphrases of later writers, but the response that it elicited survives in full. This is a long treatise that bears the long title *Response of the Teacher Abamon to the Letter of Porphyry to Anebo and the Solutions of the Problems Posed Therein*, although the Italian humanist scholar Marsilio Ficino, who in 1497 published the first Latin translation of the work, gave it the new title, *On the Mysteries of the Egyptians, Chaldaeans, and Assyrians*, by which it has generally been known ever since. The author presents himself as the teacher of Anebo responding in his stead, but the fifth-century CE Platonist Proclus believed that the real author was Iamblichus himself. The majority of modern scholars have agreed, pointing out that Proclus's testimony seems corroborated by the fact that the text presents parallels with Iamblichean teachings as known from other sources. The date of Porphyry's letter and Iamblichus's response cannot be determined with any certainty, although majority opinion currently puts the former in the late 290s CE and the latter in the early 300s.[10]

One of the questions posed by Porphyry prompted Iamblichus to devote a lengthy disquisition to the topic of sacrificial practice. "The question you raise next," he writes, "is one that is a common concern for virtually all men, both those who have given time to education and those relatively lacking

---

9. Life of Iamblichus: Clarke, Dillon, and Hershbell 2003, xviii–xxvi; Saffrey and Segonds 2013, xxxiii–xlvi. Disagreement between Porphyry and Iamblichus: Digeser 2012, 111–26; Marx-Wolf 2016, 29–37; "god talk" and "god work": Clarke, Dillon, and Hershbell 2003, xxix.

10. The best editions of Porphyry's letter and Iamblichus's response are now Saffrey and Segonds 2012 and 2013; for the latter, see also Clarke, Dillon, and Hershbell 2003, a helpful English translation with introduction and notes. On the authorship, title, and date of Iamblichus's treatise, see Clarke, Dillon, and Hershbell 2003, xxvi–xxxvii, and Saffrey and Segonds 2013, ix–xxxii.

in experience of philosophic reasoning; I mean the question of sacrifices (περὶ θυσιῶν)—what is the utility of them, or what power they have in respect of the universe or the gods, and on what principle they achieve their purpose, both suitably to those honored, and usefully for those presenting the gifts. Furthermore, there straightaway arises a contradiction as well, stemming from the fact that the priests should abstain from animal food (ἀπέχεσθαι ... ἐμψύχων), in order that the gods should not be polluted by the vapors arising from animals, since this contradicts the opinion that they are primarily attracted by odors from living things."[11] Iamblichus's strategy for solving the problem posed by Porphyry is to generalize it and address the broader question of how any kind of material offering can have any effect on divinities that are themselves immaterial. Unlike Porphyry in *On Abstinence*, he does not discuss animal sacrifice in particular, but that is because he is concerned with explicating the underlying principles of sacrificial practice or, as he himself puts it, the reasons for its efficacy.[12] He says enough, however, to make it clear that his account of sacrificial practice includes animal sacrifice, as one particular form of corporeal offerings.

Although it is not possible here to do justice to Iamblichus's complex and highly nuanced discussion, we may note a few key points. His core argument is that the efficacy of sacrifices arises from what he calls "friendship and affinity" (φιλία καὶ οἰκείωσις), the relationship that binds together an immaterial divine power with the particular part of the material world that it generated. "When therefore, under the guidance of this common principle, we comprehend that some animal or plant growing in the earth simply and purely preserves the intention of its maker, then, through this intermediary, we set in motion, in an appropriate manner, the creative cause which, without in any way compromising its purity, presides over this entity." An appropriate sacrifice is one that conforms to the divine power to which it is directed. Although all these powers are themselves immaterial, some we may reasonably describe as material insofar as they "embrace matter within themselves and impose order upon it." These material gods "have a certain communion with matter inasmuch as they preside over it" and are accordingly "responsible for those phenomena

---

11. Iambl. *Myst.* 5.1, 199.5–13; all quotations are in the translation of Clarke, Dillon, and Hershbell 2003, sometimes lightly adapted. Porphyry's question apparently focused on the contradiction noted at the end: *Aneb.* F 69 Saffrey and Segonds 2012.

12. E.g., *Myst.* 5.7, 207.6–7: "The argument therefore demands that we state in what respect sacrifices possess the capacity to produce results and connect us to the gods"; 5.8, 209.2: "causes of the efficacy of sacrifices (αἴτια τῆς ἐν ταῖς θυσίαις ἀπεργασίας)."

that arise in matter, such as divisions, impacts, and resistance, and the alteration, generation, and destruction of all material bodies." To such gods it is appropriate to make offerings that conform to these phenomena. "And so, in sacrifices, dead bodies (τὰ νεκρὰ σώματα) deprived of life, the slaughter of animals (φόνος τῶν ζῴων) and the consumption of their bodies, and every sort of change and destruction, and in general processes of dissolution are suitable to those gods who preside over matter—not to them in themselves, but because of the matter over which they rule." As he explains in a later passage, "the rule of cult, obviously, assigns like to like (τὰ ὅμοια . . . τοῖς ὁμοίοις), and extends this principle from the highest to the lowest levels, incorporeal entities to incorporeal, and bodies to bodies, apportioning to each what is conformable to its own nature." Since it is crucial that we honor all levels of the divine with appropriate offerings, it follows that we must offer animal sacrifices to those powers for whom such sacrifices are appropriate. Indeed, because we can ascend to the higher immaterial gods only after giving due honor to the lower material gods, material offerings are an indispensable stage in that ascent.[13]

Even on this cursory review, it is obvious that Porphyry and Iamblichus took radically opposed positions regarding animal sacrifice. We should not, however, allow their obvious disagreements to obscure their fundamental agreement about the overall framework of the debate. Both of them subscribe to the same general thesis that sacrificial practice should vary in conformity with the hierarchy of divine beings, on the principle of "like to like." They consequently both extend the scope of sacrificial practice beyond material offerings to encompass nonmaterial practices as well. Like many of the Christian writers discussed in Chapter 7, they deploy the terminology of sacrifice in ways that initially appear metaphorical but, in fact, supplement or even displace its original meaning. We see this most clearly in Porphyry, for example, in his assertion that the "holy sacrifice" most appropriate to the supreme God is our own striving to become like him. Since Iamblichus's chief concern is to uphold the validity of material offerings against Porphyry's attack, he naturally has less to say about nonmaterial offerings, but they are nonetheless an important part of his overall sacrificial program. Like Porphyry, he asserts that just as we must honor material gods with material offerings,

---

13. Friendship and affinity: *Myst.* 5.9, 209.9 and 11–14. Material gods: 5.14, 217.6–7 and 10–13; sacrifices of dead bodies: 5.14, 218.4–8. Like to like: 5.20, 227.13–228.2. Material gods before immaterial: 5.14, 8–10. For an outline of Iamblichus's treatment of sacrifice, see Saffrey and Segonds 2013, cxxxiv–cxxxvii; for useful discussions, see G. Shaw 1995, 146–61; E. Clarke 2001, 39–57; and Krulak 2014, 355–60.

so, too, we must honor the higher, nonmaterial gods with "appropriate gifts which are intellectual and proper to incorporeal life, such as are conferred by virtue and wisdom, and any perfect and complete goods of the soul."[14]

Most important, both writers agreed that sacrificial practice, and animal sacrifice in particular, was a topic that required serious philosophical attention. As I argued in Section 6c, the philosophers of the classical schools tended to accept sacrifice as a traditional practice without making any sustained attempt to theorize it. To the extent that they did analyze sacrificial practice, they focused on social and moral questions, especially the propriety of killing animals and the moral character of the worshiper. Even the early thinkers who rejected animal sacrifice because of a belief in metempsychosis seem otherwise to have had little interest in the practice. Porphyry's and Iamblichus's handling of the topic could hardly present a more striking contrast. For all that their views on animal sacrifice were diametrically opposed, they were alike in regarding sacrificial practice as a matter of crucial philosophical importance. Its importance, moreover, was no longer solely moral or social, although Porphyry dealt at length with such issues in his treatise on abstinence, but primarily metaphysical. It was the effects that the act of animal sacrifice had on key elements in the structure of the cosmos that rendered it for Porphyry a practice that philosophers should avoid, insofar as it reinforced their entanglement in the material world and for Iamblichus an essential first step in a hierarchy of practice that enabled philosophers to ascend the hierarchy of being. It was because both philosophers took sacrificial practice so seriously that they expressed in such strong terms their disagreement over its effects.[15]

How did such a radical change in the philosophical standing of sacrificial practice come about? As I argued in Chapter 7, it was the need to make sense of the life and death of Jesus that prompted early Christian leaders to draw on sacrificial imagery and ultimately transform the very idea of sacrifice. It is much more difficult to identify a similar impetus behind the changes in the philosophical tradition. We may, however, at least note some general parameters. First, the basic elements of the general thesis shared by Porphyry and Iamblichus, that different levels of the divine hierarchy required different types of offerings, were of long standing. The idea of a divine hierarchy extended

---

14. Porphyry: *Abst.* 2.34.3; Iamblichus: *Myst.* 5.19, 226.9–11. See further Camplani and Zambon 2002, especially 3–14 on Porphyry.

15. See further Marx-Wolf 2016, 100–25, on the trend among third-century Platonic philosophers to adopt the persona of ritual experts.

back to mythic notions about gradations of divine power, as expressed, for example, in Hesiod's insistence on the supremacy of Zeus. Plato's ontological speculations provided the materials for more analytical formulations of the idea, such as his account of *daimones* as intermediaries between the divine and mortal spheres that I noted in Section 6d. The first person to systematize Platonic ideas into an ordered hierarchy that encompassed abstract conceptions was apparently Xenocrates, head of the Academy in the late fourth century BCE, whose theories seem to have influenced Plutarch and other early imperial Platonists. By the second century CE, the formulation of divine hierarchies had become a standard element of Platonic doctrine, as we see, for example, in the summaries presented in such introductory texts as Alcinous's *Handbook of Platonism* and Apuleius's *On Plato and His Doctrine*. Plotinus developed the idea in a much more sophisticated form, with the transcendent One at the apex of several grades of being that extend down to the world of matter; it is largely the Plotinian hierarchy with which Porphyry is working.[16] Similarly, the principle of "like to like" had long played a part in determining the offerings appropriate to different divinities. As a bit of folk wisdom, it dated back to the Homeric epics, and as such was frequently cited by Plato and Aristotle. "Like to like" was apparently the ruling idea behind such traditional sacrificial practices as offering female victims to female deities or black victims to underworld deities, even though Porphyry himself seems to have been the first extant writer to develop that idea explicitly.[17]

It is more difficult to determine at what point the principle of "like to like" began to be applied to Platonic divine hierarchies along the lines that we find in Porphyry and Iamblichus, but Porphyry's own account provides some intriguing hints. As I noted earlier in this section, he presents two slightly different accounts of the divine hierarchy with which offerings must be correlated. The first begins with the supreme God, proceeds to the intelligible gods and then to the visible celestial gods, and ends with *daimones*; the second also begins with the supreme God but then proceeds to the world soul before continuing to the visible celestial gods and the invisible gods,

---

16. Xenocrates: Dillon 2003, 99–107, 121–23. Alcinous: 10 and 14–15 with Dillon 1993, xvii–xix and xxxi–xxxv; Apuleius: *De dog. Plat.* 1.5–11 (190–205). Porphyry: Johnson 2013, 53–101. See further Marx-Wolf 2016, 38–70, on the complexities and ambiguities in third-century CE attempts to construct coherent taxonomies of superhuman entities.

17. Homer: *Od.* 17.218, quoted by Plato at *Lysis* 214a; see also *Symp.* 195b; Aristotle, *Eth. Nic.* 8.1.6, 1155a32–35 and 9.3.3, 1165b17, *De an.* 1.2, 405b15. Porphyry's development of the principle: *Philos. Orac.* F 314–15 A. Smith 1993 = Euseb. *Praep. evang.* 4.8.4–9.2 and 9.3–7, with Johnson 2013, 127–30.

here identified with *daimones*. This second account, which leads directly into his discussion of good and bad *daimones*, he explicitly attributes to "certain Platonists," by which he seems to have meant philosophers of the second century CE.[18] The first account, by contrast, he does not explicitly attribute to any named individual or group. He does, however, cite an unnamed "wise man" as his authority for the idea that we must worship the supreme God only with pure thought. It has long been recognized that this "wise man" must be the first-century CE sage Apollonius of Tyana. We owe this insight to Eusebius, who, after discussing this very passage of Porphyry, goes on to quote a passage from the treatise *On Sacrifices* credited to Apollonius that presents many similarities. Speaking of the one supreme God, Apollonius asserts that we should offer him nothing perceptible; rather, "one should always use with him the superior kind of discourse, I mean that which does not issue through the mouth, but ask for his blessing with the noblest element in us, and this is mind, which needs no instrument. For these reasons one should in no way sacrifice to the great God who is above all." Despite some differences in formulation, it is generally agreed that this passage was Porphyry's immediate inspiration.[19]

With Apollonius of Tyana, we are once again on very uncertain ground. We have no firsthand evidence for this intriguing yet elusive figure but must rely on later, often much later, sources. Our main source, the account of his life written by Philostratus, dates probably to the 220s or 230s CE, more than a century after the likely period of Apollonius's death, and clearly reflects an extensive accretion of legendary elaboration. A number of letters attributed to Apollonius are also extant, but their provenance and date are very uncertain; although some may possibly be genuine, the most that we may do with confidence is to regard them as another source for traditions about Apollonius. Moreover, Apollonius seems to have inspired strong reactions, and as a result, the evidence tends either to idealize or to demonize him. Yet, despite the problems with our evidence, a few basic points seem reasonably secure. Apollonius seems to have been an itinerant teacher and wonderworker who was active in the latter part of the first century CE. He apparently presented himself as an exponent of Pythagorean tradition, a motif that pervades

---

18. First hierarchy: Porph. *Abst.* 2.34–36; second: 2.37. "Certain Platonists": 2.36.6; on their possible identity, see Bouffartigue and Patillon 1979, 35–36.

19. "Wise man": Porph. *Abst.* 2.34.2. Eusebius: *Praep. evang.* 4.13.1 (cf. *Dem. evang.* 3.3.11) = C. Jones 2006 T 22, translation lightly adapted; see Bouffartigue and Patillon 1979, 30–34, and Clark 2000, 152–53, for comparisons with the passage of Porphyry.

Philostratus's account of his life as well as many of the letters. According to the *Suda*, Apollonius even wrote a life of Pythagoras, which both Porphyry and Iamblichus apparently cite in their own accounts of Pythagoras.[20]

As we saw in Chapter 6, it is clear that by the imperial period, a refusal to eat meat or kill animals had become a defining feature of the Pythagorean way of life, and according to tradition, it was a practice that Apollonius himself consistently espoused.[21] Not surprisingly, our sources likewise credit Apollonius with the rejection of animal sacrifice. A letter to the cult personnel of Olympia, for example, insists that "the gods do not need sacrifices, so what might one do to please them? Acquire wisdom, it seems to me, and do all the good in one's power to those humans who deserve it. That is what pleases the gods, but your actions are those of atheists." Another, addressed to the priests at Delphi, declares that "priests pollute altars with blood, and then some people wonder why their cities are unfortunate when they suffer great misfortune. What ignorance!" It is worth noting that these letters frame Apollonius's rejection of animal sacrifice in terms not of abstinence from meat but of theories about sacrificial practice. Philostratus likewise portrays Apollonius as having a particular interest in the proper forms of rituals, claiming, for example, that Apollonius gave the Athenians a lecture in which he revealed "how, and at what time of night or day, to make a sacrifice, libation, or prayer in the way appropriate to each god." He elsewhere claims that prescriptions of this sort constituted the content of Apollonius's treatise *On Sacrifices*, presumably the one known to Eusebius.[22]

Although we could reasonably characterize the passage that Eusebius quotes as a prescription about how to make an appropriate sacrifice to a particular god, its content is more abstract and theological than we might expect from Philostratus's description. Coming back to Porphyry, I would tentatively propose that he based his entire first scheme for correlating the

---

20. On Philostratus and Apollonius, see in general Bowie 1978 and Dzielska 1986. Letters of Apollonius: Penella 1979, especially 23–29 on authenticity. Apollonius's life of Pythagoras: *Suda* A 3420 Adler; apparently cited by Porphyry at *Vit. Pyth.* 2 and Iamblichus at *Vit. Pyth.* 254–64; see further Lévy 1926, 104–10, and Burkert 1972 [1962], 100–101, with the counterarguments of Gorman 1985. On Apollonius's Pythagoreanism, see Bowie 1978, 1691–92, and Flinterman 2014, 253–57.

21. Phil. *Vit. Apoll.* 1.8.1, 1.21.3, 6.11.3 and 5; *Ep.* 8 and 43.

22. Letters to the priests of Olympia and Delphi: *Epp.* 26 and 27, trans. C. Jones 2006; Penella 1979, 105, rightly points out that *Ep.* 26 seems to reject all forms of sacrifice, in contrast to *Ep.* 27 and the anecdotes relayed by Philostratus (*Vit. Apoll.* 1.31.2–32.1 and 5.25.1–2). Philostratus on Apollonius's speech to the Athenians: *Vit. Apoll.* 4.19; on his treatise on sacrifices: *Vit. Apoll.* 3.41.1–2; see further Bowie 1978, 1688–90, and Dzielska 1986, 136–51.

different levels of the divine hierarchy with different types of sacrifices on the treatise *On Sacrifices* that circulated under Apollonius's name.[23] It was presumably relatively accessible, since not only was it available to Eusebius, but Philostratus claims to have found it "in many sanctuaries, many cities, and the homes of many wise men." As we have seen, it is very likely that Apollonius was the "wise man" whom Porphyry cited as his authority for the highest level of his theological/cultic hierarchy. Moreover, commentators have suggested a Pythagorean source for Porphyry's first scheme, and Apollonius was by his day recognized as an authority on Pythagorean tradition. Some scholars have identified "the theologian" whom Porphyry cites at the end of this section as Pythagoras, but it could just as well be Apollonius or, perhaps even more probably, Apollonius's "Pythagoras." There are thus grounds to suppose that the correlation of different types of sacrifices with different levels of a divine hierarchy, which appears in a developed form in Porphyry and Iamblichus, may have originated in the Pythagorean traditions associated with the figure of Apollonius of Tyana.[24]

If, for the sake of argument, we grant this hypothesis, we may ask what might have prompted Apollonius, or more likely "Apollonius," to make this innovation in the philosophical discourse on animal sacrifice. In Section 6d, I argued that a renewed interest in abstinence from animal flesh was "in the air" in the first century CE, an interest that tradition also associated with Apollonius. Such abstinence would almost inevitably have prompted reflection on the practice of animal sacrifice, which, as we have seen, played so important a sociopolitical role in the Roman Empire. Yet previous theorization of the practice had been strictly limited and perhaps no longer seemed satisfactory. Moreover, by the late first and second centuries CE, new conceptual tools were to hand: the idea of a divine hierarchy with *daimones* as intermediaries between humans and its higher levels. In these circumstances, it does not seem surprising that someone would have hit on the idea of theorizing sacrificial practice in the way later documented in Porphyry and Iamblichus. Whether that person was the historical Apollonius of Tyana we have no way of knowing, but that it was someone prior to Porphyry seems likely.

---

23. For an earlier presentation of this argument, see Rives 2011c, 196–97.

24. Philostratus's claim: *Vit. Apoll.* 3.41.2. Pythagorean influence in Porphyry's account: Bouffartigue and Patillon 1979, 9–16, 35. "The theologian": Porph. *Abst.* 2.36.3–4.

## 8c. *Animal Sacrifice and Evil* Daimones

At the same time as Pythagorean and Platonic thinkers were developing the discourse of a hierarchy of offerings correlated with a hierarchy of the divine, Christian thinkers were developing a discourse that, while involving important points of overlap, was in crucial respects strikingly different. We get a valuable glimpse of this development in its earliest stages from a passage that I discussed in Section 7b, Paul's exhortation to his Corinthian audience to avoid idolatry and accordingly *eidōlothuton*, meat from sacrificial victims. As we saw, Paul insists on this point not because idols are anything themselves but because "what [people] sacrifice, they sacrifice to *daimonia* and not to God (δαιμονίοις καὶ οὐ θεῷ). I do not want you to be partners with *daimonia*. You cannot drink the cup of the Lord and the cup of *daimonia*. You cannot partake of the table of the Lord and the table of *daimonia*." What does Paul mean by *daimonia*, and how does he understand their association with gentile sacrifice?

We may start from the fact that in making the connection between sacrifice and *daimonia*, Paul seems to be quoting from the Septuagint, the Greek version of the Judaean sacred writings. The passage in question comes from Deuteronomy, the song that the Lord instructed Moses to write shortly before his death, in which he upbraided the Israelites for turning from his worship to that of foreign gods: "They provoked me with foreign things, by their abominations they embittered me. They sacrificed to *daimonia* and not to God (δαιμονίοις καὶ οὐ θεῷ), to gods they did not know. New recent ones have come, whom their fathers did not know." Since the verbal echo can hardly be accidental in one who must have known the Septuagint very well indeed, it seems likely that one thing that Paul meant by *daimonia* were the gods of the gentiles. The word *daimonia*, in fact, often carries this meaning in the Septuagint, notably in a passage from one of the Psalms that was often quoted by later Christian writers: "because all the gods of the nations are *daimonia*, but the Lord made the heavens." The idea that the gods of the gentiles were *daimonia* coexisted, in a way that was often not very clearly worked out, with the idea that gentiles worshiped insensate idols made of metal or wood, just as we see in this passage of Paul.[25]

---

25. Deuteronomy: 31.16–22 and 30 for context, 32.16–17 for quotation, trans. *NETS*. LXX Ps. 95.5 (= 96.5), trans. *NETS*; cf. LXX Ps. 105.35–39 (= 106.35–39). *Daimonia* and idols: e.g., Rev. 9.20–21.

By Paul's day, however, Judaeans writing in Greek had begun to use *daimonion* and the related term *daimōn* with other connotations as well. For example, the translator of the tale of Tobit, writing probably in the mid- to late Hellenistic period, relates that the successive husbands of his heroine Sarra had all been killed by "the wicked *daimonion* Asmodaus." *Daimonion/ daimōn* in this sense designates a malevolent superhuman being, the same sense of the word that prevails in its modern English derivative "demon." The writers who used the word in this way were apparently translating Judaean traditions about malevolent "unclean spirits" by means of Greek philosophical speculations about *daimones*, which, as I noted in Section 6d, had begun with Plato and had become commonplace in early imperial writers such as Plutarch. The Gospel attributed to Mark, for example, includes numerous scenes of people under the control of malevolent beings who in some fashion inhabit their bodies; it is one of Jesus's most distinctive abilities, and one that he passes on to his students, that he can "cast out" these beings and so free their victims from their control. Mark often designates this kind of being as an "unclean spirit" (πνεῦμα ἀκάθαρτον), but he just as often uses *daimōn* and its derivatives as a synonym; the latter usage became increasingly standard in later Christian texts.[26] When Paul urges the Christ followers of Corinth not to be partners with *daimonia*, he is accordingly urging them not merely to avoid the worship of idols but also to shun involvement with malevolent superhuman beings. In short, his exhortation implies that gentile cult necessarily involves an association with evil *daimones*. Although this is not an implication that Paul himself paused to develop, later Christians did.

By the middle of the second century CE, Christian thinkers had elaborated the idea of *daimones* that we find in rudimentary form in Paul into a wide-ranging discourse about the true nature of the world in which people lived their lives. This discourse is amply documented in the work of a writer whom I cited in Chapter 7 but who now needs more of an introduction. Justin "Martyr," as he is traditionally designated, was born in Flavia Neapolis (modern Nablus, some 40 kilometers north of Jerusalem) in the early second century CE. A student of philosophy, especially Platonism, from an early age, he at some point, probably still in his youth, became a Christian.

---

26. Tob. 3.8. "Unclean spirits" in Mark: e.g., 1.21–28, 3.11 and 30, 6.7, 9.25. *Daimōn* as synonym: for example, Mark initially describes the man whom Jesus heals near Gerasa as a "man in an unclean spirit" (ἄνθρωπος ἐν πνεύματι ἀκαθάρτῳ, 5.2; cf. 5.8 and 13) but later (5.15–16 and 18) designates him as "the one possessed by a *daimōn*" (τὸν δαιμονιζόμενον); in their versions, Matthew (8.28–34) uses only *daimōn* and its derivatives, while Luke (8.26–39) once uses "unclean spirit" (8.29) but otherwise *daimonia* (8.27, 30, 33, 35, 36, 38).

He eventually moved to Rome, where he established a school. It was apparently there that he wrote his vindications of Christianity both against Roman authorities, the texts conventionally known as the *First* and *Second Apologies*, and against Judaean tradition, the *Dialogue with Trypho*. In the mid-160s CE, he was arrested, tried, and executed as a Christian; an account of his trial and death is extant in three different versions. When Justin became a Christian, however, he did not renounce his earlier training in philosophy; on the contrary, he became a Christian because he became convinced that Christianity was the truest and best philosophy, and as a Christian, he maintained the persona of a philosopher. His writings, especially the two *Apologies*, constitute the first robust attempt to synthesize the Greek philosophical tradition with the Judaean tradition of earliest Christianity. He not only identified Jesus Christ as the incarnation of God's Logos, for example, but believed that the great Greek philosophers had also perceived that Logos, if only dimly, through their use of reason.[27]

The *First Apology*, although clearly a literary composition, takes the form of a petition to the emperor, seeking the redress of an injustice. The injustice in question was the legal status of Christianity. Since at least the early 110s CE, there was an established precedent that Roman authorities could condemn to death anyone who had been charged before them with being a Christian and who refused to deny that identity and perform actions to confirm their denial. Such a procedure, Justin argues, is both anomalous and unjust. As he develops his argument, however, Justin goes far beyond the legal issues in order to craft a wide-ranging account of Christian beliefs and a comprehensive assertion of their truth and superiority to traditional Graeco-Roman worship.[28] It is in this context that he elaborates in much greater detail the early Christian discourse of *daimones*.

Justin's central claim is that evil *daimones* play a major role in human lives but that most people, including his imperial addressees, are oblivious

---

27. Life and thought: Minns and Parvis 2009, 32–34, 57–70. There has been much debate over the nature of the so-called *Second Apology* and its relation to the *First*; for an overview with new arguments, see Minns and Parvis 2009, 21–28. Justin's conversion and self-presentation as a philosopher: *Dial.* 1–8. Accounts of his trial and death: *BHG* 972z–974e = Musurillo 1972, no. 4.

28. Format and scope: Minns and Parvis 2009, 44–54, with a detailed outline. The legal status of Christianity prior to 250 CE has been endlessly debated; for a survey of the debate and my own views, see Rives 2011a. Scholars sometimes use the term "sacrifice test" to refer to the actions that presiding magistrates required accused Christians to perform in order to confirm their denial; although our sources suggest that the requirement was common, the specific actions varied widely, so that the term "sacrifice test" can be misleading; see Rives 2020, 180–87.

to that fact. As a result, Roman authorities do not conduct their inquiry into Christianity "with sober judgment but with senseless passion, and driven under the whip of wicked *daimones* you punish us unreflectingly. To say this," Justin insists, "is to tell the truth. Since, in ancient times, wicked *daimones* (δαίμονες φαῦλοι), in apparitions, committed adultery with women and seduced boys and made people see horrifying things, so those who did not rationally (λόγῳ) evaluate what the *daimones* were doing were stunned with terror. Carried away with fear, they named them gods, not knowing they were wicked *daimones*." In other words, the worship of traditional gods is, in reality, the worship of evil *daimones*, whose goal is "to make you their slaves and servants; and sometimes through appearances in dreams, sometimes again through magical changes, they overpower those who do not strain in every way after their salvation." They accordingly attack all those who try to undermine their power: "when Socrates attempted with true reason and judicious inquiry to bring these things into the open and to draw people away from the *daimones*, the *daimones*, using people who delight in evil, worked it that he too was killed." Their greatest enemy, however, is Christ, the incarnate Logos, and it is accordingly the evil *daimones* who stir up the persecution against his followers; Roman authorities are merely their unwitting tools.[29]

The *daimones*' domination and exploitation of humanity are not merely the result of malice, however, but are also driven by their own needs. While evil *daimones* are a recurring motif through the *First Apology*, it is in a passage of the *Second Apology* that Justin reveals their origin and motivation:

> When he made the whole universe, God made earthly things subject to human beings. . . . But providential care over human beings and of things beneath the firmament he handed over to angels whom he had established over them. But the angels transgressed this appointed order, succumbed to intercourse with women, and begot children—who are called *daimones*. They then went on to enslave the human race to themselves, partly through magical changes, partly through fear and through the punishments which they inflicted, partly through instruction about sacrifices and incense and libations (τὰ δὲ διὰ διδαχῆς θυμάτων καὶ θυμιαμάτων καὶ σπονδῶν)—things they have needed ever

---

29. Quotations from *1 Apol.* 5.1–2, 14.1, and 5.3; all quotations from Justin's *Apologies* are in the translation of Minns and Parvis 2009, lightly adapted. *Daimones* and the persecution of Christians: *1 Apol.* 10.6, 12.5, 23.3, 44.12, and generally 56–58. For a concise summary of their role in Justin's thought, see Minns and Parvis 2009, 69.

since they were enslaved by passions and desires. And they sowed amongst human beings murders, wars, adulteries, licentiousness, and every kind of evil. Hence it is that poets and storytellers, not knowing that the things which they have recorded were done to men and women and cities and nations by the angels and the *daimones* they begot, attributed these things to the god himself, and to the sons who were begotten as if from him by the sowing of seed and from those who were called his brothers and their children as well. For they—that is, the poets and storytellers—called them by the names which each of the angels gave to himself and to his children.

Justin based his account of the origin of these evil *daimones* on a passage in Genesis that describes how the sons of God slept with the daughters of men and begot the Nephilim, and even more on the elaboration of this story in Judaean texts of the Hellenistic period, which he then interpreted through the lens of Platonic speculations about *daimones*, such as we find in the works of Plutarch, writing about a generation or two before him.[30]

In his *Apologies*, Justin established the basic elements of the Christian discourse of evil *daimones* for the next century or more: their origin from the fallen angels, their responsibility for the evils that befall humanity, their masquerading as gods in order to dominate humanity, their reliance on sacrifices and other offerings for their sustenance, and their role in the persecution of Christians. This demonological discourse, as we may term it, particularly the interpretation of traditional cult and myth as the work of *daimones*, became a central element in early Christian thought and in particular in what is conventionally described as the apologetic tradition, the series of texts written to vindicate Christianity against its Graeco-Roman critics that begins in the second and extends into the fourth century CE. These include works in Greek by Tatian (probably 150s–160s CE) and Athenagoras (late 170s CE) and in Latin by Tertullian (c. 197 CE) and Minucius Felix (probably first third of the third century CE). By far the most elaborate, at least prior to the fourth century, was Origen of Alexandria's eight-volume rebuttal of an anti-Christian treatise, the *True Word*, written by a philosopher named

---

30. *2 Apol.* 4(5).2–6. Genesis: 6.1–4; Hellenistic elaboration: 1 Enoch, especially 19; for a careful analysis of Justin's origin story in its Judaean background, see Reed 2004, especially 142–53, and more broadly Martin 2010. That the recipients of traditional cult practices were *daimones* and not gods was standard doctrine in Platonic thought at least from the time of Plutarch: Timotin 2012, 163–215.

Celsus. We know of Celsus and his work only from Origen's response, but since Origen quotes Celsus's text verbatim and at considerable length, we can make some reasonably secure inferences about it. It is obvious from Celsus's arguments that his views were very much in line with the Platonism of the second century CE, and a couple of specific remarks suggest that he wrote his treatise in the late 170s CE. The fact that Origen composed his response some seventy years later, in the latter half of the 240s CE, suggests that at least some Christians continued to regard Celsus's treatise as something that required a rebuttal.[31]

All these apologists adopted Justin's demonological discourse as part of their vindication of Christianity and, despite some differences in emphasis and detail, adhered to his model very closely.[32] Thus, they all insist that the evil *daimones* promote animal sacrifice and other cult offerings because they require them for their own sustenance. Athenagoras explains that "it is these *daimones* who drag men to the images; they engross themselves in the blood from the sacrifices (τῷ ἀπὸ τῶν ἱερείων αἵματι) and lick all around them," and goes on to describe them as "*daimones* associated with matter [who] are greedy for the savor of fat and the blood of the sacrifices (τὸ τῶν ἱερείων αἷμα)." Tertullian similarly explains that "of all delusions [perpetrated by *daemones*] that is the greatest, which they use to recommend those gods [i.e., the gods of traditional cult] to the captive and outwitted minds of men—and it also serves to secure for themselves their peculiar diet of smell and blood (*pabula propria nidoris et sanguinis*), offered to their likenesses and images." So, too, Minucius Felix: "their object is to force us to worship them; they will then be in a position, when they are gorged with the reek of altars and the sacrifice of beasts (*nidore altarium vel hostiis pecudum saginati*), to appear to cure us merely by relaxing their stranglehold." The *daimones*' obsession with the blood and smoke of sacrifices is a recurring motif in Origen's treatise against Celsus, but he also sets it within a broader philosophical, and recognizably Platonic, context. Pure souls, he explains, rise to higher realms, whereas those that are weighed down by evil acts descend to the lower terrestrial realms; we must accordingly assume that those that have been tied for centuries to particular earthly shrines must necessarily be evil. "That this is the character of the *daimones* is also made clear by the fact that their bodies, nourished

---

31. Apologetic tradition: for overviews, see Grant 1988 on the Greek apologists, Price 1999 on the Latin. Celsus and Origen: Chadwick 1953, xxiv–xxix, and Frede 1999.

32. Tatian *Or. Graec.* 7, 12–13, 16–18; Athenag. *Leg.* 23–27; Tert. *Apol.* 22–23; Min. Fel. *Oct.* 26.7–27.8. For an overview, see Proctor 2022, 122–29.

by the smoke from sacrifices (ταῖς ἀπὸ τῶν θυσιῶν ἀναθυμιάσεσι) and by the portions taken from the blood and burnt offerings (ταῖς ἀπὸ τῶν αἱμάτων καὶ ὁλοκαυτωμάτων ἀποφοραῖς) in which they delight, find in this, as it were, their heart's desire, like vicious men who do not welcome the prospect of living a pure life without their bodies, but only enjoy life in the earthly body because of its physical pleasures."[33]

It is important to note that Christian theorizing about the *daimones*' sustenance was not limited to animal sacrifice but also included other types of offerings: Justin says that *daimones* taught humans about "sacrificial offerings and incense and libations" (θυμάτων καὶ θυμιαμάτων καὶ σπονδῶν), and Origen likewise mentions incense (λιβανωτός) in two different passages and wine in a third. Nevertheless, all these writers focus in particular on animal sacrifice. That may be due in part to the fact that animal sacrifice with its gore and stench had greater potential for rhetorical elaboration than the cleaner offerings of incense and libations; we may note Tertullian's claim that anyone should be able to deduce that these so-called gods are, in fact, unclean spirits simply from their food, "the blood and smoke and stinking pyres of cattle." Yet it may also reflect an assumption that the coarser materiality of flesh and blood was more suited to the nature of demonic bodies and desires.[34]

Although the evidence of Paul indicates the sources of this early Christian demonological discourse, we may nevertheless ask what prompted its extensive elaboration, such as we find in Justin and Origen. We may start with the fact that it occurs almost exclusively in apologetic texts, that is, writings ostensibly addressed to Graeco-Roman critics that sought to justify Christian practices and beliefs. One of the things that seem to have attracted these critics' particular ire was the Christian refusal to engage in traditional cult practices, especially sacrifice. As we saw in Section 7b, most Christian leaders from the start demanded that Christ followers take no part in the worship of other deities. The same had also long been true of Judaeans, but they could at least point to their own tradition of sacrifices directed to their own God, and as we saw in Section 4d, they often utilized this to promote good relations with their gentile overlords. It was in this respect that the Christian displacement

---

33. Athenag. *Leg.* 26.1 and 27.2, trans. Schoedel 1972, lightly adapted. Tert. *Apol.* 22.6, trans. T. R. Glover, Loeb; cf. 23.14. Min. Fel. *Oct.* 27.2, trans. G. Clarke 1974. Origen *Cels.* 7.5, trans. Chadwick 1953, lightly adapted; cf. *Cels.* 3.37, 4.32, 7.35, and *Mart.* 45.

34. Justin: *2 Apol.* 4(5).4. Origen: *Mart.* 45 and *Cels.* 4.32 for incense; *Cels.* 8.31 for wine. Rhetorical elaboration: Tert. *Apol.* 23.14. Demonic bodies: G. Smith 2008, especially 483–90; Marx-Wolf 2016, 24–28; and now the wide-ranging study of Proctor 2022, especially 126–29.

of animal sacrifice, which I traced in Section 7d, became a crucial factor: since the sacrificial interpretation of Jesus's life and death gradually came to leave no room for actual sacrificial practice, Christian apologists had to justify not only the exclusivity of their worship but also their complete rejection of a widely accepted and ideologically important cult practice. That is what the elaborated discourse of *daimones* enabled them to do. Athenagoras provides a good example of its utility in this regard. He begins his address by asserting that one of the chief charges brought against Christians is that of atheism. After a lengthy exposition of Christian doctrines about the nature of God, he concedes that such theological arguments are perhaps beside the point, "since the majority of those accusing us of atheism have not even the foggiest notion of the nature of God, are ignorant of and unacquainted with physical or theological doctrine, and measure piety in terms of sacrifices (θυσιῶν νόμῳ)." Accordingly, he then embarks on an even longer and somewhat digressive exposition of the reasons for their refusal to sacrifice; it is in that connection that he eventually comes around to the discourse about *daimones*.[35]

The Christian demonological discourse of sacrifice developed in the context of an ongoing dialogue between Christian and non-Christian thinkers. The very use of the Greek terms *daimones* and *daimonia* to designate the unclean spirits of Judaean tradition entails a certain blending of the two traditions, and Justin's theorizing involves even more of a synthesis. In later texts, we can document what seem to be points and counterpoints in an unfolding debate. Celsus, for example, who apparently wrote at much the same time as Athenagoras, addressed the Christian refusal to sacrifice to traditional gods in a way that directly responds to the sort of demonological discourse that Athenagoras propounded. Christians, he says, claim that the beings to whom images and shrines are dedicated "are not gods but *daimones*, and that no one who worships God ought to serve *daimones*." But this, he insists, is not a valid position. "I would ask, Why should we not worship *daimones*? Are not all things indeed administered according to God's will, and is not all providence derived from him? And whatever there may be in the universe, whether the work of God or of angels or of other *daimones* or heroes, do not all these things keep a law given by the greatest God? And has there not been appointed over each particular thing a being who has been thought worthy to be allotted power? Would not a man, therefore, who worships God rightly

---

35. Athenagoras on the charge of atheism: *Leg.* 3.1; exposition of doctrines: *Leg.* 4–12; quotation: *Leg.* 13.1, trans. Schoedel 1972, adapted. For the refusal to sacrifice as a major charge against Christians, see also Tert. *Apol.* 10.1.

worship the being who has obtained authority from him?" Using an image that apparently goes back to the Hellenistic period, Celsus compares these *daimones* to the governors and officials of the Persian or Roman emperor. Since they help to administer the world under God's authority, "we ought to believe them and sacrifice to them according to the laws (καλλιερητέον κατὰ νόμους), and pray to them that they may be kindly disposed."[36]

Some scholars have argued that Celsus wrote his treatise in response to Justin's *Apologies*; whether or not that was actually the case, we can at least say that Celsus justified the practice of sacrificing to *daimones* in a way that effectively served as a rebuttal of Justin's position. Tertullian, in turn, seems to have responded, if not specifically to Celsus, at least to the same type of argument. Most men, he points out, "hold that the control of supreme rule rests with one god, while its various functions rest with many. Plato, for instance, describes the great Jupiter in heaven accompanied by a host of gods and *daemones* together. So they hold that his procurators and prefects and presiding officers should be respected equally with him." So far, so good; but then comes the twist: "And yet what crime does he commit, who, to win Caesar's favor more securely, transfers his attention and his hope elsewhere, and does not confess that the title of God, like that of Emperor, belongs to the one supreme over all, when it is legally a capital offense to speak of another beside Caesar or even to listen to such talk?" Origen's response to Celsus's argument is less legalistic and more absolute: "Celsus fails to notice that the name of *daimones* is not morally neutral like that of men.... The name of *daimones* is always applied to evil powers without the grosser body, and they lead men astray and distract them, and drag them down from God and the world beyond the heavens to earthly things." Origen is aware that not everyone uses the term in this way but insists that those who do not are wrong. "In the view of the majority of people who hold that *daimones* exist, it is only the evil *daimones* who do not keep the law of God but transgress it. But in our opinion all *daimones* have fallen from the way to goodness, and previously they were not *daimones*; for the category of *daimones* is one of those classes of being which have fallen

---

36. Quotations of Celsus from Origen *Cels.* 7.67–68 and 8.24, trans. Chadwick 1953, lightly adapted; see further 8.2, 21, 28, and 33. *Daimones* as God's officials: 8.35; cf. Arist. *Mund.* 6, 398a–b, with Timotin 2012, 111.

away from God. That is why no one who worships God ought to worship *daimones*."[37]

The Christian demonological discourse of animal sacrifice not only developed in dialogue with the demonological theorizing of Graeco-Roman philosophers but also at times, it seems, directly influenced it. Scholars have long noted that Porphyry's theory of maleficent *daimones*, which I briefly sketched in the previous section, has much in common with Christian theories about evil *daimones*, especially in the work of Origen: the idea that these *daimones* deliberately turned away from the higher realm to the lower terrestrial realm, where they succumbed to material desires and needs; that they are responsible for many of the ills that befall humanity; that they masquerade as benevolent beings in order to obtain from humans the sacrifices and offerings that they crave. Like Origen, Porphyry also counsels his audience that those who are committed to their own salvation should avoid all interaction with such beings, especially that brought about by participation in animal sacrifice. Recent scholars have made a strong case that these similarities are due not only to the fact that both discourses drew on Platonic theorizing about *daimones* but also to the direct influence of Origen's theorizing on Porphyry's own.[38]

Despite the similarities, however, we should be clear that Origen's condemnation of *daimones* is far more absolute than Porphyry's. Whereas Porphyry was one of those who believed that there were good as well as bad *daimones*, Origen himself, as we have seen, insisted that all *daimones* were by definition evil, the common enemy of humanity. In this respect, he was following his predecessors; Tatian, for example, writing a century or so earlier, had vividly compared *daimones* with bandits. As a result, Origen's condemnation of animal sacrifice is likewise far more absolute than Porphyry's. Porphyry urges philosophers to avoid animal sacrifice but is willing to concede it to the masses and to political communities. Origen tolerates no such compromise. Far from apologizing for Christians' refusal to sacrifice, he goes on the offensive against those who do:

---

37. Celsus and Justin: Andresen 1955, especially 308–11. Tert. *Apol.* 24.3–4, trans. T. R. Glover, Loeb, adapted; cf. Pl. *Phdr.* 246e. Origen: *Cels.* 5.5 and 7.69, trans. Chadwick 1953, lightly adapted; see also 4.92 and 7.5.

38. Proctor 2014, building on Digeser 2012. I refer here to the Christian Origen; whether or not he is to be identified with the Platonist Origen is not important for my analysis; for arguments pro, see Digeser 2012, 49–51n1; *contra*, Edwards 2015.

Some give no thought to the question of *daimones* (μὴ θεωροῦντες τὸν περὶ τῶν δαιμόνων λόγον): that is to say, to the fact that these *daimones*, in order to be able to exist in the heavy atmosphere that encircles the earth, must have the nourishment of exhalations and, consequently, are always on the lookout for the savor of burnt sacrifices, blood, and incense. Since they attach no importance to the matter of sacrifice (τὸ θύειν), we would express ourselves on this subject. If men who give sustenance to robbers, murderers, and barbarian enemies of the Great King are punished as criminals against the state, how much more will they be punished justly who through offering sacrifice (διὰ τοῦ θύειν) proffer sustenance to the minions of evil and thus hold them in the atmosphere of the earth! ... In my opinion, when there is question of crimes committed by these *daimones* operating against men, they who sustain them by sacrificing to them (διὰ τοῦ θύειν θρέψαντες αὐτούς) will be held no less responsible than the *daimones* themselves that do the crimes. For the *daimones* and they that have kept them on earth, where they could not exist without the exhalations and nourishment considered vital to their bodies, work as one in doing evil to mankind.[39]

For Origen, animal sacrifice was not merely something that wise people should avoid but rather something that should be punished as a crime against humanity.

It is worth noting that the passage I have just quoted is one of the earliest examples of the Christian demonological discourse of sacrifice in a text addressed to committed Christians rather than their critics and opponents. It is an address that Origen wrote probably around 235 CE to his friend and patron Ambrose, as well as an otherwise unknown man named Protectetus, apparently after they had been arrested on a charge of being Christian, and its main purpose is to exhort them to remain steadfast and, if necessary, to die rather than engage in idolatry. To do so, Origen declares, would be to deny God and his Christ and to bear witness instead to *daimones*.[40] Origen's introduction of the demonological discourse of animal sacrifice into an

---

39. Tatian: *Or. Graec.* 18, citing the authority of Justin. Origen: *Mart.* 45, trans. O'Meara 1954, lightly adapted.

40. Date and addressees: O'Meara 1954, 10–12 with 199n3. Bearing witness to *daimones*: *Mart.* 40. The demonological discourse of sacrifice first appears in Christian narratives in the Acts of Andrew (53) and Thomas (76–77), both of which probably date to the third century CE (Proctor 2022, 124–25). It appears in the Pseudo-Clementine narratives of the fourth century CE but perhaps not in their *Grundschrift* of the third century CE (Bremmer 2022, 366–71).

exhortation to martyrdom is a harbinger of things to come. As we will see in Chapter 9, in the wake of Decius's decree requiring universal sacrifice, Christian leaders found it necessary to impress upon ordinary Christians even more than before the crucial necessity of avoiding any involvement with traditional sacrificial practice, and the demonological discourse of sacrifice, originally developed in the context of Christian apologetics, proved to be a useful tool in this endeavor.

## 8d. Conclusion

In this chapter, we have sampled some of the discursive treatments of sacrificial practice that developed over the course of the first three centuries CE. As we have seen, in addition to the many significant differences between them, there are also numerous and in some cases perhaps surprising instances of overlap. What I want to emphasize in particular is that they all share a basic orientation that distinguishes them from the treatment of sacrifice in the classical philosophical schools. First, all the writers discussed here, Christians no less than Platonists and Pythagoreans, took sacrifice extremely seriously, as a practice that had crucial and very real consequences, whether negative or positive, for those who engaged in it. No longer, it seems, was it possible for philosophers to regard sacrifice simply as an ancestral practice that was in itself largely a matter of indifference but that could be accepted on the grounds of tradition. Second, all these writers agreed that the real meaning of sacrificial practice, its true significance and value, could be grasped only within the context of a correct understanding of the cosmos. Popular perceptions of its significance, as a marker of piety to the gods and an occasion for festivities, were at best inadequate and at worst profoundly wrong and thus potentially dangerous; only someone with the requisite correct understanding of the cosmos could bring its real significance to light. Again, this was a point on which everyone from Justin Martyr to Iamblichus agreed.

It was an underlying premise of Justin's address to Antoninus Pius, for example, that neither the emperor nor his representatives truly understood what they were doing in persecuting Christians; only a philosopher like Justin could reveal to them the reality of the situation. Athenagoras, as we have seen, insists that it is because "the majority of those accusing us of atheism have not even the foggiest notion of the nature of God [and] are ignorant of and unacquainted with physical or theological doctrine (ἀμαθεῖς καὶ ἀθεώρητοι ὄντες τοῦ φυσικοῦ καὶ τοῦ θεολογικοῦ λόγου)" that they require a philosopher's insight. Such people are especially liable to demonic deceptions, he declares, because it is "when the soul is weak and docile, ignorant and unacquainted with sound teachings (ἄπειρος λόγων ἐρρωμένων), unable to contemplate the truth (ἀθεώρητος δὲ τοῦ ἀληθοῦς)," that evil *daimones* are able to trick people into thinking that idols can deliver oracles and perform miracles. Origen declares that Christians have learned (the verb is μαθεῖν) that "all the gods of the nations are *daimonia*," gluttonous *daimones* "who wander around sacrifices and blood and the portion taken from the sacrifices"; it is thanks to this knowledge that Christians shun traditional sacrificial practice. He concedes that "there are some who because of their great simplicity do not know how to explain (δοῦναι λόγον) their actions" but adds that "there are others who explain their actions with arguments which may not be lightly regarded (μετ' οὐκ εὐκαταφρονήτων λόγων) but which are profound and, as a Greek might say, esoteric and mysterious." Porphyry would have strongly disagreed with Origen that Christians had learned anything correct about the divine but would have certainly agreed that in such matters there was need for *logos*, rational argument and learned discourse. Like Athenagoras, he is highly critical of those who "circulate around the shrines" without bothering "to learn from those who are wise about the gods (παρὰ τῶν θεοσόφων μαθεῖν) how far and to what extent one should venture in this area." Similarly, it is because "the concept of *daimones* is confused and leads to serious misrepresentation" that he thought it "necessary to give a rational analysis of (διαστεῖλαι λόγῳ) their nature."[41] Iamblichus, too, would have fully agreed on the importance of correct understanding. Although he is the only thinker considered in this chapter who apparently thought that sacrificial practice was beneficial in and of itself, he clearly believed that it took a philosopher to explain why that was the case. Why else would he have undertaken to respond to Porphyry's queries in a lengthy treatise written in the persona of "Abamon the Teacher"? In short, integral to the production of these discourses of animal sacrifice were claims to social power on the part of those who shaped them, power based on their privileged insight into the true nature of the world and their consequent ability to instruct the unenlightened majority how best to live their lives.

---

41. Athenagoras: *Leg.* 13.1 and 27.2, trans. Schoedel 1972, adapted. Origen: *Cels.* 3.37, citing LXX Ps. 95.5, trans. Chadwick 1953, adapted. Porphyry: *Abst.* 2.35.1 and 38.1, trans. Clark 2000, adapted.

# *Epilogue*

In this part, I have surveyed some of the major verbal discourses that developed around sacrificial practice, and animal sacrifice in particular, extending from the early Orphic and Pythagorean rejection of animal sacrifice based on a belief in metempsychosis, through the early Christian transformation of the idea of sacrifice in interpreting the life and death of Jesus, down to the elaboration of a hierarchy of offerings correlated with divine hierarchies in the late Platonic systems of Porphyry and Iamblichus. As varied as these discourses were, we can analyze them all as manifestations of transcendent ideology, in that to varying degrees, they served to promote the social power of the people who advanced them.

A concept that scholars have often used in mapping these developments is the "spiritualization" of sacrificial practice. Robert Daly provides a good, succinct account in the introduction to his magisterial study of the early Christian theology of sacrifice: "we are using the word in the much broader sense which includes all those movements and tendencies within Judaism and Christianity which attempted to emphasize the true meaning of sacrifice, i.e. the inner, spiritual, or ethical significance of the cult over against the merely material or merely external understanding of it." He goes on to enumerate some of these "movements and tendencies": "the pious Jew's attempt to make his material sacrifice an expression of an ethically good life; the prophetic criticism of the cult, the philosophically influenced doubts about the sense of offering material sacrifice to a spiritual God; the necessity of finding substitutes for material sacrifice . . .; and finally, among Christians, the various ways in which it was understood that the old economy had been definitively superseded by the new." Other scholars with less overt theological commitments have also employed the concept. Guy Stroumsa, in the series of lectures titled "La fin du sacrifice" that he delivered at the Collège de France, uses the term "spiritualisation" to describe "le passage à un rituel sans prêtres et sans sacrifices sanglants" and goes on to equate "une religion spiritualisée" with "une religion sans sang." Stroumsa stresses the central role of Judaean tradition in this process, arguing that in rabbinic tradition, Torah study, liturgical prayer, prayers, and almsgiving replaced the earlier practice of animal sacrifice.[1]

In common with other recent scholars, I find this an unsatisfactory interpretive framework, for two main reasons.[2] First, it tends to carry with it a set of value judgments that correlate certain types of cult practices with less "spiritual" and thus inferior forms of religious life, whether these value judgments are explicit or implicit.[3] This negative value judgment is often framed in terms of an assumed dichotomy between the material and the spiritual, with the implication that practices have a spiritual dimension only to the extent that they lack a material dimension.[4] To a large extent, then, the idea of "spiritualization" merely reproduces the judgments in our sources, whose authors, as I have argued, redeployed traditional terminology in order to explain and justify their own preferred practices and, in many cases, to denigrate practices of which they did not approve. The second reason is that many scholars use the concept of "spiritualization" in such a capacious sense as to deprive it of any real analytical value; the passage from Daly again provides a good example. As I have tried to demonstrate in this part, the discursive developments that

---

1. Daly 1978, with quotation from 4–5; see also Daly 2019 for his most recent treatment of this material, with some valuable reflections on his earlier work. Stroumsa 2005, 116–25, with quotations from 117 and 118; Stroumsa more often employs the similar concept of "interiorization," e.g., 24–25, 114, 123, 128. Young 1979 makes extensive use of the term "spiritualization," although she never defines it; note, however, 98: "In general, [the spiritualization of sacrifice] meant that only prayer, charity, a life of Christian virtue, and self-offering in martyrdom were reckoned to be suitable sacrifices for the one true God." She traces the influence of both Judaean and Greek tradition (102–27). Ferguson 1980 likewise never defines what he means by "spiritual sacrifice" but uses it to encompass the same range of discourses as Young.

2. For a cogent critique, see Klawans 2002, 12–14, and Klawans 2006, especially 220–21. Ullucci 2012 focuses on the related notion of what he describes as "the critique of sacrifice model"; see especially 10 for criticism of the idea that other practices "replaced" animal sacrifice. See further Reed 2014, 137–48, and Ullucci 2015, 410–12.

3. For example, Stroumsa's claim that he uses the word "spiritualisation" "sans jugement de valeur" (2005, 117) is in tension with his no doubt deliberately provocative suggestion that the Jews properly owed thanks to Titus, since by destroying the Temple, he forced them "bien malgré eux, de se libérer, avant d'autres sociétés, du sacrifice et de sa violence rituel" (115).

4. Daly is an exception: although he notes that all the movements he describes "had in common a shift in emphasis from the material to the spiritual," he is also careful to stress that he is not using the term "spiritualization" "in the narrowly anti-material, anti-institutional sense usually ascribed to it by the liberal history-of-religions school" (1978, 5); similarly, Young 1979, 98–102.

are often lumped together as examples of "spiritualization" are in significant respects quite varied, involving markedly different conceptual frameworks, priorities, and goals. Although many of them share a tendency to extend the category of sacrifice to cover a wider range of practices than traditional conceptualizations had normally included, they do so in significantly different ways. In eliding these differences and reducing this variety to a single phenomenon, the idea of "spiritualization" offers little analytical precision.

As an alternative, I have instead focused on issues of communication and power. As we have seen, the authors and texts surveyed in this part employed a wide range of discursive strategies: some relied on a narrative mode that reflected and built on traditional myth; others made extensive use of metaphor, especially as a tool to assimilate new practices to the category of sacrifice; still others emphasized the analytical mode pioneered by pre-Socratic philosophers. Not a few employed two or more strategies in combination; this was especially common among those who emphasized the exegesis of authoritative texts, notably early Christian thinkers. Yet, despite this diversity, all the writers and thinkers surveyed here shared the same underlying strategy: to persuade others, by means of verbal discourse, to accept a particular understanding of the cosmos, one that was often at odds with what was generally accepted, and on that basis to prioritize certain values and adopt certain ways of behaving.[5] As part of this process, they shifted the cultural weight of animal sacrifice from the practice itself to discourses about the practice. No longer did its value lie in communicating and constructing the types of social relationships and identity claims that supported established elites, as I argued in Part I had traditionally been the case; it instead required exegesis by an expert, who alone could reveal its true significance with a correct understanding of the world.

The strategy of persuasion employed by the proponents of these various discourses was closely and to some extent inevitably bound up with forging forms of social power that existed apart from traditional socioeconomic and political structures. In persuading people to accept an understanding of the cosmos that did not necessarily align with received traditions, these writers and thinkers were necessarily also persuading people to accept their

---

5. The best study of this social phenomenon is Wendt 2016. Her analysis of freelance religious experts in the imperial period is broadly applicable to earlier figures as well. See, for example, Edmonds 2013, 8–9: "My definition [of Orphism] permits a re-examination of the ancient evidence that takes seriously the model ... of itinerant religious specialists competing for religious authority among a varying clientele."

own authority as individuals with privileged insight into the true nature of the world. As a result, they exercised a type of social power that did not rest upon the traditional bases of wealth, inherited status, and control of physical force. Using the terminology of Michael Mann that I outlined in Section 1d, we would classify it as a form of transcendent ideology as opposed to immanent ideology. The relationship between these self-appointed authorities and established sociopolitical authorities varied considerably, from close cooperation to mutual indifference to outright antagonism. Within their own communities, however, to the extent that they aimed at and succeeded in creating communities, they fashioned and sustained their positions of authority primarily through their powers of persuasion.

The theorization of sacrificial practice that I have surveyed here was not only bound up with new forms of social power but also had an impact on actual practice. I would argue in particular that it had the effect of undermining the traditional social and cultural role of animal sacrifice. This is readily apparent in the case of discourses that assigned it a strongly negative value. For example, the conceptual displacement of animal sacrifice in the Christian tradition by the (initially) metaphorical sacrifice of Jesus allowed for a discourse of animal sacrifice that interpreted it as a mode of sustenance for evil *daimones*. This discourse helped ensure that opposition to the practice on the part of Christian leaders tended to be adamant and uncompromising. Porphyry, who conceptualized *daimones* not as enemies of God but as entities weighed down in the material sphere of being from which philosophers are trying to escape, attached a similarly negative valence to animal sacrifice, even though it was much less absolute than it was for Christians such as Origen. Yet even those discourses that provided a positive theorization of animal sacrifice, such as we find in Iamblichus, served more subtly to undermine the actual practice, through the very process of disembedding it from its sociocultural context and rendering it the object of specialized discourse. As a result, animal sacrifice had to be interpreted, justified, understood; it acquired a "meaning" of a sort that it previously did not possess and required exegesis in a way that it previously had not needed. In short, the theorization of sacrificial practice meant that the practice itself became less important than verbal discourses about the practice and as a result shifted its ideological power from established elites to self-appointed experts. In Part III, we will examine how these new discourses interacted with changes in socioeconomic and political structures to bring about a radical transformation of the place of animal sacrifice in the Roman world.

PART III

*Transformations of Animal Sacrifice in Late Antiquity*

# *Prologue*

## THE DECREE OF DECIUS (*SB* I.443)

On the face of it, it would seem absurd to suggest that the Roman emperor Decius was a figure of pivotal historical significance; not only did his reign last less than two years, but a scarcity of sources renders him little more than a cipher for later historians. For many centuries, his one claim to fame, or rather infamy, was his secure place in Christian tradition as one of the canonical persecuting emperors. Although the text of Decius's decree does not survive, the letters and treatises of Cyprian, the bishop of Carthage, provide a firsthand account of its effects on the Christian community in his city: crowds of people were ordered to offer sacrifice and faced incarceration if they refused to do so or could not produce an official certificate, a *libellus*, to prove that they had already done so. In the later Christian imagination, Decius and his wicked decree became a favorite setting for the vivid and violent narratives that showcased Christian heroes' and heroines' fortitude in the face of imperial savagery. Decius's role as a persecutor was so well known that there was considerable interest when among the thousands of papyri unearthed in Egypt starting in the late nineteenth century, scholars began to identify actual examples of the certificates that Cyprian mentioned in connection with the Decian persecution. I quote here a representative example from the village of Theadelphia in the Fayum:

> To the commission chosen to superintend the sacrifices (τοῖς ἐπὶ τῶν θυσιῶν ᾑρημένοις). From Aurelia Ammonarion of the village of Theadelphia. I and my children, Aurelius Didymus, Aurelius Nouphius, and Aurelius Taas, have always and without interruption sacrificed and shown piety to the gods (ἀεὶ μὲν θύουσα καὶ εὐσεβοῦσα τοῖς θεοῖς [ . . . ] διατετελέκαμεν), and now in your presence in accordance with the edict's decree we have poured libations and made sacrifice

(ἐθύσαμεν) and tasted the sacred victims (τῶν ἱερείων ἐγευσάμεθα). I request you to certify this for me below. Farewell.

As the number of examples grew, people started to notice a somewhat surprising pattern: nothing in any of these certificates even hints that the people involved were Christians. On the contrary, one of them actually identifies the recipient as "priestess of the god Petesouchos, the great, the mighty, the immortal, and priestess of the gods in the Moeris quarter," a highly unlikely candidate for identification as a Christian.[1]

Continuing study of these certificates gradually resulted in a fundamental shift in the historical interpretation of Decius's decree. Scholars began increasingly to regard it not as a measure aimed primarily at Christians but rather as a general measure enforcing universal participation in the practice of animal sacrifice. Although it is highly likely that Decius was aware that Christians generally refused to participate in traditional cult practices, there is now widespread agreement that they were not his primary focus. In Section 9b, we will consider in more detail the specific provisions of, possible motivations behind, and actual effects of Decius's decree. What I want to highlight here is the way it constituted a sea change in imperial policy. The practice of animal sacrifice, as demonstrated in Part I, was closely bound up with the functioning of the Roman Empire and in that connection was an important source of ideological power. It was so well established, however, and so prominent an element in Graeco-Roman culture, that there had never been any reason to legislate regarding it. Emperors had issued decrees urging people to make offerings to the gods, but none prior to Decius, as far as we know, included provisions for enforcing universal participation in a particular cult act. By contrast, in the wake of Decius's decree, animal sacrifice became a regular focus of imperial legislation well into the fifth century CE.[2] As we will see, this legislation varied considerably: some measures required people to engage in animal sacrifice, as Decius's did, whereas others threatened punishments for those who did engage in it. How did it come about that animal sacrifice became the focus of so much imperial legislation in later antiquity? And what was the long-term effect of that legislation?

Part III is in part an attempt to answer these questions. The core of my argument is that over the course of the century and a half from the accession of Decius in 249 to the death of Theodosius I in 395, the social function and cultural significance of

---

1. Quotation: *SB* I.443, in the translation of Knipfing 1923, no. 7, slightly modified. Petesouchos: Knipfing 1923, no. 3.

2. All dates in Part III are CE unless otherwise indicated.

animal sacrifice underwent a profound transformation. This transformation was the result of many different factors that intersected in ways that defy easy analysis. The new discourses of animal sacrifice whose development I traced in Part II played a part but perhaps rather less than the scholarly focus on them might suggest. Of equal or even greater importance were major structural changes in the organization and administration of the Roman Empire, which had a significant impact on the ideological work performed by animal sacrifice. What had been one of its greatest strengths in the Roman Empire of the first through early third centuries, namely, its close interrelationship with the empire's sociopolitical structures, came to be one of its greatest weaknesses, as those structures were transformed from the mid-third century onward. It was the interplay between these changes in the sociopolitical structures of the Roman Empire and the new discourses of animal sacrifice that caused the practice to become an object of ongoing imperial legislation, ultimately resulting in a profound transformation of its social and cultural role.

Chapter 9 focuses on imperial directives that mandated participation in animal sacrifice. The decree of Decius was the first of these and seems to some extent to have provided a model for those that followed, even though later emperors, unlike Decius, were explicitly concerned with Christianity. The emperor Valerian's two directives of 257 and 258 apparently had the immediate goal of undermining Christian communities, by forcing their leaders to engage in the traditional worship of the gods and punishing them if they refused and by banning Christian assemblies and confiscating communal property. Although none of the sources mentions animal sacrifice in connection with these measures or indeed says anything at all about the specific cult acts that were required, they nevertheless suggest an underlying concern on the part of Valerian that the people of the Roman Empire conform to certain norms of worship. The same concern even more clearly underlies the "Great Persecution" that was initiated by the emperor Diocletian in 303 and maintained for some ten years by his colleagues and successors Galerius and Maximinus. In this case, initial edicts aimed at eradicating Christian institutions, similar to those of Valerian, were followed by others that tried to enforce participation in animal sacrifice, as had that of Decius.

The "Great Persecution" varied considerably in both intensity and duration in different parts of the empire but was not fully ended until 313, when Constantine's co-emperor Licinius extended to the territories newly added to his area of rule the policies already prevailing in the rest of the empire, which guaranteed to all people the right to engage in the worship of their choice. Within a decade, however, Constantine, who in his rise to power had claimed the patronage of the Christian God, began to move away from the careful neutrality articulated in Licinius's letter. He instead adopted an increasingly aggressive stance toward traditional

Graeco-Roman cult, issuing directives that restricted and marginalized the practice of animal sacrifice. The antisacrificial legislation of Constantine and his successors is the focus of Chapter 10. Whether or not Constantine himself issued a comprehensive prohibition of animal sacrifice is a much-debated question, but there is no doubt that his sons and successors Constans and Constantius II did so. His nephew Julian, by contrast, who became sole emperor in 361, although raised a Christian, had converted in his youth to the traditional Graeco-Roman worship of the gods, which he termed Hellenism, and as emperor tried to restore it to its former privileged place in the empire. Julian reigned less than two years, however, and his initiative ultimately came to nothing. Even so, his successors seem to have adopted a less aggressive policy with regard to animal sacrifice, which they more or less maintained until the early 390s, when Theodosius I enacted measures that thenceforth banned animal sacrifice and most other traditional Graeco-Roman cult acts in all contexts, both public and private.

On one level, we can analyze the developments covered in these two chapters as a series of pendulum swings between imperial endorsement and enforcement of animal sacrifice on the one hand and imperial castigation and prohibition on the other. On another level, however, I argue that we can trace a more fundamental shift in the social function and cultural significance of animal sacrifice, away from its traditional role in structuring sociopolitical hierarchies and contributing to social and cultural consensus and into a new role as a marker of personal allegiance, initially to the Roman Empire and later to a particular religion. It is this underlying transformation that I aim to map in this part.

My argument requires that we examine the specific evidence concerning animal sacrifice in the context of broader historical developments during the century and a half covered in this part. Chapters 9 and 10 accordingly include more historical summary than the earlier chapters do. These were highly eventful years, however, and in order not to distract too much from our primary focus, I have tried to keep this historical contextualization to a minimum, omitting many important figures and events and keeping my focus tightly on issues directly pertinent to animal sacrifice.[3]

---

[3]. Several excellent surveys provide broader treatments: see Potter 2014 for the entire period covered in this part, and for the third century in particular, see Hekster 2008 and Ando 2012. A. Jones 1964 remains invaluable, especially on administrative and institutional topics.

# 9

# The Obligations of Empire

## DECIUS TO THE TETRARCHS (250–313 CE)

## 9a. Introduction

The third century has long been seen as a period of crisis for the Roman Empire. During this time, its northern and eastern borders were under severe pressure from, respectively, increasingly well-organized Germanic tribes and a revitalized Persian Empire; invasions were frequent and warfare virtually endemic. Moreover, imperial leadership was shifting and uncertain, due to the frequent deaths of emperors either in combat with foreign enemies or at the hands of their own troops. Major portions of the empire in the north and east effectively broke away, as regional leaders assumed responsibility for the safety and security of their own territories. In addition, a massive and ongoing debasement of the coinage, combined with a significant increase in the number of known coin hoards, has been thought to indicate severe economic problems. In cities across the empire, there was a sudden and sharp decline in the erection of public inscriptions, commemorative statues, and new public buildings; at the same time, older inscriptions and monuments were increasingly repurposed, suggesting a shift in civic priorities and institutions. All this contributes to the long-held belief that by the mid-third century, the Roman Empire was on the verge of collapse. On this view, it was thanks only to a series of effective if short-lived soldier-emperors starting in the late 260s that the imperial government was gradually able to address these challenges, although in ways that entailed significant changes at both the local and the imperial level. These changes reached their climax with the large-scale reforms of Diocletian and Constantine in the late third and early fourth centuries, as a result of which the Roman Empire of the mid-fourth century was a significantly different polity from that of the early third century.

Over the last twenty-five years, a number of scholars have called into question various elements of this traditional narrative, with the result that many now reject the notion of "crisis" as an appropriate characterization of the third century. There is instead a very lively debate over the nature, pace, and scale of the changes that took place in this period and over the best way to assess and characterize them.[1] Much of this debate does not concern us, especially since virtually everyone agrees that the Roman world underwent significant changes in the third century, even if they disagree about how best to characterize them. I will here note just a few changes that are particularly relevant to the argument of this chapter. The first is not, in fact, associated with the "crisis" at all but instead precedes it. Probably in the year 212, the emperor Marcus Aurelius Antoninus, a son of Septimius Severus who is better known by his nickname Caracalla, issued an edict that bestowed Roman citizenship on all free inhabitants of the empire. Although there is considerable debate about both Caracalla's motivations and the practical effects of his edict, conventionally known as the Constitutio Antoniniana, for our purposes, what is most important is that it capped a long-term process of extending Roman citizenship to more and more people in the empire. In many ways, it constituted a major turning point in the transformation of the Roman Empire from an empire ruled by Rome to an empire of Romans.[2]

Equally important are changes in the established institutions of the Graeco-Roman city. As we saw in Chapter 3, local elites had long been deeply invested in the euergetic system, in which the wealthy expended their personal resources on public benefactions in return for political control and public honors. Although the system functioned effectively for many years, there was from an early date a tendency for voluntary benefactions to be codified as obligations. Already in the second century, it seems, some members of the municipal elite were starting to seek exemption from the obligations that a civic career entailed, and their numbers are likely to have increased with the economic pressures of the third century. The result was a weakening of the euergetic system. Many scholars have interpreted the decline in honorific inscriptions and statues as a symptom of that weakening. As with other

---

1. A pivotal work is Witschel 1999, with an English summary in Witschel 2004. Counterarguments: Liebeschuetz 2007. Gerhardt 2006 surveys the historiography of the third-century "crisis"; for a brief overview, see Hekster 2008, 82–86.

2. Sherwin-White 1973, 279–87, 380–93; Carrié 2005, 271–75; Hekster 2008, 45–55.

aspects of the third-century crisis, however, this narrative of a collapse in the traditional structures and values of the Graeco-Roman city has been challenged. It is now clear that in many parts of the empire, urban life not only was undiminished but even became more vital. The decline of honorific statues and inscriptions, some have suggested, had more to do with changes in the ways cities honored their benefactors than with a decline in actual benefactions; other sources make it clear that in many places, euergetism continued well into late antiquity. Yet even if we reject the picture of a collapse in traditional Graeco-Roman civic institutions, there were clearly changes in the way those institutions were modulated. The sharp decline in honorific inscriptions and statues in the mid-third century suggests at the least a shift in the priorities of local elites.[3]

There is also evidence that in regions as different as Egypt and Gaul, traditional temples and their associated cults experienced a significant decrease in wealth and influence. In Gaul, many major civic sanctuaries were abandoned in the middle to late third century, with some subsequently plundered for construction materials; few, if any, were ever restored, and even where there is evidence for continued offerings, these were on a much smaller scale than what preceded them. In Rome itself, there are likewise instances of traditional practices coming to an abrupt end. For example, the Arval Brothers continued their practice of engraving records of their cult activities on the walls of their sanctuary without any signs of slacking into the reign of Gordian III (238–244). Yet the last datable entry is from the year 241; thereafter, they abruptly cease, never to be resumed. The institutions of the public cult of deified emperors come to an end at about the same time: the last deified emperor for whom a priestly college was established was Severus Alexander (died 235), and there is no mention of any priests of deified emperors after the reign of his successor Maximinus Thrax (235–238). At the same time, there is also evidence that many traditional temples and cults continued to thrive. It is accordingly difficult to determine whether these phenomena constitute signs of a more general shift away from traditional cult practices or are local developments driven by specifically local factors.[4]

---

3. Municipal elites and exemptions from financial burdens: A. Jones 1964, 13–14, 20; later assessments of the changes in cities and their elites: Carrié 2005 and Gerhardt 2008; see now the detailed study of Pont 2020, focusing on Asia Minor. Euergetism: contrast Zuiderhoek 2009, 154–59, on its decline with Lepelley 1997 on its ongoing vitality. Shift in values: Liebeschuetz 2007, 17–18.

4. Egypt: Bagnall 1988. Gaul: Van Andringa 2014, together with the other papers in that volume. Arval Brothers: *CIL* VI.2114 = Scheid 1998, no. 115, for the last datable entry; no. 116

There is some reason to suppose that the practice of animal sacrifice was itself in decline during this period, although the lack of any readily quantifiable body of evidence makes it virtually impossible to test that hypothesis.[5] The most precise analysis is Jaś Elsner's careful survey of visual representations of cult offerings. He demonstrates in detail that starting around 200 and increasing after 230, there is a decline in the imagery of animal sacrifice in a wide range of media and a concomitant increase in the imagery of vegetal offerings. He concludes that although we cannot interpret this pattern as an index for a decline in the actual practice, it nevertheless suggests that "animal sacrifice was in fact significantly weakening at least as an ideology during the pre-Christian imperial period, from as early as 200 CE." This possible weakening in the cultural importance of animal sacrifice would fit well with the documented decline in public cults that occurred in at least some parts of the empire. It would also fit well with what some have seen as a larger shift in cult practice. In two short articles published in the middle of the last century, Martin Nilsson gathered a range of literary, epigraphic, and archaeological evidence to support his argument that over the course of the Hellenistic and imperial periods, costly but infrequent animal sacrifices were increasingly supplemented and in some cases even supplanted by daily but inexpensive offerings of incense, lamps, and hymns. We can perhaps regard as one particular example of that trend the cult of Theos Hypsistos, "the Highest God," that Stephen Mitchell has argued spread through the eastern Mediterranean world in the first through fourth centuries and that seems to have eschewed animal sacrifice for cult practices centered on lamps and prayers.[6]

It was in the context of these large-scale political, social, and cultural changes that animal sacrifice became for the first time a focus of imperial

---

is a brief dedication to Diocletian and Maximian but includes no record of cultic activity. Cult of deified emperors in Rome: Gradel 2002, 356–69, especially 358.

5. Some scholars point to Lucian's short treatise *On Sacrifices* as evidence for a turn away from animal sacrifice, but I am hesitant to attach too much importance to it, given that it continues a long-standing tradition of satirical critiques of the practice.

6. Imagery: Elsner 2012, with quotation from 163; see also Section 5c above. Incense, lamps, and hymns: Nilsson 1945 and 1950; cf. Bradbury 1995, 335–37, and Petropoulou 2008, 20–24; the latter, however, documents in detail the ongoing vitality of animal sacrifice for the period 100 BCE to 200 CE (48–106). Nilsson's thesis echoes Theophrastus's stress on continuous piety, although as I argued in Section 6d, Theophrastus's treatise seems to have had little influence. Theos Hypsistos: Mitchell 1999, especially 95, 107–8, and 127 on cult practices; see further his follow-up, Mitchell 2010, especially 174–79 on cult practices. The fact that prescriptions for appropriate aromatics accompany the *Orphic Hymns* (perhaps second century or later) may also suggest an increased focus on vegetal offerings.

policy. Decius's decree requiring all inhabitants of the empire to perform an animal sacrifice was a turning point, in that it established animal sacrifice as a cultic obligation to the empire, analogous to the financial obligation of paying taxes. Animal sacrifice thus came, in effect, to signify self-identification with the Roman Empire. Although Decius's decree was in force for barely a year, it provided a precedent for other measures to come. Just a few years later, Valerian issued his own directives that in some ways revived the Decian model. Although Valerian's main goal, it seems, was to destroy Christian communal organization, he also seems to have been keen to enforce, as Decius did, participation in certain types of cult practices as a requirement for being a Roman subject. The reign of his son and successor Gallienus saw a radical volte-face: not only did he abrogate Valerian's measures, but he also for the first time extended de facto recognition to Christian associations. As a result, he effectively severed the connection between animal sacrifice and identification with Rome that Decius, and possibly Valerian as well, had tried to enforce. The imperial government instead adopted a policy of neutrality in the matter of religious adherence and the cultic practices associated with it. After a period of some forty-three years, virtually the same cycle was repeated in the early fourth century, when Diocletian and his colleagues attempted once again to enforce the practice of animal sacrifice but then declared imperial neutrality in matters of religious allegiance. As we will see, however, the intervening period had also brought some changes.

## *9b. The Decree of Decius and Its Aftermath*

As I noted in the prologue to this part, our sources of information for the life and reign of Decius are meager in the extreme. The only surviving narrative accounts are those in late-fourth-century Latin historical epitomes and in Zosimus and Byzantine chronicles; otherwise, we rely on inscriptions, coins, and other documentary sources. After a successful military career, he became emperor in the summer of 249, when the legions he was commanding along the Danube proclaimed him emperor and he defeated the reigning emperor Philip in battle. After a few months in Rome, he returned to the Danubian provinces, where a large band of Goths had crossed the border and penetrated south into Macedonia. After some initial successes, he was defeated and killed in battle in the late spring of 251.[7]

---

7. Decius's career and reign: Birley 1998; date of accession: Worp 2017; date of death: Kovács 2015.

It was while he was in Rome, it seems, that Decius issued his decree. No Greek or Latin historical account so much as alludes to it; the only literary sources, and for many years the only sources whatsoever, are all Christian. Chief among these are letters and other documents of contemporaries, notably Cyprian of Carthage and Dionysius, the bishop of Alexandria. Neither actually refers to the decree itself, since they were, not surprisingly, more concerned with its impact on their congregations, but they provide vivid testimony to its effects. By the early fourth century, Decius had become enshrined in Christian tradition as one of the canonical "persecuting emperors," and it is in this role that we encounter him in the works of Lactantius and Eusebius as well as in various martyr acts that purport to record the trials and executions of Christians who refused to sacrifice.[8] As we have seen, it was only with the discovery of the papyrus certificates, of which forty-seven examples are now known, that scholars began to reconsider the nature and purpose of his decree. Although we have no direct evidence for its contents, the certificates, eked out by the Christian sources, allow us to deduce its key provisions with some confidence. First and foremost, it required everyone in the empire to engage in the traditional cult acts of a libation and an animal sacrifice and to swear that they had always done so. In addition, it established an elaborate bureaucratic procedure to ensure universal compliance, by requiring local officials to oversee the proceedings and to issue certificates attesting that they had witnessed the recipient performing the required cult acts. It is not clear whether the decree also included specific provisions for dealing with noncompliance, but the evidence of the contemporary Christian texts indicates that the consequences could be severe, ranging from exile and loss of property to torture and death.[9]

---

8. Cyprian: *Ep.* 5–43 and *Laps.*; Dionysius: Euseb. *Hist. eccl.* 6.40–44; Lactantius: *Mort.* 4; Eusebius: *Hist. eccl.* 6.39. Martyr acts: the only two usually regarded as having much historical basis are those of Carpus and companions and of Pionius, both discussed later in this section, but Decius is named as emperor in a number of acts now generally regarded as purely fictional; see, e.g., Ménard 2006.

9. Certificates: Knipfing 1923, to which add PSI VII.778, *SB* VI.9084, *P.Oxy.* XLI.2990 and LVIII.3929, *P.Lips.* II.152, and, most recently, P.Luther 4, for which see Claytor 2015. The wording of the certificates is, with minor variations, the same in all known examples and so must reflect the official instructions for implementing the decree in Egypt (Schubert 2016). The phrase "we have tasted the sacred victims," τῶν ἱερείων ἐγευσάμεθα, clearly implies animal sacrifice; only in the case of animal victims were participants expected to taste the offerings (my thanks to Fred Naiden for confirming this point), and the noun ἱερεῖον, "victim," refers exclusively to animal victims (Casabona 1966, 28–38). It is thus very likely that Decius's decree itself specified animal sacrifice, although the local authorities responsible for implementing it may have allowed vegetal alternatives; Cyprian seems to distinguish Christians who had offered

Scholars have long speculated on Decius's motivations in issuing this decree, although given the total absence of any direct evidence, speculating is all we can do. We may take it for granted that he wanted to win the goodwill of the gods, since that had always been the fundamental goal of animal sacrifice. Some scholars have associated his decree with the long-established practices of offering sacrifices in celebration of a new emperor's accession or the annual vows for the emperor's well-being on January 3. Both are plausible contexts, although in both cases, the process would have been unusually protracted, since in Egypt, officials were still issuing certificates in mid-July, some ten months after Decius became emperor and six months after the customary day for the vows. The underlying difficulty with explaining Decius's edict on the basis of such long-established practices, however, is that in important respects, it was entirely unprecedented. Although imperial authorities had for centuries enjoined people to make offerings to the gods in thanksgiving for particular blessings or in supplication during particular crises, no one had ever, as far as we know, established an elaborate bureaucratic procedure to ensure universal participation in a specific cult act on an individual basis. Hence recent scholars have suggested more specific motivations. Paul McKechnie proposes that Decius's immediate incentive was the contemporary Persian campaign against non-Zoroastrians within their territory, led by the priest Kartir; the aim of his own decree "was to obtain divine favor, or least counteract any advantage the Persians might be obtaining from their gods as a result of Kartir's programme." Bruno Bleckmann cogently argues that the decree constituted Decius's attempt to create loyalty among his subjects after the bloody civil war that brought him to power. Allen Brent sees it as a response to the perceived cosmic malaise of the times; Decius's goal was "to obtain the *pax deorum* following the collapse of the world into its *senectus* in order to set right a nature at variance with itself."[10] My own proposal is as follows.

Decius, I would suggest, was motivated in part by a nostalgia for the sociopolitical order of the high Roman Empire, in which animal sacrifice played so prominent a part. Born probably around 190, he was old enough to remember

---

incense (*turificati*, *Ep.* 55.2.1) from those who had actually sacrificed (*sacrificati*, *Ep.* 55.12.1 and 17.3), perhaps indicating such an alternative in Carthage. For general discussions of the decree, see Rives 1999 and G. Clarke 2005, 625–35.

10. Accession: Selinger 2004, 32–53; annual vows: G. Clarke 1984–89, 1.25 (tentatively); protracted process: Knipfing 1923, no. 20, dated July 14, 250. Motivations: McKechnie 2002, with quotation from 266; Bleckmann 2006; Brent 2010, with quotation from 178. Brent takes an approach to understanding Decius and his decree that differs fundamentally from my own; see in general Brent 2010, 144–92.

the reign of Septimius Severus, an era that in retrospect must have seemed a golden age of strength, stability, and prosperity. By the time he became emperor, however, things were very different, and he was faced with complex problems of external military threats, political instability, and social change for which there was no easy solution. In this context, it is possible that Decius was aware of the cultural shift away from animal sacrifice discussed in Section 9a and that he associated it with the increase in social and political instability. The decline in animal sacrifice may have served for him as a proxy focus of concern, not merely symbolic of but in some way contributing to the broader sociopolitical problems that were undermining the empire; he may have had some notion that by systematically enforcing the practice of animal sacrifice, he was doing something to reinforce the fabric of the empire. If so, it would have made sense for him to take steps not merely to decree offerings to the gods, as earlier emperors had done, but to ensure that all the people of the empire actually took part in a practice that had for centuries been so closely bound up with its smooth functioning.

More important than Decius's motivations, however, are the effects of his decree. Two strike me as particularly significant, of which one was certainly, and the other very likely, inadvertent. If Decius was, in fact, motivated by nostalgia for the sociopolitical order of the high Roman Empire, as I have suggested, then he fundamentally misunderstood the role that animal sacrifice played in it. As I argued in Chapter 3, it was precisely because most people could not afford to offer an animal sacrifice that it served as such a valuable tool for structuring sociopolitical hierarchies. Decius, by universalizing the practice, effectively undercut its utility in this respect. Once animal sacrifice was required of everyone, it could no longer function as a privileged marker of wealth or serve as a paradigmatic elite benefaction.[11] In this respect, Decius's decree reinforced the effects of the shift away from civic euergetism and further undermined the distinctive role of public animal sacrifice in Graeco-Roman urban life. At the same time, it also had the effect of endowing the practice of animal sacrifice with a new type of cultural significance, one that built on its long-established role as a marker of normative Graeco-Roman culture but took it in a new and more politicized direction. It is striking that

---

11. How the multitudes who complied with Decius's decree paid for their animal victims is an open question, since nothing in the available evidence provides any basis for an answer. As I noted above (n. 9), local authorities may have allowed cheaper vegetal alternatives, but it is also possible that elite benefaction was still in some way involved. I am grateful to an anonymous reader for Oxford University Press for raising this important issue.

the bureaucratic procedure that Decius established to ensure universal participation in animal sacrifice has its closest analogues in long-established procedures for issuing tax receipts, death and birth certificates, census records, and other documents that played a role in the system of taxation. Just as all inhabitants of the empire had long been required to pay their taxes and acquire receipts as proof that they had done so, they were now required to offer an animal sacrifice and acquire a certificate as proof that they had done so. In other words, by setting up a bureaucratic procedure to ensure the universal participation in the practice of animal sacrifice, Decius, in effect, transformed it into a civic obligation and thus into a marker of self-identification with the Roman Empire.[12]

Decius's decree also had a significant impact on Christians.[13] As I argued in Chapters 7 and 8, Christian leaders had come to reject the practice of animal sacrifice and to conceptualize it within a view of the cosmos in which a good God was opposed by evil *daimones*. These *daimones* had gained sway over humanity by masquerading as gods, even though they were actively working against human welfare. It was they who had instituted the practice of animal sacrifice, because they required the sustenance of the smoke and fumes that it produced. Accordingly, as Origen argued, to engage in animal sacrifice was to aid and abet the enemies of God and humanity, comparable to offering support to robbers and bandits. By the time of Decius, this demonological discourse of animal sacrifice had been extensively elaborated and was apparently broadly established among literate Christian elites. It thus comes as a surprise to learn that, as the Christian sources themselves attest, many self-identified Christians chose in varying degrees to comply with Decius's decree. Cyprian, who left Carthage and went into hiding shortly after the decree was promulgated, was aware from an early date that a considerable number of the Christians there had offered sacrifice. The numbers were so great that the question of what to do with the "lapsed," as he termed Christians who had in any way complied with the decree, became a burning issue even before he had returned to Carthage. In a pamphlet he composed in the spring of 251, he claims:

> Forthwith, at the first words of the threatening enemy, an immense number of the brothers (*maximus fratrum numerus*) betrayed their

---

12. I here summarize arguments developed more fully in Rives 1999, 147–54.

13. The remainder of this section appeared in earlier form as Rives 2020, 194–99.

faith, not laid low by the onslaught of the persecution, but they laid themselves low by a voluntary collapse. . . . Many were defeated before they joined battle, laid low without engaging the enemy, and accordingly did not even leave for themselves the appearance of having sacrificed to idols (*sacrificare idolis*) unwillingly.

In letters written many months later, he indicates that among those who had offered sacrifice were even a few bishops. Dionysius, the bishop of Alexandria, provides a similar description of the situation in his city: "of the more eminent persons, some came forward immediately through fear, others in public positions were compelled to do so by their business, and others were dragged by those around them."[14]

Why did so many Christians obey Decius's decree and offer sacrifice? Cyprian and Dionysius cite worldly considerations and take it for granted that no Christian could have possibly sacrificed without knowing full well that he or she was committing a terrible sin. They both expatiate to excellent rhetorical effect on the emotions that such people must have experienced as they performed their sacrifice: "But surely," writes Cyprian, "even if a man approached of his own accord to commit himself to this grim crime, did not his step falter, his eyes cloud, did not his heart quake, his arms go limp? Surely his blood ran cold, his tongue clove to his palate, his speech failed him?" The fact that some people devised strategies to avoid the choice between full compliance and direct refusal indicates that there were Christians who did regard animal sacrifice as an act that they should avoid: some, like Cyprian, went into hiding, and some who had the means either compelled others to sacrifice on their behalf or bribed officials to provide them with certificates without having performed a sacrifice.[15] Nevertheless, we should be wary of accepting at face value these two bishops' insistence that all true Christians regarded any involvement in animal sacrifice as a grievous sin. The rhetorical effectiveness that makes their accounts so vivid is in itself a reminder that they were concerned not with providing a neutral assessment but with advancing their own agenda.

---

14. Early date: Cypr. *Ep.* 13.1, 14.1.1, using allusive and elliptical language (e.g., 14.1.1: "infesta tempestas, quae plebem nostram ex maxima parte prostrauit"); both letters were written before mid-April 250: G. Clarke 1984–89, 1.254 and 261. Quotation: Cypr. *Laps.* 7–8; date: Clarke and Poirier 2012, 9–12. Bishops: Cypr. *Ep.* 59.10.2–3 and 65.1–3; date of the letters: G. Clarke 1984–89, 3.235–36 and 316–17. Dionysius: Euseb. *Hist. eccl.* 6.41.11, trans. J. E. L. Oulton, Loeb.

15. Quotation: Cypr. *Laps.* 8, trans. Bévenot 1971. Strategies: Brent 2010, 220–22, 240–47.

There are, in fact, good reasons to suppose that some people who identified as Christian did not regard offering a public sacrifice as such a serious offense. As Éric Rebillard has pointed out, the fact that many of those who did so clearly expected to remain part of their Christian community suggests that they did not regard their act as a repudiation of their Christian adherence.[16] Origen, in the passage I quoted in Chapter 8c, indicates that some Christians did not regard the practice of animal sacrifice with the gravity that he felt it deserved. What prompted his comparison of those who offer sacrifice to those who aid robbers and murderers was precisely the fact that "some people give no thought to the question of *daimones* [and] attach no importance to the matter of sacrifice."[17] That there were Christians who held such views seems clear enough, but since they did not explain their views in any form that has survived, we can only guess at their thinking.[18] A treatise on idolatry written some half a century earlier by Cyprian's fellow Carthaginian Tertullian, however, may provide some insight. Tertullian was concerned that most Christians unduly limited their idea of idolatry to overt cult practices such as burning incense, sacrificing victims, hosting sacrificial banquets, or holding a priesthood, whereas in reality, he insists, idolatry is far more widespread. True Christians must scrupulously avoid all public festivals and the performances associated with them, cannot hold public office that involves any association with temples or cult practices, and should not even accept blessings in the name of the gods.[19] We may infer from Tertullian's diatribe that in his day, there was disagreement among Christians, not so much over the principle of avoiding idolatry but rather over what practices actually constituted idolatry. Whereas a rigorist like Tertullian regarded as idolatrous any practice that could be construed as worship of traditional gods, there were, no doubt, many who viewed some of these practices as religiously neutral social and cultural customs. Was it possible that some Christians regarded animal sacrifice in that category? It was, after all, the emperor who issued the

---

16. Rebillard 2012, 51.

17. Origen *Mart.* 45, trans. O'Meara 1954, lightly adapted.

18. Brent 2010, 225–28, 239–40, argues that some Christians complied with Decius's decree because they had not fully divested themselves from their pagan background and so truly believed that the ritual was needed to save the empire. Rebillard 2012, 1–5, 50–54, proposes instead that because people have multiple identities that they activate in different times and in different contexts, many would have seen no inherent incompatibility between participation in a civic ritual decreed by the emperor and their personal identity as Christians.

19. Tert. *Idol.*, especially 2 on the extent of idolatry, 13–15 on festivals (cf. *Spect.*), 17 on public office, and 22 on blessings.

requirement to participate in animal sacrifice, making it a civic obligation. Moreover, there is no evidence that Decius's decree specified the deities to whom people had to offer their sacrifice; the papyrus certificates simply say "to the gods." If Christians offered sacrifices to the true God, did it constitute idolatry?[20]

Regardless of their reasons, the evidence suggests that some self-identified Christians did not regard it as such a serious offense to engage in animal sacrifice and that Decius's decree made that fact more apparent to Christian leaders than it had ever been before. Previously, there had been few, if any, systematic pressures on people to offer sacrifice on an individual basis, and consequently only rarely would professed Christians have felt an obligation to offer sacrifice or Christian leaders have had the opportunity of learning that they had done so. Decius's edict changed all that, so that for the first time, Christian leaders became keenly aware of the extent to which some Christians were willing to engage in animal sacrifice. As a result, they thereafter took steps to promulgate and enforce their own understanding of animal sacrifice as a practice incompatible with Christian adherence.

In the short term, it was important to emphasize that compliance with the decree constituted a major offense that could not lightly be forgiven. In Carthage, Cyprian insisted that the lapsed must undergo an extended period of severe penance before they could be readmitted to communion. Other members of the Carthaginian clergy, however, had been much readier to absolve those who had sacrificed and allow them to rejoin the community, and they co-opted for their cause the charismatic authority of the "confessors," those who had refused to comply with the decree and had been imprisoned as a result. It was only by means of some adroit political maneuvering that Cyprian was able to circumvent the resulting challenge to his authority and advocate for his policy at a council of African bishops that met in Carthage in spring 251. It was in preparation for this council that he composed his pamphlet on the lapsed, in which he used all his considerable rhetorical skill to impress upon his audience the seriousness of the offense. Among other tactics, he included a series of lurid anecdotes of what befell those who, having participated in the mandated sacrifices, did receive the Eucharist without having undergone penance and formal readmission to communion. One man was "unable to eat or even handle the Lord's sacred body; when he opened

---

20. It is suggestive that the author of the acts of Pionius was able to imagine the presiding official saying to the recalcitrant Christian hero, "Why are you looking at the air? Sacrifice to it" (19.10, trans. Rebillard 2017).

his hands, he found he was holding nothing but ashes"; there was also a girl who, "after the first spasms, gasping feverishly, began to choke and, a victim now not of the persecution but of her own crime, collapsed in tremors and convulsions." Such stories provided a vivid demonstration that Paul's dictum about the incompatibility of the table of the Lord and the table of *daimones* held true on a basic bodily level. Although the council ultimately adopted a policy of readmission that was somewhat less rigorous than that initially advocated by Cyprian, he nonetheless succeeded in establishing the essential point.[21]

If the disciplinary policies of bishops like Cyprian constituted the immediate response to the willingness of some Christians to engage in animal sacrifice, longer-term strategies included the crafting of narratives that illustrated the incompatibility of the practice with self-identification as a Christian. This is apparent in two martyr narratives that in some form must date back to the immediately post-Decian period, those of Pionius of Smyrna and Carpus of Pergamum. Whereas animal sacrifice had played a very minor role in accounts of earlier trials of Christians, it is a dominant theme in the acts of Pionius.[22] According to the author, Pionius knew in advance that he and his companions would be arrested and thus put chains around their necks, so that everyone would know that they, unlike others, could not be induced to eat defiled food (μιαροφαγῆσαι) but were ready to go to prison instead. The temple warden Polemon then comes with his men to haul them off to sacrifice (ἐπιθύειν) and eat defiled food, citing the emperor's edict to sacrifice to the gods. He leads them to the agora, where there occurs a series of exchanges in which demands and refusals to sacrifice are a virtual leitmotif. After a stay in prison, Polemon returns and again urges them to offer sacrifice, this time citing the example of Euctemon, a local Christian leader, who had already done so. He then takes them to the temple, where Euctemon is still in the act of worshiping idols; the author later explains that Euctemon had brought a lamb to the temple, where he had roasted and eaten some of it and had sworn by the emperor's *tyche*

---

21. Cypr. *Laps.* 26, trans. Bévenot 1971, lightly adapted; see also 15, where Cyprian actually quotes Paul's dictum (1 Cor. 10.21). Policy adopted by the council: Cypr. *Ep.* 55; see further Clarke and Poirier 2012, 74–77.

22. Animal sacrifice in earlier martyr accounts: Rives 2020, 180–87. Acts of Pionius: *BHG* 1546 = Musurillo 1972, no. 10 = Rebillard 2017, 52–79. The extant text was known to Eusebius (*Hist. eccl.* 4.15.47), giving a terminus ante quem of about 300: Rebillard 2017, 49. Although Eusebius dates the events to the reign of Marcus Aurelius, the text itself associates them with the decree of Decius, which must be correct; see Robert 1994, 2–9, and Barnes 2010, 74–76, who further argue for its historical reliability.

and the city's patron deities that he was not a Christian. Once more, there is a series of exchanges, in which Pionius and his companions again steadfastly refuse to offer sacrifice. Sacrifice reappears as a leitmotif in the narrative's final exchange, between Pionius and the proconsul, which concludes with the proconsul condemning Pionius to be burned alive. The author ends with a brief account of his death and an exhortation to the audience: "a marvelous grace shone on his face again, so that the Christians were strengthened in their faith and the unbelievers returned dismayed and with fearful consciences."[23]

In contrast to earlier martyr narratives, the account of Pionius's arrest and trial dwells almost obsessively on the act of sacrifice, to the exclusion even of the libations that seem to have featured in Decius's actual decree. Moreover, with its early and repeated references to eating defiled food, there is no doubt that the focus of concern was specifically animal sacrifice and not other types of offering. Lastly, the author pointedly and repeatedly presents the act of animal sacrifice and self-identification as a Christian as mutually exclusive alternatives. When Polemon orders Pionius to sacrifice, Pionius responds simply, "I am a Christian." He makes the same response to another official who asks him why he refuses to sacrifice. When the officials put garlands on Pionius and his companions, they tear them off and shout that they are Christians, so that the public slave who is standing nearby with a platter of sacrificial meat (εἰδωλόθυτον) does not dare to approach them but simply eats the meat himself. The import of all this for the intended audience is clear: true Christians do not engage in animal sacrifice and cannot do so without betraying their commitment to Christ.[24]

The *Acts of Carpus* presents the same lesson in an even more forceful and didactic form.[25] The account begins with Carpus and his companion Papylus brought before the Roman proconsul. The proconsul asks Carpus his name, and Carpus responds by stating that his "first and chosen name is Christian, but if you seek my worldly name, it is Carpus." The proconsul then reminds

---

23. Defiled food: *Passio Pionii* 2.4; cf. 3.5, 6.3; edict: 3.2; demands and refusals to sacrifice: 4.1, 4.13, 7.2, 7.6, 8.2, 8.4, 10.5–6; Euctemon's sacrifice: 15.2 and 18.13–14; further refusals to sacrifice: 16.1–2, 18.3–6; final exchange: 19–20; conclusion: 22.4, in the translation of Rebillard 2017.

24. "I am a Christian": *Passio Pionii* 8.2; cf. 8.4 and 16.2; public slave: 18.4–6.

25. *BHG* 293 = Musurillo 1972, no. 2A = Rebillard 2017, 38–45. The text itself does not date the events; Eusebius (*Hist. eccl.* 4.15.48) implies a date in the reign of Marcus Aurelius, whereas a Latin version dates them to the reign of Decius (*BHL* NS 1622m = Musurillo 1972, no. 2B, 1); the latter is now generally regarded as correct; see further C. Jones 2012, 262–68, who also argues for its overall historical reliability. My discussion here summarizes the analysis that I develop at greater length in Rives 2018, 79–85.

him of the imperial decrees requiring people to honor the gods and advises him to sacrifice (θῦσαι). Carpus repeats that he is a Christian, declares that he worships Christ, and states that he does not sacrifice to idols. He then continues with a brief disquisition in order to explain himself further: "it is impossible for me to sacrifice to the deceptive images of *daimones*, since those who sacrifice to them are like them." Just as those who worship the true God become like him, "so too do the men who serve these idols become alike to the folly of *daimones* and perish with them in Gehenna." And indeed, it is just that they should be destroyed along with the devil, who because of his innate wickedness has deceived humanity. "Know then, proconsul, that I do not sacrifice to these idols." After a further brief exchange in which the proconsul repeatedly presses him to sacrifice, Carpus responds with a second disquisition about the relationship between God, *daimones*, and humans. After one final refusal to sacrifice, the proconsul has him tortured and turns his attention to Papylus.[26]

As in the account of Pionius, the *Acts of Carpus* presents the conflict between the martyr and the proconsul in terms of a nonnegotiable mutual exclusivity between Christian identity and the practice of animal sacrifice: according to Carpus, his Christian allegiance is what precludes his obeying the proconsul's orders. But whereas the redactor of the account of Pionius simply presents this incompatibility as a given, the redactor of this text has his protagonist provide a detailed explanation for it. Although the various ideas that he puts in the mouth of Carpus do not all easily cohere with one another, they generally draw on the long-standing Christian demonological discourse of animal sacrifice. Compared with the account of Pionius, then, the *Acts of Carpus* has an even more obviously didactic purpose: not only does it model the way good Christians should react to animal sacrifice, but it also provides an explanation for why they should react in that way. Nevertheless, both texts make the same crucial point: in contrast to the "lapsed" of Cyprian's Carthage, true Christians must be willing to undergo the most painful of deaths rather than make any compromise with the practice of animal sacrifice.

For both Christians and non-Christians, then, Decius's decree served as a turning point in the cultural and social significance of animal sacrifice, even if its long-term effects were not fully apparent at the time. On the one hand, it hastened the decline of animal sacrifice as an integral element within the sociopolitical structure of the empire, a decline already under way as the result

---

26. Quotations from 3, 6, 7, and 8, in the translation of Rebillard 2017, lightly adapted.

of long-term economic and political developments, and instead heightened its significance as a marker of allegiance to the Roman Empire. On the other hand, it prompted Christian leaders to take more aggressive measures to persuade their followers that animal sacrifice was a practice fundamentally incompatible with Christian allegiance. It is here in particular that we can see the impact that the Christian discourse of animal sacrifice had on practice; the *Acts of Carpus* is perhaps the first text to incorporate demonological discourse into a narrative that models the utter incompatibility of Christian adherence and the practice of animal sacrifice.[27] In all these respects, Decius's decree and its aftermath set the stage for developments over the next sixty-five years.

## 9c. *Valerian and Gallienus*

Decius appears to have abandoned attempts to enforce his decree well before his final campaign and death. By the end of 250, imprisoned Christians were being released, and those who, like Cyprian, had gone into hiding were re-emerging; by early 251, Cyprian and his fellow African bishops felt secure enough to organize a large-scale council to meet in Carthage in the spring.[28] Although Christians were still subject to harassment, there seem to have been no further imperial directives concerning them until the summer of 257, when the emperor Valerian issued the first of two decrees, with the second following a year later. Although these differed from Decius's initiative in some significant ways, I argue that they maintained and reinforced the overall framework established by Decius's decree, within which animal sacrifice and other traditional cult acts functioned as markers of allegiance to the Roman Empire.

The historical record for Valerian's reign is not much better than that for Decius's. He had had a long and successful career by the time he became emperor in the summer of 253, when his predecessor Trebonianus Gallus was killed in a mutiny; shortly afterward, he appointed his older son Gallienus his co-ruler. Valerian spent most of his reign dealing with the threat posed by the renascent Persian Empire, under its aggressive and highly capable ruler Shapur I. As with Decius, it is only Christian sources that mention the actions that affected them. The most important contemporary witnesses are again Dionysius of Alexandria, whose letters are excerpted by Eusebius, and Cyprian

---

27. See Hartmann 2020 for the relative scarcity of demonological discourse in early martyrological literature.

28. G. Clarke 1984–89, 2.222–24, 3.18–22.

of Carthage. Equally important are the accounts of Cyprian's trial and execution, which are extant in both a shorter and a longer form. Many scholars believe that they both date to shortly after Cyprian's death in September 258 and are based on official records of his trial; the chief argument is that the Carthaginian deacon Pontius, who accompanied Cyprian in exile, refers to them in the account of the bishop's life and death that he wrote not long after the end of Valerian's persecution. Rebillard, however, has recently called that argument into question, so we must be cautious in assessing their historical reliability. Despite this uncertainty, however, we remain reasonably well informed about the content of Valerian's two decrees.[29]

The first, issued in August 257, directed provincial authorities to summon Christian bishops and require them to worship the gods by performing certain unspecified cult acts. Dionysius provides a detailed account of his encounter with the deputy prefect of Egypt, and the longer *Acts of Cyprian* contains a similar report of Cyprian's encounter with the proconsul of Africa. Both stress the centrality of cult acts in these exchanges, although in Dionysius's account, theological questions loom large as well; neither account specifies what cult acts are at issue. According to Dionysius, he and several colleagues were brought before the deputy prefect Aemilianus, who informed them that the emperors would release them if they were willing "to turn to that which is according to nature (τὸ κατὰ φύσιν) and worship (προσκυνεῖν) the gods that preserve their empire and forget those that are contrary to nature (παρὰ φύσιν)." Dionysius replies that not all men worship all gods and asserts that he and his colleagues worship the one God and pray to him for the emperors and their empire. Aemilianus asks why they cannot worship that god along with the others, "for you were ordered to reverence (σέβειν) gods, and gods whom all know." When Dionysius refuses, Aemilianus exiles him to a remote part of Libya. The account of Cyprian's encounter with the proconsul Paternus is similar, although in it, the standard invoked is not what is in accordance with nature but what is properly Roman. Paternus says to Cyprian, "The most sacred emperors Valerian and Gallienus have deigned to send me a letter, in which they have ordered that those who do not cultivate

---

29. Dionysius: Euseb. *Hist. eccl.* 7.10–11; Cyprian: *Ep.* 80–81 and cf. 76–79. *Acts of Cyprian*, longer version: *BHL* 2037a = Musurillo 1972, no. 11 = Rebillard 2017, 238–45 (whose numbering of the text I use in my citations); shorter version: *BHL* 2039 = Rebillard 2017, 248–51; Pontius's life of Cyprian: Rebillard 2017, 204–35. For the early date and general reliability of the *Acts*, see, e.g., Barnes 2010, 78–82; *contra*, Rebillard 2017, 198–201. On the persecution of Valerian, see the detailed study of Schwarte 1989 and, more briefly, Selinger 2004, 83–95, and G. Clarke 2005, 637–46.

Roman piety (*non Romanam religionem colunt*) should acknowledge Roman ceremonies (*Romanas caerimonias recognoscere*)." Cyprian responds that he is a Christian and a bishop and thus acknowledges only the one true God, to whom he prays for the well-being of the emperors. After ascertaining that Cyprian will not change his mind, Paternus exiles him to a small coastal town northeast of Carthage. In both texts, the Roman officials go on to inform the bishops that the emperors also forbid Christians to assemble or enter their cemeteries; later evidence indicates that cemeteries and other community property were confiscated.[30]

Two points are worth noting in connection with Valerian's initial decree. First, in contrast to the decree of Decius, there is no evidence that it affected anyone other than Christians; only Christian leaders were summoned and ordered to worship the gods. Moreover, in addition to requiring certain actions, as Decius's decree had, it also forbade Christians to engage in certain other actions, which Decius's decree had not. In both respects, Valerian's decree seems to have been explicitly anti-Christian in a way that Decius's decree was not. Its goal, we may infer, was to undermine the standing of Christians as a distinct group and to pressure them instead to reintegrate into the wider society. Second, there is no evidence for mass compliance with the decree, such as is attested for Decius's decree, perhaps because it was directed primarily at Christian leaders. No stories survive of bishops or other clergy performing the requested acts of worship. On the contrary, although both Dionysius and Cyprian went into exile as ordered, their own subsequent writings make it clear that Christians continued to maintain their communities and their sense of themselves as a distinct group.[31]

It was presumably because the decree was not achieving its intended effects that in the summer of 258, the senate wrote to Valerian, by now in the east preparing for war with Persia, to request further guidance. Cyprian had sent men to Rome to gather information, and in a letter to his fellow bishop Successus in August 258, he reported on what he had learned. Valerian had directed that all Christian clergy were to be put to death; Christian men of

---

30. Dionysius: Euseb. *Hist. eccl.* 7.11.6–11; see further Driediger-Murphy 2017, who assesses the reliability of the report and rightly stresses the theological dimension of the exchange. Cyprian: *Acta Cypr.* (*BHL* 2037a) 1, trans. Rebillard 2017; although there has been much debate over the precise meaning of the phrase *Romanas caerimonias recognoscere* (most recently, Freudenberger 1978 and Heberlein 1988), the crucial importance of Roman cult practices is clear. Assemblies and cemeteries: Euseb. *Hist. eccl.* 7.11.10–11; *Acta Cypr.* 1.7.

31. See Dionysius ap. Euseb. *Hist. eccl.* 7.11.12–17 and Cypr. *Ep.* 76–81; cf. Pont. *VCypr.* 12.2 and 13.12–13 and *Acta Cypr.* (*BHL* 2037a) 4.3; see further G. Clarke 2005, 641–42.

high social status were to forfeit their rank and property and, if they persisted in their adherence, likewise be put to death; Christian women of high status were to have their property confiscated and be exiled; Christians in the imperial household were to lose their property and be sent in chains to work the imperial estates. According to the *Acts of Cyprian*, clergy were given one last chance to comply with the initial edict before being sentenced to death. The new proconsul of Africa, Galerius Maximus, again declares to Cyprian that "the most sacred emperors have decreed that you perform the rite (*caerimoniari*)." After Cyprian steadfastly refuses to do so, the proconsul formally sentences him to death: "For a long time you have lived with a sacrilegious mind, and you have gathered around you men of a criminal conspiracy (*nefariae . . . conspirationis*), and you have set yourself up as an enemy to the Roman gods and our sacred laws, and the pious and most sacred emperors Valerian and Gallienus and Valerian the most noble Caesar have not been able to recall you to the observance of their sacred rites (*nec . . . ad sectam caerimoniarum suarum revocare potuerunt*). And therefore, since you have been arrested as the instigator and standard-bearer of a most vile crime, you yourself will serve as an example to those whom you have gathered around yourself in your wickedness: discipline shall be confirmed by your blood." The fact that Pontius quotes some of the key phrases from this speech in his life of Cyprian suggests that it may be a fairly faithful version of what the proconsul actually said. If so, it is striking how much emphasis he places on the characterization of Cyprian as the ringleader of a criminal conspiracy, one defined by a refusal to participate in normative cultic behavior.[32]

As we have seen, Valerian's decrees differed fundamentally from Decius's in that they were concerned solely with Christians; their goal was apparently to undermine Christian associations both by forcing their leaders to conform to normative forms of worship and by banning communal activities and confiscating property. At the same time, they also maintained the overall goals of Decius's decree. Valerian's measures similarly assume that the inhabitants of the empire have an obligation to engage in a certain style of worship; as with Decius, being Roman entails certain cultic obligations. The complete absence in our sources of any reference to specific cult acts makes it impossible to know exactly what it was that their interrogators wanted Dionysius and Cyprian to do. Although we may infer from this that Valerian, unlike

---

32. Valerian's second decree: Cypr. *Ep.* 80.1.1–2; date: G. Clarke 1984–89, 4.296–97. Final trial and sentence: *Acta Cypr.* (*BHL* 2037a; cf. *BHL* 2039) 3.3–5, trans. Rebillard 2017; Pontius, *VCypr.* 17.1.

Decius, did not put any special emphasis on animal sacrifice, it seems equally safe to assume that, given the Decian precedent, animal sacrifice would have been an acceptable option. As I have suggested, however, Christian leaders in the wake of Decius's decree had become much more rigorous in emphasizing the dire consequences of participation in any form of idolatry, which they insisted was tantamount to a denial of one's Christian identity. In such a context, Valerian's decrees created a situation in which Roman and Christian allegiance, as defined primarily by cult acts (although not necessarily animal sacrifice in particular), were effectively set in a mutually exclusive opposition to each other: what Roman emperors demanded Christian leaders forbade.

This stalemate, however, was soon resolved. In the summer of 260, Valerian's war with Persia ended disastrously when the emperor himself was captured in battle; later Christian writers gleefully recount the humiliations that his Persian captors inflicted on him before finally putting him to death. His son Gallienus, it seems, lost little time in repealing his father's anti-Christian measures. Our only evidence comes from Eusebius, who reports that when Gallienus became sole emperor, he "immediately" (αὐτίκα) issued edicts ending the persecution. As proof, Eusebius quotes a letter that Gallienus sent to Dionysius and other bishops, apparently in response to a request that he intervene on their behalf against people who were refusing to restore confiscated Christian property as mandated by an earlier imperial directive: "I have given my order that the benefit of my bounty should be published throughout all the world, to the intent that they [i.e., the illegal occupiers] should depart from the places of worship (ἀπὸ τῶν τόπων τῶν θρησκευσίμων), and therefore you also may use the ordinance contained in my rescript (τῆς ἀντιγραφῆς τῆς ἐμῆς τῷ τύπῳ χρῆσθαι δύνασθε), so that none may molest you. And this thing which it is within your power to accomplish has long since been conceded by me; and therefore Aurelius Quirinius, who is in charge of the Exchequer, will observe the ordinance given by me." For good measure, Eusebius also cites another imperial directive, addressed to other bishops, granting them permission to recover their cemeteries.[33]

As T. D. Barnes has argued, these documents suggest that Gallienus's actions amounted in practice to more than a simple repeal of his father's anti-Christian measures; by guaranteeing the right of Christian groups to own property and to engage in group activities without interference, Gallienus, in effect, extended official recognition to Christian associations for the first

---

33. Euseb. *Hist. eccl.* 7.13, trans. J. E. L. Oulton, Loeb.

time.[34] For our purposes, the most important implication of this recognition is that it severed the link between animal sacrifice and allegiance to Rome that Decius's decree had created. Christians, for whom the categorical rejection of animal sacrifice and other traditional cult acts had become an increasingly crucial marker of their self-identification as Christians, could now remain Roman subjects in good standing without compromising their place in their Christian community. Allegiance to the Roman Empire was made independent of religious allegiance, and animal sacrifice was consequently no longer a distinctive marker of being a good Roman.

Thanks to this policy of official neutrality in matters of religious adherence, Christians seem to have become increasingly well integrated into Roman society over the next forty years. Yet animal sacrifice remained an issue. Even if the practice was in decline, it nevertheless continued to be an unavoidable element of public life, so that Christians in public positions might be faced with difficult choices.[35] This is precisely the situation implied by an intriguing though problematic text, the canons of the council of Elvira (Latin Illiberis, modern Granada in Spain). Canons 2–4 deal with Christians who hold the position of *flamen* (a public priest, usually of the emperor) and take a very strict line on sacrifice: those who have sacrificed (*sacrificaverunt*) after baptism may never again receive communion, even at the point of death; those who have presided over games but did not actually sacrifice (*non immolaverint*) may receive communion at the point of death, provided that they have done penance; *flamines* who have been catechumens and have abstained from sacrifices (*a sacrificiis abstinuerint*) may be baptized after three years.[36] It is possible that some emperors may have made special provisions to allow Christians to hold public office while exempting them from practices they found unacceptable; Septimius Severus had done this for Judaeans about a century before.

---

34. Barnes 2010, 97–105.

35. Eusebius (*Hist. eccl.* 7.15 = Musurillo 1972, no. 16) preserves the story of a Christian soldier named Marinus, who, when he was in line for promotion to centurion, was accused by a rival of not sacrificing to the emperors and, on refusing to recant, was executed. Eusebius seems to date the episode to the reign of Gallienus (260–268), although Barnes (2010, 106–7) suggests that it may, in fact, date to the reign of Valerian.

36. Canons 2–4 of Elvira: Hefele 1907, 222–24. It is generally agreed that the council took place in the early fourth century, although the precise date is debated; the issue of dating is further complicated by a debate over the nature of the text, which some scholars see as a composite that in its current form dates to the sixth century or even later; for reviews of scholarship, see Streeter 2006 and Lázaro Sánchez 2008. I follow the analysis of Meigne 1975, especially 373–74, who identifies the first twenty-one canons as the work of the original council, which met sometime in the period 300–303 CE; for the date, see further Barnes 1981, 314n108.

Eusebius, waxing eloquent about the freedom and security that Christians enjoyed prior to the persecution of Diocletian, claims that emperors even entrusted Christians with positions as governors, while "freeing them from anxiety concerning sacrifice (τῆς περὶ τὸ θύειν ἀγωνίας)."[37] We have little to go on other than these hints, but in any case, the new order did not last very long.

## 9d. Diocletian and the Tetrarchs

When the emperor Numerian died in November 284, the head of his bodyguard, a man named Diocles, was acclaimed as his successor; he soon assumed the more suitably imperial appellation of Gaius Aurelius Valerius Diocletianus. At the time, very few observers could have predicted that he would not be simply another in what was by then a long succession of short-lived soldier-emperors but would reign for twenty years and, in the process, help bring about a fundamental transformation of the Roman Empire. As is paradoxically so often the case, the man who effected so many radical changes seems to have had markedly conservative inclinations, especially in matters of religion, and it was he and his colleagues who, after a period of more than forty years, once more made the practice of animal sacrifice a pressing issue. A brief survey of the broader historical developments will set that in its proper context.

Although Diocletian's immediate predecessors had made some headway in re-establishing the security and stability of the Roman Empire, serious challenges remained. Diocletian seems to have realized early on that it would take more than one emperor to address them effectively, and so in July 285, he proclaimed his fellow officer Maximian as Caesar, a ruler second in rank to Diocletian as Augustus. After Maximian had led several successful military campaigns, Diocletian promoted to him to Augustus. In theory, the two Augusti were equal in rank, although a distinction in seniority was implied in the epithets they assumed: Diocletian was Jovius, linking him to Jupiter, whereas Maximian was Herculius, invoking Jupiter's son Hercules. Diocletian eventually found that even two emperors were not enough to meet all threats in person, and so on March 1, 293 he established a system that modern historians conventionally describe as the Tetrarchy, the "rule of four." He and Maximian each took on a junior emperor, a Caesar, men named Galerius and Constantius, respectively, who likewise became Jovius and Herculius. The

---

37. Septimius Severus: Ulpian in *Dig.* 50.2.3.3; cf. Linder 1987, 103–6. Eusebius: *Hist. eccl.* 8.1.2.

concord of the four emperors was a key element of Tetrarchic ideology, constantly emphasized both in texts and visually in coins and monuments. The Tetrarchic system not only allowed for a more widespread imperial presence but also addressed the perennial problem of succession, since the Caesars were already in place to succeed the Augusti. In practice, the Tetrarchs divided the empire into two halves, with Maximian and Constantius in charge of the western empire and Diocletian and Galerius the eastern; over time, there was a tendency for each emperor to have a more or less defined area under his control. After some severe health issues, Diocletian put the new system to the test in 305, when on May 1, both he and Maximian abdicated. Constantius and Galerius became Augusti in turn, with men named Severus and Maximinus Daia installed as their respective Caesars.

In the absence of Diocletian's authority and force of will, however, the Tetrarchic system soon broke down, and the next several years saw a complex series of civil wars and political maneuvers as various aspirants to rule jockeyed for position. Only a few points are pertinent for our purposes. A major problem was the fact that Maximian and Constantius both had grown sons who had been excluded from the succession. Given the strength of dynastic claims, especially with the army, it is not surprising that when Constantius died in July 306, his troops immediately proclaimed his son Constantine as emperor. Troops stationed in Rome responded by doing the same for Maximian's son Maxentius. Severus was soon eliminated, but it took six years before Constantine was able to defeat Maxentius and establish himself as sole emperor of the western empire. The turmoil in the west prompted Galerius to attempt a new settlement of the empire, and in November 308, he appointed another seasoned military officer, Licinius, as a second Augustus in the east. After a long illness, Galerius himself died in spring 311, and Licinius and Maximinus divided his territories between them. By this point, Constantine and Licinius had established an alliance, and just as Constantine was eventually able to defeat Maxentius, so, too, Licinius in the spring of 313 defeated Maximinus. The empire was thus once again divided into two halves, with Constantine as ruler in the west and Licinius in the east.

Although Diocletian's Tetrarchic system did not long survive his abdication, many of the other changes he made to the administration of the empire did and were often taken further by his successors. Already in the third century, it seems, emperors had begun to subdivide provinces into smaller administrative units, and Diocletian pursued this policy systematically, so that by the early fourth century, the number of provinces had almost doubled. Not only did the number of governors increase significantly, but each governor's staff increased as well, allowing for a much higher level of direct administration by imperial bureaucrats. The multiplication of provinces in turn led to an increase in senior administrators to supervise them, just as the existence of four emperors required the existence of four separate imperial courts. In the same period, the army also significantly expanded in size, in order to meet the need for both a permanent standing border guard and a mobile strike force. The significant increase in the army and the imperial bureaucracy meant that the expenses of the central government were greater than ever, which in turn made it necessary to channel more wealth from local municipalities to the imperial government. The Christian writer Lactantius, although hardly an objective judge, claims that those receiving government funds began to exceed the number of those paying into them. Not surprisingly, many members of the local elite seem to have been keen to move from the latter to the former category.[38]

The Tetrarchic period also saw the revival of systematic attempts to suppress Christianity and promote participation in the traditional worship of the gods, in what has conventionally been termed the "Great Persecution." As with the earlier measures of Decius and Valerian, our knowledge of the events comes almost entirely from the accounts of contemporary Christian writers, Lactantius and Eusebius, supplemented by a few documentary sources and some later martyr acts. Lactantius, a native of North Africa, was summoned by Diocletian sometime before 303 to teach Latin rhetoric at his capital of Nicomedia in what is now northwestern Turkey, where he witnessed at first hand the outbreak of the persecution. Around 305, he returned to the west, although he may have returned to Nicomedia in 313; late in his life, he served as tutor to Constantine's eldest son Crispus. For our purposes, his most important work is his treatise *On the Deaths of the Persecutors*, *De Mortibus Persecutorum*, which, as the title suggests, is a polemical account of the fates of emperors who had persecuted Christians. Although Lactantius includes brief notices of earlier emperors such as Nero, Decius, and Valerian, the text is for the most part a detailed account of the Tetrarchs and their measures, and he seems to have completed it not long after the persecution ended, probably in 315. Eusebius of Caesarea, on the coast of what is now Israel, was one of the most important Christian writers of the early fourth century. He became bishop of Caesarea about the time the persecution finally ended in 313 and so was well placed to see its effects on his community and gain access to

---

38. Lact. *Mort.* 7.3. For the reign and reforms of Diocletian, the account of A. Jones 1964, 37–76, remains valuable; for a recent overview, see Rémy 2016.

copies of official documents. His *History of the Church*, which we have already encountered several times, contains a mass of information found nowhere else and is particularly valuable thanks to his practice of quoting verbatim from earlier texts that are no longer extant. The date of composition has been much debated, especially of the later books; in its current form, it must date to 324/325, although it is usually thought that Eusebius worked on it over a number of years and published more than one edition. Books 8 and 9 are devoted to his account of the Great Persecution. Also important is his much shorter treatise *On the Martyrs of Palestine*, in which he recounts the events of the persecution in his hometown of Caesarea and its environs. The latter text is found in two different forms, a longer recension that survives most fully in a Syriac translation and a shorter recension that survives in the original Greek and has some connection with Book 8 of his *History of the Church*. Both Lactantius and Eusebius quote relevant imperial decrees and letters, Eusebius in Greek translations of the original Latin, but only the later decrees that ameliorated or reversed the persecution, not the earlier ones that initiated and expanded it. For those, we have to rely on the two writers' statements about their contents and effects.[39]

The initial anti-Christian measures were limited to people in imperial service; Eusebius speaks in rather vague terms of a persecution in the army, while Lactantius includes members of the imperial household as well. He also recounts a very specific incident that, he claims, was the reason for the persecution (*causa persequendi*). When Diocletian was presiding over a sacrifice of cattle (*immolabat pecudes*), some of his attendants made the sign of the cross in order to ward away the evil *daimones* which, as we have seen, Christians believed thronged around animal sacrifices. As a result, the *haruspices*, a class of traditional diviner, were unable to read the signs in the entrails and blamed their failure on the presence of profane men. In a fury, Diocletian first ordered everyone in the court either to sacrifice (*sacrificare*) or be beaten; he then sent instructions that all soldiers offer sacrifice or face discharge. Given Lactantius's close connections with Diocletian's court, it is likely that his account reflects a story that was accepted at the time.[40]

---

39. Lactantius: e.g., Barnes 2010, 115–19. Eusebius: Johnson 2014, 18–24; date of *Hist. eccl.*: Johnson 2014, 20–21, 104–12; *Mart. Pal.*: see the very different views of Barnes 2010, 119–24, 387–92, and Johnson 2014, 108; in what follows, I cite the short recension (*BHG* 1193). For concise overviews of the whole sequence of imperial actions, see de Ste. Croix 2006 [1954], 35–38, and Mitchell 1988, 111–15.

40. Eusebius: *Hist. eccl.* 8.1.7 and 8.4.1–4. Lactantius: *Mort.* 10.1–5; cf. *Div. inst.* 4.27.4–5; "cause of persecution": *Mort.* 9.12. The date is uncertain. Eusebius provides no indication at all,

The general persecution began on February 23, 303, when Diocletian ordered his soldiers to destroy the main church in Nicomedia. On the following day, an edict was posted that ordered all church buildings destroyed, all copies of scriptures and liturgical books burned, all communal property confiscated, and all Christian assemblies banned; in addition, Christians of high status lost their legal privileges, and freedmen in imperial service were returned to slavery. A second edict followed, probably in the spring or early summer, which ordered the arrest of all Christian clergy; according to Eusebius, the prisons became so crowded with bishops and priests that there was no longer room for common criminals. A third edict, issued probably in connection with the celebration of Diocletian's *vicennalia* on November 20, 303, provided some relief by authorizing the release of clergy who performed a sacrifice. Eusebius includes a vivid description of the lengths to which presiding officials went in order to gain compliance: "one man was brought to the abominable and unholy sacrifices by the violence of others who pressed round him, and dismissed as if he had sacrificed (ὡς τεθυκώς), even though he had not; another who did not so much as approach or touch any accursed thing, when others had said that he had sacrificed, went away bearing the false accusation in silence. . . . Another stoutly maintained that he had not sacrificed, and never would. Nevertheless these also were struck on the mouth and silenced by a large band of soldiers drawn up for that purpose, and with blows on their face and cheeks driven forcibly away." Lastly, a fourth edict, issued probably in the early spring of 304, ordered that (in Eusebius's words) "everyone publicly, city by city, sacrifice and offer a libation to idols (πάντας πανδημεὶ τοὺς κατὰ πόλιν θύειν τε καὶ σπένδειν τοῖς εἰδώλοις)."[41]

Despite the ideological emphasis on the unanimity of the emperors, the extent to which they enforced the various edicts in the territories under their

---

but Lactantius locates it between the defeat of the Persian king Narses in 298 (*Mort.* 9.7) and Diocletian's spending the winter of 302/3 in Bithynia (*Mort.* 10.6; for the relevant chronology, see Barnes 1982, 55–56, 63); most scholars accept a date around 299 or 300.

41. First edict: Lact. *Mort.* 13.1 (cf. 12.1–2 for the date); Euseb. *Hist. eccl.* 8.2.4 and *Mart. Pal* pr. 1. Second and third edicts: Euseb. *Hist. eccl.* 8.2.5 and *Mart. Pal.* pr. 2; cf. *Hist. eccl.* 8.6.8–10, with the reference to the crowded prisons. *Vicennalia*: Lact. *Mort.* 17.1; cf. de Ste. Croix 2006 [1954], 37–38. Enforcement of third edict: Euseb. *Hist. eccl.* 8.3.2–4, more or less equivalent to *Mart. Pal.* 1.4–5. Fourth edict: Euseb. *Mart. Pal.* 3.1; cf. the martyrdom of Agape, Eirene, and Chione (*BHG* 34 = Musurillo 1972, no. 22), in which the presiding official repeatedly demands that they sacrifice in accordance with imperial decrees (e.g., 3.4, 5.2, 6.3) and which gives the date of Eirene's death as April 1, 304 (7.2). See Corcoran 1996, 179–82, for an overview. Schwarte 1994 argued that there was only a single edict that ordered the destruction of Christian churches and scriptures and at the same time imposed universal sacrifice, but his arguments have not been widely accepted; see *contra* Löhr 2002, 75–86.

control varied dramatically. All four emperors promulgated the first edict, although Constantius allegedly refrained from all but a token enforcement. There is general agreement that neither the second nor the third edict was promulgated in the western empire but much debate about the fourth edict. The prevailing opinion is that in the west, it was probably not promulgated and certainly not enforced, although there is some evidence to the contrary. The weightiest is an account of the martyrdom of a woman named Crispina, who was tried before the proconsul of Africa on December 5, 304. The proconsul informs her that an imperial law requires her to sacrifice (*sacrificare*) on behalf of the emperors and, on her steadfast refusal to do so, orders her to be put to death. On the whole, however, the evidence indicates that if the fourth edict was enforced at all in the west, it was on a very ad hoc basis. Moreover, by the time of Crispina's trial, the persecution in the west already seems to have been winding down; hers is, in fact, the last datable martyrdom. By the time of Diocletian's and Maximian's abdication on May 1, 305, it was effectively in abeyance. Within a few years, first Constantine and then Maxentius seem to have officially rescinded the provisions of the first edict, guaranteeing Christians freedom of worship and restitution of confiscated property.[42]

In the eastern empire, by contrast, the situation was very different. The new Caesar Maximinus Daia was an enthusiastic proponent of the persecution and seems to have breathed new life into it. Within a year of taking office, he issued new directives that, in a move reminiscent of Decian procedures, required local municipal officials to ensure that everyone offered sacrifice. Eusebius describes how in his own city of Caesarea, heralds summoned the people to the temples while officials read out individual names from rolls, perhaps those used for the census. He also preserves a letter of Phileas, the bishop of Thmuis in the Nile delta, soon to be put to death himself, describing how people were given the choice either to participate in a sacrifice (θυσία) or be executed. Two or three years later, Maximinus reiterated and expanded these orders: not only were men, women, and children again required to sacrifice, but also goods for sale in the market were defiled "with the libations from sacrifices (ταῖς ἀπὸ τῶν θυσιῶν σπονδαῖς)," and guards were stationed in front of public baths in order to defile bathers "with abominable sacrifices (ταῖς

---

42. Enforcement in the western empire: de Ste. Croix 2006 [1954], 46–59; Barnes 2010, 124–26. Constantius: Lact. *Mort.* 15.7; contrast Euseb. *Hist. eccl.* 8.13.13. Crispina: *BHL* NS 1989b = Musurillo 1972, no. 24; Barnes 2010, 136–38, argues that the proconsul of Africa, when enforcing the first edict, added on his own authority the requirement that everyone sacrifice. Persecution ended by Constantine: Lact. *Mort.* 24.9; by Maxentius: Euseb. *Hist. eccl.* 8.14.1; date: Corcoran 1996, 185.

παμμιάροις ... θυσίαις)." It was perhaps around the same time that Maximinus also began to establish a new institutional framework for the traditional worship of the gods, appointing priests in every city and over them, as provincial high priests, men with distinguished public careers, to whom he assigned military bodyguards like those of provincial governors.[43]

Not much later, however, there was a dramatic change in the situation. According to our sources, in 310, Galerius developed a terrible disease that resisted all efforts at a cure. He evidently came to conclude that his suffering was due to the Christian god and accordingly decided to end the persecution. In an edict published in Nicomedia on April 30, 311, he explained that since Christians had obstinately resisted all his attempts to bring them back to the traditions of their ancestors and were accordingly worshiping neither the traditional gods nor their own, he once more granted them the right to exist and rebuild their meeting places. Shortly thereafter, he died. Licinius, who was soon to collaborate with Constantine in advancing the Christian cause, presumably upheld Galerius's edict within his territories, leaving Maximinus as the only emperor still committed to the persecution. Although Maximinus did not openly reject Galerius's edict, he limited his promulgation of it as much as he could and soon, it seems, devised an effective workaround. He made it known that he would welcome and even reward petitions from individual cities requesting the authority to expel Christians from their communities, and he responded to them in rescripts whose virtually identical wording suggests that, as Eusebius asserts, Maximinus had orchestrated the whole process. Although increasing pressure from Constantine and Licinius eventually caused him to repeat his lukewarm assertions of noninterference with Christians, his actions soon ceased to matter one way or the other. On April 30, 313, he was roundly defeated by Licinius at a battle near Adrianople in what is now the European part of Turkey; he fled to Asia Minor and not long after committed suicide. Licinius took command of Maximinus's army, marched to the capital Nicomedia, and on June 13, 313, published a letter in which he set forth the policy that he and Constantine had agreed upon when

---

43. Maximinus's initial directives and the scene in Caesarea: Euseb. *Mart. Pal.* 4.8. Eusebius dates it to the "third year of the persecution"; since Eusebius dates the beginning of the persecution to March 303 (*Hist. eccl.* 8.2.4), the third year would begin in March 305. Letter of Phileas: Euseb. *Hist. eccl.* 8.10.2–10 (= Musurillo 1972, no. 26a); his martyrdom: Euseb. *Hist. eccl.* 8.9.7–8, and Chapter 10, n. 2. Maximinus's later directives: Euseb. *Mart. Pal.* 9.2; he seems to date them to the seventh year of the persecution, thus, March 308 to March 309. Municipal and provincial priests: Euseb. *Hist. eccl.* 8.14.8–9 and 9.4.2–3; cf. Lact. *Mort.* 36.4–5, who, however, dates this initiative after Galerius's death; Belayche 2011 argues that these measures involved a reinforcement of existing structures rather than a new organization.

they met some four months previously in Milan. This letter, conventionally but misleadingly known as the "Edict of Milan," extended to the former territory of Maximinus the policies already in place in the rest of the empire: all people, Christians and non-Christians alike, were granted "open and free permission to follow their own religion and worship as befits the peacefulness of our times, so that each man may have a free opportunity to engage in whatever worship he has chosen"; in addition, Christians were guaranteed full restitution of any property that had been confiscated. With that, the "Great Persecution" finally came to an end.[44]

What prompted the persecution in the first place is a question that has been much debated. As we have seen, the imperial government had by the early fourth century maintained a de facto policy of neutrality toward Christians for more than forty years, during which time ecclesiastical organization had expanded and Christians had become increasingly well integrated into the wider society. The motivations behind Diocletian's decision to revert to a policy of active suppression have thus long invited speculation. Without canvassing all the arguments that have been advanced, I will here note only two particular issues that loom large in the debates. One concerns who was really behind the persecution. According to Lactantius, the real motivating force was Galerius, who manipulated and pressured his senior colleague into issuing the edicts. Constantine, however, later portrayed Diocletian himself as the main instigator and says nothing about Galerius. Since both men were fairly close to the center of power, there has been little scholarly agreement on how to assess their allegations. A more important question concerns the possible impact of philosophical discourse. Several scholars have argued strongly that philosophical objections to Christianity, especially those of Porphyry, helped shape Diocletian's anti-Christian measures. The key evidence again comes from Lactantius, who claims that two anti-Christian polemicists, of whom one was a philosopher and the other a judge, played an important part in the persecution. Although he does not provide any names, scholars have long suggested that the philosopher was Porphyry, who wrote a lengthy

---

44. Galerius's illness, recantation, and edict: Lact. *Mort.* 33.1–35.1, Euseb. *Hist. eccl.* 8.16–17. Maximinus's limited promulgation: Euseb. *Hist. eccl.* 9.1.1–6, with Corcoran 1996, 148–49; contrast Lact. *Mort.* 36. Petitions and rescripts: Euseb. *Hist. eccl.* 9.1–7, who provides a translation of Maximinus's rescript to Tyre (9.7.3–14); parts of the Latin originals sent to two towns in Asia Minor are known from inscriptions: Mitchell 1988; cf. Corcoran 1996, 149–52. Pressure from Constantine and Licinius and Maximinus's response: Euseb. *Hist. eccl.* 9.9.12–13 and 9.9a.1–12, with Corcoran 1996, 187–88. Licinius's defeat of Maximinus and the "Edict of Milan": Lact. *Mort.* 47–48, Euseb. *Hist. eccl.* 10.5.2–14, with the quotation from Lact. *Mort.* 48.6, trans. Creed 1984; see further Corcoran 1996, 158–60, and Barnes 2011, 90–97.

treatise against the Christians that remained notorious for generations to come. Yet even if we grant that he played a role in promoting the persecution, it seems unlikely, given what we know about his views on animal sacrifice, that he would have been directly involved in shaping measures mandating universal participation in the practice.[45]

Whoever was ultimately responsible for the persecution and whatever their underlying motivations, we can make some reasonably secure deductions about their immediate goals from the measures themselves and, where we have them, the words of the imperial pronouncements. The initial goal, it seems, was the destruction of Christian institutions, just as it presumably had been for Valerian. The provisions of the first edict were aimed at eradicating Christian associations and making it less attractive for those of high status to self-identify as Christians, while the second aimed at eradicating Christian leadership. Starting with the third edict, however, we can also observe a concern with enforcing a particular mode of worship, which again seems to have been an underlying concern for Valerian. The extant imperial decrees confirm the importance of this concern. Since we lack the texts of the edicts that initiated the persecution, we have no direct information about the way the emperors who issued them framed their measures. We do, however, have the wording of the later decrees of Galerius and Maximinus, which gives us insight into how those emperors publicly presented their intentions, at least retrospectively. Galerius's deathbed "edict of toleration" is particularly valuable, not only because we have the original Latin text but also because Galerius, however we assess his specific role, was closely associated with Diocletian at the time the persecution began. According to Galerius, he and his colleagues had wanted "to set everything right in accordance with the ancient laws and public discipline of the Romans (*iuxta leges veteres et publicam disciplinam Romanorum*) and to ensure that the Christians too, who had abandoned the way of life of their ancestors (*parentum suorum reliquerant sectam*), should return to a sound frame of mind." Such willfulness and foolishness had taken hold of them "that they no longer followed those usages of the ancients (*illa vetera instituta*) which their own ancestors (*parentes eorundem*) perhaps had first instituted"; consequently, the emperors had issued an order "that they

---

45. Debate over the causes of the persecution: Löhr 2002, 86–95. Role of Galerius: Lact. *Mort.* 11 and 14; contrast Eusebius, who in only one passage indicates awareness of a "story" that Galerius was the one responsible (*Hist. eccl.* 8.app.1). Constantine on Diocletian: Euseb. *Vit. Const.* 2.50–51. Role of Christian polemicists: Lact. *Div. inst.* 5.2. Recent contributions to the debate over the role of Porphyry: Schott 2008, 76–78, 177–85; Digeser 2012, 164–91; Johnson 2013, 21, 286–99; Greenwood 2016.

should betake themselves to the practices of the ancients (*ad veterum se instituta conferrent*)." The focus here is on ancestral tradition, closely associated with Roman rule, from which Christians have deviated and to which the imperial decrees were meant to cause them to return. Maximinus's praetorian prefect Sabinus uses similar language in the letter he wrote to provincial governors, conveying to them Maximinus's instructions in the wake of Galerius's edict: the emperors have "for a long time determined to lead all men's thoughts into the holy and right path of life, so that those also who seemed to follow customs foreign to the Romans (ἀλλοτρίᾳ Ῥωμαίων συνηθείᾳ) should perform the acts of worship due to the immortal gods (τὰς ὀφειλομένας θρησκείας τοῖς ἀθανάτοις θεοῖς)." In his own letters, Maximinus himself seems to have laid more stress on the latter notion than on ancestral tradition. In his rescript to petitions for permission to expel Christians, he dwells at length on "how excellent and splendid and saving a thing it is to draw nigh to the worship and sacred rites of the immortal gods (τῇ θρησκείᾳ καὶ ταῖς ἱεροθρησκείαις τῶν ἀθανάτων θεῶν) with due reverence," and in his letter to Sabinus, in which under pressure from Licinius and Constantine he distances himself from the persecution, he claims that he acted as he did only because the senior emperors "rightly gave orders that all men who deserted the worship of their gods, the immortal gods (τοὺς ἀπὸ τῆς τῶν αὐτῶν θεῶν τῶν ἀθανάτων θρησκείας ἀναχωρήσαντας), should be recalled to the worship of the gods (εἰς τὴν θρησκείαν τῶν θεῶν) by open correction and punishment."[46] Much of this language is reminiscent of that in the exchanges between Dionysius and Cyprian and the Roman officials in the Valerianic persecution.

Maximinus never defines what characterizes this worship of the gods, just as Galerius does not specify what constitutes the institutions of the ancestors. Judging from their actions, however, we may reasonably suppose that for the Tetrarchs, its most characteristic and essential act was sacrifice, and animal sacrifice in particular. Lactantius and Eusebius agree on its prominent, even central, part in the enactment of the persecution, although its place in their narratives differs significantly: Lactantius portrays sacrifice as a chief concern from the very start, whereas in Eusebius's account, it comes to prominence only later. Lactantius alone includes the story of the failed cattle sacrifice that led to the order for members of the household and soldiers to sacrifice. Moreover, he begins his account of the way Galerius incited Diocletian to the

---

46. Galerius: Lact. *Mort.* 34.1–3, trans. Creed 1984; note, however, the cogent argument of Woods 2010 that the actual author of the edict was not Galerius but pro-Licinius officials in his court. Sabinus: Euseb. *Hist. eccl.* 9.1.3; Maximinus: 9.7.7 and 9.9a.1, trans. J. E. L. Oulton, Loeb.

persecution by explaining that Galerius himself was incited by his mother, a superstitious woman who used to sacrifice almost daily and offer banquets to her neighbors; she hated Christians because they ostentatiously abstained. Lactantius rounds off his account by asserting that although Galerius finally persuaded Diocletian to initiate a persecution, Diocletian nevertheless tried to moderate it by rejecting Galerius's proposal that those who refused to sacrifice be burned alive (*cum Caesar vivos cremari vellet qui sacrificio repugnassent*). If we can trust Lactantius on this detail (and it is not clear that we can), it would appear that a requirement to sacrifice was discussed as a potential component of the first edict. Animal sacrifice is thus a virtual leitmotif in Lactantius's account of the persecution's origin, whereas Eusebius has nothing to say about it at all. It is likely that Lactantius in Nicomedia knew more about the early stages of the persecution than Eusebius in Caesarea; even if he is unreliable on specific details, he gives us insight into the perceptions of contemporary observers.[47]

In contrast, Lactantius's account of the later stages of the persecution differs markedly from and is generally less detailed than that of Eusebius. Lactantius claims that Galerius, feeling that the first edict against the Christians did not go far enough, arranged for men to start a fire in the imperial palace in Nicomedia for which he then blamed the Christians and thereby manipulated Diocletian into taking further action. He describes this later stage of the persecution in vague terms, writing of widespread executions, imprisonments, and tortures, of judges scattered throughout the temples who forced everyone to sacrifice. He does, however, include one interesting detail that we can corroborate from another source. According to Lactantius, altars were placed in council chambers and before judges' tribunals, "so that litigants would first sacrifice (*sacrificarent*) and thus plead their cases." As it happens, we have a papyrus letter from Oxyrhynchus in Egypt in which a Christian named Copres explains to his "sister" Sarapias (probably his wife rather than a sister by blood) how he has learned that those appearing in court are being forced to sacrifice and that he has accordingly arranged for his brother to have power of attorney so that they can proceed with their "case about the land." Since Lactantius associates this requirement with the later stages of the persecution, we should perhaps understand it as part of the fourth edict, although it

---

47. The failed sacrifice and its consequences: Lact. *Mort.* 10.1–5 (summarized at *Div. Inst.* 4.27.4–5); Galerius's mother: 11.1–2; Galerius's proposal: 11.8.

is tempting to suppose that he was hazy on chronology and that it was instead connected with the first edict's provisions on legal privileges.[48]

Eusebius, on the other hand, very clearly demarcates the later stages of the persecution, with new imperial directives initiating different phases: the second and third edicts that focused on Christian clergy, the fourth edict that mandated universal sacrifice, and the two initiatives of Maximinus to enforce the fourth edict more systematically.[49] Although his account makes it clear how important a part sacrifice played in these measures, at least from the third edict on, it is rarely clear what precisely was meant by "sacrifice." Virtually all the textual sources use the verbs θύειν or *sacrificare*, neither of which necessarily denotes animal sacrifice as opposed to other types of offerings. In fact, the acts of Crispina depict the proconsul, after repeatedly demanding that she sacrifice, eventually explaining that he is merely asking that "in the sacred temples with bowed head you offer incense (*tura immoles*) to the gods of the Romans." Another martyr narrative, however, that of Agape, Eirene, and Chione of Thessalonica set in the early spring of 304, indicates that in this instance, "sacrifice" meant specifically animal sacrifice, since the presiding official repeatedly demands that they sacrifice to the gods and "eat the sacrificial offering (ἱερόθυτον φαγεῖν)." Since the account of Crispina is set in the western empire, where the fourth edict may have never been enforced, whereas that of Agape is set in territory directly controlled by Diocletian and Galerius (whose main residence was, in fact, in Thessalonica), the latter more likely reflects the specific requirements of the decree, although the latitude that officials had in carrying out imperial measures means that different officials no doubt felt free to interpret it in different ways.[50]

Lastly, there is evidence that in the last stages of the persecution, Maximinus was as concerned with animal sacrifice as Diocletian and Galerius,

---

48. Lactantius's account: *Mort.* 14–15, with 15.5 on sacrifices before court cases; Copres: *P.Oxy.* XXXI.2601, with Luijendijk 2008, 216–26.

49. It is worth noting that it is only in *Martyrs of Palestine* that Eusebius recounts the full sequence (*Mart. Pal.* pr. 1–2: first three edicts; 3.1: fourth edict; 4.8 and 9.2: Maximinus's initiatives); in *History of the Church*, he mentions only the first three edicts (*Hist. eccl.* 8.2.4–5 and 8.6.10).

50. Crispina: *BHL* NS 1989b = Musurillo 1972, no. 24, at 2.1. Agape and companions: *BHG* 34 = Musurillo 1972, no. 22, at 3.1; cf. 3.4 (τῶν ἱερῶν μεταλαβεῖν), 3.5, and 5.2; the text dates the death of Eirene, which closes the narrative, very precisely to April 1, 304 (7.2; cf. 1.2). Since many details conform closely to what we know of the persecution from other sources, it is generally regarded as historically reliable (e.g., Barnes 2010, 140–41), even though the names of the martyrs ("Love, Peace, and Snowy") seem a little too good to be true. Role of officials: Corcoran 1996, 245–53, 295.

according to Lactantius, had been at the start. Eusebius describes how the second of Maximinus's measures meant to enforce the fourth edict more systematically required people not only "to sacrifice and pour a libation (θύειν καὶ σπένδειν)" but also "to taste the sacrifices (ἀπογεύεσθαι θυσιῶν)." Given that Eusebius was presumably an eyewitness, writing for an audience that included other eyewitnesses, his evidence about this detail is probably reliable. Although Lactantius says nothing about these later measures, he attributes to Maximinus an almost obsessive concern with animal sacrifice: not only did he make it a practice to sacrifice in the palace on a daily basis, but he also made sure that "all the animals on which he fed were slaughtered not by cooks, but by priests before their altars (*non a coquis, sed a sacerdotibus ad aras immolarentur*), and nothing at all was laid on his table unless an offering had been made from it or it had itself been offered in sacrifice or drenched in pure wine." Although we might be tempted to dismiss this as a lurid Christian rumor, it accords well enough with traditional practice that there is no reason to regard it as far-fetched.[51]

Taken together, Lactantius and Eusebius thus provide reasonably secure evidence that animal sacrifice figured largely in the Tetrarchic persecution throughout its duration, in terms of both the personal interests of the emperors involved and the planning and enactment of the persecution. Moreover, we can find confirmation of the importance of animal sacrifice in Tetrarchic ideology in the visual sources. Although images of emperors as sacrificants had never entirely disappeared from coinage, it became increasingly sparse after the middle of the third century. In the 290s, however, it makes a sudden and notable reappearance. For example, the practice of commemorating imperial *vota* with issues of coins featuring the emperor as sacrificant, which had flourished from Hadrian to Caracalla, was revived for Diocletian's and Maximian's *decennalia* in 293, with a series of coins featuring on the reverse images of the two Augusti facing each other and pouring libations over a brazier. This image of imperial concord, one of the key components of Tetrarchic ideology, was to prove popular. The mint at Trier issued a gold series that featured the same scene on the reverse, with the legend FELICITAS TEMPORUM, "the blessedness of our times"; the mint at Ticinum used a similar image with a legend that literally spelled

---

51. Eusebius: *Mart. Pal.* 9.2. Lactantius: *Mort.* 37.1–2, trans. Creed 1984; cf. 37.5, where, in describing Maximinus's practice of confiscating people's property, he asserts that "herds of sheep and cattle were seized from the fields for daily sacrifices, by which he so corrupted his men that they spurned their grain ration."

**FIGURE 9.1.** Coin of 294–295 CE, reverse: the Tetrarchs offering a libation over a tripod (*OCRE* Antioch 33b), Münzkabinett, Staatliche Museen, Berlin.

Münzkabinett–Staatliche Museen zu Berlin/Creative Commons, CC BY-SA 4.0

out its message: CONCORDIA AVGG ET CAESS, "the concord of the Augusti and Caesars." Most striking of all, and by far the most common, was a reverse type scene that illustrates that concept precisely (see Figure 9.1): all four emperors around a tripod, two on either side, pouring libations, while the obverse features busts of all four individual emperors in rotation. This type, with various reverse legends (in the example shown here, VICTORIAE SARMATICAE, "for the victory over the Sarmatians"), was issued by mints across the empire, east as well as west (in our example, Antioch), during the period 294–299.[52]

---

52. *Decennalia*: *RIC* 5.2[1] = OCRE Diocletian and colleagues nos. 109–11, 466–67, 485–86, and 702, all *antoniniani* from the mints at Lugdunum and Trier; the revival had been anticipated by Diocletian's predecessor Carus in 283–285 (*RIC* 5.2[1] = OCRE Carus nos. 315–16 and 461). Felicitas: *RIC* 6[1] = OCRE Treveri nos. 27 and 35 (cf. no. 617, which depicts Constantius and Galerius); Concordia: *RIC* 6[1] = OCRE Ticinum no. 1. Four emperors: *RIC* 6[1] = OCRE

Equally striking is the reappearance of sacrifice scenes on major public monuments, for the first time, as far as we know, since the reign of Septimius Severus. Two such scenes are extant. In Thessalonica, as part of a monumental complex that included both his residence and his future mausoleum, the emperor Galerius constructed a highly elaborate arch with eight piers, of which only two piers survive. This arch, built probably around 300 to commemorate Galerius's victory over the Persians in 297, is densely covered with relief panels depicting the campaigns and related scenes. The panel that most concerns us depicts Galerius in military uniform pouring a libation over a lit altar; he is attended by a number of divine personifications, and the victim, a bovine, is shown to his right.[53] The other extant scene comes from Rome, where the emperors constructed a highly elaborate monument at the western end of the Forum, the ancient center of the empire, which consisted of five monumental columns capped with statues and supported by bases adorned with elaborately carved relief panels; the statues most likely represented Jupiter flanked by the four emperors. Three inscriptions, two recorded in the Renaissance but now lost, indicate that the monument was erected to celebrate the *vicennalia* of Diocletian and Maximian on November 20, 303, with which was associated the *decennalia* of Constantius and Galerius. The only surviving part of the monument is one of the column bases, with a relief that depicts two Victories carrying a shield with the inscription *Caesarum decennalia feliciter*, "the Caesars' *decennalia*, with blessings"; it is as a result conventionally known as the "Decennalia Base." On the opposite side is a scene of an emperor, presumably one of the Caesars, pouring a libation over a tripod, accompanied by two of the usual sacrificial attendants, as well as a man wearing an *apex*, a distinctively archaic Roman priestly head covering, and two figures wearing togas; the sacrificant is being crowned by Victoria and faces Mars on the opposite side of the altar (see Figure 9.2). The reliefs on the flanking side panels depict, to the right, a procession of figures wearing togas and carrying banners and, to the left, the bull, ram, and pig of the ancient rite of the *suovetaurilia*. The imagery is thus highly traditional and almost ostentatiously Roman and employs visual conventions that date back to the late republican Altar of Domitius Ahenobarbus. It is likely that the sacrificial imagery was equally

---

Treveri nos. 100–133, Ticinum nos. 12a–19, Rome nos. 10a–42b, Siscia nos. 32a–62, Heraclea nos. 1–11, Nicomedia nos. 18–20, Cyzicus nos. 4–6, Antioch nos. 31–33b, Alexandria nos. 7a–8.

53. Ryberg 1955, 139–40 with fig. 76; Rothman 1977 (the sacrifice scene is B.I.17 in her analysis).

FIGURE 9.2. Altar scene from the Decennalia Base, 303 CE, Forum, Rome.
HIP/Art Resource, NY

present on at least one of the other bases of the monument, but we know almost nothing about them.[54]

Although a scarcity of evidence does not allow us to determine how prominent a place animal sacrifice had in Tetrarchic visual imagery, the little that does survive provides some confirmation of the ideological importance that the literary sources attribute to it. Coins and monumental reliefs alike attest to the close connection that sacrificial imagery had with one of the central elements of Tetrarchic ideology, the unanimity of the four emperors, and also attest that such imagery was already well established in the decade prior to the persecution. The reliefs of the Decennalia Base further attest to its ongoing importance during the persecution itself, since the monument of which

---

54. Ryberg 1955, 117–19 with figs. 61a–b; L'Orange 1973 [1938]. Inscriptions: *CIL* VI.1203–1205 = EDCS 17700494; the two now lost read *Augustorum vicennalia feliciter* and *Imperatorum vicennalia*. Date of *vicennalia*: Lact. *Mort.* 17.1.

it formed a part was dedicated after the persecution was well under way; as noted earlier in this section, several scholars have argued that the third edict, which required Christian clergy to sacrifice and be released, was issued in connection with the celebration of the same imperial anniversary that the monument was built to commemorate. Why did animal sacrifice have such importance for the Tetrarchs, especially if in the wider society its importance was on the wane? We should first of all note that its importance for the Tetrarchs complicates any simple narrative of its decline. We may also observe that animal sacrifice was part of a larger constellation of images and practices that evoked ancestral and more specifically Roman tradition and was thus associated with the Tetrarchs' well-documented cultural and religious conservatism. I would suggest, however, that the importance of animal sacrifice in Tetrarchic ideology also resulted in part from the developments of the past half century, which caused animal sacrifice to function as a privileged signifier of self-identification with the Roman Empire and its traditions in ways that previously it had not. It is now time to summarize those developments.

## *9e. Conclusion*

It is first of all important to keep in mind the large-scale structural changes that were taking place in this period. Increasing economic pressures and an apparent shift in the priorities of municipal elites over the course of the third century are likely to have weakened the role that animal sacrifice played in structuring the socioeconomic hierarchies of Graeco-Roman cities. Diocletian's reform of the bureaucracy and the army accelerated this process further. By transferring more of the weight of imperial governance from local municipalities to centralized institutions, he significantly reduced the need for social practices that helped maintain local hierarchies and link them to imperial ones, as animal sacrifice had done. At the same time, the increasing centralization of governing structures, along with increasing economic pressures, helped encourage a shift of local elites from municipal careers to imperial ones, where they would be free of the heavy burdens that a municipal career now entailed. As a result, they not only had fewer resources to fund public animal sacrifice but less motivation to do so. In these circumstances, the organic connections that animal sacrifice had had with imperial society and culture were significantly eroded.[55]

---

55. Shift in weight of governance: e.g., Van Andringa 2014, 9: "Avec les événements du IIIe s., on est passé d'une forme historique du polythéisme à une autre qui n'était plus articulée, ou moins

Seen in this broader context, Decius's and (perhaps) Valerian's attempts to enforce animal sacrifice as the defining feature of a common standard of worship appear clearly as deeply conservative, even reactionary, measures. At the same time as animal sacrifice was losing its long-established sociopolitical role, emperors seized on its cultural significance as a marker of shared values and norms. The work that public animal sacrifice did in forging ties between local traditions and the Roman Empire, something that in the past had been left to the initiative of local elites, now became the object of an official policy that emperors tried to enforce from above. Not only did their attempts fail, however, but they also had the unintended consequence of intensifying the Christian rejection of the practice. Although demonological discourse had long provided Christian leaders with the intellectual grounds for that rejection, it was the practical challenges presented by the enforcement of Decius's and Valerian's measures that endowed it with such ideological weight; as a result, the rejection of animal sacrifice acquired increasingly important implications for the way Christians articulated their identity as Christians. Even after Gallienus's repeal of Valerian's anti-Christian measures eliminated the practical challenges, allowing Christian networks to expand and assume a more secure and prominent place in Roman society, the ideological weight attached to the rejection of animal sacrifice remained intact and perhaps, as I have argued, even increased.

In many ways, the events of 303–313 seem a repeat of those of 250–260: imperial measures aimed at enforcing animal sacrifice and other traditional cult practices as an obligation to the empire were followed by others that repealed and reversed them. Nevertheless, the larger framework had shifted in subtle yet significant ways. The greatly increased prominence of Christianity in Roman society had had the effect of reifying traditional cult as a specific religious option and no longer simply the shared practice of humanity. We can observe this most clearly in the carefully balanced phrasing used by Licinius in his letter of 313 proclaiming religious freedom: he and Constantine, he writes, have made arrangements "so that we might grant both to Christians and to all men (*et Christianis et omnibus*) freedom to follow whatever religion each one wished," "whether he wished to give his mind to the observance of the Christians or to that religion (*vel observationi Christianorum vel ei religioni*) which he felt was most fitting to himself."[56] Christianity and

---

qu'avant, sur l'organisation des cités." Shift of local elites from civic to imperial careers: A. Jones 1964, 69–70; cf. Pont 2020, 240–45, 331–34.

56. Lact. *Mort.* 48.2 and 3, trans. Creed 1984.

traditional cult here appear as two more or less equivalent alternatives, what modern observers would describe as two different religions. Thus, while we can understand the measures of Diocletian, Galerius, and Maximinus as another attempt to establish animal sacrifice as a marker of self-identification with the Roman Empire, the cultural framework within which they were operating was already shifting to one wherein animal sacrifice signaled identification with a specific religious tradition. That was a shift that Constantine, as I argue in Chapter 10, deliberately reinforced.

# 10

# From Roman to Pagan

## CONSTANTINE TO THEODOSIUS I (313–395 CE)

### 10a. Introduction

Despite the trauma that Diocletian's persecution undoubtedly inflicted on Christians throughout the empire, especially in the east, it did not result in any significant new developments in Christian discourses of animal sacrifice. Rather, it reinforced already established trends. Elite authors, for example, continued to elaborate on the demonological discourse first established by Justin Martyr. One culmination of that development was the extensive discussion of animal sacrifice that Eusebius included in his treatise *Preparation for the Gospel*, written in the years 312 to 324. Relying heavily on Porphyry, whose treatise on abstinence he quotes at length, Eusebius argues with great force and a fair amount of repetition that Greek philosophers themselves acknowledge that the beings to which they offer animal sacrifices are *daimones*, not gods, and that *daimones*, contrary to Porphyry's division of them into good and bad, are always and by definition evil; it was God's grace, working through his son the savior, that delivered humanity from the sway of these maleficent beings.[1] In addition to texts such as these, written by and for a highly educated elite audience, other texts such as martyr acts continued to signal the evils of animal sacrifice for a wider audience. Many martyr acts

---

1. Euseb. *Praep. evang.* 4.4–23; see Johnson 2014, 19, for the date and 25–46 for a concise overview of the treatise; for a more detailed treatment, see Kofsky 2002, especially 118–23 on sacrifice. The critique of animal sacrifice that Arnobius includes in the seventh and last book of his treatise *Against the Nations*, written probably in the period 302–305, provides a striking contrast, since Arnobius makes no use at all of the demonological discourse but instead relies on a critique of the anthropomorphic conception of the gods that extends back to Xenophanes: Arn. *Adv. nat.* 7.1–25, with 7.34 on anthropomorphism; date: Simmons 1995, 47–93.

featured heroes and heroines who, like those discussed in Chapter 9, vividly and dramatically enacted the principle that participation in animal sacrifice was fundamentally incompatible with self-identification as a Christian.[2] That principle accordingly became more firmly fixed and widely accepted, something that had significant consequences when Roman emperors began to ally themselves with Christian leaders and publicly identify as Christians.

At the same time, the ongoing structural changes in the organization and administration of the Roman Empire had an even more dramatic impact on the practice of animal sacrifice. As we saw in Chapter 9, the disruptions of the mid-third century likely resulted in an increase in the financial burdens of local elites and a weakening of civic euergetism. Diocletian, although in many ways quite successful in addressing the underlying challenges that beset the empire, did so in ways that further accelerated that process. His vast expansion of the army and the imperial bureaucracy greatly increased the financial needs of the central government, needs that were inevitably met by diverting wealth from local municipalities. As a result, many members of the local elites began to look more to the imperial bureaucracy than to their hometowns as the chief locus for their careers. The cumulative effect of these developments on public animal sacrifice must have been significant. Most obviously, it became more and more difficult to fund traditional local festivals with their costly sacrifices: not only did the funding provided by individual benefactors decrease, but public funds likewise became increasingly scarce. Less obvious but perhaps even more significant was the shift in power away from largely self-governing cities dominated by local elites to a centralized empire in which the most attractive roles for the wealthy and the ambitious were as agents of the imperial state. In this context, the ideological work that public animal sacrifice had traditionally done in fashioning and reinforcing local sociopolitical hierarchies became increasingly superfluous. In short, the practice of animal sacrifice, which as I argued in Chapter 3 had once been an important source of ideological power and played a valuable role in the workings of the empire, became less and less relevant.

It is within this wider context that we must consider developments under the Christian emperors of the fourth century. Animal sacrifice continued to

---

2. See, e.g., the accounts of Julius the Veteran (*BHL* 4555 = Musurillo 1972, no. 19), Irenaeus the Bishop of Sirmium (*BHL* 4466 = Musurillo 1972, no. 23), Euplus (*BHG* 629 and *BHL* 2728 = Musurillo 1972, nos. 25A and B), and Phileas (*BHG Auct.* 1513k and *BHL* 6799 = Musurillo 1972, no. 27, with Barnes 2010, 142–46, and Bremmer 2020).

be a focus of imperial policy, as it had become with Decius, but to very different ends. Beginning with Constantine, emperors issued laws that in various ways castigated, restricted, or even prohibited the practice of animal sacrifice, as part of a larger pattern of what is generally termed "anti-pagan" legislation.[3] We are fortunate that in tracing these developments, we can draw extensively on the actual texts of imperial decrees. A significant amount of imperial legislation has been preserved, more or less in the form in which it was originally issued, in the great collection of laws known as the Theodosian Code. This compilation was the product of a panel of legal scholars working at the behest of the emperor Theodosius II, who in 429 decreed that "a collection shall be made of all the laws that were issued by the renowned Constantine, by the divine emperors after him, and by us, and which rest upon the force of edicts or sacred imperial law of general force." He directed that the editors should include all laws, even those superseded by later legislation, and preserve them in their original form, with two qualifications: they were to omit rhetorical elaboration deemed irrelevant to the substance of the law, and they were to divide up laws that touched on more than one topic so as to include different passages under the relevant rubric. Theodosius renewed the initiative in 435 under a new panel of scholars, and the completed work was officially published in 438.[4]

While the Theodosian Code adds immeasurably to our knowledge of developments in the fourth and early fifth centuries, we must keep in mind its limitations. First, although the goal was a comprehensive collection of all imperial laws from the reign of Constantine to the time of publication, practical limitations meant that the reality fell short. The editors could include only laws of which they were able to find copies, but no complete archive existed anywhere in the empire. Subscriptions to some of the laws included in the Code indicate that the editors drew on both local and central records, suggesting that they attempted to be as thorough as possible, but even so, their collection was incomplete. We have unambiguous evidence for important laws that do not appear in the Code, and it is very likely that there was

---

3. Among recent surveys, Curran 2000, 161–217, and Sandwell 2005 provide good overviews of the period covered in this chapter; Delmaire 2004 and Belayche 2005 both focus on sacrifice; Corcoran 2015 surveys its broader context.

4. Original commission: *Cod. Theod.* 1.1.5; renewal: *Cod. Theod.* 1.1.6; publication: *Nov. Theod.* 1. All quotations from the Theodosian Code are in the translation of Pharr 1952, sometimes lightly adapted.

other legislation of which we now know nothing. Moreover, the emperor's instructions to omit superfluous verbiage required the editors to decide which words in a given law were mere rhetorical embellishment and which were substantive. Given that the effect of these laws was to some extent as much rhetorical as what we might regard as strictly legal, their decisions must at times have involved some nice distinctions. Another limitation has to do with the nature of imperial legislation more generally. Many of the laws included in the Theodosian Code were not the result of independent imperial initiative but rather responses to particular inquiries; such responses were, strictly speaking, applicable only to the region from which the inquiry originated. In addition, even those charged with applying the law could act on a piece of legislation only if they were aware of it, and in the conditions of the ancient world, that was a much more uncertain business than it is today. Once the imperial bureau responsible for such matters had drafted a new law, a copy had to be sent to the relevant party; if the recipient was an imperial official, he would post it in a public place and, if appropriate, send copies to lower officials for posting elsewhere. Laws were normally posted on perishable material, which meant that they had a limited life span; once the posted copy was no longer legible, interested parties had to rely on copies that they themselves or someone else had made and kept for their own reference. All this is to emphasize that we must be cautious in assuming that the effect of the laws that we encounter in this chapter was as comprehensive and systematic as that of laws in modern states.[5]

Keeping in mind these provisos, this chapter surveys imperial policy on animal sacrifice from Constantine's initial alliance with Christian leaders down to Theodosius I, who in the early 390s effectively outlawed all forms of traditional cult. The legal status of animal sacrifice fluctuated over the course of this eighty-year period. At first tolerated, then restricted and perhaps banned outright by Constantine, it was explicitly prohibited by his sons and successors. His nephew Julian, the last member of his family to rule, was an enthusiastic proponent of Greek tradition in its religious as well as cultural dimension and did his best to restore animal sacrifice to a central place in the empire. Julian's early death put an end to his program of revival, and thereafter the legal status of animal sacrifice seems to have been uncertain for about

---

[5]. See Matthews 2000 for a comprehensive study of the Theodosian Code, especially 55–71 on the process of editing, 168–99 on the life cycle of imperial legislation, and 280–93 on the sources; more briefly, Delmaire in *LRER* 1.13–35.

thirty years, until Theodosius I issued a comprehensive ban. Yet underlying these fluctuations of restriction, prohibition, and promotion, I argue, there was a steady shift in the social and cultural significance of animal sacrifice, its transformation from a marker of a particular sociopolitical identity, that of a Roman imperial subject, to a marker of a newly constructed religious identity, that of a pagan.

This argument requires a brief preliminary discussion of terminology and conceptual categories. The word "pagan," as commonly applied to people in the ancient Mediterranean world who were neither Judaeans nor Christians, denotes an inherently Christian category. Although Greeks and Romans employed a range of words to distinguish different modes or traditions of worshiping the gods, these were typically national or ethnic; they had no need of a generic term to denote all those modes collectively in distinction with some other category, for the simple reason that there was no other category. Judaeans, however, with their strong ideology of exclusive devotion to a unique god, did make such a division and denoted all non-Judaeans by a term that was translated into Greek as *ta ethnē*, "the peoples." Early Christians inherited this division but triangulated it by differentiating themselves from Judaeans as well as from *ta ethnē*. In this process, they gradually fashioned a new way of categorizing peoples less by their national or ethnic affiliation and more by their practices and beliefs about the divine, in which all the highly diverse adherents of traditional forms of worship other than Judaean were reconceptualized as a homogeneous mass to which a single collective label could be applied. The one that eventually became standard in English was the Latin *paganus*, a term that originally denoted an inhabitant of a country district or *pagus*. What we now call paganism was thus in effect a Christian construction, predicated on a distinctively Christian discourse about the cosmos as the site of a supremely good God opposed by inherently evil *daimones*; pagans, by worshiping these powers as gods, aligned themselves with cosmic evil. As Christian leaders acquired increasing political power and social influence over the course of the fourth century, the Christian division of humanity into Christians, Judaeans, and pagans, groups recognizable to modern observers as adherents of different religions, became more and more culturally dominant. Adherents of traditional modes of worship soon began to feel the need for a nonderogatory term to refer to themselves, of which the most important was "Hellene" or "Greek." Although this is a highly schematic sketch of a highly complicated development, it is enough to signal that all these terms were closely bound up with a deeply contested reconceptualization of cultural categories, a process in which animal sacrifice played a significant role. In sketching out that role, I have tried to use these labels with an awareness that they inherently reflect particular ideological assumptions and judgments.[6]

## 10b. Constantine

Constantine came to power amid the collapse of the Tetrarchy, which had functioned as well as it did largely because of Diocletian's force of will. Although Constantine's father, Constantius, succeeded Maximian as the western Augustus, he died in Britain not much more than a year later, in July 306, whereupon his troops promptly proclaimed his son Constantine Augustus. Through a series of strategic maneuvers, Constantine was able to build up his power to the point where by 310, he was in a position to challenge Maxentius, his remaining rival in the western empire, for control of Italy and North Africa. In the fall of 312, he defeated Maxentius at the battle of the Milvian Bridge north of Rome. Constantine later claimed that prior to the battle, he had had a dream in which the Christian God had guaranteed his victory.[7] Meanwhile, control of the eastern empire was being contested by Galerius's former Caesar Maximinus and former co-emperor Licinius, with whom Constantine struck an alliance. In February 313, the two met at Milan, where, among other things, they decided to extend to the eastern empire the official recognition that Christians in the territories ruled by Constantine already enjoyed. After the defeat and death of Maximinus in the spring of 313, Licinius publicly announced the new policy in the letter that is misleadingly known as the "Edict of Milan." Relations between Constantine and Licinius remained fraught, however, and after a series of conflicts and fragile reconciliations, Constantine decisively defeated Licinius in the summer of 324, at which point he took control over his territories in the east and became sole ruler of the entire empire. Constantine continued as sole emperor, supported by shifting configurations of sons and male relatives, until his death in May 337.[8]

---

6. On these developments, see the elegant article of Massa 2017. On terminology, see especially Remus 2004 and Cameron 2011, 14–32; it is important to note that the use of the term "Hellene" to mean an adherent of traditional religion is also Christian in origin.

7. The two main sources are Lact. *Mort.* 44.5 and Euseb. *Vit. Const.* 1.28–32. Among the many discussions, see most recently Barnes 2011, 74–80, and Lenski 2016, 69–71.

8. For a recent narrative account of Constantine's life and reign with exhaustive documentation, see Barnes 2011; more briefly, Lenski 2012.

The precise nature of Constantine's relationship to Christianity is one of the most debated topics in Roman history, but it is not necessary here to enter into the debate. I note only that his views seem to have evolved during the period between the defeat of Maxentius in 312 and the defeat of Licinius in 324. It is clear that from the start, he acted as a patron and ally of Christian leaders and was willing to involve himself in their disputes with one another. At the same time, he did not eschew all connections with traditional Graeco-Roman cult; traditional deities continued to appear regularly on his coinage into the 320s, and several scholars have argued cogently that he maintained an association with the personified Sun to the end of his life.[9] Starting in the 320s, however, his partiality to Christianity seems to have been increasingly matched by a hostility to traditional cult. What primarily concerns us here is the bearing that his policies and actions had on the practice of animal sacrifice. The policy outlined in the letter of Licinius, which may, in fact, reflect his own views more than those of Constantine, establishes an equality between Christians and non-Christians: both alike are guaranteed the right to pursue whatever form of worship seems best to them, without hindrance or interference. In this context, animal sacrifice, which as a result of earlier imperial measures had become so closely bound up with religious allegiance, could be neither promoted nor castigated. It was no longer a practice required of all Romans but rather an expression of personal religious self-identification. The question is how far Constantine, after his defeat of Licinius, went in the other direction, by actively restricting or even fully banning it. Although the evidence is contradictory, some points are clear enough.[10]

First of all, we know that by the mid-320s, Constantine was willing to express his abhorrence of animal sacrifice in public documents. In a letter to Macarius, the bishop of Jerusalem, dating probably to around 325, he reports that his mother-in-law had informed him that pagan cult practices were taking place at Mamre near Hebron, a site long associated with the patriarch Abraham: "Idols fit only for absolute destruction have been set up beside it, she explains, and an altar stands nearby, and foul sacrifices (θυσίας ἀκαθάρτους) are constantly conducted there."[11] Constantine orders that the idols and altar be destroyed and replaced by a Christian basilica and that anyone offering

---

9. Coinage: Christodoulou 1998; the Sun: Wallraff 2001 and Bardill 2012, especially 89–109; briefly, Lenski 2016, 48–51.

10. The following incorporates work that appeared in earlier form in Rives 2012.

11. Euseb. *Vit. Const.* 3.53.1; all passages from this text are quoted in the translation of Cameron and Hall 1999, sometimes lightly adapted. The date is certainly after the defeat of Licinius in 324 and probably before the death of Constantine's wife Fausta in 326: Cameron and Hall

sacrifice there in the future be punished. Although we might expect such condemnation in a letter to a Christian bishop, he uses equally strong language in a letter to the Persian emperor Shapur II, likewise dating probably to the mid-320s, in which he pointedly declares that in his own worship, he shuns "all abominable blood and foul hateful odors (αἷμα βδελυκτὸν καὶ ὀσμὰς ἀηδεῖς καὶ ἀποτροπαίους)."[12] Lastly, in his speech "to the Assembly of Saints," probably also dating to the mid-320s, he declares to imagined pagan auditors, "Away with you, impious ones (for this command is laid on you on account of your incorrigible sin) to the slaughter of sacrificial victims (ἐπὶ τὰς τῶν ἱερείων σφαγάς), your feasts and festivals and drunkenness, as you profess to offer worship while you devise unbridled pleasures and debaucheries, and pretend to make sacrifice (θυσίας μὲν ἐπιτελεῖν σκηπτόμενοι) while you are in thrall to your own pleasures."[13] All this suggests that by the mid-320s, Constantine's aversion to animal sacrifice was both firmly established and widely known.

It is likely that around this same time, Constantine dramatically refused to preside over an important public animal sacrifice in the city of Rome. The historian Zosimus, writing c. 500, reports that on the occasion of an ancestral festival (which he does not otherwise identify), Constantine aroused the anger of the senate and people by refusing to ascend with the army to the Capitol and perform the customary rites; although Zosimus does not say so explicitly, the context suggests that these rites included animal sacrifice. Zosimus's account may receive some confirmation from the fourth-century rhetorician Libanius, who also refers to an occasion when the people of Rome became angry at Constantine, although he says nothing about the cause.[14] The date at which this episode took place is uncertain. Zosimus dates it to 326, but since he connects it to an account of Constantine's conversion that cannot be taken at face value, some scholars have argued that he changed the date for polemical purposes. Constantine was indeed in Rome in 326 for the delayed observance of his *vicennalia* and is known to have been there on only

---

1999, 300. On cultic activities at Mamre, see further the description of Sozomen, *Hist. eccl.* 2.4, who specifies offerings of wine, incense, and animal victims.

12. Euseb. *Vit. Const.* 4.10.1; the text we have is a Greek translation of the Latin original. Date: K. Smith 2011, 45–46.

13. Constantine, *Coet. Sanct.* 11.7, in the translation of Edwards 2003, adapted; see also 16.1; our text, preserved as Book 5 of Euseb. *Vit. Const.*, is again a Greek translation of a Latin original (Euseb. *Vit. Const.* 4.32). Most scholars accept a date in the mid-320s, although Edwards himself (2003, xxiii–xxix) argues for a date shortly after Licinius's defeat of Maximinus in 313; see further Barnes 2011, 113–20.

14. Zos. 2.29.5; cf. Lib. *Or.* 19.18–19 and 20.24.

two other occasions: immediately after his defeat of Maxentius in 312 and for his *decennalia* in 315. His visit in 312 is an unlikely context for this incident, since on that occasion, relations between Constantine and the people of Rome were apparently very positive. Also weighing against a date in the 310s is the Arch of Constantine, probably begun in 312 and dedicated to mark his *decennalia* in 315, which incorporates material from earlier monuments, notably a series of reliefs honoring Trajan, Hadrian, and Marcus Aurelius that had their faces recarved to represent Constantine and his imperial colleagues. Perhaps surprisingly, some of these reused reliefs depict the emperor presiding over sacrifices. For example, a panel from a lost monument of Marcus Aurelius, discussed in Section 5c, shows the emperor making the preliminary offering for a *suovetaurilia* in a military lustration, with the three victims prominently depicted on either side of him (see Figure 10.1). We may assume that those responsible for the monument had little reason to think that Constantine would be offended by images of himself presiding over an animal sacrifice, which could hardly have been the case if he had ostentatiously refused to do so just three years earlier.[15] The reused reliefs on the arch do not preclude dating Constantine's refusal to sacrifice in 315, since by that time, it was probably nearing completion. Nevertheless, in my view, Zosimus's date of 326 is more likely to be correct, even if the narrative into which he inserts it is false; the little he says about the occasion fits well with the celebration of Constantine's *vicennalia*, and some of the details in Libanius's account fit the historical context of that year better than any other.[16] Assuming that there is any historical basis for this anecdote, it suggests an interest on the part of Constantine in publicly separating himself from the practice of animal sacrifice.

In addition to making public his own rejection of animal sacrifice, Constantine was perfectly willing to prohibit it in specific contexts. In December 320, he wrote to the prefect of Rome authorizing the public consultation of *haruspices* but added that private individuals must "abstain from domestic sacrifices, which have been specifically prohibited." In doing so, however, he was simply maintaining a long-standing prohibition of private divination, which emperors had for centuries regarded with suspicion due to its potential use in political conspiracies. More innovative are the

---

15. Date: Buttrey 1983, Pensabene and Panella 1999; iconographic program: P. Peirce 1989; those responsible: Lenski 2008.

16. Some scholars also cite Euseb. *Vit. Const.* 1.48 in support of 315, but we should be wary of interpreting too literally the highly figurative language found there. Almost every aspect of this alleged event is controversial; I rely largely on Paschoud 1971, Paschoud 1993, Wiemer 1994, and Paschoud 1997. For a more detailed account of my views, see Rives 2012, 158–60.

300 TRANSFORMATIONS OF ANIMAL SACRIFICE

**FIGURE 10.1.** Relief panel from a lost monument (an arch?) in Rome (late 170s CE?), later incorporated into the Arch of Constantine (312–315 CE): Marcus Aurelius presiding over a *suovetaurilia* in an army camp, Rome.
© Vanni Archive/Art Resource, NY

instructions that he sent in 323 to the *vicarius* of Rome, ordering that anyone who constrained a member of the clergy to participate in lustral sacrifices (*lustrorum sacrificia*) be publicly beaten with clubs or, if of higher rank, subject to a heavy fine. His purpose here, we may assume, was to keep Christian clergy pure from the contamination of a distinctively non-Christian cult practice. We may see the same purpose in his prohibition of traditional cult at the site of Mamre, which he wanted to refashion as a purely Christian site.[17] According to Eusebius, he did something similar when he refounded the ancient Greek city of Byzantium as his new capital of Constantinople in 324: "he saw fit to purge it of all idol worship, so that nowhere in it appeared those images of the supposed gods which are worshiped in temples, nor altars foul with bloody slaughter (βωμοὺς λύθροις αἱμάτων μιαινομένους), nor sacrifices offered as holocaust in fire (θυσίας ὁλοκαυτουμένας πυρί), nor feasts of *daimones* (δαιμονικὰς ἑορτάς), nor any of the other customs of the superstitious." Eusebius's account is misleading, since Constantine did not, in fact, prohibit all traditional cults in Constantinople. For example, there is good evidence that he re-established the cult of Tyche, Byzantium's chief tutelary deity, and even featured her on his coinage. At the same time, our chief source for this new cult of Tyche, the sixth-century chronographer John Malalas, specifically states that Constantine instituted it with a "bloodless sacrifice" (θυσίαν ἀναίμακτον), thereby providing some corroboration for Eusebius's assertion about the prohibition of animal sacrifice.[18] Most of these measures suggest a desire not so much to eradicate animal sacrifice altogether as to remove it from contexts that he sought to mark off as distinctively Christian. Two other specific actions, however, evince a concern to ban animal sacrifice in contexts that were not distinctively Christian: Eusebius claims that shortly after his defeat of Licinius, Constantine forbade imperial officials to offer sacrifices, and in a rescript to the Italian town of Hispellum in the mid-330s, Constantine authorized the construction of a temple in honor of his family, provided that it not be "polluted by the deceits of a contaminating superstition (*contagiosae superstitionis fraudes*)."[19] We will consider these measures in

---

17. Domestic sacrifices: *Cod. Theod.* 16.10.1; prohibition of private divination: e.g., Desanti 1990. Clergy: *Cod. Theod.* 16.2.5, with *LRER* 1.130 on date and addressee; the phrase *lustrorum sacrificia* apparently refers to the celebration of an imperial anniversary. Mamre: Euseb. *Vit. Const.* 3.51–53.

18. Constantinople: Euseb. *Vit. Const.* 3.48.2; Tyche: Malalas 13.7–8; see further Bleckmann 2012 and Lenski 2015.

19. Officials: Euseb. *Vit. Const.* 2.44. Hispellum: *CIL* XI.5265 = *ILS* 705 = EDR 136860.

more detail shortly but will turn first to the most vexed question concerning Constantine and animal sacrifice: whether he ever banned the practice altogether.

The evidence is not merely inconsistent but flat-out contradictory. Eusebius states unequivocally that Constantine prohibited sacrifice tout court: after his defeat of Licinius and assumption of rule over the eastern empire, he issued two laws (νόμοι), of which one ordered the construction of churches and the other "restricted the pollutions of idolatry . . ., so that no one should presume to set up cult objects, or practice divination or other occult arts, or even to sacrifice at all (μήτε μὴν θύειν καθόλου)." A few paragraphs later, however, Eusebius quotes at length from a public letter that Constantine issued to the people in his new territories, in which he makes statements that certainly appear to guarantee noninterference in matters of religion: "Let those in error, as well as the believers, gladly receive the benefit of peace and quiet. . . . May none molest another; may each retain what his soul desires, and practice it." Although he declares that it would be better for all to follow "the right way," "let those who hold themselves back keep if they wish their sanctuaries of falsehood (τὰ τῆς ψευδολογίας τεμένη)." He closes the letter by explicitly countering a rumor that "the customs of the temples (τῶν ναῶν . . . τὰ ἔθη) and the agency of darkness have been removed altogether. I would indeed have recommended that to all mankind, were it not that the violent rebelliousness of injurious error is so obstinately fixed in the minds of some, to the detriment of the common weal."[20] Such assurances of noninterference would seem disingenuous, to say the least, if Constantine had, in fact, just recently issued a blanket prohibition of one of those "customs of the temples" that for centuries had held a central place in traditional cult.

Later evidence merely muddies the waters further. On the one hand, a law issued by his son Constans only four years after Constantine's death threatens punishments for anyone who has dared to "perform sacrifices (*sacrificia celebrare*)" "in violation of the law (*contra legem*) of the divine emperor our father." On the other hand, the rhetorician Libanius, writing probably in the mid-380s, states just as baldly that Constantine "made absolutely no alteration in the traditional forms of worship (τῆς κατὰ νόμους . . . θεραπείας), but, though poverty reigned in the temples, one could see that all the rest of the ritual was fulfilled"; according to Libanius, it was instead Constantine's son Constantius II who first declared that sacrifices should no longer exist (μηκέτ'

---

20. Ban: Euseb. *Vit. Const.* 2.45.1; cf. 4.23 and 4.25.1. Letter to the eastern provincials: Euseb. *Vit. Const.* 2.48–60, with citations from 2.56.1–2 and 2.60.2.

εἶναι θυσίας).²¹ Not surprisingly, this dossier has led to an extended and sometimes heated debate: some insist that Constantine absolutely forbade animal sacrifice, others raise objections, and most settle for some sort of compromise, proposing that Constantine did take some sort of action but that it was more limited than Eusebius implies, or was soon abrogated, or was never really meant to be enforced.²² Although certainty is impossible, something along the lines of the last of these seems to me most likely.

More important, however, I would suggest that the whole debate is of limited significance for an overall assessment of the effect that Constantine's actions had on animal sacrifice. Since no single legal prohibition could possibly have ended the practice once and for all, it ultimately does not matter very much whether or not Constantine enacted such a prohibition. As I hope to demonstrate in the remainder of this chapter, regardless of what Constantine did, the practice of animal sacrifice did not vanish, even from the public sphere, but continued to be a living issue for decades after his death. What matters much more than any one piece of legislation is the cumulative effect of his policies, pronouncements, and priorities, not only those that were directly concerned with animal sacrifice but also, and perhaps even more important, those that were not. In order to assess the long-term effect of his reign on the place of animal sacrifice in the Roman Empire, therefore, we must broaden our view.

We may appropriately begin with what is without question the most momentous development of Constantine's reign. However we assess his personal religious commitments, there is abundant evidence that from the time of his victory over Maxentius in 312, Constantine began aggressively pursuing an alliance with Christian leaders. This alliance initiated some fundamental

---

21. Law of Constans: *Cod. Theod.* 16.10.2; the law is attributed to Constantius alone, but given that it is addressed to the *vicarius* of Italy, a region over which Constans had control, it must have originated with him: Errington 1988, 315n12. Libanius: *Or.* 30.6–7; cf. 30.37: Constantine "did not proceed against the sacrifices (οὐκ ἐπὶ τὰς θυσίας προῆλθε)"; on the value of Libanius's evidence, see further Section 10d below; all quotations from Libanius are in the Loeb translation of A. F. Norman.

22. The most forceful advocate of a blanket ban is Barnes 1981, 210–12, updated in Barnes 2011, 109–11. Objections: e.g., Cameron and Hall 1999, 20, 243–44; Curran 2000, 176–78, 185. Compromises: Errington 1988, 311–18, argues that a ban was issued but shortly thereafter rescinded; Bradbury 1994, 132–35, argues that it was issued but not meant to be strictly enforced; Sandwell 2005, 98–102, argues that it was concerned with private divination and not sacrifice as a general practice (similarly, Delmaire 2004). See most recently the balanced discussion of Lenski 2016, 231–34, who concludes that "Constantine likely did issue an edict against animal sacrifice late in 324, but one worded vaguely enough, constructed loosely enough, and enforced sporadically enough that it by no means put an immediate halt to the practice."

but highly complex changes in both the organization of the empire and the dynamics of Christian development. It gave Christian leaders access to the power of the emperor, which was more firmly based on control of economic resources and physical force and which they quickly brought to bear on their own contentious and ever-changing rivalries. Constantine was soon embroiled in these controversies, in which he consistently favored those parties whom he regarded as ideologically and institutionally the best partners for his new Roman state. The alliance between Constantine and Christian leaders also meant that Christian discourses, and the new forms of social power based on them, could now have a more direct impact on society as a whole. As we have seen, the demonological discourse of animal sacrifice, which aligned the practice very closely with the forces of cosmic evil, had motivated Christian leaders to put great emphasis on animal sacrifice as a practice incompatible with Christian adherence. Almost inevitably, then, the alliance between Roman imperial power and Christian leadership accelerated the decline of animal sacrifice in several important ways.

In the first place, Constantine not only prohibited animal sacrifice in particular contexts but also publicly castigated it. Contemporaries, in fact, may not have distinguished these two types of actions quite so sharply as we might. The structures of modern states lead us to assume that the legal prohibition of a practice entails systematic enforcement and thus has direct and immediate effects in ways that a mere expression of disapproval does not. But enforcement was generally not quite so central an aspect of imperial pronouncements in the Roman world, for the practical reason that the state lacked the means for systematic enforcement: there was no police force, no office of public prosecutors, no state-sponsored organization whose business it was to monitor compliance. (It was precisely in its mechanisms for ensuring systematic compliance that the decree of Decius had been so unusual.) Hence, the impact of laws such as the ones that we are considering here was often less immediately practical and more rhetorical, a means of communicating imperial approval and disapproval. This is not to say that such laws did not also have direct consequences but only that it was not in those consequences that their greatest impact lay.[23]

It seems likely that Constantine's strong antipathy to animal sacrifice was a matter of personal conviction as much as, or even more than, public policy.

---

23. Cf. Matthews 2000, 191: "Edicts were not only used to enact and order; they were used to announce, advise, excuse, exhort, explain, lecture, to create opinion, to respond to abuse"; see further Bradbury 1994, 134–39; Curran 2000, 165–69; Matthews 2000, 191–95.

We cannot be entirely certain of the reasons for his antipathy, however, because in the extant sources, he never explicitly states them. His tendency to emphasize the impurity of animal sacrifice and the foulness of the reeking blood certainly evokes the Christian demonological discourse.[24] Bruno Bleckmann, in contrast, has made an intriguing argument that Constantine's aversion may have owed just as much to philosophical critiques such as that of Porphyry, who similarly believed that animal sacrifice provided nourishment for maleficent *daimones*. It is thus worth noting that in none of the texts that I cited earlier in this section does Constantine explicitly refer to *daimones* in connection with animal sacrifice. Eusebius does so freely enough when referring to Constantine's actions, and he may have had reason to believe that Constantine agreed with his interpretation. Moreover, the phrase in Constantine's rescript to Hispellum cited a few paragraphs earlier, "the deceits of a contaminating superstition (*contagiosae superstitionis fraudes*)," could well be an allusion to *daimones*, whose deceitful subterfuges were so often highlighted by Christian writers and Porphyry alike.[25] It is thus likely that, one way or another, Constantine's hostility toward animal sacrifice was shaped by these contemporary discourses.

It is worth underscoring the significance of this development. Regardless of the extent to which discourses of animal sacrifice had shaped Diocletian's policy, they certainly became important under Christian emperors. The general reasons for this are obvious enough, but I would argue that there may also have been a more precise reason. To understand it clearly, we must take a slight detour to consider a law of Constantine that has no direct connection with animal sacrifice at all. Sometime in the late 310s or early 320s, Constantine wrote to the prefect of Rome to declare that those who employed magical arts against people's health or chastity are to be "punished and deservedly avenged by the most severe laws," but that charms for healing or protecting crops are not liable to criminal prosecution. As scholars have often noted, the key criterion here for determining whether a given action is licit or illicit is whether it is harmful or helpful. This was a long-established principle in Roman law and one that was maintained throughout the fourth century.

---

24. Cf. Athenag. *Leg.* 26.1 and 27.2; Tert. *Apol.* 22.6 and 23.14; Min. Fel. *Oct.* 27.2; Origen *Cels.* 3.37, 4.32, 7.5, 7.35, and *Mart.* 45.

25. Bleckmann 2012. Eusebius on *daimones*: "appeasing earthly *daimones* (χθονίους δαίμονας ἀπομειλισσόμενος)" (*Laud. Const.* 2.5); "the feasts of *daimones* (δαιμονικὰς ἑορτάς)" in his account of Constantine's prohibition of pagan cults in Constantinople (*Vit. Const.* 3.48.2). Deceits of *daimones*: Section 8c above.

Constantine's alliance with Christian leaders, however, introduced a complication. In Christian discourse, all animal sacrifice was by definition harmful, since it provided sustenance to the evil *daimones* who were the common enemies of all humanity. As we saw in Section 8c, Origen had quite logically argued that, given that fact, those who performed animal sacrifices should be equally as liable to punishment as those who provided aid and succor to brigands. Although the lack of direct evidence means that the case must remain hypothetical, we can at least identify a specific way in which Christian discourse about animal sacrifice could have had a direct impact on its legal standing.[26]

As with earlier imperial policies, however, more important than Constantine's motivations and goals are the long-term effects of his actions. For the sake of analysis, we can distinguish two ways these directly concerned sacrifice, even though in practice the distinction must have been largely blurred. First, his public disapproval of animal sacrifice in and of itself distanced animal sacrifice from what could be regarded as appropriately Roman: because the Roman emperor was in many ways the supreme embodiment of the Roman Empire, anything that he publicly abhorred would ipso facto have acquired non-Roman associations. In this regard, much more telling than his emphasis on the foulness and impurity of animal sacrifice is his characterization of it in his law decreeing punishment for those who compel clergy to sacrifice as "a ritual of an alien superstition," *ritus alienae superstitionis*. Whereas animal sacrifice had once functioned as a standard of civilization, something that could unite the varied peoples and cultures of the empire, it was now literally being "othered." We can best appreciate the implications of Constantine's language here if we contrast it with that of the proconsul in the *Acts of Cyprian*, when he explains that Valerian has ordered "that those who do not cultivate Roman religion must acknowledge Roman rites."[27]

Second, the specific actions that Constantine took against animal sacrifice worked to effect a sharp separation of animal sacrifice not only from the Christian sphere but also from the governing structures of the Roman Empire.

---

26. *Cod. Theod.* 9.16.3; for the problem of its date, see *LRER* 2.140. On the principle of harmful intent as the criterion for distinguishing between permissible and punishable acts, see Marcian at *Dig.* 48.8.3.2 and more generally Rives 2009; on its ongoing relevance in the fourth century, see, e.g., Valentinian in *Cod. Theod.* 9.16.9 (371 CE). Origen: *Mart.* 45.

27. Constantine: *Cod. Theod.* 16.2.5. Valerian: *Acta Cypr.* (*BHL* 2037a) 1.1 (*qui Romanam religionem non colunt, debere Romanas caerimonias recognoscere*).

It is in this connection that we may consider in more detail the two measures that I previously mentioned but did not discuss. According to Eusebius, shortly after his defeat of Licinius in 324, Constantine "first sent governors to the peoples in their various provinces, for the most part men consecrated to the saving faith; those who preferred Hellenic cult he forbade to sacrifice (ὅσοι δ'ἑλληνίζειν ἐδόκουν, τούτοις θύειν ἀπείρητο). The same applied also to the ranks above provincial government, the highest of all, who held office as prefects. If they were Christians, he permitted them to make public use of the name; if otherwise disposed, he instructed them not to worship idols (τὸ μὴ εἰδωλολατρεῖν)."[28] If we can accept Eusebius's account of this directive (and as we have seen, Eusebius was prone to exaggerate the anti-pagan tendencies of Constantine's measures), Constantine allowed representatives of the Roman state to present themselves publicly as Christians but not as adherents of traditional cult, at least not to the extent of presiding over animal sacrifice.

The other measure is his response to a petition from the civic leaders of Hispellum (modern Spello, in central Italy), who requested a change to the annual imperial festival that they jointly celebrated with the city of Volsinii and, in connection with that, permission to construct a new temple dedicated to the Gens Flavia, the imperial house. Constantine granted these requests but only on condition that the new temple not be polluted by the "deceits of a contaminating superstition (*contagiosae superstitionis fraudes*)."[29] There has been much debate as to whether or not Constantine was using this phrase with specific reference to animal sacrifice. Although there is no way to resolve this debate, for my purposes, it does not much matter; no one who read the phrase with any awareness of the wider context could possibly have understood it not to encompass animal sacrifice. This proviso, noted almost in passing, constituted an astonishing shift. As we saw in Section 5b, imperial cult played a crucial part in constructing the power of the Roman emperor, and it is hardly surprising that someone as savvy as Constantine appreciated its value. As we also saw, however, animal sacrifice had long played an important and distinctive part in the imagery and practices of imperial cult. Constantine now established a precedent for excising it from that context and for shaping a new version of imperial cult in which animal sacrifice had no part.

---

28. Euseb. *Vit. Const.* 2.44.

29. *CIL* XI.5265 = *ILS* 705 = EDR 136860. For important recent discussions, see Cecconi 2012 and Lenski 2016, 114–30; on the ambiguity of the term *superstitio* in the imperial legislation of the fourth century, see especially Salzman 1987.

By means of these restrictions and strategies for marginalizing the practice of animal sacrifice, Constantine effectively refashioned it as a marker no longer of public identification with Rome but of a personal allegiance to a particular religious tradition, a tradition that was rapidly losing its privileged connection with the structures of the empire. In short, animal sacrifice was coming less and less to signify "being a Roman" and more and more to signify "being a pagan." As we will see, this was a trend that would be confirmed and accelerated by all of Constantine's successors, not only committed Christians such as Constantius II and Theodosius I but also the born-again Hellene Julian. It was in this respect above all, I would argue, that the actions of Constantine that directly concerned animal sacrifice had a long-term effect on its social and cultural significance.

As I have suggested, Constantine's policies that were not directly concerned with animal sacrifice also had a significant impact, as much as or even more than those that were. In some cases, their impact is readily apparent. For example, many scholars agree that Constantine confiscated much of the wealth that temples had amassed over the years. Eusebius asserts that he stripped them of their bronze and gold ornamentation and removed their gold and silver statues; those not used to adorn Constantinople were melted down for bullion. Other sources suggest a broader confiscation of movable property that may have encompassed cash reserves and other forms of treasure. In addition, there is evidence that his confiscations also extended to the revenue-generating landholdings that we know many temples possessed. We may recall Libanius's acknowledgment that, although Constantine did not interfere with traditional cult practices, "poverty reigned in the temples." Not only did Constantine seize temple property, but he apparently also confiscated municipally owned estates. The fifth-century church historian Sozomen asserts that he appropriated the fixed revenue of civic treasuries that derived from tributary land and redirected it to the local clergy and church. Although Sozomen may have exaggerated, indirect evidence suggests that Constantine did indeed take action along these lines. Similarly, by legalizing and encouraging bequests to churches, he provided local elites with an alternative beneficiary for their munificence, one that the emperor himself ostentatiously favored. There is much about all this that remains uncertain, particularly the extent to which these developments took place in Constantine's reign as opposed to that of his sons; moreover, whatever Constantine did along these lines was more likely piecemeal and ad hoc than systematic. We can nevertheless conclude that he took actions that further undermined the ability of cities to fund their traditional local festivals and especially the associated animal sacrifices; this reduction in traditional sources of funding would have compounded the effects of the decline in civic euergetism that was apparently already under way. As Scott Bradbury has aptly noted, the more limited the funding, the more likely were available funds to be directed toward the most popular aspects of those festivals, the theatrical performances and other public spectacles, while animal sacrifice was increasingly neglected.[30]

Constantine's alliance with Christian leaders had an additional effect on animal sacrifice as well, less direct but in the long term just as significant. We need to understand this alliance not merely as a specifically religious policy but as an essential complement to his overall strategy, building on the precedent of Diocletian, of shifting the weight of governance and the allocation of resources away from local municipalities to the institutions of the centralized state. Christian leaders had by the early fourth century made considerable progress in fashioning a centralized and hierarchically organized church, with a provincial structure similar to that of the empire. Constantine further encouraged the development of this church as an ideal partner in the new empire that he was in the process of creating. It is perhaps not too much to suggest that Constantine cultivated this church as in some ways a replacement for the alliance that the imperial administration had traditionally had with local elites. The clearest indication is Constantine's ongoing policy of granting Christian clergy immunity from the burdens of serving in city councils and holding local office, which effectively structured the church as an alternative career path for local elites while at the same time shifting resources from civic to ecclesiastical institutions.[31] In these ways, Constantine and his ecclesiastical allies helped accelerate the trends that were undermining the role that animal sacrifice had traditionally played in structuring the empire.

Seen in the wider context of the cumulative effect of his actions and policies, then, the question of whether Constantine formally issued a comprehensive ban on animal sacrifice pales into relative insignificance. As I have

---

30. Eusebius: *Vit. Const.* 3.54.1–6; Libanius: *Or.* 30.6; Sozomen: *Hist. eccl.* 1.8.10; cf. Zos. 2.38.4 and, on the confiscation of precious metals and gems, *De rebus bellicis* 2; see further A. Jones 1964, 131; Delmaire 1989, 641–57; Lenski 2016, 167–78; and, for the impact of these confiscations on animal sacrifice, Bradbury 1995, 352–55. Bequests: *Cod. Theod.* 16.2.4 = *Cod. Iust.* 1.2.1.

31. Immunity to clergy: the earliest attested grant is for the province of Africa and was issued in February 313 CE, shortly after Constantine's defeat of Maxentius (Euseb. *Hist. eccl.* 10.7.1–2, with Corcoran 1996, 155; cf. *Cod. Theod.* 16.2.1 with Corcoran 1996, 162); similar grants were made to Lucania and Bruttium in southern Italy (*Cod. Theod.* 16.2.2, probably 313 CE: *LRER* 1.124–25) and the province of Numidia (*Cod. Theod.* 16.2.7, 330 CE). Shift of financial resources to the church: in general, A. Jones 1964, 894–910.

tried to demonstrate, the effect of those policies and actions was profound. His redirection of economic resources away from temples and municipalities to the centralized institutions of state and church exacerbated long-standing problems of funding public animal sacrifice. His aggrandizement of these centralized institutions over local municipalities continued the trends that were undercutting the sociopolitical significance of public animal sacrifice and rendering it increasingly otiose. Most important of all, regardless of his motivations, his public disapproval of the practice and the specific actions that he took against it furthered the process of transforming its social and cultural significance from a marker of identification with the Roman Empire to a marker of a specific religious affiliation, one that was in the process of being labeled as "pagan." In all these respects, Constantine redefined the terms of the debate over animal sacrifice for the rest of the century.

### 10c. *From the Death of Constantine to Julian*

At Constantine's death, the empire was effectively partitioned among his three sons, although the eldest of them, Constantine II, reigned only three years before he was killed in a war with his brother Constans. For the next decade, Constans ruled the western empire and Constantius II the eastern. Both maintained their father's hostility toward animal sacrifice, and indeed seem to have taken it to new levels. As we saw in the previous section, in 341, Constans issued a law to the official in charge of Italy that is both more strident in tone and more absolute in substance than anything securely attested for Constantine: "Superstition shall cease; the madness of sacrifices shall be abolished (*sacrificiorum aboleatur insania*). For if any man . . . should dare to perform sacrifices, he shall suffer the infliction of a suitable punishment and the effect of an immediate sentence." We know nothing of the circumstances that prompted Constans to issue this forceful directive, and there is no further evidence for such concerns on his part.[32]

Constans's reign lasted nine more years. In January 350, he was killed in a coup led by his general Magnentius, who assumed rule over the western empire. Although Constantius II had had no great love for his brother, he decided that his forceful replacement by a stranger was not to be tolerated, and he inflicted a massive but costly defeat on Magnentius's forces in September 351. Magnentius retreated to his power base in Gaul, abandoning Italy, and

---

32. *Cod. Theod.* 16.10.2, with n. 21 above.

after another defeat committed suicide in August 353. At some point in his brief control of Rome, Magnentius apparently issued a directive relevant to sacrifice, since a law issued to the prefect of Rome by Constantius II in November 353 states that "nocturnal sacrifices (*sacrificia nocturna*), which were permitted by the authority of Magnentius, shall be abolished, and henceforth such nefarious license shall be destroyed." We know nothing of the circumstances behind this directive, but the specification of "nocturnal sacrifices" is striking. Roman authorities had long condemned such sacrifices, which were associated with harmful magic and illicit divination, so it is difficult to imagine why Magnentius would have authorized them. Nicole Belayche has proposed that he, in fact, permitted all sacrifice and that Constantius, under the cover of recriminalizing nocturnal sacrifices in particular, actually mitigated his brother's total ban of nine years earlier by tacitly exempting sacrifices conducted during the day. Another possibility is suggested by a striking parallel from some dozen years later. In 364, after the emperors Valentinian and Valens renewed the prohibition of nocturnal sacrifices, in this case explicitly because of their association with harmful magic, the aristocratic senator Praetextatus, then proconsul of Achaea, obtained an exemption from Valentinian for Greece, so that the mysteries of Eleusis could continue to be celebrated. It is not impossible that some other member of the Roman aristocracy sought a similar exemption from Magnentius for the celebration of mysteries in Rome, of which several of those aristocrats were well-known devotees. Since Magnentius seems to have been keen to gain support from Christians and non-Christians alike, it is easy to imagine him granting such a request.[33]

Three years after his repeal of Magnentius's authorization of nocturnal sacrifices, Constantius issued two directives that reiterated his brother's total ban on sacrifice. First, in February 356, he declared that "if any persons should be proved to devote their attention to sacrifices (*operam sacrificiis dare*) or to worship images, we command that they shall be subjected to capital punishment." Then, in December of the same year, he wrote to Flavius Taurus, the praetorian prefect of Italy and Africa, ordering the immediate closure of all temples, "so as to deny to all abandoned men the opportunity to commit sin." Likewise, "it is also our will that all men shall abstain from sacrifices (*sacrificiis*

---

33. Law of Constantius: *Cod. Theod.* 16.10.5. Magnentius permitting all sacrifices: Belayche 2005, 355. Law of Valentinian: *Cod. Theod.* 9.16.7; exemption for Eleusinian mysteries: Zos. 4.3.2–3. Roman aristocrats and mysteries: e.g., Cameron 2011, 142–63. Magnentius's policy: Rubin 1998; Conti 2007.

*abstinere*)." The penalties are again dire: those found guilty "shall be struck down with the avenging sword" and their property confiscated; moreover, provincial governors who fail to take action in such cases will themselves be liable to the same punishment.[34]

Given these harsh threats, it comes as a surprise that the historian Ammianus Marcellinus, writing toward the end of the fourth century, narrates two separate anecdotes involving sacrifice from only three years later with no comment whatsoever. First, he relates that when the prefect of Rome, a man named Tertullus, was faced with a populace alarmed at the prospect of a grain shortage and on the verge of rioting, he offered a sacrifice in Ostia at the Temple of Castor and Pollux, long worshiped as protectors of seafarers; just then, the skies cleared, the seas calmed, and the grain fleet from Alexandria arrived safely and filled the granaries. Here we have the highest imperial official in Rome offering a sacrifice to traditional deities in a very public context, an act explicitly forbidden by Constantine some thirty-five years previously, apparently without any reprisals. The second anecdote concerns an elderly philosopher named Demetrius Cythras, who, amid a rash of treason trials conducted by Constantius's notoriously bloodthirsty hatchet man Paulus Catena, "Paul the Chain," was arrested on the charge of offering sacrifice to the Egyptian god Besa at his oracle at Abydos; the specific charge was clearly that of sacrificing for the purposes of illicit divination. Demetrius did not deny that he had offered sacrifice but instead insisted that he had done so his entire life, solely for the sake of propitiating the god and not with any political motivation. He was eventually released without further penalty. In this instance, we have a man who, even in a treason trial before a Roman official known to be particularly vindictive, was not punished for his practice of sacrificing to a traditional deity.[35]

It is this apparent disconnect between imperial pronouncements against sacrifice and what was actually happening that provides the strongest evidence in support of the argument that, despite what we may be inclined to

---

34. Law of February: *Cod. Theod.* 16.10.6. Law of December: *Cod. Theod.* 16.10.4 = *Cod. Iust.* 1.11.1; the date given in *Cod. Theod.* is 346, but since Taurus did not assume his office until 355, the correction to 356 is generally accepted: Belayche 2005, 355n115. Libanius (*Or.* 30.7) also asserts that it was Constantius who first banned sacrifices.

35. Tertullus: Amm. Marc. 19.10.4; Demetrius Cythras: 19.12.12; both date to 359. See also Eunapius's account of Anatolius, praetorian prefect of Illyricum in 357–60, whom he describes as "a lover of sacrifices (φιλοθύτης)" and who he says "sacrificed boldly (θύσας ... θαρσαλέως)" and went around to all the temples during a visit to Athens (*Vit. soph.* 10.6.1–10, with quotations from 10.6.3 and 8 = 490–91); date: *PLRE* Anatolius 3.

assume, the impact of such laws consisted less in their strict enforcement than in their communication of imperial disapproval.[36] As I have already argued, however, we should not for that reason underestimate their impact. These laws of Constans and Constantius II heightened the rhetoric against animal sacrifice and thereby reinforced their father's reframing of it as a non-Roman practice, the marker of an increasingly marginalized and officially castigated personal religious affiliation. It is also clear that Constantius II in particular continued and even accelerated Constantine's practice of confiscating temple property and thereby curtailing the funds needed to maintain the costly practice of animal sacrifice. We may thus fully expect that the decline of animal sacrifice continued apace, and there is evidence to indicate that this was indeed the case. The rhetorician Libanius, in defending his friend Aristophanes against the emperor Julian's anger, invoked Aristophanes's bona fides as a Hellene by recounting how he had worshiped in the temples as best he could even when it was not allowed to bring incense or a victim (ἱερεῖον) or a libation. Similarly, in his funeral oration for Julian, Libanius claimed that Julian's concern for the decline of traditional cult was his only incentive for considering the possibility of becoming emperor, because it struck his heart to see the gods' "temples in ruins, their ritual banned, their altars overturned, their sacrifices suppressed (θυσίας ἀνῃρημένας), their priests sent packing, and their property divided up between a crew of rascals."[37]

Although Libanius's claim is hardly an objective assessment of the state of traditional cults in the 350s, it certainly aligns with Julian's own perception. For example, Julian tells a story that in late 354, on his way to join Constantius at his court in Milan, he stopped to sightsee in Ilium and was so surprised to see "the altars still alight, I might almost say still blazing," in a shrine to Hector and Achilles that he asked his guide, the local bishop, whether the people of Ilium sacrifice (Ἰλιεῖς θύουσιν). As emperor, Julian several times expressed dismay at the extent to which animal sacrifice had fallen

---

36. See especially Leppin 1999, 466–74, who argues persuasively that Constantius's laws of 356 were intended to establish his anti-pagan credentials amid the "Arian" controversy of that time, since those perceived as "Arians," of whom Constantius was one, were often accused of being soft on paganism.

37. Constantius and the confiscation of temple property: Lenski 2016, 167–78. Libanius on Aristophanes: *Or.* 14.41 with Sandwell 2005, 102; on Julian: 18.21–23, quotation from 18.23, trans. A. F. Norman, Loeb. See further Bradbury 1995, 342–45. For an indirect but striking indication of the decline in the cultural importance of animal sacrifice, see Jan Bremmer's comparison of its role in the Greek novels of the earlier empire with its role in the fourth-century Heliodorus: Bremmer 2018, 216–22, 228–31.

into desuetude. While traveling from Constantinople to Antioch in the early summer of 362, he wrote to ask his friend Aristoxenus to meet him at Tyana, the old hometown of Apollonius, "and show me a genuine Hellene among the Cappadocians. For I observe that, as yet, some refuse to sacrifice, and that, though some few are zealous, they do not know how to sacrifice (οὐκ εἰδότας δὲ θύειν)." Most strikingly, in the satirical rebuke that he wrote against the people of Antioch for their hostility toward him, he relates his anticipation in visiting the great shrine of Apollo located outside the city: "I imagined in my own mind the sort of procession it would be, like a man seeing visions in a dream, beasts for sacrifice (ἱερεῖα), libations, choruses in honor of the god, incense, and the youths of your city there surrounding the shrine, their souls adorned with all holiness and themselves attired in white and splendid raiment. But when I entered the shrine I found there no incense, not so much as a cake, not a single beast for sacrifice. For the moment I was amazed and thought that I was still outside the shrine and that you were awaiting the signal from me, doing me that honor because I am supreme pontifex. But when I began to inquire what sacrifice the city intended to offer (τί μέλλει θύειν ἡ πόλις) to celebrate the annual festival in honor of the god, the priest answered, 'I have brought with me from my own house a goose as an offering to the god, but the city this time has made no preparations.'"[38]

The decline of animal sacrifice was a trend that Julian felt himself divinely appointed to reverse. His father had been a half-brother of Constantine, who, along with a number of his other male relatives, had been murdered shortly after Constantine's death in 337, when Julian was about six years old. He and his older brother Gallus were spared, presumably because of their youth, and Julian spent his childhood and youth engaged in literary and philosophical studies, far from the court. Although raised as a Christian, in his twentieth year, he apparently underwent a conversion that caused him to repudiate Christianity and adopt instead what he termed Hellenism, which he regarded as the old Greek religious tradition. Given Constantius's devotion to Christianity, however, he prudently kept this change in his devotion a secret. At about the same time, Constantius, who needed support in governing the empire while at war with the usurper Magnentius, appointed Gallus as his Caesar. Gallus proved unsatisfactory, however, and in 354, Constantius had him deposed and executed. He then turned to Julian, who was proclaimed

---

38. Ilium: Julian. *Ep.* 19 Wright 1923 = 79 Bidez 1924. Tyana: *Ep.* 35 Wright 1923 = 78 Bidez 1924. Antioch: *Mis.* 361D–362B; see further Bradbury 1995, 354–55. All quotations from Julian are in the Loeb translation of Wilmer C. Wright, sometimes adapted.

Caesar in November 355 and promptly sent to deal with incursions of Germanic tribes across the Rhine. Surprisingly, the bookish Julian proved to be a talented general, quickly racking up a number of military successes and winning the devotion of his troops. In February 360, they proclaimed him Augustus, and in the summer of 361, Julian began leading his army to Constantinople to challenge Constantius. The latter's sudden death in November of that year prevented civil war, and Julian became sole emperor. It was on his march to Constantinople that Julian came out publicly as an adherent of Hellenism, and as soon as he acquired sole rule, he quickly embarked on a set of policies aimed at restoring traditional cult to its favored place in the empire. Julian had also inherited a war with Shapur II of Persia, however, and soon decided to launch a major campaign against him. In June 362, he moved to Antioch to make preparations, and in March 363, he led his army out to the east. Despite some initial successes, the campaign did not go well, and after being wounded in a skirmish, Julian died in June 363.[39]

Not surprisingly, Julian has long attracted the attention of scholars, and there has been considerable debate over the precise nature of his personal beliefs and the extent to which they informed his policies. A few points are clear enough. At the time of his conversion, he was studying philosophy under Maximus of Ephesus, a philosopher in the Iamblichean tradition (Maximus's teacher Aedesius had been one of Iamblichus's star pupils), and it is generally agreed that Maximus played a key role in shaping Julian's outlook; certainly, Julian remained devoted to Maximus for the rest of his life, and his own writings bear considerable traces of an Iamblichean understanding of the cosmos.[40] For the purposes of my argument, however, the chief thing to note is that Julian's identification with Hellenism resulted from a deliberate commitment to a discourse, that is, a belief system articulated in philosophical terms, analogous to that of the Christianity in which he was raised, and not from participation in cult practices that were integrated into the rhythms of daily life and pervasive social and political structures, such as we explored in Part I. In Julian's Hellenism, cult practices and philosophical principles were inextricably bound together, although the latter always took precedence. The priority of philosophy in Julian's Hellenism emerges clearly in a

---

39. For a brief account of Julian's life and reign, see, e.g., R. Smith 1995, 1–9. Conversion in his twentieth year: Julian. *Ep.* 47 Wright 1923 = 111 Bidez 1924, 434D; see further R. Smith 1995, 180–89.

40. Debate over Julian's beliefs and policies: Greenwood 2021, 10–16. Maximus: Eunap. *Vit. soph.* 7 = 473–81; Julian's devotion: Lib. *Or.* 18.155–56 and Amm. Marc. 22.7.3.

fragmentary letter he wrote laying down guidelines for priests in the new hierarchy he established, modeled to some extent on the organization of the Christian church. Although he includes recommendations for cult practices (for example, priests ought to sacrifice every day at dawn and dusk), he has far more to say about how they ought to behave and what they ought to believe and profess.[41] We can likewise see Julian's orientation toward discourse over practice, albeit in a different guise, in his directive forbidding Christians to teach the classic texts of Greek literature and philosophy, on the grounds that teachers ought not to set the bad example of expounding to their pupils things that they themselves do not believe.[42]

In recommending that the members of his new priestly hierarchy sacrifice every day at dawn and dusk, Julian was only encouraging them to adopt his own practice. In a letter to Libanius written on his march to the east, Julian notes that while stopping at Batnae, "I sacrificed (ἔθυσα) in the evening and again at early dawn, as I am in the habit of doing practically every day." Whether he actually slaughtered an animal victim twice every day is not clear. Although practical considerations would suggest that a vegetal offering was more likely, we know from other evidence that Julian placed a great deal of stress on animal sacrifice in particular. In a letter to Maximus that he wrote en route to Constantinople in the fall of 361, he declares, "I worship the gods openly, and the whole mass of the troops who are returning with me worship the gods; we sacrifice cattle in public (φανερῶς βουθυτοῦμεν), we have offered to the gods many hecatombs (ἑκατόμβας πολλάς) as thank offerings." Here there can be no doubt that Julian meant animal sacrifice in particular.[43]

Yet despite Julian's admiration of Greek tradition, there was one respect in which his manner of conducting a sacrifice was strikingly at odds

---

41. The extant portion of the letter to a priest (Wright 1913, 293–339 = *Ep.* 89b Bidez 1924) was at some point incorporated into Julian's letter to Themistius but was identified as a separate text by an early modern scholar; guidelines for cult practice: 302B–C; for beliefs: 299B–302A. As one who himself came to the worship of the gods through texts, Julian devotes particular attention to designing a reading list: the archaic iambic poets, Old Comedy, Epicurus, and the Skeptics are out; Pythagoras, Plato, Aristotle, the early Stoics, and hymns are in.

42. *Ep.* 36 Wright 1923 = *Ep.* 61c Bidez 1924, with Amm. Marc. 22.10.7 and 25.4.20, Rufin. *Eccl. hist.* 10.33, Sozom. *Hist. eccl.* 5.18, Theodoret *Hist. eccl.* 3.8; see further R. Smith 1995, 212–14, and Belayche 2001, 469–70. Note also Libanius's assertion that Julian considered literature and the rites of the gods as "brothers" (*Or.* 18.157: ὁ ... νομίζων ἀδελφὰ λόγους τε καὶ θεῶν ἱερά).

43. Daily sacrifices: *Ep.* 58 Wright 1923 = 98 Bidez 1924, 401B; also noted by Libanius, *Or.* 12.80 and 18.127. In offering sacrifice at dusk and dawn, Julian may have been following the recommendation of Hesiod (*Op.* 338–39). Sacrifice on the march: *Ep.* 8 Wright 1923 = 26 Bidez 1924, 415C.

with established norms. As we saw in Part I, it was common in both Greek and Roman tradition for the sacrificant to be assisted by an attendant, called a *mageiros* in Greek and a *victimarius* in Latin, who was responsible for the specialized and bloody business of slaughtering and butchering the victim. According to Libanius, however, Julian himself assumed these duties: "he performs the sacrifice in person (αὐτουργεῖ); he busies himself on the preparations, gets the wood, wields the knife (μάχαιραν δέχεται), opens the birds, and inspects their entrails. The proof of this is in his fingers which bear the evidence therefrom." Ammianus mentions that the people of Antioch mockingly called him a *victimarius* rather than a sacrificant (*sacricola*), a joke that suggests that they, too, were struck by Julian's eccentricity in his sacrificial practice. I would suggest that this odd detail provides us with valuable insight into Julian's conception of animal sacrifice: rather than an act embedded in sociopolitical structures, as it had been in ages past, it was for him a form of personal communion with the divine in which he was unwilling to suffer any intermediaries.[44]

Julian's passion for animal sacrifice made a lasting impression on his contemporaries. Libanius, in a speech to Theodosius I more than fifteen years after Julian's death, made much of his predecessor's piety to the gods: "If Hector deserved to be lamented by Zeus because of his many sacrifices, if Zeus is accused by Athena during the wanderings of Odysseus for neglecting a man who had sacrificed to him, what were the remarks they made about Julian, do you think, since he in ten years offered more sacrifices (θυσίας) than all the rest of the Greeks put together?" Libanius perhaps especially had in mind his preparations for the war against Persia. In a speech in honor of Julian's fourth consulship that he delivered in the emperor's presence in Antioch on January 1, 363, Libanius asserts that what really caused alarm among the Persians was not the Romans' military might but "the many sacrifices (αἱ πυκναὶ θυσίαι), the frequent blood offerings (αἷμα τὸ πολύ), the clouds of incense, the feasting of gods and spirits." In a later speech, he declares that Julian was so convinced of the importance of the soldiers' offering sacrifice during this time that he actually bribed them to do so.[45] Ammianus, who was present in Antioch in this period, depicts Julian's actions there in much more negative terms: he "drenched the altars with the blood of an excessive number of

---

44. Libanius: *Or.* 12.82; Ammianus: 22.14.3. For the interpretation offered here, see especially Belayche 2001, 467–69.

45. Speech to Theodosius: Lib. *Or.* 24.35; speech in Antioch: *Or.* 12.79; bribery: *Or.* 18.167–72.

victims, sometimes offering up a hundred bulls at once, with countless flocks of various other animals and with white birds hunted out by land and sea; to such a degree that almost every day his soldiers, who gorged themselves on the abundance of meat, living boorishly and corrupted by their eagerness for drink, were carried through the squares to their lodgings on the shoulders of passersby from the public temples, where they indulged in banquets that deserved punishment rather than indulgence." Ammianus's sharply negative tone is all the more striking given the fact that he was generally a devoted admirer of Julian. Indeed, in the almost adulatory assessment of Julian's character that he appends to his account of Julian's death, the only faults he can come up with were that he was sometimes inconsistent, was a terrible chatterbox, and sacrificed so many cattle that he seemed superstitious rather than properly devout.[46]

Scholars have puzzled over this apparent obsession with animal sacrifice, especially in one who was personally inclined to a rather austere way of life and had a marked distaste for ostentation. Indeed, although Julian reported to Libanius that he was very pleased to see victims ready for sacrifice on his stop at Batnae, he nevertheless added that the preparations seemed a bit overdone: "it looked to me like overheated zeal and alien to proper reverence for the gods."[47] Julian's own theorizing about animal sacrifice in his extant writings does little to explain it. In a passage from his treatise *Against the Galileans* (his preferred term for Christians), he explains God's rejection of Cain's offering by arguing that "since of things on the earth some have souls (ἔμψυχα) and others lack them (ἄψυχα), and those that have souls are more precious than those that lack them to the living God who is also the cause of life (τῷ ζῶντι καὶ ζωῆς αἰτίῳ θεῷ), inasmuch as they also have a share of life and a soul more akin to his," God was more inclined to accept Abel's offering of a lamb.[48] Given his training and philosophical affinities, Julian was undoubtedly familiar with the Platonic theory of a hierarchy of sacrificial practices

---

46. Sacrifices in Antioch: Amm. Marc. 22.12.6; Julian's faults: 25.4.16–17 (*superstitiosus magis quam sacrorum legitimus observator, innumeras sine parsimonia pecudes mactans, ut aestimaretur, si revertisset de Parthis, boves iam defuturos*). All translations from Ammianus are in the Loeb translation of John C. Rolfe.

47. *Ep.* 58 Wright 1923 = 98 Bidez 1924, 400C–D. For studies that focus on Julian's engagement with animal sacrifice, see especially Bradbury 1995 and Belayche 2001.

48. *Contra Galileos* 347C. Julian's argument here has some affinities with one of the arguments in favor of animal sacrifice advanced by Sallustius (16), although his striking use of the Pythagorean terminology of *empsychos*, "ensouled," and *apsychos*, "soulless," in such a blatantly non-Pythagorean argument seems unique to him.

correlated with a hierarchy of divine entities, and he several times refers to the idea that the supreme God set *daimones* as governors over individual cities and peoples. He may well have believed, as we saw Celsus did, that animal sacrifice was the most appropriate offering for these lower-ranking officials of the divine world, even though he never says anything to that effect in his extant writings.[49] Yet although Platonism may have provided a satisfactory philosophical justification for the appropriateness of animal sacrifice in particular contexts, it did not attribute to it any overriding importance.

Some scholars have attributed Julian's enthusiasm for animal sacrifice to his loathing of Christianity, since animal sacrifice was more anathema to Christians than any other traditional cult practice.[50] This interpretation seems to me on the right track, although I would argue that there was more to it than mere malevolent pleasure in offending Christian sensibilities; it had an important positive function as well. Just as Christian leaders had fashioned animal sacrifice in particular as the practice most incompatible with Christian adherence, so, too, Julian now promoted it as the most potent marker of adherence to Hellenism. We have already seen indications of the extent to which Julian regarded animal sacrifice as the signature ritual of Hellenism. For example, his report to Maximus that he and his troops were openly sacrificing cattle on their march to Constantinople is a boast of his coming out publicly as a Hellene. Similarly, it was apparently his friend Aristoxenus's knowledge of how to perform a proper sacrifice that allowed him to be "a genuine Hellene among the Cappadocians." Although the people of Batnae may have been overzealous in their provisions for animal sacrifice, these provisions were nevertheless what prompted Julian to report to Libanius that "its name is barbarous but the place is Hellenic."[51]

At the same time, it was important to Julian that animal sacrifice was not limited to Hellenism; it was also, he liked to point out, a practice that it had

---

49. *Letter to Themistius* 258A–259A; cf. *Contra Galileos* 115D–116A, 143A–B, and 148B–C; on Celsus, see further Section 8c above.

50. Bradbury 1995, 346–47; Greenwood 2021, 17–18. Paula Fredriksen has suggested to me (personal communication) that Julian's enthusiasm for large-scale sacrifices may also reflect his bookishness, in that he took the heroic holocausts of the Homeric epics as setting the standard for real-world expressions of piety.

51. To Maximus: *Ep.* 8 Wright 1923 = 26 Bidez 1924, 415C. To Aristoxenus: *Ep.* 35 Wright 1923 = 78 Bidez 1924. To Libanius: *Ep.* 58 Wright 1923 = 98 Bidez 1924, 400C. See also *Ep.* 10 Wright 1923 = 29 Bidez 1924, to his confidant Eutherius, asking him to make thank offerings to the gods on Julian's behalf: "you will sacrifice not on behalf of a single man, but of the community of Hellenes."

in common with Judaism. In his treatise *Against the Galileans*, he hammers away at the theme that although Christians deserted Hellenism in order to align themselves with Judaism, they do not, in fact, follow Judaean practice, either, but have abandoned much of Mosaic law, including animal sacrifice. Why have they done this? He anticipates the obvious rebuttal—"No doubt some sharp-sighted person will answer, 'Judaeans too do not sacrifice' "—and is ready with his response: Judaeans do, in fact, sacrifice in their homes, but the destruction of the Temple prevents their offering communal sacrifice. But since Christians have invented a new kind of sacrifice (τὴν καινὴν θυσίαν) and have no need of Jerusalem, what prevents them from sacrificing? His main point here is that apart from the eccentric Judaean belief in only one god, everything else they have in common with Hellenes: "temples, sanctuaries, altars, purifications, and certain precepts. For as to these we differ from one another either not at all or in trivial matters."[52] According to the church historians of the early fifth century, it was Julian's eagerness for Judaeans to resume their sacrificial practice that led him to undertake the costly measure of rebuilding the Temple in Jerusalem. Although no contemporary source attests to this as his key motivation, given Julian's overall advocacy of animal sacrifice, it seems plausible. He certainly did not do it out of a deep love of Judaeans and their cult, since for Julian, despite his perhaps sincere assertions of devotion to the Judaean god, Judaean tradition was valuable primarily as a stick with which he could beat Christians.[53]

That Julian placed a very different valuation on animal sacrifice than did his uncle and cousins is obvious and, given his commitment to Hellenism and his loathing of Christianity, only to be expected. In that respect, we can see his policies as part of an extended swing of the pendulum from one extreme (the Tetrarchs's demand for animal sacrifice) to another (Constantius's prohibition of animal sacrifice) and back again. Seen from another angle,

---

52. *Contra Galileos* 299A–C + 305B, D + 306A–B (= Loeb 3.402–6); I have quoted from 305D and 306B. In claiming that Judaeans still sacrifice in their own homes, Julian seems to have had in mind the ritualized slaughter required to produce kosher meat: Finkelstein 2018, 71, 76–78.

53. Early church historians: Rufin. *Hist. eccl.* 10.38–40, Sozom. *Hist. eccl.* 5.22, Socrates *Hist. eccl.* 3.20, Theodoret *Hist. eccl.* 3.20; a similar account in the fifth-century Syriac *Martyrdom and History of Blessed Simeon bar Ṣabbaʿe* (K. Smith 2014, 90); see also Brock 1976. Julian himself, in a letter to Judaean leaders, indicates his intention to rebuild Jerusalem on his return from Persia (*Ep.* 51 Wright 1923, 398; see further Finkelstein 2018, 145–48). According to Ammianus (23.1.2–3), work actually began on the foundations while Julian was still in Antioch but was abandoned as a result of balls of flame that burst forth from the earth. Julian's use of Judaism: Belayche 2001, 476–79, and Greenwood 2021, 111–13; a more detailed and nuanced discussion: Finkelstein 2018.

however, and to my mind a more interesting one, Julian's policies regarding animal sacrifice actually display a marked continuity with those of his uncle and cousins. Although diametrically opposed to them in his religious allegiance, Julian operated squarely within the same conceptual framework: he promoted animal sacrifice as a crucial marker of adherence to Hellenism, just as they had castigated it as a crucial marker of a marginalized pagan adherence. Yet he went still further and tried to refashion animal sacrifice more broadly as a marker of mainstream religion, something that Hellenism shared with Judaism; for Julian, the rejection of animal sacrifice was what marked Christianity as the deviant form of religion that he considered it to be. In this respect, Julian appears as the mirror image of Constantius II: the same shape, merely reversed.[54]

It is tempting to think that Julian, in trying to re-establish animal sacrifice as a marker of normative religion, was reviving the cultural norms of the high empire, when animal sacrifice, as we saw in Section 4b, constituted a "Graeco-Roman" practice par excellence, a practice that helped to define the standards of civilized life in the Roman world. But the world had changed too much for such a revival to be a real option. The bonds that had integrated animal sacrifice so tightly into the social and cultural structures of the Roman Empire had been unraveling for a century or more by the time Julian came to the throne, as a result both of gradual changes in underlying socioeconomic structures and of imperial policies that increasingly marginalized the practice of animal sacrifice and redefined it as a marker of a specific religious affiliation. Although Julian could try to shift the valuation of that affiliation, he could not recreate, nor did he probably even fully understand, the social and cultural structures of the earlier period, within which animal sacrifice had its distinctive place. This is by no means the same as saying that Julian's attempt to restore traditional Graeco-Roman religion to a central place in the empire was doomed to failure; it does not seem absurd to me to speculate that had Julian reigned for more than thirty years as Constantine had done instead of less than three as he, in fact, did, he may well have succeeded in establishing

---

54. My analysis here has obvious affinities with Greenwood's analysis of Julian's goal as a recapitulation and overwriting of Constantine's Christianized empire (Greenwood 2021, especially 17–18, 39–40, 122–23), although I place more emphasis on continuity. There is, however, a significant complication that I do not address here: Julian tried to enforce a conceptualization of Hellenism in which traditional cult and Greek culture were inextricably linked, whereas many Christian intellectuals had been working hard to separate culture from cult, in order to integrate the former into Christian tradition while marginalizing the latter as deviant.

Hellenism as a viable religious tradition for centuries to come. My point is rather that even if this had been the case, the Hellenism that he established, and the role of animal sacrifice within it, would necessarily have been different from what it had been two centuries earlier.

### 10d. *From the Death of Julian to Theodosius I*

When Julian died on his eastern campaign in June 363, he left behind no children, no Caesar, and no successor. The empire, and more immediately the army, needed a new leader quickly. His officers met and, after their first choice refused, proclaimed as the new emperor Julian's senior staff officer, a Christian named Jovian. Jovian concluded a hasty peace with Persia, led back the army, assumed the consulship on January 1, 364, and within two months was dead. At that point, a group of senior officials and generals elected a military officer named Valentinian, also a Christian. Since the army demanded that he have a colleague, a month or so after his own elevation, he proclaimed his younger brother Valens as co-emperor, and during the summer of 364, the two made arrangements for an effective division of the empire, with Valentinian taking the western half and Valens the eastern. In 367, after a serious illness, Valentinian bestowed the title of Augustus on his son Gratian as well, despite the fact that Gratian was only eight at the time. After spending much of his reign dealing with external threats on the northern frontier, Valentinian died suddenly in November 375, leaving the sixteen-year-old Gratian as senior emperor of the western empire. Meanwhile, in the eastern empire, increasing pressure from the Goths across the Danube was developing into a major problem; a mismanaged attempt to resolve it by allowing large numbers of Goths to settle in Roman territory resulted in the disastrous Battle of Adrianople in August 378, in which Valens, along with two-thirds of his army, was killed. In this crisis, the young Gratian turned to a man named Theodosius, a successful military leader who at the time was living in retirement on his estates in Spain. Theodosius was officially proclaimed emperor in January 379, taking over rule of the eastern empire, and reigned until his death in January 395; since by that point, both Gratian and his younger brother Valentinian II were dead, Theodosius's two sons assumed rule of the empire, Arcadius in the east and Honorius in the west.

Julian's early death, and even more the fact that all his successors were Christians, effectively ended his program for establishing Hellenism as the favored religion of the empire. His successors, however, rather than pursuing strongly pro-Christian and anti-pagan measures, seem instead to have adopted a more neutral, laissez-faire policy in religious matters. Although Jovian hardly reigned long enough to develop a real policy, he was apparently inclined to avoid taking sides in religious controversies. We have good evidence for his approach in a speech delivered by the philosopher and rhetorician Themistius celebrating Jovian's assumption of the consulship.[55] Valentinian seems to have adopted a similar strategy. Although he quickly reversed some of Julian's measures that penalized Christians, notably the ban on Christians teaching the classics, or that benefited traditional cults, such as an increase in the privileges of municipal priests, he also issued proclamations at the start of his reign guaranteeing freedom of worship.[56] We lack comparable evidence for Valens, but there is no reason to think that in these matters he differed from his brother. As a negative indication, it is worth noting that the compilers of the Theodosian Code found no laws from their reigns that they deemed appropriate for inclusion in the section that dealt with pagans. Valentinian, indeed, seems to have gone to some lengths to authorize traditional cult practices. As we have already seen, the historian Zosimus claims that when Valentinian banned nocturnal sacrifices, the aristocratic Roman senator Praetextatus, at the time governor of Achaea, complained that this hindered the celebration of traditional mysteries and that as a result, Valentinian exempted Greece from the ban. He likewise explicitly authorized traditional public haruspicy, even though a recent series of treason trials in Rome had involved forbidden private consultation of *haruspices*.[57]

Did this official policy of neutrality in matters of religion extend to animal sacrifice? The evidence is again contradictory, making certainty impossible. One of the most important sources is the speech of Libanius conventionally known as "For the Temples." I have already cited this speech in my discussion of Constantine, where Libanius served as star witness for

---

55. Themistius: *Or.* 5, with Errington 2000, 873–78; Heather and Moncur 2001, 154–58; and Marcos 2014, who makes a detailed argument that Jovian issued a formal edict of toleration near the start of his reign.

56. Christian teachers: *Cod. Theod.* 13.3.6, with *LRER* 2.350–53 (June 11, 364); privileges of priests: *Cod. Theod.* 12.1.60 with *LRER* 2.304–7 (September 12, 364). Freedom of worship: *Cod. Theod.* 9.16.9 with *LRER* 2.150–52 (May 371); note that some of the phrasing is very similar to that of the "edict of Milan" in the version of Lact. *Mort.* 48.2 and 6. Ammianus (30.9.5) likewise praises Valentinian's moderation in matters of religion; see further Rougé 1987.

57. Nocturnal sacrifices: Zos. 4.3.2–3 (364); although the law of Valentinian does not survive, an equivalent law issued by Valens does: *Cod. Theod.* 9.16.7, with *LRER* 2.148–49 (September 9, 364). Public haruspicy: *Cod. Theod.* 9.16.9; treason trials: Amm. Marc. 28.1, especially sections 8, 14, 19–22, and 29.

the case that Constantine did not prohibit animal sacrifice. It is now time to examine it more closely. Libanius was a distinguished rhetorician from Antioch, where he held an official chair of rhetoric from 354 until his death in c. 393. Although he was an adherent of traditional Hellenic cult, his literary distinction, along with his tendency to avoid political controversies, allowed him to maintain imperial goodwill from one regime to the next. In the mid-380s, however, a series of attacks on traditional temples, conducted by gangs of monks and tacitly condoned by imperial officials, moved him to compose a speech pleading the injustice of these actions. The speech, which Libanius wrote probably around the year 386, is addressed to Theodosius I but was not delivered in his presence and probably not even widely circulated until a couple of years later.

Libanius opens with a brief review of legislation affecting traditional religion. As we have already seen, he asserts that Constantine made no change to traditional practice but that Constantius II was the first to prohibit sacrifice. Julian then restored it, and following his death, animal sacrifice continued for some time (μένει μέν τινα τὸ θύειν ἱερεῖα χρόνον), until after some disturbances, Valentinian and Valens banned it (ἐκωλύθη παρὰ τοῖν ἀδελφοῖν); they did, however, make an exception for offerings of incense, which Theodosius himself confirmed. Libanius goes on to complain that despite official policy, gangs of marauding monks, egged on by the local bishop, have been attacking and destroying temples. As justification, they claim that worshipers there engage in animal sacrifice. That, Libanius asserts, is a lie. It is true, he admits, that people slaughtered animals for a feast, but "no altar received the blood offering, no single part of the victim was burned, no offering of meal began the ceremony, nor did libations follow it. If people assemble in some beauty spot, slaughter a calf or a sheep or both, and boil or roast it, and then lie down on the ground and eat it, I do not see that they have broken the laws at all." This is a point on which Libanius insists: "even if they were in the habit of drinking together amid the scent of every kind of incense, they broke no law, nor yet if in their toasts they sang hymns and invoked the gods, unless indeed you intend to use a man's private life as grounds for accusation." His argument is significant, because Libanius concedes that the authorities could legally confiscate property where animal sacrifices have taken place. Indeed, Peter Van Nuffelen makes a persuasive case that Libanius's primary concern in the speech is, in fact, "the threat of confiscation of estates and the loss of revenue on the grounds that sacrifice had been practiced there." Libanius thus provides vivid testimony that by the mid-380s, people in the region of Antioch regarded animal sacrifice, although not other forms of traditional cult practice, as strictly prohibited and that they were moreover aware that violating this prohibition would result in a loss of property.[58]

To what extent does other evidence bear out Libanius's account of imperial policy on sacrifice? As we have seen, as regards Constantine, it does not do so at all: both Eusebius and Constans's law of 341 indicate that Constantine did, in fact, make substantial changes to traditional practice, although, as I suggested, there are various ways of squaring that particular circle. Similar issues arise in the case of Jovian. Whereas Libanius asserts that animal sacrifice continued for some time after Julian's death, which would surely include Jovian's brief reign, the church historian Socrates, writing in the 430s or 440s, declares categorically that "the pollution that came about publicly through blood (ὁ δι' αἵματος δημοσίᾳ γινόμενος μολυσμός), which under Julian people had employed to the point of satiety, was brought to an end" by Jovian. In this case, Themistius may help to resolve the contradiction. In describing how Jovian cracked down on magic, he noted that "while allowing lawful sacrifices (θυσίας ἐννόμους ἀφιείς), he did not bestow indemnity on those practicing sorcery." As we have now repeatedly seen, it was long-standing policy for emperors to ban sacrifice in connection with magic and illicit divination. If that is what Jovian did, Socrates may well have read more into his action than was intended at the time, just as Eusebius may have done with Constantine. On the other hand, Themistius does not explain what precisely constituted "lawful sacrifices." Given the ambiguity of the word *thusia*, it is perfectly possible that Jovian did, in fact, prohibit animal sacrifices while allowing other types of offerings.[59]

There is likewise no other evidence to support Libanius's assertion that Valentinian and Valens forbade animal sacrifice but allowed incense. It is again possible that whatever action he had in mind may originally have had a more limited force. Libanius says that the ban occurred in the wake of certain unspecified disturbances (νεωτέρων ... τινων συμβάντων). The Greek word he uses, *neōtera*, literally "newer things," was commonly used to denote revolutionary or conspiratorial activities, and in the fourth century, as

---

58. Date and circumstances of *Or.* 30: Nesselrath et al. 2011, 33–38. Review of legislation: *Or.* 30.6–8, with quotations from 7. Claims of animal sacrifice and Libanius's defense: *Or.* 30.12, 15–23, and 47, with quotations from 17–18. Libanius goes on to claim that sacrifices still occur in Rome and Alexandria (*Or.* 30.31–35), although it is not clear whether he is speaking of animal sacrifice in particular. Libanius's primary concern: Van Nuffelen 2014, 300–312, quotation from 295–96.

59. Socrates: *Hist. eccl.* 3.24.6. Themistius: *Or.* 5, 70b–c; cf. Marcos 2014, 165. On Eusebius and Constantine, see Section 10b above.

we have seen, accusations of illicit divination, often involving sacrifice, were a common feature of treason trials. Later in their reigns, both Valentinian and Valens were deeply concerned with the threat posed by ambitious men who resorted to magic and divination to attain their ends, causing Valentinian to order the prefect of Rome to preside in person over the trial of senators who were "touched by the hateful accusation of practicing magic." Moreover, near the start of their reigns, as we have seen, both emperors, presumably acting out of similar concerns, had apparently already issued laws forbidding people to conduct "wicked prayers or magic preparations or funereal sacrifices" at night. Given all this, we could perhaps explain the tensions in the evidence by supposing that Libanius had in mind a prohibition against sacrifice in the context of magic and divination that people then interpreted more broadly. On the other hand, given his insistence that any acts not specifically forbidden were allowed, we might expect him to be equally precise about distinguishing the different contexts, some lawful and some not, in which a sacrifice might take place. Moreover, the detail that those who engaged in animal sacrifice stood to forfeit their property, on which he puts so much emphasis, seems too specific for a generalized anxiety about practicing animal sacrifice.[60]

Theodosius reiterated the ban on sacrifices in the context of magic and divination in two measures of the early and mid-380s, but there is no evidence for a more general prohibition of animal sacrifice from that period. In a directive to the Roman governor of Osrhoene, a province in northern Mesopotamia, probably in response to a petition for permission to close or destroy a major temple (its exact identity is not specified), Theodosius decrees that it shall, in fact, remain open and that public festivals shall continue to take place there, "but in such a way that the performance of sacrifices forbidden therein (*illic prohibitorum usus sacrificiorum*) may not be supposed to be permitted under the pretext of such access to the temple." It is once again worth noting the ambiguity of this proviso. Does the reference to forbidden sacrifices imply that some types of sacrifices were not forbidden? And if so, what kind of sacrifices were they: vegetal offerings or any public sacrifices not connected with magic or divination? The latter is likely enough, given his law

---

60. "Newer things": LSJ νεώτερος s.v. II.2. Treason trials: Amm. Marc. 28.1.11–24 for Valentinian, from 369 to 371 CE, and 29.1–2 for Valens, from 371 CE. Prefect of Rome: *Cod. Theod.* 9.16.10, with *LRER* 2.152–54 (December 6, 371). Funereal sacrifice: *Cod. Theod.* 9.16.7, with *LRER* 2.148–49, a law of Valens from September 9, 364; for Valentinian, see Zos. 4.3.2.

on that issue of just a year previously, but we cannot be certain, and perhaps neither could the original recipients.[61]

Lastly, to balance Libanius's careful acknowledgment that animal sacrifice was prohibited, we may note two other anecdotes, neither precisely datable but both probably referring to the 370s or 380s, that indicate that sacrifice was still taking place, even in public contexts. The first is a story that Eunapius tells about his old teacher Chrysanthius, like Maximus a pupil of the Iamblichean philosopher Aedesius. A Roman official named Justus, newly arrived in the province of Asia, announced a public sacrifice in the city of Sardis and summoned all the learned men there resident to attend. After the victim (τὸ ἱερεῖον) had been slaughtered, he asked them what was portended by the position in which it had fallen; not surprisingly, all the learned men were stumped, except for Chrysanthius, who gave a wise response and earned Justus's admiration. The second is a passage from a letter of Symmachus, one of the leading pagan senators of Rome, to his friend Praetextatus. Symmachus writes that he is deeply concerned "because, despite numerous sacrifices (*sacrificiis multiplicibus*), and these often repeated by each of the authorities, the prodigy of Spoleto has not yet has been expiated in the public name. For the eighth sacrificial victim (*mactatio*) scarcely appeased Jupiter and for the eleventh time honor was paid to Fortuna Publica with multiple sacrificial victims (*multiiugis hostiis*) in vain." In both cases, it is clearly animal sacrifice that is in question and not merely offerings of incense or the like.[62]

It is impossible on the basis of this inconsistent evidence to reach any certainty about the legal status of animal sacrifice in the period from the death of Julian to the end of the 380s. None of the references to lawful and forbidden sacrifices explain the criteria for determining which practices fall into which category; the latter certainly included sacrifices associated with private divination and magic, but beyond that, matters are highly uncertain. I would suggest that this uncertainty is not merely the result of incomplete and tendentious evidence but also a reflection of the contemporary state of

---

61. Magic and divination: *Cod. Theod.* 16.10.7 and 9, from December 21, 381, and May 25, 285, respectively. Osrhoene: *Cod. Theod.* 16.10.8, with *LRER* 1.436–37, from November 30, 382; it is generally assumed that the temple in question was the main temple in Edessa, the capital of Osrhoene, which was, in fact, destroyed a few years later, but others are possible.

62. Eunapius: *Vit. soph.* 23.4.1–9 = 503–4; we can infer the date from the fact that Eunapius describes Chrysanthius, who was born c. 345 and died in 396/397, as an old man; see further Bradbury 1995, 344n38. Symmachus: *Ep.* 1.49, in the translation of Salzman and Roberts 2011, 106–7; see further Salzman 2011, 169–70, who suggests that these sacrifices may, in fact, have been private.

affairs. Not only was the wording of individual laws ambiguous and thus open to differing interpretations, but also, as we saw in the introduction to this chapter, legislation was in general much less comprehensive and fixed in its effects than we would expect in a modern state. Such a situation was bound to generate uncertainty. Nevertheless, it must at least have been widely known that participation in animal sacrifice could result in trouble. In such a situation, most people, regardless of how much they knew about the relevant imperial legislation, would have preferred to be cautious; that much we can safely infer from Libanius's speech on the temples. Yet if there was uncertainty about the legal status of animal sacrifice in the years after Julian's death, that changed dramatically during the final years of Theodosius's reign, when a series of new pronouncements helped establish a much less ambiguous and much more comprehensive policy.

First came a set of three laws in 391 that specifically concerned people of high status. The first was issued on February 24 and was apparently applicable to Italy and perhaps other parts of the western empire: "No person shall pollute himself with sacrificial animals (*nemo se hostiis polluat*); no person shall slaughter an innocent victim (*insontem victimam*); no person shall approach the shrines, shall wander through the temples, or revere the images formed by mortal labor, lest he become guilty by divine and human laws." Although the prohibition is stated in general terms, the penalties that follow specify only imperial officeholders, who have to pay fines according to their rank, from fifteen pounds of gold for those of the highest rank down to four pounds of gold for those of the lowest. The second, issued on June 9, was sent to Nicomachus Flavianus, the praetorian prefect of Italy, and specifically targets apostates: anyone who has either attained or was born into high rank shall lose it if they are found to "have deserted the cult and worship of the sacrosanct religion and have given themselves over to sacrifices (*sacrificiis*)." The third, issued just a few days later on June 16, was directed to the two imperial officials in charge of Egypt and was virtually identical with the law of February: "No person shall be granted the right to perform sacrifices; no person shall go around the temples; no person shall revere the shrines." Once again, although the prohibition is framed in general terms, the penalties specify fines for imperial officials. What prompted these directives is not clear, although we might associate the last with the unrest in Alexandria that culminated in the destruction of the great Temple of Serapis in the winter of 391–92. In general, they seem to be a response to scenarios such as that recorded by Eunapius, with imperial officials seen to be endorsing traditional cult through their actions. In any case, in spirit, they are strongly reminiscent of Constantine's attempt of some seventy years before to separate animal sacrifice from the administration of the empire.[63]

On November 8, 392, a new directive, issued to Flavius Rufinus as praetorian prefect of the eastern empire, extended those of the previous year in two ways. First, it was much more careful in insisting that the prohibitions contained therein applied to people of every rank: "No person at all, of any class or order whatsoever of men or of dignities, whether he occupies a position of power or has completed such honors, whether he is powerful by the lot of birth or is humble in lineage, legal status, and fortune, shall sacrifice an innocent victim to senseless images in any place at all or in any city." Second, the prohibitions themselves were much more comprehensive, specifically covering acts of worship that took place in homes as well as in public and covering vegetal offerings as well as animal sacrifice: "he shall not, by more secret wickedness, venerate his *lar* with fire, his *genius* with wine, his *penates* with fragrant odors; he shall not burn lights to them, place incense before them, or suspend wreaths for them." The law further specifies that these acts are culpable even if they do not involve inquiries about the emperor. Those found guilty forfeit to the imperial treasuries the property in which they performed the act; if they did so on property other than their own, they are subject to a fine of twenty-five pounds of gold. It also details specific procedures to be followed in prosecuting such cases: judges who do not take action are themselves liable to a fine of thirty pounds of gold. It is worth noting that the penalties specified in this law, as in those of the previous year, are less severe but also much more precise than Constantius's vague threats of being "struck down with the avenging sword." That in itself suggests that Theodosius was more interested in actual enforcement than in yet another largely rhetorical denunciation.[64]

---

63. February 24: *Cod. Theod.* 16.10.10; the letter is addressed to the prefect of Rome (although his title is incorrectly given as praetorian prefect), but since it specifies provincial governors, it must have had a wider range: *LRER* 1.438–41. July 9: *Cod. Theod.* 16.7.5, with *LRER* 1.362–65 on the date. July 16: *Cod. Theod.* 16.10.11; see further *LRER* 1.440–42 on its association with the destruction of the Serapeion, on which see also Errington 2006, 249–51. Penalties: Curran 2000, 215–16.

64. Law of 392: *Cod. Theod.* 16.10.12; Van Nuffelen 2014, 305–6, suggests that we can understand the provision in Theodosius's law that substitutes a fine for confiscation of property as addressing the concern that Libanius raises in *Or.* 30. Note that since the law is addressed to the praetorian prefect of the east, it, strictly speaking, applied only to that part of the empire and not the west as well. "Avenging sword": *Cod. Theod.* 16.10.4. On Theodosius's legislation, see further Errington 2006, 233–37, and Cameron 2011, 59–74.

Theodosius's law of November 392 stands as the effective climax of imperial legislation against animal sacrifice. Although emperors continued to issue laws reiterating the prohibition of animal sacrifice well into the fifth century, they often framed them as supplements. In the eastern empire, for example, Arcadius issued a directive some seven months after his father's death that reaffirmed all of Theodosius's recent laws on religious matters. In the western empire, Honorius issued a series of laws in 399 that allowed temples to remain standing as public monuments and festivals to continue as entertainment, with the constant proviso that there be no sacrifices. Lastly, Theodosius II issued two laws, one in 426 and another in 435, that reaffirmed previously established penalties for any surviving pagans who engage in prohibited practices. We can interpret these reiterations in two rather different ways. Some have argued that they attest to the ineffectiveness of the legislation and the ongoing tenacity of traditional cult practice. By contrast, it seems equally plausible that such measures functioned as public demonstrations of imperial piety and severity, displays of righteous anger directed against increasingly absent opponents. They may well have involved some of both.[65]

## *10e. Conclusion*

The imperial program of marginalizing and suppressing traditional cult practices that culminated in the legislation of Theodosius I in the early 390s was by no means concerned solely with animal sacrifice. The evidence that I have cited regularly refers to other traditional cult practices as well: rituals centered on idols, entry into temples, the pouring of libations, the burning of incense, and so forth. Moreover, since the Greek and Latin terms *thusia* and *sacrificium* encompassed a range of offerings that extended beyond animal sacrifice, legislation that used those terms was far more wide-ranging in effect. As we have seen, however, animal sacrifice had come to be a particularly charged practice in terms of marking religious affiliation, and so it is no surprise that it had a particularly prominent place in the suppression of traditional cult.

The cultic use of incense provides an instructive contrast. As we have seen, Libanius, in his speech for the temples, concedes that animal sacrifice has been prohibited but claims that offerings of incense are still allowed, "so that

---

[65]. Arcadius: *Cod. Theod.* 16.10.13. Honorius: *Cod. Theod.* 16.10.15, 17, and 18. Theodosius II: *Cod. Theod.* 16.10.23 and 25. On the tenacity of traditional cult practices, see, e.g., Harl 1990 and Trombley 1995, especially 1.1–97.

we do not so much lament what we have lost as show gratitude for the concession we have obtained.... From the temples and altars you have banished neither fire nor incense nor the offerings of other perfumes." Similarly, in Rome, the staunchly pagan senator Symmachus seems to have considered the possibility that he and his fellows could maintain the city's traditional public cults by shifting the focus away from animal sacrifice to non-blood offerings.[66] Christians had long opposed the cultic use of incense along with other pagan practices, and as we have seen, Theodosius ultimately banned incense and offerings of wine or garlands as well as animal sacrifice. Nevertheless, such vegetal offerings never inspired the same degree of disgust as animal sacrifice and never figured so centrally in demonological discourse; it seems to have been more the context than the offerings themselves that inspired Christian hostility. A striking indication of this difference is the fact that when Theodosius banned the use of incense in the context of traditional cult, it was already starting to be incorporated into Christian cult. The pilgrim Egeria, who visited Jerusalem in the late fourth century, describes the use of incense in the liturgy there, and by the fifth century, it was apparently becoming more widespread. The association of incense with idolatry thus seems to have been much less indissoluble than that of animal sacrifice.[67]

Although there are many uncertainties about imperial policy regarding animal sacrifice in the fourth century, a few points seem relatively secure. Constantine castigated the practice and may have issued a more comprehensive ban, although if he did, its effects must have been fairly limited. His sons certainly issued categorical prohibitions, although they did not result in the eradication of animal sacrifice even from public contexts. Julian reversed course and actively promoted the practice, presenting himself as a model of sacrificial piety. Its legal status in the thirty years after his death is now uncertain and perhaps was so even at the time; there is evidence that some people continued to perform animal sacrifices in more or less public contexts, whereas others regarded it as forbidden. In the early 390s, however, Theodosius put an end to such uncertainty, and thereafter animal sacrifice was consistently marked as a criminal activity.

---

66. Libanius: *Or.* 30.7–8. Symmachus: Salzman 2011, 174–77; see further Elsner 2012, 126–33, for the emphasis on vegetal offerings in late Roman art.

67. Egeria 24.10: *thimiateria inferuntur intro spelunca Anastasis, ut tota basilica Anastasis repleatur odoribus*; see further Caseau 2012, 543–49, and for a broader discussion of incense in fourth- and fifth-century Christianity, Harvey 2006, 75–83. The contrast between the eventual Christian acceptance of incense and rejection of animal sacrifice was already noted by Naiden 2013, 288–89.

# *Epilogue*

In this part, I have focused on imperial policy concerning animal sacrifice, tracing its shifts over a period of a century and a half. As I have argued, these shifts ultimately resulted in a radical transformation of the social function and cultural significance of animal sacrifice. Beginning with Decius, Roman emperors tried to enforce the practice in a way that earlier emperors never had and in the process transformed it from an integral part of the empire's sociopolitical structure into an imperially mandated signifier of identification with the Roman Empire. Their actions provoked a powerful reaction on the part of Christian leaders, who used all the resources at their disposal to propagate among their followers the belief that animal sacrifice was fundamentally incompatible with Christian identity. Imperial insistence on animal sacrifice, matched by the equally insistent rejection of Christian leaders, effectively rendered Roman and Christian identity mutually exclusive options. Although Gallienus's de facto legal recognition of Christian associations and institutions temporarily resolved that standoff, Christian leaders did not relax their vigilance regarding animal sacrifice. Their heightened concern with the practice ultimately had the effect of recasting it as a particularly potent signifier of the religious traditions that they were in the process of rebranding as "paganism." After Constantine effected his alliance between Roman imperial power and Christian authority, he incorporated this shift in the social and cultural role of animal sacrifice into imperial policy. Thereafter, all his successors accepted animal sacrifice as a marker of self-identification not with Rome but with a particular religion, whether they approved of that religion, as did Julian, or disapproved of it, as did the majority. As emperors gradually evolved a policy of suppressing paganism, they inevitably came to restrict, castigate, and ultimately prohibit animal sacrifice with greater zeal than other traditional cult practices.

In closing, I return to the questions that I posed in the prologue to this part. Why did animal sacrifice become the focus of so much imperial concern? What factors drove this transformation in its social and cultural role? In answering these questions, it is tempting to assign too much weight to the new discourses of animal sacrifice that developed in the imperial period, which I traced in Chapters 7 and 8. The temptation arises in part from the fact that these are developments for which we have abundant evidence and which we can effectively chart; as such, they attract our attention and simultaneously distract us from other factors that are more difficult to document. In the case of animal sacrifice, I would argue that large-scale changes in the political and economic structures of the empire were ultimately of greater significance.

That is by no means to say that the new discourses of animal sacrifice did not play a part in its transformation. On the contrary, their impact, especially in the Christian tradition, was profound. As I argued in Section 7c, the developing discourse of Jesus as sacrificial victim eventually came to displace traditional sacrificial practice from Christian cult and thereby laid the essential foundations for elaborating the demonological discourse of animal sacrifice. Yet this demonological discourse did not directly or immediately determine the behavior of all those who identified as Christians: even as late as the mid-third century, our evidence indicates that at least some Christians complied with Decius's order that all inhabitants of the empire engage in animal sacrifice. It required ongoing interventions on the part of Christian leaders to establish firmly the principle that animal sacrifice was in all cases incompatible with Christian identity and to attach sufficient ideological weight to its rejection. It was as a result of their determined opposition and discursive maneuvering that when a Roman emperor eventually espoused the Christian cause, the conceptual transformation of animal sacrifice into a signifier of pagan identity was ready at hand for him to adopt. I have argued that Constantine's views on animal sacrifice may have been influenced by arguments such as those of Origen, who insisted that providing sustenance to evil *daimones* by means of animal sacrifice was just as damaging to the political community as aiding and abetting bandits. More important than the impact of specific discourses on specific policies, however, was the general perception of animal sacrifice as a distinctively pagan cult practice, a perception that was the direct result of many decades of discursive work on the part of Christian leaders.

For the proponents of animal sacrifice, on the other hand, the importance of these new discourses is much less clear. This is partly an issue of evidence, since, in contrast to Christian leaders, we have little direct insight into the motivations and thinking of the emperors who tried to impose animal sacrifice on the people of the empire. There is indirect evidence for a general concern with Roman tradition on the part of Valerian and Diocletian and more direct evidence in the case of Galerius. Some scholars have argued strongly that Porphyry played a significant part in instigating and shaping the Tetrarchs' persecution of Christians, but his influence on their policies on animal sacrifice remains highly uncertain. The issue is not, however, merely one of evidence: broader considerations of communication and power suggest that these new discourses did, in fact, have less impact on Roman authorities than on Christian leaders. The latter had from the start established their authority within their communities on the basis of claims to privileged knowledge about the nature of the cosmos and their ability to persuade others of its truth. Traditional elites, in contrast, derived their social power from other sources, above all the control of economic resources. As a result, discourse was simply much less important to them. For example, although I have suggested that the development of discourses of sacrificial practice helped disembed it from its traditional sociocultural context, this is likely to have affected only a small proportion of the population, those with both the resources and the inclination to interest themselves in such matters. Animal sacrifice did indeed become increasingly disembedded from its traditional sociocultural context, but that was primarily the result of very different forces.

Among the factors from which the scholarly focus on discourse tends to distract us are the large-scale changes in the sociopolitical organization of the empire. In the Roman Empire of the first through early third centuries, which was to a large extent a fairly loose network of self-governing cities, animal sacrifice had played a valuable role in articulating and reinforcing sociopolitical structures based on wealth and enabling the elites of populations recently brought under Roman hegemony to negotiate a place for themselves within those structures. In the new empire of the fourth century, in which the centralized and hierarchical institutions of the Roman imperial state and the imperially authorized Christian church played a dominant role, the practice of animal sacrifice had much less to contribute. As Daniel Ullucci has aptly put it, "it no longer made sense to people as a thing to do."[1] These changes in the sociopolitical structures of the empire were already under way by the mid-third century and were perhaps already undermining the place of animal sacrifice in the culture of the empire, even though their effect is not easy to document. Decius's decree, I have suggested, may have been a response to these developments. Yet the attempts of Decius and the emperors who followed him to re-establish the

---

[1]. Ullucci 2012, 136; his larger point is that "in a social context where religious power derived from intellectual production and textual mastery, animal sacrifice, tied as it was to agricultural production and landownership, was simply an incoherent practice." I largely agree, although I posit additional factors as well.

social and cultural importance of animal sacrifice on a new basis had instead the effect of undermining the richness, nuance, and flexibility of its traditional role, as I analyzed it in Part I, and reducing it to a simple marker of identification with the Roman Empire. Without this earlier transformation of the social function and cultural significance of animal sacrifice, Constantine's crucial reconceptualization of it as a signifier of paganism would not have been possible.

# 11

# The End of Animal Sacrifice?

## 11a. Introduction

In this book, I have traced the transformation of animal sacrifice from a normative practice tightly bound up with the functioning of the Roman Empire into a particularly potent marker of the "paganism" that Christian leaders and Roman authorities increasingly marginalized and suppressed. Already seriously weakened by the time of Theodosius's legislation in the early 390s CE, traditional Graeco-Roman animal sacrifice thereafter largely disappears from view. Yet the end of animal sacrifice as a ritualized practice did not entail its disappearance from Christian and later European culture; on the contrary, it left traces that remain vivid to this day. Somewhat paradoxically, many of these traces are to be found in the Christian tradition. As we saw in Section 7d, although early Christian thinkers rejected the practice of animal sacrifice as fundamentally incompatible with Christian identity, they nevertheless retained and transformed the idea of sacrifice, reworking it as a central if often contested element in Christian theology. Christ's life and death became the paradigmatic sacrifice, the standard according to which other actions could also be regarded as sacrifices, if always to a lesser degree. In this way, the Christian idea of sacrifice came to include both ritualized practices, most notably the Eucharist, as well as nonritualized types of behavior characterized by charity, devotion, and self-denial. Some Christians even adopted ritualized practices involving the slaughter of animals, although those who have done so have been careful to conceptualize them as non-sacrifices. In this final chapter, I trace some of these Christian transformations of animal sacrifice, whose influence in certain cases extends far beyond specifically Christian contexts. Before turning to the Christian tradition, however, I must first briefly note a very different way in which animal sacrifice continues to have a place in European culture.

## 11b. Animal Sacrifice and the Primitive

As we saw in Section 8c, early Christian leaders reconceptualized animal sacrifice as a practice that served the needs of the evil *daimones* who opposed God and preyed on humanity. Anyone who engaged in it was thus by definition either ignorant of the salvation brought by Christ or, worse, deliberately rejected or violated it. In this way, animal sacrifice became over time a prominent marker of the non-Christian "other": heathen barbarians and savages, on the one hand, people in need of correction by the more enlightened, and, on the other hand, people who deliberately chose to side with the forces of cosmic evil and thus deserved punishment.[1] It continued to function in this way for as long as those with social power equated civilization with Christianity. With the fracturing of western European Christendom in the Protestant Reformation and the growth of a secular worldview in the Enlightenment, this view of animal sacrifice became increasingly attenuated, although it still retains some hold on the European imagination. European scholars instead increasingly came to regard animal sacrifice in more neutral terms as a cultural practice, a ritual.[2] Yet even so, it continued to signify "the other." Implicitly accepting the standards of a civilization that had long marginalized animal sacrifice, such scholars associated it with the primitive and the exotic, the practice of peoples separated from themselves by significant temporal or geographical distance. Just as the elite of the Graeco-Roman world had accepted animal sacrifice as a normative marker of civilization, so, too, later European elites accepted its absence as a marker of civilization. Its presence, consequently, required explanation. We may here briefly consider a few of the explanations offered by scholars over the last 150 years.

The English scholar E. B. Tylor (1832–1917), one of the founders of modern anthropology, analyzed sacrificial practice in terms of the evolutionary scheme of human culture that he developed most fully in his *Primitive*

---

1. In some ways, animal sacrifice came to function in the later European imagination much as human sacrifice had in the earlier Graeco-Roman imagination (see Rives 1995a), although human sacrifice continues to be an even more powerful signifier of the other: e.g., Frankfurter 2006, especially 73–128.

2. On the reconceptualization of sacrifice as a ritual, see Naiden 2013, 276–316, with the additional analysis of Bremmer 2018, 232–36.

*Culture* (1871). For Tylor, the cultures of contemporary tribal societies in the Americas, Africa, Oceania, and elsewhere represented earlier phases of human cultural development, out of which the higher cultures of Europe and Asia had long ago evolved; they thus provided European scholars with an opportunity to study "primitive" culture at first hand. Tylor distinguished three dominant modes of sacrificial practice. "The ruder conception that the deity takes and values the offering for itself, gives place on the one hand to the idea of mere homage expressed by a gift, and on the other to the negative view that the virtue lies in the worshiper depriving himself of something prized." He labeled these ideas as respectively "the gift-theory, the homage-theory, and the abnegation-theory." Animal sacrifice constituted one of the most primitive forms of sacrificial practice. "When the deity is considered to take actual possession of the food or other objects offered, this may be conceived to happen by abstraction of their life. . . . Among this group of conceptions, the most materialized is that which carries out the obvious primitive world-wide doctrine that the life is the blood. Accordingly, the blood is offered to the deity."[3]

Another early theorist of sacrificial practice was the Scottish scholar William Robertson Smith (1846–1894), who developed his ideas most fully in his *Lectures on the Religion of the Semites* (1889). Under the influence of contemporary anthropological thought, Smith believed that the most primitive form of religion is totemism, in which a social group defines itself through identification with a natural object, most often an animal. In ordinary circumstances, the totemic animal is sacrosanct and hedged around with taboos. In times of crisis, however, there is a perception that the group's relationship to its totem has been disrupted. The solution is animal sacrifice, in which the members of the group restore their connection with the totem and reinforce their collective identity by killing and communally consuming the totemic animal. "In the oldest sacrifices . . . the ritual exactly corresponds with the primitive ideas that holiness means kinship to the worshipers and their god, that all sacred relations and all moral obligations depend on physical unity of life, and that unity of physical life can be created or reinforced by common participation in living flesh and blood."[4] Smith's ideas about the origin and essential nature of sacrifice had considerable influence on the sacrificial theories of such pivotal thinkers as Sigmund Freud (in *Totem und Tabu*, 1913) and Émile Durkheim (in *Les formes élémentaires de la vie religieuse*, 1915),

---

3. Carter 2003, 12–38, for an overview and extract, with quotations from 14 and 18.

4. Carter 2003, 53–75, with quotations from 62–63.

both of whom, in significantly different ways, interpreted animal sacrifice as an act arising from the most primitive level of human cultural development.

An emphasis on the primitive is not limited to scholars of a century or more ago but also characterizes the ideas of two of the most influential theorists of animal sacrifice of the last fifty years, Walter Burkert (1931–2015) and René Girard (1923–2015), both of whom coincidentally published their crucial books on the subject in the same year, 1972. Burkert, in *Homo necans: Interpretationen altgriechischer Opferriten und Mythen*, traced the origins of animal sacrifice back to the Paleolithic period, when groups of hunters learned to cooperate by redirecting their inherently aggressive tendencies toward their prey instead of each other; its slaughter, however, inspired feelings of guilt, which they assuaged through such ritual means as arranging the animal's bones and skin in order to recreate it after death. So powerful were the psychological and sociological needs that these practices met that societies maintained them even as they transitioned from hunting and gathering to agriculture, in the process transforming them into the ritual of animal sacrifice. Girard, in *La violence et le sacré*, likewise located the origin of animal sacrifice in fundamental psychological and sociological needs. According to Girard, an underlying motivating force in human behavior is mimetic desire, the desire to have something simply because another person desires it. Mimetic desire inevitably leads to aggression, as people ultimately seek to obtain their desires by killing their rivals, and the aggression inevitably becomes cyclical, as each act of aggression inspires an act of counter-aggression. The only way to break the cycle is to transfer the aggression to a surrogate victim, a scapegoat, whose death provides a safe outlet for the violent tendencies inherent in any group.[5] From Tylor to Burkert and Girard, then, animal sacrifice has played a significant role in European thinking about the primordial stages of human cultural development.

## *IIc. Animal Offerings in Christian Tradition*

Turning now to sacrifice in the Christian tradition, we may begin with practices that in form have much in common with ancient Mediterranean animal sacrifice. Starting in the early fourth century CE and continuing into the present day, some Christian groups have engaged in ritualized practices that involve the slaughter of animals. Although scholars have been describing

---

5. Burkert and Girard: Carter 2003, 210–38, 239–75.

these practices as animal sacrifice for more than a century, the Christian leaders who endorse them have typically been at pains to differentiate them from "real" animal sacrifices.[6] I note here a few well-attested examples.

According to Paulinus, the bishop of the town of Nola outside Naples, people from the surrounding regions regularly vowed animals to Nola's patron saint Felix; they would slaughter these animals at his shrine and then use the meat in a feast for the poor. In the poem that he wrote for the saint's festival day in 406 CE, Paulinus relates at length three miraculous tales featuring animals who, under divine inspiration, played an active role in realizing their owners' vows. In a similar case, an anonymous account of the construction of the great church of Hagia Sophia in Constantinople, dating probably to the eighth or ninth century, relates that the emperor Justinian, as part of the elaborate festivities celebrating its dedication in 537 CE, "sacrificed (ἔθυσε) a thousand bulls, six thousand sheep, six hundred deer, a thousand swine, birds and cocks ten thousand each, and gave it out to the poor and needy. He also dispensed thirty thousand measures of grain. He was distributing all this until three o'clock of the same day. . . . On the following day he celebrated the opening of the church, offering the same and even more abundant whole-burnt sacrifices (τοσαῦτα καὶ πλείονα ὁλοκαυτώματα θύσας) and up to the holy Epiphany, during fifteen days, he was giving feasts to all, distributing alms, and bringing thanksgivings to the Lord." Although scholars have long questioned the historicity of this account, Ekaterina Kovaltchuk has argued convincingly that it may well reflect an awareness on the part of both author and audience that ritualized slaughter could play a role in Christian festivals.[7]

Turning to the modern period, we may note the *kourbánia* that are celebrated in Greek villages down to the present day. These are festivals organized around the slaughter of domestic animals in honor of the local saint and the collective consumption of the meat by the villagers. The slaughter normally takes place outside the village church before, during, or after the festival mass, and the victim, most often funded by the community as a whole, is consecrated by the local priest. The focal point of the festival is not the slaughter itself but the consumption of the meat, which is most often cooked

---

6. The earliest scholarly study of "Christian animal sacrifice" known to me is Conybeare 1903, the most recent is Hutt 2018–19. Kovaltchuk 2008 provides a valuable survey of the Christian material; Hutt 2018–19 also includes late ancient Judaism and early Islam.

7. Paulinus: *Carmen* 20, with Trout 1995 and Grottanelli 2005. Justinian: Kovaltchuk 2008, 159–62, 191–98, with quotations from her translation on 158–59; text from Vitti 1986, 464.

and eaten on the spot in a communal feast. Another well-known contemporary example of a Christian ritual involving the slaughter of an animal is the practice of *matał* or *matagh* in the Armenian Church, which according to tradition dates back to the church's founding in the early fourth century and continues to be one of its official practices. According to the website of the Mother See of Holy Etchmiadzin, the mother cathedral of the worldwide Armenian Church, *matagh* is an offering whose "main meaning is giving a gift to God and giving alms to the poor." "One needs two elements for offering a sacrifice: an animal and salt. The animal must be male. It can be a cow, sheep, chicken or dove. When a cow is killed, its meat is distributed to 40 houses, a lamb, to 7 houses, a chicken, to 3 houses. The meat must not be left until the next day.... First, the salt must be blessed. The salt is the element which purifies the *matagh* and makes it different from the pagan sacrifice. The meat is cooked only in salted water."[8]

Historical evidence suggests that in at least some cases, practices such as these originated as the result of a deliberate strategy on the part of Christian leaders to adapt pre-Christian sacrificial practices to a Christian framework. The most explicit statement of such a policy occurs in a letter that Pope Gregory the Great wrote in 601 CE to the abbot Mellitus, whom he had recently sent to Britain to aid in the process of converting the Anglo-Saxons. Gregory proposed a policy of maintaining the external forms to which the people were accustomed but transforming their content. "Because they are in the habit of slaughtering much cattle as sacrifices to demons (*in sacrificio daemonum*), some solemnity ought to be given them in exchange for this. So on the day of the dedication or the festival of the holy martyrs, whose relics are deposited there, let them make themselves huts from the branches of trees around the churches which have been converted out of shrines, and let them celebrate the solemnity with religious feasts (*religiosis conviviis*). Do not let them sacrifice animals to the devil (*nec diabolo iam animalia immolent*), but let them slaughter (*occidant*) animals for their own food to the praise of God, and let them give thanks to the Giver of all things for His bountiful provision. Thus while some outward rejoicings are preserved, they will be able more easily to share in inward rejoicings." As in the modern Greek *kourbánia*,

---

8. *Kourbánia*: Georgoudi 1979. *Matał*: quotations from https://www.armenianchurch.org/index.jsp?sid=1&id=5819&pid=2429; on the historical background, see Conybeare 1903 and Kovaltchuk 2008, 175–79.

the slaughter and the feasting would continue but no longer constitute a sacrifice.[9]

Whether or not it is appropriate to describe such practices as animal sacrifice depends on one's definition of the term, since they display both similarities to and differences from pre-Christian animal sacrifice.[10] One striking similarity, beyond the popular appeal that feasting on meat has had across cultures, is the ongoing utility of rituals that redistribute animal resources in ways that communicate and construct social structures and cultural norms. That is as true of these Christian practices as it was of ancient Graeco-Roman animal sacrifice, even though the structures and norms involved often differ from those analyzed in Chapters 3 and 4. In a few cases, notably in the tradition about Justinian's largesse at the dedication of Hagia Sophia, Christian practices serve to reinforce social hierarchies in a manner very similar to that of animal sacrifice in Graeco-Roman euergetism. The modern Greek *kourbánia*, by contrast, seem instead to emphasize egalitarian community. The most striking difference from traditional Graeco-Roman practice is that the party to whom the sacrifice is offered does not receive any portion of the victim: no part of the animal is burned on an altar or otherwise consigned to the figure to whom it was vowed.[11] Accordingly, by the definition of animal sacrifice that I have used throughout this book, these do not constitute animal sacrifices; although they are ritualized practices involving the slaughter of animals, no part of the victims is offered to perceived superhuman powers.[12]

---

9. The letter is preserved by Bede, *Hist. eccl.* 1.30, trans. Colgrave and Mynors 1969, lightly adapted; cf. Trout 1995, 297; Grottanelli 2005, 403–4; Kovaltchuk 2008, 171–72. Broadly similar strategies of transforming traditional animal sacrifice into a Christian ritual are attributed to Gregory the Illuminator in Armenia in the early fourth century CE (Conybeare 1903, 62–63) and to Nicholas of Hagia Sion in Lycia in the first half of the sixth century (Trombley 1985, 339; cf. Trout 1995, 298n72). Note, however, that the similarities of the modern Greek *kourbánia* to pre-Christian animal sacrifice do not mean that we should understand the former simply as a survival of the latter: Georgoudi 1979, especially 287–90.

10. See, for example, Grottanelli 2005 responding to Trout 1995 over the relative degree of continuity and change in the animal offerings to Saint Felix of Nola.

11. This is a point rightly emphasized by Georgoudi 1979, 299–301, in connection with the modern Greek *kourbánia*, but it seems equally true of the Armenian *matał* and the various historical practices noted here. The one exception may be in the account of Justinian's offerings, depending on what the author had in mind by "whole-burnt offerings" (ὁλοκαυτώματα), although the context suggests that he is using the term loosely.

12. Libanius would presumably have agreed, since he made precisely the same point in arguing that no one had broken the law by offering animal sacrifices at the temples he was trying to protect; they may have slaughtered an animal and held a feast and even burned incense and sang hymns, but since "no altar received the blood offering, no single part of the victim was burned,"

The sources instead regularly present these practices as a form of charity, since in many cases, all the meat from the victims goes toward the sustenance of the poor. Paulinus repeatedly stresses that the purpose behind the practice of vowing animals to Saint Felix was to feed the poor and drives home this point in the first and longest of his three tales of miraculous animals. A man who had vowed a pig to the saint duly slaughtered it at the shrine but then attempted to fob off the less desirable bits on the poor while he loaded his horse with all the good meat to take back to his own household. On his return journey, however, the horse threw him to the ground, left him there incapable of walking, and returned riderless to the shrine; his master was taken by his relatives back to the shrine, where he confessed his misdeed and ordered the meat distributed to the poor, whereupon he was promptly healed by the saint.[13] In these practices, it seems that what the worshiper actually offers to God or the saint is not the animal victim itself but rather the act of charity that results from its slaughter. In this respect, they align less with the Graeco-Roman practice of animal sacrifice than with its Christian reconceptualization, to which we turn next.

### 11d. Christian Reconceptualizations of Sacrifice

As we saw in Section 7c, Christians at an early date began to use sacrificial terminology to make sense of Jesus's life and death. By the third century CE, it had become widely established that this constituted the one perfect and paradigmatic sacrifice.[14] In tandem with that development, some Christian thinkers also began to apply the terminology of sacrifice to the practices of his devotees. We may briefly consider two of the most prominent cases.

One of the practices to which sacrificial terminology has been applied is the ritual of the Eucharist, which Christian writers began to describe as a sacrifice already in the early second century. The author (or compiler) of the Didache instructs his readers that when they gather on Sundays to break bread and give thanks, they must first confess their misdeeds, "so that your

---

what they did was not an animal sacrifice (Lib. *Or.* 30.16–18, trans. A. F. Norman, Loeb); see further Section 10d above.

13. Paulinus, *Carmen* 20.62–300; see also 312–20 and 389–94. The Byzantine legend about Justinian's offerings at the dedication of Hagia Sophia stresses the same point, as does the Armenian practice of *matał* (Kovaltchuk 2008, 177; see also the website cited in n. 8 above).

14. Young 1979, 139–217; cf. Section 7c above. On the Christian transformation of the idea of sacrifice, see in general the wide-ranging paper of Muñiz Grijalvo 2003.

sacrifice may be pure (ὅπως καθαρὰ ἡ θυσία ὑμῶν ᾖ)." If they are involved in quarrels, they should be reconciled before they join, "so that your sacrifice may not be profaned (ἵνα μὴ κοινωθῇ ἡ θυσία ὑμῶν)." "For this," he explains, "is the sacrifice mentioned by the Lord: 'In every place and time, bring me a pure sacrifice. For I am a great King, says the Lord, and my name is considered marvelous among the Gentiles.'" The quotation here comes from a passage of the prophet Malachi, which the author has carefully edited to serve his purposes; its implications in its original context were very different.[15] This passage became a favorite proof text among later Christian writers, who used it to demonstrate that the Christian Eucharist had replaced the sacrifices of the Jerusalem Temple as the only sacrifices acceptable to God. Justin Martyr, for example, in his dialogue with the Judaean Trypho, after another carefully selected quotation from this passage, concludes that God, "by making reference to the sacrifices which we gentiles offer to him (περὶ δὲ τῶν . . . προσφερομένων αὐτῷ θυσιῶν) in every place, namely, the bread of the Eucharist and the chalice of the Eucharist, predicted that we should glorify his name, but that you Judaeans should profane it."[16]

On what basis did these writers conceptualize the Eucharist as a sacrifice, one that they could equate with those previously offered in the Jerusalem Temple? On the surface, the two practices had very little in common. A likely answer is that they did so because they identified the Eucharist with the sacrifice of Christ. Justin, for example, after describing Eucharistic practice in his apology, asserts that "we do not receive these things as common bread or common drink. But, just as Jesus Christ our Savior was made flesh by means of a word of God, and had flesh and blood for our salvation, just so we have been taught that the food which has been Eucharistized (τὴν . . . εὐχαριστηθεῖσαν τροφήν) through a word of prayer which comes from him is the flesh and blood of that Jesus who was made flesh—from which food our blood and flesh are nourished by metabolic process." He then supports this interpretation of the ritual by summarizing the events of the Last Supper.[17] By the third century, these ideas had come to cohere into an established doctrine that was more and more widely accepted. We find evidence for this in one of the earliest extended discussions of the meaning of the Eucharist, a letter of

---

15. Did. 14.1–3, with the quotation from 14.3, trans. Bart D. Ehrman, Loeb. The passage of Malachi is 1.6–14, where the prophet berates priests for sacrificing blind, lame, or sick animals.

16. *Dial.* 41.3, trans. Falls 2003, lightly adapted; cf. 117.1–5.

17. Just. *Apol.* 1.66.2–3, trans. Minns and Parvis 2009.

Cyprian dating probably to the mid-250s. Cyprian writes to his fellow bishop Caecilius, who had apparently been celebrating the Eucharist with water only, and argues at considerable length that the cup must also contain wine; wine, Cyprian insists, is the element in the ritual that constitutes the blood of Christ. In support, he cites and interprets many passages of scripture, which make it evident, he declares, "that the blood of Christ is not offered if there is no wine in the cup, and that the Lord's sacrifice (*sacrificium dominicum*) is not duly consecrated and celebrated unless the offering and sacrifice we make (*oblatio et sacrificium nostrum*) corresponds with His passion." For Cyprian, it seems, the Eucharist was a sacrifice because in some way it re-embodied the sacrifice of Christ.[18]

In Christian tradition, then, the Eucharist became the only true form of ritual sacrifice, one that reproduced in ritual form the paradigmatic sacrifice of Christ. This continues to be the case for many Christians today, even though there has been considerable disagreement, starting with the Protestant Reformation, about the precise sense in which the Eucharist constitutes a sacrifice. I describe the Eucharist as specifically a ritual sacrifice, because another early Christian reconceptualization of sacrifice removed it from the sphere of ritual altogether. While the ongoing debate over the nature of the Eucharist is important primarily for theologians, this other reconceptualization has had much broader influence in contemporary society. Here I can sketch only its earliest stages.

In his letter to the Christ followers in Rome, Paul urges his audience "to present your bodies as a living sacrifice (θυσίαν ζῶσαν), holy and acceptable to God, which is your reasonable act of worship." Paul here demonstrates once again his genius for devising compelling if enigmatic images. In traditional animal sacrifice, it was essential that the bodies of the animals that the worshipers presented to the divine be dead; their slaughter was an indispensable part of the ritual. How, then, would his audience have understood his exhortation to present their own living bodies as a sacrifice? Although we have no evidence for what they made of it, we may note that Paul continues by emphasizing the importance of, first, community among believers ("we, who are many, are one body in Christ") and then the virtues of love, compassion, and humility: "love one another with mutual affection; outdo one another in showing honor; do not lag in zeal; be ardent in spirit; serve the Lord; rejoice

---

18. Cypr. *Ep.* 63, with the quotation from 9.3, trans. G. Clarke 1984–89; cf. 1.1, 4.1, 5.1, 12.1, 14.1, and 16.2; date: G. Clarke 1984–89, 3.287–88. On celebrating the Eucharist with water alone, see McGowan 1999a, especially 204–11 on this letter.

in hope; be patient in affliction; persevere in prayer; contribute to the needs of the saints; pursue hospitality to strangers; bless those who persecute you." As he does so often, Paul leaves it to his audience to make the connections between his ideas, but he seems to be suggesting that it is through the way they live their lives that they can present their bodies to God as a living sacrifice.[19]

Paul was not the only early Christian writer to use sacrifice as a metaphor in this way. The author of the letter traditionally known as 1 Peter develops a complex figurative scheme, one that in its richness is worthy of Paul himself, in which he represents his addressees as both the stones of the temple and the priests who serve there. In the course of this scheme, he urges them to "come to him [Christ], a living stone, though rejected by mortals yet chosen and precious in God's sight, and like living stones let yourselves be built into a spiritual house, to be a holy priesthood, to offer spiritual sacrifices ($\pi\nu\epsilon\upsilon\mu\alpha\tau\iota\kappa\grave{\alpha}\varsigma$ $\theta\upsilon\sigma\acute{\iota}\alpha\varsigma$) acceptable to God through Jesus Christ." Like Paul in his letter to the Christ followers in Rome, the author then goes on to exhort his audience to live lives of discipline, obedience, and passive endurance, following the example of Christ himself:

> Beloved, I urge you as aliens and exiles to abstain from the desires of the flesh that wage war against the soul. Conduct yourselves honorably among the gentiles, so that, though they malign you as evildoers, they may see your honorable deeds and glorify God when he comes to judge. For the Lord's sake be subject to every human authority, whether to the emperor as supreme or to governors as sent by him to punish those who do wrong and to praise those who do right. For it is God's will that by doing right you should silence the ignorance of the foolish. As servants of God, live as free people, yet do not use your freedom as a pretext for evil. Honor everyone. Love the family of believers. Fear God. Honor the emperor.[20]

The author of the letter to the Hebrews makes a similar point more explicitly and concisely. As we saw in Section 7d, he devotes most of his treatise to elaborating on the idea of Christ as simultaneously the supreme high priest and the supreme sacrificial victim. Near the end, however, he applies the metaphor of sacrifice to the actions of Christ's followers as well: "Let us

---

19. Rom. 12, with quotations from 1, 5, and 10–14, NRSV.
20. 1 Peter 2, with quotations from 4–5 and 11–17, NRSV.

continually offer a sacrifice of praise (θυσίαν αἰνέσεως) to God, that is, the fruit of lips that confess his name. Do not neglect to do good and to share what you have, for such sacrifices are pleasing to God (τοιαύταις γὰρ θυσίαις εὐαρεστεῖται ὁ θεός)."[21] What he here terms "sacrifices" are clearly the doing of good deeds (εὐποιΐα) and community spirit (κοινωνία) that he has just urged them to observe.

All these writers extend the meaning of the term "sacrifice" to denote a virtuous life, especially one modeled on Jesus's own life. We can trace here similarities with the earlier insistence, expressed in somewhat difference ways by both Greek philosophers and Israelite prophets, that the divine is more interested in worshipers' moral behavior and true devotion than in their material offerings.[22] The difference is that the earlier philosophers and prophets saw these moral qualities as essential elements of a properly conducted ritual sacrifice, whereas these early Christian thinkers applied the term "sacrifice" to the moral qualities alone and dispensed with the actual ritual altogether.

Just as these writers described a virtuous life as a sacrifice, other writers so described a virtuous death. In the early Christian context, the paradigmatic virtuous death was one that resulted from steadfast self-identification as a Christian in the face of persecution, which came to be termed a martyrdom.[23] We find an early example of this usage in the letters written by Ignatius, the bishop of Antioch, during his journey to Rome after being condemned to death by exposure to wild beasts in the arena there. One of his chief concerns in his letter to the Christians in Rome is to entreat them not to take any actions that would hinder his execution. In a passage dense with figurative language, he first describes himself as the wheat of God, to be ground by the teeth of wild beasts so that he may become the pure bread of Christ, and then asks them to "petition Christ on my behalf, that I may be found a sacrifice (θυσία) through these instruments of God." Similarly, the author of a letter preserved by Eusebius describing a persecution of Christians in the Gallic cities of Lugdunum and Vienna (modern Lyons and Vienne), probably in 177,

---

21. Hebrews 13.15–16, NRSV.

22. Ullucci 2012, 31–64.

23. Recent scholarship consistently emphasizes that the concept of martyrdom resulted from a complex process of development over the course of Mediterranean antiquity, although there is considerable debate over the contours of that development; key discussions include Bowersock 1995, Boyarin 1999, Barnes 2010, Moss 2010b, and Moss 2012. On the role of sacrifice in the conceptualization of martyrdom, see especially Castelli 2004, 50–67; Heyman 2007, 161–218, provides a wide-ranging discussion, although one that relies on a notably broad and loose definition of "sacrifice."

several times says of his heroes that after suffering many tortures, they "were finally sacrificed (τοὔσχατον ἐτύθησαν)."[24] The image is more elaborately developed in the account of the martyrdom of Polycarp, the bishop of Smyrna, who was burned at the stake probably in the late 150s; although the account is usually thought to be the work of an eyewitness, recent scholars have argued that it more likely dates to the third century CE:

> They did not nail him down, but they tied him. With his hands placed behind him and bound, like a ram marked out from a great flock for an offering (εἰς προσφοράν), prepared as a burnt offering acceptable to God (ὁλοκαύτωμα δεκτὸν τῷ θεῷ), he looked up to heaven and said: "Lord, God Almighty, Father of your beloved and blessed son Jesus Christ, through whom we have received knowledge of you . . ., I bless you because you have found me worthy of this day and hour, to receive, among the number of your martyrs, a share in the cup of your Christ for the resurrection of eternal life, both of soul and body, in the immortality of the Holy Spirit. May I be accepted among these in your presence today, in a rich and acceptable sacrifice (ἐν θυσίᾳ πίονι καὶ προσδεκτῇ), as you, the truthful and true God, have prepared, revealed beforehand, and fulfilled."[25]

None of these writers explains why they describe the death of martyrs as a "sacrifice," but the basic point of comparison is obvious enough: the martyr is slaughtered just as the victims in an animal sacrifice were, something that the author of the martyrdom of Polycarp makes explicit in his simile likening his hero to a ram chosen for an offering. Yet he also suggests a connection with the sacrifice of Jesus by having Polycarp give thanks for being found worthy to share in the cup of Christ, an image that the authors of the Synoptic Gospels several times use regarding his suffering and death. Describing martyrs as sacrifices, then, evokes not just the obvious point of comparison but also the idea that they were in some sense imitating the paradigmatic sacrifice of

---

24. Ignatius: *Rom.* 4.1–2, trans. Bart D. Ehrman, Loeb; cf. 2.2, where he similarly asks that they allow him to be poured out as a libation to God (σπονδισθῆναι θεῷ). Lugdunum: Euseb. *Hist. eccl.* 5.1 (= Musurillo 1972, no. 5 = Rebillard 2017, 145–73, with quotation from 5.1.40, cf. 51 and 56; Eusebius dates the events to 177 CE (*Hist. eccl.* 5.*praef*.1), and it is usually assumed that the letter was written by an eyewitness.

25. Martyrdom of Polycarp: *BHG* 1556–60 = Musurillo 1972, no. 1 = Rebillard 2017, 90–105; quotation from 14.1–2, trans. Rebillard 2017. Date of martyrdom: Barnes 2010, 367–78; date of text: Moss 2010a; cf. Rebillard 2017, 84.

Christ.[26] This was an idea that Origen, in his treatise on martyrdom, developed more systematically, drawing not on the image of the cup of Christ but on the presentation of Christ in the letter to the Hebrews as simultaneously the perfect high priest and the perfect sacrificial victim:

> We learn that as the High Priest Jesus Christ offered Himself in sacrifice (θυσίαν ἑαυτὸν προσήνεγκεν), so the priests, whose leader He is, also offer themselves in sacrifice; for this reason one sees them at the altar as their proper place. But while some of the priests were without blemish and offered victims without blemish and so performed the divine service, others had blemishes such as are listed by Moses in Leviticus, and were kept away from the altar. Who then is the priest without blemish who can offer a victim without blemish, if not he who bears witness to the last and fulfills every requirement of the concept of martyrdom (ὁ τοῦ μαρτυρίου λόγος)?[27]

In death as well as in life, then, Christ's sacrifice served as a model for the sacrifices of Christians.

These metaphors completely remove the idea of sacrifice from the sphere of ritual and apply it instead to a person's actions more generally. For all these writers, the true sacrifice that Christians offer to God, following the example of Christ, is their obedience, their service, and their devotion, if need be to the point of death. Over the centuries, this early Christian reconceptualization of sacrifice, which divorces it so fully from its original reference to a ritualized practice involving the slaughter of animals, has become increasingly independent of a specifically Christian worldview and permeates the English language much more broadly. We now readily say that parents make sacrifices for their children, that people with high ideals sacrifice themselves for a cause, that soldiers killed in battle have made the ultimate sacrifice. For many people in the contemporary world, the term "sacrifice" refers no longer to a ritualized practice but to self-sacrifice, the action of a person who voluntarily gives up something of value to himself or herself for the sake of something

---

26. Cup of Christ: Mark 10.38–40, with the parallel at Matt. 20.22–23; Mark 14.36, with parallels at Matt. 26.39 and Luke 22.42. Martyrs as imitators of Christ: Moss 2010b.

27. Origen *Mart.* 30, trans. O'Meara 1954.

else, whether an individual, a group, or a cause. For many people, this is what a sacrifice "really" is.[28]

## 11e. Envoi

We thus return to the point with which I began this chapter, since these Christianizing assumptions about what constitutes "real" sacrifice played an important part in shaping the ideas of the late-nineteenth- and early-twentieth-century European scholars who pioneered the modern study of ritual sacrifice. Given that I, too, am steeped in the assumptions of Christian and European culture, I have no doubt that they have likewise shaped my own analyses in this book. Nevertheless, I have attempted to compensate for them, in two ways.

In the first place, I have tried to demystify animal sacrifice, by treating it not as the expression of timeless and profound truths, whether theological or psychological or moral, but rather as a practice in which a range of social and cultural forces intersected and interacted. Although I am conscious of the irony involved in saying so at the end of this lengthy study, in my view, there is nothing particularly special about animal sacrifice. It does not provide us with unique insights into the human condition or a unique key to understanding the ancient Mediterranean world. The reason I have found it to be a subject worthy of sustained attention is instead precisely the fact that it intersected and interacted in such a range of ways with so many aspects of Roman imperial society and culture. It is the density of those interconnections that makes it useful for a case study of cultural transformation in the ancient Mediterranean.[29]

---

28. For a thoughtful and wide-ranging exploration of the shifts in the meaning of the term "sacrifice," see Auffarth 2023; I am grateful to Professor Auffarth for sharing with me an advance copy of his book.

29. Cf. Reed 2014, 146–47, who argues that, instead of "assuming that the 'cessation' of animal sacrifice occurred *in essence* already at an early stage (whether with the biblical prophets or the destruction[s] of the Jerusalem Temple or the birth of Christianity or the rise of the 'holy man') and was inevitable thereafter, ... we might better seek, for instance, multivalent and culturally-specific factors ... —further inquiring, for instance, into the possible after-effects of the spatial displacements of meat-production (e.g., public vs. private, urban vs. local, religious vs. secular), transitions in the political structuring of societies and in the strategies of governmental coercion, shifts in the hierarchies of social stratification, and changing views of the ideals of 'civilization' inscribed onto and with the bodies of the animal and the human." An in-depth study of the ecological and economic dimensions of animal sacrifice, topics that I have only lightly touched on, remains a desideratum.

Second, I have tried to acknowledge the complexity of that cultural transformation. Throughout the book, I have insisted on the stubborn particularities of the evidence, its insufficiencies and uncertainties and inconsistencies. Yet the complexity is not merely a byproduct of the data; it is not something that would disappear if only we had better data. On the contrary, the stubbornness of the evidence is an effective index of the complexity of the social and cultural developments that produced it. In attempting to catalog and analyze some of the traces that the practice of animal sacrifice has left in the historical record, I hope that I have given some sense of the range of factors involved in shaping its social function and cultural significance as these developed and shifted over time. The complexity of these changes, in what was, after all, only one specific practice in the Roman Empire, suggests how much more complicated, and even less susceptible to analysis, were the wider cultural transformations with which the shifting fortunes of animal sacrifice were so closely bound up.

# References

Aldhouse-Green, Miranda. 2010. *Caesar's Druids: Story of an Ancient Priesthood*. New Haven, CT: Yale University Press.

Allison, Dale C., Jr. 2010. *Constructing Jesus: Memory, Imagination, and History*. Grand Rapids, MI: Baker Academic.

Ando, Clifford. 2000. *Imperial Ideology and Provincial Loyalty in the Roman Empire*. Berkeley: University of California Press.

Ando, Clifford. 2005. "*Interpretatio Romana*." *Classical Philology* 100, no. 1: 41–51.

Ando, Clifford. 2007. "Exporting Roman Religion." In *A Companion to Roman Religion*, edited by Jörg Rüpke, 429–45. Malden, MA: Blackwell.

Ando, Clifford. 2008. *The Matter of the Gods: Religion and the Roman Empire*. Berkeley: University of California Press.

Ando, Clifford. 2012. *Imperial Rome AD 193 to 284: The Critical Century*. Edinburgh: Edinburgh University Press.

Ando, Clifford. 2017. "City, Village, Sacrifice: The Political Economy of Religion in the Early Roman Empire." In *Mass and Elite in the Greek and Roman World: From Sparta to Late Antiquity*, edited by Richard Evans, 118–36. New York: Routledge.

Andresen, Carl. 1955. *Logos und Nomos: Die Polemik des Kelsos wider das Christentum*. Berlin: De Gruyter.

Asad, Talal. 1983. "Anthropological Conceptions of Religion: Reflections on Geertz." *Man* 48: 237–59.

Asad, Talal. 1993. "The Construction of Religion as an Anthropological Category." In *Genealogies of Religion: Discipline and Reasons of Power in Christianity and Islam*, 27–54. Baltimore: Johns Hopkins University Press.

Auffarth, Christoph. 2023. *Opfer: Eine europäische Religionsgeschichte*. Göttingen: Vandenhoeck & Ruprecht.

Bagnall, Roger S. 1988. "Combat ou vide: Christianisme et paganisme dans l'Égypte romaine tardive." *Ktèma* 13: 285–96.

Balberg, Mira. 2017. *Blood for Thought: The Reinvention of Sacrifice in Early Rabbinic Literature*. Berkeley: University of California Press.

Barclay, John M. G. 1996. *Jews in the Mediterranean Diaspora from Alexander to Trajan (323 BCE–117 CE)*. Edinburgh: T&T Clark.

Barclay, John M. G. 2007. *Flavius Josephus: Translation and Commentary*, Vol. 10: *Against Apion*. Leiden: Brill.

Bardill, Jonathan. 2012. *Constantine, Divine Emperor of the Christian Golden Age*. Cambridge: Cambridge University Press.

Barnes, Timothy D. 1981. *Constantine and Eusebius*. Cambridge, MA: Harvard University Press.

Barnes, Timothy D. 1982. *The New Empire of Diocletian and Constantine*. Cambridge, MA: Harvard University Press.

Barnes, Timothy D. 2010. *Early Christian Hagiography and Roman History*. Tübingen: Mohr Siebeck.

Barnes, Timothy D. 2011. *Constantine: Dynasty, Religion and Power in the Later Roman Empire*. Malden, MA: Wiley-Blackwell.

Barton, Carlin A., and Daniel Boyarin. 2016. *Imagine No Religion: How Modern Abstractions Hide Ancient Realities*. New York: Fordham University Press.

Baudy, Dorothea. 1998. *Römische Umgangsriten: Eine ethologische Untersuchung der Funktion von Wiederholung für religiöses Verhalten*. Berlin: De Gruyter.

Beard, Mary. 2007. *The Roman Triumph*. Cambridge, MA: Harvard University Press.

Beckmann, Martin. 2012. "The Column of Marcus Aurelius." In *A Companion to Marcus Aurelius*, edited by Marcel van Ackeran, 251–63. Malden, MA: Wiley-Blackwell.

Belayche, Nicole. 2001. "'Partager la table des dieux': L'empereur Julien et les sacrifices." *Revue de l'Histoire des Religions* 218, no. 4: 457–86.

Belayche, Nicole. 2005. "*Realia versus leges*: Les sacrifices de la religion d'état au IVe siècle." In *La cuisine et l'autel: Les sacrifices en questions dans les sociétés de la Méditerranée ancienne*, edited by Stella Georgoudi, Renée Koch Piettre, and Francis Schmidt, 343–70. Turnhout: Brepols.

Belayche, Nicole. 2011. "Le politique religieuse 'païenne' de Maximin Daia: De l'historiographie à l'histoire." In *Politiche religiose nel mondo antico e tardoantico: Atti del Convegno Internazionale di Studi (Firenze, 24–26 settembre 2009)*, edited by Giovanni A. Cecconi and Chantal Gabrielli, 235–59. Bari: Edipuglia.

Bell, Catherine. 1997. *Ritual: Perspectives and Dimensions*. Oxford: Oxford University Press.

Bernabé, Alberto. 2002. "La toile de Pénélope: A-t-il existé un mythe orphique sur Dionysos et les Titans?" *Revue de l'Histoire des Religions* 219, no. 4: 401–33.

Bernabé, Alberto. 2004–5. *Poetae epici Graeci: Testimonia et fragmenta, Pars II, Fasciculi 1 et 2: Orphicorum et Orphicis similium testimonia et fragmenta*. Munich: K. G. Saur.

Bernstein, Frank. 1998. *Ludi publici: Untersuchungen zur Entstehung und Entwicklung der öffentlichen Spiele im republikanischen Rom*. Stuttgart: Franz Steiner.

Bernstein, Frank. 2007. "Complex Rituals: Games and Processions in Republican Rome." In *A Companion to Roman Religion*, edited by Jörg Rüpke, 249–61. Malden, MA: Blackwell.

Betegh, Gábor. 2014. "Pythagoreans, Orphism and Greek Religion." In *A History of Pythagoreanism*, edited by Carl A. Huffman, 149–66. Cambridge: Cambridge University Press.

Bévenot, Maurice, trans. 1971. *Cyprian: De Lapsis and De Ecclesiae Catholicae Unitate.* Oxford: Clarendon Press.

Bidez, Joseph, ed. and trans. 1924. *L'empereur Julien: Oeuvres complètes, Tome 1.2: Lettres et fragments.* Paris: Les Belles Lettres.

Billows, Richard A. 1993. "The Religious Procession of the Ara Pacis Augustae: Augustus' Supplicatio in 13 B.C." *Journal of Roman Archaeology* 6: 80–92.

Birley, A. R. 1998. "Decius Reconsidered." In *Les empereurs illyriens: Actes du colloque de Strasbourg (11–13 octobre 1990)*, edited by Edmond Frézouls and Hélène Jouffroy, 57–80. Strasbourg: AECR.

Bleckmann, Bruno. 2006. "Zu Motiven der Christenverfolgung des Decius." In *Deleto paene imperio Romano: Transformationsprozesse des römischen Reiches im 3. Jahrhundert und ihre Rezeption in der Neuzeit*, edited by Klaus-Peter Johne, Thomas Gerhardt, and Udo Hartmann, 57–71. Stuttgart: Franz Steiner.

Bleckmann, Bruno. 2012. "Konstantin und die Kritik des blutigen Opfers." In *Costantino prima e dopo Costantino/Constantine before and after Constantine*, edited by Giorgio Bonamente, Noel Lenski, and Rita Lizzi Testa, 165–80. Bari: Edipuglia.

Boatwright, Mary T. 2000. *Hadrian and the Cities of the Roman Empire.* Princeton, NJ: Princeton University Press.

Boschung, Dietrich. 1993. *Die Bildnisse des Augustus.* Das römische Herrscherbild 1.2. Berlin: Gebrüder Mann.

Boschung, Dietrich. 2012. "The Reliefs: Representation of Marcus Aurelius' Deeds." In *A Companion to Marcus Aurelius*, edited by Marcel van Ackeran, 305–14. Malden, MA: Wiley-Blackwell.

Bouffartigue, Jean, and Michel Patillon, eds. and trans. 1977. *Porphyre: De l'abstinence, Introduction, Livre I.* Paris: Les Belles Lettres.

Bouffartigue, Jean, and Michel Patillon, eds. and trans. 1979. *Porphyre: De l'abstinence, Livres II et III.* Paris: Les Belles Lettres.

Bowersock, Glen W. 1995. *Martyrdom and Rome.* Cambridge: Cambridge University Press.

Bowie, Ewan Lyall. 1978. "Apollonius of Tyana: Tradition and Reality." *Aufstieg und Niedergang der römischen Welt* 2.16.2: 1652–99.

Boyarin, Daniel. 1999. *Dying for God: Martyrdom and the Making of Christianity and Judaism.* Stanford, CA: Stanford University Press.

Boyarin, Daniel. 2004. *Border Lines: The Partition of Judaeo-Christianity.* Philadelphia: University of Pennsylvania Press.

Bradbury, Scott. 1994. "Constantine and the Problem of Anti-Pagan Legislation in the Fourth Century." *Classical Philology* 89, no. 2: 120–39.

Bradbury, Scott. 1995. "Julian's Pagan Revival and the Decline of Blood Sacrifice." *Phoenix* 49, no. 4: 331–56.

Bradshaw, Paul. F. 2002. *The Search for the Origins of Christian Worship: Sources and Methods for the Study of Early Liturgy.* 2nd ed. Oxford: Oxford University Press.

Bremmer, Jan N. 2005. "The Sacrifice of Pregnant Animals." In *Greek Sacrificial Ritual: Olympian and Chthonian*, edited by Robin Hägg and Brita Alroth, 155–65. Stockholm: Svenska Institutet I Athen. Reprinted with updates in Jan N. Bremmer, *The World of Greek Religion and Mythology: Collected Essays II*, 337–48. Tübingen: Mohr Siebeck, 2019.

Bremmer, Jan N. 2018. "Transformations and Decline of Sacrifice in Imperial Rome and Late Antiquity." In *Transformationen paganer Religion in der römischen Kaiserzeit: Rahmenbedingungen und Konzepte*, edited by Michael Blömer and Benedikt Eckhardt, 215–56. Berlin: De Gruyter.

Bremmer, Jan N. 2019a. "Ancient Teetotallers: From Homer via the Early Christian Eucharist to Late Antique Monks." In *"Zu Tisch bei den Heiligen . . .": Askese, Nahrung und Individualisierung im spätantiken Mönchtums*, edited by Daniel Albrecht and Katharina Waldner, 69–80. Stuttgart: Franz Steiner.

Bremmer, Jan N. 2019b. "Animal Sacrifice." In *The World of Greek Religion and Mythology: Collected Essays II*, 303–35. Tübingen: Mohr Siebeck.

Bremmer, Jan N. 2020. "Roman Judge vs. Christian Bishop: The Trial of Phileas during the Great Persecution." In *Desiring Martyrs: Locating Martyrs in Space and Time*, edited by Harry O. Maier and Katharina Waldner, 81–118. Berlin: De Gruyter.

Bremmer, Jan N. 2021. "The Place, Date and Author of the Ignatian Letters: An Onomastic Approach." In *Die Datierung neutestamentlicher Pseudepigraphen: Herausforderungen und neuere Lösungsansätze*, edited by Wolfgang Grünstäudl and Karl Matthias Schmidt, 405–33. Tübingen: Mohr Siebeck.

Bremmer, Jan N. 2022. "Third- and Fourth-Century Aspects of the *Homilies*: Bishops, Statues and Sacrifice." In *In Search of Truth in the Pseudo-Clementine Homilies*, edited by Benjamin M. J. De Vos and Danny Praet, 351–74. Tübingen: Mohr Siebeck.

Brent, Allen. 2010. *Cyprian and Roman Carthage*. Cambridge: Cambridge University Press.

Breytenbach, Cilliers. 1993. "Zeus und der lebendige Gott: Anmerkungen zur Apostelgeschichte 14.11–17." *New Testament Studies* 39: 396–413.

Briand-Ponsart, Claude. 1999. "*Summa Honoraria* et ressources des cités d'Afrique." In *Il capitolo delle entrate nelle finanze municipali in Occidente ed in Oriente: Actes de la Xe Rencontre Franco-Italienne sur l'Épigraphie du Monde Romain, Rome, 27–29 mai 1996*, 217–34. Rome: Università degli Studi di Roma La Sapienza.

Brink, C. O. 1956. "Οἰκείωσις and Οἰκειότης: Theophrastus and Zeno on Nature in Moral Theory." *Phronesis* 1, no. 2: 123–45.

Brock, Sebastian P. 1976. "The Rebuilding of the Temple under Julian: A New Source." *Palestine Exploration Quarterly* 108: 103–7.

Brown, Raymond E. 1994. *The Death of the Messiah: From Gethsemane to the Grave*, Vol. 1: *A Commentary on the Passion Narratives in the Four Gospels*. New York: Doubleday.

Brubaker, Rogers, and Frederick Cooper. 2000. "Beyond 'Identity.'" *Theory and Society* 29, no. 1: 1–47. Reprinted in Rogers Brubaker, *Ethnicity without Groups*, 28–63. Cambridge, MA: Harvard University Press, 2004.

Brunaux, Jean-Louis. 2000. *Les religions gauloises, Ve–Ier siècles av. J-C: Nouvelles approches sur les rituels celtiques de la Gaule indépendante*. Paris: Editions Errance.

Brunaux, Jean-Louis. 2006. *Les druides: Des philosophes chez les barbares*. Paris: Editions du Seuil.

Brunaux, Jean-Louis, and Claude Malagoli. 2003. "La France du Nord (Champagne-Ardenne, Île-de-France, Nord, Basse-Normandie, Haute-Normandie, Pas-de-Calais, Picardie)." *Gallia* 60: 9–73.

Brunaux, Jean-Louis, Patrice Méniel, and François Poplin. 1985. *Gournay I: Les fouilles sur le sanctuaire et l'oppidum (1974–1984)*. Revue Archéologique de Picardie, special issue. Amiens: Société des Antiquités de Picardie.

Buckler, W.-H. 1913. "Monuments de Thyatire." *Revue de Philologie* 37: 289–331.

Buraselis, Kostas. 2012. "Appended Festivals: The Coordination and Combination of Traditional Civic and Ruler Cult Festivals in the Hellenistic and Roman East." In *Greek and Roman Festivals: Content, Meaning, and Practice*, edited by J. Rasmus Brandt and Jon W. Iddeng, 247–66. Oxford: Oxford University Press.

Burkert, Walter. 1972 [1962]. *Lore and Science in Ancient Pythagoreanism*. Translated by Edwin L. Minar Jr., with revisions. Cambridge, MA: Harvard University Press. First published as *Weisheit und Wissenschaft: Studien zu Pythagoras, Philolaos und Platon*. Nuremberg: H. Carl, 1962.

Burkert, Walter. 1983 [1972]. *Homo Necans: The Anthropology of Ancient Greek Sacrificial Ritual and Myth*. Translated by Peter Bing. Berkeley: University of California Press. First published as *Homo necans: Interpretationen altgriechischer Opferriten und Mythen*. Berlin: De Gruyter, 1972.

Buttrey, Theodore V. 1983. "The Dates of the Arches of 'Diocletian' and Constantine." *Historia* 32, no. 3: 375–83.

Cameron, Alan. 2011. *The Last Pagans of Ancient Rome*. Oxford: Oxford University Press.

Cameron, Averil, and Stuart G. Hall. 1999. *Eusebius: Life of Constantine: Introduction, Translation, and Commentary*. Oxford: Clarendon Press.

Camia, Francesco. 2011. "Spending on the *Agones*: The Financing of Festivals in the Cities of Roman Greece." *Tyche: Beiträge zur Alten Geschichte, Papyrologie und Epigraphik* 26: 41–76.

Camia, Francesco. 2012. "*Theoi Olympioi* e *Theoi Sebastoi*: Alcune considerazioni sull'associazione tra culto imperiale e culti tradizionali in Grecia." In *Forme della memoria e dinamiche identitarie nell'antichità greco-romana*, edited by Elena Franchi and Giorgia Proietti, 93–110. Trento: Università degli Studi di Trento.

Camia, Francesco. 2016. "Between Tradition and Innovation: Cults for Roman Emperors in the Province of Achaia." In *Kaiserkult in den Provinzen des römischen Reiches: Organisation, Kommunikation und Repräsentation*, edited by Anne Kolb and Marco Vitale, 255–83. Berlin: De Gruyter.

Camia, Francesco, and Maria Kantiréa. 2010. "The Imperial Cult in the Peloponnese." In *Roman Peloponnese III: Society, Economy and Culture under the Roman Empire: Continuity and Innovation*, edited by Athanasios D. Rizakis and Claudia E.

Lepenioti, 375–406. Athens: National Hellenic Research Foundation, Institute for Greek and Roman Antiquity.

Campbell, Douglas A. 2022. "Chronology." In *T&T Clark Handbook to the Historical Paul*, edited by Ryan S. Schellenberg and Heidi Wendt, 265–86. London: T&T Clark.

Camplani, Alberto, and Marco Zambon. 2002. "Il sacrificio come problema in alcune correnti filosofiche di età imperiale." *Annali di Storia dell'Esegesi* 19, no. 1: 59–99.

Carboni, Romina. 2016. "Unusual Sacrificial Victims: Fish and Their Value in the Context of Sacrifices." In *Animals in Greek and Roman Religion and Myth: Proceedings of the Symposium Grumentinum, Grumento Nova (Potenza), 5–7 June 2013*, edited by Patricia A. Johnston, Attilio Mastrocinque, and Sophia Papaioannou, 255–80. Newcastle upon Tyne: Cambridge Scholars Publishing.

Carrié, Jean-Michel. 2005. "Developments in Provincial and Local Administration." In *The Cambridge Ancient History*, Vol. 12: *The Crisis of Empire, AD 193–337*, edited by Alan Bowman, Averil Cameron, and Peter Garnsey, 269–312. 2nd ed. Cambridge: Cambridge University Press.

Carter, Jeffrey, ed. 2003. *Understanding Religious Sacrifice: A Reader*. London: Continuum.

Casabona, Jean. 1966. *Recherches sur le vocabulaire des sacrifices en grec des origines à la fin de l'époque classique*. Aix-en-Provence: Editions Ophrys.

Caseau, Béatrice. 2012. "Constantin et l'encens: Constantin a-t-il procédé à une révolution liturgique?" In *Costantino prima e dopo Costantino/Constantine before and after Constantine*, edited by Giorgio Bonamente, Noel Lenski, and Rita Lizzi Testa, 535–49. Bari: Edipuglia.

Castelli, Elizabeth A. 2004. *Martyrdom and Memory: Early Christian Culture Making*. New York: Columbia University Press.

Cecconi, Giovanni Alberto. 2012. "Il rescritto di Spello: Prospettive recenti." In *Costantino prima e dopo Costantino/Constantine before and after Constantine*, edited by Giorgio Bonamente, Noel Lenski, and Rita Lizzi Testa, 273–90. Bari: Edipuglia.

Chadwick, Henry, trans. 1953. *Origen: Contra Celsum*. Cambridge: Cambridge University Press.

Chaniotis, Angelos. 1995. "Sich selbst feiern? Städtische Feste des Hellenismus im Spannungsfeld von Religion und Politik." In *Stadtbild und Bürgerbild im Hellenismus*, edited by Paul Zanker and Michael Wörrle, 147–72. Munich: C. H. Beck.

Chastagnol, André. 1984a. "Les fêtes décennales de Septime-Sévère." *Bulletin de la Société Nationale des Antiquaires de France* 1984: 91–107.

Chastagnol, André. 1984b. "Les jubilés décennaux et vicennaux des empereurs sous les Antonins at les Sévères." *Revue Numismatique* 26: 104–24.

Christodoulou, Demetrios N. 1998. Οι μορφές των αρχαίων θεών στην νομισματοκοπία του Μεγάλου Κωνσταντίνου (306–326 μ. X.) = *The Figures of Ancient Gods on the Coinage of Constantine the Great (306–326 AD)*. Athens: Hellenic Numismatic Society.

Clark, Gillian, trans. 2000. *Porphyry: On Abstinence from Killing Animals*. Ithaca, NY: Cornell University Press.

Clarke, Emma C. 2001. *Iamblichus' De Mysteriis: A Manifesto of the Miraculous*. Aldershot, UK: Ashgate.

Clarke, Emma C., John M. Dillon, and Jackson P. Hershbell, trans. 2003. *Iamblichus: On the Mysteries*. Atlanta: Society of Biblical Literature.

Clarke, Graeme W., trans. 1974. *The Octavius of Marcus Minucius Felix*. New York: Newman Press.

Clarke, Graeme W., trans. 1984–89. *The Letters of St. Cyprian of Carthage*. 4 vols. New York: Newman Press.

Clarke, Graeme W. 2005. "Third-Century Christianity." In *The Cambridge Ancient History*, Vol. 12: *The Crisis of Empire, AD 193–337*, edited by Alan Bowman, Averil Cameron, and Peter Garnsey, 589–671. 2nd ed. Cambridge: Cambridge University Press.

Clarke, Graeme W., and Michel Poirier, eds. 2012. *Cyprien de Carthage: Ceux qui sont tombés (De lapsis)*. Paris: Éditions du Cerf.

Claytor, W. Graham. 2015. "A Decian *Libellus* at Luther College (Iowa)." *Tyche: Beiträge zur Alten Geschichte, Papyrologie und Epigraphik* 30: 13–18.

Cohen, Shaye J. D. 1987. "Pagan and Christian Evidence on the Ancient Synagogue." In *The Synagogue in Late Antiquity*, edited by Lee I. Levine, 159–81. Philadelphia: American Schools of Oriental Research.

Colgrave, Bertram, and R. A. B. Mynors, eds. and trans. 1969. *Bede's Ecclesiastical History of the English People*. Oxford: Oxford University Press.

Conti, Stefano. 2007. "Religione e usurpazione: Magnenzio tra cristianesimo e paganesimo." In *Antidoron: Studi in onore di Barbara Scardigli Forster*, edited by Paolo Desideri, Mauro Moggi, and Mario Pani, 105–19. Pisa: ETS.

Conybeare, Fred C. 1903. "The Survival of Animal Sacrifices inside the Christian Church." *American Journal of Theology* 7, no. 1: 62–90.

Corcoran, Simon. 1996. *The Empire of the Tetrarchs: Imperial Pronouncements and Government, AD 284–324*. Oxford: Clarendon Press.

Corcoran, Simon. 2015. "From Unholy Madness to Right-Mindedness: Or How to Legislate Religious Conformity from Decius to Justinian." In *Conversion in Late Antiquity: Christianity, Islam, and Beyond*, edited by Arietta Papaconstantinou with Neil McLynn and Daniel Schwartz, 67–94. Aldershot, UK: Ashgate.

Cornwell, Hannah. 2015. "The King Who Would Be Prefect: Authority and Identity in the Cottian Alps." *Journal of Roman Studies* 105: 41–72.

Crawford, Michael H., ed. 1996. *Roman Statutes*. London: Institute of Classical Studies.

Creed, J. L., ed. and trans. 1984. *Lactantius: De Mortibus Persecutorum*. Oxford: Clarendon Press.

Curran, John. 2000. *Pagan City and Christian Capital: Rome in the Fourth Century*. Oxford: Clarendon Press.

Daly, Robert J. 1978. *Christian Sacrifice: The Judaeo-Christian Background before Origen*. Washington, DC: Catholic University of America Press.

Daly, Robert J. 2019. *Sacrifice in Pagan and Christian Antiquity*. London: T&T Clark.

Danby, Herbert, trans. 1933. *The Mishnah*. Oxford: Clarendon Press.

D'Andrea, Bruno. 2018. *Bambini nel "limbo": Dati e proposte interpretive sui tofet fenici e punici*. Rome: École Française de Rome.

De Cazanove, Olivier. 1987. "*Exesto*: L'incapacité sacrificielle des femmes à Rome." *Phoenix* 41, no. 2: 159–73.

Degrassi, Attilio, ed. 1963. *Inscriptiones Italiae 13.2: Fasti anni Numani et Iuliani*. Rome: Libreria dello Stato.

Delamarre, J. 1896. "Inscriptions d'Amorgos." *Revue Archéologique*: 73–84.

Delano Smith, Catherine. 1979. *Western Mediterranean Europe: A Historical Geography of Italy, Spain, and Southern France since the Neolithic*. London: Academic Press.

Delmaire, Roland. 1989. *Largesses sacrées et res privata: L'Aerarium impérial et son administration du IVe au VIe siècle*. Rome: École Française de Rome.

Delmaire, Roland. 2004. "La législation sur les sacrifices au IVe siècle: Un essai d'interprétation." *Revue Historique de Droit Français et Étranger* 82, no. 3: 319–33.

De Maria, Sandro. 1988. *Gli archi onorari di Roma e dell'Italia romana*. Rome: "L'Erma" di Bretschneider.

Derks, Ton. 1998. *Gods, Temples and Ritual Practices: The Transformation of Religious Ideas and Values in Roman Gaul*. Amsterdam: Amsterdam University Press.

Desanti, Lucetta. 1990. *Sileat omnibus perpetuo divinandi curiositas: Indovini e sanzioni nel diritto romano*. Milan: Giuffrè.

De Ste. Croix, G. E. M. 1981. *The Class Struggle in the Ancient Greek World from the Archaic Age to the Arab Conquests*. Ithaca, NY: Cornell University Press.

De Ste. Croix, G. E. M. 2006 [1954]. "Aspects of the 'Great' Persecution." Reprinted with updated notes in G. E. M. de Ste. Croix, *Christian Persecution, Martyrdom, and Orthodoxy*, edited by Michael Whitby and Joseph Streeter, 35–78. Oxford: Oxford University Press. First published in *Harvard Theological Review* 47, no. 2: 75–113.

Detienne, Marcel. 1977. *Dionysos mis à mort*. Paris: Gallimard.

Detienne, Marcel. 1979a. "Pratiques culinaires et esprit de sacrifice." In *La cuisine du sacrifice en pays grec*, edited by Marcel Detienne and Jean-Pierre Vernant, 7–35. Paris: Gallimard.

Detienne, Marcel. 1979b. "Violentes 'eugénies'. En pleines Thesmophories des femmes couvertes du sang." In *La cuisine du sacrifice en pays grec*, edited by Marcel Detienne and Jean-Pierre Vernant, 183–214. Paris: Gallimard.

Detienne, Marcel. 2007 [1972]. *Les jardins d'Adonis: La mythologie des parfums et des aromates en Grèce*. New ed. Paris: Gallimard. First edition 1972.

De Vaux, Roland. 1964. *Studies in Old Testament Sacrifice*. Cardiff: University of Wales Press.

Digeser, Elizabeth DePalma. 2012. *A Threat to Public Piety: Christians, Platonists, and the Great Persecution*. Ithaca, NY: Cornell University Press.

Dillon, John, trans. 1993. *Alcinous: The Handbook of Platonism*. Oxford: Oxford University Press.

Dillon, John. 2003. *The Heirs of Plato: A Study of the Old Academy (347–274 BC)*. Oxford: Oxford University Press.

Dolansky, Fanny. 2011. "Celebrating the Saturnalia: Religious Ritual and Roman Domestic Life." In *A Companion to Families in the Greek and Roman Worlds*, edited by Beryl Rawson, 488–503. Malden, MA: Blackwell.

Domingo Gygax, Marc. 2016. *Benefactions and Rewards in the Ancient Greek City: The Origins of Euergetism*. Cambridge: Cambridge University Press.

Donahue, John F. 2017. *The Roman Community at Table during the Principate*. New and expanded ed. Ann Arbor: University of Michigan Press.

Driediger-Murphy, Lindsay G. 2017. "God(s) Contrary to Nature: A Theological Debate between Pagans and Christians." *Greek, Roman, and Byzantine Studies* 57, no. 3: 660–86.

Duncan-Jones, R. P. 1982. *The Economy of the Roman Empire: Quantitative Studies*. 2nd ed. Cambridge: Cambridge University Press.

Dzielska, Maria. 1986. *Apollonius of Tyana in Legend and History*. Rome: "L'Erma" di Bretschneider.

Eberhart, Christian A. 2013. *Kultmetaphorik und Christologie: Opfer- und Sühneterminologie im Neuen Testament*. Tübingen: Mohr Siebeck.

Eberhart, Christian A., and Donald Schweitzer. 2019. "The Unique Sacrifice of Christ According to Hebrews 9: A Study in Theological Creativity." *Religions* 10, no. 1: https://doi.org/10.3390/rel10010047.

Eck, Werner. 1997. "Der Euergetismus im Funktionszusammenhang der kaiserzeitlichen Städte." In *Actes du Xe Congrès International d'Epigraphie Grecque et Latine, Nîmes, 4–9 octobre 1992*, edited by Michel Christol and Olivier Masson, 305–31. Paris: Publications de la Sorbonne.

Edelstein, Ludwig, and I. G. Kidd, eds. 1972. *Posidonius*, Vol. 1: *The Fragments*. Cambridge: Cambridge University Press.

Edmonds, Radcliffe G., III. 1999. "Tearing Apart the Zagreus Myth: A Few Disparaging Remarks on Orphism and 'Original Sin.'" *Classical Antiquity* 18, no. 1: 35–73.

Edmonds, Radcliffe G., III. 2013. *Redefining Ancient Orphism: A Study in Greek Religion*. Cambridge: Cambridge University Press.

Edmondson, Jonathan. 2006. "Cities and Urban Life in the Western Provinces of the Roman Empire, 30 BCE–250 CE." In *A Companion to the Roman Empire*, edited by David S. Potter, 250–80. Malden, MA: Blackwell.

Edwards, Mark, trans. 2003. *Constantine and Christendom: The Oration to the Saints, The Greek and Latin Accounts of the Discovery of the True Cross, The Edict of Constantine to Pope Sylvester*. Liverpool: Liverpool University Press.

Edwards, Mark. 2015. "One Origen or Two? The *Status Quaestionis*." *Symbolae Osloenses* 89, no. 1: 81–103.

Ekroth, Gunnel. 2005. "Blood on the Altars? On the Treatment of Blood at Greek Sacrifices and the Iconographical Evidence." *Antike Kunst* 48: 9–29.

Ekroth, Gunnel. 2007. "Meat in Ancient Greece: Sacrificial, Sacred or Secular?" In *Sacrifices, marché de la viande et pratiques alimentaires dans les cités du monde romain*, edited by William Van Andringa. *Food & History* 5, no. 1: 249–72.

Ekroth, Gunnel. 2014a. "Animal Sacrifice in Antiquity." In *The Oxford Handbook of Animals in Classical Thought and Life*, edited by Gordon Lindsay Campbell, 324–54. Oxford: Oxford University Press.

Ekroth, Gunnel. 2014b. "Castration, Cult and Agriculture: Perspectives on Greek Animal Sacrifice." *Opuscula: Annual of the Swedish Institutes at Athens and Rome* 7: 153–74.

Ekroth, Gunnel. 2017. "Holocaustic Sacrifices in Ancient Greek Religion: Some Comments on Practice and Theory." In *Animal Sacrifice in Ancient Greece: Proceedings of the First International Workshops in Kraków (12–14.11.2015)*, edited by Krzysztof Bielawksi, 45–66. Warsaw: Global Scientific Platform.

Ekroth, Gunnel. 2018. "Holocaustic Sacrifices in Ancient Greek Religion and the Ritual Relations to the Levant." In *Change, Continuity, and Connectivity: North-Eastern Mediterranean at the Turn of the Bronze Age and in the Early Iron Age*, edited by Łukasz Niesiołowski-Spanò and Marek Węcowski, 308–26. Wiesbaden: Harrassowitz.

Elsner, Jaś. 1991. "Cult and Sculpture: Sacrifice in the Ara Pacis Augusta." *Journal of Roman Studies* 81: 50–61.

Elsner, Jaś. 2012. "Sacrifice in Late Roman Art." In *Greek and Roman Animal Sacrifice: Ancient Victims, Modern Observers*, edited by Christopher A. Faraone and F. S. Naiden, 120–63. Cambridge: Cambridge University Press.

Erdkamp, Paul, and Claire Holleran, eds. 2019. *The Routledge Handbook of Diet and Nutrition in the Roman World*. London: Routledge.

Errington, R. Malcolm. 1988. "Constantine and the Pagans." *Greek, Roman and Byzantine Studies* 29, no. 3: 309–18.

Errington, R. Malcolm. 2000. "Themistius and His Emperors." *Chiron* 30: 864–901.

Errington, R. Malcolm. 2006. *Roman Imperial Policy from Julian to Theodosius*. Chapel Hill: University of North Carolina Press.

Falls, Thomas B., trans. 2003. *St. Justin Martyr: Dialogue with Trypho*. Revised and with a new introduction by Thomas P. Halton. Edited by Michael Slusser. Washington, DC: Catholic University of America Press.

Feldman, Louis H. 1993. *Jew and Gentile in the Ancient World*. Princeton, NJ: Princeton University Press.

Fercoq du Leslay, Gérard, and Sébastien Lepetz. 2008. "Manger dans les sanctuaires: Salaisons et viande fraîche à Ribemont-sur-Ancre." In *Archéologie du sacrifice animal en Gaule romaine: Rituels et pratiques alimentaires*, edited by Sébastien Lepetz and William Van Andringa, 201–6. Montagnac, France: Monique Mergoil.

Ferguson, Everett. 1980. "Spiritual Sacrifice in Early Christianity and Its Environment." *Aufstieg und Niedergang der römischen Welt* 2.23.2: 1151–89.

Fink, R. O., A. S. Hoey, and W. F. Snyder. 1940. "The Feriale Duranum." *Yale Classical Studies* 7: 1–222.

Finkelstein, Ari. 2018. *Specter of the Jews: Emperor Julian and the Rhetoric of Ethnicity in Syrian Antioch*. Berkeley: University of California Press.

Finley, M. I. 1985. *The Ancient Economy*. 2nd ed. Berkeley: University of California Press.

Fishwick, Duncan. 1987–92. *The Imperial Cult in the Latin West: Studies in the Ruler Cult of the Western Provinces of the Roman Empire*, Vols. 1–2. Leiden: Brill.

Fishwick, Duncan. 2002–5. *The Imperial Cult in the Latin West: Studies in the Ruler Cult of the Western Provinces of the Roman Empire*, Vol. 3: *Provincial Cult*. Leiden: Brill.

Fishwick, Duncan. 2007. "*Numen Augustum*." *Zeitschrift für Papyrologie und Epigraphik* 160: 247–55.

Fitzmyer, Joseph A. 2008. *First Corinthians: A New Translation with Introduction and Commentary*. Anchor Yale Bible. New Haven, CT: Yale University Press.

Flemming, Rebecca. 2007. "Festus and the Role of Women in Roman Religion." In *Verrius, Festus and Paul: Lexicography, Scholarship, and Society*, edited by Fay Glinister and Clare Woods, 87–108. London: Institute of Classical Studies.

Flinterman, Jaap-Jan. 2014. "Pythagoreans in Rome and Asia Minor around the Turn of the Common Era." In *A History of Pythagoreanism*, edited by Carl A. Huffman, 341–59. Cambridge: Cambridge University Press.

Flower, Harriet I. 2017. *The Dancing Lares and the Serpent in the Garden: Religion at the Roman Street Corner*. Princeton, NJ: Princeton University Press.

Fortenbaugh, William W. 2003. "Theophrastus: Piety, Justice and Animals." In *Theophrastean Studies*, 173–92. Stuttgart: Franz Steiner.

Fossey, John M. 1979. "The Cities of the Kopaïs during the Roman Period." *Aufstieg und Niedergang der römischen Welt* 2.17.1: 549–91.

Foxhall, Lin. 1990. "The Dependent Tenant: Land Leasing and Labour in Italy and Greece." *Journal of Roman Studies* 80: 97–114.

Foxhall, Lin, and H. A. Forbes. 1982. "Σιτομετρεία: The Role of Grain as a Staple Food in Antiquity." *Chiron* 12: 41–90.

Frankfurter, David. 2006. *Evil Incarnate: Rumors of Demonic Conspiracy and Satanic Abuse in History*. Princeton, NJ: Princeton University Press.

Frankfurter, David. 2011. "Egyptian Religion and the Problem of the Category 'Sacrifice.'" In *Ancient Mediterranean Sacrifice*, edited by Jennifer Wright Knust and Zsuzsanna Várhelyi, 75–93. Oxford: Oxford University Press.

Frankfurter, David. 2015. "Review of Brent Nongbri, *Before Religion* (2013)." *Journal of Early Christian Studies* 23, no. 4: 632–34.

Frankfurter, David. 2021. "Religion in the Mirror of the Other: The Discursive Value of Cult-Atrocity Stories in Mediterranean Antiquity." *History of Religions* 60, no. 3: 188–208.

Frayn, Joan M. 1982. *Sheep-Rearing and the Wool Trade in Italy during the Roman Period*. Liverpool: Francis Cairns.

Frede, Michael. 1999. "Origen's Treatise *Against Celsus*." In *Apologetics in the Roman Empire: Pagans, Jews, and Christians*, edited by Mark Edwards, Martin Goodman, and Simon Price, 131–55. Oxford: Oxford University Press.

Fredriksen, Paula. 2010. "Judaizing the Nations: The Ritual Demands of Paul's Gospel." *New Testament Studies* 56, no. 2: 232–52.

Fredriksen, Paula. 2015. "Arms and the Man: A Response to Dale Martin's 'Jesus in Jerusalem: Armed and Not Dangerous.'" *Journal for the Study of the New Testament* 37, no. 3: 312–25.

Fredriksen, Paula. 2017. *Paul: The Pagans' Apostle*. New Haven, CT: Yale University Press.

Fredriksen, Paula. 2018. *When Christians Were Jews: The First Generation*. New Haven, CT: Yale University Pres.

Freudenberger, Rudolf. 1978. "Romanas caerimonias rocognoscere." In *Donum gentilicium: New Testament Studies in Honour of David Daube*, edited by Ernst Bammel, Charles Kingsley Barrett, and William David Davies, 238–54. Oxford: Clarendon Press.

Friesen, Steven. 1993. *Twice Neokoros: Ephesus, Asia and the Cult of the Flavian Imperial Family*. Leiden: Brill.

Frija, Gabrielle. 2012. *Les prêtres des empereurs: Le culte impérial civique dans la province romaine d'Asie*. Rennes: Presses Universitaires de Rennes.

Frija, Gabrielle. 2019. "Cultes impériales and pouvoir impérial: Diffusion et circulation des cultes des empereurs dans le monde romain." *Pallas: Revue d'Études Antiques* 111: 77–94.

Gabba, Emilio. 1991. *Dionysius and the History of Archaic Rome*. Berkeley: University of California Press.

Garnsey, Peter. 1971a. "Honorarium decurionatus." *Historia: Zeitschrift für Alte Geschichte* 20, nos. 2/3: 309–25.

Garnsey, Peter. 1971b. "*Taxatio* and *Pollicitatio* in Roman Africa." *Journal of Roman Studies* 61: 116–29.

Garnsey, Peter. 1991. "The Generosity of Veyne." *Journal of Roman Studies* 81: 164–68.

Garnsey, Peter. 1999. *Food and Society in Classical Antiquity*. Cambridge: Cambridge University Press.

Gascou, Jacques. 1987. "Les *Sacerdotes Cererum* de Carthage." *Antiquités Africaines* 20: 105–20.

Gasperini, Lidio. 2008. "L'Augusteo di 'Forum Clodii.'" In *Nuove ricerche sul culto imperiale in Italia: Atti dell'Incontro di Studio, Ancona, 31 gennaio 2004*, edited by Lidio Gasperini and Gianfranco Paci, 91–134. Tivoli: Edizioni Tored.

Gauthier, Philippe. 1985. *Les cités grecques et leurs bienfaiteurs (IVe–Ier siècle avant J.C.): Contribution à l'histoire des institutions*. Paris: De Boccard.

Georgoudi, Stella. 1979. "L'égorgement sanctifié en Grèce moderne: Les 'kourbania' des saints.'" In *Le cuisine du sacrifice en pays grec*, edited by Marcel Detienne and Jean-Pierre Vernant, 271–307. Paris: Gallimard.

Georgoudi, Stella. 2017. "Reflections on Sacrifice and Purification in the Greek World." In *Animal Sacrifice in the Ancient Greek World*, edited by Sarah Hitch and Ian Rutherford, 105–35. Cambridge: Cambridge University Press.

Gerhardt, Thomas. 2006. "Zur Geschichte des Krisenbegriffs." In *Deleto paene imperio Romano: Transformationsprozesse des römischen Reiches im 3. Jahrhundert und ihre Rezeption in der Neuzeit*, edited by Klaus-Peter Johne, Thomas Gerhardt, and Udo Hartmann, 381–410. Stuttgart: Franz Steiner.

Gerhardt, Thomas. 2008. "Die Städte." In *Die Zeit der Soldatenkaiser: Krise und Transformation des römischen Reiches im 3. Jahrhundert n. Chr. (235-284)*, edited by Klaus-Peter Johne, Udo Hartmann, and Thomas Gerhardt, 1.691–712. Berlin: Akademie.

Girard, René. 1977 [1972]. *Violence and the Sacred*. Translated by Patrick Gregory. Baltimore: Johns Hopkins University Press. First published as *La violence et le sacré*. Paris: B. Grasset, 1972.

Gleason, Maud W. 2006. "Greek Cities under Roman Rule." In *A Companion to the Roman Empire*, edited by David S. Potter, 228–49. Malden, MA: Blackwell.

González, Julián. 1986. "The Lex Irnitana: A New Copy of the Flavian Municipal Law." *Journal of Roman Studies* 76: 147–243.

Goodman, Martin. 1987. *The Ruling Class of Judaea: The Origins of the Jewish Revolt against Rome, A.D. 66–70*. Cambridge: Cambridge University Press.

Gordon, Richard. 1990. "The Veil of Power: Emperors, Sacrificers and Benefactors." In *Pagan Priests*, edited by Mary Beard and John North, 219–31. Ithaca, NY: Cornell University Press.

Gorman, Peter. 1985. "The 'Apollonios' of the Neoplatonic Biographies of Pythagoras." *Mnemosyne* 38, nos. 1–2: 130–44.

Grabbe, Lester L. 2004–8. *A History of the Jews and Judaism in the Second Temple Period*, Vol. 1: *Yehud: A History of the Persian Province of Judah*. Vol. 2: *The Coming of the Greeks: The Early Hellenistic Period (335–175 BCE)*. London: T&T Clark.

Gradel, Ittai. 2002. *Emperor Worship and Roman Religion*. Oxford: Clarendon Press.

Grant, Robert M. 1988. *Greek Apologists of the Second Century*. Philadelphia: Westminster Press.

Greenwood, David Neal. 2016. "Porphyry, Rome, and Support for Persecution." *Ancient Philosophy* 36, no. 1: 197–206.

Greenwood, David Neal. 2021. *Julian and Christianity: Revisiting the Constantinian Revolution*. Ithaca, NY: Cornell University Press.

Griebel, Johannes. 2013. *Der Kaiser im Krieg: Die Bilder der Säule des Marc Aurel*. Berlin: De Gruyter.

Grottanelli, Cristiano. 2005. "Tuer des animaux pour la fête de Saint Félix." In *La cuisine et l'autel: Les sacrifices en questions dans les sociétés de la Méditerranée ancienne*, edited by Stella Georgoudi, Renée Koch Piettre, and Francis Schmidt, 387–407. Turnhout: Brepols.

Hachlili, Rachel. 1998. *Ancient Jewish Art and Archaeology in the Diaspora*. Leiden: Brill.
Harl, K. W. 1990. "Sacrifice and Pagan Belief in Fifth- and Sixth-Century Byzantium." *Past and Present* 128: 7–27.
Harland, Philip A. 2003. *Associations, Synagogues, and Congregations: Claiming a Place in Ancient Mediterranean Society*. Minneapolis: Fortress Press.
Harrill, J. Albert. 2012. *Paul the Apostle: His Life and Legacy in Their Roman Context*. Cambridge: Cambridge University Press.
Hartmann, Nicole. 2020. "On Demons in Early Martyrology." In *Demons in Late Antiquity: Their Perception and Transformation in Different Literary Genres*, edited by Eva Elm and Nicole Hartmann, 61–80. Berlin: De Gruyter.
Harvey, Susan Ashbrook. 2006. *Scenting Salvation: Ancient Christianity and the Olfactory Imagination*. Berkeley: University of California Press.
Heather, Peter, and David Moncur. 2001. *Politics, Philosophy, and Empire in the Fourth Century: Select Orations of Themistius*. Liverpool: Liverpool University Press.
Heberlein, Friedrich. 1988. "Eine philologische Anmerkung zu 'Romanas caerimonias recognoscere' (Acta Cypriani 1)." In *Festschrift für Paul Klopsch*, edited by Udo Kindermann, Wolfgang Maaz, and Fritz Wagner, 83–100. Göppingen: Kümmerle.
Hefele, Karl Joseph von. 1907. *Histoire des conciles d'après les documents originaux*, Vol. 1, Part 1. Translated and revised by Henri Leclercq. Paris: Letouzey.
Hekster, Olivier. 2008. *Rome and Its Empire, AD 193–284*. With Nicholas Zair. Edinburgh: Edinburgh University Press.
Hellholm, David, and Dieter Sänger, eds. 2017. *The Eucharist—Its Origins and Contexts: Sacred Meal, Communal Meal, Table Fellowship in Late Antiquity, Early Judaism, and Early Christianity*. Tübingen: Mohr Siebeck.
Henrichs, Albert. 2000. "Drama and Dromena: Bloodshed, Violence, and Sacrificial Metaphor in Euripides." *Harvard Studies in Classical Philology* 100: 173–88.
Henrichs, Albert. 2011. "Dionysos Dismembered and Restored to Life: The Earliest Evidence (*OF* 59 I–II)." In *Tracing Orpheus: Studies of Orphic Fragments in Honour of Alberto Bernabé*, edited by Miguel Herrero de Jáuregui, 61–68. Berlin: De Gruyter.
Hermary, Antoine, Martine Leguilloux, Véronique Chankowski, and Angeliki Petropoulou. 2004. "Les sacrifices dans le monde grec." In *Thesaurus cultus et rituum antiquorum*, edited by Jean Ch. Balty et al., Vol. 1, 59–134. Los Angeles: J. Paul Getty Museum.
Heyman, George. 2007. *The Power of Sacrifice: Roman and Christian Discourses in Conflict*. Washington, DC: Catholic University of America Press.
Hingley, Richard. 2005. *Globalizing Roman Culture: Unity, Diversity and Empire*. London: Routledge.
Hodkinson, Stephen. 1988. "Animal Husbandry in the Greek Polis." In *Pastoral Economies in Classical Antiquity*, edited by C. R. Whittaker, 35–74. Proceedings of the Cambridge Philological Society Supplement 14. Cambridge: Cambridge Philological Society.

Hopkins, Keith. 1978. "Divine Emperors or the Symbolic Unity of the Roman Empire." In *Conquerors and Slaves*, 197–242. Cambridge: Cambridge University Press.

Horden, Peregrine, and Nicholas Purcell. 2000. *The Corrupting Sea: A Study of Mediterranean History*. Malden, MA: Blackwell.

Howe, Timothy. 2008. *Pastoral Politics: Animals, Agriculture, and Society in Ancient Greece*. Publications of the Association of Ancient Historians 9. Claremont, CA: Regina Books.

Howe, Timothy. 2014. "Value Economics: Animals, Wealth and the Market." In *The Oxford Handbook of Animals in Classical Thought and Life*, edited by Gordon Lindsay Campbell, 136–55. Oxford: Oxford University Press.

Hubert, Henri, and Marcel Mauss. 1968 [1899]. "Essai sur la nature et la fonction du sacrifice." In Marcel Mauss, *Oeuvres, 1: Les fonctions sociales du sacré*, edited by Viktor Karády, 193–307. Paris: Minuit, 1968. First published in *L'Année Sociologique* 2 (1899): 29–138.

Huet, Valérie, Francesca Prescendi, Anne Viola Siebert, William Van Andringa, and Stéphanie Wyler. 2004. "Les sacrifices dans le monde romain." In *Thesaurus cultus et rituum antiquorum*, edited by Jean Ch. Balty et al., Vol. 1, 183–235. Los Angeles: J. Paul Getty Museum.

Huffman, Carl A. 2009. "The Pythagorean Conception of the Soul from Pythagoras to Philolaus." In *Body and Soul in Ancient Philosophy*, edited by Dorothea Frede and Burkhard Reis, 21–44. Berlin: De Gruyter.

Huffman, Carl A., ed. 2014a. *A History of Pythagoreanism*. Cambridge: Cambridge University Press.

Huffman, Carl A. 2014b. "The Peripatetics on the Pythagoreans." In *A History of Pythagoreanism*, edited by Carl A. Huffman, 274–95. Cambridge: Cambridge University Press.

Hutt, Curtis. 2018–19. "A Threefold Heresy: Reassessing Jewish, Christian, and Islamic Animal Sacrifice in Late Antiquity." *History of Religions* 58, no. 3: 251–76.

Inwood, Brad. 2001. *The Poem of Empedocles: A Text and Translation with an Introduction*. Rev. ed. Toronto: University of Toronto Press.

Isager, Signe, and Jens Erik Skydsgaard. 1992. *Ancient Greek Agriculture: An Introduction*. London: Routledge.

Isenberg, M. 1975. "The Sale of Sacrificial Meat." *Classical Philology* 70, no. 4: 271–73.

Jameson, Michael H. 2014 [1988]. "Sacrifice and Animal Husbandry in Classical Greece." In Michael H. Jameson, *Cults and Rites in Ancient Greece: Essays on Religion and Society*, edited by Allaire B. Stallsmith, 198–231. Cambridge: Cambridge University Press. First published in *Pastoral Economies in Classical Antiquity*, edited by C. R. Whittaker, 87–119. *Proceedings of the Cambridge Philological Society* Supplement 14. Cambridge: Cambridge Philological Society, 1988.

Johnson, Aaron P. 2013. *Religion and Identity in Porphyry of Tyre: The Limits of Hellenism in Late Antiquity*. Cambridge: Cambridge University Press.

Johnson, Aaron P. 2014. *Eusebius*. London: I. B. Tauris.

Johnston, Sarah Iles, ed. 2004. *Religions of the Ancient World: A Guide*. Cambridge, MA: Harvard University Press.

Jones, A. H. M. 1964. *The Later Roman Empire, 284–602: A Social, Economic, and Administrative Survey*. Oxford: Basil Blackwell.

Jones, Brian W. 1992. *The Emperor Domitian*. London: Routledge.

Jones, Christopher P., ed. and trans. 2006. *Philostratus, Apollonius of Tyana: Letters of Apollonius, Ancient Testimonia, Eusebius' Reply to Hierocles*. Loeb Classical Library 458. Cambridge, MA: Harvard University Press.

Jones, Christopher P. 2012. "Notes on the *Acts of Carpus* and Some Related Martyr-Acts." In *Pignora amicitiae: Scritti di storia antica e di storiografia offerti a Mario Mazzai*, edited by Margherita Cassia et al., Vol. 1, 259–68. Acireale: Bonanno.

Joseph, Simon J. 2017. "'I Have Come to Abolish Sacrifices' (Epiphanius, *Pan.* 30.16.5): Re-examining a Jewish Christian Text and Tradition." *New Testament Studies* 63: 92–110.

Kahn, Charles H. 2001. *Pythagoras and the Pythagoreans: A Brief History*. Indianapolis: Hackett.

Kajava, Mika. 1998. "*Visceratio.*" *Arctos* 32: 109–31.

Kannicht, Richard, ed. 2004. *Tragicorum Graecorum Fragmenta*, Vol. 5: *Euripides*. Göttingen: Vandenhoeck & Ruprecht.

Kazen, Thomas. 2017. "Sacrificial Interpretation in the Narratives of Jesus' Last Meal." In *The Eucharist—Its Origins and Contexts: Sacred Meal, Communal Meal, Table Fellowship in Late Antiquity, Early Judaism, and Early Christianity*, edited by David Hellholm and Dieter Sänger, 477–502. Tübingen: Mohr Siebeck.

Keil, Josef, and Anton von Premerstein. 1911. "Bericht über eine zweite Reise in Lydien." *Denkschriften der kaiserlichen Akademie der Wissenschaften in Wien, philosophisch-historische Klasse* 54.

Kenyon, F. G. 1909. "Two Greek School-Tablets." *Journal of Hellenic Studies* 29: 29–40.

King, Anthony. 1999. "Diet in the Roman World: A Regional Inter-Site Comparison of Mammal Bones." *Journal of Roman Archaeology* 12: 168–202.

Klawans, Jonathan. 2002. "Interpreting the Last Supper: Sacrifice, Spiritualization, and Anti-Sacrifice." *New Testament Studies* 48: 1–17.

Klawans, Jonathan. 2006. *Purity, Sacrifice, and the Temple: Symbolism and Supersessionism in the Study of Ancient Judaism*. Oxford: Oxford University Press.

Knipfing, John R. 1923. "The Libelli of the Decian Persecution." *Harvard Theological Review* 16, no. 4: 345–90.

Knust, Jennifer Wright, and Zsuzsanna Várhelyi. 2011. "Introduction: Images, Acts, Meanings and Ancient Mediterranean Sacrifice." In *Ancient Mediterranean Sacrifice*, edited by Jennifer Wright Knust and Zsuzsanna Várhelyi, 3–31. Oxford: Oxford University Press.

Kofsky, Aryeh. 2002. *Eusebius of Caesarea against Paganism*. Leiden: Brill.

Koortbojian, Michael. 2013. *The Divinization of Caesar and Augustus: Precedents, Consequences, Implications*. Cambridge: Cambridge University Press.

Köster, Isabel K. 2021. "Flamingos and Perverted Sacrifices in Suetonius' *Life of Caligula*." *Mnemosyne* 74: 299–317.

Kovács, Péter. 2015. "Einige Bemerkungen zum Todesdatum von Decius (AÉp 2003, 1415)." *Acta Archaeologica Academiae Scientiarum Hungaricae* 66, no. 2: 305–14.

Kovaltchuk, Ekaterina. 2008. "The Encaenia of St. Sophia: Animal Sacrifice in Christian Context." In *Scrinium 4 = Patrologia Pacifica: Selected Papers Presented to the Western Pacific Rim Patristics Society, 3rd Annual Conference (Nagoya, Japan, September 29–October 1, 2006) and Other Patristic Studies*, edited by Vladimir Baranov and Basil Lourié, 158–200. Piscataway, NJ: Gorgias Press.

Kron, Geoffrey. 2014. "Animal Husbandry." In *The Oxford Handbook of Animals in Classical Thought and Life*, edited by Gordon Lindsay Campbell, 109–35. Oxford: Oxford University Press.

Krulak, Todd C. 2014. "Θυσία and Theurgy: Sacrificial Theory in Fourth- and Fifth-Century Platonism." *Classical Quarterly* n.s. 64, no. 1: 353–82.

Kuttner, Ann L. 1995. *Dynasty and Empire in the Age of Augustus: The Case of the Boscoreale Cups*. Berkeley: University of California Press.

Lambrinudakis, Wassilis. 1984. "Apollon, M: Apollon mit anderen Göttern identifiziert." *Lexicon iconographicum mythologiae classicae*, edited by John Boardman et al., 2.1: 243–48. Zurich: Artemis.

Lapin, Hayim. 2017. "Feeding the Jerusalem Temple: Cult, Hinterland, and Economy in First-Century Palestine." *Journal of Ancient Judaism* 8, no. 3: 410–53.

Larsen, Jennifer. 2017. "Venison for Artemis? The Problem of Deer Sacrifice." In *Animal Sacrifice in the Ancient Greek World*, edited by Sarah Hitch and Ian Rutherford, 48–62. Cambridge: Cambridge University Press.

Lasserre, François, ed. 1966. *Eudoxus: Die Fragmente*. Berlin: De Gruyter.

Last, Hugh. 1949. "Rome and the Druids: A Note." *Journal of Roman Studies* 39: 1–5.

Latham, Jacob A. 2016. *Performance, Memory, and Processions in Ancient Rome: The Pompa Circensis from the Republic to Late Antiquity*. Cambridge: Cambridge University Press.

Laurence, Ray, Simon Esmonde Cleary, and Gareth Sears. 2011. *The City in the Roman West, c. 250 BC–c. AD 250*. Cambridge: Cambridge University Press.

Law, Timothy Michael, and Charles Halton, eds. 2014. Jew and Judean: A Marginalia Forum on Politics and Historiography in the Translation of Ancient Texts. https://themarginaliareview.com/jew-judean-forum/.

Lázaro Sánchez, Miguel J. 2008. "L' état actuel de la recherche sur le concile d'Elvire." *Revue des Sciences Religieuses* 82, no. 4: 517–46.

Lenski, Noel. 2008. "Evoking the Pagan Past: *Instinctu Divinitatis* and Constantine's Capture of Rome." *Journal of Late Antiquity* 1, no. 2: 204–57.

Lenski, Noel. 2012. "The Reign of Constantine." In *The Cambridge Companion to the Age of Constantine*, edited by Noel Lenski, 59–90. Rev. ed. Cambridge: Cambridge University Press.

Lenski, Noel. 2015. "Constantine and the Tyche of Constantinople." In *Contested Monarchy: Integrating the Roman Empire in the Fourth Century AD*, edited by Johannes Wienand, 330–53. Oxford: Oxford University Press.

Lenski, Noel. 2016. *Constantine and the Cities: Imperial Authority and Civic Politics*. Philadelphia: University of Pennsylvania Press.

Lepelley, Claude. 1997. "Évergétisme et épigraphie dans l'antiquité tardive: Les provinces de langue Latine." In *Actes du Xe Congrès International d'Épigraphie Grecque et Latine, Nîmes, 4–9 octobre 1992*, edited by Michel Christol and Olivier Masson, 335–52. Paris: Éditions de la Sorbonne.

Lepetz, Sébastien, and Patrice Méniel. 2008. "Des sacrifices sans consommation: Les dépôts d'animaux non consommés en Gaule romain." In *Archéologie du sacrifice animal en Gaule romaine: Rituels et pratiques alimentaires*, edited by Sébastien Lepetz and William Van Andringa, 155–64. Montagnac, France: Monique Mergoil.

Leppin, Hartmut. 1999. "Constantius II. und das Heidentum." *Athenaeum* 87: 457–80.

Letta, Cesare. 2006–7. "Per una rilettura storica del fregio dell'arco di Susa." *Atti della Pontificia Accademia Romana di Archeologia, Serie 3: Rendiconti* 79: 343–64.

Lévy, Isidore. 1926. *Recherches sur les sources de la légende de Pythagore*. Paris: Ernest Leroux.

Lewin, John, and Jamie Woodward. 2009. "Karst Geomorphology and Environmental Change." In *The Physical Geography of the Mediterranean*, edited by Jamie Woodward, 287–317. Oxford: Oxford University Press.

Liebeschuetz, Wolf. 2007. "Was There a Crisis of the Third Century?" In *Crises and the Roman Empire*, edited by Olivier Hekster, Gerda de Kleijn, and Daniëlle Slootjes, 11–20. Leiden: Brill.

Lightfoot, J. L., ed. and trans. 2009. *Hellenistic Collection*. Loeb Classical Library 508. Cambridge, MA: Harvard University Press.

Linder, Amnon, ed. 1987. *The Jews in Roman Imperial Legislation*. Detroit: Wayne State University Press.

Lindsay, Wallace M., ed. 1913. *Sexti Pompei Festi de verborum significatu quae supersunt cum Pauli epitome*. Leipzig: Teubner.

Linforth, Ivan M. 1941. *The Arts of Orpheus*. Berkeley: University of California Press.

Liver, Jacob. 1963. "The Half-Shekel Offering in Biblical and Post-Biblical Literature." *Harvard Theological Review* 56, no. 3: 173–98.

Llewelyn, Stephen R., and Dionysia Van Beek. 2010. "Reading the Temple Warning as a Greek Visitor." *Journal for the Study of Judaism* 41: 1–22.

Lloyd, Geoffrey. 2014. "Pythagoras." In *A History of Pythagoreanism*, edited by Carl A. Huffman, 24–45. Cambridge: Cambridge University Press.

Löhr, Winrich A. 2002. "Some Observations on Karl-Heinz Schwarte's 'Diokletian's Christengesetz.'" *Vigiliae Christianae* 56, no. 1: 75–95.

L'Orange, Hans-Peter. 1973 [1938]. "Ein tetrarchisches Ehrendenkmal auf dem Forum Romanum." In *Likeness and Icon: Selected Studies in Classical and Early Medieval Art*, 131–57. Odense: Odense University Press. First published in *Mitteilungen des Deutschen Archäologischen Instituts, Römische Abteilung* 53: 1–34.

Luijendijk, AnneMarie. 2008. *Greetings in the Lord: Early Christians and the Oxyrhynchus Papyri*. Cambridge, MA: Harvard Theological Studies.

Mackey, Jacob L. 2022. *Belief and Cult: Rethinking Roman Religion*. Princeton, NJ: Princeton University Press.

MacKinnon, Michael. 2004. *Production and Consumption of Animals in Roman Italy: Integrating the Zooarchaeological and Literary Evidence*. Portsmouth, RI: Journal of Roman Archaeology.

MacKinnon, Michael. 2023. "Animals in Roman Religion: The Economics behind the Rituals." In *The Economy of Roman Religion*, edited by Andrew Wilson, Nick Ray, and Angela Trentacoste, 198–223. Oxford: Oxford University Press.

Macris, Constantinos. 2018. "Pythagore de Samos." In *Dictionnaire des philosophes antiques*, edited by Richard Goulet, Vol. 7, 681–850, 1025–1174. Paris: Éditions du Centre National de la Recherche Scientifique.

Madsen, Jesper. 2009. *Eager to Be Roman: Greek Response to Roman Rule in Pontus and Bithynia*. London: Duckworth.

Magness, Jodi. 2016. "Were Sacrifices Offered at Qumran? The Animal Bone Deposits Reconsidered." *Journal of Ancient Judaism* 7, no. 1: 5–34.

Manders, Erika. 2012. *Coining Images of Power: Patterns in the Representation of Roman Emperors on Imperial Coinage, AD 193–284*. Leiden: Brill.

Mann, Michael. 2012 [1986]. *The Sources of Social Power*, Vol. 1: *A History of Power from the Beginning to AD 1760*. 2nd ed. Cambridge: Cambridge University Press. First published 1986.

Marco Simón, Francisco. 2007. "Celtic Ritualism from the (Graeco)-Roman Point of View." In *Rites et croyances dans les religions du monde romain*, edited by John Scheid, 149–177. Geneva: Fondation Hardt.

Marcos, Mar. 2014. "Emperor Jovian's Law of Religious Tolerance (a. 363)." In *Política, religión y legislación en el Imperio Romano (ss. IV y V d.c.)*, edited by María Victoria Escribano Paño and Rita Lizzi Testa, 153–77. Bari: Edipuglia.

Marghitan, L., and Constantin C. Petolescu. 1976. "*Vota Pro Salute Imperatoris* in an Inscription at Ulpia Traiana Sarmizegetusa." *Journal of Roman Studies* 66: 84–86.

Martens, Peter W. 2008. "Revisiting the Allegory/Typology Distinction: The Case of Origen." *Journal of Early Christian Studies* 16, no. 3: 283–317.

Martin, Dale B. 2010. "When Did Angels Become Demons?" *Journal of Biblical Literature* 129, no. 4: 657–77.

Martins, Pedro Ribeiro. 2018. *Der Vegetarismus in der Antike im Streitgespräch: Porphyrios' Auseinandersetzung mit der Schrift "Gegen die Vegetarier."* Berlin: De Gruyter.

Marx, Alfred. 2005. *Systèmes sacrificiels de l'Ancien Testament: Formes et fonctions du culte sacrificiel à Yhwh*. Leiden: Brill.

Marx-Wolf, Heidi. 2016. *Spiritual Taxonomies and Ritual Authority: Platonists, Priests, and Gnostics in the Third Century C.E.* Philadelphia: University of Pennsylvania Press.

Maschek, Dominik. 2018. "Not *Census* but *Deductio*: Reconsidering the '*Ara* of Domitius Ahenobarbus.'" *Journal of Roman Studies* 108: 27–52.

Mason, Steve. 2007. "Jews, Judeans, Judaizing, Judaism: Problems of Categorization in Ancient History." *Journal for the Study of Judaism* 38, nos. 4–5: 1–56. Reprinted in Steve Mason, *Josephus, Judea, and Christian Origins: Methods and Categories*, 141–84. Peabody, MA: Hendrickson, 2009.

Massa, Francesco. 2017. "Nommer et classer les religions aux IIe–IVe siècles: La taxonomie 'paganisme, judaïsme, christianisme.'" *Revue de l'Histoire des Religions* 234, no. 4: 689–715.

Matthews, John. 2000. *Laying Down the Law: A Study of the Theodosian Code*. New Haven, CT: Yale University Press.

Mattingly, David J., ed. 1997. *Dialogues in Roman Imperialism. Journal of Roman Archaeology* Supplementary Series 23. Portsmouth, RI: Journal of Roman Archaeology.

Mattingly, Harold. 1950. "The Imperial 'Vota.'" *Proceedings of the British Academy* 36: 155–95.

Mattingly, Harold. 1951. "The Imperial 'Vota' (Second Part)." *Proceedings of the British Academy* 37: 219–69.

McCarty, Matthew M. 2017. "Africa Punica? Child Sacrifice and Other Invented Traditions in Early Roman Africa." *Religion in the Roman Empire* 3, no. 3: 393–428.

McClymond, Kathryn. 2008. *Beyond Sacred Violence: A Comparative Study of Ritual*. Baltimore: Johns Hopkins University Press.

McDonough, Christopher Michael. 2004. "The Pricing of Sacrificial Meat: *Eidolothuton*, the Ara Maxima, and Useful Misinformation from Servius." In *Augusto augurio: Rerum humanarum et divinarum commentationes in honorem Jerzy Linderski*, edited by Christoph F. Konrad, 69–76. Stuttgart: Franz Steiner.

McGowan, Andrew B. 1994. "Eating People: Accusations of Cannibalism against the Christians in the Second Century." *Journal of Early Christian Studies* 2, no. 4: 413–42.

McGowan, Andrew B. 1999a. *Ascetic Eucharists: Food and Drink in Early Christian Ritual Meals*. Oxford: Oxford University Press.

McGowan, Andrew B. 1999b. "'Is There a Liturgical Text in This Gospel?': The Institution Narratives and Their Early Interpretive Communities." *Journal of Biblical Literature* 118, no. 1: 73–87.

McGowan, Andrew B. 2010. "Rethinking Eucharistic Origins." *Pacifica* 23: 173–91.

McGowan, Andrew B. 2014. *Ancient Christian Worship: Early Church Practices in Social, Historical, and Theological Perspectives*. Grand Rapids, MI: Baker Academic.

McGowan, Andrew. 2015. "The Myth of the 'Lord's Supper': Paul's Eucharistic Meal Terminology and Its Ancient Reception." *Catholic Biblical Quarterly* 77: 502–20.

McInerney, Jeremy. 2010. *The Cattle of the Sun: Cows and Culture in the World of the Ancient Greeks*. Princeton, NJ: Princeton University Press.

McKechnie, Paul. 2002. "Roman Law and the Laws of the Medes and Persians: Decius' and Valerian's Persecutions of Christianity." In *Thinking Like a Lawyer: Essays on*

*Legal History and General History for John Crook on His Eightieth Birthday*, edited by Paul McKechnie, 253–69. Leiden: Brill.

McPherran, Mark L. 2000. "Does Piety Pay? Socrates and Plato on Prayer and Sacrifice." In *Reason and Religion in Socratic Philosophy*, edited by Gregory Vlastos, Thomas C. Brickhouse, Mark L. McPherran, Nicholas D. Smith, and Paul B. Woodruff, 89–114. Oxford: Oxford University Press.

Meigne, Maurice. 1975. "Concile ou collection d'Elvire." *Revue d'Histoire Ecclésiastique* 70: 361–87.

Ménard, Hélène. 2006. "La persécution de Dèce d'après le récit de la *Passio sancti Saturnini*: 'Vnxit ad tauri latus iniugati plebs furibunda.'" In *La "crise" de l'empire romain de Marc Aurèle à Constantin: Mutations, continuités, ruptures*, edited by Marie-Henriette Quet, Andrea Giardina, and Michel Christol, 497–510. Paris: Université de Paris–Sorbonne.

Méniel, Patrice. 1992. *Les sacrifices d'animaux chez les Gaulois*. Paris: Editions Errance.

Méniel, Patrice. 2008. "Sacrifices d'animaux, traditions gauloises et influences romains." In *Archéologie du sacrifice animal en Gaule romaine: Rituels et pratiques alimentaires*, edited by Sébastien Lepetz and William Van Andringa, 147–54. Montagnac, France: Monique Mergoil.

Migeotte, Léopold. 2014. *Les finances des cités grecques*. Epigraphica 8. Paris: Les Belles Lettres.

Mikalson, Jon D. 2010. *Greek Popular Religion in Greek Philosophy*. Oxford: Oxford University Press.

Millar, Fergus. 1993. "The Greek City in the Roman Period." In *The Ancient Greek City-State*, edited by Mogens Herman Hansen, 232–60. Copenhagen: Munksgaard.

Minns, Denis, and Paul Parvis, eds. and trans. 2009. *Justin, Philosopher and Martyr: Apologies*. Oxford: Oxford University Press.

Mitchell, Stephen. 1988. "Maximinus and the Christians in A.D. 312: A New Latin Inscription." *Journal of Roman Studies* 78: 105–24.

Mitchell, Stephen. 1990. "Festivals, Games, and Civic Life in Roman Asia Minor." *Journal of Roman Studies* 80: 183–93.

Mitchell, Stephen. 1999. "The Cult of Theos Hypsistos between Pagans, Jews, and Christians." In *Pagan Monotheism in Late Antiquity*, edited by Polymnia Athanassiadi and Michael Frede, 81–148. Oxford: Clarendon Press.

Mitchell, Stephen. 2010. "Further Thoughts on the Cult of Theos Hypsistos." In *One God: Pagan Monotheism in the Roman Empire*, edited by Stephen Mitchell and Peter Van Nuffelen, 167–208. Cambridge: Cambridge University Press.

Moser, Claudia. 2016. "The Architecture of Changing Sacrificial Practices in Pre-Roman and Roman Gaul." In *Beyond Boundaries: Connecting Visual Cultures in the Provinces of Ancient Rome*, edited by Susan E. Alcock, Mariana Egri, and James F. D. Frakes, 174–89. Los Angeles: Getty Publications.

Moss, Candida R. 2010a. "On the Dating of Polycarp: Rethinking the Place of the Martyrdom of Polycarp in the History of Christianity." *Early Christianity* 4, no. 1: 539–74.

Moss, Candida R. 2010b. *The Other Christs: Imitating Jesus in Ancient Christian Ideologies of Martyrdom*. Oxford: Oxford University Press.

Moss, Candida R. 2012. *Ancient Christian Martyrdom: Diverse Practices, Theologies, and Traditions*. New Haven, CT: Yale University Press.

Muñiz Grijalvo, Elena. 2003. "El sacrificio cristiano como factor de autoexclusión." *Studia Historica/Historia Antigua* 21: 139–57.

Musurillo, Herbert. 1972. *The Acts of the Christian Martyrs*. Oxford: Clarendon Press.

Naiden, Fred S. 2013. *Smoke Signals for the Gods: Ancient Greek Sacrifice from the Archaic through the Roman Periods*. Oxford: Oxford University Press.

Naiden, Fred S., and James B. Rives. 2016. "Sacrifice." *Oxford Bibliographies*. https://doi.org/10.1093/obo/9780195389661-0209.

Nash, Daphne. 1976. "Reconstructing Poseidonios' Celtic Ethnography: Some Considerations." *Britannia* 7: 111–26.

Nesselrath, Heinz-Günther, et al. 2011. *Für Religionsfreiheit, Recht und Toleranz: Libanios' Rede für den Erhalt der heidnischen Tempel*. Tübingen: Mohr Siebeck.

Nilsson, Martin P. 1906. *Griechische Feste von religiöser Bedeutung, mit Ausschluss der attischen*. Leipzig: B. G. Teubner.

Nilsson, Martin P. 1945. "Pagan Divine Service in Late Antiquity." *Harvard Theological Review* 38, no. 1: 63–69.

Nilsson, Martin P. 1950. "Lampen und Kerzen im Kult der Antike." *Skrifter Utgivna av Svenska Institutet i Rom*, 40, XIII = *Opuscula Archaeologica* 6: 96–111.

Nongbri, Brent. 2013. *Before Religion: A History of a Modern Concept*. New Haven, CT: Yale University Press.

Obbink, Dirk. 1988. "The Origin of Greek Sacrifice: Theophrastus on Religion and Cultural History." In *Theophrastean Studies: On Natural Science, Physics and Metaphysics, Ethics, Religion and Rhetoric*, edited by William W. Fortenbaugh and Robert W. Sharples, 272–95. New Brunswick, NJ: Transaction Books.

Obbink, Dirk. 1996. *Philodemus: On Piety*. Oxford: Clarendon Press.

Öhler, Markus. 2014. "Cultic Meals in Associations and the Early Christian Eucharist." *Early Christianity* 5, no. 4: 475–502.

Oliver, James H. 1971. "Epaminondas of Acraephia." *Greek, Roman and Byzantine Studies* 12: 221–37.

Olson, S. Douglas, and Alexander Sens, eds. 2000. *Archestratos of Gela: Greek Culture and Cuisine in the Fourth Century BCE*. Oxford: Oxford University Press.

O'Meara, John J., trans. 1954. *Origen: Prayer/Exhortation to Martyrdom*. New York: Newman Press.

Osborne, Robin. 1993. "Women and Sacrifice in Classical Greece." *Classical Quarterly* 43, no. 2: 392–405.

Parker, Robert C. T. 1996. *Athenian Religion: A History*. Oxford: Oxford University Press.

Parker, Robert C. T. 2010. "Eating Unsacrificed Meat." In *Paysage et religion en Grèce antique: Mélanges offerts à Madeleine Jost*, edited by Pierre Carlier and Charlotte Lerouge-Cohen, 137–45. Paris: De Boccard.

Parker, Robert C. T. 2014. "Review of Radcliffe G. Edmonds III, *Redefining Ancient Orphism: A Study in Greek Religion* (2013)." *Bryn Mawr Classical Review*. https://bmcr.brynmawr.edu/2014/2014.07.13/.

Paschoud, François. 1971. "'Zosime 2,29 et la version païenne de la conversion de Constantin." *Historia* 20, nos. 2–3: 334–53. Reprinted in François Paschoud, *Cinq études sur Zosime*, 24–62. Paris: Les Belles Lettres, 1976.

Paschoud, François. 1993. "Ancora sul rifiuto di Costantino di salire al Campidoglio." In *Costantino il Grande dall'antichità all'umanesimo*, edited by Giorgio Bonamente and Franca Fusco, 2.737–48. Macerata: Università degli Studi di Macerata.

Paschoud, François. 1997. "Zosime et Constantin: Nouvelles controverses." *Museum Helveticum* 54: 9–28.

Peels, Saskia. 2016. *Hosios: A Semantic Study of Greek Piety*. Leiden: Brill.

Peirce, Charles S. 1998. *The Essential Peirce: Selected Philosophical Writings, Volume 2 (1893–1913)*, edited by the Peirce Edition Project. Bloomington: Indiana University Press.

Peirce, Philip. 1989. "The Arch of Constantine: Propaganda and Ideology in Late Roman Art." *Art History* 12, no. 4: 387–418.

Penella, Robert J. 1979. *The Letters of Apollonius of Tyana: A Critical Text with Prolegomena, Translation and Commentary*. Leiden: Brill.

Pensabene, Patrizio, and Clementina Panella, eds. 1999. *Arco di Costantino tra archeologia e archeometria*. Rome: "L'Erma" di Bretschneider.

Pervo, Richard I. 2006. *Dating Acts: Between the Evangelists and the Apologists*. Santa Rosa, CA: Polebridge Press.

Pervo, Richard I. 2009. *Acts: A Commentary*. Hermeneia Commentaries. Minneapolis: Fortress Press.

Petropoulou, Maria-Zoe. 2008. *Animal Sacrifice in Ancient Greek Religion, Judaism, and Christianity, 100 BC to AD 200*. Oxford: Oxford University Press.

Pfeiffer, Rudolf, ed. 1949. *Callimachus*, Vol. 1: *Fragmenta*. Oxford: Clarendon Press.

Pharr, Clyde, trans. 1952. *The Theodosian Code and Novels, and the Sirmondian Constitutions*, in collaboration with Theresa Sherrer Davidson and Mary Brown Pharr. Princeton: Princeton University Press.

Piggott, Stuart. 1968. *The Druids*. London: Thames & Hudson.

Piotrkowski, Meron M. 2019. *Priests in Exile: The History of the Temple of Onias and Its Community in the Hellenistic Period*. Berlin: De Gruyter.

Pollini, John. 1987. *The Portraiture of Gaius and Lucius Caesar*. New York: Fordham University Press.

Pollini, John. 2012. *From Republic to Empire: Rhetoric, Religion, and Power in the Visual Culture of Ancient Rome*. Norman: University of Oklahoma Press.

Pont, Anne-Valérie. 2020. *La fin de la cité grecque: Métamorphoses et disparition d'un modèle politique et institutionnel local en Asie Mineure, de Dèce à Constantin*. Geneva: Droz.

Potter, David S. 2014. *The Roman Empire at Bay, AD 180–395*. 2nd ed. Abingdon, UK: Routledge.

Price, Simon R. F. 1980. "Between Man and God: Sacrifice in the Roman Imperial Cult." *Journal of Roman Studies* 70: 28–43.

Price, Simon R. F. 1984. *Rituals and Power: The Roman Imperial Cult in Asia Minor*. Cambridge: Cambridge University Press.

Price, Simon R. F. 1999. "Latin Christian Apologists: Minucius Felix, Tertullian, and Cyprian." In *Apologetics in the Roman Empire: Pagans, Jews, and Christians*, edited by Mark Edwards, Martin Goodman, and Simon Price, 105–29. Oxford: Oxford University Press.

Proctor, Travis W. 2014. "Daemonic Trickery, Platonic Mimicry: Traces of Christian Daemonological Discourse in Porphyry's *De abstinentia*." *Vigiliae Christianae* 68, no. 4: 416–49.

Proctor, Travis W. 2022. *Demonic Bodies and the Dark Ecologies of Early Christian Culture*. Oxford: Oxford University Press.

Quass, Friedemann. 1993. *Die Honoratiorenschicht in den Städten des griechischen Ostens: Untersuchungen zur politischen und sozialen Entwicklung in hellenistischer und römischer Zeit*. Stuttgart: Franz Steiner.

Rachat, Marguerite. 1980. "Decennalia et vicennalia sous la dynastie des Antonins." *Revue des Études Anciennes* 82: 200–35.

Rebillard, Éric. 2012. *Christians and Their Many Identities in Late Antiquity, North Africa, 200–450 CE*. Ithaca, NY: Cornell University Press.

Rebillard, Éric. 2017. *Greek and Latin Narratives about the Ancient Martyrs*. Oxford: Oxford University Press.

Reed, Annette Yoshiko. 2004. "The Trickery of the Fallen Angels and the Demonic Mimesis of the Divine: Aetiology, Demonology, and Polemics in the Writings of Justin Martyr." *Journal of Early Christian Studies* 12, no. 2: 141–71.

Reed, Annette Yoshiko. 2014. "From Sacrifice to the Slaughterhouse: Ancient and Modern Approaches to Meat, Animals, and Civilization." *Method and Theory in the Study of Religion* 26: 111–58.

Rehak, Paul. 2001. "Aeneas or Numa? Rethinking the Meaning of the Ara Pacis Augustae." *Art Bulletin* 83, no. 2: 190–208.

Remus, Harold. 2004. "The End of 'Paganism'?" *Studies in Religion/Sciences Religieuses* 33, no. 2: 191–208.

Rémy, Bernard. 2016. *Dioclétien: L'empire restauré*. Paris: Armand Colin.

Reynolds, Joyce M. 1962. "*Vota Pro Salute Principis*." *Papers of the British School at Rome* n.s. 17: 33–36.

Reynolds, Joyce M. 1965. "Notes on Cyrenaican Inscriptions." *Papers of the British School at Rome* n.s. 20: 52–54.

Riedweg, Christoph. 2005. *Pythagoras: His Life, Teaching, and Influence*. Translated by Steven Rendall with Christoph Riedweg and Andreas Schatzmann. Ithaca, NY: Cornell University Press.

Rigsby, Kent J. 1996. *Asylia: Territorial Inviolability in the Hellenistic World*. Berkeley: University of California Press.

Ritchie, Hannah. 2021. "If the World Adopted a Plant-Based Diet We Would Reduce Global Agricultural Land Use from 4 to 1 Billion Hectares." Our World in Data, March 4. https://ourworldindata.org/land-use-diets.

Rives, James B. 1995a. "Human Sacrifice among Pagans and Christians." *Journal of Roman Studies* 85: 65–85.

Rives, James B. 1995b. *Religion and Authority in Roman Carthage from Augustus to Constantine*. Oxford: Clarendon Press.

Rives, James B. 1999. "The Decree of Decius and the Religion of Empire." *Journal of Roman Studies* 89: 135–54.

Rives, James B. 2009. "Magic, Religion, and Law: The Case of the Lex Cornelia *de sicariis et veneficiis*." In *Religion and Law in Classical and Christian Rome*, edited by Clifford Ando and Jörg Rüpke, 47–67. Stuttgart: Franz Steiner.

Rives, James B. 2011a. "The Persecution of Christians and Ideas of Community in the Roman Empire." In *Politiche religiose nel mondo antico e tardoantico: Atti del Convegno Internazionale di Studi (Firenze, 24–26 settembre 2009)*, edited by Giovanni Alberto Cecconi and Chantal Gabrielli, 199–217. Bari: Edipuglia.

Rives, James B. 2011b. "Roman Translation: Tacitus and Ethnographic Interpretation." In *Travel and Religion in Antiquity*, edited by Philip A. Harland, 165–83. Waterloo, ON: Wilfrid Laurier Press.

Rives, James B. 2011c. "The Theology of Animal Sacrifice in the Ancient Greek World: Origins and Developments." In *Ancient Mediterranean Sacrifice*, edited by Jennifer Wright Knust and Zsuzsanna Várhelyi, 187–202. Oxford: Oxford University Press.

Rives, James B. 2012. "Between Orthopraxy and Orthodoxy: Constantine and Animal Sacrifice." In *Costantino prima e dopo Costantino / Constantine before and after Constantine*, edited by Giorgio Bonamente, Noel Lenski, and Rita Lizzi Testa, 153–63. Bari: Edipuglia.

Rives, James B. 2013. "Women and Animal Sacrifice in Public Life." In *Women and the Roman City in the Latin West*, edited by Emily Hemelrijk and Greg Woolf, 129–46. Leiden: Brill.

Rives, James B. 2014. "Animal Sacrifice and Political Identity in Rome and Judaea." In *Jews and Christians in the First and Second Centuries: How to Write Their History*, edited by Peter J. Tomson and Joshua Schwartz, 105–25. Compendia Rerum Iudaicarum ad Novum Testamentum 13. Leiden: Brill.

Rives, James B. 2018. "Cult Practice, Social Power, and Religious Identity: The Case of Animal Sacrifice." In *Juden, Christen, Heiden? Religiöse Inklusion und Exklusion in Kleinasien bis Decius*, edited by Stefan Alkier and Hartmut Leppin, 71–88. Tübingen: Mohr Siebeck.

Rives, James B. 2019a. "Animal Sacrifice and Euergetism in the Hellenistic and Roman Polis." In *Transformations of Value: Lived Religion and the Economy*, edited by Claudia Moser and Christopher Smith, 83–102. Religion in the Roman Empire 5, no. 1. Tübingen: Mohr Siebeck.

Rives, James B. 2019b. "Roman Empire and Roman Emperor: Animal Sacrifice as an Instrument of Religious Convergence." In *Religious Convergence in the Ancient Mediterranean*, edited by Sandra Blakely and Billie Jean Collins, 523–40. Atlanta: Lockwood Press.

Rives, James B. 2019c. "Sacrifice and 'Religion': Modeling Religious Change in the Roman Empire." *Religions* 10, no. 1. https://doi.org/10.3390/rel10010016.

Rives, James B. 2020. "Animal Sacrifice and the Roman Persecution of Christians (2nd–3rd Centuries CE)." In *Religious Violence in the Ancient World from Classical Athens to Late Antiquity*, edited by Jitse Dijkstra and Christian Raschle, 177–202. Cambridge: Cambridge University Press.

Robert, Louis. 1935. "Études sur les inscriptions et la topographie de la Grèce centrale, VI: Decrets d'Akraiphia." *Bulletin de Correspondance Héllenique* 59: 438–52. Reprinted in Louis Robert, *Opera Minora Selecta* I, 279–93. Amsterdam: A. M. Hakkert, 1969.

Robert, Louis. 1948. "Inscriptions de Thyatire." In *Hellenica: Receuil d'épigraphie de numismatique et d'antiquités grecques* 6, 70–79. Limoges: Bontemps.

Robert, Louis. 1994. *Le martyre de Pionios, prêtre de Smyrne*. Updated and completed by Glen W. Bowersock and Christopher P. Jones. Washington, DC: Dumbarton Oaks.

Rogers, Guy McLean. 1991. "Demosthenes of Oenoanda and Models of Euergetism." *Journal of Roman Studies* 81: 91–100.

Roos, A. G. 1938. "Lesefrüchte, II, 9." *Mnemosyne* 6: 174–78.

Rose, Valentin, ed. 1886. *Aristotelis qui ferebantur librorum fragmenta*. Stuttgart: Teubner.

Rosenblum, Jordan D. 2013. "Home Is Where the Hearth Is? A Consideration of Jewish Household Sacrifice in Antiquity." In *"The One Who Sows Bountifully": Essays in Honor of Stanley K. Stowers*, edited by Caroline Johnson Hodge, Saul M. Olyen, Daniel Ullucci, and Emma Wasserman, 153–63. Providence, RI: Brown Judaic Studies.

Rosivach, Vincent. 1994. *The System of Public Sacrifice in Fourth-Century Athens*. American Classical Studies 34. Atlanta: Scholars Press.

Rossini, Orietta. 2008. *Ara Pacis*. Comune di Roma, Assessorato alle Politiche Culturali/Sovraintendenza ai Geni Culturali. Milan: Mondadori Electa.

Rothman, Margret S. Pond. 1977. "The Thematic Organization of the Panel Reliefs on the Arch of Galerius." *American Journal of Archaeology* 81, no. 4: 427–54.

Rougé, Jean. 1987. "Valentinien et la religion: 364–365." *Ktèma* 12: 286–97.

Roymans, Nico. 1990. *Tribal Societies in Northern Gaul: An Anthropological Perspective*. Amsterdam: University of Amsterdam Press.

Rubin, Zeev. 1998. "Pagan Propaganda during the Usurpation of Magnentius (350–353)." *Scripta Classica Israelica* 17: 124–41.

Rudhardt, Jean. 1992 [1958]. *Notions fondamentales de la pensée religieuse et actes constitutifs du culte dans la Grèce classique.* 2nd ed. Paris: Picard. First edition Geneva: Droz, 1958.

Rüpke, Jörg. 1995. *Kalender und Öffentlichkeit: Die Geschichte der Repräsentation und religiösen Qualifikation von Zeit in Rom.* Berlin: De Gruyter.

Rüpke, Jörg. 2006. "Religion in the Lex Ursonensis." In *Religion and Law in Classical and Christian Rome*, edited by Clifford Ando and Jörg Rüpke, 34–46. Stuttgart: Franz Steiner.

Rüpke, Jörg. 2011. *The Roman Calendar from Numa to Constantine: Time, History, and the Fasti.* Malden, MA: Blackwell.

Rutherford, Ian. 2017. "The Reception of Egyptian Animal Sacrifice in Greek Writers: Ethnic Stereotyping or Transcultural Discourse?" In *Animal Sacrifice in the Ancient Greek World*, edited by Sarah Hitch and Ian Rutherford, 253–66. Cambridge: Cambridge University Press.

Ryberg, Inez Scott. 1955. *Rites of the State Religion in Roman Art.* Memoirs of the American Academy in Rome 22. Rome: American Academy in Rome.

Saffrey, Henri Dominique, and Alain-Philippe Segonds, eds. 2012. *Porphyre: Lettre à Anébon l'Égyptien.* Paris: Les Belles Lettres.

Saffrey, Henri Dominique, and Alain-Philippe Segonds, eds. 2013. *Jamblique: Réponse à Porphyre (De Mysteriis).* Paris: Les Belles Lettres.

Safrai, Shmuel. 1981. *Die Wallfahrt im Zeitalter des Zweiten Tempels.* Neukirchen-Vluyn, Germany: Neukirchener Verlag.

Şahin, Sencer. 1995. "Studien zu den Inschriften von Perge II: Der Gesandte Apollonios und seine Familie." *Epigraphica Anatolica* 25: 1–23.

Sallares, Robert. 2009. "Environmental History." In *A Companion to Ancient History*, edited by Andrew Erskine, 164–74. Malden, MA: Blackwell.

Salzman, Michele Renee. 1987. "'Superstitio' in the Codex Theodosianus and the Persecution of Pagans." *Vigiliae Christianae* 41, no. 2: 172–88.

Salzman, Michele Renee. 2011. "The End of Public Sacrifice: Changing Definitions of Sacrifice in Post-Constantinian Rome and Italy." In *Ancient Mediterranean Sacrifice*, edited by Jennifer Wright Knust and Zsuzsanna Várhelyi, 167–84. Oxford: Oxford University Press.

Salzman, Michele Renee, and Michael Roberts, trans. 2011. *The Letters of Symmachus: Book 1.* Atlanta: Society of Biblical Literature.

Sanders, E. P. 1992. *Judaism: Practice and Belief, 63 BCE–66 CE.* Philadelphia: Trinity Press International.

Sanders, E. P. 2015. *Paul: The Apostle's Life, Letters, and Thought.* Minneapolis: Fortress Press.

Sandwell, Isabella. 2005. "'Outlawing 'Magic' or Outlawing 'Religion'? Libanius and the Theodosian Code as Evidence for Legislation against 'Pagan' Practices." In *The Spread of Christianity in the First Four Centuries*, edited by William V. Harris, 88–123. Leiden: Brill.

Saquete Chamizo, José Carlos, Salvador Ordóñez Agulla, and Sergio García-Dils de la Vega. 2011. "Una *votorum nuncupatio* en Colonia Augusta Firma (Écija-Sevilla)." *Zeitschrift für Papyrologie und Epigraphik* 176: 281–90.

Schachter, Albert. 1981. *Cults of Boiotia, 1: Acheloos to Hera*. Bulletin of the Institute of Classical Studies Supplement 38. London: Institute of Classical Studies.

Schäfer, Peter. 1997. *Judeophobia: Attitudes toward the Jews in the Ancient World*. Cambridge, MA: Harvard University Press.

Scheid, John. 1985. "Sacrifice et banquet à Rome: Quelques problèmes." *Mélanges de l'École Française de Rome: Antiquité* 97: 193–206.

Scheid, John. 1990. *Romulus et ses frères: Le collège des frères arvales, modèle du culte public dans la Rome des empereurs*. Rome: École Française de Rome.

Scheid, John. 1995. "Graeco Ritu: A Typically Roman Way of Honoring the Gods." *Harvard Studies in Classical Philology* 97: 15–31.

Scheid, John. 1998. *Recherches archéologiques à la Magliana: Commentarii Fratrum Arvalium qui supersunt: Les copies épigraphiques des protocoles annuels de la confrérie arvale (21 av.–304 ap. J.-C.)*, with contributions by Paola Tassini and Jörg Rüpke. Rome: École Française de Rome, Soprintendenza Archeologica di Roma.

Scheid, John. 1999. "Aspects religieux de la municipalisation: Quelques réflexions générales." In *Cités, municipes, colonies: Les processus de municipalisation en Gaule et en Germanie sous le Haut Empire romain*, edited by Monique Dondin-Payre and Marie-Thérèse Raepsaet-Charlier, 381–423. Paris: Publications de la Sorbonne.

Scheid, John. 2005. *Quand faire, c'est croire: Les rites sacrificiels des Romains*. Paris: Aubier.

Scheid, John. 2007. "Le statut de la viande à Rome." In *Sacrifices, marché de la viande et pratiques alimentaires dans les cités du monde romain*, edited by William Van Andringa. *Food & History* 5, no. 1: 19–28.

Scheid, John. 2019 [2011]. "Les offrandes végétales dans les rites sacrificiels des Romains." In *Rites et religion à Rome*, 151–64. Paris: CNRS Éditions. First published in *"Nourrir les dieux?": Sacrifice et représentation du divin*, edited by Vinciane Pirenne-Delforge and Francesca Prescendi, 105–15. *Kernos* Supplement 26. Liège: Centre International d'Étude de la Religion Grecque Antique, 2011.

Schellenberg, Ryan S., and Heidi Wendt, eds. 2022. *T&T Clark Handbook to the Historical Paul*. London: T&T Clark.

Schlumberger, Daniel, Louis Robert, André Dupont-Sommer, and Émile Benveniste. 1958. "Une bilingue gréco-araméenne d'Asoka." *Journal Asiatique* 246: 1–48.

Schmidt, Johanna. 1948. "Tyrimnos." In *Paulys Real-encyclopädie der classischen Altertumswissenschaft*, edited by August Pauly, Georg Wissowa, and Wilhem Kroll, 7A.2: 1867–68. Munich: A. Druckenmüller.

Schmitt Pantel, Pauline. 1992. *La cité au banquet: Histoire des repas publics dans les cités grecques*. Rome: École Française de Rome.

Schoedel, William R., ed. and trans. 1972. *Athenagoras: Legatio and De Resurrectione*. Oxford: Clarendon Press.

Schörner, Günther. 2011. "Sacrifice East and West: Experiencing Ritual Difference in the Roman Empire." In *Ritual Dynamics and the Science of Ritual*, Vol. IV: *Reflexivity, Media and Visuality*, edited by Axel Michaels, 81–99. Wiesbaden: Harrassowitz.

Schott, Jeremy M. 2008. *Christianity, Empire, and the Making of Religion in Late Antiquity*. Philadelphia: University of Pennsylvania Press.

Schubert, Paul. 2016. "On the Form and Content of the Certificates of Pagan Sacrifice." *Journal of Roman Studies* 106: 172–98.

Schultz, Celia E. 2010. "The Romans and Ritual Murder." *Journal of the American Academy in Rome* 78, no. 2: 516–41.

Schultz, Celia E. 2016. "Roman Sacrifice, Inside and Out." *Journal of Roman Studies* 106: 58–76.

Schwarte, Karl-Heinz. 1989. "Die Christengesetze Valerians." In *Religion und Gesellschaft in der römischen Kaiserzeit: Kolloquium zu Ehren von Friedrich Vittinghoff*, edited by Werner Eck, 103–63. Cologne: Böhlau.

Schwarte, Karl-Heinz. 1994. "Diocletians Christengesetz." In *E fontibus haurire: Beiträge zur römischen Geschichte und zu ihren Hilfswissenschaften*, edited by Rosmarie Günther and Stefan Rebenich, 203–40. Paderborn, Germany: Schöningh.

Schwartz, Daniel R. 1992. "On Sacrifice by Gentiles in the Temple of Jerusalem." In *Studies in the Jewish Background of Christianity*, 102–16. Tübingen: Mohr Siebeck.

Schwartz, Daniel R. 2014. *Judeans and Jews: Four Faces of Dichotomy in Ancient Jewish History*. Toronto: University of Toronto Press.

Schwartz, Joshua. 2014. "Sacrifice without the Rabbis: Ritual and Sacrifice in the Second Temple Period according to Contemporary Sources." In *The Actuality of Sacrifice: Past and Present*, edited by Alberdina Houtman, Marcel Poorthuis, Joshua Schwartz, and Joseph Turner, 123–48. Leiden: Brill.

Schwartz, Seth. 2010. *Were the Jews a Mediterranean Society? Reciprocity and Solidarity in Ancient Judaism*. Princeton, NJ: Princeton University Press.

Scullard, H. H. 1981. *Festivals and Ceremonies of the Roman Republic*. Ithaca, NY: Cornell University Press.

Selinger, Reinhard. 2004. *The Mid-Third Century Persecutions of Decius and Valerian*. Rev. ed. Frankfurt am Main: Peter Lang.

Seyrig, Henri. 1929. "Inscriptions de Gythion." *Revue Archéologique* 29: 84–106.

Shaw, Brent D. 2016. "Lambs of God: An End of Human Sacrifice." *Journal of Roman Archaeology* 29: 259–91.

Shaw, Gregory. 1995. *Theurgy and the Soul: The Neoplatonism of Iamblichus*. University Park: Pennsylvania State University Press.

Sherwin-White, A. N. 1973. *The Roman Citizenship*. 2nd ed. Oxford: Clarendon Press.

Simmons, Michael Bland. 1995. *Arnobius of Sicca: Religious Conflict and Competition in the Age of Diocletian*. Oxford: Clarendon Press.

Smallwood, E. Mary, ed. and trans. 1961. *Philo: Legatio ad Gaium*. Leiden: Brill.

Smith, Andrew. 1993. *Porphyrii philosophi fragmenta*. Stuttgart: Teubner.

Smith, Gregory A. 2008. "How Thin Is a Demon?" *Journal of Early Christian Studies* 16, no. 4: 479–512.

Smith, Kyle. 2011. *Constantine and the Captive Christians of Persia: Martyrdom and Religious Identity in Late Antiquity*. Berkeley: University of California Press.

Smith, Kyle. 2014. *The Martyrdom and History of Blessed Simeon bar Ṣabbaʿe*. Piscataway, NJ: Gorgias Press.

Smith, Rowland. 1995. *Julian's Gods: Religion and Philosophy in the Thought and Action of Julian the Apostate*. London: Routledge.

Sobocinski, Melanie Grunow, and Elizabeth Wolfram Thill. 2018. "Dismembering a Sacred Cow: The Extispicium Relief in the Louvre." In *Roman Artists, Patrons, and Public Consumption: Familiar Works Reconsidered*, edited by Brenda Longfellow and Ellen E. Perry, 38–62. Ann Arbor: University of Michigan Press.

Sorabji, Richard. 1993. *Animal Minds and Human Morals: The Origins of the Western Debate*. Ithaca, NY: Cornell University Press.

Spannagel, Martin. 1999. *Exemplaria principis: Untersuchungen zu Entstehung und Ausstattung des Augustusforums*. Heidelberg: Verlag Archäologie und Geschichte.

Spannagel, Martin. 2017. "'Micat inter omnis . . .': Zur Kolossalstatue des Divus Iulius im Augustusforum." In *Augustus ist tot—Lang lebe der Kaiser! Internationales Kolloquium anlässlich des 2000. Todesjahres des römischen Kaisers vom 20.–22. November 2014 in Tübingen*, edited by Manuel Flecker, Stefan Krmnicek, Johannes Lipps, Richard Posamentir, and Thomas Schäfer, 205–71. Rahden, Germany: Leidorf.

Stangl, Thomas, ed. 1912. *Ciceronis orationum scholiastae*. Vienna: F. Tempsky.

Stepper, Ruth. 2003. *Augustus et sacerdos: Untersuchungen zum römischen Kaiser als Priester*. Stuttgart: Franz Steiner.

Stowers, Stanley K. 1994. *A Rereading of Romans*. New Haven, CT: Yale University Press.

Stowers, Stanley K. 2011a. "Kinds of Myths, Meals, and Power: Paul and the Corinthians." In *Redescribing Paul and the Corinthians*, edited by Ron Cameron and Merrill P. Miller, 105–49. Atlanta: Society of Biblical Literature.

Stowers, Stanley K. 2011b. "The Religion of Plant and Animal Offerings versus the Religion of Meanings, Essences, and Textual Mysteries." In *Ancient Mediterranean Sacrifice*, edited by Jennifer Wright Knust and Zsuzsanna Várhelyi, 35–56. Oxford: Oxford University Press.

Streeter, Joseph. 2006. "The Date of the Council of Elvira." In G. E. M. de Ste. Croix, *Christian Persecution, Martyrdom, and Orthodoxy*, edited by Michael Whitby and Joseph Streeter, 99–104. Oxford: Oxford University Press.

Stroumsa, Guy G. 2005. *La fin du sacrifice: Les mutations religieuses de l'antiquité tardive*. Paris: Odile Jacob.

Swain, Simon. 1996. *Hellenism and Empire: Language, Classicism, and Power in the Greek World, AD 50–250*. Oxford: Oxford University Press.

Thomas, Oliver. 2017. "Sacrifice and the *Homeric Hymn to Hermes* 112–41." In *Animal Sacrifice in the Ancient Greek World*, edited by Sarah Hitch and Ian Rutherford, 181–99. Cambridge: Cambridge University Press.

Threpsiades, John Ch. 1939. "Decree in Honor of Euthydemos of Eleusis." *Hesperia* 8, no. 2: 177–80.

Thurmond, David L. 2006. *A Handbook of Food Processing in Classical Rome: For Her Bounty No Winter*. Leiden: Brill.

Tierney, J. J. 1960. "The Celtic Ethnography of Posidonius." *Proceedings of the Royal Irish Academy* 60: 189–275.

Timotin, Andrei. 2012. *La démonologie platonicienne: Histoire de la notion de daimōn de Platon aux derniers néoplatoniciens*. Leiden: Brill.

Trombley, Frank R. 1985. "Paganism in the Greek World at the End of Antiquity: The Case of Rural Anatolia and Greece." *Harvard Theological Review* 78, nos. 3–4: 327–52.

Trombley, Frank R. 1995. *Hellenic Religion and Christianization, c. 370–529*. 2nd ed. Leiden: Brill.

Trout, Dennis. 1995. "Christianizing the Nolan Countryside: Animal Sacrifice at the Tomb of St. Felix." *Journal of Early Christian Studies* 3, no. 3: 281–98.

Ullucci, Daniel C. 2012. *The Christian Rejection of Animal Sacrifice*. Oxford: Oxford University Press.

Ullucci, Daniel C. 2015. "Sacrifice in the Ancient Mediterranean: Recent and Current Research." *Currents in Biblical Research* 13, no. 3: 388–439.

Van Andringa, William. 2002. *La religion en Gaule romaine: Piété et politique (Ier–IIIe siècle apr. J.-C)*. Paris: Éditions Errance.

Van Andringa, William. 2007. "Du sanctuaire au macellum: Sacrifices, commerce et consummation de la viande à Pompéi." In *Sacrifices, marché de la viande et pratiques alimentaires dans les cités du monde romain*, edited by William Van Andringa. *Food & History* 5, no. 1: 47–72.

Van Andringa, William. 2008. "La cuisine du sacrifice en pays gallo-romaine." In *Archéologie du sacrifice animal en Gaule romaine: Rituels et pratiques alimentaires*, edited by Sébastien Lepetz and William Van Andringa, 27–42. Montagnac, France: Monique Mergoil.

Van Andringa, William. 2014. "Les dieux changent en Occident (IIIe–IVe s. apr. J.-C.): Archéologie et mutations religieuses de l'Antiquité tardive." In *La fin des dieux: Les lieux de culte du polythéisme dans la pratique religieuse du IIIe au Ve siècle apr. J.-C. (Gaules et provinces occidentales)*, edited by William Van Andringa and Marie-Thérèse Raepsaet-Charlier, 3–10. *Gallia* 71, no.1. Paris: Centre de la Recherche Scientifique.

Van der Lans, Birgit, and Jan N. Bremmer. 2017. "Tacitus and the Persecution of the Christians: An Invention of Tradition?" *Eirene* 53, nos. 1–2: 299–331.

Van Haeperen, Françoise. 2002. *Le collège pontifical (3ème s. a. C.–4ème s. p. C.): Contribution à l'étude de la religion publique romaine*. Brussels: Institut Historique Belge de Rome.

Van Nijf, Onno. 2001. "Local Heroes: Athletics, Festivals and Elite Self-Fashioning in the Roman East." In *Being Greek under Rome: Cultural Identity, the Second Sophistic and the Development of Empire*, edited by Simon Goldhill, 306–34. Cambridge: Cambridge University Press.

Van Nuffelen, Peter. 2014. "Not the Last Pagan: Libanius between Elite Rhetoric and Religion." In *Libanius: A Critical Introduction*, edited by Lieve Van Hoof, 293–314. Cambridge: Cambridge University Press.

Van Straten, Folkert T. 1995. *Hierà kalá: Images of Animal Sacrifice in Archaic and Classical Greece*. Leiden: Brill.

Vernant, Jean-Pierre. 1979. "À la table des hommes: Mythe de fondation du sacrifice chez Hésiode." In *La cuisine du sacrifice en pays grec*, edited by Marcel Detienne and Jean-Pierre Vernant, 37–132. Paris: Gallimard.

Veyne, Paul. 1976. *Le pain et le cirque: Sociologie d'un pluralisme politique*. Paris: Du Seuil.

Veyne, Paul. 1990. *Bread and Circuses: Historical Sociology and Political Pluralism*. Translated by Brian Pearce, abridged by Oswyn Murray. London: Allan Lane.

Villing, Alexandra. 2017. "Don't Kill the Goose That Lays the Golden Egg? Some Thoughts on Bird Sacrifices in Ancient Greece." In *Animal Sacrifice in the Ancient Greek World*, edited by Sarah Hitch and Ian Rutherford, 63–102. Cambridge: Cambridge University Press.

Vitti, Evangelia. 1986. *Die Erzählung über den Bau der Hagia Sophia in Konstantinopel: Kritische Edition mehrerer Versionen*. Amsterdam: Adolf M. Hakkert.

Wallraff, Martin. 2001. "Constantine's Devotion to the Sun after 324." *Studia Patristica* 34: 256–69.

Watson, Alasdair. 2007. *Religious Acculturation and Assimilation in Belgic Gaul and Aquitania from the Roman Conquest until the End of the Second Century CE*. British Archaeological Reports International Series 1624. Oxford: Archaeopress.

Weddle, Candace. 2013. "The Sensory Experience of Blood Sacrifice in the Roman Imperial Cult." In *Making Senses of the Past: Toward a Sensory Archaeology*, edited by Jo Day, 137–59. Carbondale: Southern Illinois University Press.

Wehrli, Fritz. 1967a. *Die Schule des Aristoteles: Texte und Kommentar, Heft 1: Dikaiarchos*. 2nd ed. Basel: Schwabe.

Wehrli, Fritz. 1967b. *Die Schule des Aristoteles: Texte und Kommentar, Heft 2: Aristoxenus*. 2nd ed. Basel: Schwabe.

Wehrli, Fritz. 1969. *Die Schule des Aristoteles: Texte und Kommentar, Heft 7: Herakleides Pontikos*. 2nd ed. Basel: Schwabe.

Wendt, Heidi. 2016. *At the Temple Gates: The Religion of Freelance Religious Experts in the Roman Empire*. Oxford: Oxford University Press.

West, M. L., ed. 1966. *Hesiod: Theogony*. Oxford: Clarendon Press.

White, K. D. 1970. *Roman Farming*. Ithaca, NY: Cornell University Press.

White, L. Michael, and G. Anthony Keddie. 2018. *Jewish Fictional Letters from Hellenistic Egypt: The Epistle of Aristeas and Related Literature*. Atlanta: Society of Biblical Literature.

Whitehead, David. 1983. "Competitive Outlay and Community Profit: φιλοτιμια in Democratic Athens." *Classica et Mediaevalia* 34: 55–74.

Wiemer, Hans-Ulrich. 1994. "Libanios und Zosimus über den Rom-Besuch Konstantins I. im Jahre 326." *Historia* 43, no. 4: 469–94.

Wightman, Edith Mary. 1985. *Gallia Belgica.* Berkeley: University of California Press.
Wissowa, Georg. 1912. *Religion und Kultus der Römer.* 2nd ed. Munich: C. H. Beck.
Witschel, Christian. 1999. *Krise, Rezession, Stagnation? Der Westen des römischen Reiches im 3. Jahrhundert n. Chr.* Frankfurt am Main: Marthe Clauss.
Witschel, Christian. 2004. "Re-evaluating the Roman West in the 3rd Century AD." *Journal of Roman Archaeology* 17: 251–81.
Woods, David. 2010. "The Deathbed Conversion of Galerius Maximianus to Religious Tolerance: Fact or Fraud?" *Studia Patristica* 44: 85–89.
Woodward, Jamie, ed. 2009. *The Physical Geography of the Mediterranean.* Oxford: Oxford University Press.
Woolf, Greg. 1994. "Becoming Roman, Staying Greek: Culture, Identity and the Civilizing Process in the Roman East." *Proceedings of the Cambridge Philological Society* 40: 116–43.
Woolf, Greg. 1998. *Becoming Roman: The Origins of Provincial Civilization in Gaul.* Cambridge: Cambridge University Press.
Woolf, Greg. 2009. "Found in Translation: The Religion of the Roman Diaspora." In *Ritual Dynamics and Religious Change in the Roman Empire: Proceedings of the Eighth Workshop of the International Network Impact of Empire (Heidelberg, July 5–7, 2007),* edited by Olivier Hekster, Sebastian Schmidt-Hofner, and Christian Witschel, 239–52. Leiden: Brill.
Worp, Klaas A. 2017. "Notes on Papyri: The Earliest Papyrological Attestation of the Emperor Decius." *Bulletin of the American Society of Papyrologists* 54: 257–60.
Wörrle, Michael. 1988. *Stadt und Fest im kaiserzeitlichen Kleinasien: Studien zu einer agonistischen Stiftung aus Oinoanda.* Munich: C. H. Beck.
Wright, Wilmer C., ed. and trans. 1913. *The Works of the Emperor Julian,* Vol. 2. Loeb Classical Library 29. Cambridge, MA: Harvard University Press.
Wright, Wilmer C., ed. and trans. 1923. *The Works of the Emperor Julian,* Vol. 3. Loeb Classical Library 157. Cambridge, MA: Harvard University Press.
Young, Frances M. 1979. *The Use of Sacrificial Ideas in Greek Christian Writers from the New Testament to John Chrysostom.* Cambridge, MA: Philadelphia Patristic Foundation.
Zeitlin, Froma. 1965. "The Motif of Corrupted Sacrifice in Aeschylus' *Oresteia.*" *Transactions of the American Philological Association* 96: 463–508.
Zetterholm, Magnus. 2009. *Approaches to Paul: A Student's Guide to Recent Scholarship.* Minneapolis: Fortress Press.
Ziehen, Ludwig. 1939. "Opfer." In *Paulys Real-encyclopädie der classischen Altertumswissenschaft,* edited by August Pauly, Georg Wissowa, and Wilhem Kroll, 18: 579–627. Munich: A. Druckenmüller.
Zuiderhoek, Arjan. 2009. *The Politics of Munificence in the Roman Empire: Citizens, Elites and Benefactors in Asia Minor.* Cambridge: Cambridge University Press.
Zuiderhoek, Arjan, and Wouter Vanacker. 2017. "Introduction: Imperial Identities in the Roman World." In *Imperial Identities in the Roman World,* edited by Wouter Vanacker and Arjan Zuiderhoek, 1–15. London: Routledge.

# Index

*For the benefit of digital users, indexed terms that span two pages (e.g., 52–53) may, on occasion, appear on only one of those pages.*

Figures are indicated by *f* following the page number

abstinence from animal flesh, 158–70, 184–85, 215–16, 226, 227
Acca Larentia, 69
Acharnae, 46
Acraephia, 47–49, 53–55, 119–22
Acts of the Apostles, 153–55, 188–89, 190–92, 193–94, 201
*adventus*, 143–45
Aedesius, 315–16, 327
aediles, 67, 71–72, 75
Aeneas, 127–29
Aesop, 32–33
　*Life of*, 69–71
Agape and companions, martyrs, 276n.41, 283
Agonalia, 64–65
agonothete, 48, 51–53, 56–57, 121
agoranomos, 47–48
agropastoralism, 35n.24
Alcinous, Platonic philosopher, 223–24
Alexandria
　Christians in, 260
　on coins of Hadrian, 143–45
　Judaeans in, 102–3, 105, 110–11, 110n.61, 145–46
　temple of Serapis in, 328–29

Alexis, Greek comic playwright, 163–64
altar
　of Augustan Peace (Ara Pacis Augustae) in Rome, 116–17, 125–29
　of Claudius in Rome, 133
　of 'Domitius Ahenobarbus' in Rome, 77–79, 126–27, 131, 286–87
　of Fortuna Redux in Rome, 116–17
　of the Numen Augusti in Narbo, 118–19, 123
　of the Numen Augustum in Forum Clodii, 60–63, 118–19, 123
　of the Temple in Jerusalem, 103–4, 190–91
　of the 'Temple of Vespasian' in Pompeii, 1–4
Ameria, 73
Ammianus Marcellinus
　on Constantius II, 312
　on Julian, 316–18, 320n.53
　on Valentinian, 323n.56
Amorgos, 47
Angerona, 64–65
animal husbandry, 26, 28–30, 34–36

animal sacrifice
    in early Christianity, 189–95, 211–13
    Constantine's prohibition of, 302–3, 309–10
    in the decree of Decius, 247–48, 255–56
    defined, 4–9
    economic aspects of, 37–40
    and euergetism, 53–55, 59–60, 63–64, 71, 76–77
    as a Graeco-Roman practice, 83–88
    in imperial cult, 115–16, 121–25
    in Judaean-Roman relations, 108–12
    as a marker of the primitive, 337–39
    philosophical theorization of, 181–83, 222–23
    'spiritualization' of, 241–43
    in Tetrarchic policy, 281–88
animate vs. inanimate food, 158–70
Antioch
    Christians in, 186–87
    Julian in, 313–15, 316–18
    Libanius in, 323–25
Antiphanes, Greek comic playwright, 160n.6, 163–64, 180
Antoninus Pius, 136–38, 141n.40, 206, 239–40
Apion, 107–8, 110–11
Apollo, 73, 179–80
    at Antioch, 314–15
    of the Lyrbotai, 58
    in Oenoanda, 56–57, 119–20
    Ptoios, 47–49, 98–99, 119–20
    in Rome, 67–68, 85–86
    Tyrimnos, 51–54, 98–99, 119–20
Apollonios of Kalindoia, 51
Apollonius of Tyana, 224–27
Apuleius, 223–24
Ara Pacis Augustae. See altar: of Augustan Peace
Arcadius, 322, 330

arch
    of Constantine at Rome, 138–39, 298–99
    of Cottius at Segusio, 129–31
    of Galerius at Thessalonica, 286–87
    of Marcus Aurelius at Rome, 138–39, 298–99
    of Septimius Severus at Lepcis Magna, 138–39
    of Titus at Rome, 133
    of Trajan at Beneventum, 134–36
Archestratus, 164
Aristeas, Letter of, 109–10
Aristophanes, 159–60
Aristophon, Greek comic playwright, 163–64
Aristotle
    on animal sacrifice, 175–76
    on 'like to like', 223–24
    on pigs, 32–33
    on Pythagoreans, 162–63, 169n.25
Aristoxenus, associate of Aristotle, 163–64
Aristoxenus, friend of Julian, 314–15
Armenian Church, 340–41
Arnobius, 291n.1
Artemis, 58–59
Arval Brothers, 65, 117–18, 123, 253
Asad, Talal, 11n.14
Asklepios, 39n.35, 119–20
Aśoka, 168n.24
Athena, 21–23, 47
Athenaeus, 163n.11, 164
Athenagoras, 232–36, 239–40
Athens, 37n.29, 45–46
augury, 127
Augustus
    cults of, 51, 60–62, 73, 116–17, 118–20
    depicted as sacrificant, 127–31
    Divus, 123, 133–34
    on druids, 97–98
    priesthoods of, 125–26

## Index

and sacrifices in the Jerusalem
  temple, 110–11
and spending on *ludi* in Rome, 67–68
Augustus, as imperial title, 272–73. *See also* Tetrarchy
Aurelian, 139n.38
Avelius Priscus, Quintus, 62–63

Balberg, Mira, 106n.48, 112–13, 211–12
Barnabas, in Acts of the Apostles, 153–55, 193–94
Barnabas, Letter of, 188–89, 201, 210
Barnes, T. D., 270–71
Baruch, 109–10
Batnae, 316, 318–19
Belayche, Nicole, 310–11
Beneventum, 134–36
Bennecourt, 92–93, 95–96
Besa, Egyptian god, 312
birds, as sacrificial victims, 92–93, 316–18
  chickens, 39n.35
  doves, 190–91
  flamingoes, 87–88n.6
  geese, 39n.35, 313–14
Bleckmann, Bruno, 257, 304–5
Boeotia, 47–49
Boscoreale cups, 131–33
bovines. *See* cattle/bovines
Bradbury, Scott, 308–9
Brent, Allen, 257, 261n.18
Brunaux, Jean-Louis, 90–91
bulls, as sacrificial victims, 21–23, 73, 153–55, 167–68, 174, 317–18. *See also* suovetaurilia
  in Greek festivals, 48, 56–57
  in imperial cult, 1–3, 60, 119–20, 121, 123
  in Judaean cult, 108n.55, 109–10
  prestige of, 37–38
Burkert, Walter, 7n.8, 9n.13, 339

Caesar, as imperial title, 272–73. *See also* Tetrarchy

Caesar. *See* Julius Caesar, Gaius
Caesarea, 274–75, 277–78
Caligula
  and Judaeans, 110–11, 145–46
  as sacrificant, 133–34
*capite velato*, 77–78, 84–86, 127–31, 133–38
Caracalla, 52n.23, 136–38, 139n.38, 252
Carpus, martyr, 264–66
Carthage, Punic, 87
Carthage, Roman, 73–75, 247, 256–57n.9, 259–60, 262–63, 266
Carus, 285–86n.52
Cascellius Labeo, Quintus, 61–63
Castor and Pollux, 312
Cato, the elder, 31–32, 36
cattle/bovines. *See also* bulls; heifers; oxen
  prestige of, as sacrificial victims, 1–3, 23, 37–38, 180
  production and consumption of, 28–29, 30–31, 33–34, 35–36, 39–40
  sacrificed for emperors, 116–18, 121, 123, 143–45
  sacrificed by emperors, 131–33, (Tiberius), 133–34 (Caligula), 134–36 (Trajan), 136–38 (Hadrian), 138–39, 140f (Marcus Aurelius), 275 (Diocletian), 286–87 (Galerius), 284n.51 (Maximinus), 316, 318–19 (Julian)
  as sacrificial victims, 67–68, 91–93, 178, 341–42
  as victims in Graeco-Roman tradition, 84, 85, 87
Celsus, 232–33, 235–37
Ceres, 66–67, 74–75
Christian, origin and use of term, 186–87
Chrysanthius, 327
Cicero, 32–33, 181n.52, 182–83

city, Graeco-Roman
  in Gaul, 95, 96–97
  in Greek east, 55–56
  importance to Roman empire, 55–56, 80, 82–83
  public animal sacrifice in, 23–24, 53–55, 75–77, 147–48, 181–82, 217
  in Roman west, 71–72
  shift of emphasis away from, 252–53, 258–59, 288, 292, 308–9
Claudius, 97–98, 123, 133
Claudius Gothicus, 139n.38
Columella, 28–29, 31–33
column
  of Marcus Aurelius, 138–39
  of Tetrarchs, 286–87
  of Trajan, 134–36
Commodus, 138n.35
Concordia, 284–85
Constans, 249–50, 302–3, 310–11
Constantine
  career, 273, 296–97
  on Diocletian's role in the persecution, 279–80
  effects of his policies on animal sacrifice, 306–9, 332, 334–35
  ends persecution of Christians, 278–79, 289–90
  hostility to animal sacrifice, 297–302, 304–6
  prohibition of animal sacrifice, 302–3, 324–25, 331
Constantinople, 299–302, 340
Constantius I, 272–73, 276–77, 286–87, 296
Constantius II
  career, 310–11, 314–15
  prohibition of animal sacrifice, 249–50, 302–3, 311–13, 324–25
Constitutio Antoniniana, 252
consuls, 65–66, 67–68, 116–17
Copres, 282–83

Corfinium, 62–63
Corinth, Christians in, 187–88, 193, 196, 197–98, 204
Cottius, Marcus Julius, 129–31
crisis of the 3rd century, 251–53
Crispina, martyr, 276–77, 283
Cumae, 73, 118–19, 123
Cyprian
  and Decius' decree, 247, 256–57n.9, 259–60, 262–63, 266
  on the Eucharist, 344–45
  and Valerian's decrees, 266–70

*daimones/daimonia*
  Christian demonological discourse, 228–39, 244, 259, 264–65, 275, 295–96, 341–42
  Empedocles on, 168n.24
  Eusebius on, 291–92, 304–5
  Justin Martyr on, 229–33
  Paul on, 193, 228, 262–63
  Plato on, 185, 223–24
  Porphyry on, 217, 218–19, 224–25, 237, 244
  possible role in Constantine's thought, 304–6, 333
  possible role in Julian's thought, 318–19
Daly, Robert, 241–42
Darius, 109–10
*decemviri sacris faciundis*, 67–68
*decennalia*, 136–38, 284–85, 286–87, 298–99
'Decennalia Base', 286–87
Decius
  career, 255
  effects of decree, 258–59, 265–66, 289, 334–35
  effects of decree on Christians, 259–66, 275
  motivations behind decree, 257–58, 334–35

## Index

provisions of decree, 247–48, 256, 268–69, 304
termination of decree, 266
decurions, 43–44, 61–62, 71–72, 73–74, 76–77, 96–97
Demetrius Cythras, 312
demons. See *daimones*
Demosthenes of Oenoanda, 56–57, 119–20
Derks, Ton, 95
Detienne, Marcel, 9n.12, 9n.13, 38–39, 170n.30
Deuteronomy, 228
Didache, 188–89, 193–94, 205–6, 206n.41, 343–44
Digeser, Elizabeth DePalma, 216–17n.4, 237n.38
Diocletian
  career, 272–73
  images of animal sacrifice, 284–87
  motivations behind persecution, 279–83
  persecution of Christians, 249, 275–79
  reforms of, 273–74, 288, 292
Diodorus of Aspendus, 164
Diodorus Siculus, 89–90, 93–94, 162
Dionysius of Alexandria, 256, 260, 266–68, 270
Dionysius of Halicarnassus, 67–68, 85
Dionysios of Thyatira, 51–53
Dionysus, 46, 160–61
discourse
  defined, 13–15, 155
  impact on practice, 243–44, 248–49, 265–66, 279–80, 304–5, 332–34
  Julian's Hellenism as, 315–16
  narrative vs. analytical, 157–58, 168–69
  and social power, 183–84, 187–88, 239–40, 241, 243–44
divination. *See also* augury; *haruspices*
  philosophical interest in, 171n.32

prohibitions of, 299–302, 303n.22, 310–11, 312, 325–27
role of *daimones* in, 185
*divus*, 61–62, 122–23
dogs, as sacrificial victims, 87, 92–93, 95–96
Domingo Gygax, Marc, 42
Domitian, 58–59, 133–34
Donahue, John, 62–63
druids, 93–94, 97–98
*duoviri/duumviri*, 60, 61–62, 71–72, 73–74, 75, 96–97, 119
Dura-Europus, 112–13, 118, 211–12
Durkheim, Émile, 338–39

Edmonds, Radcliffe, 161n.8, 243n.5
Egeria, 330–31
Egypt, 88, 102–3, 247, 253, 257, 282–83, 312
*eidōlothuton*, 192–95, 228, 264
Elagabalus, 138n.35
Eleusis, 46, 310–11
Elsner, Jaś, 254
Elvira, canons of, 271–72
Empedocles, 158–59, 160–61, 165–68, 170
emperor
  civic cults for, in Gaul, 96–97
  civic cults for, in Greek east, 48, 51, 53–54
  civic cults for, in Italy, 60–62, 65, 73
  ideological role of, 22, 114–16
  Judaean sacrifices for, 110–12
  as sacrificant, 125–42
  sacrifices for, 116–25
Epaminondas of Acraephia, 48, 122
Ephesus, 141n.40, 187–88
Epictetus, 175–76, 181–82
Epicurus, 176–77
Epinomides of Minoa, 47
*epulum Iovi*, 69
Eucharist, 204–7, 210–11, 262–63, 343–45. *See also* Last Supper

Eudoxus, 164
euergetism
    animal sacrifice and, 41–42, 79–80
    decline of, 252–53, 258–59, 292, 308–9
    sacrificial euergetism in Greek east, 49, 53–55, 59–60
    sacrificial euergetism in Latin west, 63–64, 76–77, 79
    sacrificial euergetism in Judaean tradition, 102n.37, 106
    role in Roman empire, 11–12, 23–24, 42–45
Eunapius, 312n.35, 327
Euripides, 159–60
Eusebius
    on animal sacrifice, 291–92
    on Apollonius of Tyana, 224–25
    career and writings, 274–75
    on Constantine, 299–302, 304–5, 306–7, 308
    on Decius, 256
    on Gallienus and the 'peace of the church', 270, 271–72
    on the 'Great Persecution', 275, 276, 277–79, 281–82, 283–85
    on the martyrs of Lyons and Vienne, 347–48
Euthydemos of Eleusis, 46
Extispicium Relief, 135n.32
Ezra, book of, 109–10

Felicitas, 123, 284–85
*feriale*
    of Ameria, 73
    of Cumae, 73, 118–19, 123
    Duranum, 118, 119, 123
Fesques, 92n.15, 95–96
festivals, Greek, ideological role of, 53–55
Festus, 69–71
Flora, 66–67
Fordicidia, 64–65
Fortuna, 73, 116–17, 327

Forum of Augustus, 129–31
Forum Clodii, 60–62, 118–19, 123
Fredriksen, Paula, 319n.50
Freud, Sigmund, 338–39
Friesen, Steven, 123–24

Gaius Caesar, grandson of Augustus, 129–31
Galerius
    Arch of, 286–87
    career, 272–73, 278–79
    'edict of toleration', 280–81
    role in the persecution of Christians, 249, 279–80, 281–83
Gallienus
    coinage of, 139n.38
    co-ruler with Valerian, 266–67
    support of Christian associations, 270–71
Gallus, older brother of Julian, 314–15
games, Roman. *See* ludi
Gauls/Gaul
    and animal sacrifice, 89–100, 113, 147–48
    decline of sanctuaries in, 253
    and human sacrifice, 87
Genesis, 208–9, 232
*genius*
    of Augustus, 129n.23
    defined, 122–23
    of the emperor, sacrifices to, 61, 123
    of the emperor, on coinage, 136–38
    offerings to, banned, 329
Geta, 138n.35
Girard, René, 7n.8, 339
goats
    production of, 31–32
    as sacrificial victims, 67–68, 87, 175–76
Goodman, Martin, 97–98
Gordan, Richard, 45n.11, 125n.18
Gordian III, 139n.38, 253
Gournay-sur-Aronde, 89–93, 95–96

Gradel, Ittai, 123–24
*Graeco ritu*, 85–86
Graeco-Roman culture
    animal sacrifice as a marker of, 84–88
    defined, 24, 81–83
Gratian, 322
Gregory the Great, 341–42
gymnasiarch, 50
Gythium, 119–20

Hadrian, 58–59, 136–38, 141, 141n.40, 143–45, 298–99
*haruspices*, 74–75, 275, 299–302, 322–23
Hebrews, letter to the, 188–89, 208–10, 346–47
heifers, as sacrificial victims, 21–23, 64–65, 67–68, 117, 123
Hellenism, 249–50, 296n.6, 314–16, 319, 320–21
Herakles/Hercules, 50, 85–86, 122, 272–73
Hermes, 50, 122, 153–54, 158n.3
Hesiod, 30–31, 157–58, 223–24, 316n.43
*hilasmos / hilaskomai / hilastērion*, 196–97, 202n.32, 209n.46
Hispellum, 299–302, 304–5, 307
holocausts, 7–8, 104–5, 106, 107n.49, 319n.50
Homer, 21–23, 35–36, 85, 172–73, 223–24, 319n.50
Honorius, 322, 330
Horden, Peregrine, 34–35
horses
    production of, 31n.12, 35
    as sacrificial victims, 91–93, 95–96
Howe, Timothy, 29–30, 46
Hubert, Henri, 8–9
human sacrifice, 87, 93, 97–98, 178, 337n.1
Hygieia, 119–20

Iamblichus
    citing Apollonius, 225–26
    dispute with Porphyry, 216–17n.4, 220–21
    influence on Julian, 315–16
    life and thought, 219–20
    and the primacy of discourse, 239–40
    on sacrificial practice, 221–23, 244
identity, as a term of analysis, 12–13
ideology, 11–12, 147–48, 241, 243–44
idolatry, 107–8, 192–93, 210–11, 238–39, 261–62, 269–70, 302. *See also* *eidōlothuton*
Ignatius of Antioch, 188–89, 204–5, 347–48
Ilium, 313–14
imperial cult, 114–15, 116–25, 307. *See also* emperor
incense. *See also praefatio*; *supplicatio*
    as an alternative to animal sacrifice, 6–7, 102, 167–68, 254
    as an alternative to animal sacrifice for Christians, 256–57n.9, 283
    in Christian cult, 330–31
    as offering to *daimones*, 231–32, 234, 238
    in the policies of Christian emperors, 312–13, 324–26, 329, 330–31
*interpretatio Romana*, 99n.31
Irenaeus of Lyons, 193–94
Irni, 72, 73–74
Isaiah, 201

Jerusalem
    'Council of', 193–94
    destruction of Temple and end of Judaean sacrifice, 112–13, 194–95, 207–8, 211–12, 242n.3
    Egeria in, 330–31
    funding of Temple, 105
    Judaean sacrifice in Temple, 102–3, 111–12, 189–92, 194–95, 343–44
    Julian's proposed rebuilding of Temple, 112–13, 319–20

Jesus
  casting out *daimones*, 229
  as high priest, 276–77, 349
  historical, 187 (*see also* Last Supper)
  and Judaean sacrificial cult, 189–91, 192n.11
  as a sacrificial victim, 195–203, 208–9, 211–13, 234–35, 244, 333, 343, 348–49
John, Gospel of, 187n.3, 188–89, 190, 199–201, 203n.34
John, letters of, 202–3
John Malalas, 299–302
John of Patmos, 188–89, 193–94, 200
Josephus, 100–1, 104–5, 106, 107–9, 110–12, 145–46
Jovian, 322, 323–24, 325
Judaean
  animal sacrifice, 100–13, 189–92, 194–95, 211–12
  Christian defined in contrast to, 207–8, 212
  contrasted with gentile, 295–96
  displacement of animal sacrifice, 241–42
  exempted from pagan cult practices, 271–72
  Julian on, 319–20
  references to *daimones*, 228–29, 232, 235–36
  sacrifices for the emperor, 110–12, 145–46
  as translation of *Ioudaios*, 89n.9
Julian
  career, 314–15
  beliefs, 315–16, 318–19
  on the decline of animal sacrifice, 313–14
  enthusiasm for animal sacrifice, 294–95, 316–18
  and Judaean tradition, 112–13, 319–20
  significance of policies, 319–22

Julius Caesar, Gaius, 89–90, 93–94
Juno, 72, 75, 117, 123
Jupiter
  cults in Rome, 65–67, 69, 117, 123, 138–39
  cults in cities of the Latin west, 70n.59, 72, 73, 75, 327
  in Tetrarchic ideology, 272–73, 286–87
Justin Martyr
  and Celsus, 236–37
  on Christ as Passover lamb, 202–3
  on *daimones*, 230–33, 234
  on *eidōlothuton*, 194–95
  on the Eucharist, 206, 343–45
  on the importance of correct understanding, 239–40
  on Judaean sacrifice, 210–11
  life, 229–30
Justinian, 340, 342

Kalindoia, 51
Knossos, 75
*kourbánia*, 340–41, 342
Kovaltchuk, Ekaterina, 340
Kuttner, Ann, 131–33

Lactantius
  on animal sacrifice in the 'Great Persecution', 281–83
  on Decius, 256
  on Diocletian's reforms, 273–74
  on Diocletian's persecution in the army, 275
  on impetus for the 'Great Persecution', 279–80
  life, 274–75
  on Maximinus' role in the 'Great Persecution', 283–84
lamb
  as metaphor for Jesus, 196, 199–203
  as sacrificial victim, 37–38, 91–92, 190–91, 263–64, 318–19

as victim at Passover, 102–3, 104–5,
     198–99, 212
Lamptrae, 46
*lar*, 329
Last Supper, 104–5, 197–99, 200–1, 204,
     206, 212, 344–45
Latona, 67–68
Leontopolis, 102–3
Lepcis Magna, 138–39
Leviticus, 100–1, 104n.43, 349
Libanius
  on animal sacrifice, 323–26, 329n.64,
     342–43n.12
  on Constantine, 298–99, 302–
     3, 308–9
  on incense, 324–25, 330–31
  and Julian, 312–13, 316–18
libation. See also *patera*; *praefatio*
  as alternative to animal
     sacrifice, 167–68
  associated with animal sacrifice in
     images, 1, 77–78, 133–34, 136–38,
     143–45, 286–87
  associated with animal sacrifice in
     texts, 172–73, 175–76, 226, 231–32,
     234, 312–13, 324–25
  and *daimones*, 231–32, 234
  in decree of Decius, 247–48, 256, 264
  defined, 6–7
  in 'Great Persecution', 276, 277–
     78, 283–84
  prohibited by Christian emperors, 330
  Theophrastus on, 178n.46
  as visual metonymy for animal
     sacrifice, 129–31, 139, 284–85
Licinius
  career, 273, 278–79, 296
  'Edict of Milan', 249–50, 278–79,
     289–90, 296–97
Livia, 61, 118–20, 123
Longueil-Sainte-Marie, 95–96
Lucian, 254n.5

*ludi*. See also *pompa*
  animal sacrifice in, 67–69
  in cities of the western Empire, 45n.10,
     67–71, 72–76, 271–72
  in Rome, 66–67, 85–86, 133–34
Luke, Gospel of, 188–89, 190–91, 198–99
Lystra, 153–55

Macarius, 297–98
Macomades, 62–63
Macrinus, 139n.38
*mageiros*, 8–9, 316–17
magic, as criminal offense, 305–6, 310–
     11, 325–26
Magna Mater, 66–67, 68n.52
Magnentius, 310–11
Malachi, 206n.39, 211n.51, 343–44
Mamre, 297–98, 299–302
Mann, Michael, 10–12, 243–44
Marcus Aurelius, 138–39, 298–99
Marinus, martyr, 271n.35
Mark, Gospel of, 188–89, 190, 198–99, 229
Mars, 65–66, 77–78, 98–99, 123, 286–87
martyrs and martyr acts, 256, 291–92
  Agape and companions, 276n.41, 283
  Carpus, 264–66
  Crispina, 276–77, 283
  Cyprian, 266–69
  Euplus, 292n.2
  Irenaeus of Sirmium, 292n.2
  Julius the Veteran, 292n.2
  of Lyons and Vienne, 347–48
  Marinus, 271n.35
  of Palestine, 274–75, 276, 277–78,
     283n.49
  Phileas, 277–78, 292n.2
  Pionius, 262n.20, 263–64, 265
  Polycarp, 347–49
martyrdom
  Origen's exhortation to, 237–39, 261–
     62, 305–6, 348–49
  as sacrifice, 347–49

*matal / matagh*, 340–41, 342n.11, 343n.13
Matthew, Gospel of, 188–89, 190–91, 198–99, 229n.26
Mauss, Marcel, 8–9
Maxentius, 273, 276–77, 296
Maximian, 272–73, 284–87
Maximinus Daia
    career, 272–73, 278–79, 296
    persecution of Christians, 249, 277–79, 280–81, 283–84
Maximinus Thrax, 253
Maximus of Ephesus, 315–16
McKechnie, Paul, 257
meat. *See also* abstinence from animal flesh; cattle/bovines; *eidolōthuton*; pigs; sheep
    absence from early Christian meals, 206–7, 212
    from Judaean sacrifices, 104–5
    production and consumption, 28–30, 38–40
    sold in markets, 69–71
Mediterranean, environmental features of, 26–28
*megalophrosynē*, 42–43, 48, 51
Menander, 176–77, 180
Menas of Sestos, 49–51, 54
Mercury, 73
metempsychosis. *See* transmigration of souls
Minerva, 72, 75, 117, 123, 133–34
Minoa, 47
Minucius Felix, 232–34
Mishnah, 100–1, 102, 103n.41, 108–9
Mitchell, Stephen, 254
Mnesimachus, 163–64
Moser, Claudia, 99–100
Mouas of Perge, 58–59

Narbo, 118–19, 123
Nebuchadnezzar, 109–10
Nero, 123, 268
Nestor, 21–23

Nicomedia, 274–75, 276, 278–79, 282–83
Nilsson, Martin, 254
Numa Pompilius, 127–29
*numen*, 61, 118–19, 122–23

Oenoanda, 56–58, 119–21
Onesicritus, 164, 169n.27
Origen
    on *daimones*, 233–40, 259, 261–62, 305–6, 333
    treatise against Celsus, 232–33
    treatise on martyrdom, 238–39, 348–49
Orpheus, Orphic tradition, 159–61, 168–70, 173n.35
Orphic Hymns, 254n.6
Ostia, 312
Ovid, 64–65, 116–17, 162, 184–85
oxen. *See also* cattle/bovines
    use in agriculture, 30–31, 33–34
    as sacrificial victims, 65–66, 67–68, 106, 117, 123
Oxyrhynchus, 281–82

pagan, paganism
    animal sacrifice as a marker of, 308, 309–10, 320–21, 332, 333
    use of the term, 16–17, 295–96
Passover, 102–3, 104–5, 108n.56, 190–91, 196, 198–201, 202–3. *See also* lamb
*patera*, 77–78, 127–31. *See also* libation
Paul
    in Acts of the Apostles, 153–55, 191–92, 193–94
    application of sacrificial metaphors to Christ, 196–97
    on Christians as a living sacrifice, 345–46
    on *daimonia*, 193, 228–29, 262–63
    and Judaean sacrificial cult, 191–92, 194–95
    letters of, 187–88
    on the Lord's Supper, 197–98, 204
    on sacrificial meat, 69–71, 192–93

Paulinus of Nola, 340, 343
Paulus Catena, 312
Peirce, C. S., 59–60
*penates*, 329
Pergamum, 49–50, 193–94, 263–64
Perge, 58–59
Pertinax, 138n.35
Pescennius Niger, 139
Peter, letters attributed to, 202–3, 346
Philadelphia, 122
Phileas, martyr, 277–78, 292n.2
Philip, apostle, 201
Philip, Roman emperor, 139n.38, 255
Philippi, 187–88, 191–92
Philo of Alexandria, 100–1, 103n.40, 105, 110–11
Philodemus, 176–77
*philodoxia*, 42–43, 48, 50–51
Philokedes of Acharnae, 46
Philostratus, 225–27
*philotimia*, 42–43, 46–47, 51
Pietas, 100–1, 139
pigs. See also *suovetaurilia*
　production and consumption of, 32–33, 35–36, 39–40
　as sacrificial victims, 37–38, 84, 91–93, 95–96, 106–7, 127–29, 178
Pionius, martyr, 262n.20, 263–64, 265
Plato
　on *daimones*, 185, 223–24
　on 'like to like', 223–24
　on the Orphic life, 159–60
　on sacrifice, 171–74, 181–82
Pliny, the elder, 32n.16, 37–38, 87, 97–98
Pliny, the younger, 69–71, 117–18, 194n.18, 206n.40
Plotinus, 215–16, 223–24
Plutarch
　on *daimones*, 185, 223–24, 232
　on Epicurus, 176–77
　on the Orphic myth of Dionysus, 160–61
　as a vegetarian, 184–85

Pluto, 62–63
Polycarp, martyr, 347–49
*pompa*
　*circensis*, 67–68, 73–74
　*theatralis*, 68n.53, 74n.67
Pompeii, 1, 70n.61, 75
*pontifex maximus*, 61, 64–65, 125–26, 313–14
*pontifices*, 64–65, 71–72, 74–75, 116–17
Pontius, 266–67, 268–69
Porphyry
　citing Apollonius, 224–26
　dispute with Iamblichus, 219–20
　on divine hierarchies, 223–25, 226–27
　on Empedocles, 167–68, 167n.20
　and the 'Great Persecution', 279–80
　on the importance of correct understanding, 239–40
　life and thought, 215–16
　relationship to Origen, 237
　on sacrificial practice, 216–19, 222–23, 244, 304–5
　on Theophrastus, 177–79, 180
　used by Eusebius, 291–92
Posidonius, 89–90
power, as term of analysis, 10–13
practice, as term of analysis, 13–14, 23, 79, 86–87, 123–25, 244
*praefatio*, in Roman sacrificial practice, 77–78, 84–85, 131–33, 134–38
Praeneste, 73
Praetextatus, 310–11, 322–23, 327
praetors, 67–68
Price, Simon, 123–24
priests, priesthoods. See also Arval Brothers; *decemviri sacris faciundis*; druids; *pontifices*; Vestal Virgins
　of emperors, 51, 96–97, 119, 121, 253, 271–72
　in Greek east, 51, 121, 153–55, 226, 248, 313–14

priests, priesthoods (*cont.*)
    Judaean, 103–5, 106, 109–11, 190–91, 196–97, 206n.39
    Julian's hierarchy of, 315–16, 322–23
    in Latin west, 71–72, 74–75, 96–97, 119
    Maximinus' hierarchy of, 277–78
    as metaphor for Jesus, 208–10, 346–47, 348–49
    pagan, forbidden to Christians, 271–72
    Roman, 64–65, 85–86, 116–17, 125, 253, 271–72, 286–87
    role of, in Graeco-Roman tradition, 8–9, 14
Prometheus, 157–58
Purcell, Nicholas, 34–35
Pythagorean tradition
    and abstinence from animal flesh, 162–65, 168–70
    and Apollonius of Tyana, 225–27
    and Empedocles, 165, 166
    fluidity of, 158–59
    historical Pythagoras, 161–62
    in Rome, 184–85
    and Julian, 318n.48

Qumran, 102–3

rabbis, 102–3, 104n.43, 106n.48, 107n.50, 108n.56, 112–13, 211–12, 241–42. *See also* Mishnah
rams, as sacrificial victims, 108n.55, 109–10
Rebillard, Éric, 261–62, 266–67
Reed, Annette Yoshiko, 350n.29
religion, as term of analysis, 15–17, 289–90, 295–96. *See also* Hellenism; pagan, paganism
Ribemont-sur-Ancre, 92–93, 95–96
ritual, as term of analysis, 4, 337–39
Roma, 125–26
Romanization, 88n.7
Rome, city of. *See also* altars; arches; Arval Brothers; columns; 'Decennalia Base'; priests
    public sacrifice in, 64–71, 298–99
Romulus, 125–26, 127–29

sacrificant
    benefactors as, 23–24, 53–55, 79
    defined, 8–9
    emperors as, 115–16, 125–42, 145, 147–48, 284–87
    in Gallic tradition, 93–94, 97–98
    in Graeco-Roman tradition, 84–85
    in Judaean tradition, 103–4
    Julian as, 316–17
    magistrates as, 74–75, 76–79
    philosophical stress on moral character of, 180–82
Salus, 117
Sardis, 141n.40, 327
Saturnalia, 64–65
Schwartz, Seth, 106
Sebastoi, cult of, 121
Segusio, 129–31
Seneca, 184–85
Septimius Severus, 138–39, 141n.40, 271–72
Serapis, 328–29
Servius, 69–71
Sestos, 49–51, 54
Severus, tetrarch, 272–73
Severus Alexander, 123, 139n.38, 253
Sextius, Roman philosopher, 184–85
Sextus Empiricus, 165–67, 183n.55
Shapur I, 266–67
Shapur II, 297–98, 314–15
sheep. *See also* lamb; rams; *suovetaurilia*
    production and consumption of, 28–29, 31–32, 35–36, 39–40

as sacrificial victims, 37–38, 84, 92–93, 95–96, 109–10, 116–17, 126, 175–76
Smith, William Robertson, 338–39
Smyrna, 204–5, 263–64, 347–48
Socrates, church historian, 325
Socrates, philosopher
  in Justin Martyr, 230–31
  in Plato, 171–74, 185
  in Xenophon, 175
Sotion, 184–85
Sozomen, 308–9
'spiritualization' of sacrificial practice, 241–43
Stoics, 175–76, 181n.52
Stowers, Stanley, 14n.17, 196–97
Strabo, 87, 93–94
Stroumsa, Guy, 241–42
Suetonius, 97–98
*summa honoraria*, 43–44, 75, 76–77
*suovetaurilia*, 65–66, 77–78, 129–31, 134–36, 138–39, 286–87, 298–99
*supplicatio*, offering of wine and incense, 73, 118–19, 123, 127n.21
Symmachus, 327, 330–31

Tatian, 232–33, 237
Tertullian, 73–75, 169n.26, 232–34, 236–37, 261–62
Tetrarchy, 272–73, 284–88
Tetricus, 139n.38
Themistius, 322–23, 325
Theodosian Code, 292–94
Theodosius I
  career, 9–10, 322
  and Libanius, 317–18, 323–24
  prohibition of animal sacrifice, 249–50, 326–27, 328–31
Theodosius II, 292–93, 330
Theophrastus, 107n.49, 177–81, 182, 254n.6
Theopompus, 180

Theos Hypsistos, 254
Thessalonica, 187–88, 283, 286–87
Thyatira, 51–54, 119–20, 193–94
Tiberius
  cults of, 60–62, 119–20
  and druids, 97–98
  as sacrificant, 131–33
Timaeus, historian, 164
Titans, 160–61
Titus, Arch of, 133
Titus Tatius, 127–29
Tobit, 229
Trajan, 117–18, 134–38, 298–99
transmigration of souls, metempsychosis, 162, 166–67, 168–69, 184–85
triumph, 66n.48, 131–33, 134–36, 138–39
Tyche, 263–64, 299–302
Tylor, E. B., 337–38

Ullucci, Daniel, 186n.1, 242n.2, 334–35
Ulpian, 31
Urso, 72–75

Valens
  career, 322
  policies on religious practices, 310–11, 322–23, 324–26
Valentinian,
  career, 322
  policies on religious practices, 310–11, 322–23, 324–26
Valentinian II, 322
Valerian
  career, 266–67, 270
  provisions and goals of decrees, 249, 254–55, 267–70, 289
Valerius Valentinus, Gaius, 62–63
Van Andringa, William, 99–100
Van Nuffelen, Peter, 324–25
Varro, 31–33

vegetal offerings. *See also* incense; libations
  as characteristic of an idealized past, 159–60, 166–67, 178
  contrasted with animal sacrifice, 6–8, 37
  increased emphasis on in the third century CE, 254
  prohibited, 329, 330–31
vegetarianism. *See* abstinence from animal flesh
Venus, 72
Vertault, 92–93
Vespasian, 66n.48, 100–1, 102–3, 133, 134n.30
Vesta, 73
Vestal Virgins, 116–17, 126
*vicennalia*, 136–38, 276, 286–87, 298–99

*victimarius*, 4, 316–17
vows, *vota*. *See also decennalia*; *vicennalia*
  for the emperor, 117–18, 136–38, 143–45, 257, 284–85
  for the Republic, 65–66, 117
  to St. Felix, 340, 343

Whitehead, David, 46
women, as sacrificants, 9n.12

Xenocrates, 185, 223–24
Xenophon, 175

Zeno, 175–76
Zeus, 48, 51, 153–55, 157–58, 160–61, 173–74, 223–24, 317–18
Zosimus, 255, 298–99, 322–23